Massachusetts Bank Commissioners

Annual Report of the Board of Commissioners of Savings Banks

1881

Massachusetts Bank Commissioners

Annual Report of the Board of Commissioners of Savings Banks
1881

ISBN/EAN: 9783337249700

Printed in Europe, USA, Canada, Australia, Japan

Cover: Foto ©Suzi / pixelio.de

More available books at **www.hansebooks.com**

PUBLIC DOCUMENT. No. 8.

ANNUAL REPORT

OF THE

BOARD OF COMMISSIONERS

OF

SAVINGS BANKS.

1881.

BOSTON:
Rand, Avery, & Co., Printers to the Commonwealth,
117 Franklin Street.
1882.

Commonwealth of Massachusetts.

OFFICE OF THE COMMISSIONERS OF SAVINGS BANKS,
STATE HOUSE, BOSTON, Jan. 4, 1882.

To the Honorable Senate and House of Representatives.

THE Commissioners of Savings Banks respectfully present their Sixth Annual Report for the consideration of the Legislature.

The number of savings banks now doing business in the Commonwealth is one hundred and sixty-five, one more than last year.

The Brockton Savings Bank of Brockton, which was incorporated by the last Legislature, commenced business in May last, under favorable circumstances. The bank supplies an urgent need in this large manufacturing community, which had been deprived of the facilities of a savings bank since the failure of the North Bridgewater Savings Bank, in 1877.

There are now twelve banks in the hands of receivers. The final dividend of ten per cent has been allowed, by decree of the Supreme Judicial Court, in the West Boston Savings Bank of Boston.

There have been six dividends in all allowed by the Court, amounting to eighty-five per cent of the principal of the deposits.

The final account of the receivers of the Rockport Savings Bank has been presented to the Supreme Judicial Court, and a dividend of about fourteen per cent will probably be allowed, which, with the three previous dividends, will return to the depositors about eighty-four per cent of the principal of their deposits.

The receivers of the Mercantile Savings Institution of Boston and the Hyannis Savings Bank expect to present their final accounts to the Court during the winter. The final dividends to the depositors will probably be payable early in the spring.

The receivers of the remaining eight banks expect to close

up their affairs during this year, should there be a fair market for the sale of real estate.

The officers of the Emigrant Savings Bank, who are closing up its affairs, expect to make the final disposition of its assets during this year, completing the list of fifteen savings banks which will have been wound up, under decrees of the Supreme Judicial Court, since the failures began in 1875. They had nominally assets of $12,271,783.24. The amount due depositors was $11,958,833.42, and the number of depositors was 37,505. The loss to the depositors on the principal of their deposits will be about $1,900,000, calculated upon the basis of the estimates of the amount to be realized from the remaining assets made by the receivers in their last returns.

On the opposite page is a table giving some statistics relative to banks in the hands of receivers.

The Foxborough Savings Bank, which had been subject to the provisions of the Act of 1877, regulating and limiting the payments of deposits, was temporarily enjoined by the Supreme Judicial Court at the expiration of that act, as the officers were not confident that the bank could with safety resume in full. It is the expectation of the officers that the bank will be in condition to resume payment in full before July 1, 1882.

The amount of deposits in the savings banks doing business Oct. 31, 1881, was $230,444,479.10, being $12,396,556.73 more than at the same date of the previous year.

The surplus was $4,890,600.67, showing an increase of $132,-405.79 for the year.

The guaranty fund was $3,341,062.35, which is an increase of $670,909.50 for the year.

The number of open accounts was 738,951, an increase of 32,556 for the year; which would make the average of the accounts $311.85, an increase from the average of the previous year of $3.17.

The amount of deposits during the year was $48,223,496.86, — $5,471,939.43 more than the previous year, and the number of deposits (615,514) increased 82,920. The average of deposits was $78.35. The average the previous year was $80.27, being a decrease of $1.92 for the year. The total of withdrawals was $40,212,786.44, showing an increase of $5,809,358.21 from that of the previous year. The number of withdrawals was 419,959, — 30,184 more than the previous year.

Banks in the Hands of Receivers.

NAME.	Location.	Date of Perpetual Injunction.	Nominal Value of Assets delivered to the Receivers.	Amount due Depositors at Date of Injunction.	Amount of Dividends.	Per Centum.	Balance of Assets in Hands of the Receivers convertible for future Dividends.
Barnstable Savings Bank .	Barnstable .	May 23, 1878,	$1,274,040 81	$1,287,614 04	$901,166 60	70	$212,526 74
Dorchester Savings Bank,*	Boston . .	Feb. 26, 1878,	412,124 27	398,161 65	368,883 87	$92\frac{65}{100}$	–
Hyannis Savings Bank .	Hyannis .	Sept. 3, 1878,	529,058 64	524,617 05	327,885 65	$62\frac{1}{2}$	121,773 85
Lancaster Savings Bank .	Lancaster .	Dec. 30, 1875,	1,030,523 27	973,390 36	517,928 09	$53\frac{1}{3}$	282,988 10
Lexington Savings Bank .	Lexington .	Dec. 13, 1878,	101,209 89	95,222 52	71,416 89	75	31,696 78
Mechanics' Savings Bank,†	Boston . .	Feb. 1, 1877,	421,960 33	428,934 92	309,502 45	$72\frac{1}{5}$	–
Mercantile Inst. for Sav'gs,	Boston . .	Feb. 20, 1878,	3,519,294 70	3,298,390 08	2,143,739 48	65	683,805 51
Needham Savings Bank .	Needham .	March 4, 1879,	23,623 37	23,354 17	17,513 58	75	7,473 19
N. Bridgewater Sav. B'k .	Brockton .	Nov. 13, 1877,	450,840 40‡	551,360 28	441,088 23	80	102,566 49
Reading Savings Bank .	Reading .	April 11, 1879,	113,212 81	155,345 69	42,563 13	$27\frac{1}{2}$	75,806 15§
Rockport Savings Bank † .	Rockport .	Feb. 26, 1878,	194,459 71	182,415 58	127,624 61	$84\frac{7}{10}$	–
Sandwich Savings Bank .	Sandwich .	Jan. 29, 1878,	109,586 22	108,145 35	81,107 81	75	15,822 66
Scituate Savings Bank .	Scituate .	July 9, 1880,	125,486 44	127,261 53	51,251 00	40	71,325 48‖
West Boston Sav. Bank † .	Boston . .	Jan. 9, 1878,	1,939,897 59	1,822,015 83	1,548,713 44	85	–
Totals	. . .	. . . . .	$10,245,318 45	$9,976,229 05	$6,950,384 83	. .	$1,605,784 95

* Final dividend allowed by the Supreme Judicial Court Oct. 1, 1880; the receivers have paid the balance due depositors to the treasurer of the Commonwealth, under provisions of chap. 70 of the Acts of 1881.

† The receivers of these banks are paying the final dividend.

‡ In addition to this amount is the sum of $68,091.84 due from the late treasurer, E. Southworth.

§ This is the balance of assets after paying the dividend of fifteen per cent, Nov. 23, 1881.

‖ This is the balance of assets after paying the dividend of twenty per cent, Nov. 15, 1881.

The average of the withdrawals was $95.75, an increase of $7.49 from the previous year, when it was $88.26.

Investments in United States bonds have increased $1,522,-667.21.

State and municipal bonds have increased $44,895.80. Loans on public funds have decreased $602,003. Investments in bank stock have increased $859,222.18.

Loans on bank stock have increased $108,616.83.

Investments in railroad bonds have increased $790,852.33.

Loans on mortgages of real estate have increased $86,083.81, and $1,169,894.92 have been deducted from real estate acquired by foreclosure, which is $8,052,450.79.

Loans on personal security have increased $17,612,461.20. The deposits in banks bearing interest are $11,770,415.27, a decrease from the previous year of $4,486,361.71.

The percentage of assets in the various classes of investments is about seventeen and one-sixth per cent in public funds, and loans on public funds; ten and eighty-six one-hundredths per cent in bank stock, and loans on same; three and twenty-six one-hundredths per cent in railroad bonds; thirty-four and one-half per cent in loans on mortgages of real estate; four and forty-three one-hundredths per cent invested in real estate, including foreclosures; twenty and twenty-three one-hundredths per cent in loans on personal security; three and sixty-three one-hundredths per cent in loans to counties, cities, and towns; four and ninety-two one-hundredths per cent in deposits in banks on interest.

The earnings of the banks were $12,285,345.35, — $390,634.75 more than the previous year. The amount of dividends was $8,293,774.37, an increase of $335,887.28.

Seven banks paid the highest rate of dividend of interest allowed, — five per cent; thirty-two banks paid dividends between four and five per cent; one hundred and ten banks paid four per cent dividends; four banks paid three and three-fourths per cent dividends; three banks paid three and one-half per cent dividends; four banks paid three per cent dividends; two banks paid one dividend of two per cent; three banks paid no dividend of interest, but of these, two were temporarily enjoined by decrees of the Supreme Judicial Court, and the other was organized during the previous year.

The average rate of ordinary dividends was four per cent.

The previous year the average was three and ninety-three one-hundredths per cent. The slight increase of seven one-hundredths of one per cent in the average of dividends is due mainly to the fact that all the banks but one which had been temporarily enjoined were relieved from injunction, and have resumed the payment of ordinary dividends of interest.

The large increase in deposits, while it indicates the complete restoration of the public confidence in savings banks, embarrasses many of them with a surplus of money seeking investment at a time when securities which they are authorized to hold command high premiums.

The last Legislature increased the classes of securities in which investments might be made; but as yet the relief has been small. In our opinion, as suggested in our last Annual Report, the most effectual remedy for this embarrassment is to be found in the refusal of the banks to receive large deposits from persons not properly beneficiaries of these institutions.

Three years ago we called the attention of the Legislature to the doubtful character of the shares of national banks as an investment of the deposits of savings banks, on account of the liability of stockholders, in case of loss, to assessments amounting to one hundred per cent of the par value of the stock; also to the difficulty of convertibility in times of stress, as they were based upon commercial or personal credits, which are liable to be seriously affected by financial disturbances.

Recent events have confirmed us more strongly in this opinion; and, if authority to invest in these stocks is to be continued, we recommend that investments be limited to one-quarter of the deposits of any one bank.

Loan and Trust Companies.

There are now six loan and trust companies doing business in the Commonwealth.

One, the American Loan and Trust Company of Boston, was chartered by the last Legislature, and commenced business in May last, with a paid-up capital of one million dollars.

The trust departments of these institutions are of minor importance. Only three of them have opened such departments, and in only one of them does there appear to be much interest exhibited by the management in extending this class of business.

The business of these institutions is generally such as banks, bankers, or merchandise-brokers ordinarily pursue.

We respectfully renew the recommendation made in our last Annual Report, that a general law be enacted granting the same powers and privileges to each and all of them, and subjecting them to the same duties, liabilities, and limitations.

The last Legislature, in amending the charter of the Massachusetts Hospital Life Insurance Company, made it the duty of the Commissioners of Savings Banks to examine into its affairs, once in each year at least.

It also required an annual return of its affairs to be made by the institution to the Commissioners. The return for last year is published in this Report with the returns of the loan and trust companies.

At the official examination we found its affairs to be in good condition, and prudently managed.

This venerable institution, incorporated Feb. 24, 1818, is more essentially a trust company than any other of these corporations. $14,717,391.76 of its assets were invested in trust for beneficiaries, to whom it now pays four per cent income per annum. In the past, when higher rates of interest were obtainable, it paid larger rates.

It has also during its existence paid to the Massachusetts General Hospital more than $400,000, in accordance with a provision of its charter, that it shall pay one-third part of its net profits to said institution.

The original charter required an annual return to be made to the Secretary of State. As there appears to be no necessity for two returns, we recommend that the provision of the act requiring a return to be made annually to the Secretary of State be repealed.

Co-operative Saving Fund and Loan Associations.

There are now eighteen of these associations doing business in the Commonwealth, an increase of two during the fiscal year, — the West Roxbury Association of Boston, incorporated July 1, 1881, and the New Bedford Association, incorporated July 8, 1881.

The assets of all the associations have risen during the year from $372,462.31 to $653,142.80, an increase of $280,680.49, which indicates a marked degree of prosperity.

NAME.	Location.	Date of Incorporation.	Number of Shares now in Force.	Present Number of Members.	Present Number of Borrowers.	Assets.	Increase of Assets from Previous Year.
Cambridge	East Cambridge	Sept. 5, 1877,	296	50	14	$6,285 19	$1,265 22
Campello	Brockton	Oct. 3, 1877,	1,982	412	72	62,212 66	18,173 52
Equitable	Lynn	Oct. 2, 1877,	752	176	26	14,542 82	5,817 66
Fitchburg	Fitchburg	Oct. 27, 1877,	2,124	282	78	54,982 26	21,795 73
Haverhill	Haverhill	Aug. 20, 1877,	1,034	255	31	22,984 80	7,576 11
Holyoke	Holyoke	July 24, 1880,	717	120	4	8,423 32	7,199 58
Homestead	Boston	Sept. 11, 1877,	3,133	600	66	58,909 17	23,732 09
Mechanics'	Taunton	Sept. 14, 1877,	3,065	481	105	76,807 30	14,526 58
New Bedford	New Bedford	July 8, 1881,	826	137	5	2,795 74	2,795 74
Pioneer	Boston	July 26, 1877,	4,037	794	96	93,579 43	30,336 01
Security	Brockton	Dec. 17, 1877,	1,602	324	53	49,876 02	14,790 74
Somerville	Somerville	May 4, 1880,	728	174	7	8,789 51	7,428 13
Taunton	Taunton	March 2, 1880.	2,969	480	44	53,332 54	32,186 64
Troy	Fall River	July 10, 1880,	2,252	434	21	23,512 55	20,087 76
Waltham	Waltham	Oct. 13, 1880,	3,365	474	26	35,315 81	33,054 81
West Roxbury	Boston	Feb. 1, 1881,	452	109	3	2,587 52	2,587 52
Worcester	Worcester	Oct. 19, 1877,	2,637	479	68	59,182 15	23,805 41
Workingmen's	Boston	June 9, 1880,	1,574	284	12	19,024 01	13,521 24
Totals			33,545	6,065	731	$653,142 80	$280,680 49

The last Legislature amended the general law relative to these associations in several of its sections, so as to make the investments more secure, and the division of the profits more equitable.

On the preceding page is a table showing the general condition of each association.

Following these remarks may be found the Public Statutes relative to Savings Banks.

Respectfully submitted.

J. GATCHELL,
C. CURRY,
Commissioners of Savings Banks.

[P. S., Chapter 116.]

OF SAVINGS BANKS AND INSTITUTIONS FOR SAVINGS.

COMMISSIONERS OF SAVINGS BANKS.

Appointment and tenure of office of board. 1866, 192, §§ 1, 2. 1876, 231, §§ 1-3.

SECTION 1. The board of commissioners of savings banks shall consist of two commissioners appointed by the governor with the advice and consent of the council, and subject to removal in like manner, each of whom shall be sworn, and shall hold office for the term of three years unless sooner removed. Upon the occurrence of a vacancy before the expiration of a term, an appointment shall be made for the remainder of the term.

Compensation and allowances. 1879, 124, § 1. 1879, 293, § 3. 1880, 161, § 5.

SECT. 2. The annual salary of each of said commissioners shall be two thousand eight hundred dollars; and the board shall be allowed a sum not exceeding one thousand six hundred dollars a year for clerical assistance, and also the actual expenses incurred in travelling in the discharge of its official duties.

The board to visit and examine every bank annually. 1866, 192, § 2. 1876, 231, § 3.

SECT. 3. The commissioners shall visit once in every year, and as much oftener as they deem expedient, every savings bank and institution for savings incorporated by authority of this commonwealth. At such visits they shall have free access to the vaults, books, and papers, and shall thoroughly inspect and examine all the affairs of each of said corporations, and make such inquiries as may be necessary to ascertain its condition and ability to fulfil all its engagements, and whether it has complied with the provisions of law. They shall preserve in a permanent form a full record of their proceedings, including a statement of the condition of each of said corporations.

may summon and examine officers, etc.; penalty for refusing to obey summons, or obstructing commissioner. 1866, 192, § 3. 1876, 231, § 3.

SECT. 4. Either of the commissioners may summon all trustees, officers, or agents of any such corporation, and such other witnesses as he thinks proper, in relation to the affairs, transactions, and condition of the corporation, and for that purpose may administer oaths; and whoever refuses, without justifiable cause, to appear and testify when thereto required, or obstructs a commissioner in the discharge of his duty, shall be punished by fine not exceeding one thousand dollars, or imprisonment not exceeding one year.

The board shall examine bank on request of five officers or creditors, etc. 1866, 192, § 4. 1876, 231, § 3.

SECT. 5. Upon the certificate under oath of any five or more officers, trustees, creditors, or depositors of any such corporation, setting forth their interest and the reasons for making such examination, directed to the commissioners and requesting them to examine such corporation, they shall forthwith make a full investigation of its affairs in the manner before provided.

proceedings by, when bank insolvent, or in

SECT. 6. The commissioners, if upon such examination any such corporation appears to be insolvent, or its condition such as to render its further proceeding hazardous to the public or to those having funds in his custody, shall apply, or, if such corporation appears to have exceeded its powers or failed to comply with any rule, restriction, or condition provided by law, they may apply to a justice of the supreme judicial court to issue an injunction restraining such corporation in whole or in part from further proceeding with its business until a hearing can be had. Such justice may, with or without previous notice, issue such injunction, and, after a full hearing, may dissolve or modify it or make it perpetual, and may make such orders and decrees according to the course of proceedings in equity to restrain or prohibit the further prosecution of the business of the corporation as may be needful in the premises; and may appoint one or more receivers to take possession of its property and effects, subject to such directions as may from time to time be prescribed by the court or a justice thereof.

a hazardous condition. 1866, 192, § 5. 1876, 231, § 3.

SECT. 7. When receivers are so appointed, the treasurer of the corporation shall make a schedule of all its property; and its treasurer, board of investment, and other officers transferring its property to the receivers shall make oath that said schedule sets forth all the property which the corporation owns or is entitled to. The treasurer shall deliver said schedule to the receivers and a copy thereof to the commissioners, who may at any time examine under oath such treasurer, board of investment, or other officers, in order to determine whether or not all the property which the corporation owns or is entitled to has been transferred to the receivers.

Schedule of effects to be made, sworn to, and delivered to receivers. Officers may be examined under oath. 1878, 253, § 5.

SECT. 8. The commissioners, or one of them, shall at least once in every year, and as much oftener as they deem expedient, examine the accounts and doings of all such receivers; and shall carefully examine and report upon all accounts and reports of receivers made to the supreme judicial court and referred to the commissioners by the court; and, for the purposes of this section, shall have free access to the books and papers relating to the transactions of such receivers, and may examine them under oath relative to such transactions.

Commissioners to examine the accounts, etc., of receivers. 1878, 253, §§ 1, 2, 3.

SECT. 9. The commissioners, if in their opinion any such corporation or its officers or trustees have violated any law in relation to savings banks or institutions for savings, shall forthwith report the same, with such remarks as they deem expedient, to the attorney-general, who shall forthwith institute a prosecution for such violation, in behalf of the commonwealth.

to report violations of law. 1866, 192, § 7. 1876, 231, § 3. 1878, 253, § 6.

SECT. 10. The commissioners, whenever in their opinion any such receiver has violated his duty, shall present the facts to the supreme judicial court.

to report violations of law by receivers. 1878, 253, § 4

SAVINGS BANKS AND INSTITUTIONS FOR SAVINGS.

Savings banks and institutions for savings, powers and duties of. 1876, 203, § 1.

SECT. 11. All savings banks or institutions for savings, incorporated under the authority of this commonwealth, may exercise the powers, and shall be governed by the rules, and subject to the duties, liabilities, and provisions, contained in the following sections, so far as the same are consistent with the provisions of their respective charters; and any such corporation may, by vote at its annual meeting or at a meeting called for the purpose, accept any provision of said sections which is inconsistent with its charter.

Power of general court over same. Penalty for obstructing investigation. G. S. 57, §§ 102, 103, 155. 1876, 203, § 27.

SECT. 12. The general court may make other or further regulations for the government of such corporations, or may take away their corporate powers; and every such corporation and its officers shall be subject to examination by any committee of the general court appointed for the purpose, who may examine into the doings of the corporation, and shall have free access to its books and vaults. An officer of such corporation, or other person having charge of its books and property, who refuses or neglects to exhibit them to such committee, or who in any way obstructs its examination thereof, shall be punished by fine not exceeding ten thousand dollars, or imprisonment not exceeding three years.

OFFICERS AND MEETINGS.

Officers of such corporations. 1876, 203, §§ 2, 3.

SECT. 13. The officers of every such corporation shall consist of a president, one or more vice-presidents, a board of not less than nine trustees, a treasurer, clerk, and such other officers as it may find necessary for the management of its affairs. The president, vice-presidents, and trustees shall be chosen from the members, and no person shall hold any office in two such corporations at the same time. Such officers shall be sworn, and shall hold their several offices until others are chosen and qualified in their stead, except in the cases hereinafter provided otherwise.

Treasurer's bond, and duty of trustees and board concerning same. 1876, 203, § 3, 1880, 162.

SECT. 14. The treasurer shall give bond for the faithful discharge of his duties to the satisfaction of the trustees, and they shall file a copy of the bond with the commissioners, and shall notify them of any change thereafter made therein. The commissioners shall keep a record showing when said bonds expire and the changes so notified, and, whenever in their judgment it is necessary for the security of the depositors, shall require a new bond, in such amount and with such sureties as they may approve.

SECT. 15. The officers of every such corporation, except the treasurer, shall be chosen at its annual meetings, to be holden at such time as the by-laws direct, any thing in its charter to the contrary notwithstanding. The treasurer shall be appointed by the trustees, and shall hold his office during their pleasure. If an office becomes vacant during the year, the trustees may appoint a person to fill the same until it is filled at the next annual meeting; and if a person chosen or appointed does not within thirty days thereafter take the oath, his office shall thereupon become vacant. The person acting as clerk at such meeting shall, within ten days thereafter, notify all persons elected to an office, and within thirty days thereafter shall publish in some newspaper published within the county a list of all persons who have taken the oath of office to which they were elected. A clerk neglecting to make such notification or publication, or making a false publication, and any person who knowingly publishes or circulates, or knowingly causes to be published or circulated, a printed notice containing the name of a person as an officer of any such corporation who has not taken the oath of office, shall be liable to a penalty of fifty dollars.

Choice and appointment of officers. Vacancies. Not taking oath, to vacate office. Clerk to notify persons elected, and publish list. Penalty. 1876, 203, § 4.

SECT. 16. Every such corporation may at any time hold special meetings by order of its trustees; and its treasurer shall also notify special meetings upon the requisition in writing of any ten members of the corporation. Notice of all meetings shall be given by public advertisement in some newspaper of the county where the corporation is established, or by seasonably mailing to each member a written or printed notice of such meeting.

Special meetings, how called and notified. 1876, 203, § 5.

SECT. 17. Every such corporation may, at a legal meeting, elect by ballot any citizen of this commonwealth to be a member thereof; and any person may, at an annual meeting, cease to be a member, if he has filed with the treasurer a written notice of his intention so to do three months at least before such meeting. No person shall continue to be a member after removing from the commonwealth.

Members of the corporation. 1876, 203, § 6.

SECT. 18. A regular meeting of the board of trustees of every such corporation shall be held as often as once in three months, for the purpose of receiving the report of its treasurer, and for the transaction of other business. A quorum shall consist of not less than seven trustees, but less than a quorum may adjourn from time to time or until the next regular meeting. At each regular meeting the trustees shall cause to be prepared a statement showing the condition of the corporation as it appears upon its books, in the form of a trial-balance of its

Regular meetings of trustees to be held once in three months. Quorum. Statement of condition of bank. Record of each meeting, and names of trustees present. Office of trustee, how vacated, and proceedings thereon. 1876, 203, § 7.

accounts, and such statement shall be posted in a conspicuous place in its banking-room, and there remain until the next regular meeting of said board. A record shall be made at each meeting of the transactions of the trustees and the names of those present. If a trustee fails to attend the regular meetings of the board, or to perform any of the duties devolved upon him as such trustee, for six consecutive months, his office shall thereupon become vacant. A record of such vacancy shall be entered upon the books of the corporation, and a transcript of such record shall be sent by mail to the person whose office is thus made vacant.

DEPOSITS, LOANS, AND INVESTMENTS.

Limit to amount of deposits from any person, and interest. 1876, 203, § 8.

SECT. 19. Every such corporation may receive deposits from any person until they amount to one thousand dollars; and may allow interest upon such deposits, and upon the interest accumulated thereon, until the principal, with the accrued interest, amounts to sixteen hundred dollars; and thereafter upon no greater sum than sixteen hundred dollars; but the limitations contained in this section shall not apply to deposits by religious or charitable corporations.

Deposits, etc., how invested. 1876, 203, § 9.

SECT. 20. Deposits and the income derived therefrom shall be invested only as follows: —

First mortgages of real estate. 1876, 203, § 9, cl. 1.

First, On first mortgages of real estate, situated in this commonwealth, to an amount not to exceed sixty per cent of the valuation of such real estate: but not exceeding seventy per cent of the whole amount of deposits shall be so invested; and no loan on mortgage shall be made except upon the report of not less than two members of the board of investment, who shall certify to the value of the premises to be mortgaged, according to their best judgment, and such report shall be filed and preserved with the records of the corporation.

Public funds. 1872, 203, § 9, cl. 3. 1880, 177, § 1. 1881, 214, § 2.

Second, In the public funds of the United States, of any of the New England states, or of the state of New York, in the bonds or notes of any city, county, or town of this commonwealth, or of any city of the states of Maine, New Hampshire, Vermont, Rhode Island, or Connecticut, whose net indebtedness does not exceed five per cent of the last preceding valuation of the property therein, for the assessment of taxes; or of any county or town thereof whose net indebtedness does not exceed three per cent of such valuation; or in the notes of any citizen of this commonwealth, with a pledge of any of the aforesaid securities at no more than the par value thereof.

Third, In the first mortgage bonds of any railroad company incorporated under the authority of any of the New England states and whose road is located wholly or in part in the same, and which is in possession of and operating its own road, and has earned and paid regular dividends for the two years next preceding such investment; or in the first mortgage bonds, guaranteed by any such railroad company, of any railroad company so incorporated whose road is thus located; or in the bonds or notes of any railroad company incorporated under the laws of this commonwealth, and whose road is located wholly or in part therein, and is unencumbered by mortgage, and which has paid a dividend of not less than five per cent per annum for two years next preceding such investment; or in the notes of any citizen of this commonwealth, with a pledge as collateral of any of the aforesaid securities at no more than eighty per cent of the par value thereof; but street railway companies shall not be considered railroad companies within the meaning of this section. Railroad bonds. 1881, 214, §§ 1, 4.

Fourth, In the stock of any bank incorporated under the authority of this commonwealth, or the stock of any banking association located in the New England states, and incorporated under the authority of the United States, or on the notes of any citizen of this commonwealth, with a pledge as collateral of any of the aforesaid securities at no more than eighty per cent of the market value and not exceeding the par value thereof: *provided*, that such corporation shall not hold, both by way of investment and as security for loans, more than one-quarter of the capital stock of any one bank or banking association, nor invest more than ten per cent of its deposits, nor more than one hundred thousand dollars, in the capital stock of any one such bank or association. Savings banks may deposit sums not to exceed twenty per cent of the amount of their deposits, on call, in such banks or banking associations, or in any trust company incorporated under the laws of this commonwealth which provides the same security as banking associations incorporated under the authority of the United States, and may receive interest for the same. Bank stocks, and deposits in banks, etc. 1876, 203, § 9, cl. 4. 1881, 214, § 3.

Fifth, In loans upon the personal notes of the depositors of the corporation, but not exceeding one-half of the amount of his deposit to a depositor; and in each such case the deposit and the book of the depositor shall be held by the corporation as collateral security for the payment of such loan. Loans to depositors. 1879, 57, § 1.

Sixth, If such deposits and income cannot be conveniently invested in the modes hereinbefore prescribed, not exceeding Personal securities. 1876, 203, § 9, cl. 5.

one-third part thereof may be invested in bonds or other personal securities, payable at a time not exceeding one year, with at least two sureties, if the principal and sureties are all citizens of this commonwealth and resident therein.

Corporation building and site. 1876, 203, § 9, cl. 6.

Seventh, Ten per cent of the deposits of any such corporation, but not exceeding two hundred thousand dollars, may be invested in the purchase of a suitable site and the erection or preparation of a suitable building for the convenient transaction of its business.

Real estate acquired by foreclosure, etc. 1876, 203, § 26. See c. 13, § 20.

Eighth, Any such corporation may hold real estate acquired by the foreclosure of any mortgage owned by it, or by purchase at sales made under the provisions of any such mortgage, or upon judgments for debts due it, or in settlements effected to secure such debts; but all such real estate shall be sold by it within five years after the title thereto is vested in the corporation.

Pledges of securities as collateral to remain valid. 1876, 203, § 30. 1878, 94, § 1.

Ninth, The provisions of this chapter shall not be construed to invalidate or in any manner impair the title of any corporation to any securities which have been or may be held by it in pledge or as security for a loan or indebtedness; and the same shall be held for the purposes for which they were pledged; and nothing herein contained shall require any such corporation to change any of its investments made before the first day of October in the year eighteen hundred and seventy-six.

No officer, etc., to borrow the funds of the corporation, or become surety. 1876, 203, § 10.

SECT. 21. No member of a committee or board of investment, or officer of such corporation charged with the duty of investing its funds, shall borrow or use any portion thereof, be surety for loans to others, or in any manner, directly or indirectly, be an obligor for money borrowed of the corporation; and if such member or officer becomes the owner of real estate upon which a mortgage is held by the corporation, his office shall become vacant at the expiration of sixty days thereafter, unless he has ceased to be the owner thereof, or has caused said mortgage to be discharged. Only one of the persons holding the offices of president, clerk, and treasurer shall at the same time be a member of the investing committee.

Savings banks, etc., not to receive brokerage, etc., on acount of a loan. Penalties. 1876, 203, § 11.

SECT. 22. No such corporation, nor any person acting in its behalf, shall negotiate, take, or receive a fee, brokerage, commission, gift, or other consideration for or on account of a loan made by or on behalf of such corporation, other than appears on the face of the note or contract by which such loan purports to be made; but nothing herein contained shall apply to any reasonable charge for services in the examination of titles and preparation of conveyances to such corporation as security for its loans. Whoever violates a provision of this section shall be punished by fine of not less than one hundred nor more than one thousand dollars. All sums paid for services, fees, or otherwise to a member of the board of trustees shall be reported in detail at each regular meeting of the trustees.

SECT. 23. All applications for loans shall be made in writing, through the treasurer of the corporation, who shall keep a record thereof, showing the date, name of applicant, amount asked for, and the security offered, and he shall cause the same to be presented to the board of investment.

Applications for loans to be in writing, and record kept. 1876, 203, § 12.

DIVIDENDS AND PAYMENTS.

SECT. 24. Every such corporation shall, at the time of making each semi-annual dividend, reserve as a guaranty fund, from the net profits which have accumulated during the six months then next preceding, not less than one-eighth nor more than one-fourth of one per cent of the whole amount of deposits, until such fund amounts to five per cent of the whole amount of deposits, which fund shall be thereafter maintained and held to meet losses in its business from depreciation of its securities, or otherwise.

Guaranty fund to be created and maintained. 1876, 203, § 13.

SECT. 25. The income or profit of every such corporation, after a deduction of all reasonable expenses incurred in the management thereof and the guaranty fund, shall be divided among its depositors or their legal representatives at times fixed by its by-laws in the following manner: Ordinary dividends shall be made every six months, and shall not exceed two and one-half per cent on all sums which have been on deposit for six months preceding, or one and one-fourth per cent on all sums which have been on deposit for three months preceding; and no ordinary dividend shall be declared or paid except as above provided, nor upon a deposit of less than three months' standing; and any such corporation may, by its by-laws, provide that no dividends shall be declared or paid on a less sum than three dollars, or on the fractional part of a dollar.

Net profit to be divided among depositors, and in what manner. 1876, 203, § 14.

SECT. 26. If, at the time provided by the by-laws for making ordinary dividends, the net profits for the six months preceding, over and above the sum to be added to the guaranty fund, do not amount to one and one-half per cent of the deposits, no dividend of the profits shall be declared or paid, except such as shall be approved in writing by the commissioners.

Dividend not to be paid unless net profits are one and one-half per cent, except, etc. 1876, 203, § 15. 1880, 150.

SECT. 27. Once in every term of three years, if the net profits accumulated over and above said guaranty fund and dividends amount to one per cent of the deposits which have

Extra dividends may be paid once in every three years, when, etc. 1876, 203, § 16.

remained in such corporation for one year then next preceding, such net profits shall be divided among the depositors whose deposits have remained therein for one year at least then next preceding, in proportion to the amount of dividends which have been declared on their deposits during the three years then next preceding.

No dividend to be declared or paid, until, etc. 1876, 203, § 17.

SECT. 28. No dividend shall be declared until the trustees cause an examination to be made, and find that the amount thereof has actually accrued; and no dividend or interest shall be paid unless authorized by a vote of the trustees after such examination.

Deposits, how withdrawn. Payments to minors. 1876, 203, § 18. 127 Mass. 183.

SECT. 29. The principal deposits in such corporations may be withdrawn at such time and in such manner as the by-laws direct, but the deposits so withdrawn shall be deducted in each case from the amounts last deposited. Money deposited in the name of a minor may, at the discretion of the trustees or committee of investment, be paid to such minor or to the person making such deposit; and the same shall be a valid payment.

Depositor may set off the amount of his deposit in proceedings by the corporation. 1878, 201, § 1.

SECT. 30. A person indebted to any such corporation, whether his indebtedness is secured or not, may, in any proceeding for the collection thereof or for the enforcement of any security therefor, set off the amount of a deposit held and owned by him at the time of the commencement of such proceeding, and of the interest due thereon, except a deposit purchased or acquired from another after the commencement of proceedings in equity to restrain the corporation from doing its usual business.

When deposits are claimed by a person other than plaintiff, claimants may be made defendants, etc. Deposits may remain or be paid into court, etc. 1876, 203, § 19. 1877, 179.

SECT. 31. In actions against any such corporation for money on deposit therewith, if it appears that the same fund is claimed by another party than the plaintiff, whether by the husband or wife of such plaintiff, or otherwise, the court in which such action is pending, on the petition of the corporation and on such notice as the court considers proper to the plaintiff and to such claimants, may order the proceedings to be amended by making such claimants parties defendant thereto; and thereupon the rights and interests of the several parties in and to said funds shall be heard and determined. Such deposits may remain with the corporation until final judgment, and shall be paid in accordance with the order of the court, or may be paid into court to await final judgment; and, when so paid into court, the corporation shall be stricken out as a party to the action, and its liability for such deposit shall cease. The taxable costs of the corporation in such actions shall be in the discretion of the court, and may be charged upon the fund.

SECT. 32. When a deposit is made in such corporation by any one in trust for another, the name and residence of the person for whom it is made shall be disclosed, and it shall be credited to the depositor as trustee for such person; and if no other notice of the existence and terms of a trust has been given in writing to the corporation, in the event of the death of the trustee, the deposit with the interest thereon may be paid to the person for whom such deposit was made, or to his legal representative.

When a deposit is made in trust, name, etc., of person for whom made, to be disclosed; to whom payable in case of death. 1876, 203, § 20.

SECT. 33. The treasurer of every such corporation, upon making up each semi-annual dividend, shall send written notice by mail to each depositor who for six months then next preceding has not been entitled to a dividend on the whole amount standing to his credit, because the same exceeds the amount on which interest is allowed, specifying the amount not entitled to dividend.

Depositor to be notified when amount entitled to dividend is exceeded. 1876, 203, § 21.

SECT. 34. Every such corporation shall once in five years publish, in some newspaper of the county where it is established, a list of the amounts standing to the credit of depositors who have not been entitled to dividends on the whole amounts standing to their credit for two years then next preceding, because the same exceed the amount on which interest is allowed, with the names and last known residences of the persons to whose credit such amounts stand; which publication shall be continued in three successive papers.

List of amounts due depositors not entitled to dividend to be published once in five years. 1876, 203, § 22.

SPECIAL TRUST FUNDS.

SECT. 35. Any such corporation may receive on deposit to any amount funds in trust for the purpose of setting out shade-trees in streets and parks, and improving the same; for purchasing land for parks, and improving the same; for maintaining cemeteries or cemetery lots; and for erecting and maintaining drinking fountains in public places, or for any or all of said purposes. Such funds shall be placed on interest in such corporation, and the interest and dividends arising therefrom shall be paid semi-annually to such city, town, or cemetery authorities as may be designated by the donors of said funds or the will of the person bequeathing the same, and shall be expended by such authorities within their respective cities, towns, or cemeteries for any or all of said purposes, as may be specified by such donors or such will. No part of the principal of such funds shall be withdrawn or expended, and the same shall be exempt from attachment or levy on execution.

Funds in trust for parks, shade-trees, cemeteries, and drinking fountains. Principal not to be withdrawn, and to be exempt from attachment. 1875, 174, § 1.

Probate court may authorize executors, etc., to deposit funds in trust for such purposes. 1877, 162.

SECT. 36. A judge of the probate court, after due notice and a hearing, if in his judgment it is expedient so to do, may authorize an executor, administrator, or trustee holding money or other personal property for any of the purposes mentioned in the preceding section, to deposit such moneys or the avails arising from such personal property in any such corporation designated by the judge, to be held by it in the manner and for the uses and purposes mentioned in said section, and upon the trusts upon which said executor, administrator, or trustee held the same; and upon the deposit of such money and its receipt and acceptance by such corporation, the said executor, administrator, or trustee shall be discharged from further care and responsibility therefor.

Statement of the amount thereof to be made every third year, etc. 1875, 174, § 2.

SECT. 37. The funds held in accordance with the two preceding sections shall be known as the "Shade-Tree and Cemetery Fund," and the treasurer of the corporation in which they are deposited shall give a certificate of gift to each donor of such funds. and shall send by mail or deliver in the month of January in every third year after the first deposit, to the mayor of any city or the chairman of the selectmen of any town within the limits of which the interests and dividends of any such fund are to be expended, a written statement, signed by such treasurer, of the amount of funds on deposit for the purposes aforesaid, which statement shall be recorded in the office of the clerk of such city or town.

If the corporation ceases to do business, these funds to be deposited in another. 1875, 174, § 3.

SECT. 38. If a corporation holding such funds surrenders its charter or ceases to do business, the supreme judicial court may order said funds to be transferred and deposited in some other such corporation upon the same trusts as aforesaid; and if the laws authorizing such corporations are repealed, the court may order said funds to be transferred and deposited in such banking institution as it may deem proper, to be held upon the trusts aforesaid.

BOOKS AND RETURNS.

Board may prescribe manner of keeping and auditing books, etc. 1880, 228, § 1.

SECT. 39. The commissioners may prescribe the manner and form of keeping and auditing the books and accounts of any such corporation.

Treasurer to make annual report to board. Particulars to be stated in same. 1876, 203, § 23. 1877, 159.

SECT. 40. The treasurer of every such corporation shall annually within fifteen days after the last business day of October make a report to the commissioners, showing accurately the condition thereof at the close of business on said day. The report shall be in such form as the commissioners shall prescribe, and shall specify the following particulars: namely,

Name of corporation, and number of corporators; place where located; amount of deposits; amount of each item of other liability; public funds, including all United States, state, county, city, and town bonds, stating each particular kind, the par value, estimated market value, and amount invested in each; loans on public funds, stating amount on each; bank stock, stating par value, estimated market value, and amount invested in each; loans on bank stock, stating amount on each; railroad bonds, stating par value, estimated market value, and amount invested in each; loans on railroad bonds, stating amount on each; estimated value of real estate, and amount invested therein; loans on mortgage of real estate; loans to counties, cities, or towns; loans on personal security; cash on deposit in banks, with the names of such banks, and the amount deposited in each; cash on hand; the whole amount of interest or profits received or earned, and the rate and amount of each semi-annual dividend for the previous year; the times for dividends fixed by the by-laws; the average annual per cent of dividends for the term ending at the time of and including the last extra dividend; the rates of interest received on loans; the total amount of loans bearing each specified rate of interest; the number of outstanding loans which are of an amount not exceeding three thousand dollars each, and the aggregate amount of the same; the number of open accounts; also the number and amount of deposits received; the number of deposits received of three hundred dollars or more at one time; the number and amount of withdrawals; the number of accounts opened, and the number of accounts closed, severally, for the previous year; and the annual expenses of the corporation; all of which shall be certified and sworn to by the treasurer. And five or more of the trustees shall certify and make oath that the report is correct according to their best knowledge and belief.

Additional statements may be required by the board. 1880, 228, § 2.

SECT. 41. Such annual reports shall also, when so required by the commissioners, state the number and amount of open accounts of fifty dollars and less, of those exceeding fifty dollars and not more than one hundred dollars, of those exceeding one hundred dollars and not more than two hundred dollars, of those exceeding two hundred dollars and not more than five hundred dollars, of those of one thousand dollars or more; and of those to the credit of women, both adult and minor, guardians, religious and charitable associations, and in trust, respectively.

Blank forms of reports to be furnished.

SECT. 42. The commissioners shall furnish blank forms of reports to every such corporation, and shall prepare annually

Commissioners to report to the general court. 1866, 192, § 6. 1876, 203, § 24. 1878, 253, § 2.

from such reports, and communicate to the general court on or before the first Wednesday in January, a statement of the condition of each corporation from which a report has been received for the preceding year, and shall include therein a statement of the affairs of such corporations in the hands of receivers, and shall make such suggestions as they may deem expedient relative to the general conduct and condition of each of the corporations visited by them.

Treasurer to inform overseers of poor of deposits to the credit of a pauper. 1876, 203, § 25.

SECT. 43. The treasurer of every such corporation shall, upon a written request signed by an overseer of the poor of a city or town, inform him of the amount, if any, deposited in the corporation to the credit of any person named in such request, who is a charge upon the commonwealth or upon a city or town therein as a pauper; and a treasurer who unreasonably refuses to give such information, or wilfully renders false information, shall forfeit fifty dollars for every such offence, to the use of the city or town upon which such pauper is a charge, or to the commonwealth if the pauper is a charge upon the commonwealth.

Receivers to deposit unclaimed moneys, etc., with treasurer. 1881, 70.

SECT. 44. Receivers of any savings bank or institution for savings having unclaimed moneys or dividends remaining in their hands for one year after final settlement ordered by the court shall deposit the same, with a schedule of the names and residences so far as known of the parties entitled thereto, with the treasurer of the commonwealth, who shall receive and hold the same in trust, and pay over the same to such parties or their representatives, upon proper demand made therefor, and upon evidence satisfactory to him of the identity of the claimant and the justice of the claim.

ABSTRACT OF ANNUAL REPORTS

OF THE

SAVINGS BANKS, TRUST COMPANIES, AND CO-OPERATIVE SAVING-FUND AND LOAN ASSOCIATIONS,

SHOWING THEIR

CONDITION AT THE CLOSE OF BUSINESS ON THE 31st OF OCTOBER, 1881.

ABINGTON SAVINGS BANK — ABINGTON.

Incorporated 1853. Number of corporators, 53.

N. WHITMARSH, *President*. *Treasurer*, JUDSON N. FARRAR.

STATEMENT.

LIABILITIES.		ASSETS.	
Deposits	$982,723 36	Public funds	$98,062 50
Earnings undivided	20,166 98	Bank stock	149,282 87
Guaranty fund	11,250 00	Loans on bank stock	4,100 00
		Railroad bonds	45,061 08
		Real estate by foreclosure	2,549 91
		Loans on real estate	609,419 11
		Loans on personal security,	56,506 89
		Loans to counties, cities, or towns	12,200 00
		Deposit in bank on interest,	35,512 80
		Expense account	23 08
		Suspense account	353 47
		Individual tax	21 45
		Cash on hand	447 18
	$1,014,140 34		$1,014,140 34

Loans on Bank Stock: —

On 61 shares Abington National Bank . . . $4,100 00

Cash on Deposit in Bank: —

Abington National Bank $35,512 80

Amount of real estate held by foreclosure . . $2,549 91

Assessed value of the same 2,350 00

Amount of income received from the same . . 108 00

Amount of municipal tax on real estate . . . 36 00

Whole amount of interest or profits received or earned . . . $57,392 18

Rate and amount of each semi-annual dividend for previous year . . . 2¼ per cent . 19,900 81; 2¼ per cent . 20,917 68

Times for the dividends fixed by the by-laws: first Tuesday in April and October.

Average annual per cent of dividends for the term ending at time of and including last extra dividend: 7½ per cent.

The total amount of loans, with each specified rate of interest: $139,700, 5 per cent; $5,000, 5½ per cent; $573,426, 6 per cent.

Number of outstanding loans which are of an amount not exceeding $3,000 each 439

Aggregate amount of the same 396,001 00

Number of open accounts 2,666

Number and amount of deposits received for previous year, 1,487 176,692 88

Number and amount of deposits of and exceeding $300 at any one time for the previous year 160 89,639 05

Number and amount of withdrawals. 1,140 123,533 41

Number of accounts opened the previous year 429

Number of accounts closed the previous year 225

Amount of expenses of the corporation during previous year . 1,025 87

Amount of treasurer's bond 15,000 00

Date of examination by commissioner: Aug. 19.

PUBLIC FUNDS.

	Par Value.	Estimated Market Value.	Amount Invested.
United States bond	$5,000	$5,045 00	$5,000 00
City and town bonds: —			
City of Boston	$15,000	$15,400 00	$15,000 00
of Meriden, Conn.	20,000	23,725 00	21,000 00
of Fall River	25,000	31,000 00	27,407 50
of Portland, Me.	7,000	7,854 00	7,000 00
of Bangor, Me.	9,000	10,200 00	7,605 00
of Holyoke	5,000	5,900 00	5,000 00
of Lynn	1,000	1,000 00	1,000 00
Town of Abington	9,000	9,180 00	9,050 00
	$96,000	$109,304 00	$98,062 50

BANK STOCK.

	Par Value.	Estimated Market Value.	Amount Invested.
Abington Nat'l Bank, Abington	$13,600	$18,360 00	$14,810 00
Boston Nat'l Bank, Boston	7,400	9,472 00	7,400 00
Blackstone Nat'l Bank, Boston	7,500	8,625 00	7,500 00
Central Nat'l Bank, Boston	1,200	1,440 00	1,200 00
Continental Nat'l Bank, Boston	2,500	2,950 00	2,500 00
Eliot Nat'l Bank, Boston	5,900	7,080 00	5,900 00
Eagle Nat'l Bank, Boston	1,900	2,281 00	1,900 00
Freeman's Nat'l Bank, Boston	1,500	1,785 00	1,500 00
First Nat'l Bank, Danvers	2,850	3,600 00	3,452 87
First Nat'l Bank, Adams	4,000	6,750 00	4,000 00
Globe Nat'l Bank, Boston	5,000	5,550 00	5,500 00
Howard Nat'l Bank, Boston	15,000	19,500 00	15,000 00
Hamilton Nat'l Bank, Boston	5,000	6,150 00	5,500 00
Hide and Leather Nat'l B'k, Boston,	6,800	7,888 00	6,800 00
Mount Vernon Nat'l Bank, Boston	3,800	4,826 00	3,800 00
Merchants' Nat'l Bank, Boston	10,000	14,600 00	13,000 00
North Nat'l Bank, Boston	2,200	3,102 00	2,600 00
Old Colony Nat'l Bank, Plymouth	200	280 00	240 00
Republic Nat'l Bank, Boston	4,500	5,895 00	4,500 00
Redemption Nat'l Bank, Boston	11,000	14,850 00	14,280 00
Second Nat'l Bank, Boston	5,000	7,550 00	7,200 00
Shoe and Leather Nat'l B'k, Boston,	1,000	1,130 00	1,000 00
State Nat'l Bank, Boston	3,200	4,000 00	3,200 00
Traders' Nat'l Bank, Boston	5,800	5,916 00	5,800 00
Third Nat'l Bank, Boston	2,000	2,120 00	2,000 00
Webster Nat'l Bank, Boston	4,700	5,217 00	4,700 00
Metropolitan Nat'l Bank, Boston	4,000	4,800 00	4,000 00
	$137,550	$175,717 00	$149,282 87

RAILROAD BONDS.

	Par Value.	Estimated Market Value.	Amount Invested.
Eastern Railroad Company	$50,000	$55,000 00	$40,261 08
Old Colony Railroad Company	5,000	6,250 00	5,400 00
	$55,000	$61,250 00	$45,661 08

AMHERST SAVINGS BANK — AMHERST.

Incorporated 1864. Number of corporators, 13.

ENOS F. COOK, *President.* *Treasurer,* SAMUEL C. CARTER.

STATEMENT.

LIABILITIES.		ASSETS.	
Deposits	$675,484 84	Public funds	$90,696 25
Earnings undivided	19,340 41	Loans on public funds	1,500 00
Guaranty fund	8,481 32	Bank stock	101,733 89
		Railroad bonds	67,260 42
		Real estate	15,000 00
		Loans on real estate	292,779 64
		Loans on personal security,	63,621 18
		Loans to counties, cities, or towns	36,700 00
		Deposit in bank on interest,	28,887 11
		Cash on hand	5,128 08
	$703,306 57		$703,306 57

Loans on Public Funds: —

On $1,500 United States 4s . . $1,500 00

Cash on Deposit in Bank: —

First National Bank, Amherst $28,887 11

Amount invested in real estate (for banking purposes) . . $15,000 00
Estimated value of the same 15,000 00
Amount of municipal tax on real estate 118 04

Whole amount of interest or profits received or earned . . . $38,823 50
Rate and amount of each semi-annual dividend for previous year: 2½ per cent . 13,512 39; 2 per cent . 12,307 65
Times for the dividends fixed by the by-laws: January and July.
Average annual per cent of dividends for the term ending at time of and including last extra dividend: 5½ per cent.
The total amount of loans, with each specified rate of interest: $28,331, 5 per cent; $7,000, 5½ per cent; $298,783, 6 per cent; $60,486, 7 per cent.
Number of outstanding loans which are of an amount not exceeding $3,000 each 257
Aggregate amount of the same 228,929 00
Number of open accounts 2,516
Number and amount of deposits received for previous year, 1,687 151,263 21
Number and amount of deposits of and exceeding $300 at any one time for the previous year 114 70,811 00
Number and amount of withdrawals 1,236 119,489 17
Number of accounts opened the previous year 350
Number of accounts closed the previous year 275
Amount of expenses of the corporation during previous year . 1,856 76
Amount of treasurer's bond 5,000 00
Date of examination by commissioner: July 14.

Public Funds.

	Par Value.	Estimated Market Value.	Amount Invested.
United States 3½s	$37,000	$37,370 00	$37,000 00
" " 4½s	10,000	11,300 00	11,296 25
City bonds: —			
City of Bangor, Me., 6s . . .	$20,000	$22,400 00	$20,500 00
of Rockland, Me., 6s . .	5,000	5,000 00	5,025 00
of Bath, Me., 6s . . .	5,000	5,050 00	5,000 00
of Fall River 6s . . .	8,000	10,000 00	8,680 00
of Pawtucket, R.I., 5s . .	3,000	3,600 00	3,195 00
	$88,000	$94,720 00	$90,696 25

Bank Stock.

	Par Value.	Estimated Market Value.	Amount Invested.
Suffolk Nat'l Bank, Boston . .	$1,000	$1,220 00	$1,210 00
First Nat'l Bank, Easthampton .	9,400	11,950 00	10,724 00
First Nat'l Bank, Northampton .	12,900	17,544 00	17,176 00
First Nat'l Bank, Holyoke . .	10,000	12,000 00	10,800 00
Hampshire Co. N'l B'k, Northampt'n,	7,900	10,270 00	8,963 00
Conway Nat'l Bank, Conway . .	4,400	5,500 00	5,012 00
Northampton N'l B'k, Northampt'n,	13,300	22,175 00	13,504 00
Crocker Nat'l Bank, Turner's Falls,	8,400	9,660 00	8,664 39
Agawam Nat'l Bank, Springfield .	7,300	9,198 00	8,966 00
Chapin Nat'l Bank, Springfield .	2,000	2,520 00	2,515 00
City Nat'l Bank, Worcester . .	4,000	4,800 00	5,120 00
Mechanics' Nat'l Bank, Worcester .	1,000	1,200 00	1,250 00
Citizens' Nat'l Bank, Worcester .	2,500	3,000 00	3,062 50
First Nat'l Bank, Barre . . .	3,000	3,750 00	3,660 00
Hide and Leather Nat'l B'k, Boston,	1,000	1,190 00	1,107 00
	$88,100	$115,977 00	$101,733 89

Railroad Bonds.

	Par Value.	Estimated Market Value.	Amount Invested.
New London & Northern R.R. 7s, reg.	$25,000	$31,250 00	$25,000 00
New London & Northern R.R. 6s .	3,500	4,305 00	3,500 00
Vermont and Massachusetts Railroad,	2,000	2,060 00	2,000 00
Boston and Revere Beach Railroad .	25,000	29,500 00	26,268 75
Boston and Lowell Railroad . .	10,000	11,300 00	10,491 67
	$65,500	$78,415 00	$67,260 42

ANDOVER SAVINGS BANK—ANDOVER.

Incorporated April 2, 1834. Number of corporators, 55.

MOSES FOSTER, *President*. *Treasurer*, JOHN F. KIMBALL.

STATEMENT.

LIABILITIES.		ASSETS.	
Deposits	$1,336,424 95	Public funds	$468,250 00
Earnings undivided	42,050 26	Bank stock	160,700 00
Guaranty fund	26,000 00	Loans on bank stock	500 00
		Loan on savings bank book	100 00
		Railroad bonds	174,000 00
		Real estate by foreclosure	40,296 35
		Loans on real estate	406,089 28
		Loans on personal security,	132,635 32
		Loans to counties, cities, or towns	10,000 00
		Deposit in banks on interest,	9,219 67
		Cash on hand	2,684 59
	$1,404,475 21		$1,404,475 21

Loans on Bank Stock:—

On 6 shares Andover National Bank $500 00

Cash on Deposit in Banks, amount in each:—

Andover National Bank, Andover $4,477 13
Blackstone National Bank, Boston 4,742 54

Amount of real estate held by foreclosure . $40,296 35
Assessed value of the same 79,119 00
Amount of income received from the same . 1,130 00
Amount of municipal tax on real estate . . 1,159 51

Whole amount of interest or profits received or earned . . . $85,003 60
Rate and amount of each semi-annual dividend for previous year . . . . { 2 per cent . 25,929 65; 2 per cent . 26,314 99 }
Times for the dividends fixed by the by-laws: third Wednesday in June and December.
The total amount of loans, with each specified rate of interest: $25,000, 4 per cent; $25,000, 4½ per cent; $84,500, 5 per cent; $236,942.15, 6 per cent; $4,500, 6¼ per cent; $163,382.45, 7 per cent.
Number of outstanding loans which are of an amount not exceeding $3,000 each 188
Aggregate amount of the same 251,605 00
Amount of investments from which no income is received . . 8,000 00
Number of open accounts 3,447
Number and amount of deposits received for previous year, 1,910 139,635 33
Number and amount of deposits of and exceeding $300 at any one time for the previous year 130 65,704 00
Number and amount of withdrawals 1,381 195,533 58

Number of accounts opened the previous year	431	
Number of accounts closed the previous year	349	
Amount of expenses of the corporation during previous year .		$2,100 00
Amount of treasurer's bond		30,000 00

Date of examination by commissioner: April 18.

PUBLIC FUNDS.

	Par Value.	Estimated Market Value.	Amount Invested.
United States $3\frac{1}{2}$s and 4s	$76,250	$79,500 00	$76,250 00
City and town bonds: —			
City of Bangor, Me.	$25,000	$25,000 00	$25,000 00
of Belfast, Me.	17,000	17,000 00	17,000 00
of Chelsea	27,000	30,000 00	27,000 00
of Cambridge	12,000	13,000 00	12,000 00
of Dover, N.H.	25,500	28,500 00	25,500 00
of Fall River	10,000	11,000 00	10,000 00
of Holyoke	18,000	21,000 00	18,000 00
of Lynn	30,000	35,000 00	30,000 00
of Lewiston, Me.	7,000	7,500 00	7,000 00
of Lowell	5,000	5,500 00	5,000 00
of Nashua, N.H.	5,000	5,500 00	5,000 00
of Newburyport	20,000	23,000 00	20,000 00
of Norwich, Conn.	35,000	40,000 00	35,000 00
of Portland, Me.	22,000	24,000 00	22,000 00
of Portsmouth, N.H. . . .	32,500	35,000 00	32,500 00
of Salem	20,000	21,000 00	20,000 00
of Somerville	10,000	10,000 00	10,000 00
of Worcester	5,000	5,000 00	5,000 00
Town of Melrose	15,000	17,000 00	15,000 00
of Northampton	33,000	36,000 00	33,000 00
of Tolland	10,000	11,500 00	10,000 00
of Wakefield	8,000	8,000 00	8,000 00
	$468,250	$509,000 00	$468,250 00

BANK STOCK.

Andover Nat'l Bank, Andover .	$31,200	$37,000 00	$31,200 00
Bay State Nat'l Bank, Lawrence .	7,500	10,000 00	7,500 00
Blackstone Nat'l Bank, Boston .	10,800	12,000 00	10,800 00
Continental Nat'l Bank, Boston .	10,000	11,500 00	10,000 00
Commonwealth Nat'l Bank, Boston,	15,000	18,000 00	15,000 00
Everett Nat'l Bank, Boston . .	4,500	5,000 00	4,500 00
Hide and Leather N'l Bank, Boston,	10,000	11,500 00	10,000 00
Merchants' Nat'l Bank, Boston .	2,500	3,300 00	2,500 00
Republic Nat'l Bank, Boston . .	22,500	28,000 00	22,500 00
Revere Nat'l Bank, Boston . .	26,300	30,000 00	26,300 00
Webster Nat'l Bank, Boston . .	15,400	17,500 00	15,400 00
Wachusett Nat'l Bank, Fitchburg .	5,000	10,000 00	5,000 00
	$160,700	$193,800 00	$160,700 00

RAILROAD BONDS.

	Par Value.	Estimated Market Value.	Amount Invested.
Boston and Maine Railroad 7s .	$50,000	$60,000 00	$50,000 00
Boston and Lowell Railroad 7s .	64,000	77,800 00	64,000 00
Old Colony Railroad 7s . . .	20,000	24,000 00	20,000 00
New Bedford Railroad 7s . .	10,000	12,000 00	10,000 00
Worcester and Nashua Railroad 5s .	5,000	5,000 00	5,000 00
Agricultural Branch Railroad 6s .	25,000	25,000 00	25,000 00
	$174,000	$203,800 00	$174,000 00

ARLINGTON FIVE CENTS SAVINGS BANK — ARLINGTON.

Incorporated April 2, 1860. Number of corporators, 36.

ALBERT WINN, *President.* *Treasurer,* ABEL R. PROCTOR.

STATEMENT.

LIABILITIES.		ASSETS.	
Deposits	$656,300 10	Public funds	$40,792 75
Earnings undivided	12,240 82	Bank stock	19,866 25
Guaranty fund	12,181 06	Railroad bonds	5,050 00
		Real estate	26,396 59
		Real estate by foreclosure	44,719 80
		Loans on real estate	391,513 56
		Loans on personal security,	25,916 19
		Loans to counties, cities, or towns	94,300 00
		Deposit in bank on interest,	30,122 47
		Expense account	373 73
		Tax account	1,424 10
		Insurance account	152 00
		Cash on hand	94 54
	$680,721 98		$680,721 98

Cash on Deposit in Bank: —

Faneuil Hall National Bank, Boston $30,122 47

Amount invested in real estate (for banking purposes)		$26,396 59
Estimated value of the same		26,396 59
Amount of real estate held by foreclosure		44,719 80
Assessed value of the same		56,150 00
Amount of income received from the same		4,062 89
Amount of municipal tax on real estate		1,424 10
Whole amount of interest or profits received or earned		$35,107 50
Rate and amount of each semi-annual dividend for previous year	2 per cent	12,187 58
	2 per cent	12,373 06

Times for the dividends fixed by the by-laws: January and July.

Average annual per cent of dividends for the term ending at time of and including last extra dividend: $4\frac{9}{32}$ per cent.

The total amount of loans, with each specified rate of interest: $30,122.47, 3 per cent; $46,000, 4 per cent; $13,000, 4½ per cent; $41,000, 5 per cent; $171,550, 6 per cent; $32,000, 6½ per cent; $207,579.75, 7 per cent; $600, 8 per cent.

Number of outstanding loans which are of an amount not exceeding $3,000 each	243	
Aggregate amount of the same		229,336 18
Number of open accounts	2,361	
Number and amount of deposits received for previous year,	2,037	137,924 75
Number and amount of deposits of and exceeding $300 at any one time for the previous year	77	45,770 57
Number and amount of withdrawals	1,090	93,768 37
Number of accounts opened the previous year	538	
Number of accounts closed the previous year	405	

Amount of expenses of corporation during previous year . . $1,432 08
Amount of treasurer's bond 10,000 00
Date of examination by commissioner: May 25.

PUBLIC FUNDS.

	Par Value.	Estimated Market Value.	Amount Invested.
United States 4s, coupons .	$450	$526 50	$492 75
City and town bonds: —			
City of Portland, Me., 6s . .	$20,000	$24,000 00	$20,100 00
of Lawrence 6s . . .	6,000	7,320 00	5,000 00
of Holyoke 6s	5,000	6,500 00	4,167 00
Town of Woburn 6s . . .	7,000	8,400 00	5,833 00
of North Adams 6s . .	5,000	5,850 00	5,200 00
	$43,450	$52,596 50	$40,792 75

BANK STOCK.

Redemption Nat'l Bank, Boston .	$1,000	$1,350 00	$1,353 75
Republic Nat'l Bank, Boston . .	3,300	4,323 00	4,281 50
North America Nat'l Bank, Boston .	2,500	2,875 00	2,975 00
Union National Bank, Boston . .	1,200	1,840 50	1,644 00
Continental Nat'l Bank, Boston .	5,000	5,931 25	5,955 75
Faneuil Hall Nat'l Bank, Boston .	1,000	1,307 50	1,310 00
First Ward Nat'l Bank, Boston .	2,200	2,552 00	2,346 25
	$16,200	$20,179 25	$19,866 25

RAILROAD BONDS.

Eastern Railroad	$5,500	$6,105 00	$5,050 00

ATHOL SAVINGS BANK — ATHOL.

Incorporated 1867. Number of corporators, 36.

CHARLES C. BASSETT, *President*. *Treasurer*, ALPHEUS HARDING.

STATEMENT.

LIABILITIES.		ASSETS.	
Deposits	$919,215 34	Public funds	$89,000 00
Earnings undivided	11,053 92	Bank stock	9,800 00
Guaranty fund	13,725 00	Loans on bank stock	14,875 00
		Real estate by foreclosure	6,745 43
		Loans on real estate	333,231 20
		Loans on personal security,	240,362 74
		Loans to counties, cities, or towns	79,180 00
		Deposit in banks on interest,	168,000 00
		Expense account	707 50
		Accrued interest	1,201 55
		Cash on hand	890 84
	$943,994 26		$943,994 26

Loans on Bank Stock, amount on each: —

On 23 shares Athol National Bank	$2,075 00
On 33 shares Miller's River National Bank	2,800 00
On 100 shares South Reading National Bank	10,000 00

Cash on Deposit in Banks, amount in each: —

Athol National Bank	$5,000 00
First National Bank, Leominster	35,000 00
Central National Bank, Boston	25,000 00
Continental National Bank, Boston	20,000 00
Westminster National Bank	10,000 00
Franklin County National Bank	10,000 00
Miller's River National Bank, Athol	48,000 00
National Bank of the Commonwealth, Boston	15,000 00

Amount of real estate held by foreclosure	$6,745 43
Assessed value of the same	8,125 00
Amount of income received from the same	603 00
Amount of municipal tax on real estate	119 90

Whole amount of interest or profits received or earned	$47,587 75
Rate and amount of each semi-annual dividend for previous year: 2 per cent	16,989 77
2 per cent	17,167 06

Times for the dividends fixed by the by-laws: January and July.

Average annual per cent of dividends for the term ending at time of and including last extra dividend: $5\frac{5}{8}$ per cent.

The total amount of loans, with each specified rate of interest: $76,500, 4 per cent; $36,500, $4\frac{1}{4}$ per cent; $50,000, $4\frac{1}{2}$ per cent; $104,828.34, 5 per cent; $394,820.60, 6 per cent; $5,000, 7 per cent.

Number of outstanding loans which are of an amount not exceeding $3,000 each . . . 319

Aggregate amount of the same		$264,351 60
Number of open accounts	3,352	
Number and amount of deposits received for previous year,	8,000	174,652 32
Number and amount of deposits of and exceeding $300 at any one time for the previous year	136	62,298 22
Number and amount of withdrawals	1,304	130,209 72
Number of accounts opened the previous year	567	
Number of accounts closed the previous year	280	
Amount of expenses of the corporation during previous year .		2,338 42
Amount of treasurer's bond		10,000 00

Date of examination by commissioner: June 23.

Public Funds.

	Par Value.	Estimated Market Value.	Amount Invested.
United States 6s, currency .	$10,000	$13,000 00	$10,000 00
State, city, and town bonds:—			
State of New Hampshire . .	$14,000	$14,700 00	$14,000 00
City of Cambridge	15,000	15,900 00	15,000 00
of Charlestown . . .	10,000	10,100 00	10,000 00
of Lynn	10,000	10,700 00	10,000 00
of Newton	10,000	11,000 00	10,000 00
of Portland, Me. . . .	5,000	5,350 00	5,000 00
Town of Meriden, Conn. . .	14,000	14,700 00	14,000 00
of Haverhill	1,000	1,100 00	1,000 00
	$89,000	$96,550 00	$89,000 00

Bank Stock.

Blackstone Nat'l Bank, Boston .	$1,100	$1,265 00	$1,100 00
Eliot Nat'l Bank, Boston . .	1,000	1,120 00	1,000 00
Eagle Nat'l Bank, Boston . .	5,000	5,900 00	5,000 00
Miller's River Nat'l Bank, Athol .	2,700	4,320 00	2,700 00
	$9,800	$12,605 00	$9,800 00

ATTLEBOROUGH SAVINGS BANK — NORTH ATTLEBOROUGH.

Incorporated 1860. Number of corporators, 68.

ABIEL CODDING, *President*. *Treasurer*, EDWARD R. PRICE.

STATEMENT.

LIABILITIES.		ASSETS.	
Deposits	$424,170 03	Public funds	$25,000 00
Earnings undivided	10,444 34	Bank stock	5,079 00
Guaranty fund	7,200 00	Loans on real estate	230,672 00
		Loans on personal security,	82,871 25
		Loans to counties, cities, or towns	33,000 00
		Deposit in banks on interest,	61,244 02
		Expense account	98 46
		Cash on hand	3,849 64
	$441,814 37		$441,814 37

Cash on Deposit in Banks, amount in each: —

Maverick National Bank, Boston		$61,244 02
Attleborough National Bank, North Attleborough		3,849 64
Whole amount of interest or profits received or earned		$22,168 46
Rate and amount of each semi-annual dividend for previous year	2½ per cent	8,362 20
	2½ per cent	9,196 88

Times for the dividends fixed by the by-laws: April 1 and Oct. 1.

The total amount of loans, with each specified rate of interest: $25,000, 3½ per cent; $5,000, 4 per cent; $35,500, 5 per cent; $162,221.25, 6 per cent; $143,572, 7 per cent; $250, 8 per cent.

Number of outstanding loans which are of an amount not exceeding $3,000 each	194	
Aggregate amount of the same		192,722 25
Number of open accounts	1,448	
Number and amount of deposits received for previous year,	1,485	164,656 25
Number and amount of deposits of and exceeding $300 at any one time for the previous year	133	79,785 41
Number and amount of withdrawals	418	83,346 13
Number of accounts opened the previous year	328	
Number of accounts closed the previous year	113	
Amount of expenses of the corporation during previous year		1,475 20
Amount of treasurer's bond		20,000 00

Date of examination by commissioner: May 4.

PUBLIC FUNDS.

	Par Value.	Estimated Market Value.	Amount Invested.
United States 6s, regist'd extended	$25,000	$25,375 00	$25,000 00

BANK STOCK.

First Nat'l Bank, Attleborough	$5,100	$5,100 00	$5,079 00

BARRE SAVINGS BANK — BARRE.

Incorporated May, 1869. Number of corporators, 51.

CHARLES BRIMBLECOM, *President*. *Treasurer*, HARDING WOODS.

STATEMENT.

LIABILITIES.		ASSETS.	
Deposits	$228,550 45	Bank stock	$126,893 54
Earnings undivided .	13,669 44	Railroad bonds	6,060 00
Guaranty fund . .	3,150 00	Real estate by foreclosure .	4,000 00
		Loans on real estate . .	67,081 98
		Loans on personal security,	33,995 79
		Deposit in bank on interest,	7,100 07
		Expense account . . .	238 51
	$245,369 89		$245,369 89

Cash on Deposit in Bank: —

First National Bank, Barre $7,100 07

Amount of real estate held by foreclosure .	$4,000 00
Assessed value of the same	3,300 00
Amount of income received from the same .	356 36
Amount of municipal tax on real estate . .	52 12

Whole amount of interest or profits received or earned $13,874 04

Rate and amount of each semi-annual dividend for previous year . . . . { 2 per cent . 4,167 52; 2 per cent . 4,254 55 }

Times for the dividends fixed by the by-laws: Jan. 15 and July 15.

Average annual per cent of dividends for the term ending at time of and including last extra dividend: 5⅛ per cent.

The total amount of loans, with each specified rate of interest: $20,000, 6 per cent; $5,000, 6½ per cent; $45,398.67, 7 per cent; $1,360.79, 7½ per cent; $20,318.31, 8 per cent.

Number of outstanding loans which are of an amount not exceeding $3,000 each	48	
Aggregate amount of the same		37,759 46
Amount of investments from which no income is received . .		16,818 31
Number of open accounts	841	
Number and amount of deposits received for previous year .	355	31,456 13
Number and amount of deposits of and exceeding $300 at any one time for the previous year	26	11,591 42
Number and amount of withdrawals	301	26,233 68
Number of accounts opened the previous year	136	
Number of accounts closed the previous year	82	
Amount of expenses of the corporation during previous year .		745 78
Amount of treasurer's bond		15,000 00

Date of examination by commissioner: July 6.

BANK STOCK.

	Par Value.	Estimated Market Value.	Amount Invested.
Atlas Nat'l Bank, Boston . .	$1,200	$1,500 00	$1,469 00
Blackstone Nat'l Bank, Boston .	4,200	4,830 00	5,722 59
Boston Nat'l Bank, Boston . .	6,400	8,192 00	7,975 27
Boylston Nat'l Bank, Boston . .	2,000	2,560 00	2,785 33
Continental Nat'l Bank, Boston .	1,700	2,015 62	2,018 56
Eliot Nat'l Bank, Boston . .	2,500	3,006 25	2,991 00
First Nat'l Bank, Boston . .	7,000	14,542 50	12,615 25
Mechanics' Nat'l Bank, Boston .	2,800	3,640 00	3,500 00
Nat'l Bank of Commerce, Boston .	3,200	4,024 00	5,316 00
Nat'l Bank of N. America, Boston,	2,500	2,875 00	2,718 75
Nat'l Bank of Redemption, Boston.	4,600	6,215 75	6,263 50
Exchange Nat'l Bank, Boston .	1,800	2,592 00	2,977 50
Hide and Leather Nat'l B'k, Boston,	2,500	2,912 50	2,912 70
Revere Nat'l Bank, Boston . .	900	1,098 00	1,185 00
Webster Nat'l Bank, Boston . .	3,300	3,679 50	3,462 63
Old Boston Nat'l Bank, Boston .	3,500	4,270 00	5,407 50
Second Nat'l Bank, Boston . .	3,400	5,151 00	5,032 35
Shoe and Leather Nat'l B'k, Boston,	2,000	2,250 00	2,800 00
Suffolk Nat'l Bank, Boston . .	3,000	3,656 25	3,753 75
Tremont Nat'l Bank, Boston . .	6,100	7,442 00	7,837 25
Market Nat'l Bank, Brighton . .	5,000	6,625 00	7,660 00
Ware Nat'l Bank, Ware . . .	700	840 00	901 25
Central Nat'l Bank, Worcester .	5,500	7,700 00	8,050 00
Citizens' Nat'l Bank, Worcester .	2,100	2,415 00	2,961 00
City Nat'l Bank, Worcester . .	5,000	5,650 00	6,830 00
First Nat'l Bank, Worcester . .	2,000	3,200 00	2,700 00
First Nat'l Bank, Barre . . .	7,400	9,176 00	10,042 00
	$92,300	$122,058 37	$127,888 18
Less interest earned at date of purchase	–	–	994 64
	$92,300	$122,058 37	$126,893 54

RAILROAD BONDS.

Eastern Railroad $4\frac{1}{2}$s . .	$5,000	$5,500 00	$5,200 00
Rutland Railroad 5s . .	1,000	890 00	860 00
	$6,000	$6,390 00	$6,060 00

BASS RIVER SAVINGS BANK — SOUTH YARMOUTH.

Incorporated April 20, 1874. Number of corporators, 31.

DAVID KELLEY, *President.* *Treasurer,* DAVID D. KELLEY.

STATEMENT.

LIABILITIES.		ASSETS.	
Deposits	$222,255 49	Public funds	$36,746 44
Earnings undivided	4,879 90	Loans on public funds	4,680 00
Guaranty fund	1,585 82	Bank stock	95,188 38
		Loans on bank stock	275 00
		Railroad bonds	10,000 00
		Real estate by foreclosure	728 04
		Loans on real estate	24,832 68
		Loans on personal security,	41,350 78
		Deposit in bank on interest,	1,510 99
		Loans on mill stock *	2,500 00
		Sagamore Manufacturing Company *	5,754 81
		Border City Manufacturing Company *	4,559 54
		Cash on hand	594 55
	$228,721 21		$228,721 21

Loans on Public Funds:—

On $5,250 United States bonds, with principal and two sureties . $4,680 00

Loans on Bank Stock:—

On 3 shares First National Bank, Yarmouth $275 00

Cash on Deposit in Bank:—

In Maverick National Bank, Boston $1,510 99

Amount of real estate held by foreclosure		$728 04
Assessed value of the same		670 00
Amount of municipal tax on real estate		11 82
Whole amount or interest or profits received or earned		$11,076 28
Rate and amount of each semi-annual dividend for previous year	2 per cent	3,473 83
	2 per cent	3,899 68

Times for the dividends fixed by the by-laws: April 1 and Oct. 1.

The total amount of loans, with each specified rate of interest: $11,035, 5 per cent; $19,680, 5½ per cent; $20,360.46, 6 per cent; $800, 6½ per cent; $21,763, 7 per cent.

Number of outstanding loans which are of an amount not exceeding $3,000 each	105	
Aggregate amount of the same		48,958 46
Amount of investments from which no income is received		728 04
Number of open accounts	976	
Number and amount of deposits received for previous year	496	81,121 36
Number and amount of deposits of and exceeding $300 at any one time for the previous year	68	35,633 13
Number and amount of withdrawals	346	38,242 71

* Taken to secure indebtedness.

Number of accounts opened the previous year 209
Number of accounts closed the previous year 140
Amount of expenses of the corporation during previous year . $602 07
Amount of treasurer's bond 10,000 00
Date of examination by commissioner: June 18.

PUBLIC FUNDS.

	Par Value.	Estimated Market Value.	Amount Invested.
United States 3½s, registered . .	$10,000	$10,100 00	$10,000 00
City and town bonds:—			
City of Boston 4s	$10,000	$10,450 00	$10,000 00
of Providence, R.I., 5s . .	10,000	11,875 00	11,746 44
Town of Beverly 4s . . .	5,000	5,137 50	5,000 00
	$35,000	$37,562 50	$36,746 44

BANK STOCK.

	Par Value.	Estimated Market Value.	Amount Invested.
Nat'l Bank of the Republic, Boston,	$8,200	$10,742 00	$9,731 88
Faneuil Hall Nat'l Bank, Boston .	5,500	7,397 50	6,877 75
Eagle Nat'l Bank, Boston . .	2,100	2,514 75	2,297 50
Old Boston Nat'l Bank, Boston .	700	854 00	770 00
Everett Nat'l Bank, Boston . .	6,300	7,378 87	6,803 25
Atlas Nat'l Bank, Boston . .	3,000	3,750 00	3,660 00
Nat'l Bank of Redemption, Boston .	5,000	6,756 25	6,500 00
Boston Nat'l Bank, Boston . .	3,000	3,840 00	3,270 00
Merchants' Nat'l Bank, Boston .	5,600	9,176 00	7,840 00
Exchange Nat'l Bank, Boston . .	5,000	7,200 00	6,750 00
Second Nat'l Bank, Boston . .	4,900	7,405 12	7,105 00
Suffolk Nat'l Bank, Boston . .	1,000	1,218 75	1,000 00
Manufacturers' Nat'l Bank, Boston,	10,500	11,576 25	11,182 50
Blackstone Nat'l Bank, Boston .	800	920 00	800 00
Tremont Nat'l Bank, Boston . .	7,300	9,271 00	8,448 50
State Nat'l Bank, Boston . .	1,500	1,882 50	1,770 00
Shawmut Nat'l Bank, Boston . .	2,500	3,081 25	2,750 00
Market Nat'l Bank, Boston . .	1,300	1,439 75	1,357 00
First Nat'l Bank, New Bedford .	2,400	3,240 00	2,400 00
Citizens' Nat'l Bank, New Bedford,	2,000	2,300 00	2,000 00
First Nat'l Bank, Yarmouth . .	1,500	1,950 00	1,875 00
	$80,100	$103,893 99	$95,188 38

RAILROAD BONDS.

	Par Value.	Estimated Market Value.	Amount Invested.
Old Colony Railroad 7s	$4,000	$5,000 00	$4,000 00
Old Colony Railroad 6s	3,000	3,450 00	3,000 00
New Bedford Railroad 7s . . .	3,000	3,600 00	3,000 00
	$10,000	$12,050 00	$10,000 00

BENJAMIN FRANKLIN SAVINGS BANK — FRANKLIN.

Incorporated Feb. 23, 1871. Number of corporators, 40.

DAVIS THAYER, JUN., *President*. *Treasurer*, C. W. STEWART.

STATEMENT.

LIABILITIES.		ASSETS.	
Deposits . . .	$256,724 01	Public funds . . .	$21,223 50
Earnings undivided .	3,521 81	Bank stock	51,640 12
Guaranty fund . .	3,070 78	Real estate by foreclosure .	20,774 24
		Loans on real estate . .	125,751 00
		Loans on personal security,	31,436 22
		Loans to counties, cities, or towns	10,000 00
		Deposit in banks on interest,	107 65
		Expense account . . .	592 01
		Furniture account . .	562 31
		Suspense account . .	402 66
		Cash on hand . . .	826 89
	$263,316 60		$263,316 60

Cash on Deposit in Banks, amount in each: —

Franklin National Bank, Franklin	$17 01
Maverick National Bank, Boston	4 94
International Trust Company, Boston *	84 80

Amount of real estate held by foreclosure . .	$20,774 24
Assessed value of the same	22,270 00
Amount of income received from the same . .	837 44
Amount of municipal tax on real estate . . .	410 11

Whole amount of interest or profits received or earned . . . $12,894 46

Rate and amount of each semi-annual dividend for previous year . . . . { 2 per cent . 4,619 97; 2 per cent . 4,750 32 }

Times for the dividends fixed by the by-laws: the first Monday in January and July.

Average annual per cent of dividends for the term ending at time of and including last extra dividend: 4 per cent.

The total amount of loans, with each specified rate of interest: $10,400, 4 per cent; $12,800, 5 per cent; $68,742.22, 6 per cent; $74,070, 7 per cent; $575, 8 per cent.

Number of outstanding loans which are of an amount not exceeding $3,000 each	141	
Aggregate amount of the same		117,787 22
Amount of investments from which no income is received . .		2,600 00
Number of open accounts	1,208	
Number and amount of deposits received for previous year .	722	56,374 13
Number and amount of deposits of and exceeding $300 at any one time for the previous year	30	16,167 88
Number and amount of withdrawals	604	47,791 02

* The Attorney-General has given an opinion that deposits by savings banks in this trust company are legal.

Number of accounts opened the previous year	168	
Number of accounts closed the previous year	140	
Amount of expenses of the corporation during previous year .		$1,225 83
Amount of treasurer's bond		5,000 00

Date of examination by commissioner: Aug. 24.

PUBLIC FUNDS.

	Par Value.	Estimated Market Value.	Amount Invested.
United States 4½s, registered . .	$16,000	$17,920 00	$16,312 50
City bonds:—			
City of Bath, Me.	$2,000	$2,000 00	$1,815 00
of Lewiston, Me. . . .	3,000	3,240 00	3,096 00
	$21,000	$23,160 00	$21,223 50

BANK STOCK.

Wrentham Nat'l Bank, Wrentham .	$630	$720 00	$990 00
Franklin Nat'l Bank, Franklin .	12,900	14,835 00	15,255 00
Tremont Nat'l Bank, Boston . .	3,100	3,906 00	3,902 37
Hide and Leather Nat'l B'k, Boston,	900	1,080 00	1,032 75
Howard Nat'l Bank, Boston . .	2,500	3,275 00	2,902 50
Washington Nat'l Bank, Boston .	2,300	3,220 00	3,266 00
Eliot Nat'l Bank, Boston . .	7,000	8,470 00	8,887 50
Market Nat'l Bank, Boston . .	1,000	1,130 00	1,100 00
Revere Nat'l Bank, Boston . .	1,600	2,016 00	1,776 00
Commerce Nat'l Bank, Boston .	2,700	3,510 00	3,456 00
Shoe and Leather Nat'l B'k, Boston,	800	928 00	1,137 00
Columbian Nat'l Bank, Boston .	1,400	2,044 00	1,845 00
North America Nat'l Bank, Boston,	1,500	1,800 00	1,680 00
Hamilton Nat'l Bank, Boston . .	3,000	3,720 00	3,790 00
Continental Nat'l Bank, Boston .	500	610 00	620 00
	$41,830	$51,264 00	$51,640 12

BERKSHIRE COUNTY SAVINGS BANK — PITTSFIELD.

Incorporated 1847. Number of corporators, 46.

HON. JULIUS ROCKWELL, *President*. *Treasurer*, ROBERT W. ADAM.

STATEMENT.

LIABILITIES.		ASSETS.	
Deposits	$1,768,936 92	Public funds	$590,500 00
Earnings undivided .	18,745 52	Bank stock	94,120 00
Guaranty fund . .	22,500 00	Loans on bank stock . .	21,900 00
		Railroad bonds . . .	10,000 00
		Real estate by foreclosure .	90,983 40
		Loans on real estate . .	691,873 30
		Loans on personal security,	190,195 66
		Loans to counties, cities, or towns	45,000 00
		Deposit in banks on interest,	27,859 89
		Expense account . . .	4,657 00
		Premium account . .	26,571 50
		Cash on hand, and in banks not on interest . . .	16,521 69
	$1,810,182 44		$1,810,182 44

Loans on Bank Stock, amount on each:—

On 160 shares Pittsfield National Bank	$19,000 00
On 19 shares Agricultural National Bank	2,500 00
On 5 shares Third National Bank, Pittsfield	400 00

Cash on Deposit in Banks, amount in each:—

Revere National Bank, Boston	$24,845 01
National Bank of the Commonwealth, Boston	14 88
North Adams Savings Bank*	1,000 00
South Adams Savings Bank*	2,000 00
Agricultural National Bank, Pittsfield	5,418 91
Pittsfield National Bank, Pittsfield	8,759 32

Amount of real estate held by foreclosure		$90,983 40
Assessed value of the same		56,050 00
Amount of income received from the same		2,891 00
Amount of municipal tax on real estate		590 22
Whole amount of interest or profits received or earned		$87,571 35
Rate and amount of each semi-annual dividend for previous year	2 per cent .	31,914 41
	2 per cent .	33,362 31

Times for the dividends fixed by the by-laws: first Thursday in January and July.

Average annual per cent of dividends for the term ending at time of and including last extra dividend: 6½ per cent.

The total amount of loans, with each specified rate of interest: $6,000, 4 per cent; $20,000, 4½ per cent; $2,000, 5½ per cent; $830,968.30, 6 per cent; $85,000, 7 per cent.

Number of outstanding loans which are of an amount not exceeding $3,000 each	200	
Aggregate amount of the same		261,851 00
Amount of investments from which no income is received . .		5,900 00
Number of open accounts	6,182	
Number and amount of deposits received for previous year,	5,159	359,780 29

* Deposits taken for foreclosed real estate sold.

Number and amount of deposits of and exceeding $300 at any one time for the previous year	213	$104,322 57
Number and amount of withdrawals	3,407	321,792 49
Number of accounts opened the previous year	1,197	
Number of accounts closed the previous year	738	
Amount of expenses of the corporation during previous year		5,672 50
Amount of treasurer's bond		50,000 00

Date of examination by commissioner: August 3.

PUBLIC FUNDS.

	Par Value.	Estimated Market Value.	Amount Invested.
United States $3\frac{1}{4}$s, extended	$50,000	$50,500 00	$51,562 50
" " 4s, registered	285,000	330,600 00	301,000 00
" " 6s, currency	55,000	71,500 00	55,000 00
State, city, and town bonds: —			
State of Connecticut 6s	$5,000	$6,000 00	$5,000 00
City of Boston 4s	30,000	33,000 00	30,000 00
of Charlestown 6s	5,000	5,500 00	5,000 00
of Bath, Me., 6s	12,000	12,000 00	13,667 50
of Pawtucket, R.I., 5s	20,000	22,000 00	21,300 00
of Providence, R.I., 5s	27,000	29,700 00	30,360 00
Town of Watchemoket, R.I., 5s	26,500	29,000 00	28,970 00
of Pittsfield 6s	50,000	60,000 00	50,000 00
of Adams 6s	25,000	28,000 00	25,000 00
	$590,500	$677,800 00	$616,860 00

BANK STOCK.

Blackstone Nat'l Bank, Boston	$4,100	$4,715 00	$4,100 00
Howard Nat'l Bank, Boston	3,200	4,176 00	3,200 00
Shawmut Nat'l Bank, Boston	2,000	2,550 00	2,000 00
North Nat'l Bank, Boston	3,500	4,970 00	3,500 00
Atlantic Nat'l Bank, Boston	4,500	6,885 00	4,500 00
Merchants' Nat'l Bank, Boston	6,800	9,928 00	6,800 00
Boston Nat'l Bank, Boston	10,000	12,800 00	10,000 00
Revere Nat'l Bank, Boston	12,000	14,640 00	12,000 00
Webster Nat'l Bank, Boston	8,000	8,920 00	8,000 00
Eagle Nat'l Bank, Boston	8,000	9,520 00	8,000 00
Hide and Leather Nat'l B'k, Boston	2,500	2,912 00	2,500 00
Bank of Commerce, Boston	6,000	7,500 00	6,000 00
Atlas Nat'l Bank, Boston	900	1,125 00	1,111 50
Hadley Falls Nat'l Bank, Holyoke	2,000	3,500 00	2,000 00
Adams Nat'l Bank, North Adams	200	275 00	200 00
Chicopee First Nat'l Bank, Chicopee	6,000	10,000 00	6,000 00
Agricultural Nat'l Bank, Pittsfield	3,200	6,000 00	3,200 00
Pittsfield Nat'l Bank, Pittsfield	4,500	5,700 00	4,500 00
Lee Nat'l Bank, Lee	6,720	8,000 00	6,720 00
	$94,120	$124,116 00	$94,331 50

RAILROAD BONDS.

Worcester and Nashua Railroad	$10,000	$10,000 00	$10,000 00

BEVERLY SAVINGS BANK — BEVERLY.

Incorporated 1867. Number of corporators, 42.

WILLIAM ENDICOTT, *President*. *Treasurer*, R. G. BENNETT.

STATEMENT.

LIABILITIES.		ASSETS.	
Deposits	$573,931 99	Loans on public funds	$35,000 00
Earnings undivided	3,365 35	Bank stock	137,490 00
Gauranty fund	8,000 00	Loans on bank stock	6,200 00
		Railroad bonds	2,000 00
		Real estate by foreclosure	19,412 91
		Loans on real estate	238,599 00
		Loans on personal security,	2,125 00
		Loans to counties, cities, or town	105,000 00
		Deposit in banks on interest,	15,000 00
		Expense account	2 50
		Premium account	15,000 00
		Cash on hand	9,467 93
	$585,297 34		$585,297 34

Loans on Public Funds: —

On $35,000 United States 3½s $35,000 00

Loans on Bank Stock: —

On 63 shares Beverly National Bank $6,200 00

Cash on Deposit in Banks, amount in each: —

National Exchange Bank, Boston $15,000 00

Beverly National Bank, Beverly 9,467 93

Amount of real estate held by foreclosure $19,412 91

Assessed value of the same 21,850 00

Amount of income received from the same 1,854 16

Amount of municipal tax on real estate 378 03

Whole amount of interest or profits received or earned . . . $31,402 78

Rate and amount of each semi-annual dividend for previous year . . . { 2 per cent . 9,967 03; 2 per cent . 10,638 61 }

Times for the dividends fixed by the by-laws: fourth Wednesday in April and October.

The total amount of loans, with each specified rate of interest: $37,500, 4 per cent; $5,000, 4½ per cent; $97,500, 5 per cent; $246,924, 6 per cent.

Number of outstanding loans which are of an amount not exceeding $3,000 each 244

Aggregate amount of the same 231,274 00

Amount of investments from which no income is received . . 855 35

Number of open accounts 1,972

Number and amount of deposits received for previous year. 5,405 145,957 66

Number and amount of deposits of and exceeding $300 at any one time for the previous year 116 64,581 19

Number and amount of withdrawals	1,116	$87,559 06
Number of accounts opened the previous year	264	
Number of accounts closed the previous year	191	
Amount of expenses of the corporation during previous year .		969 26
Amount of treasurer's bond		15,000 00

Date of examination by commissioner: Aug. 13.

Bank Stock.

	Par Value.	Estimated Market Value.	Amount Invested.
Atlas Nat'l Bank, Boston . .	$5,000	$6,250 00	$5,000 00
City Nat'l Bank, Boston . . .	10,000	12,300 00	10,000 00
Continental Nat'l Bank, Boston .	5,000	5,950 00	5,000 00
Eagle Nat'l Bank, Boston . .	5,000	6,000 00	5,000 00
Freeman's Nat'l Bank, Boston .	5,000	5,950 00	5,000 00
Massachusetts Nat'l Bank, Boston .	10,000	12,400 00	10,000 00
North Nat'l Bank, Boston . .	5,000	7,150 00	5,000 00
Hide and Leather Nat'l B'k, Boston,	5,000	5,800 00	5,000 00
Howard Nat'l Bank, Boston . .	5,000	6,500 00	5,000 00
Merchandise Nat'l Bank, Boston .	3,000	3,300 00	3,000 00
Republic Nat'l Bank, Boston . .	5,000	6,250 00	5,000 00
Revere Nat'l Bank, Boston . .	3,800	4,630 00	3,800 00
Shoe and Leather Nat'l B'k, Boston,	5,000	5,650 00	5,000 00
Traders' Nat'l Bank, Boston . .	10,000	10,200 00	10,000 00
Tremont Nat'l Bank, Boston . .	5,000	6,100 00	5,000 C0
Webster Nat'l Bank, Boston . .	5,000	5,500 00	5,000 00
First Nat'l Bank, Lynn . . .	5,000	6,000 00	5,000 00
Grand Nat'l Bank, Marblehead .	1,800	2,160 00	1,800 00
Asiatic Nat'l Bank, Salem . .	2,190	2,920 00	2,190 00
Exchange Nat'l Bank, Salem . .	3,300	3,960 00	3,300 00
First Nat'l Bank, Salem . . .	4,700	5,640 00	4,700 00
Mercantile Nat'l Bank, Salem . .	3,700	4,440 00	3,700 00
Salem Nat'l Bank, Salem . .	5,000	6,000 00	5,000 00
Beverly Nat'l Bank, Beverly . .	20,000	25,000 00	20,000 00
	$137,490	$166,050 00	$137,490 00

Railroad Bonds.

Eastern Railroad . . .	$2,000	$2,200 00	$2,000 00

BOSTON FIVE CENTS SAVINGS BANK — BOSTON.

Incorporated 1854. Number of corporators, 47.

ALONZO H. EVANS, *President*. *Treasurer*, CURTIS C. NICHOLS.

STATEMENT.

LIABILITIES.		ASSETS.	
Deposits	$9,612,566 75	Public funds	$1,367,000 00
Earnings undivided	255,364 28	Loans on public funds	2,650 00
Guaranty fund	139,528 48	Bank stock	357,587 50
		Loans on bank stock	29,200 00
		Railroad bonds	140,000 00
		Real estate	139,601 21
		Real estate by foreclosure	177,063 50
		Loans on real estate	4,134,365 28
		Loans on personal security,	2,463,500 00
		Loans to counties, cities, or towns	508,000 00
		Deposit in banks on interest,	668,869 65
		Expense account	103 49
		Cash on hand	19,518 88
	$10,007,459 51		$10,007,459 51

Loans on Public Funds, amount on each:—

On $1,500 United States bonds On $1,300 State of Maine bonds	$2,650 00

Loans on Bank Stock, amount on each:—

On 146 shares Maverick National Bank	$14,600 00
On 11 shares Old Colony National Bank, Plymouth	1,100 00
On 40 shares National Bank of Redemption On 40 shares Everett National Bank On 25 shares Atlas National Bank	10,500 00
On 30 shares Blackstone National Bank	3,000 00

Cash on Deposit in Banks, amount in each:—

National Bank of the Commonwealth	$34,524 01
Merchandise National Bank	10,340 09
Blackstone National Bank	109 38
Maverick National Bank	65,958 53
First National Bank	115 07
Traders' National Bank	100,000 00
Mount Vernon National Bank	50,000 00
Central National Bank	150,414 78
National Exchange Bank	90,407 79
National Security Bank	100,000 00
First National Bank, Newburyport	67,000 00

Amount invested in real estate (for banking purposes)	$139,601 21
Estimated value of the same	175,000 00
Amount of real estate held by foreclosure	177,063 50
Assessed value of the same	245,150 00
Amount of income received from the same	10,000 00
Amount of municipal tax on real estate	6,333 96

Whole amount of interest or profits received or earned $515,043 97

Rate and amount of each semi-annual dividend for previous year . . . . { 2 per cent . 168,025 83; $1\frac{3}{4}$ per cent . 151,788 93 }

Times for the dividends fixed by the by-laws: second Wednesday in April and October.

Average annual per cent of dividends for the term ending at time of and including last extra dividend: 7 per cent.

The total amount of loans, with each specified rate of interest: $95,000, 3 per cent; $192,000, $3\frac{1}{2}$ per cent; $30,000, $3\frac{3}{4}$ per cent; $245,000, 4 per cent; $181,600, $4\frac{1}{2}$ per cent; $585,000, $4\frac{3}{4}$ per cent; $1,846,600, 5 per cent; $45,300, $5\frac{1}{4}$ per cent; $610,000, $5\frac{1}{2}$ per cent; $1,126,130.48, 6 per cent; $35,000, $6\frac{1}{4}$ per cent; $564,650, $6\frac{1}{2}$ per cent; $819,236.60, 7 per cent.

Number of outstanding loans which are of an amount not exceeding $3,000 each 258

Aggregate amount of the same 450,450 00

Amount of investments from which no income is received . . 49,638 50

Number of open accounts 70,350

Number and amount of deposits received for previous year, 55,373 3,013,731 43

Number and amount of deposits of and exceeding $300 at any one time for the previous year 1,887 1,068,572 00

Number and amount of withdrawals 36,363 2,086,107 67

Number of accounts opened the previous year . . 8,415

Number of accounts closed the previous year . . . 3,340

Amount of expenses of the corporation during previous year . 29,876 29

Amount of treasurer's bond 25,000 00

Date of examination by commissioner: April 28.

Public Funds.

	Par Value.	Estimated Market Value.	Amount Invested.
United States bonds	$600,000	$762,500 00	$600,000 00
State and city bonds:—			
State of Massachusetts	$100,000	$101,000 00	$100,000 00
of Maine	50,000	54,500 00	50,000 00
City of Boston	219,000	247,000 00	219,000 00
of Chelsea	50,000	56,000 00	50,000 00
of Newton	50,000	50,000 00	50,000 00
of Somerville	198,000	202,680 00	198,000 00
of Salem	100,000	108,000 00	100,000 00
	$1,367,000	$1,581,680 00	$1,367,000 00

Bank Stock.

Third Nat'l Bank, Springfield .	$10,000	$15,600 00	$10,000 00
Boston Nat'l Bank, Boston . .	15,000	18,900 00	15,287 50
Hide and Leather Nat'l B'k, Boston,	32,500	37,700 00	32,500 00
Republic Nat'l Bank, Boston . .	15,000	18,750 00	15,000 00

BANK STOCK — Concluded.

	Par Value.	Estimated Market Value.	Amount Invested.
Second Nat'l Bank, Boston . .	$12,000	$17,520 00	$12,000 00
First Nat'l Bank, Boston . .	25,000	50,750 00	25,000 00
Blackstone Nat'l Bank, Boston .	41,100	47,265 00	41,100 00
Suffolk Nat'l Bank, Boston . .	17,100	20,862 00	17,100 00
Shawmut Nat'l Bank, Boston . .	10,000	12.500 00	10,000 00
Tremont Nat'l Bank, Boston . .	29,500	36,285 00	29,500 00
Continental Nat'l Bank, Boston .	10,000	11,600 00	10.000 00
Rockland Nat'l Bank, Boston . .	20,000	26,400 00	20.000 00
Washington Nat'l Bank, Boston .	15,000	20,400 00	15,000 00
Howard Nat'l Bank, Boston . .	20,000	25.000 00	20.000 00
Revere Nat'l Bank, Boston . .	22,500	27,000 00	22,500 00
Merchants' Nat'l Bank, Boston .	4,700	6,815 00	4,700 00
Webster Nat'l Bank, Boston . .	7,500	8,250 00	7,500 00
Commonwealth Nat'l Bank, Boston,	28,000	34,440 00	28.000 00
Merchandise Nat'l Bank, Boston .	10,000	11,000 00	10,000 00
Commerce Nat'l Bank, Boston .	12,400	15,252 00	12,400 00
	$357,300	$462,289 00	$357,587 50

RAILROAD BONDS.

Eastern Railroad	$140,000	$152,600 00	$140,000 00

BOSTON PENNY SAVINGS BANK — BOSTON.

Incorporated 1864. Number of corporators, 100.

EBEN HOWES, *President*. *Treasurer*, HENRY R. REYNOLDS.

STATEMENT.

LIABILITIES.		ASSETS.	
Deposits . . .	$753,790 34	Public funds . . .	$22,450 00
Earnings undivided .	9,170 01	Bank stock	103,690 50
Guaranty fund . .	12,089 05	Loans on bank stock . .	500 00
		Railroad bonds . . .	6,225 00
		Real estate	115,000 00
		Real estate by foreclosure .	4,315 69
		Loans on real estate . .	363,450 00
		Loans on personal security,	60,000 00
		Deposit in banks on interest,	79,111 28
		Expense account. . .	358 60
		Accrued interest . . .	8,936 32
		Cash on hand . . .	11,012 01
	$775,049 40		$775,049 40

Loan on Bank Stock: —

On 5 shares Mechanics' National Bank, Boston $500 00

Cash on Deposit in Banks, amount in each: —

Maverick National Bank	$22,563 22
Hide and Leather National Bank	6,548 06
Mount Vernon National Bank	50,000 00

Amount invested in real estate (for banking purposes)	$115,000 00
Estimated value of the same	100,000 00
Amount of real estate held by foreclosure	4,315 69
Assessed value of the same	4,400 00
Amount of income received from the same	300 00
Amount of municipal tax on real estate	1,166 21

Whole amount of interest or profits received $37,862 16

Rate and amount of each semi-annual dividend for previous year . . . . { 1½ per cent . 10,538 04; 1½ per cent . 10,467 71 }

Times for the dividends fixed by the by-laws: second Wednesday in April and October.

Average annual per cent of dividends for the term ending at time of and including last extra dividend: 7 per cent.

The total amount of loans, with each specified rate of interest: $10,000, 4 per cent; $50,000, 4½ per cent; $39,500, 5 per cent; $3,500, 5½ per cent; $217,500, 6 per cent; $15,500, 6½ per cent; $77,750, 7 per cent; $6,200, 7½ per cent.

Number of outstanding loans which are of an amount not exceeding $3,000 each 37

Aggregate amount of the same 66,250 00

Number of open accounts 5,674

Number and amount of deposits received for previous year,	5,031	$202,590 09
Number and amount of deposits of and exceeding $300 at any one time for the previous year	113	63,602 24
Number and amount of withdrawals	2,954	187,556 41
Number of accounts opened the previous year	748	
Number of accounts closed the previous year	655	
Amount of expenses of the corporation during previous year		4,350 29
Amount of treasurer's bond		10,000 00

Date of examination by commissioner: Feb. 23.

Public Funds.

	Par Value.	Estimated Market Value.	Amount Invested.
United States 4s	$20,000	$23,225 00	$22,450 00

Bank Stock.

	Par Value.	Estimated Market Value.	Amount Invested.
Everett Nat'l Bank, Boston	$15,000	$17,568 75	$16,725 00
Hide and Leather Nat'l B'k, Boston,	10,000	11,650 00	11,550 00
North America Nat'l Bank, Boston,	5,000	5,750 00	5,525 00
Atlas Nat'l Bank, Boston	5,000	6,250 00	6,300 00
Manufacturers' Nat'l Bank, Boston,	5,000	5,512 50	5,325 00
Merchants' Nat'l Bank, Boston	2,500	3,650 00	3,600 00
Fourth Nat'l Bank, Boston	5,000	5,500 00	5,175 00
Boston Nat'l Bank, Boston	5,000	6,400 00	6,050 00
Tremont Nat'l Bank, Boston	4,100	5,002 00	5,084 00
Webster Nat'l Bank, Boston	4,800	5,352 00	5,448 00
Atlantic Nat'l Bank, Boston	4,200	6,447 00	6,384 00
State Nat'l Bank, Boston	1,100	1,380 50	1,402 50
First Nat'l Bank, Boston	7,000	14,542 50	14,210 00
Howard Nat'l Bank, Boston	5,000	6,506 25	6,250 00
Commerce Nat'l Bank, Boston	3,700	4,763 75	4,662 00
	$82,400	$106,275 25	$103,690 50

Railroad Bonds.

	Par Value.	Estimated Market Value.	Amount Invested.
Boston and Maine 7s	$5,000	$6,356 25	$6,225 00

BRAINTREE SAVINGS BANK — SOUTH BRAINTREE.

Incorporated March 21, 1870. Number of corporators, 22.

E. A. HOLLINGSWORTH, *President*. *Treasurer*, C. H. HOBART.

STATEMENT.

LIABILITIES.		ASSETS.	
Deposits . . .	$89,292 96	Public funds . . .	$19,571 63
Earnings undivided .	3,203 93	Bank stock	28,219 74
Guaranty fund . .	945 40	Real estate by foreclosure .	2,921 32
		Loans on real estate . .	41.240 00
		Deposit in bank on interest,	1,311 24
		Expense account . . .	53 36
		Cash on hand . . .	125 00
	$93,442 29		$93,442 29

Cash on Deposit in Bank: —
Shawmut National Bank, Boston $1,311 24

Amount of real estate held by foreclosure		$2,921 32
Amount of income received from the same		200 00
Amount of municipal tax on real estate		33 36
Whole amount of interest or profits received or earned . . .		$4,777 45
Rate and amount of each semi-annual dividend for previous year	2 per cent .	1,504 99
	2 per cent .	1,551 28
Times for the dividends fixed by the by-laws: Jan. 1 and July 1.		
The total amount of loans, with each specified rate of interest: $25,530, 6 per cent; $13,310, 7 per cent; $2,400, 7½ per cent.		
Number of outstanding loans which are of an amount not exceeding $3,000 each	39	
Aggregate amount of the same		41,240 00
Number of open accounts	392	
Number and amount of deposits received for previous year .	294	27,211 74
Number and amount of deposits of and exceeding $300 at any one time for the previous year	21	11,930 42
Number and amount of withdrawals	180	20,619 76
Number of accounts opened the previous year	50	
Number of accounts closed the previous year	45	
Amount of expenses of the corporation during previous year .		248 73
Amount of treasurer's bond		5,000 00

Date of examination by commissioner: June 28.

PUBLIC FUNDS.

	Par Value.	Estimated Market Value.	Amount Invested.
United States 4s, coupon	$1,500	$1,740 00	$1,498 13
" " $3\frac{1}{2}$s, registered	4,000	4,080 00	4,095 00
City and town bonds:—			
City of New Bedford 5s	$3,000	$3,360 00	$3,090 00
of Fall River 6s	1,000	1,075 00	1,088 50
of Boston 6s	2,000	2,320 00	2,320 00
of Worcester $4\frac{1}{2}$s	2,000	2,170 00	2,170 00
of Manchester, N.H., 4s	2,000	2,070 00	2,070 00
Town of Brookline 5s	3,000	3,300 00	3,240 00
	$18,500	$20,115 00	$19,571 63

BANK STOCK.

	Par Value.	Estimated Market Value.	Amount Invested.
Merchants' Nat'l Bank, Boston	$700	$1,022 00	$920 50
Union Nat'l Bank, Weymouth	2,200	2,591 50	2,591 50
Manufacturers' Nat'l Bank, Boston,	2,000	2,200 00	2,096 25
Union Market N'l B'k, Watertown	3,200	3,520 00	3,021 50
State Nat'l Bank, Boston	1,500	1,875 00	1,616 25
Blackstone Nat'l Bank, Boston	3,100	3,627 00	3,295 37
North America Nat'l Bank, Boston	1,000	1,140 00	1,138 75
Shawmut Nat'l Bank, Boston	2,000	2,498 75	2,498 75
Commonwealth Nat'l Bank, Boston,	1,800	2,250 00	1,982 25
Hide and Leather Nat'l B'k, Boston,	1,000	1,150 00	1,150 00
Merchandise Nat'l Bank, Boston	1,300	1,472 25	1,472 25
Brockton Nat'l Bank, Brockton	2,500	2,609 37	2,609 37
Freeman's Nat'l Bank, Boston	800	1,002 00	1,002 00
Shoe and Leather Nat'l B'k, Boston,	2,500	2,825 00	2,825 00
	$25,600	$29,782 87	$28,219 74

BRIDGEWATER SAVINGS BANK — BRIDGEWATER.

Incorporated March 19, 1872. Number of corporators, 20.

LLOYD PARSONS, *President*. *Treasurer*, SAMUEL P. GATES.

STATEMENT.

LIABILITIES.		ASSESS.	
Deposits	$191,335 41	Public funds	$11,000 00
Earnings undivided	2,197 99	Bank stock	34,057 49
Guaranty fund	3,185 00	Railroad bonds	1,000 00
Suspense account	31 00	Real estate by foreclosure	9,500 00
		Loans on real estate	101,509 00
		Loans on personal security,	36,733 71
		Loans to counties, cities, or towns	1,500 00
		Deposit in bank on interest,	700 48
		Cash on hand	748 72
	$196,749 40		$196,749 40

Cash on Deposit in Bank: —

First National Bank, Boston $700 48

Amount of real estate held by foreclosure $9,500 00
Assessed value of the same 7,250 00
Amount of income received from the same 540 33
Amount of municipal tax on real estate 105 30

Whole amount of interest or profits received or earned $11,144 83
Rate and amount of each semi-annual dividend for previous year . . . 2 per cent . . 3,393 10; 2 per cent . . 3,552 19
Times for the dividends fixed by the by-laws: April 1 and Oct. 1.
Average annual per cent of dividends for the term ending at time of and including last extra dividend: $4\frac{9}{10}$ per cent.
The total amount of loans, with each specified rate of interest: $1,500, $4\frac{1}{2}$ per cent; $9,300, 5 per cent; $70,576.30, 6 per cent; $2,200, $6\frac{1}{2}$ per cent; $48,964, 7 per cent; $800, $7\frac{1}{2}$ per cent; $5,702.41, 8 per cent.
Number of outstanding loans which are of an amount not exceeding $3,000 each 114
Aggregate amount of the same 97,742 71
Amount of investments from which no income is received . . 700 00
Number of open accounts 800
Number and amount of deposits received for previous year . 610 59,818 75
Number and amount of deposits of and exceeding $300 at any one time for the previous year 45 29,086 35
Number and amount of withdrawals 534 51,637 44
Number of accounts opened the previous year 147
Number of accounts closed the previous year 85
Amount of expenses of the corporation during previous year . . 668 45
Amount of treasurer's bond 10,000 00
Date of examination by commissioner: July 8.

PUBLIC FUNDS.

	Par Value.	Estimated Market Value.	Amount Invested.
United States 4s	$2,000	$2,320 00	$2,000 00
City bonds: —			
City of Boston 5s, gold . . .	$5,000	$5,900 00	$5,000 00
of Fall River 6s . . .	4,000	5,040 00	4,000 00
	$11,000	$13,260 00	$11,000 00

BANK STOCK.

Blackstone Nat'l Bank, Boston .	$7,000	$8,050 00	$7,000 00
Merchants' Nat'l Bank, Boston .	1,000	1,460 00	1,391 24
Washington Nat'l Bank, Boston .	300	420 00	300 00
Boylston Nat'l Bank, Boston . .	1,300	1,664 00	1,300 00
Eagle Nat'l Bank, Boston . .	1,200	1,428 00	1,200 00
Globe Nat'l Bank, Boston . .	900	999 00	900 00
Fourth Nat'l Bank, Boston . .	1,500	1,650 00	1,500 00
Blue Hill Nat'l Bank, Boston . .	1,700	1,870 00	2,218 75
Security Nat'l Bank, Boston . .	600	1,080 00	1,042 50
Shawmut Nat'l Bank, Boston . .	1,100	1,397 00	1,320 50
Freeman's Nat'l Bank, Boston .	2,000	2,400 00	2,382 50
Brighton Nat'l Bank, Boston . .	3,900	4,173 00	3,900 00
Faneuil Hall Nat'l Bank, Boston	1,000	1,300 00	1,250 00
Howard Nat'l Bank, Boston . .	2,000	2,600 00	2,395 00
Home Nat'l Bank, Brockton . .	2,200	2,464 00	2,200 00
Brockton Nat'l Bank, Brockton .	2,000	2,100 00	2,000 00
Bristol County Nat'l Bank, Taunton,	1,100	1,760 00	1,757 00
	$30,800	$36,815 00	$34,057 49

RAILROAD BONDS.

Boston and Maine	$1,000	$1,267 50	$1,000 00

BRIGHTON FIVE CENT SAVINGS BANK — WARD 25, BOSTON.

Incorporated March, 1861. Number of corporators 98.

HORACE W. JORDAN, *President*. *Treasurer*, WILLIAM A. FISKE.

STATEMENT.

LIABILITIES.		ASSETS.	
Deposits	$172,129 37	Public funds	$3,000 00
Earnings undivided .	14,529 09	Bank stock	31,266 25
Guaranty fund . .	3,309 88	Real estate by foreclosure .	58,508 73
		Loans on real estate . .	93,682 15
		Deposit in banks on interest,	1,907 75
		Expense account . . .	491 13
		Suspense account (accrued interest)	974 57
		Cash on hand . . .	137 76
	$189,968 34		$189,968 34

Cash on Deposit in Bank: —

National Bank of Brighton	$1,907 75

Amount of real estate held by foreclosure	$58,508 73
Assessed value of the same	41,900 00
Amount of income received from the same	2,662 24
Amount of municipal tax on real estate	550 54

Whole amount of interest or profits received or earned		$7,477 53
Rate and amount of each semi-annual dividend for previous year	2 per cent .	3,548 02
	2 per cent .	3,314 22

Times for the dividends fixed by the by-laws: January and July.

Average annual per cent of dividends for the term ending at time of and including last extra dividend: $6\frac{1}{3}$ per cent.

The total amount of loans, with each specified rate of interest: $21,700, 6 per cent; $15,000, $6\frac{1}{2}$ per cent; $44,382.15, 7 per cent; $3,600, $7\frac{3}{10}$ per cent; $9,000, 8 per cent.

Number of outstanding loans which are of an amount not exceeding $3,000 each	43	
Aggregate amount of the same		56,798 00
Amount of investments from which no income is received . .		4,053 00
Number of open accounts	821	
Number and amount of deposits received for previous year .	382	20,175 34
Number and amount of deposits of and exceeding $300 at any one time for the previous year	15	9,880 00
Number and amount of withdrawals	463	37,574 80
Number of accounts opened the previous year	117	
Number of accounts closed the previous year	145	
Amount of expenses of the corporation during previous year .		1,487 19
Amount of treasurer's bond		10,000 00

Date of examination by commissioner: March 28.

PUBLIC FUNDS.

	Par Value.	Estimated Market Value.	Amount Invested.
City of Fall River water bonds .	$3,000	$3,765 00	$3,000 00

BANK STOCK.

	Par Value.	Estimated Market Value.	Amount Invested.
Brighton Nat'l Bank, Boston . .	$7,900	$8,453 00	$9,537 00
Market Nat'l B'k, Boston (Brighton)	3,000	3,975 00	5,205 00
Freeman's Nat'l Bank, Boston .	500	596 25	670 00
Eliot Nat'l Bank, Boston . .	1,500	1,803 75	1,732 50
Shawmut Nat'l Bank, Boston . .	400	509 00	400 00
State Nat'l Bank, Boston . .	1,000	1,255 00	1,132 50
Central Nat'l Bank, Boston . .	500	600 00	500 00
Metropolitan Nat'l Bank, Boston .	1,200	1,443 00	1,236 00
Suffolk Nat'l Bank, Boston . .	1,000	1,218 75	1,208 25
Webster Nat'l Bank, Boston . .	8,900	9,923 50	9,645 00
	$25,900	$29,777 25	$31,266 25

BRISTOL COUNTY SAVINGS BANK — TAUNTON.

Incorporated March 2, 1846. Number of corporators, 113.

——— ———, *President.** *Treasurer*, N. C. PLACE.

STATEMENT.

LIABILITIES.		ASSETS.	
Deposits	$2,653,917 76	Public funds	$224,000 00
Earnings undivided .	25,158 99	Loans on public funds .	1,000 00
Guaranty fund . .	55,000 00	Bank stock	138,400 00
Rents	2,000 00	Loans on bank stock . .	5,500 00
		Railroad bonds . . .	55,000 00
		Railroad stock† . . .	40,000 00
		Loans on railroad stock .	500 00
		Real estate	25,000 00
		Real estate by foreclosure .	269,002 97
		Loans on real estate . .	1,504,802 00
		Loans on personal security,	423,623 38
		Loans on bank books . .	4,440 00
		Deposit in banks on interest,	35,936 33
		Deposit in banks not on interest	1,519 00
		Expense account . . .	520 57
		Suspense account . .	1,554 98
		Cash on hand . . .	5,277 52
	$2,736,076 75		$2,736,076 75

Loan on Public Funds: —

On $1,000 United States 4½s	$1,000 00

Loans on Bank Stock, amount on each: —

On 38 shares Taunton National Bank, Taunton	$4,300 00
On 10 shares Machinists' National Bank, Taunton	1,000 00
On 2 shares Bristol County National Bank, Taunton	200 00

Loan on Railroad Stock: —

On 5 shares Boston and Albany Railroad	$500 00

Cash on Deposit in Banks, amount in each: —

Bristol County National Bank, Taunton	$1,519 00
Machinists' National Bank, Taunton	768 79
Maverick National Bank, Boston	35,167 54

Amount invested in real estate (for banking purposes)	$25,000 00
Estimated value of the same	45,000 00
Amount of real estate held by foreclosure	269,002 97
Assessed value of the same	231,808 00
Amount of income received from the same	16,956 81
Amount of municipal tax on real estate	3,918 76

* Office vacant by death of president.

† This is preferred stock in the Boston, Clinton, Fitchburg, and New Bedford Railroad, taken to secure indebtedness.

Whole amount of interest or profits received or earned . . . $149,072 23
Rate and amount of each semi-annual dividend for previous year . . . . { 2 per cent . 49,948 00; 2 per cent . 51,005 17 }
Times for the dividends fixed by the by-laws: April and October.
The total amount of loans, with each specified rate of interest: $10,000, 4½ per cent; $89,045.85, 5 per cent; $5,000, 5½ per cent; $1,835,819.53, 6 per cent.
Number of outstanding loans which are of an amount not exceeding $3,000 each 1,291
Aggregate amount of the same 1,115,381 46
Amount of investments from which no income is received . . 23,550 73
Number of open accounts 8,001
Number and amount of deposits received for previous year, 4,529 555,190 93
Number and amount of deposits of and exceeding $300 at any one time for the previous year 334 190,016 00
Number and amount of withdrawals 4,581 456,755 91
Number of accounts opened the previous year 1,139
Number of accounts closed the previous year 895
Amount of expenses of the corporation during previous year . . 8,399 73
Amount of treasurer's bond 20,000 00
Date of examination by commissioner: June 20.

PUBLIC FUNDS.

	Par Value.	Estimated Market Value.	Amount Invested.
United States continued 5s, funded loan of 1881 at 3½	$70,000	$71,400 00	$70,000 00
United States 4s	15,000	17,400 00	15,000 00
" " 4½s	45,000	49,850 00	45,000 00
State, city, and town bonds: —			
State of New Hampshire . .	$10,000	$12,500 00	$10,000 00
City of Providence, R.I. . . .	30,000	35,100 00	30,000 00
of Dover, N.H.	10,000	12,000 00	10,000 00
of Fall River	7,000	9,290 00	7,000 00
of Springfield	6,000	6,550 00	6,000 00
of Portsmouth, N.H. . .	5,000	6,000 00	5,000 00
of Boston	4,000	4,800 00	4,000 00
of Cambridge	1,000	1,260 00	1,000 00
of Taunton	1,000	1,240 00	1,000 00
Town of Brockton	20,000	22,000 00	20,000 00
	$224,000	$249,390 00	$224,000 00

BANK STOCK.

Machinists' Nat'l Bank, Taunton .	$16,200	$29,970 00	$16,200 00
Bristol County Nat'l Bank, Taunton,	4,500	7,650 00	4,500 00
Taunton Nat'l Bank, Taunton .	700	1,134 00	700 00
Fairhaven Nat'l Bank, Fairhaven .	2,000	1,840 00	2,000 00
Third Nat'l Bank, Springfield .	10,000	17,000 00	10,000 00

BANK STOCK — Concluded.

	Par Value.	Estimated Market Value.	Amount Invested.
First Nat'l Bank, Boston . .	$10,000	$20,700 00	$10,000 00
Boston Nat'l Bank, Boston . .	4,000	5,120 00	4,000 00
Hide and Leather Nat'l Bank, Boston,	1,500	1,740 00	1,500 00
Metropolitan Nat'l Bank, Boston .	4,000	4,800 00	4,000 00
Merchants' Nat'l Bank, Boston .	10,000	14,600 00	10,000 00
Exchange Nat'l Bank, Boston .	3,200	4,608 00	3,200 00
North Nat'l Bank, Boston . .	10,000	14,200 00	10,000 00
Mount Vernon Nat'l Bank, Boston .	2,000	2,540 00	2,000 00
North America Nat'l Bank, Boston .	2,000	2,300 00	2,000 00
Rockland Nat'l Bank, Roxbury .	4,300	6,020 00	4,300 00
Columbian Nat'l Bank, Boston .	5,000	7,100 00	5,000 00
Atlantic Nat'l Bank, Boston . .	2,500	3,825 00	2,500 00
Second Nat'l Bank, Boston . .	2,000	3,020 00	2,000 00
Redemption Nat'l Bank, Boston .	10,000	13,500 00	10,000 00
Commerce Nat'l Bank, Boston .	5,200	6,656 00	5,200 00
Tremont Nat'l Bank, Boston . .	5,000	6,100 00	5,000 00
Everett Nat'l Bank, Boston . .	5,200	6,084 00	5,200 00
State Nat'l Bank, Boston . .	10,000	12,500 00	10,000 00
Faneuil Hall Nat'l Bank, Boston .	1,000	1,300 00	1,000 00
Eagle Nat'l Bank, Boston . .	1,000	1,190 00	1,000 00
Howard Nat'l Bank, Boston . .	2,700	3,510 00	2,700 00
People's Nat'l Bank, Boston . .	1,200	1,944 00	1,200 00
Union Nat'l Bank, Boston . .	2,800	4,284 00	2,800 00
Shawmut Nat'l Bank, Boston . .	400	508 00	400 00
	$138,400	$205,743 00	$138,400 00

RAILROAD BONDS.

Boston, Revere Beach, and Lynn Railroad first mortgage . .	$15,000	$17,550 00	$15,000 00
Boston, Clinton, Fitchburg, and New Bedford Railroad first mort. .	40,000	42,450 00	40,000 00
	$55,000	$60,000 00	$55,000 00

BROADWAY SAVINGS BANK — LAWRENCE.

Incorporated 1872. Number of corporators, 28.

JOHN FALLON *President.* *Treasurer,* GILBERT E. HOOD.

STATEMENT.

LIABILITIES.		ASSETS.	
Deposits	$549,678 37	Public funds	$150,000 00
Earnings undivided	34,731 93	Bank stock	127,900 00
Guaranty fund	8,500 00	Loans on bank stock	1,500 00
Balance of Smith guaranty fund	54,090 06	Real estate by foreclosure	121,150 00
		Loans on real estate	155,901 00
		Loans on personal security,	30,500 00
		Deposit in bank on interest,	58,979 06
		Cash on hand	1,070 30
	$647,000 36		$647,000 36

Loan on Bank Stock:—

On 15 shares of Lawrence National Bank . . $1,500 00

Cash on Deposit in Bank:—

In Lawrence National Bank . . $58,979 06

Amount of real estate held by foreclosure	$121,150 00
Assessed value of the same	92,425 00
Amount of income received from the same	5,832 53
Amount of municipal tax on real estate	1,426 96

Whole amount of interest or profits received or earned $31,142 07

Rate and amount of each semi-annual dividend for previous year . . . { 2 per cent . 10,274 60; 2 per cent . 10,432 43 }

Times for the dividends fixed by the by-laws: third Wednesday in April and October.

The total amount of loans, with each specified rate of interest: $54,000, 6 per cent; $4,800, 6½ per cent; $129,101, 7 per cent.

Number of outstanding loans which are of an amount not exceeding $3,000 each	139	
Aggregate amount of the same		109.901 00
Amount of investments from which no income is received		150 00
Number of open accounts	1,840	
Number and amount of deposits received for previous year.	1,084	104,193 39
Number and amount of deposits of and exceeding $300 at any one time for the previous year	100	74,754 70
Number and amount of withdrawals	915	123,584 95
Number of accounts opened the previous year	240	
Number of accounts closed the previous year	357	
Amount of expenses of the corporation during previous year		2,532 13
Amount of treasurer's bond		20,000 00

Date of examination by commissioner: March 29.

PUBLIC FUNDS.

	Par Value.	Estimated Market Value.	Amount Invested.
United States 4s	$150,000	$175,500 00	$150,000 00

BANK STOCK.

	Par Value.	Estimated Market Value.	Amount Invested.
Bay State Nat'l Bank, Lawrence .	$4,850	$7,360 00	$6,400 00
City Nat'l Bank, Boston . . .	4,400	5,280 00	4,400 00
Commerce Nat'l Bank, Boston .	10,000	12,800 00	10,000 00
Eagle Nat'l Bank, Boston . .	5,000	6,000 00	5,000 00
Eliot Nat'l Bank, Boston . .	5,000	6,000 00	5,000 00
Everett Nat'l Bank, Boston . .	5,000	5,800 00	5,000 00
Globe Nat'l Bank, Boston . .	3,300	3,630 00	3,300 00
Hamilton Nat'l Bank, Boston . .	5,000	5,050 00	5,000 00
Hide and Leather Nat'l Bank, Boston,	1,500	1,700 00	1,500 00
Howard Nat'l Bank, Boston . .	5,000	6,500 00	5,000 00
Lawrence Nat'l Bank, Lawrence .	7,800	8,500 00	7,800 00
Manufacturers' Nat'l Bank, Boston,	5,000	5,500 00	5,000 00
Market Nat'l Bank, Boston . .	5,000	5,500 00	5,000 00
North America Nat'l Bank, Boston .	5,000	5,700 00	5,000 00
State Nat'l Bank, Boston . .	5,000	6,300 00	5,000 00
Shawmut Nat'l Bank, Boston . .	7,600	9,500 00	7,600 00
Shoe and Leather Nat'l Bank, Boston,	10,000	11,200 00	10,000 00
Suffolk Nat'l Bank, Boston . .	10,000	12,100 00	10,000 00
Tremont Nat'l Bank, Boston . .	16,900	20,800 00	16,900 00
Webster Nat'l Bank, Boston . .	5,000	5,550 00	5,000 00
	$126,350	$151,370 00	$127,900 00

BROCKTON SAVINGS BANK — BROCKTON.

Incorporated March 3, 1881. Number of corporators, 51.

SANFORD WINTER, *President*. *Treasurer*, C. R. FILLEBROWN.

STATEMENT.

Liabilities.		Assets.	
Deposits	$50,901 01	Public funds	$2,040 00
Earnings undivided	101 14	Railroad bonds	2,100 00
		Loans on real estate*	38,400 00
		Loans on personal security	4,275 00
		Expense account	143 04
		Cash on hand	4,044 11
	$51,002 15		$51,002 15

Cash on Deposit in Bank:—
Brockton National Bank, Brockton $2,732 57

Whole amount of interest or profits received or earned		$101 14
Times for the dividends fixed by the by-laws: April 15 and Oct. 15.		
The total amount of loans, with each specified rate of interest: $2,040, 4 per cent; $2,100, 5 per cent; $34,475, 6 per cent; $5,350, 6½ per cent; $2,850, 7 per cent.		
Number of outstanding loans which are of an amount not exceeding $3,000 each	34	
Aggregate amount of the same		30,815 00
Number of open accounts	363	
Number and amount of deposits received for previous year	544	58,328 01
Number and amount of deposits of and exceeding $300 at any one time for the previous year	52	27,065 00
Number and amount of withdrawals	102	7,427 00
Number of accounts opened the previous year	408	
Number of accounts closed the previous year	45	
Amount of expenses of the corporation during previous year		143 04
Amount of treasurer's bond		10,000 00
Date of examination by commissioner: July 7.		

PUBLIC FUNDS.

	Par Value	Estimated Market Value.	Amount Invested.
Town of Brockton	$2,000	$2,040 00	$2,040 00

RAILROAD BONDS.

Newport and Richford Railroad	$2,000	$2,100 00	$2,100 00

* This bank has been notified that the amount of loans on real estate exceeded the legal limit.

BROOKFIELD SAVINGS BANK — BROOKFIELD.

Incorporated April 12, 1872. Number of corporators, 35.

HENRY D. FALES, *President*. *Treasurer*, HIRAM P. GERALD.

STATEMENT.

LIABILITIES.		ASSETS.	
Deposits	$31,381 78	Loans on real estate	$22,050 00
Earnings undivided	1,055 03	Loans on personal security,	10,400 00
Guaranty fund	470 93	Deposit in bank on interest,	152 49
		Expense account	155 25
		Furniture account	150 00
	$32,907 74		$32,907 74

Cash on Deposit in Bank: —

First National Bank, Worcester		$152 49
Whole amount of interest or profits received or earned		$1,787 62
Rate and amount of each semi-annual dividend for previous year	2 per cent	672 52
	2 per cent	601 73

Times for the dividends fixed by the by-laws: Jan. 1 and July 1.

Average annual per cent of dividends for the term ending at time of and including last extra dividend: 5⅙ per cent.

The total amount of loans, with each specified rate of interest: $9,000, 4 per cent; $1,500, 5 per cent; $21,950, 6 per cent.

Number of outstanding loans which are of an amount not exceeding $3,000 each	39	
Aggregate amount of the same		32,450 00
Number of open accounts	223	
Number and amount of deposits received for previous year	141	5,027 11
Number and amount of deposits of and exceeding $300 at any one time for the previous year	38	18,087 66
Number and amount of withdrawals	123	9,737 46
Number of accounts opened the previous year	25	
Number of accounts closed the previous year	25	
Amount of expenses of the corporation during previous year		160 25
Amount of treasurer's bond		10,000 00

Date of examination by the commissioner: July 5.

6

BROOKLINE SAVINGS BANK — BROOKLINE.

Incorporated Feb. 24, 1871. Number of corporators, 59.

WILLIAM H. LINCOLN, *President.* *Treasurer,* WILLIAM E. LINCOLN.

STATEMENT.

LIABILITIES.		ASSETS.	
Deposits	$135,997 38	Public funds	$14,241 25
Earnings undivided	3,080 55	Bank stock	28,301 63
Guaranty fund	1,293 25	Real estate by foreclosure	7,857 11
S. E. Gardner	10 00	Loans on real estate	71,487 50
		Loans on personal security,	10,000 00
		Deposit in bank on interest,	3,683 42
		Expense account	375 51
		Accrued interest	2,377 44
		Premium on public funds,	1,402 08
		Cash on hand	655 24
	$140,381 18		$140,381 18

Cash on Deposit in Bank: —

Central National Bank	$3,683 42

Amount of real estate held by foreclosure		$7,857 11
Assessed value of the same		5,100 00
Amount of income received from the same		400 00
Amount of municipal tax on real estate		55 08
Whole amount of interest or profits received or earned		$6,798 76
Rate and amount of each semi-annual dividend for previous year	2 per cent	1,951 63
	2 per cent	2,156 12

Times for the dividends fixed by the by-laws: second Monday in January and July.

The total amount of loans, with each specified rate of interest: $31,287.50, 6 per cent; $19,500, 6½ per cent; $17,900, 7 per cent; $2,800, 8 per cent.

Number of outstanding loans which are of an amount not exceeding $3,000 each	35	
Aggregate amount of the same		38,987 50
Amount of investments from which no income is received		1,416 78
Number of open accounts	1,036	
Number and amount of deposits received for previous year,	1,902	53,497 94
Number and amount of deposits of and exceeding $300 at any one time for the previous year	23	11,420 60
Number and amount of withdrawals	576	28,303 34
Number of accounts opened the previous year	333	
Number of accounts closed the previous year	125	
Amount of expenses of the corporation during previous year		1,060 00
Amount of treasurer's bond		5,000 00

Date of examination by commissioner: Dec. 5.

PUBLIC FUNDS.

	Par Value.	Estimated Market Value.	Amount Invested.
Brookline water scrip 7s, 1898 .	$4,000	$5,093 33	$3,691 25
Brookline water scrip 4½s, 1893 .	10,000	10,550 00	10,550 00
	$14,000	$15,643 33	$14,241 25

BANK STOCK.

	Par Value.	Estimated Market Value.	Amount Invested.
City Nat'l Bank, Boston . . .	$8,500	$10,540 00	$9,192 50
Central Nat'l Bank, Boston . .	7,500	9,000 00	8,088 00
Merchandise Nat'l Bank, Boston .	5,000	5,500 00	5,000 00
Revere Nat'l Bank, Boston . .	3,700	4,514 00	4,057 00
Tremont Nat'l Bank, Boston . .	1,800	2,196 00	1,964 13
	$26,500	$31,750 00	$28,301 63

CAMBRIDGEPORT SAVINGS BANK — CAMBRIDGE.

Incorporated March 16, 1853. Number of corporators, 11.

BENJAMIN TILTON, *President*. *Treasurer*, EDWARD HYDE.

STATEMENT.

LIABILITIES.		ASSETS.	
Deposits	$2,207,619 19	Public funds	$351,100 00
Earnings undivided .	40,269 40	Bank stock	98,100 00
Guaranty fund . .	30,000 00	Loan on railroad bonds * .	10,000 00
		Real estate by foreclosure .	84,745 75
		Loans on real estate . .	1,085,837 13
		Loans on personal security,	314,958 63
		Deposit in banks on interest,	327,792 87
		Expense account . . .	3,449 89
		Cash on hand . . .	1,904 32
	$2,277,888 59		$2,277,888 59

Loan on Railroad bonds: —

Union Pacific Railroad . . . $10,000 00

Cash on Deposit in Banks, amount in each: —

Exchange National Bank, Boston	$270,000 00
First National Bank, Cambridge	37,081 87
Cambridgeport National Bank, Cambridge . .	20,711 00

Amount of real estate held by foreclosure . .	$84,745 75
Assessed value of the same	120,800 00
Amount of income received from the same . .	7,575 74
Amount of municipal tax on real estate . . .	1,835 40

Whole amount of interest or profits received $116,209 12

Rate and amount of each semi-annual dividend for previous year . . . . { 2 per cent . { 38,920 00; 2 per cent . 40,958 33 }

Times for the dividends fixed by the by-laws: third Wednesday in January and July.

The total amount of loans, with each specified rate of interest: $25,000, 3 per cent; $75,000, 3¼ per cent; $50,000, 3½ per cent; $44,661.91, 4 per cent; $25,000, 4¼ per cent; $20,000, 4½ per cent; $20,000, 5 per cent; $136,665.63, 5½ per cent; $533,321.09, 6 per cent; $389,505, 6½ per cent; $54,717.13, 7 per cent; $20,350, 7-3/10 per cent; $16,575, 7½ per cent.

Number of outstanding loans which are of an amount not exceeding $3,000 each	297	
Aggregate amount of the same		391,915 00
Number of open accounts	6,509	
Number and amount of deposits received for previous year,	6,302	431,215 12
Number and amount of deposits of and exceeding $300 at any one time for the previous year	326	185,946 00
Number and amount of withdrawals	4,139	326,090 62

* This loan is made with a principal and two sureties.

Number of accounts opened the previous year . . . 1,056
Number of accounts closed the previous year 563
Amount of expenses of the corporation during previous year . $6,000 00
Amount of treasurer's bond 20,000 00
Date of examination by commissioner: April 26.

PUBLIC FUNDS.

	Par Value.	Estimated Market Value.	Amount Invested.
United States 4s, coupons . .	$75,000	$86,812 50	$75,000 00
" " 4s, registered . .	275,000	305,525 00	275,000 00
" " 4½s, registered . .	1,100	1,243 00	1,100 00
	$351,100	$393,580 50	$351,100 00

BANK STOCK.

Eliot Nat'l Bank, Boston . .	$4,000	$4,810 00	$4,000 00
Webster Nat'l Bank, Boston . .	7,500	8,362 50	7,500 00
Commerce Nat'l Bank, Boston .	5,600	7,238 00	5,600 00
Blackstone Nat'l Bank, Boston .	5,000	5,750 00	5,000 00
Washington Nat'l Bank, Boston .	5,000	7,000 00	5,000 00
Hamilton Nat'l Bank, Boston . .	10,000	12,325 00	10,000 00
Tremont Nat'l Bank, Boston . .	10,000	12,200 00	10,000 00
Suffolk Nat'l Bank, Boston . .	15,000	18,150 00	15,000 00
Globe Nat'l Bank, Boston . .	5,000	5,600 00	5,000 00
Union Nat'l Bank, Boston . .	20,600	31,672 50	20,600 00
Cambridge City N'l B'k, Cambridge,	1,400	2,310 00	1,400 00
Cambridgeport N'l B'k, C'bridgep't,	4,000	6,600 00	4,000 00
First Nat'l Bank, Cambridge . .	5,000	8,250 00	5,000 00
	$98,100	$130,268 00	$98,100 00

CAMBRIDGE SAVINGS BANK — CAMBRIDGE.

Incorporated April 2, 1834. Number of corporators, 74.

CHARLES W. SEVER, *President*. *Treasurer*, JAMES M. THURSTON.

STATEMENT.

LIABILITIES.		ASSETS.	
Deposits . . .	$1,818,418 99	Public funds . . .	$271,191 25
Earnings undivided .	37,740 88	Bank stock	287,934 73
Guaranty fund . .	25,300 00	Loans on bank stock . .	18,400 00
		Real estate by foreclosure .	155,273 46
		Loans on real estate . .	706,251 00
		Loans on personal security,	296,917 00
		Deposit in banks on interest,	142,508 97
		Expense account . . .	1,409 65
		Cash on hand . . .	1,573 81
	$1,881,459 87		$1,881,459 87

Loans on Bank Stock, amount on each: —

On 4 shares Merchants' National Bank, Boston $400 00

On 200 shares American Loan and Trust Company, Boston * . . 18,000 00

Cash on Deposit in Banks, amount in each: —

Charles River National Bank, Cambridge $15,648 88

Maverick National Bank, Boston 111,764 29

Manufacturers' National Bank, Boston 9,558 92

National Bank of Redemption, Boston 5,536 88

Amount of real estate held by foreclosure $155,273 46

Assessed value of the same 164,000 00

Amount of income received from the same 7,900 00

Amount of municipal tax on real estate 2,481 16

Whole amount of interest or profits received or earned $90,070 13

Rate and amount of each semi-annual dividend for previous year . . . . { 2 per cent . 32,602 53; 2 per cent . 33,813 33 }

Times for the dividends fixed by the by-laws: fourth Thursday in January and July.

The total amount of loans, with each specified rate of interest: $155,000, 3¾ per cent; $133,000, 4 per cent; $20,000, 4½ per cent; $8,000, 5 per cent; $200, 5½ per cent; $213,826, 6 per cent; $126,417, 6½ per cent; $248,750, 7 per cent; $112,375, 7½ per cent; $9,000, 8 per cent.

Number of outstanding loans which are of an amount not exceeding $3,000 each 323

Aggregate amount of the same 446,321 00

Number of open accounts 5,177

Number and amount of deposits received for previous year, 4,697 328,115 10

Number and amount of deposits of and exceeding $300 at any one time for the previous year 259 147,303 77

* The attention of this bank was called to the illegality of this loan.

Number and amount of withdrawals	3,438	$288,109 45
Number of accounts opened the previous year . . .	816	
Number of accounts closed the previous year	537	
Amount of expenses of the corporation during previous year .		5,000 00
Amount of treasurer's bond		20,000 00

Date of examination by commisioner: April 28.

Public Funds.

	Par Value.	Estimated Market Value.	Amount Invested.
United States 3½s	$100,000	$102,000 00	$103,718 75
State, city, and town bonds:—			
State of Massachusetts 5s . .	$4,000	$4,300 00	$4,000 00
City of Newburyport 6s . . .	18,000	20,000 00	18,090 00
of Fitchburg 6s	25,000	28,000 00	25,125 00
of Fall River 6s	20,000	22,000 00	19,000 00
of Lowell 6s	20,000	23,000 00	19,400 00
of Providence, R.I., 5s . .	22,000	24,500 00	24,035 00
of Cambridge 6s . . .	22,000	25,500 00	21,932 50
of Boston 4s	1,000	1,100 00	1,000 00
of Boston 6s	15,000	19,000 00	17,775 00
of Boston 5s	2,000	2,200 00	2,240 00
Town of Westborough 5s . .	14,000	15,000 00	14,875 00
	$263,000	$286,600 00	$271,191 25

Bank Stock.

Atlas Nat'l Bank, Boston . .	$15,900	$19,716 00	$19,054 25
Boston Nat'l Bank, Boston . .	26,500	29,680 00	29,134 37
Continental Nat'l Bank, Boston .	1,800	2,038 50	2,203 25
Eliot Nat'l Bank, Boston . .	10,700	12,010 75	12,489 12
Faneuil Hall Nat'l Bank, Boston .	4,200	5,502 00	5,484 75
Freeman's Nat'l Bank, Boston .	900	1,062 25	997 25
Globe Nat'l Bank, Boston . .	6,900	7,659 00	8,919 26
Hamilton Nat'l Bank, Boston . .	9,300	11,000 00	11,590 00
Howard Nat'l Bank, Boston . .	11,400	14,934 00	12,831 49
Market Nat'l Bank, Boston . .	5,800	6,264 00	6,280 63
Merchants' Nat'l Bank, Boston .	13,400	19,430 00	18,207 25
Shawmut Nat'l Bank, Boston . .	1,000	1,260 00	1,206 25
State Nat'l Bank, Boston . .	5,000	6,250 00	5,481 25
Suffolk Nat'l Bank, Boston . .	14,500	17,545 00	17,836 50
Third Nat'l Bank, Boston . .	20,000	21,300 00	20,598 12
Traders' Nat'l Bank, Boston . .	10,000	10,200 00	11,515 88
Tremont Nat'l Bank, Boston . .	11,700	14,274 00	14,003 25
Commerce Nat'l Bank, Boston .	12,500	16,000 00	15,309 99
Exchange Nat'l Bank, Boston . .	1,100	1,585 00	1,575 75
Eagle Nat'l Bank, Boston . .	1,100	1,300 00	1,241 88
Hide and Leather Nat'l B'k, Boston,	2,800	3,220 00	3,144 00
Revere Nat'l Bank, Boston . .	14,600	17,812 00	17,499 99
Union Nat'l Bank, Boston . .	500	765 00	719 00

BANK STOCK — Concluded.

	Par Value.	Estimated Market Value.	Amount Invested.
Charles River Nat'l B'k, Cambridge,	$2,500	$4,375 00	$2,526 00
Newton Nat'l Bank, Newton . .	4,600	4,968 00	5,880 00
Rockland Nat'l Bank, Roxbury .	3,000	4,200 00	4,625 25
Naumkeag Nat'l Bank, Salem .	5,000	9,750 00	7,800 00
First Nat'l Bank, New Bedford .	6,000	7,500 00	7,420 00
Commerce Nat'l Bank, New Bedford,	5,000	6,250 00	6,160 00
First Nat'l Bank, Leominster . .	10,000	11,000 00	11,200 00
S. Framingham N'l B'k, S. Fram'm,	5,000	5,000 00	5,000 00
	$242,700	$293,850 50	$287,934 73

CANTON INSTITUTION FOR SAVINGS — CANTON.

Incorporated 1835. Number of corporators, 31.

CHARLES H. FRENCH, *President*. *Treasurer*, FRANCIS W. DEANE.

STATEMENT.

LIABILITIES.		ASSETS.	
Deposits . . .	$411,896 48	Public funds . . .	$37,000 00
Earnings undivided .	9,966 97	Bank stock	55,300 00
Guaranty fund . .	9,511 90	Loans on bank stock . .	5,400 00
		Railroad bonds . . .	22,500 00
		Real estate by foreclosure .	18,995 00
		Loans on real estate . .	191,786 00
		Loans on personal security,	18,875 00
		Loans to counties, cities, or towns	51,109 00
		Deposit in bank on interest,	30,188 16
		Expense account . . .	222 19
	$431,375 35		$431,375 35

Loans on Bank Stock, amount on each:—

On 40 shares First National Bank, Easton $4,000 00

On 14 shares Neponset National Bank, Canton 1,400 00

Cash on Deposit in Bank:—

Neponset National Bank, Canton $30,188 16

Amount of real estate held by foreclosure . . . $18,995 00

Assessed value of the same 18,000 00

Amount of income received from the same . . . 1,383 57

Amount of municipal tax on real estate 285 08

Whole amount of interest or profits received or earned . . . $22,875 88

Rate and amount of each semi-annual dividend for previous year . . . . } 2 per cent . 7,373 44; 2 per cent . 7,716 78

Times for the dividends fixed by the by-laws: first Tuesday in April and October.

Average annual per cent of dividends for the term ending at time of and including last extra dividend: 5 per cent.

The total amount of loans, with each specified rate of interest: $30,109, 4 per cent; $10,000, 4½ per cent; $15,000, 5 per cent; $191,086, 6 per cent; $14,975, 7 per cent.

Number of outstanding loans which are of an amount not exceeding $3,000 each 199

Aggregate amount of the same 204,070 00

Number of open accounts 1,477

Number and amount of deposits received for previous year, 1,001 81,169 00

Number and amount of deposits of and exceeding $300 at any one time for the previous year 59 29,901 00

Number and amount of withdrawals 552 58,638 84

Number of accounts opened the previous year 241

Number of accounts closed the previous year 148
Amount of expenses of the corporation during previous year. . $1,189 35
Amount of treasurer's bond 10,000 00
Date of examination by commissioner: Aug. 8.

PUBLIC FUNDS.

	Par Value.	Estimated Market Value.	Amount Invested.
United States 4s, consols, registered,	$20,000	$23,200 00	$20,000 00
City and town bonds: —			
City of Providence, R.I., 5s . .	$10,000	$11,200 00	$10,000 00
of Lynn 6s	2,000	2,160 00	2,000 00
of Lynn 5s	1,000	1,000 00	1,000 00
Town of Wakefield 6s . . .	4,000	4,080 00	4,000 00
	$37,000	$41,640 00	$37,000 00

BANK STOCK.

	Par Value.	Estimated Market Value.	Amount Invested.
Neponset Nat'l Bank, Canton . .	$11.300	$15,455 00	$11,300 00
North Nat'l Bank, Boston . .	1,700	2,314 00	1,700 00
Globe Nat'l Bank, Boston . .	3.300	3,679 50	3,300 00
Shoe and Leather Nat'l B'k, Boston,	2,500	2,812 50	2,500 00
Atlas Nat'l Bank, Boston . .	2,500	3,125 00	2,500 00
Freeman's Nat'l Bank, Boston .	4,000	4,800 00	4,000 00
Central Nat'l Bank, Boston . .	2,500	3,000 00	2,500 00
Blackstone Nat'l Bank, Boston .	2,500	2,875 00	2,500 00
Market Nat'l Bank, Boston . .	5,000	5,487 50	5,000 00
Pacific Nat'l Bank, Boston . .	10,000	10,500 00	10,000 00
North America Nat'l Bank, Boston.	5,000	5,750 00	5,000 00
Eagle Nat'l Bank, Boston . .	2,500	3,000 00	2,500 00
Webster Nat'l Bank, Boston . .	2,500	2,787 50	2,500 00
	$55,300	$65,586 00	$55,300 00

RAILROAD BONDS.

	Par Value.	Estimated Market Value.	Amount Invested.
Boston and Albany Railroad 7s .	$12,000	$15,240 00	$12,000 00
Boston and Maine Railroad 7s . .	5,000	6,350 00	5,000 00
Eastern Railroad 4½s	5,500	6,036 25	5,500 00
	$22,500	$27,626 25	$22,500 00

CAPE ANN SAVINGS BANK — GLOUCESTER.

Incorporated 1846. Number of corporators, 50.

ADDISON GILBERT, *President*. *Treasurer*, GEORGE J. MARSH.

STATEMENT.

Liabilities.		Assets.	
Deposits . . .	$1,161,642 04	Public funds . . .	$77,000 00
Earnings undivided .	11,813 20	Loans on public funds .	4,000 00
Guaranty fund . .	34,000 00	Bank stock . . .	201,400 00
Surplus . . .	13,695 82	Loans on bank stock . .	18,000 00
Sundry accounts . .	1,096 34	Railroad bonds . . .	31,875 00
		Real estate	6,000 00
		Real estate by foreclosure .	8,053 68
		Loans on real estate . .	473,443 00
		Loans on personal security,	283,700 00
		Loans to counties, cities, or towns	105,500 00
		Deposit in banks on interest,	10,320 52
		Expense account . . .	6 86
		Sundry accounts . . .	323 97
		Cash on hand . . .	2,624 37
	$1,222,247 40		$1,222,247 40

Loans on Public Funds, amount on each: —

On $4,000 United States 4s, coupon bonds	$4,000 00

Loans on Bank Stock, amount on each: —

On 53 shares City National Bank, Gloucester	$8,000 00
On 9 shares Salem National Bank, Salem	
On 10 shares Hide and Leather National Bank, Boston . . .	
On 5 shares National Bank of the Commonwealth, Boston . .	
On 2 shares Mechanics' National Bank, Boston	
On 9 shares Rockport National Bank, Rockport	
On 100 shares City National Bank, Gloucester	10,000 00

Cash on Deposit in Banks, amount in each: —

Cape Ann National Bank, Gloucester	$1,239 90
National Bank of Redemption, Boston	2,320 52
Maverick National Bank, Boston	8,000 00

Amount invested in real estate (for banking purposes) . . .	$6,000 00
Estimated value of the same	7,000 00
Amount of real estate held by foreclosure	8,053 68
Assessed value of the same	10,000 00
Amount of income received from the same	1,087 57
Amount of municipal tax on real estate	317 78

Whole amount of interest or profits received or earned . . .		$67,194 55
Rate and amount of each semi-annual dividend for previous year	2 per cent .	19,674 47
	2 per cent .	21,124 89

Times for the dividends fixed by the by-laws: April 1 and Oct. 1.

Average annual per cent of dividends for the term ending at time of and including last extra dividend: $5\frac{3}{10}$ per cent.

The total amount of loans, with each specified rate of interest: $63,000, 4 per cent; $20,000, $4\frac{1}{4}$ per cent; $24,000, $4\frac{1}{2}$ per cent; $25,000, $4\frac{3}{4}$ per cent; $226,000, 5 per cent; $40,000, $5\frac{1}{4}$ per cent; $2,000 $5\frac{1}{2}$ per cent; $118,050, 6 per cent; $339,968, 7 per cent; $26,625, $7\frac{3}{10}$ per cent.

Number of outstanding loans which are of an amount not exceeding $3,000 each	423	
Aggregate amount of the same		$339,243 00
Number of open accounts	4,330	
Number and amount of deposits received for previous year,	3,862	277,295 32
Number and amount of deposits of and exceeding $300 at any one time for the previous year	159	132,616 00
Number and amount of withdrawals	3,048	178,704 46
Number of accounts opened the previous year	985	
Number of accounts closed the previous year	568	
Amount of expenses of the corporation during previous year		3,358 28
Amount of treasurer's bond		20,000 00

Date of examination by commissioner: July 26.

Public Funds.

	Par Value.	Estimated Market Value.	Amount Invested.
United States 4s, registered	$5,000	$5,850 00	$5,000 00
City and town bonds:—			
City of Charlestown, 1891	$12,000	$13,800 00	$12,000 00
of Cambridge, 1894	10,000	11,500 00	10,000 00
of Fall River, 1891	8,000	9,200 00	8,000 00
of Lowell, 1890	15,000	17,250 00	15,000 00
of Lawrence, 1894	5,000	5,750 00	5,000 00
of Northampton, 1892	5,000	5,750 00	5,000 00
of Salem, 1891 and 1882	2,000	2,300 00	2,000 00
of Somerville, 1884	10,000	11,500 00	10,000 00
Town of Brookline, 1889	5,000	6,100 00	5,000 00
	$77,000	$89,000 00	$77,000 00

Bank Stock.

Atlas Nat'l Bank, Boston	$10,000	$13,000 00	$10,000 00
Atlantic Nat'l Bank, Boston	10,000	15,500 00	10,000 00
Blackstone Nat'l Bank, Boston	11,200	14,560 00	11,200 00
Cape Ann Nat'l Bank, Gloucester	8,500	12,750 00	8,500 00
City Nat'l Bank, Gloucester	10,000	12,000 00	10,000 00
City Nat'l Bank, Boston	5,000	6,350 00	5,000 00
Central Nat'l Bank, Boston	5,000	6,100 00	5,000 00
Commerce Nat'l Bank, Boston	10,000	13,000 00	10,000 00
Eagle Nat'l Bank, Boston	10,000	12,100 00	10,000 00
Everett Nat'l Bank, Boston	3,000	3,540 00	3,000 00

BANK STOCK — Concluded.

	Par Value.	Estimated Market Value.	Amount Invested.
Freeman's Nat'l Bank, Boston . .	$5,000	$6,350 00	$5,000 00
Exchange Nat'l Bank, Boston . .	5,000	7,400 00	5,000 00
Gloucester Nat'l Bank, Gloucester .	5,000	6,500 00	5,000 00
Georgetown Nat'l B'k, Georgetown .	5,000	5,000 00	5,000 00
Globe Nat'l Bank, Boston . .	200	228 00	200 00
Howard Nat'l Bank, Boston . .	5,000	6,550 00	5,000 00
Hamilton Nat'l Bank, Boston . .	5,000	6,200 00	5,000 00
Merchants' Nat'l Bank, Boston .	10,000	15,000 00	10,000 00
North Nat'l Bank, Boston . .	10,000	14,400 00	10,000 00
North America Nat'l Bank, Boston .	10,000	12,000 00	10,000 00
New England Nat'l Bank, Boston .	4,000	6,120 00	4,000 00
Old Boston Nat'l Bank, Boston .	2,500	3,250 00	2,500 00
Redemption Nat'l Bank, Boston .	16,600	22,576 00	16,600 00
Republic Nat'l Bank, Boston . .	5,000	6,600 00	5,000 00
Rockport Nat'l Bank, Rockport .	5,400	7,290 00	5,400 00
Second Nat'l Bank, Boston . .	5,000	7,700 00	5,000 00
Shawmut Nat'l Bank, Boston . .	10,000	12,600 00	10,000 00
State Nat'l Bank, Boston . .	5,000	6,400 00	5,000 00
Tremont Nat'l Bank, Boston . .	5,000	6,300 00	5,000 00
	$201,400	$267,364 00	$201,400 00

RAILROAD BONDS.

Eastern Railroad, 1906 . .	$42,500	$40,750 00	$31,875 00

CAPE COD FIVE CENTS SAVINGS BANK—HARWICH.

Incorporated 1855. Number of corporators, 78.

SAMUEL H. GOULD, *President*. *Treasurer*, MARSHALL S. UNDERWOOD.

STATEMENT.

LIABILITIES.		ASSETS.	
Deposits	$231,032 96	Bank stock	$47,151 00
Earnings undivided	5,388 51	Real estate	1,635 33
Guaranty fund	840 56	Real estate (to secure indebtedness)	21,413 00
		Real estate by foreclosure	4,992 00
		Loans on real estate	63,565 69
		Loans on personal security,	70,574 12
		Loans to counties, cities, or towns	10,887 50
		Deposit in bank on interest,	16,157 33
		Cash on hand	886 06
	$237,262 03		$237,262 03

Cash on Deposit in Bank:—

Cape Cod National Bank, Harwich	$16,157 33

Amount invested in real estate (for banking purposes)	$1,635 33
Estimated value of the same	1,635 33
Amount of real estate held by foreclosure	4,992 00
Assessed value of the same	3,500 00
Amount of income received from the same	190 00
Amount of municipal tax on real estate	275 00

Whole amount of interest or profits received or earned		$20,347 56
Rate and amount of each semi-annual dividend for previous year	2 per cent	4,096 48
	2 per cent	4,217 08

Times for the dividends fixed by the by-laws: second Wednesday in April and October.

The total amount of loans, with each specified rate of interest: $5,500, 5 per cent; $20,975, 6 per cent; $11,556.81, 6½ per cent; $106,995.50, 7 per cent.

Number of outstanding loans which are of an amount not exceeding $3,000 each	313	
Aggregate amount of the same		115,558 31
Number of open accounts	1,710	
Number and amount of deposits received for previous year	455	62,999 90
Number and amount of deposits of and exceeding $300 at any one time for the previous year	57	27,097 29
Number and amount of withdrawals	625	45,076 60
Number of accounts opened the previous year	169	
Number of accounts closed the previous year	263	
Amount of expenses of the corporation during previous year		1,000 00
Amount of treasurer's bond		10,000 00

Date of examination by commissioner: June 21.

BANK STOCK.

	Par Value.	Estimated Market Value.	Amount Invested.
Cape Cod Nat'l Bank, Harwich . .	$7,100	$9,940 00	$9,798 00
First Nat'l Bank, Yarmouthport .	6,300	8,190 00	8,064 00
Nat'l Bank of the Republic, Boston,	1,500	1,965 00	1,950 00
Shawmut Nat'l Bank, Boston . .	3,200	4,080 00	3,952 00
Hide and Leather Nat'l B'k, Boston,	2,000	2,365 00	2,380 00
Blackstone Nat'l Bank, Boston .	2,700	3,105 00	3,138 00
Nat'l Bank of Commerce, Boston .	1,700	2,189 00	2,129 00
Revere Nat'l Bank, Boston . .	3,000	3,660 00	3,675 00
Nat'l Bank of N. America, Boston .	1,600	1,840 00	1,836 00
State Nat'l Bank, Boston . .	4,400	5,522 00	5,544 00
Everett Nat'l Bank, Boston . .	4,000	4,685 00	4,685 00
	$37,500	$47,541 00	$47,151 00

CENTRAL SAVINGS BANK — LOWELL.

Incorporated March 3, 1871. Number of corporators, 91.

OLIVER H. MOULTON, *President*. *Treasurer*, SAMUEL A. CHASE.

STATEMENT.

LIABILITIES.		ASSETS.	
Deposits	$1,031,655 53	Public funds	$23,000 00
Earnings undivided .	21,558 24	Loans on public funds .	7,000 00
Guaranty fund . .	14,185 90	Bank stock	200,333 75
Interest . . .	202 00	Real estate by foreclosure .	175,250 00
		Loans on real estate . .	463,098 00
		Loans on personal security,	87,950 00
		Deposit in banks on interest,	110,284 28
		Expense account . . .	15 50
		Cash on hand . . .	670 14
	$1,067,601 67		$1,067,601 67

Loans on Public Funds, amount on each:—

On $5,000 United States 4s and 4½s	$5,000 00
On $1,000 City of Chelsea 6s and $1,000 City of Lawrence 6s .	2,000 00

Cash on Deposit in Banks, amount in each:—

Old Lowell National Bank, Lowell	$102,738 72
Merchants' National Bank, Lowell	7,545 56

Amount of real estate held by foreclosure		$175,250 00
Assessed value of the same		186,800 00
Amount of income received from the same		15,731 90
Amount of municipal tax on real estate		3,343 81
Whole amount of interest or profits received or earned		$59,460 89
Rate and amount of each semi-annual dividend for previous year	2 per cent .	16,602 05
	2 per cent .	18,108 62
Times for the dividends fixed by the by-laws: first Saturday in May and November.		
The total amount of loans, with each specified rate of interest: $27,000, 4½ per cent; $37,800, 5 per cent; $21,250, 5½ per cent; $385,148, 6 per cent; $14,250, 6½ per cent; $71,400, 7 per cent; $1,200, 8 per cent.		
Number of outstanding loans which are of an amount not exceeding $3,000 each	100	
Aggregate amount of the same		149,928 00
Number of open accounts	2,986	
Number and amount of deposits received for previous year,	2,557	281,069 36
Number and amount of deposits of and exceeding $300 at any one time for the previous year	274	160,271 00
Number and amount of withdrawals	1,954	191,290 56
Number of accounts opened the previous year	732	
Number of accounts closed the previous year	486	

Amount of expenses of the corporation during previous year . . $3,936 91
Amount of treasurer's bond 20,000 00
Date of examination by commissioner: July 19.

PUBLIC FUNDS.

	Par Value.	Estimated Market Value.	Amount Invested.
City and town bonds:—			
City of Haverhill 6s . . .	$4,000	$4,300 00	$4,000 00
Town of Methuen	19,000	20,500 00	19,000 00
	$23,000	$24,800 00	$23,000 00

BANK STOCK.

	Par Value.	Estimated Market Value.	Amount Invested.
Atlantic Nat'l Bank, Boston . .	$10,000	$15,100 00	$14,000 00
Blackstone Nat'l Bank, Boston .	8,700	10,392 00	11,100 00
Boston Nat'l Bank, Boston . .	5,000	6,500 00	6,000 00
Central Nat'l Bank, Boston . .	20,000	24,000 00	20,000 00
City Nat'l Bank, Boston . . .	10,000	12,400 00	12,000 00
Commerce Nat'l Bank, Boston .	9,800	12,446 00	9,800 00
Eliot Nat'l Bank, Boston . .	9,500	11,335 00	11,000 00
Hide and Leather Nat'l Bank, Boston,	1,500	1,755 00	1,600 00
Market Nat'l Bank, Boston . .	5,000	5,550 00	5,500 00
Maverick Nat'l Bank, Boston . .	1,000	2,500 00	1,217 50
Merchants' Nat'l Bank, Boston .	5,000	7,350 00	6,756 25
Metropolitan Nat'l Bank, Boston .	2,000	2,440 00	2,000 00
Redemption Nat'l Bank, Boston .	6,000	7,980 00	8,000 00
Republic Nat'l Bank, Boston . .	2,700	3,560 00	3,415 50
Second Nat'l Bank, Boston . .	7,000	10,570 00	10,000 00
Shawmut Nat'l Bank, Boston . .	6,300	7,869 00	8,086 00
Suffolk Nat'l Bank, Boston . .	5,000	6,150 00	6,112 50
Shoe and Leather Nat'l B'k, Boston,	4,200	4,788 00	5,000 00
Webster Nat'l Bank, Boston . .	2,400	2,762 00	2,400 00
Appleton Nat'l Bank, Lowell . .	10,000	17,000 00	16,962 50
First Nat'l Bank, Lowell . .	2,000	3,000 00	2,740 00
Merchants' Nat'l Bank, Lowell .	15,000	19,500 00	18,350 00
Old Lowell Nat'l Bank, Lowell .	4,700	5,875 00	6,092 00
Prescott Nat'l Bank, Lowell . .	1,000	1,400 00	1,000 00
Railroad Nat'l Bank, Lowell . .	1,000	1,200 00	1,201 50
Georgetown Nat'l Bank, Georgetown,	10,000	10,500 00	10,000 00
	$164,800	$213,922 00	$200,333 75

CHARLESTOWN FIVE CENTS SAVINGS BANK — BOSTON.

Incorporated 1854. Number of corporators, 124.

P. J. STONE, *President.* *Treasurer*, AMOS STONE.

STATEMENT.

LIABILITIES.		ASSETS.	
Deposits	$2,134,995 20	Public funds	$200,000 00
Earnings undivided	135,080 31	Loans on public funds	2,500 00
Guaranty fund	50,000 00	Bank stock	602,000 00
		Loans on bank stock	500 00
		Real estate	80,000 00
		Real estate by foreclosure	377,500 00
		Loans on real estate	948,826 00
		Loans on personal security,	18,850 00
		Deposit in banks on interest,	85,211 28
		Cash on hand	4,688 23
	$2,320,075 51		$2,320,075 51

Loan on Public Funds:

On $2,500 United States 4s . $2,500 00

Loans on Bank Stock:—

On 5 shares Monument National Bank, Boston $500 00

Cash on Deposit in Banks, amount in each:—

Monument National Bank, Boston . $66,384 49

Maverick National Bank, Boston . 18,826 79

Amount invested in real estate (for banking purposes) . $80,000 00

Assessed value of the same . 90,300 00

Amount of real estate held by foreclosure . 377,500 00

Assessed value of the same . 382,850 00

Amount of income received from the same . 24,587 76

Amount of municipal tax on real estate . 8,513 29

Whole amount of interest or profits received or earned . $160,289 94

Rate and amount of each semi-annual dividend for previous year . 2½ per cent . 52,938 24; 2½ per cent . 53,162 52

Times for the dividends fixed by the by-laws: third Wednesday in April and October.

Average annual per cent of dividends for the term ending at time of and including last extra dividend: 7½ per cent.

The total amount of loans, with each specified rate of interest: $6,900, 5 per cent; 3,100, 5½ per cent; $543,694, 6 per cent; $94,880, 6½ per cent; $307,582, 7 per cent; $200, 7$\frac{3}{10}$ per cent; $9,400, 7½ per cent; $5,000, 8 per cent.

Number of outstanding loans which are of an amount not exceeding $3,000 each. . 361

Aggregate amount of the same . 605,626 00

Amount of investments from which no income is received . 6,000 00

Number of open accounts . 7,099

Number and amount of deposits received for previous year, 3,321 234,953 19

Number and amount of deposits of and exceeding $300 at any one time for the previous year . 224 134,366 38

Number and amount of withdrawals . 3,882 407,684 60

Number of accounts opened the previous year 675
Number of accounts closed the previous year 1,145
Amount of expenses of the corporation during previous year . $5,583 60
Amount of treasurer's bond 30,000 00
Date of examination by commissioner: April 12.

PUBLIC FUNDS.

	Par Value.	Estimated Market Value.	Amount Invested.
United States 4½s	$200,000	$225,000 00	$200,000 00

BANK STOCK.

Boylston Nat'l Bank, Boston . .	$9,300	$11,904 00	$9,300 00
Continental Nat'l Bank, Boston .	44,000	51,920 00	44,000 00
North Nat'l Bank, Boston . .	14,000	19,880 00	14,000 00
Hide and Leather Nat'l B'k, Boston,	37,000	42,920 00	37,000 00
Revere Nat'l Bank, Boston . .	20,700	25,254 00	20,700 00
Shoe and Leather Nat'l B'k, Boston,	16,100	18,032 00	16,000 00
Eliot Nat'l Bank, Boston . .	30,000	36,000 00	30,000 00
Redemption Nat'l Bank, Boston .	20,000	27,000 00	20,000 00
Maverick Nat'l Bank, Boston . .	13,200	33,000 00	12,900 00
Webster Nat'l Bank, Boston . .	17,100	18,981 00	17,100 00
Howard Nat'l Bank, Boston . .	30,400	39,520 00	30,400 00
Republic Nat'l Bank, Boston . .	24,200	31,460 00	24,200 00
Market Nat'l Bank, Boston . .	8,600	9,460 00	8,600 00
Third Nat'l Bank, Boston . .	10,000	10,600 00	10,000 00
Suffolk Nat'l Bank, Boston . .	18,500	22,385 00	18,500 00
State Nat'l Bank, Boston . .	16,100	20,125 00	16,100 00
City Nat'l Bank, Boston . . .	9,000	11,430 00	9,000.00
Washington Nat'l Bank, Boston. .	11,900	16,660 00	11,900 00
Tremont Nat'l Bank, Boston . .	12,000	14,640 00	12,000 00
First Nat'l Bank, Boston . . .	2,000	4,140 00	2,000 00
Atlas Nat'l Bank, Boston . .	35,800	44,750 00	35,800 00
Commerce Nat'l Bank, Boston .	26,300	33,664 00	26,300 00
Blackstone Nat'l Bank, Boston .	9,400	10,810 00	9,400 00
Metropolitan Nat'l Bank, Boston .	4,800	5,856 00	4,800 00
Freeman's Nat'l Bank, Boston .	10,000	12,000 00	9,300 00
Columbian Nat'l Bank, Boston .	5,000	7,100 00	5,000 00
Pacific Nat'l Bank, Boston . .	20,000	20,900 00	20,000 00
First Ward Nat'l Bank, E. Boston .	15,000	17,400 00	14,800 00
Blue Hill Nat'l Bank, Dorchester .	5,300	5,830 00	5,300 00
Bunker Hill Nat'l B'k, Charlestown,	25,000	43,750 00	25,000 00
Monument Nat'l Bank, Charlestown,	7,000	14,350 00	7,000 00
Market Nat'l Bank, Brighton . .	2,700	3,564 00	2,700 00
Brighton Nat'l Bank, Brighton .	5,300	5,671 00	5,100 00
First Nat'l Bank, Lynn . . .	21,700	27,125 00	21,700 00
Newton Nat'l Bank, Newton . .	2,400	2,736 00	2,200 00
Andover Nat'l Bank, Andover .	2,400	2,880 00	2,400 00
Wachusett Nat'l Bank, Fitchburg .	7,500	15,000 00	7,500 00
Railroad Nat'l Bank, Lowell . .	15,000	18,000 00	15,000 00
Home Nat'l Bank, Brockton . .	15,000	16,200 00	15,000 00
Conway Nat'l Bank, Conway . .	4,000	5,320 00	4,000 00
	$603,700	$778,217 00	$602,000 00

CHELSEA SAVINGS BANK — CHELSEA.

Incorporated April 25, 1854. Number of corporators, 250.

JOHN H. OSGOOD, *President.* *Treasurer,* JOHN F. FELLOWS.

STATEMENT.

LIABILITIES.		ASSETS.	
Deposits	$1,333,210 37	Public funds	$349,555 75
Earnings undivided	15,975 57	Bank stock	110,689 55
Guaranty fund	15,515 00	Railroad bonds	11,225 00
		Real estate	13,241 54
		Real estate by foreclosure	27,395 88
		Loans on real estate	581,204 66
		Loans on personal security,	8,375 00
		Loans to counties, cities, or towns	187,060 00
		Deposit in bank on interest,	66,071 60
		Expense account	2,101 00
		Cash on hand	7,780 96
	$1,364,700 94		$1,364,700 94

Cash on Deposit in Bank:—

Hamilton National Bank, Boston $66,071 60

Amount invested in real estate (for banking purposes) . . $13,241 54
Estimated value of the same 13,500 00
Amount of real estate held by foreclosure 27,395 88
Assessed value of the same 37,600 00
Amount of income received from the same 1,419 00
Amount of municipal tax on real estate 697 30

Whole amount of interest or profits received or earned . . . $58,310 56
Rate and amount of each semi-annual dividend for previous year . . . { 2 per cent . . 22,567 05; 2 per cent . . 23,934 52 }
Times for the dividends fixed by the by-laws: second Wednesday in April and October.
Average annual per cent of dividends for the term ending at time of and including last extra dividend: 6¼ per cent.
The total amount of loans, with each specified rate of interest: $147,060, 4½ per cent; $10,000, 5 per cent; $15,000, 5½ per cent; $604,579.66, 6 per cent.
Number of outstanding loans which are of an amount not exceeding $3,000 each 345
Aggregate amount of the same 439,779 66
Number of open accounts 6,249
Number and amount of deposits received for previous year, 8,092 402,687 95
Number and amount of deposits of and exceeding $300 at any one time for the previous year 372 154,885 00
Number and amount of withdrawals 4,724 290,344 59
Number of accounts opened the previous year 1,256
Number of accounts closed the previous year 720
Amount of expenses of the corporation during previous year . . 4,839 02
Amount of treasurer's bond 25,000 00
Date of examination by commissioner: April 21.

PUBLIC FUNDS.

	Par Value.	Estimated Market Value.	Amount Invested.
United States bonds	$30,000	$33,862 50	$31,068 75
State, city, and town bonds: —			
State of Maine	$47,600	$54,859 00	$47,600 00
of New Hampshire	9,200	11,592 00	10,635 75
of Rhode Island	2,000	2,020 00	1,935 00
City of Chelsea	12,000	14,160 00	13,880 00
of Boston	44,000	55,430 00	51,136 25
of Charlestown	10,000	11,500 00	11,190 00
of Fitchburg	2,000	2,320 00	2,280 00
of Worcester	21,000	21,340 00	22,660 00
of Somerville	10,000	10,400 00	10,000 00
of Lynn	6,000	6,960 00	7,050 00
of Cambridge	19,000	21,850 00	20,790 00
of Lowell	4,000	4,560 00	4,542 50
of Fall River	5,000	7,250 00	5,550 00
of Lawrence	36,000	44,530 00	40,527 50
of Taunton	2,000	2,340 00	2,340 00
of Manchester, N.H.	4,000	4,320 00	4,000 00
of Lewiston, Me.	16,000	16,800 00	16,480 00
of Burlington, Vt.	2,500	2,700 00	2,500 00
of Providence, R.I.	15,000	15,900 00	15,525 00
of Hartford, Conn.	1,000	1,160 00	1,172 50
Town of Woburn	5,000	5,700 00	5,412 50
of Winthrop	11,000	11,660 00	11,165 00
of Everett	1,000	1,130 00	1,170 00
of Provincetown	1,000	1,030 00	1,000 00
of Brookline	5,000	5,600 00	5,625 00
of Danvers	2,000	2,200 00	2,320 00
	$323,300	$373,173 50	$349,555 75

BANK STOCK.

	Par Value.	Estimated Market Value.	Amount Invested.
North Nat'l Bank, Boston	$1,500	$2,160 00	$1,664 55
Howard Nat'l Bank, Boston	3,600	4,608 00	3,811 50
Massachusetts Nat'l Bank, Boston	6,750	8,370 00	9,122 40
Continental Nat'l Bank, Boston	4,000	4,720 00	4,845 70
Commerce Nat'l Bank, Boston	700	903 00	700 00
Traders' Nat'l Bank, Boston	7,000	7,140 00	7,556 13
Exchange Nat'l Bank, Boston	1,400	2,026 00	1,763 05
North America Nat'l Bank, Boston,	500	580 00	518 75
Boylston Nat'l Bank, Boston	2,500	3,200 00	2,776 50
Atlas Nat'l Bank, Boston	8,400	10,416 00	9,819 35
State Nat'l Bank, Boston	2,500	3,125 00	2,934 00
Suffolk Nat'l Bank, Boston	700	847 00	845 85
City Nat'l Bank, Boston	4,300	5,332 00	4,956 15
Eagle Nat'l Bank, Boston	1,800	2,124 00	2,002 95
Shawmut Nat'l Bank, Boston	500	620 00	602 50
Boston Nat'l Bank, Boston	2,000	2,560 00	2,329 37
Market Nat'l Bank, Boston	600	660 00	646 50

BANK STOCK — Concluded.

	Par Value.	Estimated Market Value.	Amount Invested.
Commonwealth Nat'l Bank, Boston,	$2,500	$3,125 00	$3,000 00
Webster Nat'l Bank, Boston . .	2,500	2,750 00	2,750 00
Republic Nat'l Bank, Boston . .	10,000	12,800 00	13,137 50
Mechanics' Nat'l Bank, Boston .	900	1,143 00	1,170 00
Atlantic Nat'l Bank, Boston . .	3,800	5,814 00	5,804 50
Everett Nat'l Bank, Boston . .	3,800	4,375 00	4,422 25
Third Nat'l Bank, Boston . .	5,000	5,300 00	5,381 25
Redemption Nat'l Bank, Boston .	6,300	8,316 00	8,410 50
First Nat'l Bank, Chelsea . .	6,600	8,250 00	6,671 30
First Nat'l Bank, South Weymouth,	2,000	2,500 00	2,420 50
Exchange Nat'l Bank, Salem . .	500	590 00	626 50
	$92,650	$114,354 00	$110,689 55

RAILROAD BONDS.

Salem and Lowell Railroad .	$10,000	$11,300 00	$11,225 00

CHICOPEE FALLS SAVINGS BANK — CHICOPEE FALLS.

Incorporated March 20, 1875. Number of corporators, 41.

JOSIAH W. OSGOOD, *President.* *Treasurer*, EDGAR T. PAIGE.

STATEMENT.

LIABILITIES.		ASSETS.	
Deposits . . .	$81,227 78	Public funds . . .	$3,050 00
Guaranty fund . .	513 46	Bank stock	16,535 00
Profit and loss . .	517 10	Loans on real estate . .	42,017 00
Interest . . .	31 60	Loans on personal security,	17,882 97
		Cash on hand . . .	2,804 97
	$82,289 94		$82,289 94

Cash on Deposit in Bank: —
City National Bank, Springfield . . . $2,694 97

Whole amount of interest or profits received or earned		$4,025 91
Rate and amount of each semi-annual dividend for previous year	2¼ per cent .	1,396 39
	2¼ per cent .	1,591 39

Times for the dividends fixed by the by-laws: January and July.

Average annual per cent of dividends for the term ending at time of and including last extra dividend: 4½ per cent.

The total amount of loans, with each specified rate of interest: $5,465, 5 per cent; $4,200, 5½ per cent; $5,000, 5¾ per cent; $43,730.19, 6 per cent; $425, 6½ per cent; $1,079.78, 7 per cent.

Number of outstanding loans which are of an amount not exceeding $3,000 each	56	
Aggregate amount of the same		49,434 97
Number of open accounts	339	
Number and amount of deposits received for previous year .	586	35,949 51
Number and amount of deposits of and exceeding $300 at any one time for the previous year	24	16,023 59
Number and amount of withdrawals	256	24,098 70
Number of accounts opened the previous year	83	
Number of accounts closed the previous year	81	
Amount of expenses of the corporation during previous year .		79 40
Amount of treasurer's bond		5,000 00

Date of examination by commissioner: Oct. 19.

PUBLIC FUNDS.

	Par Value.	Estimated Market Value.	Amount Invested.
United States 4s . . .	$3,050	$3,538 00	$3,050 00

BANK STOCK.

	Par Value.	Estimated Market Value.	Amount Invested.
City Nat'l Bank, Springfield . .	$5,000	$6,250 00	$5,000 00
Palmer Nat'l Bank, Palmer . .	1,000	1,200 00	1,120 00
Hadley Falls Nat'l Bank, Holyoke .	4,000	7,000 00	6,785 00
Chapin Nat'l Bank, Springfield .	3,000	3,900 00	3,630 00
	$13,000	$18,350 00	$16,535 00

CHICOPEE SAVINGS BANK — CHICOPEE.

Incorporated 1845. Number of corporators, 54.

JOHN B. WOOD, *President*. *Treasurer*, H. H. HARRIS.

STATEMENT.

LIABILITIES.		ASSETS.	
Deposits	$487,959 70	Public funds	$1,000 00
Earnings undivided	5,295 97	Bank stock	25,000 00
Guaranty fund	5,373 29	Loans on bank stock	13,400 00
Bills payable	10,000 00	Railroad bonds	17,000 00
Special deposit	42 87	Loans on real estate	316,566 25
		Loans on personal security,	65,280 57
		Loans to counties, cities, or towns	41,900 00
		Deposit in banks on interest,	24,677 40
		Cash on hand	3,847 61
	$508,671 83		$508,671 83

Loans on Bank Stock, amount on each:—

On 20 shares Third National Bank, Springfield	$2,000 00
On 67 shares First National Bank, Springfield }	11,400 00
On 47 shares Chicopee National Bank, Springfield }	

Cash on Deposit in Banks, amount in each:—

National Bank of the Commonwealth	$10,677 40
Hampshire County National Bank	14,000 00

Whole amount of interest or profits received or earned		$27,262 52
Rate and amount of each semi-annual dividend for previous year	2 per cent	8,790 87
	2 per cent	8,853 36
Times for the dividends fixed by the by-laws: Jan. 1 and July 1.		
The total amount of loans, with each specified rate of interest: $8,000, 4 per cent; $5,000, 4½ per cent; $127,950, 5 per cent; $5,500, 5¼ per cent; $304,096.82, 6 per cent.		
Number of outstanding loans which are of an amount not exceeding $3,000 each	257	
Aggregate amount of the same		201,111 82
Number of open accounts	1,397	
Number and amount of deposits received for previous year,	1,516	172,745 30
Number and amount of deposits of and exceeding $300 at any one time for the previous year	102	82,666 89
Number and amount of withdrawals	1,198	148,133 73
Number of accounts opened the previous year	276	
Number of accounts closed the previous year	204	
Amount of expenses of the corporation during previous year		2,139 06
Amount of treasurer's bond		10,000 00
Date of examination by commissioner: Oct. 19.		

Public Funds.

	Par Value.	Estimated Market Value.	Amount Invested.
United States 4s	$1,000	$1,100 00	$1,000 00

Bank Stock.

First Nat'l Bank, Chicopee . .	$10,000	$15,000 00	$10,000 00
Chapin Nat'l Bank, Springfield .	6,600	7,260 00	6,600 00
City Nat'l Bank, Springfield . .	3,000	3,300 00	3,000 00
Palmer Nat'l Bank, Palmer . .	3,000	3,150 00	3,000 00
Maverick Nat'l Bank, Boston . .	1,200	2,400 00	2,400 00
	$23,800	$31,110 00	$25,000 00

Railroad Bonds.

Boston and Albany Railroad . .	$12,000	$13,200 00	$12,000 09
Boston, Revere Beach, and Lynn R.R.	5,000	5,500 00	5,000 00
	$17,000	$18,700 00	$17,000 00

CITIZENS' SAVINGS BANK — FALL RIVER.

Incorporated 1851. Number of corporators, 56.

JOSEPH OSBORN, *President*. *Treasurer*, E. E. HATHAWAY.

STATEMENT.

LIABILITIES.		ASSETS.	
Deposits	$1,960,783 24	Bank stock	$285,791 50
Earnings undivided .	68,127 07	Real estate by foreclosure .	10,711 42
Guaranty fund . .	24,013 04	Loans on real estate . .	970,302 00
		Loans on personal security,*	773,804 87
		Expense account . . .	1,369 12
		Cash on hand . . .	10,944 44
	$2,052,923 35		$2,052,923 35

Cash on Deposit in Bank: —

Pocasset National Bank		$8,775 29
Amount of real estate held by foreclosure		$10,711 42
Assessed value of the same		6,700 00
Amount of income received from the same		387 31
Amount of municipal tax on real estate		127 30
Whole amount of interest or profits received or earned		$103,286 83
Rate and amount of each semi-annual dividend for previous year	2½ per cent .	42,384 29
	2½ per cent .	44,843 39

Times for the dividends fixed by the by-laws: June and December.

The total amount of loans, with each specified rate of interest: $213,000, 4 per cent; $64,500, 4½ per cent; $1,406,606.87, 5 per cent.

Number of outstanding loans which are of an amount not exceeding $3,000 each	219	
Aggregate amount of the same		314,642 00
Amount of investments from which no income is received . .		14,000 00
Number of open accounts	3,448	
Number and amount of deposits received for previous year,	8,606	467,838 55
Number and amount of deposits of and exceeding $300 at any one time for the previous year	379	249,592 51
Number and amount of withdrawals	2,155	267,371 85
Number of accounts opened the previous year	910	
Number of accounts closed the previous year	491	
Amount of expenses of the corporation during previous year .		5,979 05
Amount of treasurer's bond		15,000 00

Date of examination by commissioner: July 18.

* This bank has been notified that these loans have exceeded the legal limit.

BANK STOCK.

	Par Value.	Estimated Market Value.	Amount Invested.
First Nat'l Bank, Boston . . .	$25,000	$51,937 50	$25,000 00
Second Nat'l Bank, Fall River .	18,000	20,700 00	18,000 00
Hide and Leather Nat'l B'k, Boston,	22,500	26,212 50	22,500 00
Commerce Nat'l Bank, Boston .	7,500	9,636 25	7,500 00
Fall River Nat'l Bank, Fall River .	14,400	19,440 00	13,012 50
Pocasset Nat'l Bank, Fall River .	80,000	108,000 00	80,000 00
Maverick Nat'l Bank, Boston . .	5,400	13,500 00	4,779 00
Howard Nat'l Bank, Boston . .	14,000	18,217 50	14,000 00
Eliot Nat'l Bank, Boston . . .	7,900	9,499 75	7,900 00
Metacomet Nat'l Bank, Fail River .	28,700	35,875 00	28,700 00
Revere Nat'l Bank, Boston . .	28,100	34,282 00	28,100 00
Union Nat'l Bank, Fall River . .	15,500	17,060 00	15,500 00
Merchants' Nat'l Bank, Boston .	5,000	7,312 50	5,000 00
Redemption Nat'l Bank, Boston .	6,700	9,053 37	6,700 00
Railroad Nat'l Bank, Lowell . .	2,500	3,062 50	2,500 00
Massasoit Nat'l Bank, Fall River .	5,200	9,100 00	5,200 00
Washington Nat'l Bank, Boston .	1,400	1,960 00	1,400 00
	$287,800	$395,448 87	$285,791 50

CITY FIVE CENTS SAVINGS BANK — HAVERHILL.

Incorporated 1870. Number of corporators, 49.

JOHN B. NICHOLS, *President.* *Treasurer*, GEORGE W. NOYES.

STATEMENT.

LIABILITIES.		ASSETS.	
Deposits . . .	$510,074 49	Public funds . . .	$30,000 00
Earnings undivided .	121,776 80	Loans on public funds .	2,725 00
Guaranty fund . .	4,775 00	Bank stock	45,598 33
		Loans on bank stock . .	950 00
		Railroad bonds . . .	77,000 00
		Real estate by foreclosure .	178,831 20
		Loans on real estate . .	231,013 00
		Loans on personal security,	13,553 00
		Loans to counties, cities, or towns	13,000 00
		Deposit in bank on interest,	4,925 60
		Premium account . .	3,664 35
		Profit and loss account .	35,365 81
	$636,626 29		$636,626 29

Loans on Public Funds: —

On $4,500 United States bonds $2,725 00

Loans on Bank Stock, amount on each: —

On 5 shares Monument National Bank, Charlestown $650 00

On 3 shares First National Bank, Haverhill 300 00

Cash on Deposit in Bank: —

First National Bank, Haverhill $4,925 60

Amount of real estate held by foreclosure		$178,831 20
Assessed value of the same		114,600 00
Amount of income received from the same		6,980 75
Amount of municipal tax on real estate		1,095 41
Whole amount of interest or profits received		$37,290 52
Rate and amount of each semi-annual dividend for previous year	$1\frac{1}{2}$ per cent .	9,895 00
	2 per cent .	10,521 60

Times for the dividends fixed by the by-laws: first Wednesday in June and December.

The total amount of loans, with each specified rate of interest: $2,000, 4 per cent; $18,815, 5 per cent; $185,463, 6 per cent; $44,063, 7 per cent; $4,400, 8 per cent.

Number of outstanding loans which are of an amount not exceeding $3,000 each	131	
Aggregate amount of the same		140,928 00
Amount of investments from which no income is received . .		10,117 44
Number of open accounts	2,960	

Number and amount of deposits received for previous year	675	$62,740 99
Number and amount of deposits of and exceeding $300 at any one time for the previous year	38	19,093 70
Number and amount of withdrawals	2,223	304,808 48
Number of accounts opened the previous year	242	
Number of accounts closed the previous year	1,479	
Amount of expenses of the corporation during previous year		2,271 17
Amount of treasurer's bond		15,000 00

Date of examination by commissioner: April 30.

Public Funds.

	Par Value.	Estimated Market Value.	Amount Invested.
City and town bonds: —			
City of Lawrence	$10,000	$11,400 00	$10,000 00
of Haverhill	11,000	11,700 00	11,000 00
Town of Marlborough	5,000	5,400 00	5,000 00
of Provincetown	4,000	4,040 00	4,000 00
	$30,000	$32,540 00	$30,000 00

Bank Stock.

	Par Value.	Estimated Market Value.	Amount Invested.
First Nat'l Bank, Haverhill	$19,400	$25,220 00	$24,143 08
Merrimack Nat'l Bank, Haverhill	500	750 00	690 00
Tremont Nat'l Bank, Boston	3,000	3,660 00	3,783 75
Massachusetts Nat'l Bank, Boston	3,000	3,720 00	3,660 00
Merchants' Nat'l Bank, Boston	2,500	3,650 00	3,173 75
Continental Nat'l Bank, Boston	7,400	8,778 00	9,247 75
Commerce Nat'l Bank, Boston	900	1,161 00	900 00
	$36,700	$46,939 00	$45,598 33

Railroad Bonds.

	Par Value.	Estimated Market Value.	Amount Invested.
Boston and Maine Railroad 7s	$54,000	$68,715 00	$54,000 00
Old Colony Railroad 7s	13,000	16,250 00	13,000 00
Old Colony Railroad 6s	10,000	11,750 00	10,000 00
	$77,000	$96,715 00	$77,000 00

CITY INSTITUTION FOR SAVINGS – LOWELL.

Incorporated 1837. Number of corporators, 68.

N. ALLEN, *President.* *Treasurer,* F. A. BUTTRICK.

STATEMENT.

LIABILITIES.		ASSETS.	
Deposits	$3,343,009 20	Public funds . . .	$161,600 00
Earnings undivided .	132,573 71	Bank stock	673,480 00
Guaranty fund . .	55,000 00	Loans on bank stock . .	25,847 00
		Railroad bonds . . .	223,500 00
		Loans on real estate . .	1,520,516 63
		Loans on personal security,	603,472 22
		Loans to counties, cities, or towns	294,000 00
		Deposit in bank on interest,	24,755 71
		Expense account . . .	1,893 20
		Cash on hand . . .	1,518 15
	$3,530,582 91		$3,530,582 91

Loans on Bank Stock, amount on each:—

On 200 shares Appleton National Bank, Lowell	$19,647 00
On 46 shares First National Bank, Lowell	3,200 00
On 10 shares Merchants' National Bank, Lowell	1,000 00
On 25 shares Wamesit National Bank, Lowell . . . . . } On 9 shares Hide and Leather National Bank, Boston . . }	2,000 00

Cash on Deposit in Bank:—

Appleton National Bank, Lowell	$24,755 71

Whole amount of interest or profits received		$216,733 02
Rate and amount of each semi-annual dividend for previous years	2 per cent .	57,598 11
	2 per cent .	61,264 40

Times for the dividends fixed by the by-laws: January and July.

Average annual per cent of dividends for the term ending at time of and including last extra dividend: January, 1881, 5 per cent.

The total amount of loans, with each specified rate of interest: $32,250, 4 per cent; $25,000, 4½ per cent; $1,207,936.52, 5 per cent: $38,000, 5¼ per cent; $222,000, 5½ per cent; $877,949.33, 6 per cent; $8,600, 6¼ per cent; $40,000, 6 $\frac{45}{100}$ per cent; $60,000, 6½ per cent; $904,680, 7 per cent; $40,000, 7½ per cent; $46,000, 9 per cent.

Number of outstanding loans which are of an amount not exceeding $3,000 each	146	
Aggregate amount of the same		208,504 33
Number of open accounts	8,894	
Number and amount of deposits received for previous year,	7,800	788,201 75
Number and amount of deposits of and exceeding $300 at any one time for the previous year	360	210,781 16
Number and amount of withdrawals	4,158	483,577 90
Number of accounts opened the previous year	1,847	
Number of accounts closed the previous year	1,048	
Amount of expenses of the corporation during previous year .		6,990 13
Amount of treasurer's bond		60,000 00

Date of examination by commissioner: June 14.

PUBLIC FUNDS.

	Par Value.	Estimated Market Value.	Amount Invested.
City and town bonds: —			
City of Hartford, Conn.	$10,000	$11,800 00	$10,000 00
of Haverhill	6,000	6,600 00	5,100 00
of Haverhill	40,000	54,000 00	40,000 00
of Lowell	3,000	3,600 00	3,000 00
of Lynn	5,000	5,000 00	3,500 00
of Lynn	10,000	11,500 00	10,000 00
Town of Pittsfield	50,000	53,250 00	50,000 00
of Plymouth	20,000	21,300 00	20,000 00
of Plymouth	20,000	24,000 00	20,000 00
	$164,000	$191,050 00	$161,600 00

BANK STOCK.

Appleton Nat'l Bank, Lowell . .	$40,000	$70,000 00	$44,970 00
Atlantic Nat'l Bank, Boston . .	8,000	12,280 00	10,000 00
Atlas Nat'l Bank, Boston . .	18,000	22,500 00	18,000 00
Bay State Nat'l Bank, Lawrence .	1,875	3,125 00	1,875 00
Blackstone Nat'l Bank, Boston .	30,700	35,305 00	30,700 00
Boston Nat'l Bank, Boston . .	20,000	25,600 00	20,000 00
Boylston Nat'l Bank, Boston . .	12,400	15,872 00	12,400 00
Bunker Hill Nat'l Bank, Boston .	3,400	6,120 00	3,400 00
City Nat'l Bank, Boston . . .	5,300	6,731 00	5,300 00
Columbian Nat'l Bank, Boston .	13,800	19,665 00	16,560 00
Continental Nat'l Bank, Boston .	11,200	13,272 00	11,200 00
Eliot Nat'l Bank, Boston . .	10,000	12,025 00	10,000 00
Everett Nat'l Bank, Boston . .	500	585 50	500 00
First Nat'l Bank, Boston . .	20,000	41,550 00	20,000 00
First Nat'l Bank, Lowell . .	3,400	5,134 00	3,400 00
Globe Nat'l Bank, Boston . .	15,000	16,725 00	15,000 00
Hamilton Nat'l Bank, Boston . .	10,000	12,375 00	10,000 00
Howard Nat'l Bank, Boston . .	13,500	17,566 87	13,500 00
Market Nat'l Bank, Boston . .	10,000	11,075 00	10,000 00
Merchants' Nat'l Bank, Boston .	4,400	6,424 00	4,400 00
Metropolitan Nat'l Bank, Boston .	4,000	4,820 00	5,000 00
Commerce Nat'l Bank, Boston .	15,000	19,312 50	20,000 00
North America Nat'l Bank, Boston.	25,000	28,750 00	25,000 00
Redemption Nat'l Bank, Boston .	40,000	54,050 00	50,700 00
Republic Nat'l Bank, Boston . .	40,000	52,400 00	42,825 00
Eagle Nat'l Bank, Boston . .	3,000	3,592 50	3,000 00
Exchange Nat'l Bank, Boston . .	5,000	7,200 00	5,000 00
Hide and Leather Nat'l Bank, Boston,	10,000	11,650 00	10,000 00
Pemberton Nat'l Bank, Lawrence .	11,000	14,850 00	11,000 00
Revere Nat'l Bank, Boston . .	37,500	45,750 00	37,500 00
Union Nat'l Bank, Boston . .	3,600	5,526 00	3,600 00
Webster Nat'l Bank, Boston . .	10,500	11,707 50	10,500 00
New England Nat'l Bank, Boston .	6,500	9,685 00	8,450 00
North Nat'l Bank, Boston . .	16,700	23,672 25	16,700 00
Old Boston Nat'l Bank, Boston .	3,950	4,819 00	3,950 00
Prescott Nat'l Bank, Lowell . .	22,000	30,800 00	22,450 00

BANK STOCK — Concluded.

	Par Value.	Estimated Market Value.	Amount Invested.
Railroad Nat'l Bank, Lowell . .	$9,700	$12,028 00	$10,100 00
Second Nat'l Bank, Boston . .	26,500	40,147 50	26,500 00
Shawmut Nat'l Bank, Boston . .	10,000	12,750 00	10,000 00
State Nat'l Bank, Boston . .	2,000	2,510 00	2,000 00
Suffolk Nat'l Bank, Boston . .	20,500	24,984 37	20,500 00
Third Nat'l Bank, Boston . .	40,000	42,600 00	40,000 00
Tremont Nat'l Bank, Boston . .	23,600	28,792 00	23,600 00
Washington Nat'l Bank, Boston .	3,900	5,460 00	3,900 00
	$641,425	$851,786 99	$673,480 00

RAILROAD BONDS.

Boston and Lowell Railroad Co. .	$127,500	$158,737 50	$127,500 00
Eastern Railroad Company . .	92,000	102,120 00	46,000 00
Old Colony and Newport R.R. Co. .	50,000	58,750 00	50,000 00
	$269,500	$319,607 50	$223,500 00

CLINTON SAVINGS BANK — CLINTON.

Incorporated 1851. Number of corporators, 44.

CHARLES L. SWAN, *President*. *Treasurer*, C. L. S. HAMMOND.

STATEMENT.

LIABILITIES.		ASSETS.	
Deposits . . .	$788,781 58	Public funds . . .	$69,020 00
Earnings undivided .	427 37	Loans on public funds .	400 00
Guaranty fund . .	10,000 00	Bank stock	79,690 00
		Loans on bank stock . .	6,480 87
		Railroad bonds . . .	28,900 00
		Real estate by foreclosure .	12,372 65
		Loans on real estate . .	415,020 54
		Loans on personal security,	155,900 00
		Loans to counties, cities, or towns	20,000 00
		Premium	7,218 59
		Cash on hand . . .	4,206 30
	$799,208 95		$799,208 95

Loans on Public Funds: —

On $1,000 United States 4s $400 00

Loans on Bank Stock, amount on each: —

On 92 shares First National Bank, Clinton $4,880 87

On 16 shares Merchants' National Bank, New Bedford 1,600 00

Amount of real estate held by foreclosure $12,372 65

Assessed value of the same 13,550 00

Amount of income received from the same 984 80

Amount of municipal tax on real estate 198 24

Whole amount of interest or profits received or earned $39,524 77

Rate and amount of each semi-annual dividend for previous year . . . . { 2 per cent . 13,932 40; 2 per cent . 14,771 83 }

Times for the dividends fixed by the by-laws: second Monday in April and October.

The total amount of loans, with each specified rate of interest: $20,000, 4 per cent; $20,000, 4½ per cent; $231,930.87, 5 per cent; $17,000, 5½ per cent; $222,164.54, 6 per cent; $72,906, 7 per cent.

Number of outstanding loans which are of an amount not exceeding $3,000 each 221

Aggregate amount of the same 152,839 41

Amount of investments from which no income is received . . 13,800 00

Number of open accounts 2,849

Number and amount of deposits received for previous year, 2,840 256,897 78

Number and amount of deposits of and exceeding $300 at any one time for the previous year 179 78,537 19

Number and amount of withdrawals 1,537 166,575 86

Number of accounts opened the previous year 674

Number of accounts closed the previous year 409

Amount of expenses of the corporation during previous year . . 2,548 15

Amount of treasurer's bond 20,000 00

Date of examination by commissioner: May 24.

PUBLIC FUNDS.

	Par Value.	Estimated Market Value.	Amount Invested.
City and town bonds: —			
City of Taunton	$8,000	$8,800 00	$8,620 00
Town of Clinton	60,400	66,440 00	60,400 00
	$68,400	$75,240 00	$69,020 00

BANK STOCK.

First Nat'l Bank, Clinton . .	$30,000	$37,500 00	$30,490 00
Orange Nat'l Bank, Orange . .	5,000	5,500 00	5,000 00
First Nat'l Bank, Leominster . .	3,000	3,300 00	3,000 00
First Nat'l Bank, New Bedford .	5,000	6,250 00	5,000 00
Commerce Nat'l B'k, New Bedford,	5,000	6,250 00	5,000 00
Metropolitan Nat'l Bank, Boston .	2,000	2,405 00	2,000 00
Howard Nat'l Bank, Boston . .	1,600	2,082 00	1,600 00
Webster Nat'l Bank, Boston . .	10,500	11,707 50	10,500 00
City Nat'l Bank, Boston . . .	500	635 00	500 00
Boston Nat'l Bank, Boston . .	200	256 00	200 00
Atlas Nat'l Bank, Boston . .	1,400	1,750 00	1,400 00
North America Nat'l Bank, Boston,	4,200	4,830 00	4,200 00
Market Nat'l Bank, Boston . .	2,000	2,195 00	2,000 00
Traders' Nat'l Bank, Boston . .	800	816 00	800 00
Central Nat'l Bank, Boston . .	2,000	2,400 00	2,000 00
Manufacturers' Nat'l Bank, Boston,	5,000	5,512 50	5,000 00
Hide and Leather Nat'l B'k, Boston,	1,000	1,165 00	1,000 00
	$79,200	$94,554 00	$79,690 00

RAILROAD BONDS.

Fitchburg Railroad 7s	$13,000	$16,250 00	$13,000 00
Old Colony Railroad 7s	5,000	6,250 00	5,900 00
Old Colony Railroad 6s	10,000	11,750 00	10,000 00
	$28,000	$34,250 00	$28,900 00

COHASSET SAVINGS BANK — COHASSET.

Incorporated 1845. Number of corporators, 34.

MARTIN LINCOLN, *President*. *Treasurer*, LEVI N. BATES.

STATEMENT.

LIABILITIES.		ASSETS.	
Deposits . . .	$323,879 93	Bank stock . . .	$56,500 00
Earnings undivided .	4,053 36	Railroad bonds . . .	25,000 00
Guaranty fund . .	5,000 00	Real estate by foreclosure .	6,000 00
		Loans on real estate . .	170,645 00
		Loans on personal security,	5,000 00
		Loans to counties, cities, or towns	30,152 52
		Deposit in banks on interest,	39,180 68
		Cash on hand . . .	455 09
	$332,933 29		$332,933 29

Cash on Deposit in Banks, amount in each: —

Maverick National Bank, Boston	$12,593 43
Boston National Bank, Boston	6,587 25
Hingham National Bank, Hingham	20,000 00

Amount of real estate held by foreclosure	$6,000 00
Assessed value of the same	4,800 00
Amount of income received from the same	490 00
Amount of municipal tax on real estate	66 72

Whole amount of interest or profits received or earned . . .		$19,315 75
Rate and amount of each semi-annual dividend for previous years	2 per cent .	6,049 96
	2 per cent .	6,162 56

Times for the dividends fixed by the by-laws: first Tuesday in January and July.

Average annual per cent of dividends for the term ending at time of and including last extra dividend: 4 per cent.

The total amount of loans, with each specified rate of interest: $23,152.52, 4 per cent; $38,000, 5 per cent; $144,645, 6 per cent.

Number of outstanding loans which are of an amount not exceeding $3,000 each	73	
Aggregate amount of the same		52,645 00
Number of open accounts	822	
Number and amount of deposits received for previous year .	271	28,363 00
Number and amount of deposits of and exceeding $300 at any one time for the previous year	29	13,665 00
Number and amount of withdrawals	327	24,910 94
Number of accounts opened the previous year	75	
Number of accounts closed the previous year	49	
Amount of expenses of the corporation during previous year .		1,026 44
Amount of treasurer's bond		9,000 00

Date of examination by commissioner: May 23.

Bank Stock.

	Par Value.	Estimated Market Value.	Amount Invested.
Atlas Nat'l Bank, Boston . .	$3,000	$3,750 00	$3,000 00
Blackstone Nat'l Bank, Boston .	2,000	2,280 00	2,000 00
Boston Nat'l Bank, Boston . .	4,500	5,850 00	4,500 00
City Nat'l Bank, Boston . . .	4,300	5,375 00	4,300 00
Columbian Nat'l Bank, Boston .	2,000	2,840 00	2,000 00
Continental Nat'l Bank, Boston .	4,000	4,720 00	4,000 00
Eagle Nat'l Bank, Boston . .	1,800	2,088 00	1,800 00
Everett Nat'l Bank, Boston . .	2,000	2,300 00	2,000 00
Hide and Leather N'l B'k, Boston .	2,500	2,975 00	2,500 00
Market Nat'l Bank, Boston . .	3,000	3,300 00	3,000 00
Maverick Nat'l Bank, Boston . .	1,300	3,250 00	1,300 00
Merchants' Nat'l Bank, Boston .	2,300	3,358 00	2,300 00
North Nat'l Bank, Boston . .	1,200	1,704 00	1,200 00
Republic Nat'l Bank, Boston . .	2,200	2,838 00	2,200 00
Revere Nat'l Bank, Boston . .	4,500	5,490 00	4,500 00
Shawmut Nat'l Bank, Boston. .	3,200	3,936 00	3,200 00
State Nat'l Bank, Boston . .	3,800	4,750 00	3,800 00
Tremont Nat'l Bank, Boston . .	2,300	2,829 00	2,300 00
Union Nat'l Bank, Boston . .	1,500	2,295 00	1,500 00
Washington Nat'l Bank, Boston .	1,000	1,370 00	1,000 00
Webster Nat'l Bank, Boston . .	4,100	4,592 00	4,100 00
	$56,500	$71,890 00	$56,500 00

Railroad Bonds.

Eastern Railroad $4\frac{1}{2}$s, new . .	$16,000	$17,600 00	$16,000 00
Old Colony Railroad 7s . . .	9,000	11,250 00	9,000 00
	$25,000	$28,850 00	$25,000 00

CROCKER INSTITUTION FOR SAVINGS — TURNER'S FALLS.

Incorporated April 3, 1869. Number of corporators, 16.

GEORGE O. PEABODY, *President*. *Treasurer*, D. P. ABERCROMBIE.

STATEMENT.

LIABILITIES.		ASSETS.	
Deposits	$291,312 32	Public funds	$36,000 00
Earnings undivided	2,024 57	Bank stock	32,600 75
Guaranty fund	2,050 00	Loans on bank stock	1,000 00
		Railroad bonds	10,000 00
		Real estate	9,117 48
		Loans on real estate	157,678 15
		Loans on personal security,	26,520 00
		Loans to counties, cities, or towns	4,500 00
		Deposit in bank on interest,	4,600 00
		Expense account	169 26
		Loan to fire district	1,500 00
		Interest	120 00
		Premiums	6,505 00
		Cash in bank	5,076 25
	$295,386 89		$295,386 89

Loans on Bank Stock: —

On 13 shares Crocker National Bank	$1,000 00

Cash on Deposit in Bank: —

Crocker National Bank	$9,676 25

Amount invested in real estate (for banking purposes)		$9,117 48
Estimated value of the same		9,967 48
Amount of municipal tax on real estate		23 40
Whole amount of interest or profits received or earned		$15,124 50
Rate and amount of each semi-annual dividend for previous year	2 per cent 2 per cent	4,390 83 5,080 36
Times for the dividends fixed by the by-laws: January and July.		
Average annual per cent of dividends for the term ending at time of and including last extra dividend: 5 $\frac{9}{16}$ per cent.		
The total amount of loans, with each specified rate of interest: $6,000, 5 per cent; $149,108.15, 6 per cent; $36,000, 6½ per cent.		
Number of outstanding loans which are of an amount not exceeding $3,000 each	149	
Aggregate amount of the same		126,798 15
Number of open accounts	903	
Number and amount of deposits received for previous year.	1,170	108,635 92
Number and amount of deposits of and exceeding $300 at any one time for the previous year	85	47,964 56
Number and amount of withdrawals	478	52,947 50
Number of accounts opened the previous year	323	
Number of accounts closed the previous year	145	
Amount of expenses of the corporation during previous year		547 78
Amount of treasurer's bond		25,000 00

Date of examination by commissioner: Aug. 10.

PUBLIC FUNDS.

	Par Value.	Estimated Market Value.	Amount Invested.
State and city bonds: —			
State of Maine 6s	$3,000	$3,500 00	$3,000 00
of Massachusetts 5s . .	10,000	11,800 00	10,000 00
City of Boston 6s	6,000	7,400 00	6,000 00
of Boston 5s	4,000	4,800 00	4,000 00
of Lowell 6s	3,000	3,500 00	3,000 00
of Providence, R.I., 5s . .	5,000	5,900 00	5,000 00
of Somerville 5s . . .	5,000	5,400 00	5,000 00
	$36,000	$42,300 00	$36,000 00

BANK STOCK.

	Par Value.	Estimated Market Value.	Amount Invested.
Crocker Nat'l Bank, Turner's Falls,	$5,700	$7,125 00	$5,925 00
Conway Nat'l Bank, Conway . .	6,000	7,200 00	6,930 00
Commonwealth Nat'l Bank, Boston,	2,000	2,400 00	2,192 50
Atlantic Nat'l Bank, Boston . .	700	1,070 50	1,017 00
Pacific Nat'l Bank, Boston . .	1,000	1,050 00	1,120 00
Central Nat'l Bank, Boston . .	1,000	1,200 00	1,056 25
Boston Nat'l Bank, Boston . .	500	640 00	545 00
Continental Nat'l Bank, Boston .	4,000	4,720 00	4,704 25
Merchandise Nat'l Bank, Boston .	1,000	1,100 00	1,062 50
New England Nat'l Bank, Boston .	1,000	1,450 00	1,465 00
Columbian Nat'l Bank, Boston .	700	995 00	1,014 50
Howard Nat'l Bank, Boston . .	500	650 00	636 25
Webster Nat'l Bank, Boston . .	1,000	1,110 00	1,155 00
Eliot Nat'l Bank, Boston . .	1,000	1,200 00	1,242 50
Commerce Nat'l Bank, Boston .	1,000	1,280 00	1,292 50
Tremont Nat'l Bank, Boston . .	1,000	1,220 00	1,242 50
	$28,100	$34,410 00	$32,600 75

RAILROAD BONDS.

	Par Value.	Estimated Market Value.	Amount Invested.
Boston, Revere Beach, and Lynn R.R.	$10,000	$11,600 00	$100,00 00

DANVERS SAVINGS BANK — DANVERS.

Incorporated 1850. Number of corporators, 53.

ISRAEL H. PUTNAM, *President*. *Treasurer*, WILLIAM L. WESTON.

STATEMENT.

LIABILITIES.		ASSETS.	
Deposits . . .	$965,188 43	Public funds . . .	$47,105 00
Earnings undivided .	24,431 53	Loans on public funds .	5,000 00
Guaranty fund . .	19,250 00	Bank stock	120,621 00
		Loans on bank stock . .	2,835 00
		Real estate by foreclosure .	95,007 18
		Loans on real estate . .	405,205 00
		Loans on personal security,	301,702 15
		Loans to counties, cities, or towns	15,820 83
		Deposit in banks on interest,	4,181 46
		Cash in bank not on interest,	11,392 34
	$1,008,869 96		$1,008,869 96

Loans on Public Funds: —

On $5,000 United States bonds $5,000 00

Loans on Bank Stock: —

On 31 shares First National Bank, Danvers $2,835 00

Cash on Deposit in Banks, amount in each: —

Maverick National Bank	$3.082 20
National Bank of Redemption	1,099 26
First National Bank, Danvers	11,392 34

Amount of real estate held by foreclosure	95.007 18
Assessed value of the same	86.300 00
Amount of income received from the same	4,020 00
Amount of municipal tax on real estate	1,182 00

Whole amount of interest or profits received or earned $53.475 14

Rate and amount of each semi-annual dividend for previous year . . . . { 2 per cent . 18.179 30; 2 per cent . 18,432 65 }

Times for the dividends fixed by the by-laws: April 1 and Oct. 1.

The total amount of loans, with each specified rate of interest: $55,820, 4 per cent; $45.000, 4½ per cent; $75,000, 5 per cent; $60,000, 5½ per cent; $245.495, 6 per cent; $10.800, 6½ per cent; $1.737.57, 7 per cent; $800, 7½ per cent; $52.436, 8 per cent.

Number of outstanding loans which are of an amount not exceeding $3,000 each 234

Aggregate amount of the same 211,848 00

Amount of investments from which no income is received (secured by 16 Huntington Avenue certificates) 52,446 65

Number of open accounts 2,847

Number and amount of deposits received for previous year, 1,375 104,937 97

Number and amount of deposits of and exceeding $300 at any one time for the previous year 98 53,007 00

Number and amount of withdrawals 1,184 $116,078 20
Number of accounts opened the previous year 321
Number of accounts closed the previous year 270
Amount of expenses of the corporation during previous year . . 2,304 42
Amount of treasurer's bond 25,000 00
Date of examination by commissioner: June 4.

PUBLIC FUNDS.

	Par Value.	Estimated Market Value.	Amount Invested.
United States 4s, 1907 . . .	$17,500	$20,300 00	$17,500 00
City and town bonds: —			
City of Boston 6s, 1894 . . .	$10,000	$12,200 00	$9,775 00
of Boston 4s	10,000	10,300 00	10,000 00
of Hartford, Conn., 6s . .	2,000	2,180 00	1,830 00
Town of Danvers 5s, 1906 . .	8,000	9,280 00	8,000 00
	$47,500	$54,260 00	$47,105 00

BANK STOCK.

	Par Value.	Estimated Market Value.	Amount Invested.
Tremont Nat'l Bank, Boston . .	$2,000	$2,430 00	$2,000 00
Traders' Nat'l Bank, Boston . .	2,800	2,856 00	2,800 00
Commerce Nat'l Bank, Boston .	6,000	7,400 00	6,000 00
Exchange Nat'l Bank, Boston . .	6,500	9,360 00	6,500 00
Howard Nat'l Bank, Boston . .	6,800	8,704 00	6,800 00
Revere Nat'l Bank, Boston . .	7,500	9,075 00	7,500 00
Washington Nat'l Bank, Boston .	2,500	3,450 00	2,500 00
Atlas Nat'l Bank, Boston . .	5,000	6,250 00	5,675 00
Globe Nat'l Bank, Boston . .	8,500	9,430 00	10,612 50
Merchants' Nat'l Bank, Boston .	5,000	7,300 00	6,475 00
Redemption Nat'l Bank, Boston .	6,500	8,645 00	7,901 25
State Nat'l Bank, Boston . .	5,000	6,250 00	5,356 25
Continental Nat'l Bank, Boston .	1,000	1,180 00	1,080 00
North America Nat'l Bank, Boston,	3,100	3,565 00	3,148 75
Blackstone Nat'l Bank, Boston .	300	345 00	300 00
Salem Nat'l Bank, Salem . .	2,500	3,000 00	2,862 50
First Nat'l Bank, Salem . . .	700	875 00	700 00
Naumkeag Nat'l Bank, Salem .	500	800 00	500 00
Asiatic Nat'l Bank, Salem . .	8,100	11,502 00	8,100 00
Commerce Nat'l B'k, New Bedford,	7,500	10,425 00	8,962 50
First Nat'l Bank, New Bedford .	12,500	16,875 00	14,947 25
Warren Nat'l Bank, Peabody . .	2,000	2,800 00	2,000 00
First Nat'l Bank, Danvers . .	6,900	7,555 00	6,900 00
Rockport Nat'l Bank, Rockport .	1,000	1,300 00	1,000 00
	$110,200	$141,372 00	$120,621 00

DEDHAM INSTITUTION FOR SAVINGS — DEDHAM.

Incorporated May 1, 1831. Number of corporators, 82.

WALDO COLBURN, *President.* *Treasurer,* CALVIN GUILD.

STATEMENT.

LIABILITIES.		ASSETS.	
Deposits	$1,384,393 35	Public funds	$272,000 00
Earnings undivided	74,214 99	Bank stock	75,600 00
Guaranty fund	33,474 04	Loans on bank stock	900 00
		Railroad bonds	123,292 50
		Real estate by foreclosure	68,452 45
		Loans on real estate	640,771 80
		Loans on personal security,	251,775 00
		Loans to counties, cities, or towns	19,850 00
		Deposit in banks on interest,	39,440 63
	$1,492,082 38		$1,492,082 38

Loans on Bank Stock: —

On 10 shares Dedham National Bank $900 00

Cash on Deposit in Banks, amount in each: —

In Dedham National Bank $19.440 63

In Maverick National Bank 20,000 00

Amount of real estate held by foreclosure $68.452 45

Assessed value of the same 66.854 00

Amount of income received from the same 4.505 00

Amount of municipal tax on real estate 1,136 41

Whole amount of interest or profits received or earned . . . $71.713 38

Rate and amount of each semi-annual dividend for previous year { 2 per cent . 23.884 36; 2 per cent . 25.414 93 }

Times for the dividends fixed by the by-laws: May 1 and Nov. 1.

Average annual per cent of dividends for the term ending at time of and including last extra dividend: $6\frac{63}{100}$ per cent.

The total amount of loans, with each specified rate of interest: $10.000, 4 per cent; $50.000. 4½ per cent; $187.000. 5 per cent; $491.271.80. 6 per cent; $9.850. 6½ per cent; $157.275, 7 per cent; $4.500. 7½ per cent; $3.400. 8 per cent.

Number of outstanding loans which are of an amount not exceeding $3.000 each 351

Aggregate amount of the same 392.046 80

Amount of investments from which no income is received . . . 1.000 00

Number of open accounts 4.135

Number and amount of deposits received for previous year, 2.292 217.129 72

Number and amount of deposits of and exceeding $300 at any one time for the previous year 186 90.844 62

Number and amount of withdrawals 1.967 127.434 05

Number of accounts opened the previous year 615

Number of accounts closed the previous year 304

Amount of expenses of the corporation during previous year . 3.301 84

Amount of treasurer's bond 15.000 00

Date of examination by commissioner: April 11.

PUBLIC FUNDS.

	Par Value.	Estimated Market Value.	Amount Invested.
United States 6s, 1879	$10,000	$13,300 00	$10,000 00
" " 4½s, 1891	10,000	11,250 00	10,000 00
" " 4s, 1907	20,000	23,250 00	20,000 00
" " 3½s, 6s extended	20,000	20,250 00	20,000 00
City and town bonds: —			
City of Fall River	$5,000	$5,800 00	$5,000 00
of Manchester, N.H.	18,000	20,700 00	18,000 00
of Augusta, Me.	5,000	5,350 00	5,000 00
of Biddeford, Me.	4,000	4,160 00	4,000 00
of Worcester	10,000	10,700 00	10,000 00
of Charlestown	6,000	6,960 00	6,000 00
of Portland, Me.	9,000	10,440 00	9,000 00
of Boston 6s	10,000	12,600 00	} 110,000 00
of Boston 4s	100,000	106,000 00	
of Providence, R.I.	20,000	21,400 00	20,000 00
of Lynn	1,000	1,100 00	1,000 00
Town of Malden	10,000	11,600 00	10,000 00
of Melrose	5,000	6,350 00	5,000 00
of Woburn	5,000	5,800 00	5,000 00
of Lincoln	2,000	2,300 00	2,000 00
of Natick	2,000	2,120 00	2,000 00
	$272,000	$301,430 00	$272,000 00

BANK STOCK.

	Par Value.	Estimated Market Value.	Amount Invested.
Dedham Nat'l Bank, Dedham	$14,600	$18,250 00	$14,600 00
Howard Nat'l Bank, Boston	4,000	5,200 00	4,000 00
Blackstone Nat'l Bank, Boston	7,500	8,625 00	7,500 00
State Nat'l Bank, Boston	2,500	3,125 00	2,500 00
Union Nat'l Bank, Boston	2,500	3,825 00	2,500 00
Globe Nat'l Bank, Boston	2,500	2,775 00	2,500 00
Traders' Nat'l Bank, Boston	5,000	5,100 00	5,000 00
People's Nat'l Bank, Boston	6,000	9,600 00	6,000 00
Commerce Nat'l Bank, Boston	7,500	9,000 00	7,500 00
Atlas Nat'l Bank, Boston	10,000	12,500 00	10,000 00
Webster Nat'l Bank, Boston	8,500	9,435 00	8,500 00
Shawmut Nat'l Bank, Boston	5,000	6,300 00	5,000 00
	$75,600	$94,335 00	$75,600 00

RAILROAD BONDS.

	Par Value.	Estimated Market Value.	Amount Invested.
Worcester and Nashua Railroad 5s	$10,000	$10,000 00	$9,700 00
Boston and Maine Railroad 7s	23,000	29,210 00	23,000 00
Boston and Lowell Railroad 7s	7,000	8,400 00	7,000 00
Boston and Lowell Railroad 6s	11,000	12,650 00	11,000 00
Boston and Lowell Railroad 5s	5,000	5,350 00	5,000 00
Old Colony Railroad 7s	5,000	6,250 00	5,000 00
Boston, Clin., Fitch., & N. B. R.R. 5s,*	35,000	36,400 00	35,000 00
Eastern Railroad 4½s	29,500	32,302 50	27,502 50
	$125,500	$140,562 50	$123,202 50

* This bank has been notified that this investment is illegal.

EAST BOSTON SAVINGS BANK — EAST BOSTON.

Incorporated April 26, 1848. Number of corporators, 28.

GEORGE T. SAMPSON, *President.* *Treasurer,* WILLIAM B. PIGEON.

STATEMENT.

LIABILITIES.		ASSETS.	
Deposits . . .	$1,070,623 49	Bank stock . . .	$260,820 15
Earnings undivided .	117,377 31	Loans on bank stock . .	10,086 00
Guaranty fund . .	15,144 58	Real estate	24,732 11
		Real estate by foreclosure .	252,940 32
		Loans on real estate . .	565,010 84
		Loans on personal security,	48,128 04
		Deposit in bank on interest .	16,088 36
		Expense account . . .	1,456 86
		Accrued interest . . .	18,697 16
		Cash on hand . . .	5,185 54
	$1,203,145 38		$1,203,145 38

Loans on Bank Stock, amount on each:—

On 100 shares First National Bank, Chelsea	$10,000 00
On 1 share State National Bank	86 00

Cash on Deposit in Bank:—

First Ward National Bank, East Boston	$16,088 36

Amount invested in real estate (for banking purposes) . .	$24,732 11
Estimated value of the same	25,000 00
Amount of real estate held by foreclosure	252,940 32
Assessed value of the same	255,600 00
Amount of income received from the same	22,308 00
Amount of municipal tax on real estate	3,849 30

Whole amount of interest or profits received or earned $60,474 00

Rate and amount of each semi-annual dividend for previous years . . . . } 2 per cent . 21,874 23; 2 per cent . 20,442 42

Times for the dividends fixed by the by-laws: third Wednesday in January and July.

Average annual per cent of dividends for the term ending at time of and including last extra dividend: 4 per cent.

The total amount of loans, with each specified rate of interest: $96,400, 5 per cent; $306,655.70, 6 per cent; $3,500, 6½ per cent; $179,245, 7 per cent; $2,000, 7½ per cent; $31,851, 8 per cent.

Number of outstanding loans which are of an amount not exceeding $3,000 each	252	
Aggregate amount of the same		359,165 16
Number of open accounts	4,292	
Number and amount of deposits received for previous year.	2,567	222,162 70
Number and amount of deposits of and exceeding $300 at any one time for the previous year	136	75,220 00
Number and amount of withdrawals	2,893	312,700 37

Number of accounts opened the previous year	720	
Number of accounts closed the previous year	984	
Amount of expenses of the corporation during previous year .	.	$4,608 82
Amount of treasurer's bond	.	20,000 00

Date of examination by commissioner: April 20.

BANK STOCK.

	Par Value.	Estimated Market Value.	Amount Invested.
Atlas Nat'l Bank, Boston . .	$1,000	$1,270 00	$1,100 32
Boston Nat'l Bank, Boston . .	20,000	25,600 00	22,596 66
Blackstone Nat'l Bank, Boston .	3,800	4,408 00	4,717 31
Boylston Nat'l Bank, Boston . .	4,100	5,248 00	5,766 50
Continental Nat'l Bank, Boston .	10,000	12,100 00	11,173 40
Commerce Nat'l Bank, Boston .	13,700	17,707 25	15,706 24
Eagle Nat'l Bank, Boston . .	10,000	12,075 00	10,874 15
Eliot Nat'l Bank, Boston. . .	11,500	13,828 75	13,153 00
Freeman's Nat'l Bank, Boston .	25,000	31,312 50	30,916 24
Globe Nat'l Bank, Boston . .	20,000	22,400 00	25,212 00
Hide and Leather Nat'l B'k, Boston,	6,700	8,023 25	7,489 98
Howard Nat'l Bank, Boston . .	7,200	9,369 00	7,700 97
Market Nat'l Bank, Boston . .	5,000	5,637 50	5,443 10
Merchandise Nat'l Bank, Boston .	2,400	2,616 00	2,400 00
Mount Vernon Nat'l Bank, Boston .	2,400	3,066 00	3,064 25
Massachusetts Nat'l Bank, Boston .	3,000	3,750 00	3,490 83
North America Nat'l Bank, Boston .	15,000	18,037 50	15,940 02
Revere Nat'l Bank, Boston . .	10,000	12,500 00	11,301 06
Republic Nat'l Bank, Boston . .	5,000	6,550 00	5,541 10
Suffolk Nat'l Bank, Boston . .	10,000	12,500 00	11,917 88
State Nat'l Bank, Boston . .	10,000	12,450 00	10,509 57
Shoe and Leather Nat'l B'k, Boston,	6,400	7,200 00	8,103 13
Traders' Nat'l Bank, Boston . .	5,000	5,212 50	5,496 75
Tremont Nat'l Bank, Boston . .	5,000	6,100 00	5,908 19
Union Market Nat'l B'k, Watertown,	13,300	14,630 00	15,297 50
	$225,500	$273,591 25	$260,820 15

EAST BRIDGEWATER SAVINGS BANK — EAST BRIDGEWATER.

Incorporated 1870. Number of corporators, 50.

K. E. SHELDON, *President.* *Treasurer*, I. N. NUTTER.

STATEMENT.

LIABILITIES.		ASSETS.	
Deposits	$206,851 70	Public funds	$20,257 50
Earnings undivided	3,927 20	Bank stock	33,468 00
Guaranty fund	2,572 56	Railroad bonds	15,000 00
		Loans on real estate	105,263 78
		Loans on personal security,	38,400 16
		Deposit in bank on interest,	73 00
		Expense account	246 52
		Interest account	642 50
	$213,351 46		$213,351 46

Cash on Deposit in Bank: —
National Bank of the Commonwealth $73 00

Whole amount of interest or profits received or earned . . . $9,578 67
Rate and amount of each semi-annual dividend for previous year . . . . { 2½ per cent . 3,770 33; 2¼ per cent . 3,735 49 }
Times for the dividends fixed by the by-laws: Jan. 1 and July 1.
Average annual per cent of dividends for the term ending at time of and including last extra dividend: 4¾ per cent.
The total amount of loans, with each specified rate of interest: $5,000, 4 per cent; $8,000, 4½ per cent; $28,500, 5 per cent; $3,450.16, 5½ per cent; $104,366.61, 6 per cent; $1,150, 6½ per cent; $28,454.67, 7 per cent.
Number of outstanding loans which are of an amount not exceeding $300 each 132
Aggregate amount of the same 94,513 78
Number of open accounts 832
Number and amount of deposits received for previous year . 743 77,788 62
Number and amount of deposits of and exceeding $300 at any one time for the previous year 72 37,982 10
Number and amount of withdrawals 451 39,071 30
Number of accounts opened the previous year 203
Number of accounts closed the previous year 80
Amount of expenses of the corporation during previous year . . 536 15
Amount of treasurer's bond 10,000 00
Date of examination by commissioner: Oct. 7.

PUBLIC FUNDS.

	Par Value.	Estimated Market Value.	Amount Invested.
United States 4½s	$3,000	$3,339 00	$3,000 00
" " 4s	5,000	5,800 00	5,000 00
State, city, and town bonds: —			
State of New Hampshire 6s	$3,000	$3,690 00	$3,322 50
City of Rockland, Me., 6s	500	500 00	455 00
of Cambridge 6s	2,000	2,160 00	1,940 00
of Bath, Me., 6s	4,000	4,000 00	4,140 00
Town of Woburn 6s	2,000	2,200 00	1,900 00
of Amesbury 5s	500	500 00	500 00
	$20,000	$22,189 00	$20,257 50

BANK STOCK.

	Par Value.	Estimated Market Value.	Amount Invested.
City Nat'l Bank, Boston	$2,000	$2,540 00	$2,276 75
Commonwealth Nat'l B'k, Boston	1,000	1,200 00	1,225 00
Fourth Nat'l Bank, Boston	3,000	3,300 00	3,000 00
Hamilton Nat'l Bank, Boston	1,000	1,130 00	1,250 00
Hide and Leather Nat'l B'k, Boston,	1,700	1,980 50	1,700 00
Market Nat'l Bank, Boston	2,000	2,200 00	2,317 50
Merchandise Nat'l Bank, Boston	2,000	2,200 00	2,000 00
Shawmut Nat'l Bank, Boston	1,000	1,275 00	1,167 50
State Nat'l Bank, Boston	2,200	2,750 00	2,471 25
Traders' Nat'l Bank, Boston	3,000	3,060 00	3,000 00
Tremont Nat'l Bank, Boston	3,000	3,660 00	3,480 00
Webster Nat'l Bank, Boston	4,000	4,460 00	4,000 00
Home Nat'l Bank, Brockton	4,000	4,600 00	4,580 00
Brockton Nat'l Bank, Brockton	1,000	1,050 00	1,000 00
	$30,900	$35,405 50	$33,468 00

RAILROAD BONDS.

	Par Value.	Estimated Market Value.	Amount Invested.
Old Colony Railroad 6s	$6,000	$7,050 00	$6,000 00
Eastern Railroad 4½s	5,000	5,500 00	5,000 00
Vermont and Massachusetts R.R. 6s,	1,000	1,050 00	1,000 00
Boston, Rev. Beach, & Lynn R.R. 6s,	3,000	3,510 00	3,000 00
	$15,000	$17,110 00	$15,000 00

EAST CAMBRIDGE FIVE CENTS SAVINGS BANK — CAMBRIDGE.

Incorporated 1854. Number of corporators, 46.

GEORGE STEVENS, *President*. *Treasurer*, SAMUEL SLOCOMB.

STATEMENT.

LIABILITIES.		ASSETS.	
Deposits	$896,973 59	Public funds	$21,000 00
Earnings undivided	5,951 48	Bank stock	129,900 00
Guaranty fund	19,856 52	Loans on bank stock	12,179 21
Premiums	2,864 84	Railroad bonds	19,000 00
Profit and loss	2,500 00	Real estate	7,000 00
		Real estate by foreclosure	44,418 67
		Loans on real estate	537,914 48
		Loans on personal security,	82,200 00
		Loans to counties, cities, or towns	15,000 00
		Deposit in banks on interest,	56,815 27
		Cash on hand	2,718 80
	$928,146 43		$928,146 43

Loans on Bank Stock, amount on each: —

On 75 shares Lechmere National Bank $9,379 21
On 28 shares Pacific National Bank 2,800 00

Cash on Deposit in Banks, amount in each: —

Lechmere National Bank $26,815 27
International Trust Company* 30,000 00

Amount invested in real estate (for banking purposes) $7,000 00
Estimated value of the same 7,000 00
Amount of real estate held by foreclosure 44,418 67
Assessed value of the same 52,500 00
Amount of income received from the same (per month) . . . 360 00
Amount of municipal tax on real estate 956 08

Whole amount of interest or profits received or earned . . . $47,526 27
Rate and amount of each semi-annual dividend for previous year . . . . { 2½ per cent . 19,367 56; 2 per cent . 16,231 39 }
Times for the dividends fixed by the by-laws: April 15 and Oct. 15.
The total amount of loans, with each specified rate of interest: $15,000, 3½ per cent; $40,000, 4½ per cent; $62,150, 5 per cent; $324,073.13, 6 per cent; $100,770.56, 6½ per cent; $104,700, 7 per cent; $600, 8 per cent.
Number of outstanding loans which are of an amount not exceeding $3,000 each 262
Aggregate amount of the same 284,914 48
Amount of investments from which no income is received: 60 shares Cambridge Land Company, par value $100 per share (charged off to profit and loss).
Number of open accounts 3,809
Number and amount of deposits received for previous year, 5,954 215,287 98
Number and amount of deposits of and exceeding $300 at any one time for the previous year 131 73,567 21

* The Attorney-General has given an opinion that deposits by savings banks in this trust company are legal.

Number and amount of withdrawals	2,946	$165,830 48
Number of accounts opened the previous year	928	
Number of accounts closed the previous year	620	
Amount of expenses of the corporation during previous year . .		2,016 69
Amount of treasurer's bond		20,000 00

Date of examination by commissioner: March 1.

PUBLIC FUNDS.

	Par Value.	Estimated Market Value.	Amount Invested.
City bonds: —			
City of Cambridge 6s	$19,000	$20,710 00	$19,000 00
of Boston.	2,000	2,000 00	2,000 00
	$21,000	$22,710 00	$21,000 00

BANK STOCK.

Atlas Nat'l Bank, Boston . .	$700	$870 00	$700 00
Blackstone Nat'l Bank, Boston .	5,400	6,200 00	5,400 00
Boston Nat'l Bank, Boston . .	6,300	7,760 00	6,300 00
Bunker Hill Nat'l Bank, Boston .	4,100	7,380 00	4,100 00
Commerce Nat'l Bank, Boston .	6,700	8,570 00	6,700 00
Commonwealth Nat'l Bank, Boston .	4,000	5,960 00	4,000 00
Continental Nat'l Bank, Boston .	3,000	3,540 00	3,000 00
Eliot Nat'l Bank, Boston . . .	1,200	1,440 00	1,200 00
Exchange Nat'l Bank, Boston . .	1,600	2,304 00	1,600 00
Faneuil Hall Nat'l Bank, Boston .	2,000	2,680 00	2,000 00
First Ward Nat'l Bank, Boston .	5,000	6,000 00	4,000 00
Globe Nat'l Bank, Boston . .	2,100	2,330 00	2,100 00
Hide and Leather Nat'l B'k, Boston,	11,500	13,340 00	11,500 00
Howard Nat'l Bank, Boston . .	6,000	7,800 00	6,000 00
Massachusetts Nat'l Bank, Boston .	500	620 00	500 00
Merchants' Nat'l Bank, Boston .	5,000	7,300 00	5,000 00
Metropolitan Nat'l Bank, Boston .	1,600	1,920 00	1,600 00
New England Nat'l Bank, Boston .	2,000	2,980 00	2,000 00
North Nat'l Bank, Boston . .	1,900	2,670 00	1,900 00
North America Nat'l Bank, Boston .	500	570 00	500 00
Redemption Nat'l Bank, Boston .	1,000	1,350 00	1,000 00
Republic Nat'l Bank, Boston . .	5,800	7,590 00	5,800 00
Revere Nat'l Bank, Boston . .	3,800	4,630 00	3,800 00
Third Nat'l Bank, Boston . .	11,000	11,660 00	11,000 00
Tremont Nat'l Bank, Boston . .	7,600	9,270 00	7,600 00
Union Nat'l Bank, Boston . .	500	660 00	500 00
Webster Nat'l Bank, Boston . .	6,700	7,430 00	6,700 00
Cambridge City N'l B'k, Cambridge,	2,600	4,100 00	2,600 00
Charles River Nat'l B'k, Cambridge,	2,400	4,000 00	2,400 00
Lechmere Nat'l Bank, Cambridge .	7,600	11,400 00	7,600 00
Newton Nat'l Bank, Newton . .	1,300	1,560 00	1,300 00
Concord Nat'l Bank, Concord . .	3,300	4,290 00	3,300 00
Fall River Nat'l Bank, Fall River .	1,100	1,100 00	1,100 00
First Nat'l Bank, Malden . .	2,500	2,500 00	2,500 00
First Nat'l Bank, Marlborough .	2,000	2,000 00	2,000 00
Merchants' Nat'l B'k, Newburyport,	600	600 00	600 00
	$130,900	$166,374 00	$129,900 00

Railroad Bonds.

	Par Value.	Estimated Market Value.	Amount Invested.
Eastern Railroad	$8,500	$9,350 00	$4,000 00
Boston and Albany Railroad . .	15,000	19,050 00	15,000 00
	$23,500	$28,400 00	$19,000 00

EASTHAMPTON SAVINGS BANK — EASTHAMPTON.

Incorporated Feb. 10, 1869. Number of corporators, 30.

JOHN MAYHER, *President*. *Treasurer*, SAMUEL T. SEELYE.

STATEMENT.

LIABILITIES.		ASSETS.	
Deposits	$291,927 58	Bank stock	$69,169 25
Earnings undivided .	1,130 88	Loans on bank stock . .	1,550 00
Guaranty fund . .	5,000 00	Loans on real estate . .	153,275 00
		Loans on personal security,	72,785 00
		Expense account . . .	175 00
		Cash on hand . . .	1,104 21
	$298,058 46		$298,058 46

Loans on Bank Stock: —
On 17 shares First National Bank, Easthampton . . . $1,550 00

Cash on Deposit in Bank: —
First National Bank, Easthampton $1,104 21

Whole amount of interest or profits received or earned . . . $17,814 00
Rate and amount of each semi-annual dividend for previous year . . . . { 2¼ per cent . 5,766 19; 2¼ per cent . 6,083 48 }
Times for the dividends fixed by the by-laws: Jan. 23 and July 23.
Average annual per cent of dividends for the term ending at time of and including last extra dividend: 6½ per cent.
The total amount of loans, with each specified rate of interest: $10,000, 5 per cent; $15,000, 5½ per cent; $127,555, 6 per cent; $75,055, 6½ per cent.
Number of outstanding loans which are of an amount not exceeding $3,000 each 166
Aggregate amount of the same 125,985 00
Number of open accounts 1,137
Number and amount of deposits received for previous year, 1,213 71,115 90
Number and amount of deposits of and exceeding $300 at any one time for the previous year 51 24,883 94
Number and amount of withdrawals 587 60,809 61
Number of accounts opened the previous year 243
Number of accounts closed the previous year 154
Amount of expenses of the corporation during previous year . . 718 25
Amount of treasurer's bond 10,000 00
Date of examination by commissioner: July 13.

BANK STOCK.

	Par Value.	Estimated Market Value.	Amount Invested.
First Nat'l Bank, Easthampton .	$29,800	$37,250 00	$34,092 00
First Nat'l Bank, Northampton .	9,700	12,610 00	12,125 00
First Nat'l Bank, Lynn . . .	4,400	5,280 00	5,256 00
Holyoke Nat'l Bank, Holyoke . .	8,200	9,184 00	8,200 00
Blackstone Nat'l Bank, Boston .	2,200	2,640 00	2,200 00
Second Nat'l Bank, Boston . .	2,000	3,000 00	3,018 75
North Nat'l Bank, Boston . .	2,000	2,900 00	2,447 50
Commerce Nat'l Bank, Boston .	700	910 00	700 00
Hampshire Co. N'l B'k, Northampt'n,	1,000	1,150 00	1,130 00
	$60,000	$74,924 00	$69,169 25

EAST WEYMOUTH SAVINGS BANK — EAST WEYMOUTH.

Incorporated 1872. Number of corporators, 30.

JOHN P. LOVELL, *President*. *Treasurer*, JOSEPH A. CUSHING.

STATEMENT.

LIABILITIES.		ASSETS.	
Deposits	$212,811 92	Public funds	$24,950 00
Earnings undivided	60 77	Bank Stock	8,500 00
Guaranty fund	3,125 80	Railroad bonds	2,000 00
		Real estate by foreclosure	1,071 38
		Loans on real estate	154,613 83
		Loans on personal security,	5,006 00
		Loans to counties, cities, or towns	9,850 00
		Deposit in bank on interest,	9,860 12
		Cash on hand	147 16
	$215,998 49		$215,998 49

Cash on Deposit in Bank: —

Manufacturers' National Bank, Boston	$9,860 12

Amount of real estate held by foreclosure	$1,071 38
Assessed value of the same	1,025 00
Amount of income received from the same	74 88
Amount of municipal tax on real estate	18 10

Whole amount of interest or profits received or earned		$10,881 71
Rate and amount of each semi-annual dividend for previous year	2½ per cent	4,380 97
	2 per cent	3,881 50

Times for the dividends fixed by the by-laws: April and October.

Average annual per cent of dividends for the term ending at time of and including last extra dividend: $5\frac{4}{10}$ per cent.

The total amount of loans, with each specified rate of interest: $9,850, 5 per cent; $72,420.83, 6 per cent; $24,750, 6½ per cent; $62,449, 7 per cent.

Number of outstanding loans which are of an amount not exceeding $3,000 each	136	
Aggregate amount of the same		116,619 83
Number of open accounts	855	
Number and amount of deposits received for previous year	846	60,494 73
Number and amount of deposits of and exceeding $300 at any one time for the previous year	54	26,106 32
Number and amount of withdrawals	328	33,338 55
Number of accounts opened the previous year	230	
Number of accounts closed the previous year	99	
Amount of expenses of the corporation during previous year		960 83
Amount of treasurer's bond		20,000 00

Date of examination by commissioner: May 23.

PUBLIC FUNDS.

	Par Value.	Estimated Market Value.	Amount Invested.
State and city bonds: —			
State of Maine	$4,000	$4,000 00	$4,000 00
City of Boston	8,000	8,800 00	8,000 00
of Charlestown	7,000	9,100 00	7,950 00
of Portland, Me.	3,000	3,300 00	3,000 00
of Chelsea	1,000	1,000 00	1,000 00
of Salem	1,000	1,000 00	1,000 00
	$24,000	$27,200 00	$24,950 00

BANK STOCK.

	Par Value.	Estimated Market Value.	Amount Invested.
Union Nat'l Bank, Boston . .	$4,500	$5,400 00	$4,500 00
Central Nat'l Bank, Boston . .	1,000	1,090 00	1,000 00
Merchandise Nat'l Bank, Boston .	1,000	1,090 00	1,000 00
Manufacturers' Nat'l Bank, Boston .	2,000	2,100 00	2,000 00
	$8,500	$9,680 00	$8,500 00

RAILROAD BONDS.

	Par Value.	Estimated Market Value.	Amount Invested.
Old Colony Railroad	$2,000	$2,600 00	$2,000 00

ELIOT FIVE CENTS SAVINGS BANK — BOSTON.

Incorporated Feb. 4, 1864. Number of corporators, 74.

WILLIAM C. APPLETON, *President*. *Treasurer*, GEORGE C. LEACH.

STATEMENT.

LIABILITIES.		ASSETS.	
Deposits . .	$1,260,358 36	Public funds . . .	$433,600 00
Earnings undivided .	13,036 58	Bank stock	53,100 00
Guaranty fund . .	17,701 72	Loans on bank stock . .	7,700 00
Tax account . .	4,440 00	Railroad bonds . . .	64,000 00
Suspense account .	48 78	Real estate by foreclosure .	28,000 00
		Loans on real estate . .	491,450 00
		Loans on personal security,	187,400 00
		Expense account . . .	447 23
		Tax titles to real estate .	206 27
		Cash on hand . . .	29,681 94
	$1,295,585 44		$1,295,585 44

Loans on Bank Stock, amount on each: —

On 71 shares People's National Bank, Boston $6,700 00

On 10 shares Exchange National Bank, Boston 1,000 00

Cash on Deposit in Bank: —

People's National Bank, Boston $29,172 68

Amount of real estate held by foreclosure $28,000 00

Assessed value of the same 25,800 00

Amount of income received from the same 1,998 13

Amount of municipal tax on real estate 358 62

Whole amount of interest or profits received or earned . . . $65,417 72

Rate and amount of each semi-annual dividend for previous year . . . . { 2 per cent . 21,662 72; 2 per cent . 22,649 51 }

Times for the dividends fixed by the by-laws: second Wednesday in April and October.

Average annual per cent of dividends for the term ending at time of and including last extra dividend: 8 per cent.

The total amount of loans, with each specified rate of interest: $25,000, 3 per cent; $15,000, $3\frac{1}{4}$ per cent; $50,000, $3\frac{1}{2}$ per cent; $29,300, 4 per cent; $36,000, $4\frac{1}{2}$ per cent; $122,000, 5 per cent; $23,500, $5\frac{1}{2}$ per cent; $263,750, 6 per cent; 5,900, $6\frac{1}{2}$ per cent; $86,000, 7 per cent; $10,000, $7\frac{3}{10}$ per cent; $7,500, $7\frac{1}{2}$ per cent; $12,600, 8 per cent,

Number of outstanding loans which are of an amount not exceeding $3,000 each 91

Aggregate amount of the same 148,400 00

Number of open accounts 5,314

Number and amount of deposits received for previous year, 5,888 380,868 57

Number and amount of deposits of and exceeding $300 at any one time for the previous year 259 130,105 00

Number and amount of withdrawals	3,281	$231,950 72
Number of accounts opened the previous year . . .	1,002	
Number of accounts closed the previous year	576	
Amount of expenses of the corporation during previous year . .		6,061 12
Amount of treasurer's bond		5,000 00

Date of examination by commissioner: March 19.

PUBLIC FUNDS.

	Par Value.	Estimated Market Value.	Amount Invested.
United States bonds	$125,000	$137,500 00	$125,000 00
State, city, and town bonds :—			
State of Maine.	$1,000	$1,160 00	$1,000 00
of New Hampshire. . . .	2,600	3,036 00	2,600 00
City of Bangor, Me.	4,000	4,380 00	4,000 00
of Providence, R.I.	25,000	27,800 00	25,000 00
of Lynn	15,000	16,600 00	15,000 00
of Portsmouth, N.H. . . .	10,000	10,700 00	10,000 00
of Dover, N.H.	5,000	5,400 00	5,000 00
of Springfield	20,000	25,000 00	20,000 00
of Taunton	20,000	23,000 00	20,000 00
of Somerville	10,000	10,800 00	10,000 00
of Lowell.	13,000	14,600 00	13,000 00
of Lawrence	15,000	16,900 00	15,000 00
of Cambridge	10,000	11,800 00	10,000 00
of Fall River	10,000	11,200 00	10,000 00
of Portland, Me.	5,000	5,500 00	5,000 00
of Chelsea	15,000	17,000 00	15,000 00
of Boston.	100,000	112,300 00	100,000 00
of Manchester, N.H . . .	10,000	11,000 00	10,000 00
Town of Woburn	8,000	9,200 00	8,000 00
of Beverly	10,000	10,200 00	10,000 00
	$433,600	$485,076 00	$433,600 00

BANK STOCK.

People's Nat'l Bank, Boston . .	$13,000	$18,850 00	$13,000 00
Atlantic Nat'l Bank, Boston . .	1,000	1,350 00	1,000 00
Atlas Nat'l Bank, Boston . .	7,000	7,910 00	7,000 00
Columbian Nat'l Bank, Boston .	2,000	2,800 00	2,000 00
Continental Nat'l Bank, Boston .	5,000	5,500 00	5,000 00
Eagle Nat'l Bank, Boston . .	1,000	1,100 00	1,000 00
Eliot Nat'l Bank, Boston. . .	1,000	1,070 00	1,000 00
Howard Nat'l Bank, Boston . .	1,300	1,365 00	1,300 00
Market Nat'l Bank, Boston .	3,000	3,250 00	3,000 00
Merchants' Nat'l Bank, Boston .	3,000	3,900 00	3,000 00
Mount Vernon Nat'l Bank, Boston .	6,100	7,200 00	6,100 00
State Nat'l Bank, Boston . .	1,400	1,700 00	1,400 00
Shawmut Nat'l Bank, Boston . .	4,300	4,800 00	4,300 00
Naumkeag Nat'l Bank, Salem .	1,000	1,500 00	1,000 00
North America Nat'l Bank, Boston.	1,000	1,150 00	1,000 00
Redemption Nat'l Bank, Boston .	2,000	2,600 00	2,000 00
	$53,100	$66,045 00	$53,100 00

RAILROAD BONDS.

	Par Value.	Estimated Market Value.	Amount Invested.
Boston and Lowell Railroad . .	$29,000	$35,380 00	$29,000 00
Boston, Clinton, Fitchburg, and New Bedford Railroad * . . .	25,000	25,750 00	25,000 00
Newport and Richford Railroad, guaranteed by the Connecticut River and Passumpsic Railroad .	10,000	10,500 00	10,000 00
	$64,000	$71,630 00	$64,000 00

* This bank has been notified that this investment is illegal.

EMIGRANT SAVINGS BANK* — BOSTON.

Incorporated May, 1870. Number of corporators, 26.

THOMAS RUSSELL, *President*. *Treasurer*, JOHN W. MCDONALD.

STATEMENT.

LIABILITIES.		ASSETS.	
Deposits	$872,375 47	Real estate	$290,322 95
Earnings undivided	18,209 38	Real estate by foreclosure	281,222 35
Guaranty fund	9,019 67	Loans on real estate	220,346 70
Profit and loss	121,250 80	Loans on personal security,	204,700 00
Suspense account	621 27	Deposit in bank on interest,	7,097 78
		Expense account	2,639 69
		Fixtures and safe	11,691 91
		Cash on hand	3,455 21
	$1,021,476 59		$1,021,476 59

Cash on Deposit in Bank: —

Maverick National Bank		$7,097 78
Amount invested in real estate (for banking purposes)		$290,322 95
Estimated value of the same		250,000 00
Amount of real estate held by foreclosure		281,222 35
Assessed value of the same		217,350 00
Amount of income received from the same		13,672 43
Amount of municipal tax on real estate		2,798 07
Whole amount of interest or profits received or earned		$47,902 51

Times for the dividends fixed by the by-laws: May and November.

The total amount of loans, with each specified rate of interest: $200,000, 5 per cent; $148,425, 6 per cent; $13,000, 6½ per cent; $35,071.70, 7 per cent; $22,250, 7½ per cent; $6,300, 8 per cent.

Number of outstanding loans which are of an amount not exceeding $3,000 each	59	
Aggregate amount of the same		80,496 70
Amount of investments from which no income is received		18,660 67
Number of open accounts	6,491	
Number and amount of withdrawals	11,310	388,248 14
Amount of expenses of the corporation during previous year		5,586 74
Amount of treasurer's bond		20,000 00

Date of examination by commissioner: Feb. 12.

* This bank was temporarily enjoined by decree of Supreme Judicial Court, April 16, 1878, and is now being wound up by its officers by permission of the court.

ESSEX SAVINGS BANK — LAWRENCE.

Incorporated March 12, 1847. Number of corporators, 47.

JOSEPH SHATTUCK, *President.* *Treasurer*, JAMES H. EATON.

STATEMENT.

LIABILITIES.		ASSETS.	
Deposits	$3,734,602 82	Public funds	$536,000 00
Earnings undivided	30,878 67	Bank stock	293,225 00
Guaranty fund	50,000 00	Loans on bank stock	10,360 00
		Railroad bonds	303,500 00
		Real estate by foreclosure	105,000 00
		Loans on real estate	1,708,891 16
		Loans on personal security,	748,890 00
		Loans to counties, cities, or towns	106,000 00
		Deposit in banks on interest,	18 48
		Cash on hand	3,596 85
	$3,815,481 49		$3,815,481 49

Loans on Bank Stock, amount on each:—

On 40 shares Lawrence National Bank	$2,700 00
On 35 shares Pacific National Bank	2,700 00
On 23 shares Pemberton National Bank	2,300 00
On 8 shares Hide and Leather National Bank	660 00
On 24 shares Old Lowell National Bank	2,000 00

Cash on Deposit in Banks, amount in each:—

Hide and Leather National Bank, Boston	$18 48
Bay State National Bank, Lawrence	480 69

Amount of real estate held by foreclosure	$105,000 00
Assessed value of the same	147,300 00
Amount of income received from the same	6,561 37
Amount of municipal tax on real estate	1,920 47

Whole amount of interest or profits received or earned . . $202,612 16

Rate and amount of each semi-annual dividend for previous year: 2 per cent . 64,354 50; 2 per cent . 68,670 50

Times for the dividends fixed by the by-laws: third Wednesday in April and October.

Average annual per cent of dividends for the term ending at time of and including last extra dividend: $7\frac{23}{100}$ per cent.

The total amount of loans, with each specified rate of interest: $75,000, 4 per cent; $248,000, 4½ per cent; $642,250, 5 per cent; $116,600, 5½ per cent; $1,289,831.16, 6 per cent; $86,100, 7 per cent.

Number of outstanding loans, which are of an amount not exceeding $3,000 each	426	
Aggregate amount of the same		512,175 00
Number of open accounts	11,600	
Number and amount of deposits received for previous year,	15,331	1,000,409 54
Number and amount of deposits of and exceeding $300 at any one time for the previous year	742	418,087 76
Number and amount of withdrawals	6,717	715,144 22

Number of accounts opened the previous year 3,108
Number of accounts closed the previous year 1,923
Amount of expenses of the corporation during previous year . . $7,722 98
Amount of treasurer's bond $25.000 00
Date of examination by commissioner: June 9.

PUBLIC FUNDS.

	Par Value.	Estimated Market Value.	Amount Invested.
United States 6s, currency . .	$80,000	$104.000 00	$80,000 00
" " 4½s	200,000	226,000 00	200,000 00
" " 4s	100,000	116,000 00	100,000 00
City bonds: —			
City of Boston . .	$10,000	$10,300 00	$10.000 00
of Lawrence . .	16,000	16,000 00	16,000 00
of Somerville . .	25,000	26,000 00	25,000 00
of Fall River . .	25,000	30,000 00	25.000 00
of Lynn . . .	50,000	61,000 00	50.000 00
of Rockland, Me. .	14,000	14,000 00	14,000 00
of Newton . .	16,000	19,000 00	16,000 00
	$536,000	$622.300 00	$536,000 00

BANK STOCK.

	Par Value.	Estimated Market Value.	Amount Invested.
Atlas Nat'l Bank, Boston . .	$13,000	$16,500 00	$13,000 00
Atlantic Nat'l Bank, Boston . .	4,000	6,000 00	4,000 00
Bay State Nat'l Bank, Lawrence .	24.975	33,000 00	24,975 00
Boston Nat'l Bank, Boston . .	3,000	3,800 00	3,000 00
Commonwealth Nat'l Bank, Boston,	4,000	5,100 00	4,000 00
Commerce Nat'l Bank, Boston .	7,500	9,500 00	7,500 00
Continental Nat'l Bank, Boston .	2,000	2,400 00	2,000 00
City Nat'l Bank, Boston . . .	13,000	16,000 00	13,000 00
Eliot Nat'l Bank, Boston . .	8.000	9,400 00	8,000 00
Everett Nat'l Bank, Boston . .	10,000	11,500 00	10,000 00
Howard Nat'l Bank, Boston . .	23,200	29,600 00	23,200 00
Hide and Leather Nat'l B'k, Boston,	10,000	11.700 00	10,000 00
Massachusetts Nat'l Bank, Boston .	3,750	4,600 00	3,750 00
Maverick Nat'l Bank, Boston . .	5.100	12.400 00	5,100 00
Merchants' Nat'l Bank, Boston .	20,000	29,400 00	20,000 00
North America Nat'l Bank, Boston,	15,000	17,500 00	15,000 00
North Nat'l Bank, Boston . .	10,000	14,000 00	10,000 00
Revere Nat'l Bank, Boston . .	22.500	27,600 00	22,500 00
Republic Nat'l Bank, Boston . .	25,000	32.000 00	25,000 00
Shawmut Nat'l Bank, Boston . .	2,700	3.300 00	2,700 00
Suffolk Nat'l Bank, Boston . .	9,000	10,900 00	9,000 00
State Nat'l Bank, Boston . .	9,900	12,400 00	9,900 00
Tremont Nat'l Bank, Boston . .	10,000	12,300 00	10,000 00
Traders' Nat'l Bank, Boston . .	7,000	7,200 00	7,000 00
Union Nat'l Bank, Boston . .	1,000	1,500 00	1,000 00
Webster Nat'l Bank, Boston . .	25,000	28.000 00	25,000 00
Mount Vernon Nat'l Bank, Boston .	4.600	5,700 00	4,600 00
	$293,225	$373,300 00	$293,225 00

RAILROAD BONDS.

	Par Value.	Estimated Market Value.	Amount Invested.
Boston and Maine Railroad . .	$200,000	$254,000 00	$200,000 00
Boston and Lowell Railroad . .	50,000	62,000 00	50,000 00
Eastern Railroad	53,500	59,000 00	53,500 00
	$303,500	$375,000 00	$303,500 00

FAIRHAVEN INSTITUTION FOR SAVINGS — FAIRHAVEN.

Incorporated 1832. Number of corporators, 52.

GEORGE H. TABER, *President*. *Treasurer*, CHARLES DREW.

STATEMENT.

LIABILITIES.		ASSETS.	
Deposits	$525,756 93	Public funds	$38,500 00
Earnings undivided	8,358 43	Bank stock	179,940 00
Guaranty fund	7,771 67	Loans on bank stock	400 00
		Real estate (banking house),	4,809 36
		Real estate	7,512 29
		Real estate by foreclosure	101,776 77
		Loans on real estate	84,550 00
		Loans on personal security,	83,452 75
		Deposit in bank on interest,	20,000 00
		Oak Bluff bonds *	10,320 20
		Cash on hand	10,625 66
	$541,887 03		$541,887 03

Loans on Bank Stock, amount on each: —

On 3 shares National Bank of Commerce, Boston	$200 00
On 5 shares National Bank, Fairhaven	200 00

Cash on Deposit in Bank: —

National Bank, Fairhaven	$30,540 81

Amount invested in real estate (for banking purposes)	$4,809 36
Estimated value of the same	4,809 36
Amount of real estate held by foreclosure	101,776 77
Assessed value of the same †	58,233 00
Amount of income received from the same	1,216 61
Amount of municipal tax on real estate	843 98

Whole amount of interest or profits received or earned $40,815 16

Rate and amount of each semi-annual dividend for previous year: 2 per cent, 11,473 51; 2 per cent, 10,333 68

Times for the dividends fixed by the by-laws: last Monday in April and October.

The total amount of loans, with each specified rate of interest: $20,000, 3 per cent; $44,000, 5 per cent; $105,788.75, 6 per cent; $9,275, 6½ per cent; $9,339, 7 per cent.

Number of outstanding loans which are of an amount not exceeding $3,000 each	55	
Aggregate amount of the same		41,202 75
Amount of investments from which no income is received		42,012 29
Number of open accounts	1,078	
Number and amount of deposits received for previous year	103	44,830 11
Number and amount of deposits of and exceeding $300 at any one time for the previous year	30	18,922 72
Number and amount of withdrawals	914	172,248 07

* Taken to secure indebtedness. † Unable to give whole of assessed value.

Number of accounts opened the previous year 41
Number of accounts closed the previous year 315
Amount of expenses of the corporation during previous year . . . $2,409 18
Amount of treasurer's bond 5,000 00
Date of examination by commissioner: Sept. 19.

PUBLIC FUNDS.

	Par Value.	Estimated Market Value.	Amount Invested.
City and town bonds:—			
City of Bath, Me.	$5,000	$5,100 00	$5,000 00
of Belfast, Me. . . .	6,500	6,500 00	6,500 00
Town of Fairhaven	27,000	32,400 00	27,000 00
	$38,500	$44,000 00	$38,500 00

BANK STOCK.

	Par Value.	Estimated Market Value.	Amount Invested.
Fairhaven Nat'l Bank, Fairhaven .	$24,640	$24,640 00	$24,640 00
First Nat'l Bank, New Bedford .	10,400	14,092 00	10,400 00
Citizens' Nat'l Bank, New Bedford .	8,000	9,380 00	8,000 00
Commerce Nat'l B'k, New Bedford,	4,000	5,400 00	4,000 00
Mechanics' Nat'l B'k, New Bedford,	6,800	10,234 00	6,800 00
Commerce Nat'l Bank, Boston .	15,000	19,312 50	15,000 00
Merchants' Nat'l Bank, Boston .	8,000	11,700 00	8,000 00
Eliot Nat'l Bank, Boston . .	10,000	12,025 00	10,000 00
North Nat'l Bank, Boston . .	5,600	7,959 00	5,600 00
Traders' Nat'l Bank, Boston . .	10,500	10,710 00	10,500 00
Webster Nat'l Bank, Boston . .	6,500	7,312 50	6,500 00
Boston Nat'l Bank, Boston . .	10,000	12,800 00	10,000 00
Republic Nat'l Bank, Boston . .	8,000	10,480 00	8,000 00
State Nat'l Bank, Boston . .	10,000	12,525 00	10,000 00
Howard Nat'l Bank, Boston . .	10,000	13,012 50	10,000 00
North America Nat'l Bank, Boston .	10,000	11,500 00	10,000 00
Continental Nat'l Bank, Boston .	5,000	5,912 50	5,000 00
Metropolitan Nat'l Bank, Boston .	4,000	4,810 00	4,000 00
Manufacturers' Nat'l Bank, Boston .	3,500	3,858 75	3,500 00
Wachusett Nat'l Bank, Fitchburg .	10,000	20,700 00	10,000 00
	$179,940	$228,363 75	$179,940 00

FALL RIVER FIVE CENTS SAVINGS BANK — FALL RIVER.

Incorporated April 10, 1855. Number of corporators, 70.

WALTER C. DURFEE, *President.* *Treasurer*, CHARLES J. HOLMES.

STATEMENT.

LIABILITIES.		ASSETS.	
Deposits	$1,065,515 44	Public funds	$100,000 00
Earnings undivided	38,579 71	Bank stock	200,900 00
Guaranty fund	13,362 58	Railroad bonds	70,000 00
		Real estate	45,000 00
		Loans on real estate	426,750 00
		Loans on personal security,	247,641 63
		Expense account	1,353 78
		Border City Manufacturing Company *	20,200 00
		Cash on hand	5,612 32
	$1,117,457 73		$1,117,457 73

Amount invested in real estate (for banking purposes)		$45,000 00
Estimated value of the same		45,000 00
Amount of municipal tax on real estate		845 50
Whole amount of interest or profits received or earned		$59,773 64
Rate and amount of each semi-annual dividend for previous year	2¼ per cent	23,113 16
	2¼ per cent	23,128 49

Times for the dividends fixed by the by-laws: second Monday in June and December.

The total amount of loans, with each specified rate of interest: $54,000, 4 per cent; $45,000, 4½ per cent; $421,375, 5 per cent; $46,000, 5½ per cent; $78,175, 6 per cent.

Number of outstanding loans which are of an amount not exceeding $3,000 each	89	
Aggregate amount of the same		109,050 00
Amount of investments from which no income is received		13,192 70
Number of open accounts	4,605	
Number and amount of deposits received for previous year,	10,356	215,729 91
Number and amount of deposits of and exceeding $300 at any one time for the previous year	149	98,890 00
Number and amount of withdrawals	2,060	209,876 68
Number of accounts opened the previous year	578	
Number of accounts closed the previous year	499	
Amount of expenses of the corporation during previous year		3,663 46
Amount of treasurer's bond		20,000 00

Date of examination by commissioner: July 21.

* Taken to secure indebtedness.

PUBLIC FUNDS.

	Par Value.	Estimated Market Value.	Amount Invested.
United States 6s, currency . .	$100,000	$134,000 00	$100,000 00

BANK STOCK.

	Par Value.	Estimated Market Value.	Amount Invested.
Atlantic Nat'l Bank, Boston . .	$1,300	$1,989 00	$1,300 00
Atlas Nat'l Bank, Boston . .	3,000	3,750 00	3,000 00
Blackstone Nat'l Bank, Boston .	12,000	13,800 00	12,000 00
Boston Nat'l Bank, Boston . .	3,200	4,096 00	3,200 00
Broadway Nat'l Bank, Boston . .	5,500	5,390 00	5,500 00
Eliot Nat'l Bank, Boston . .	1,500	1,800 00	1,500 00
First Nat'l Bank, Boston . . .	5,000	10,400 00	5,000 00
Howard Nat'l Bank, Boston . .	13,300	17,290 00	13,300 00
Maverick Nat'l Bank, Boston . .	2,200	5,500 00	2,200 00
Monument Nat'l Bank, Boston .	8,500	17,765 00	8,500 00
City Nat'l Bank, Boston . . .	10,000	12,700 00	10,000 00
Commerce Nat'l Bank, Boston .	700	903 00	700 00
Exchange Nat'l Bank, Boston . .	4,000	5,760 00	4,000 00
Hide and Leather Nat'l B'k, Boston,	7,500	8,737 50	7,500 00
North America Nat'l Bank, Boston .	8,400	9,660 00	8,400 00
Revere Nat'l Bank, Boston . .	7,500	9,150 00	7,500 00
Shawmut Nat'l Bank, Boston . .	6,700	8,542 50	6,700 00
Webster Nat'l Bank, Boston . .	3,000	3,330 00	3,000 00
First Nat'l Bank, Chelsea . .	30,000	37,500 00	30,000 00
First Nat'l Bank, Malden . .	10,000	12,000 00	10,000 00
First Nat'l Bank, Oxford . .	2,000	2,240 00	2,000 00
Metacomet Nat'l Bank, Fall River .	9,400	11,750 00	9,400 00
Union National Bank, Fall River .	5,000	5,750 00	5,000 00
Second Nat'l Bank, Fall River .	41,200	47,380 00	41,200 00
	$200,900	$257,183 00	$200,900 00

RAILROAD BONDS.

	Par Value.	Estimated Market Value.	Amount Invested.
Rutland Railroad equipment . .	$100,000	$85,000 00	$70,000 00

FALL RIVER SAVINGS BANK — FALL RIVER.

Incorporated 1828. Number of corporators, 124.

J. B. FRENCH, *President*. *Treasurer*, C. A. BASSETT.

STATEMENT.

LIABILITIES.		ASSETS.	
Deposits . . .	$4,181,740 99	Public funds . . .	$700,000 00
Earnings undivided .	120,123 94	Bank stock . . .	641,200 00
Guaranty fund . .	68,500 00	Loans on bank stock . .	20,700 00
		Real estate	50,000 00
		Real estate by foreclosure .	32,500 00
		Loans on real estate . .	1,417,608 46
		Loans on personal security,	1,416,732 00
		Deposit in banks on interest,	20,200 00
		Expense account	923 57
		Tax account	913 90
		Stocks and bonds * . .	69,050 00
		Cash on hand . . .	537 00
	$4,370,364 93		$4,370,364 93

Loans on Bank Stock, amount on each:—

On 200 shares Metacomet National Bank, Fall River . . . $20,000 00
On 10 shares Pocasset National Bank, Fall River . . . 700 00

Cash on Deposit in Banks, amount in each:—

Metacomet National Bank, Fall River $3,000 00
Maverick National Bank, Boston 5,000 00
National Bank of North America, Boston . . . 5,000 00
National Bank of Redemption, Boston 2,200 00
Revere National Bank, Boston 5,000 00

Amount invested in real estate (for banking purposes) $50,000 00
Estimated value of the same 45,400 00
Amount of real estate held by foreclosure 32,500 00
Assessed value of the same 33,000 00
Amount of income received from the same 1,588 56
Amount of municipal tax on real estate 1,489 60

Whole amount of interest or profits received or earned $249,476 98
Rate and amount of each semi-annual dividend for previous year . . . . { $2\frac{1}{4}$ per cent . 93,475 59; $2\frac{1}{4}$ per cent . 92,403 27 }

Times for the dividends fixed by the by-laws: first Monday in April and October.

The total amount of loans, with each specified rate of interest: $332,500, 4 per cent; $306,550, 4½ per cent; $1,872,450, 5 per cent; $220,025, 5½ per cent; $114,515.46, 6 per cent.

Number of outstanding loans which are of an amount not exceeding $3,000 each 269
Aggregate amount of the same 355,633 00
Number of open accounts 9,558

* Taken to secure indebtedness.

Number and amount of deposits received for previous year,	4,210	$498,736 49
Number and amount of deposits of and exceeding $300 at any one time for the previous year	478	289,343 54
Number and amount of withdrawals	6,721	788,744 23
Number of accounts opened the previous year	1,198	
Number of accounts closed the previous year	1,455	
Amount of expenses of the corporation during previous year		10,280 98
Amount of treasurer's bond		25,000 00

Date of examination by commissioner: July 21.

PUBLIC FUNDS.

	Par Value.	Estimated Market Value.	Amount Invested.
United States 4½s, registered	$450,000	$508,500 00	$450,000 00
" " 4s, registered	250,000	290,000 00	250,000 00
	$700,000	$798,500 00	$700,000 00

BANK STOCK.

Fall River Nat'l Bank, Fall River	$66,300	$89,505 00	$66,300 00
Metacomet Nat'l Bank, Fall River	93,500	116,875 00	93,500 00
Massasoit Nat'l Bank, Fall River	42,200	75,960 00	42,200 00
Second Nat'l Bank, Fall River	15,000	17,250 00	15,000 00
Union Nat'l Bank, Fall River	18,000	20,700 00	18,000 00
First Nat'l Bank, New Bedford	50,000	67,500 00	50,000 00
Commerce Nat'l Bank, New Bedford,	42,000	57,540 00	42,000 00
Merchants' Nat'l B'k, New Bedford,	22,000	35,200 00	22,000 00
Eliot Nat'l Bank, Boston	15,000	18,000 00	15,000 00
Faneuil Hall Nat'l Bank, Boston	40,000	53,600 00	40,000 00
First Nat'l Bank, Boston	33,000	68,310 00	33,000 00
Howard Nat'l Bank, Boston	30,000	39,000 00	30,000 00
Merchants' Nat'l Bank, Boston	16,000	23,360 00	16,000 00
Second Nat'l Bank, Boston	23,200	35,032 00	23,200 00
Washington Nat'l Bank, Boston	20,000	28,000 00	20,000 00
Hide and Leather Nat'l B'k, Boston,	25,000	29,000 00	25,000 00
Revere Nat'l Bank, Boston	30,000	36,000 00	30,000 00
Commerce Nat'l Bank, Boston	20,000	25,600 00	20,000 00
North America Nat'l Bank, Boston	40,000	46,000 00	40,000 00
	$641,200	$883,032 00	$641,200 00

FITCHBURG SAVINGS BANK—FITCHBURG.

Incorporated Feb. 12, 1846. Number of corporators, 61.

THORNTON K. WARE, *President*. *Treasurer*, CHARLES J. BILLINGS.

STATEMENT.

LIABILITIES.		ASSETS.	
Deposits	$1,906,625 97	Public funds	$135,222 50
Earnings undivided	36,012 85	Bank stock	215,810 00
Guaranty fund	38,500 00	Loans on bank stock	9,500 00
		Railroad bonds	2,700 00
		Real estate	150,000 00
		Real estate by foreclosure	81,340 00
		Loans on real estate	752,516 00
		Loans on personal security,	433,333 00
		Loans to counties, cities, or towns	10,000 00
		Deposit in banks on interest,	183,843 82
		Expense account	396 62
		Cash on hand	6,476 88
	$1,981,138 82		$1,981,138 82

Loans on Bank Stock, amount on each:—

On 50 shares Fitchburg National Bank	$5,000 00
On 57 shares Safety Fund National Bank	4,500 00

Cash on Deposit in Banks, amount in each:—

Fitchburg National Bank	$50,000 00
Safety Fund National Bank	15,000 00
First National Bank, Leominster	20,000 00
Townsend National Bank	55,000 00
Westminster National Bank	20,000 00
Conway National Bank	15,000 00
Maverick National Bank	12,826 28
Shawmut National Bank	1,017 54

Amount invested in real estate (for banking purposes)	$150,000 00
Estimated value of the same	150,000 00
Amount of real estate held by foreclosure	81,340 00
Assessed value of the same	69,225 00
Amount of income received from the same	5,173 00
Amount of municipal tax on real estate	3,331 05

Whole amount of interest or profits received or earned		$113,317 74
Rate and amount of each semi-annual dividend for previous year	2 per cent	35,734 41
	2 per cent	36,487 16

Times for the dividends fixed by the by-laws: Jan. 1 and July 1.

The total amount of loans, with each specified rate of interest: $1,017.54, 2½ per cent; $57,826.28, 3 per cent; $13,000, 3½ per cent; $158,500, 4 per cent; $158,000, 4½ per cent; $311,700, 5 per cent; $40,400, 5½ per cent; $612,503.50, 6 per cent; $89,276, 6½ per cent; $79,192, 7 per cent.

Number of outstanding loans which are of an amount not exceeding $3,000 each . . . 255

Aggregate amount of the same		$332,150 54
Amount of investments from which no income is received . .		52,300 00
Number of open accounts	5,316	
Number and amount of deposits received for previous year,	2,844	574,802 08
Number and amount of deposits of and exceeding $300 at any one time for the previous year	524	371,023 15
Number and amount of withdrawals	2,283	499,084 65
Number of accounts opened the previous year . . .	1,118	
Number of accounts closed the previous year	936	
Amount of expenses of the corporation during previous year . .		4,364 88
Amount of treasurer's bond		25,000 00

Date of examination by commissioner: May 13.

Purlic Funds.

	Par Value.	Estimated Market Value.	Amount Invested.
United States bonds	$63,000	$71,192 50	$63,000 00
City and town bonds: —			
City of Fitchburg	$50,000	$58,500 00	$46,625 00
of Norwich, Conn. . . .	17,000	22,100 00	17,935 00
of Portland, Me. . . .	5,000	5,750 00	4,602 50
Town of Tolland	2,000	2,060 00	2,000 00
of Sandisfield . . .	1,000	1,030 00	1,000 00
	$138,000	$160,632 50	$135,222 50

Bank Stock.

Fitchburg Nat'l Bank, Fitchburg .	$13,500	$20,925 00	$14,000 00
Rollstone Nat'l Bank, Fitchburg .	11,300	18,419 00	12,210 00
Safety Fund Nat'l Bank, Fitchburg,	17,000	18,700 00	18,050 00
First Nat'l Bank, Leominster . .	20,000	21,000 00	22,550 00
Townsend Nat'l Bank, Townsend .	500	675 00	500 00
Crocker Nat'l Bank, Turner's Falls,	20,000	25,000 00	20,000 00
City Nat'l Bank, Worcester . .	10,000	11,400 00	10,000 00
Quinsigamond Nat'l B'k, Worcester,	3,000	3,360 00	3,000 00
Merchants' Nat'l Bank, Boston .	20,000	29,000 00	20,000 00
Howard Nat'l Bank, Boston . .	15,000	19,500 00	15,000 00
Boston Nat'l Bank, Boston . .	13,300	17,024 00	13,300 00
North Nat'l Bank, Boston . .	11,600	16,472 00	11,600 00
Revere Nat'l Bank, Boston . .	15,000	18,150 00	15,000 00
Hide and Leather Nat'l B'k, Boston,	10,000	11,500 00	11,600 00
North America Nat'l Bank, Boston,	6,600	7,524 00	6,600 00
Commerce Nat'l Bank, New Bedford,	10,000	13,900 00	12,400 00
Citizens' Nat'l Bank, New Bedford,	10,000	11,725 00	10,000 00
	$206,800	$264,274 00	$215,810 00

Railroad Bonds.

Agricultural Branch Railroad . .	$3,000	$3,030 00	$2,700 00

FLORENCE SAVINGS BANK — FLORENCE.

Incorporated 1873. Number of corporators, 39.

A. T. LILLY, *President*. *Treasurer*, M. W. BOND.

STATEMENT.

LIABILITIES.		ASSETS.	
Deposits . . .	$128,496 83	Real estate by foreclosure .	$1,713 64
Earnings undivided .	1,272 36	Loans on real estate . .	63,736 20
Guaranty fund . .	1,308 30	Loans on personal security,*	52,282 00
		Deposit in bank on interest,	12,209 84
		Expense account . . .	63 56
		Cash on hand . . .	1,072 25
	$131,077 49		$131,077 49

Cash on Deposit in Bank: —

Hampshire County National Bank . . . $12,209 84

Amount of real estate held by foreclosure . $1,713 64
Assessed value of the same 2,600 00
Amount of income received from the same . 108 32
Amount of municip l tax on real estate . . 11 67

Whole amount of interest or profits received or earned . . . $6,646 44
Rate and amount of each semi-annual dividend for previous year . . . . { 2 per cent . 2,089 66; 2 per cent . 2,314 76 }
Times for the dividends fixed by the by-laws: second Tuesday in April and October.
Average annual per cent of dividends for the term ending at time of and including last extra dividend: 6½ per cent.
The total amount of loans, with each specified rate of interest: $15,000, 5 per cent; $101,018.20. 6 per cent.
Number of outstanding loans which are of an amount not exceeding $3.000 each 103
Aggregate amount of the same 68.518 20
Number of open accounts 730
Number and amount of deposits received for previous year . 997 51,488 34
Number and amount of deposits of and exceeding $300 at any one time for the previous year 23 15.857 14
Number and amount of withdrawals 342 30.607 52
Number of accounts opened the previous year 168
Number of accounts closed the previous year 104
Amount of expenses of the corporation during previous year . 798 67
Amount of treasurer's bond 10,000 00
Date of examination by commissioner: July 12.

* This bank has been notified that these loans exceed the legal limit.

FOXBOROUGH SAVINGS BANK* — FOXBOROUGH.

Incorporated April 1855. Number of corporators, 60.

CHARLES W. HODGES, *President*. *Treasurer*, ELI PHELPS.

STATEMENT.

LIABILITIES.		ASSETS.	
Deposits . . .	$134,425 17	Public funds . . .	$4,000 00
Earnings undivided .	2,191 54	Bank stock	10,150 00
Guaranty fund . .	1,800 00	Real estate by foreclosure .	15,600 00
		Loans on real estate . .	74,585 00
		Loans on personal security,	6,505 29
		Deposit in bank on interest,	26,955 12
		Cash on hand . . .	621 30
	$138,416 71		$138,416 71

Cash on Deposit in Bank: —
Merchandise National Bank, Boston $26,955 12

Amount of real estate held by foreclosure		$15,600 00
Assessed value of the same		17,360 00
Amount of income received from the same		1,284 95
Amount of municipal tax on real estate		303 32

Whole amount of interest or profits received or earned $6,856 78

Times for the dividends fixed by the by-laws: May and November.

Average annual per cent of dividends for the term ending at time of and including last extra dividend: 6½ per cent.

The total amount of loans, with each specified rate of interest: $67,210.29, 6 per cent; $1,500, 6½ per cent; $12,380, 7 per cent.

Number of outstanding loans which are of an amount not exceeding $3,000 each	115	
Aggregate amount of the same		73,590 29
Amount of investments from which no income is received . .		2,044 15
Number of open accounts	838	
Number and amount of withdrawals	1	100 00
Number of accounts closed the previous year	1	
Amount of expenses of the corporation during previous year. .		497 18
Amount of treasurer's bond		13,000 00

Date of examination by commissioner: Dec. 3.

* An order regulating the payments of deposits for one year, limiting them to an amount not exceeding ten per cent each six months, was issued April 30, 1878, and extended for one year, April 30, 1879, to pay ten per cent of remainder of deposits each six months. This order was so modified April 30, 1880, that from this date until March 21, 1881, the bank was restricted from making any payments to depositors, except those due under the previous orders. The bank was temporarily enjoined by order of the Supreme Judicial Court, March 18, 1881.

PUBLIC FUNDS.

	Par Value.	Estimated Market Value.	Amount Invested.
City of Boston 5s of 1883 . .	$4,000	$4,070 00	$4,000 00

BANK STOCK.

	Par Value.	Estimated Market Value.	Amount Invested.
Boylston Nat'l Bank, Boston . .	$1,500	$1,825 00	$1,500 00
Webster Nat'l Bank, Boston . .	1,000	1,120 00	1,000 00
Faneuil Hall Nat'l Bank, Boston .	800	1,048 00	800 00
Hide and Leather Nat'l B'k, Boston,	1,500	1,755 00	1,500 00
Merchandise Nat'l Bank, Boston .	5,000	5,500 00	5,000 00
Wrentham Nat'l Bank, Wrentham .	350	350 00	350 00
	$10,150	$11,598 00	$10,150 00

FRAMINGHAM SAVINGS BANK — FRAMINGHAM.

Incorporated 1846. Number of corporators, 40.

L. F. Fuller, *President.* *Treasurer,* C. S. Adams.

Statement.

Liabilities.		Assets.	
Deposits	$1,247,801 91	Public funds	$153,500 00
Earnings undivided	51,792 19	Loans on public funds	500 00
Guaranty fund	16,600 00	Bank stock	164,800 00
		Loans on bank stock	42,429 00
		Loans on bank books	400 00
		Railroad bonds	43,000 00
		Loans on railroad bonds	3,000 00
		Real estate by foreclosure	16,200 00
		Loans on real estate	711,227 00
		Loans on personal security,	86,901 08
		Deposit in banks on interest,	45,000 00
		Expense account	3,610 11
		Premium account	13,326 00
		Safe, vault, etc.	2,000 00
		Cash on hand and in bank,	30,300 91
	$1,316,194 10		$1,316,194 10

Loans on Public Funds: —

On $500 United States 4s	$500 00

Loans on Bank Stock, amount on each: —

On 79 shares Framingham National Bank	$6,829 00
On 120 shares Natick National Bank and 100 shares Spencer National Bank	20,000 00
On 100 shares Boston National Bank and 104 shares National Bank of Redemption	15,000 00
On 6 shares Waltham National Bank	600 00
On Framingham Savings Bank book	100 00
On Natick Savings Bank book *	300 00

Loans on Railroad Bonds: —

On $3,000 Agricultural Railroad	$3,000 00

Cash on Deposit in Banks, amount in each: —

Framingham National Bank	$17,996 68
South Framingham National Bank	21,213 00
Boston Safe Deposit and Trust Company †	25,045 61

Amount of real estate held by foreclosure	$16,200 00
Assessed value of the same	17,600 00
Amount of income received from the same	1,788 98
Amount of municipal tax on real estate	387 72

Whole amount of interest or profits received or earned	$74,889 36

* This bank has been notified that this loan is illegal.

† The Attorney-General has given an opinion that, under the provisions of sect. 3, chap. 214 of the Acts of 1881, deposits by savings banks in this trust company are legal.

Rate and amount of each semi-annual dividend for previous year	2½ per cent 2½ per cent	$26,920 57 27,881 08

Times for the dividends fixed by the by-laws: first Saturday in May and November.

The total amount of loans, with each specified rate of interest: $48,700, 4 per cent; $795,257.08, 6 per cent.

Number of outstanding loans which are of an amount not exceeding $3,000 each	535	
Aggregate amount of the same		608,977 57
Amount of investments from which no income is received		6,500 00
Number of open accounts	4,823	
Number and amount of deposits received for previous year,	1,860	238,510 57
Number and amount of deposits of and exceeding $300 at any one time for the previous year	239	147,023 09
Number and amount of withdrawals	1,263	170,151 58
Number of accounts opened the previous year	824	
Number of accounts closed the previous year	319	
Amount of expenses of the corporation during previous year		3,610 11
Amount of treasurer's bond		20,000 00

Date of examination by commissioner: May 16.

Public Funds.

	Par Value.	Estimated Market Value.	Amount Invested.
United States bonds	$14,500	$16,400 00	$14,500 00
State and city bonds: —			
State of Maine	$21,000	$22,300 00	$21,000 00
City of Boston	24,000	26,400 00	24,000 00
of Providence, R.I.	30,000	35,300 00	30,000 00
of Worcester	25,000	27,500 00	25,000 00
of Norwalk, Conn.	30,000	32,400 00	30,000 00
of Lewiston, Me.	9,000	11,300 00	9,000 00
	$153,500	$171,600 00	$153,500 00

Bank Stock.

Atlas Nat'l Bank, Boston	$600	$875 00	$600 00
Boston Nat'l Bank, Boston	3,300	3,800 00	3,300 00
Blackstone Nat'l Bank, Boston	1,900	2,100 00	1,900 00
Commerce Nat'l Bank, Boston	11,900	15,400 00	11,900 00
Central Nat'l Bank, Boston	10,000	10,000 00	10,000 00
Continental Nat'l Bank, Boston	10,000	11,800 00	10,000 00
Eliot Nat'l Bank, Boston	15,500	18,200 00	15,500 00
Framingham N'l B'k, Framingham,	2,000	3,000 00	2,000 00
First Nat'l Bank, Boston	16,500	34,100 00	16,500 00
Freeman's Nat'l Bank, Boston	3,000	3,700 00	3,000 00
Globe Nat'l Bank, Boston	1,500	1,650 00	1,500 00
Hide and Leather Nat'l B'k, Boston	18,000	21,500 00	18,000 00
Howard Nat'l Bank, Boston	13,600	17,500 00	13,600 00

BANK STOCK — Concluded.

	Par Value.	Estimated Market Value.	Amount Invested.
North America Nat'l Bank, Boston .	$1,000	$1,150 00	$1,000 00
Market Nat'l Bank, Boston . .	3,000	3,250 00	3,000 00
Mount Vernon Nat'l Bank, Boston .	8,500	10,600 00	8,500 00
Nat'l Bank of the Republic, Boston,	9,000	11,250 00	9,000 00
Shoe and Leather Nat'l B'k, Boston,	5,000	5,850 00	5,000 00
Second Nat'l Bank, Boston . .	3,000	4,850 00	3,000 00
Traders' Nat'l Bank, Boston . .	11,000	11,450 00	11,000 00
Webster Nat'l Bank, Boston . .	6,500	7,200 00	6,500 00
S. Framingham N'l B'k, S. Fra'ham,	10,000	10,150 00	10,000 00
	$164,800	$209,375 00	$164,800 00

RAILROAD BONDS.

	Par Value.	Estimated Market Value.	Amount Invested.
Fitchburg Railroad	$20,000	$22,400 00	$20,000 00
Salem and Lowell Railroad . .	20,000	23,000 00	20,000 00
Lowell Railroad	3,000	3,200 00	3,000 00
	$43,000	$48,600 00	$43,000 00

FRANKLIN SAVINGS BANK — BOSTON.

Incorporated March, 1861. Number of corporators, 78.

OSMYN BREWSTER, *President*. *Treasurer*, HENRY WHITTEMORE.

STATEMENT.

LIABILITIES.		ASSETS.	
Deposits . . .	$3,048,412 82	Public funds . . .	$255,021 87
Earnings undivided .	143,370 36	Loans on public funds .	24,650 00
Guaranty fund . .	36,319 57	Bank stock	79,617 83
		Real estate by foreclosure .	297,967 53
		Loans on real estate . .	1,978,997 76
		Loans on personal security,	316,575 00
		Loans to counties, cities, or towns	216,975 00
		Deposit in banks on interest,	44,849 08
		Expense account . . .	3,465 18
		Cash on hand . . .	9,983 50
	$3,228,102 75		$3,228,102 75

Loans on Public Funds, amount on each: —

On $2,000 United States 6s, currency	$2,000 00
On $14,050 United States 4s	14,050 00
On $8,600 United States 4½s	8,600 00

Cash on Deposit in Banks, amount in each: —

Continental National Band	$34,164 54
Revere National Bank	10,684 54

Amount of real estate held by foreclosure		$297,967 53
Assessed value of the same		295,800 00
Amount of income received from the same		16,102 72
Amount of municipal tax on real estate		4,909 20
Whole amount of interest or profits received or earned . . .		$159,315 36
Rate and amount of each semi-annual dividend for previous year	2 per cent .	55,852 16
	2 per cent .	57,602 67

Times for the dividends fixed by the by-laws: Feb. 1 and Aug. 1.

Average annual per cent of dividends for the term ending at time of and including last extra dividend: 5⅝ per cent.

The total amount of loans, with each specified rate of interest: $200,000, 3¼ per cent; $50,000, 3½ per cent; $51,650, 4 per cent; $150,000, 4¼ per cent; $115,000, 4½ per cent; $600,760, 5 per cent; $93,800, 5½ per cent; $835,312.76, 6 per cent; $127,750, 6½ per cent; $69,850, 7 per cent; $17,100, 7½ per cent.

Number of outstanding loans which are of an amount not exceeding $3,000 each	67	
Aggregate amount of the same		181,021 40
Amount of investments from which no income is received . .		30,405 50
Number of open accounts	7.813	
Number and amount of deposits received for previous year,	5.075	658.898 05
Number and amount of deposits of and exceeding $300 at any one time for the previous year	539	306,949 83

Number and amount of withdrawals	4,862	$513,350 21
Number of accounts opened the previous year . . .	1,130	
Number of accounts closed the previous year	954	
Amount of expenses of the corporation during previous year . .		12,428 32
Amount of treasurer's bond		10,000 00

Date of examination by commissioner: Feb. 19.

Public Funds.

	Par Value.	Estimated Market Value.	Amount Invested.
United States 4s	$20,000	$23,250 00	$18,193 75
" " $4\frac{1}{2}$s	225,000	254,250 00	236,828 12
	$245,000	$277,500 00	$255,021 87

Bank Stock.

	Par Value.	Estimated Market Value.	Amount Invested.
Continental Nat'l Bank, Boston .	$23,500	$27,876 87	$22,237 75
Revere Nat'l Bank, Boston . .	19,900	24,178 50	20,114 38
Webster Nat'l Bank, Boston . .	3,100	4,394 25	2,905 75
New England Nat'l Bank, Boston .	4,000	5,940 00	4,170 00
Atlas Nat'l Bank, Boston . .	5,500	6,875 00	5,520 00
Second Nat'l Bank, Boston . .	5,500	8,332 50	5,602 95
North Nat'l Bank, Boston . .	14,600	20,768 50	14,067 00
Third Nat'l Bank, Springfield .	5,000	8,000 00	5,000 00
	$81,100	$106,365 62	$79,617 83

FRANKLIN SAVINGS INSTITUTION — GREENFIELD.

Incorporated 1834. Number of corporators, 20.

SAMUEL O. LAMB, *President*. *Treasurer*, WILLIAM H. ALLEN.

STATEMENT.

LIABILITIES.		ASSETS.	
Deposits	$2,779,434 00	Public funds	$1,293,900 00
Earnings undivided	24,213 03	Bank stock	69,530 00
Guaranty fund	28,000 00	Loans on bank stock	39,120 00
		Railroad bonds	182,500 00
		Real estate by foreclosure	9,773 28
		Loans on real estate	625,210 19
		Loans on personal security,	302,755 51
		Loans to counties, cities, or towns	180,823 05
		Deposit in banks on interest,	119,951 63
		Expense account	619 67
		Premium account	5,000 00
		Interest unpaid	310 00
		Cash on hand	2,153 70
	$2,831,647 03		$2,831,647 03

Loans on Bank Stock, amount on each:—

On 62 shares First National Bank, Northampton	$5,500 00
On 10 shares City National Bank, Worcester	800 00
On 10 shares Crocker National Bank, Turner's Falls	1,000 00
On 21 shares City National Bank, Worcester }	4,900 00
On 28 shares Ware National Bank, Ware }	
On 6 shares Shelburne Falls National Bank	600 00
On 14 shares Franklin County National Bank, Greenfield	520 00
On 24 shares First National Bank, Greenfield	2,700 00
On 10 shares Packard National Bank, Greenfield	700 00
On 70 shares Railroad National Bank, Lowell	7,000 00
On 50 shares National Bank of Redemption, Boston }	10,000 00
On 50 shares Railroad National Bank, Lowell }	
On 54 shares Franklin County National Bank, Greenfield	5,400 00

Cash on Deposit in Banks, amount in each:—

Hide and Leather National Bank, Boston	$29,854 13
First National Bank, Greenfield	53,097 50
Franklin County National Bank, Greenfield	20,000 00
Packard National Bank, Greenfield	17,000 00

Amount of real estate held by foreclosure	$9,773 28
Assessed value of the same	9,926 00
Amount of income received from the same	617 16
Amount of municipal tax on real estate	38 61

Whole amount of interest or profits received or earned		$155,736 08
Rate and amount of each semi-annual dividend for previous year	2 per cent	54,094 47
	2 per cent	54,527 88

Times for the dividends fixed by the by-laws: Jan. 1 and July 1.

Average annual per cent of dividends for the term ending at time of and including last extra dividend: 7 per cent.

The total amount of loans, with each specified rate of interest: $17,000, 4 per cent; $230,823.05, 4½ per cent; $900,085.70, 5 per cent.

Number of outstanding loans which are of an amount not exceeding $3,000 each	510	
Aggregate amount of the same		$434,693 00
Amount of investments from which no income is received		835 35
Number of open accounts	6,865	
Number and amount of deposits received for previous year,	3,163	250,237 01
Number and amount of deposits of and exceeding $300 at any one time for the previous year	202	103,771 24
Number and amount of withdrawals	2,962	337,253 13
Number of accounts opened the previous year	734	
Number of accounts closed the previous year	669	
Amount of expenses of the corporation during previous year		4,859 99
Amount of treasurer's bond		50,000 00

Date of examination by commissioner: Aug. 10.

Public Funds.

	Par Value.	Estimated Market Value.	Amount Invested.
United States bonds	$245,000	$255,650 00	$245,000 00
City and town bonds: —			
City of Nashua, N.H.	$75,000	$96,750 00	$75,000 00
of Worcester	18,000	21,495 00	18,000 00
of Springfield	44,000	56,402 00	44,000 00
of Lawrence	30,000	38,500 00	30,000 00
of Fitchburg	13,000	15,340 00	13,000 00
of Somerville	35,000	37,639 00	35,000 00
of Boston	72,000	88,930 00	72,000 00
of Lynn	10,000	12,400 00	10,000 00
of Cambridge	75,000	85,580 00	75,000 00
of Holyoke	80,000	92,718 00	80,000 00
of Lowell	46,000	53,360 00	46,000 00
of Portland, Me.	5,000	5,625 00	5,000 00
of Fall River	70,000	77,215 00	70,000 00
of Brockton	28,000	32,618 00	28,000 00
of Providence, R.I.	125,000	158,917 00	125,000 00
of Taunton	1,000	1,250 00	1,000 00
Town of Adams	25,000	30,250 00	25,000 00
of Malden	60,000	72,650 00	60,000 00
of Stockbridge	5,000	5,250 00	5,000 00
of Hyde Park	20,000	20,136 00	20,000 00
of Brookline	101,400	121,067 00	101,400 00
of Everett	25,000	29,750 00	25,000 00
of Amherst	50,000	60,166 00	50,000 00
of Greenfield	12,500	13,479 00	12,500 00
of Gill	10,000	10,766 00	10,000 00
of Chicopee	13,000	13,000 00	13,000 00
	$1,293,900	$1,506,903 00	$1,293,900 00

BANK STOCK.

	Par Value.	Estimated Market Value.	Amount Invested.
First Nat'l Bank, Greenfield . .	$9,800	$17,640 00	$9,800 00
First Nat'l Bank, Northampton .	4,900	6,125 00	4,900 00
Commerce Nat'l Bank, Boston .	15,300	19,698 00	15,300 00
Faneuil Hall Nat'l Bank, Boston .	500	653 00	500 00
North America Nat'l Bank, Boston,	8,700	10,005 00	8,700 00
Revere Nat'l Bank, Boston . .	12,500	15,250 00	12,500 00
Traders' Nat'l Bank, Boston . .	1,500	1,530 00	1,500 00
Webster Nat'l Bank, Boston . .	10,200	11,373 00	10,200 00
Adams Nat'l Bank, North Adams .	1,000	1,450 00	1,450 00
Pittsfield Nat'l Bank, Pittsfield .	3,000	4,680 00	4,680 00
	$67,400	$88,404 00	$69,530 00

RAILROAD BONDS.

	Par Value.	Estimated Market Value.	Amount Invested.
Connecticut River Railroad . .	$50,000	$50,000 00	$50,000 00
Eastern Railroad	57,500	62,962 00	57,500 00
Boston and Albany Railroad . .	25,000	32,300 00	25,000 00
Vermont and Massachusetts Railroad,	50,000	66,500 00	50,000 00
	$182,500	$211,762 00	$182,500 00

GARDNER SAVINGS BANK — GARDNER.

Incorporated 1868. Number of corporators, 81.

JOHN EDGELL, *President*. *Treasurer*, JOHN D. EDGELL.

STATEMENT.

LIABILITIES.		ASSETS.	
Deposits	$677,715 91	Public funds	$18,450 00
Earnings undivided	1,381 52	Bank stock	102,577 50
Guaranty fund	10,756 49	Loans on bank stock	23,600 00
Interest account	3,368 75	Railroad bonds	24,600 00
		Real estate by foreclosure	3,299 29
		Loans on real estate	306,471 97
		Loans on personal security,	69,910 48
		Loans to counties, cities, or towns	86,040 00
		Deposit in banks on interest,	50,000 00
		Expense account	154 12
		Cash on hand	8,119 31
	$693,222 67		$693,222 67

Loans on Bank Stock, amount on each:—

On 223 shares First National Bank, Gardner	$21,600 00
On 40 shares First National Bank, Winchendon	2,000 00

Cash on Deposit in Banks, amount in each:—

Maverick National Bank, Boston	$25,000 00
National Bank of the Commonwealth, Boston	15,000 00
Pacific National Bank, Boston	5,000 00
Westminster National Bank, Westminster	5,000 00

Amount of real estate held by foreclosure	$3,299 29
Assessed value of the same	3,000 00
Amount of income received from the same	96 00
Amount of municipal tax on real estate	39 14

Whole amount of interest or profits received or earned . . . $33,944 98

Rate and amount of each semi-annual dividend for previous year: 2 per cent, 12,189 07; 2 per cent, 12,528 44

Times for the dividends fixed by the by-laws: Jan. 1 and July 1.

Average annual per cent of dividends for the term ending at time of and including last extra dividend: 4 per cent.

The total amount of loans, with each specified rate of interest: $50,000, 4 per cent; $28,520, 4½ per cent; $8,000, 5 per cent; $399,502.45, 6 per cent.

Number of outstanding loans which are of an amount not exceeding $3,000 each	429	
Aggregate amount of the same		288,514 47
Amount of investments from which no income is received		600 00
Number of open accounts	2,237	
Number and amount of deposits received for previous year,	5,733	151,966 32
Number and amount of deposits of and exceeding $300 at any one time for the previous year	102	42,343 27
Number and amount of withdrawals	912	107,041 58
Number of accounts opened the previous year	342	
Number of accounts closed the previous year	163	

Amount of expenses of the corporation during previous year . $1,645 11
Amount of treasurer's bond 20,000 00
Date of examination by commissioner: June 23.

PUBLIC FUNDS.

	Par Value.	Estimated Market Value.	Amount Invested.
United States 6s, 1881, continued .	$15,600	$15,756 00	$15,600 00
" " 4s, 1907 . . .	1,100	1,276 00	1,100 00
" " 4½s, 1891 . . .	750	847 50	750 00
Bath, Me., municipal 6s . .	$1,000	$1,050 00	$1,000 00
	$18,450	$18,929 50	$18,450 00

BANK STOCK.

	Par Value.	Estimated Market Value.	Amount Invested.
Mechanics' Nat'l Bank, Worcester .	$5,000	$5,750 00	$5,250 00
Citizens' Nat'l Bank, Worcester .	2,000	2,120 00	2,000 00
First Nat'l Bank, Gardner . .	6,700	8,710 00	7,370 00
Orange Nat'l Bank, Orange . .	10,000	11,000 00	10,000 00
Crocker Nat'l Bank, Turner's Falls,	10,000	10,700 00	10,000 00
Rollstone Nat'l Bank, Fitchburg .	1,200	1,920 00	1,800 00
First Nat'l Bank, Ashburnham .	2,000	2,077 50	2,077 50
Metropolitan Nat'l Bank, Boston .	400	500 00	400 00
Central Nat'l Bank, Boston . .	1,000	1,200 00	1,000 00
Howard Nat'l Bank, Boston . .	2,500	3,250 00	2,500 00
Boston Nat'l Bank, Boston . .	12,500	16,375 00	12,500 00
Continental Nat'l Bank, Boston .	1,500	1,815 00	1,500 00
Merchandise Nat'l Bank, Boston .	5,000	5,600 00	5,000 00
State Nat'l Bank, Boston . .	5,000	6,350 00	5,150 00
Hide and Leather Nat'l B'k, Boston,	5,000	6,000 00	5,000 00
Eagle Nat'l Bank, Boston . .	1,100	1,320 00	1,155 00
Commonwealth Nat'l Bank, Boston,	5,000	6,500 00	5,150 00
Republic Nat'l Bank, Boston . .	5,000	6,550 00	5,150 00
Exchange Nat'l Bank, Boston . .	1,600	2,368 00	1,840 00
New England Nat'l Bank, Boston .	500	660 00	535 00
Mechanics' Nat'l Bank, Boston .	1,500	1,800 00	1,575 00
Merchants' Nat'l Bank, Boston .	2,000	3,000 00	2,100 00
Blackstone Nat'l Bank, Boston .	5,000	5,850 00	5,150 00
Everett Nat'l Bank, Boston . .	500	585 00	500 00
Eliot Nat'l Bank, Boston . .	5,000	6,000 00	5,250 00
Shoe and Leather Nat'l B'k, Boston,	2,500	2,900 00	2,625 00
	$99,500	$120,900 50	$102,577 50

RAILROAD BONDS.

	Par Value.	Estimated Market Value.	Amount Invested.
Boston and Albany 7s . . .	$8,000	$10,000 00	$8,000 00
Boston and Maine 7s . . .	5,000	6,250 00	5,000 00
Vermont and Massachusetts 6s .	1,600	1,696 00	1,600 00
Boston and Lowell 5s . . .	10,000	10,500 00	10,000 00
	$24,600	$28,446 00	$24,600 00

GEORGETOWN SAVINGS BANK — GEORGETOWN.

Incorporated 1868. Number of corporators, 64.

JEREMIAH P. JONES, *President*. *Treasurer*, ORLANDO B. TENNEY.

STATEMENT.

LIABILITIES.		ASSETS.	
Deposits . . .	$198,486 25	Public funds . . .	$19,300 00
Earnings undivided .	1,261 97	Bank stock	16,300 00
Guaranty fund . .	2,700 00	Real estate by foreclosure .	7,240 57
		Loans on real estate . .	131,414 95
		Loans on personal security,	18,149 00
		Deposit in banks on interest,	6,190 54
		Interest due	978 84
		Cash on hand . . .	2,874 32
	$202,448 22		$202,448 22

Cash on Deposit in Banks, amount in each: —

Blackstone National Bank, Boston		$6,190 54
Georgetown National Bank, Georgetown		2,440 27
Amount of real estate held by foreclosure		$7,240 57
Assessed value of the same		7,300 00
Amount of income received from the same		817 83
Amount of municipal tax on real estate		95 41
Whole amount of interest or profits received or earned . . .		$11,281 52
Rate and amount of each semi-annual dividend for previous year	2½ per cent .	4,352 89
	2 per cent .	3,702 86

Times for the dividends fixed by the by-laws: third Wednesday in April and October.

The total amount of loans, with each specified rate of interest: $5,000, 5 per cent; $51,764, 6 per cent; $3,200, 6½ per cent; $71,450.95, 7 per cent.

Number of outstanding loans which are of an amount not exceeding $3,000 each	180	
Aggregate amount of the same		114,543 95
Number of open accounts	670	
Number and amount of deposits received for previous year .	389	34,061 61
Number and amount of deposits of and exceeding $300 at any one time for the previous year	27	16,423 13
Number and amount of withdrawals	272	20,111 74
Number of accounts opened the previous year	79	
Number of accounts closed the previous year	47	
Amount of expenses of the corporation during previous year .		400 00
Amount of treasurer's bond		10,000 00

Date of examination by commissioner: May 4.

Public Funds.

	Par Value.	Estimated Market Value.	Amount Invested.
City and town bonds:—			
City of Bath, Me., 6s . . .	$2,500	$2,550 00	$2,500 00
of Bangor, Me , 5s . . .	2,000	2,100 00	2,000 00
of Bangor, Me., 7s . . .	2,000	2,200 00	2,000 00
of Portland, Me., 6s . .	1,500	1,650 00	1,500 00
of Belfast, Me., 6s . . .	6,000	6,240 00	6,000 00
of Rockland, Me., 6s . .	3,000	3,060 00	3,000 00
Town of Melrose 7s . . .	2,000	2,500 00	2,300 00
	$19,000	$20,300 00	$19,300 00

Bank Stock.

Georgetown Nat'l B'k, Georgetown .	$8,000	$8,000 00	$8,000 00
Columbian Nat'l Bank, Boston .	1,300	1,820 00	1,300 00
Market Nat'l Bank, Boston . .	1,000	1,100 00	1,000 00
Manufacturers' Nat'l Bank, Boston,	3,000	3,100 00	3,000 00
State Nat'l Bank, Boston . .	3,000	3,600 00	3,000 00
	$16,300	$17,620 00	$16,300 00

GRAFTON SAVINGS BANK — GRAFTON.

Incorporated March 13, 1869. Number of corporators, 50.

GEORGE K. NICHOLS, *President*. *Treasurer*, HENRY F. WING.

STATEMENT.

LIABILITIES.		ASSETS.	
Deposits	$160,660 24	Public funds	$20,834 37
Earnings undivided	8,307 08	Bank stock	38,648 49
Guaranty fund	2,000 00	Loans on real estate	50,980 00
		Loans on personal security,	37,730 14
		Loans to counties, cities, or towns	20,000 00
		Cash on hand	2,774 32
	$170,967 32		$170,967 32

Cash on Deposit in Bank: —
Grafton National Bank $2,774 32

Whole amount of interest or profits received or earned . . . $8,524 13

Rate and amount of each semi-annual dividend for previous year . . . . { 2 per cent . 2,824 40; 2 per cent . 3,010 00 }

Times for the dividends fixed by the by-laws: January and July.

Average annual per cent of dividends for the term ending at time of and including last extra dividend: 4 per cent.

The total amount of loans, with each specified rate of interest: $13,335, 4 per cent; $5,000, 4½ per cent; $24,005.14, 5 per cent; $30,590, 6 per cent; $31,380, 6½ per cent; $4,400, 7 per cent.

Number of outstanding loans which are of an amount not exceeding $3,000 each	62	
Aggregate amount of the same		69,063 04
Number of open accounts	561	
Number and amount of deposits received for previous year	343	29,864 01
Number and amount of deposits of and exceeding $300 at any one time for the previous year	27	12,033 80
Number and amount of withdrawals	212	15,004 60
Number of accounts opened the previous year	92	
Number of accounts closed the previous year	48	
Amount of expenses of the corporation during previous year		100 00
Amount of treasurer's bond		10,000 00

Date of examination by commissioner: May 19.

PUBLIC FUNDS.

	Par Value.	Estimated Market Value.	Amount Invested.
United States 4½s, 1891	$15,000	$16,950 00	$15,634 37
" " 5s, 1881, 3½s contin'd,	5,000	5,100 00	5,200 00
	$20,000	$22,050 00	$20,834 37

BANK STOCK.

	Par Value.	Estimated Market Value.	Amount Invested.
Redemption Nat'l Bank, Boston .	$3,000	$4,065 00	$4,187 75
Revere Nat'l Bank, Boston . .	3,000	3,600 00	3,814 00
State Nat'l Bank, Boston . .	2,000	2,520 00	2,040 00
Shawmut Nat'l Bank, Boston . .	1,000	1,230 00	1,222 75
Webster Nat'l Bank, Boston . .	1,300	1,450 00	1,476 12
Howard Nat'l Bank, Boston . .	1,500	1,957 00	1,744 50
North Nat'l Bank, Boston . .	1,000	1,425 00	1,206 25
Market Nat'l Bank, Boston . .	3,800	4,180 00	4,276 00
Traders' Nat'l Bank, Boston . .	1,600	1,600 00	1,885 50
Maverick Nat'l Bank, Boston . .	1,000	2,500 00	1,237 50
Massachusetts Nat'l Bank, Boston .	500	620 00	677 12
City Nat'l Bank, Boston . . .	300	369 00	363 25
North America Nat'l Bank, Boston .	2,800	3,192 00	3,200 25
Eliot Nat'l Bank, Boston . .	1,000	1,225 00	1,230 00
Manufacturers' Nat'l Bank, Boston,	500	550 00	550 00
Fourth Nat'l Bank, Boston . .	500	550 00	500 00
Spencer Nat'l Bank, Spencer . .	1,000	1,050 00	1,000 00
First Nat'l Bank, Grafton . .	1,300	1,462 50	1,462 50
Grafton Nat'l Bank, Grafton . .	6,300	6,930 00	6,575 00
	$33,400	$40,475 50	$38,648 49

GREAT BARRINGTON SAVINGS BANK — GREAT BARRINGTON.

Incorporated Feb. 23, 1869. Number of corporators, 58.

EGBERT HOLLISTER, *President*. *Treasurer*, CHARLES J. TAYLOR.

STATEMENT.

LIABILITIES.		ASSETS.	
Deposits	$207,588 25	Public funds	$1,000 00
Earnings undivided .	15,993 39	Bank stock	74,508 53
Guaranty fund . .	3,206 31	Loans on bank stock . .	825 60
		Loans on real estate . .	113,280 17
		Loans on personal security,	31,899 16
		Deposit in banks on interest,	2,046 85
		Expense account . . .	619 23
		Cash on hand and in bank,	2,608 41
	$226,787 95		$226,787 95

Loans on Bank Stock: —

On 10 shares Mahaiwe National Bank $825 60

Cash on Deposit in Banks, amount in each: —

Mahaiwe National Bank, Great Barrington $2,164 98

National Bank of Redemption, Boston 2,046 85

Whole amount of interest or profits received or earned $11,431 76

Rate and amount of each semi-annual dividend for previous year . . . . { 2 per cent . . 3,572 65 ; 2 per cent . . 3,763 57 }

Times for the dividends fixed by the by-laws: January and July.

The total amount of loans, with each specified rate of interest: $131,054 46, 6 per cent; $14,950.47, 7 per cent.

Number of outstanding loans which are of an amount not exceeding $3,000 each 126

Aggregate amount of the same 90,877 21

Amount of investments from which no income is received . . 628 68

Number of open accounts 1,136

Number and amount of deposits received for previous year, 2,681 61,218 66

Number and amount of deposits of and exceeding $300 at any one time for the previous year 41 20,134 00

Number and amount of withdrawals. 567 42,606 73

Number of accounts opened the previous year 213

Number of accounts closed the previous year 218

Amount of expenses of the corporation during previous year . 1,708 65

Amount of treasurer's bond 10,000 00

Date of examination by commissioner: Aug. 1.

PUBLIC FUNDS.

	Par Value.	Estimated Market Value.	Amount Invested.
United States 4½s, coupons . .	$1,000	$1,130 00	$1,000 00

BANK STOCK.

Mahaiwe N'l Bank, Gt. Barrington .	$3,800	$4,940 00	$5,445 20
Lee Nat'l Bank, Lee . . .	5,110	6,205 00	6,152 00
Pittsfield Nat'l Bank, Pittsfield .	300	405 00	405 00
First Nat'l Bank, Adams . .	1,000	1,300 00	1,280 00
Housatonic Nat'l Bank, Stockbridge,	300	450 00	450 00
Faneuil Hall Nat'l Bank, Boston .	1,000	1,300 00	1,500 00
Suffolk Nat'l Bank, Boston . .	1,300	1,560 00	1,703 00
Redemption Nat'l Bank, Boston .	15,900	20,670 00	23,104 13
North America Nat'l Bank, Boston,	4,200	4,746 00	4,835 25
Hamilton Nat'l Bank, Boston . .	1,900	2,223 00	2,227 75
Atlantic Nat'l Bank, Boston . .	1,000	1,480 00	1,345 00
New England Nat'l Bank, Boston .	7,600	11,020 00	11,400 00
Shoe and Leather Nat'l B'k, Boston,	6,600	7,375 00	9,248 50
Union Nat'l Bank, Boston . .	1,400	1,960 00	2,020 20
Merchants' Nat'l Bank, Boston .	2,500	3,625 00	3,392 50
	$53,910	$69,259 00	$74,508 53

GREENFIELD SAVINGS BANK — GREENFIELD.

Incorporated 1869. Number of corporators, 17.

JOHN SANDERSON, *President*. *Treasurer*, ALBERT M. GLEASON.

STATEMENT.

LIABILITIES.		ASSETS.	
Deposits	$945,909 90	Public funds . . .	$138,000 00
Earnings undivided .	1,784 75	Loans on public funds .	200 00
Guaranty fund . .	11,375 00	Bank stock	103,800 00
		Loans on bank stock . .	8,500 00
		Railroad bonds . . .	10,500 00
		Real estate by foreclosure .	13,382 23
		Loans on real estate . .	357,614 22
		Loans on personal security,	98,771 05
		Loans to counties, cities, or towns	12,075 00
		Deposit in banks on interest,	164,244 40
		Expense account . . .	3,701 85
		Interest due	4,759 26
		Premium paid . . .	40,213 56
		Furniture and fixtures .	1,795 12
		Cash on hand . . .	1,512 96
	$959,069 65		$959,069 65

Loans on Public Funds: —

On $1,000 United States 5s $200 00

Loans on Bank Stock, amount on each: —

On 45 shares Franklin County National Bank, Greenfield . . $4,400 00
On 25 shares Conway National Bank, Conway 2,500 00
On 10 shares Adams National Bank, North Adams 1,000 00
On 6 shares First National Bank, Greenfield 600 00

Cash on Deposit in Banks, amount in each: —

Franklin County National Bank, Greenfield $90,000 00
Packard National Bank, Greenfield 6,744 40
International Trust Company, Boston * 32,500 00
Agawam National Bank, Springfield 20,000 00
Crocker National Bank, Turner's Falls 5,000 00
Conway National Bank, Conway 10,000 00

Amount of real estate held by foreclosure $13,382 23
Assessed value of the same 9,050 00
Amount of income received from the same 938 22
Amount of municipal tax on real estate 115 59

Whole amount of interest or profits received or earned . . . $55,716 11
Rate and amount of each semi-annual dividend for previous year . . . . { 2 per cent . 17,537 09; $1\frac{3}{4}$ per cent . 16,022 17 }
Times for the dividends fixed by the by-laws: Jan. 1 and July 1.
The total amount of loans, with each specified rate of interest: $2,500, 3 per cent; $5,000, 4 per cent; $156,900, $4\frac{1}{2}$ per cent; $470,260.27, 5 per cent.
Number of outstanding loans which are of an amount not exceeding $3,000 each 310

* The Attorney-General has given his opinion that deposits by savings banks in this trust company are legal.

Aggregate amount of the same		$245,550 22
Number of open accounts	2,297	
Number and amount of deposits received for previous year,	1,335	157,320 55
Number and amount of deposits of and exceeding $300 at any one time for the previous year	167	92,912 19
Number and amount of withdrawals	1,079	142,746 92
Number of accounts opened the previous year	431	
Number of accounts closed the previous year	243	
Amount of expenses of the corporation during previous year .		3,865 12
Amount of treasurer's bond		25,000 00

Date of examination by commissioner: Aug. 10.

PUBLIC FUNDS.

	Par Value.	Estimated Market Value.	Amount Invested.
City and town bonds: —			
City of Burlington, Vt.	$25,000	$26,250 00	$26,250 00
of Springfield	8,000	9,437 50	9,437 50
Town of Pittsfield	65,000	67,015 00	67,015 00
of Rutland, Vt. . . .	40,000	40,000 00	40,000 00
	$138,000	$142 702 50	$142,702 50

BANK STOCK.

Market Nat'l Bank, Boston . .	$1,800	$1,975 50	$2,180 12
Eliot Nat'l Bank, Boston . .	4,200	5,040 00	4,850 32
Merchants' Nat'l Bank, Boston .	3,300	4,818 00	3,984 25
Hamilton Nat'l Bank, Boston . .	3,500	3,955 00	4,204 20
Second Nat'l Bank, Boston . .	1,000	1,500 00	1,557 50
Washington Nat'l Bank, Boston .	300	420 00	423 43
Metropolitan Nat'l Bank, Boston .	2,000	2,400 00	2,000 00
Hide and Leather Nat'l B'k, Boston,	1,300	1,500 00	1,550 25
Redemption Nat'l Bank, Boston .	5,200	7,000 00	7,006 50
Revere Nat'l Bank, Boston . .	4,800	5,850 00	5,328 00
City Nat'l Bank, Boston . . .	600	760 00	641 89
Agawam Nat'l Bank, Springfield .	500	625 00	720 00
Chicopee Nat'l Bank, Springfield .	300	480 00	510 00
Third Nat'l Bank, Springfield .	11,000	19,617 50	19,617 50
First Nat'l Bank, Springfield . .	5,000	7,500 00	7,500 00
City Nat'l Bank, Springfield . .	2,500	2,800 00	2,500 00
First Nat'l Bank, Chicopee . .	1,200	1,920 00	1,920 00
Holyoke Nat'l Bank, Holyoke . .	13,800	16,800 00	15,180 00
Hadley Falls Nat'l Bank, Holyoke .	1,400	2,380 00	2,380 00
Palmer Nat'l Bank, Palmer . .	5,000	6,000 00	5,000 00
Franklin Co Nat'l Bank, Greenfield,	14,000	21,055 83	21,055 83
First Nat'l Bank, Greenfield . .	3,400	6,200 00	4,076 00
Conway Nat'l Bank, Conway . .	4,000	4,800 00	4,509 00
Athol Nat'l Bank, Athol . .	3,700	4,000 00	3,806 00
Orange Nat'l Bank, Orange . .	5,000	5,500 00	5,000 00
First Nat'l Bank, Westfield . .	5,000	7,000 00	7,000 00
	$103,800	$141,896 83	$134,500 79

RAILROAD BONDS.

Eastern Railroad	$10,500	$11,550 00	$10,500 00

GROVELAND SAVINGS BANK — GROVELAND.

Incorporated 1869. Number of corporators, 31.

MOSES FOSTER, *President*. *Treasurer*, N. H. GRIFFITH.

STATEMENT.

LIABILITIES.		ASSETS.	
Deposits . .	$39,221 94	Public funds . . .	$2,500 00
Earnings undivided .	543 21	Bank stock	3,820 00
Guaranty fund . .	500 00	Railroad bonds . . .	4,780 00
		Real estate by foreclosure .	550 00
		Loans on real estate . .	21,975 00
		Loans on personal security,	1,410 00
		Loans to counties, cities, or towns	500 00
		Deposit in bank on interest,	4,000 00
		Cash on hand . . .	730 15
	$40,265 15		$40,265 15

Cash on Deposit in Bank: —
First National Bank, Merrimac $4,000 00

Amount of real estate held by foreclosure $550 00
Assessed value of the same 650 00
Amount of income received from the same 11 00
Amount of municipal tax on real estate 10 67

Whole amount of interest or profits received or earned $2,487 83
Rate and amount of each semi-annual dividend for previous year . . . . { 2 per cent . 710 53; 2 per cent . 723 85 }
Times for the dividends fixed by the by-laws: April and October.
The total amount of loans, with each specified rate of interest: $4,500, 4 per cent; $10,490, 7 per cent; $12,895, $7\frac{3}{10}$ per cent.
Number of outstanding loans which are of an amount not exceeding $3,000 each 49
Aggregate amount of the same 27,885 00
Number of open accounts 180
Number and amount of deposits received for previous year . 100 9,778 94
Number and amount of deposits of and exceeding $300 at any one time for the previous year 10 5,644 00
Number and amount of withdrawals 81 8,910 49
Number of accounts opened the previous year 28
Number of accounts closed the previous year 26
Amount of expenses of the corporation during previous year . 56 50
Amount of treasurer's bond 5,000 00
Date of examination by commissioner: May 4.

PUBLIC FUNDS.

	Par Value.	Estimated Market Value.	Amount Invested.
United States bonds . . .	$2,500	$2,750 00	$2,500 00

BANK STOCK.

	Par Value.	Estimated Market Value.	Amount Invested.
First Ward Nat'l Bank, Boston .	$600	$700 00	$600 00
Fourth Nat'l Bank, Boston . .	500	550 00	490 00
Manufacturers' Nat'l Bank, Boston,	1,500	1,650 00	1,570 00
Mechanics' Nat'l B'k, Newburyport,	900	1,100 00	1,035 00
Merchants' Nat'l B'k, Newburyport,	100	125 00	125 00
	$3,600	$4,125 00	$3,820 00

RAILROAD BONDS.

	Par Value.	Estimated Market Value.	Amount Invested.
Boston and Maine Railroad . .	$3,000	$3,750 00	$3,750 00
Fitchburg Railroad	1,000	1,125 00	1,030 00
	$4,000	$4,875 00	$4,780 00

HAMPDEN SAVINGS BANK — SPRINGFIELD.

Incorporated 1852. Number of corporators, 47.

ELIPHALET TRASK, *President*. *Treasurer*, PETER S. BAILEY.

STATEMENT.

Liabilities.		Assets.	
Deposits . . .	$1,646,794 54	Public funds . . .	$268,158 00
Earnings undivided .	13,187 50	Loans on public funds .	24,200 00
Guaranty fund . .	22,000 00	Bank stock	273,529 00
		Loans on bank stock . .	17,200 00
		Loans on railroad stock .	2,700 00
		Real estate by foreclosure .	190,408 85
		Loans on real estate . .	659,480 00
		Loans on personal security,	225,984 69
		Deposit in bank on interest,	10 000 00
		Expense account . .	1,494 08
		Taxes paid on bank stock .	354 96
		Cash on hand . . .	8,472 46
	$1,681,982 04		$1,681,982 04

Loans on Public Funds, amount on each: —

On $20,500 United States 4½s	$20,200 00
On $2,000 United States 4s	2,000 00
On $2,000 Springfield 7s	2,000 00

Loans on Bank Stock, amount on each: —

On 110 shares Agawam National Bank	$10,000 00
On 30 shares City National Bank	3,000 00
On 15 shares John Hancock National Bank	700 00
On 62 shares Chapin National Bank	3,150 00
On 5 shares Pynchon National Bank	350 00

Loans on Railroad Stock, amount on each: —

On 15 shares Connecticut River Railroad	$1,500 00
On 20 shares Boston and Albany Railroad *	1,200 00

Cash on Deposit in Bank: —

Agawam National Bank	$10,000 00

Amount of real estate held by foreclosure	$190,408 85
Assessed value of the same	137,500 00
Amount of income received from the same	10,734 00
Amount of municipal tax on real estate	1,714 00

Whole amount of interest or profits received or earned	$92,344 17
Rate and amount of each semi-annual dividend for previous year . . . . 2 per cent .	30,139 99
2 per cent .	31,116 39

Times for the dividends fixed by the by-laws: Feb. 15 and Aug. 15.

Average annual per cent of dividends for the term ending at time of and including last extra dividend: 7 per cent.

* This loan has been changed to conform to the provisions of the statute.

The total amount of loans, with each specified rate of interest: $20,000, 4 per cent; $24,100, 5 per cent; $885,464, 6 per cent.

Number of outstanding loans which are of an amount not exceeding $3,000 each	206	
Aggregate amount of the same		$2,649 80
Amount of investments from which no income is received		22,000 00
Number of open accounts	3,494	
Number and amount of deposits received for previous year,	3,897	419,700 92
Number and amount of deposits of and exceeding $300 at any one time for the previous year	330	2,189 28
Number and amount of withdrawals	2,174	318,554 61
Number of accounts opened the previous year	725	
Number of accounts closed the previous year	649	
Amount of expenses of the corporation during previous year		6,000 00
Amount of treasurer's bond		10,000 00

Date of examination by commissioner: Oct. 16.

PUBLIC FUNDS.

	Par Value.	Estimated Market Value.	Amount Invested.
United States 4s	$250,000	$290,625 00	$268,158 00

BANK STOCK.

	Par Value.	Estimated Market Value.	Amount Invested.
First Nat'l Bank, Chicopee	$4,000	$6,400 00	$5,030 00
First Nat'l Bank, Boston	2,800	5,796 00	2,800 00
Hide and Leather Nat'l B'k, Boston,	7,500	8,850 00	7,500 00
Hadley Falls Nat'l Bank, Holyoke	4,000	6,000 00	4,732 00
Merchants' Nat'l Bank, Boston	23,000	33,810 00	27,210 00
Monson Nat'l Bank, Monson	2,000	3,000 00	2,200 00
Commerce Nat'l Bank, Boston	7,500	9,600 00	10,865 00
Third Nat'l Bank, Springfield	7,400	12,580 00	11,560 00
Revere Nat'l Bank, Boston	7,500	9,150 00	7,500 00
Webster Nat'l Bank, Boston	4,000	4,480 00	4,292 00
Ware Nat'l Bank, Ware	7,500	9,750 00	10,050 00
Holyoke Nat'l Bank, Holyoke	15,000	18,000 00	15,000 00
Hampshire Co. N'l B'k, Northampt'n,	4,100	4,920 00	4,100 00
Pynchon Nat'l Bank, Springfield	6,500	11,375 00	10,985 00
First Nat'l Bank, Northampton	3,000	4,200 00	3,000 00
Wachusett Nat'l Bank, Fitchburg	5,000	10,500 00	5,000 00
First Nat'l Bank, Springfield	5,000	7,000 00	6,525 00
Chapin Nat'l Bank, Springfield	23,000	28,750 00	24,700 00
Republic Nat'l Bank, Boston	5,000	6,550 00	6,300 00
Suffolk Nat'l Bank, Boston	3,700	4,477 00	4,500 00
Continental Nat'l Bank, Boston	5,000	5,900 00	5,300 00
Redemption Nat'l Bank, Boston	5,000	6,750 00	6,700 00
Freeman's Nat'l Bank, Boston	5,000	5,950 00	5,900 00
State Nat'l Bank, Boston	5,000	6,250 00	5,900 00
North America Nat'l Bank, Boston	5,000	5,750 00	5,700 00
Eliot Nat'l Bank, Boston	5,000	6,000 00	6,100 00
Shawmut Nat'l Bank, Boston	6,300	8,000 00	7,600 00
Agawam Nat'l Bank, Springfield	50,000	65,000 00	56,480 00
	$233,800	$314,788 00	$273,529 00

HAMPSHIRE SAVINGS BANK — NORTHAMPTON.

Incorporated May, 1869. Number of corporators, 28.

LUTHER BODMAN, *President*. *Treasurer*, LEWIS WARNER.

STATEMENT.

LIABILITIES.		ASSETS.	
Deposits	$555,826 98	Bank stock	$197,614 42
Earnings undivided .	8,846 17	Loans on bank stock . .	1,500 00
Guaranty fund . .	6,400 00	Real estate by foreclosure .	4,600 00
		Loans on real estate .	216,937 53
		Loans on personal security,	37,199 64
		Loans to counties, cities, or towns	500 00
		Deposit in bank on interest,	111,738 44
		Expense account . . .	983 12
	$571,073 15		$571,073 15

Loans on Bank Stock, amount on each: —

On 12 shares Hampshire County National Bank $1,200 00

On 3 shares Northampton National Bank 300 00

Cash on Deposit in Bank: —

Hampshire County National Bank, Northampton $111,738 44

Amount of real estate held by foreclosure $4,600 00

Assessed value of the same 3,000 00

Amount of income received from the same 276 00

Amount of municipal tax on real estate 38 48

Whole amount of interest or profits received or earned $28,350 72

Rate and amount of each semi-annual dividend for previous year . . . . { 2 per cent . 9,004 93; 2 per cent . 10,724 88 }

Times for the dividends fixed by the by-laws: May 15 and Nov. 15.

Average annual per cent of dividends for the term ending at time of and including last extra dividend: 4 per cent.

The total amount of loans, with each specified rate of interest: $4,500, 5 per cent; $223,637.17, 6 per cent; $24,000, 7 per cent.

Number of outstanding loans which are of an amount not exceeding $3,000 each	176	
Aggregate amount of the same		102,337 17
Number of open accounts	1,696	
Number and amount of deposits received for previous year .	983	149,430 52
Number and amount of deposits of and exceeding $300 at any one time for the previous year	130	79,719 33
Number and amount of withdrawals	814	88,265 16
Number of accounts opened the previous year	342	
Number of accounts closed the previous year	224	
Amount of expenses of corporation during previous year . .		983 12
Amount of treasurer's bond		10,000 00

Date of examination by commissioner: July 12.

BANK STOCK.

	Par Value.	Estimated Market Value.	Amount Invested.
Hampshire Co. N'l B'k, Northampt'n,	$44,500	$57,850 00	$52,010 00
Northampton N'l B'k, Northampt'n,	7,800	14,040 00	11,857 50
First Nat'l Bank, Northampton .	4,100	5,535 00	5,488 00
First Nat'l Bank, Easthampton .	10,000	13,000 00	12,450 00
John Hancock Nat'l B'k, Springfield,	3,400	4,420 00	3,898 00
Chicopee Nat'l Bank, Springfield .	500	800 00	800 00
Agawam Nat'l Bank, Springfield .	800	1,120 00	1,088 00
Mechanics' Nat'l Bank, Worcester .	2,500	3,500 00	3,395 00
Ware Nat'l Bank, Ware . . .	1,200	1,624 00	1,624 00
Union Nat'l Bank, Weymouth .	1,300	1,560 00	1,592 50
First Nat'l Bank, Chicopee . .	2,400	3,960 00	3,755 00
Blackstone Nat'l Bank, Boston .	2,200	2,596 00	3,247 50
Pacific Nat'l Bank, Boston . .	3,000	3,300 00	3,300 00
North Nat'l Bank, Boston . .	10,000	14,300 00	12,661 00
Howard Nat'l Bank, Boston . .	3,300	4,323 00	3,695 00
Shawmut Nat'l Bank, Boston . .	3,500	4,445 00	4,477 50
Hide and Leather Nat'l B'k, Boston,	3,200	3,840 00	3,797 00
Nat'l Bank of Commerce, Boston .	1,500	1,950 00	2,505 00
Tremont Nat'l Bank, Boston . .	4,200	5,334 00	5,386 00
Continental Nat'l Bank, Boston .	3,500	4,270 00	4,030 00
Republic Nat'l Bank, Boston . .	800	1,032 00	1,032 00
North America Nat'l Bank, Boston,	1,000	1,200 00	1,147 50
Market Nat'l Bank, Boston . .	3,500	3,850 00	4,219 37
Mount Vernon Nat'l Bank, Boston .	700	896 00	896 00
Commonwealth Nat'l Bank, Boston,	4,000	5,200 00	4,635 00
Merchants' Nat'l Bank, Boston .	3,000	4,380 00	4,260 00
Atlantic Nat'l Bank, Boston . .	900	1,395 00	1,221 75
Atlas Nat'l Bank, Boston . .	3,300	4,290 00	3,902 75
Eliot Nat'l Bank, Boston . .	3,600	4,500 00	4,640 00
Hamilton Nat'l Bank, Boston . .	700	868 00	906 00
Massachusetts Nat'l Bank, Boston .	1,500	1,905 00	1,920 00
Suffolk Nat'l Bank, Boston . .	3,000	3,900 00	3,870 00
Revere Nat'l Bank, Boston . .	2,200	2,772 00	2,802 00
Shoe and Leather Nat'l B'k, Boston,	1,000	1,180 00	1,436 25
Globe Nat'l Bank, Boston . .	4,400	5,016 00	5,651 87
Third Nat'l Bank, Boston . .	3,000	3,240 00	3,600 93
Second Nat'l Bank, Boston . .	5,000	7,700 00	7,900 00
Eagle Nat'l Bank, Boston . .	1,200	1,464 00	1,476 00
Manufacturers' Nat'l Bank, Boston,	1,000	1,130 00	1,040 00
	$156,700	$207,685 00	$197,614 42

HAVERHILL SAVINGS BANK — HAVERHILL.

Incorporated 1829. Number of corporators, 20.

JOHN A. APPLETON, *President.* *Treasurer,* A. B. JAQUES.

STATEMENT.

LIABILITIES.		ASSETS.	
Deposits	$3,393,432 31	Public funds	$933,300 00
Earnings undivided	13,420 62	Loans on public funds	8,800 00
Guaranty fund	54,697 12	Bank stock	510,450 00
		Loans on bank stock	61,000 00
		Railroad bonds	96,000 00
		Loans on real estate	989,575 00
		Loans on personal security,	724,530 00
		Loans to counties, cities, or towns	15,000 00
		Deposit in bank on interest,	115,000 00
		Expense account	36 62
		Cash on hand	7,858 43
	$3,461,550 05		$3,461,550 05

Loans on Public Funds, amount on each:—

On $8,300 United States bonds	$8,300 00
On $1,000 County of Washington, Me., bonds	500 00

Loans on Bank Stock, amount on each:—

On 216 shares Essex National Bank, Haverhill	$19,800 00
On 153 shares First National Bank, Haverhill	15,000 00
On 120 shares First National Bank, Boston	12,000 00
On 87 shares Haverhill National Bank	8,400 00
On 20 shares Shoe and Leather National Bank, Boston }	
On 10 shares Merrimack National Bank, Haverhill }	3,600 00
On 6 shares Haverhill National Bank, Haverhill }	
On 12 shares First National Bank, Merrimac	1,200 00
On 10 shares National Bank, Methuen	1,000 00

Cash on Deposit in Bank:—

Haverhill National Bank	$115,000 00

Whole amount of interest or profits received or earned	$187,838 08
Rate and amount of each semi-annual dividend for previous year { 2 per cent	77,401 52
{ 2 per cent	64,590 00

Times for the dividends fixed by the by-laws: third Wednesday in April and October.

Average annual per cent of dividends for the term ending at time of and including last extra dividend: 7½ per cent.

The total amount of loans, with each specified rate of interest: $50,000, 3½ per cent; $85,000, 3¾ per cent; $449,230, 4 per cent; $135,000, 4½ per cent; $113,900, 5 per cent; $965,775, 6 per cent.

Number of outstanding loans which are of an amount not exceeding $3,000 each . . . 541

Aggregate amount of the same		$698,280 00
Number of open accounts	9,218	
Number and amount of deposits received for previous year,	6,323	484,356 00
Number and amount of deposits of and exceeding $300 at any one time for the previous year	441	202,874 00
Number and amount of withdrawals	4,984	380,895 23
Number of accounts opened the previous year . . .	1,565	
Number of accounts closed the previous year	804	
Amount of expenses of the corporation during previous year .		4,703 26
Amount of treasurer's bond		20,000 00

Date of examination by commissioner: June 13.

PUBLIC FUNDS.

	Par Value.	Estimated Market Value.	Amount Invested.
United States bonds . . .	$395,000	$424,412 50	$395,000 00
City and town bonds: —			
City of Haverhill	$88,500	$93,723 00	$88,500 00
of Boston	30,000	31,800 00	30,000 00
of Lynn	15,000	17,400 00	15,000 00
of Portsmouth, N.H. . . .	51,500	58,710 00	51,500 00
of Fall River	50,000	55,565 00	50,000 00
of Dover, N.H.	46,300	52,782 00	46,300 00
of Cambridge	45,000	49,050 00	45,000 00
of Nashua, N.H.	35,000	39,550 00	35,000 00
of Portland, Me.	15,000	16,350 00	15,000 00
of Lawrence	28,000	30,500 00	28,000 00
of Somerville	30,000	31,500 00	30,000 00
of Chelsea	1,000	1,015 00	1,000 00
of Charlestown	10,000	11,000 00	10,000 00
Town of Winthrop	20,000	24,000 00	20,000 00
of Natick	20,000	20,800 00	20,000 00
of Winchester	13,000	13,520 00	13,000 00
of Manchester	5,000	5,150 00	5,000 00
of Bradford	13,000	13,560 00	13,000 00
of Brookline	22,000	26,180 00	22,000 00
	$933,300	$1,016,567 50	$933,300 00

BANK STOCK.

	Par Value.	Estimated Market Value.	Amount Invested.
Haverhill Nat'l Bank, Haverhill .	$37,500	$55,500 00	$37,500 00
Merrimack Nat'l Bank, Haverhill .	27,500	42,625 00	27,500 00
Essex Nat'l Bank, Haverhill .	16,700	20,875 00	16,700 00
First Nat'l Bank, Haverhill .	13,000	16,900 00	13,000 00
Methuen Nat'l Bank, Methuen .	10,000	12,000 00	10,000 00
First Nat'l Bank, Malden . .	10,000	12,800 00	10,000 00
Bay State Nat'l Bank, Lawrence .	3,750	6,250 00	3,750 00
Andover Nat'l Bank, Andover .	3,200	3,744 00	3,200 00
Boston Nat'l Bank, Boston . .	26,700	35,244 00	26,700 00
North America Nat'l Bank, Boston .	26,700	32,040 00	26,700 00

BANK STOCK — Concluded.

	Par Value.	Estimated Market Value.	Amount Invested.
Redemption Nat'l Bank, Boston .	$25,400	$34,544 00	$25,400 00
Republic Nat'l Bank, Boston . .	22,500	20,700 00	22,500 00
Hide and Leather Nat'l B'k, Boston,	20,000	24,000 00	20,000 00
Atlas Nat'l Bank, Boston . .	20,000	26,000 00	20,000 00
Blackstone Nat'l Bank, Boston .	20,000	23,600 00	20,000 00
Exchange Nat'l Bank, Boston . .	15,000	22,200 00	15,000 00
Shawmut Nat'l Bank, Boston . .	15,000	18,900 00	15,000 00
North Nat'l Bank, Boston . .	15,000	21,600 00	15,000 00
Suffolk Nat'l Bank, Boston . .	15,000	18,750 00	15,000 00
City Nat'l Bank, Boston . . .	15,000	19,050 00	15,000 00
Howard Nat'l Bank, Boston . .	15,000	19,650 00	15,000 00
Faneuil Hall Nat'l Bank, Boston .	10,000	13,500 00	10,000 00
Maverick Nat'l Bank, Boston . .	10,000	25,000 00	10,000 00
Traders' Nat'l Bank, Boston . .	10,000	10,500 00	10,000 00
Continental Nat'l Bank, Boston .	10,000	12,200 00	10,000 00
Globe Nat'l Bank, Boston . .	10,000	11,400 00	10,000 00
Manufacturers' Nat'l Bank, Boston .	10,000	11,200 00	10,000 00
Eagle Nat'l Bank, Boston . .	10,000	12,100 00	10,000 00
Shoe and Leather Nat'l B'k, Boston,	7,500	8,700 00	7,500 00
Hamilton Nat'l Bank, Boston . .	7,500	9,300 00	7,500 00
Columbian Nat'l Bank, Boston .	5,000	7,300 00	5,000 00
Webster Nat'l Bank, Boston . .	5,000	5,650 00	5,000 00
First Nat'l Bank, Boston . .	5,000	10,750 00	5,000 00
State Nat'l Bank, Boston . .	5,000	6,400 00	5,000 00
Third Nat'l Bank, Boston . .	10,000	11,000 00	10,000 00
Fourth Nat'l Bank, Boston . .	7,500	8,325 00	7,500 00
Central Nat'l Bank, Boston . .	5,000	6,100 00	5,000 00
Everett Nat'l Bank, Boston . .	5,000	5,900 00	5,000 00
Eliot Nat'l Bank, Boston . .	5,000	6,050 00	5,000 00
	$510,450	$677,347 00	$510,450 00

RAILROAD BONDS.

	Par Value.	Estimated Market Value.	Amount Invested.
Boston and Maine Railroad . .	$75,000	$95,250 00	$75,000 00
Old Colony and Newport Railroad .	15,000	18,300 00	15,000 00
West Amesbury Branch Railroad .	6,000	7,200 00	6,000 00
	$96,000	$120,750 00	$96,000 00

HAYDENVILLE SAVINGS BANK—HAYDENVILLE.

Incorporated March 17, 1869. Number of corporators, 81.

ELNATHAN GRAVES, *President*. *Treasurer*, B. S. JOHNSON.

STATEMENT.

LIABILITIES.		ASSETS.	
Deposits	$201,088 27	Public funds	$19,094 55
Earnings undivided	9,442 13	Bank stock	13,469 00
Guaranty fund	2,562 63	Railroad bonds	5,737 50
		Real estate by foreclosure	4,000 00
		Loans on real estate	95,299 58
		Loans on personal security,	47,571 17
		Loans to counties, cities, or towns	6,800 00
		Deposit in banks on interest,	19,935 39
		Expense account	360 10
		Cash on hand	825 74
	$213,093 03		$213,093 03

Cash on Deposit in Banks, amount in each:—

Hampshire County National Bank, Northampton	$19,541 74
First National Bank, Northampton	320 56
Conway National Bank, Conway	73 09

Amount of real estate held by foreclosure		$4,000 00
Assessed value of the same		2,243 00
Amount of income received from the same		184 08
Amount of municipal tax on real estate		15 92
Whole amount of interest or profits received or earned		$12,506 61
Rate and amount of each semi-annual dividend for previous year	2¼ per cent	4,261 07
	2 per cent	3,937 87

Times for the dividends fixed by the by-laws: second Tuesday in January and July.

Average annual per cent of dividends for the term ending at time of and including last extra dividend: $6\frac{6}{11}$ per cent.

The total amount of loans, with each specified rate of interest: $5,000, 5 per cent; $144,670.75, 6 per cent.

Number of outstanding loans which are of an amount not exceeding $3,000 each	221	
Aggregate amount of the same		136,970 75
Amount of investments from which no income is received		11,340 91
Number of open accounts	798	
Number and amount of deposits received for previous year,	1,235	50,823 51
Number and amount of deposits of and exceeding $300 at any one time for the previous year	39	21,849 55
Number and amount of withdrawals	460	46,998 67
Number of accounts opened the previous year	150	
Number of accounts closed the previous year	125	
Amount of expenses of the corporation during previous year		1,277 54
Amount of treasurer's bond		20,000 00

Date of examination by commissioner: July 12.

PUBLIC FUNDS.

	Par Value.	Estimated Market Value.	Amount Invested.
City of Holyoke 7s	$15,000	$19,094 55	$19,094 55

BANK STOCK.

	Par Value.	Estimated Market Value.	Amount Invested.
Conway Nat'l Bank, Conway . .	$6,900	$8,004 00	$7,834 00
Hampshire Co. N'l B'k, Northampt'n,	300	375 00	345 00
Easthampton N'l B'k, Easthampton,	4,300	5,590 00	5,290 00
	$11,500	$13,969 00	$13,469 00

RAILROAD BONDS.

	Par Value.	Estimated Market Value.	Amount Invested.
Boston and Albany Railroad 7s .	$5,000	$6,350 00	$5,737 50

HINGHAM INSTITUTION FOR SAVINGS — HINGHAM.

Incorporated April 2, 1834. Number of corporators, 72.

DANIEL BASSET, *President.* *Treasurer,* HENRY C. HARDING.

STATEMENT.

LIABILITIES.		ASSETS.	
Deposits	$1,665,216 18	Public funds	$98,500 00
Earnings undivided	13,984 64	Bank stock	144,300 00
Guaranty fund	20,070 18	Loans on bank stock	7,430 00
		Railroad bonds	45,000 00
		Loans on railroad stock	500 00
		Real estate	3,000 00
		Real estate by foreclosure	99,120 16
		Loans on real estate	856,955 13
		Loans on personal security,	376,850 00
		Loans to counties, cities, or towns	45,700 00
		Deposit in banks on interest,	8,215 82
		Expense account	2,237 12
		Loans on deposit	100 00
		Manufacturing Co.'s stock (to secure indebtedness)	3,300 00
		Cash on hand	8,062 77
	$1,699,271 00		$1,699,271 00

Loans on Bank Stock, amount on each:—

On 5 shares Hingham National Bank	$250 00
On 3 shares Mount Wollaston National Bank	180 00
On 70 shares Freeman's National Bank	7,000 00

Loans on Railroad Stock:—

On 6 shares Boston and Providence Railroad	$500 00

Cash on Deposit in Banks, amount in each:—

Shoe and Leather National Bank, Boston	$8,215 82
Webster National Bank, Boston	3,019 19
Hingham National Bank, Hingham	2,666 29

Amount invested in real estate (for banking purposes)	$3,000 00
Estimated value of the same	3,000 00
Amount of real estate held by foreclosure	99,120 16
Assessed value of the same	100,400 00
Amount of income received from the same	4,519 08
Amount of municipal tax on real estate	1,467 01

Whole amount of interest or profits received or earned		$94,382 03
Rate and amount of each semi-annual dividend for previous year	2 per cent	31,574 37
	2 per cent	32,105 93

Times for the dividends fixed by the by-laws; first Tuesday in January and July.

The total amount of loans, with each specified rate of interest; $157,000, 4 per cent; $32,100, 4½ per cent; $396,100, 5 per cent; $546,437.13, 6 per cent; $38,150, 6½ per cent; $106,468, 7 per cent; $3,350, 7³⁄₁₀ per cent; $6,980, 7½ per cent; $950, 8 per cent.

Number of outstanding loans which are of an amount not exceeding $3,000 each	326	
Aggregate amount of the same		$281,393 00
Number of open accounts	3,687	
Number and amount of deposits received for previous year,	1,288	161,767 63
Number and amount of deposits of and exceeding $300 at any one time for the previous year	164	97,045 27
Number and amount of withdrawals	1,384	167,377 27
Number of accounts opened the previous year	361	
Number of accounts closed the previous year	287	
Amount of expenses of the corporation during previous year		3,250 93
Amount of treasurer's bond		20,000 00

Date of examination by commissioner: May 26.

PUBLIC FUNDS.

	Par Value.	Estimated Market Value.	Amount Invested.
United States 6s, extended	$48,500	$48,985 00	$48,500 00
City of Boston 4s	$50,000	$51,250 00	$50,000 00
	$98,500	$100,235 00	$98,500 00

BANK STOCK.

	Par Value.	Estimated Market Value.	Amount Invested.
Hingham Nat'l Bank, Hingham	$11,900	$11,900 00	$11,800 00
Abington Nat'l Bank, Abington	1,500	2,100 00	1,500 00
Brockton Nat'l Bank, Brockton	2,000	2,000 00	2,000 00
Old Colony Nat'l Bank, Plymouth	1,600	2,160 00	1,600 00
Union Nat'l Bank, Weymouth	2,800	3,304 00	2,800 00
First Nat'l Bank, Chelsea	3,000	3,720 00	3,000 00
Atlantic Nat'l Bank, Boston	3,800	5,700 00	3,800 00
Atlas Nat'l Bank, Boston	7,500	9,375 00	7,500 00
City Nat'l Bank, Boston	5,400	6,696 00	5,400 00
Commerce Nat'l Bank, Boston	8,200	10,578 00	8,200 00
Eagle Nat'l Bank, Boston	10,000	11,900 00	10,000 00
First Nat'l Bank, Boston	5,000	10,350 00	5,000 00
Globe Nat'l Bank, Boston	4,000	4,520 00	4,000 00
Hamilton Nat'l Bank, Boston	4,200	4,746 00	4,200 00
Market Nat'l Bank, Boston	3,600	3,924 00	3,600 00
Massachusetts Nat'l Bank, Boston	2,000	2,480 00	2,000 00
Merchants' Nat'l Bank, Boston	7,500	11,175 00	7,500 00
New England Nat'l Bank, Boston	2,000	2,900 00	2,000 00
North America Nat'l Bank, Boston	8,000	9,200 00	8,000 00
Republic Nat'l Bank, Boston	7,500	9,300 00	7,500 00
Revere Nat'l Bank, Boston	11,200	13,664 00	11,200 00
Shoe and Leather Nat'l B'k, Boston,	6,500	7,345 00	6,500 00
State Nat'l Bank, Boston	2,600	3,250 00	2,600 00
Suffolk Nat'l Bank, Boston	3,600	4,356 00	3,600 00
Tremont Nat'l Bank, Boston	8,000	9,080 00	8,000 00
Union Nat'l Bank, Boston	5,000	7,050 00	5,000 00
Webster Nat'l Bank, Boston	6,000	6,660 00	6,000 00
	$144,400	$180,633 00	$144,300 00

RAILROAD BONDS.

	Par Value.	Estimated Market Value.	Amount Invested.
Boston and Albany 7s	$10,000	$12,700 00	$10,000 00
Boston and Lowell 7s	10,000	12,400 00	10,000 00
Boston and Maine 7s	10,000	12,650 00	10,000 00
Old Colony 7s	10,000	12,400 00	10,000 00
Eastern 4½s	5,000	5,450 00	5,000 00
	$45,000	$55,600 00	$45,000 00

HOLLISTON SAVINGS BANK — HOLLISTON.

Incorporated February, 1872. Number of corporators, 50.

SETH THAYER *President.* *Treasurer,* ORRIN THOMSON.

STATEMENT.

LIABILITIES.		ASSETS.	
Deposits . . .	$373,078 62	Public funds . . .	$12,968 75
Earnings undivided .	8,887 57	Bank stock	36,428 50
Guaranty fund . .	3,791 35	Loans on bank stock . .	2,700 00
		Railroad bonds . . .	11,400 00
		Real estate by foreclosure .	13,000 00
		Loans on real estate . .	218,070 00
		Loans on personal security,	14,918 09
		Loans to counties, cities, or towns	18,540 00
		Deposit in banks on interest,	55,758 90
		Expense account . . .	754 21
		Loan on silver coin . .	200 00
		Cash on hand . . .	1,019 09
	$385,757 54		$385,757 54

Loans on Bank Stock: —

On 42 shares Holliston National Bank, Holliston	$2,700 00

Cash on Deposit in Banks, amount in each: —

Holliston National Bank, Holliston	$29,498 04
Maverick National Bank, Boston	16,839 30
Pacific National Bank, Boston	5,000 00
National Bank of the Commonwealth, Boston	4,421 56

Amount of real estate held by foreclosure . . .	$13,000 00
Assessed value of the same	15,800 00
Amount of income received from the same . . .	1,002 00
Amount of municipal tax on real estate	202 95

Whole amount of interest or profits received or earned		$21,658 32
Rate and amount of each semi-annual dividend for previous year . . . . 2¼ per cent .		7,567 02
2 per cent .		6,987 61

Times for the dividends fixed by the by-laws: June and December.

The total amount of loans, with each specified rate of interest: $14,300, 4½ per cent; $236,048, 6 per cent; $4,000, 7 per cent.

Number of outstanding loans which are of an amount not exceeding $3,000 each	243	
Aggregate amount of the same		191,263 09
Number of open accounts	1,151	
Number and amount of deposits received for previous year .	893	100,460 48
Number and amount of deposits of and exceeding $300 at any one time for the previous year	91	48,997 13
Number and amount of withdrawals	835	72,549 92

Number of accounts opened the previous year 202
Number of accounts closed the previous year 148
Amount of expenses of the corporation during previous year . $1,300 00
Amount of treasurer's bond 20,000 00
Date of examination by commissioner: May 23.

PUBLIC FUNDS.

	Par Value.	Estimated Market Value.	Amount Invested.
United States 4s, registered . .	$4,000	$4,640 00	$4,000 00
State and city bonds: —			
State of New Hampshire 6s . .	$2,000	$2,200 00	$2,145 00
City of Lewiston, Me., 5s . .	2,000	2,200 00	2,090 00
of Providence, R.I., 4½s . .	1,000	1,100 00	1,033 75
of Worcester 6s . . .	4,000	4,600 00	3,700 00
	$13,000	$14,740 00	$12,968 75

BANK STOCK.

Holliston Nat'l Bank, Holliston .	$12.800	$16,000 00	$15,290 00
Traders' Nat'l Bank, Boston . .	3,000	3,060 00	3,408 75
Old Boston Nat'l Bank, Boston .	2,000	2,470 00	2,470 00
Commonwealth Nat'l Bank, Boston,	1,700	2,040 00	1,530 00
Blackstone Nat'l Bank, Boston .	700	805 00	644 00
State Nat'l Bank, Boston . .	2,400	3,000 00	2,727 00
Market Nat'l Bank, Boston . .	1,400	1,540 00	1,365 00
Blue Hill Nat'l Bank, Boston . .	1,500	1,650 00	1,383 75
S. Framingham N'l B'k, S. Fram'm,	3,000	3,100 00	3,000 00
Home Nat'l Bank, Brockton . .	3,000	3,300 00	3,000 00
Franklin Nat'l Bank, Franklin .	1,400	1,610 00	1,610 00
	$32,900	$38,575 00	$36,428 50

RAILROAD BONDS.

Eastern Railroad	$5,000	$5,500 00	$5,000 00
Salem and Lowell, guaranteed .	5,700	6,400 00	6,400 00
	$10,700	$11,900 00	$11,400 00

HOLYOKE SAVINGS BANK — HOLYOKE.

Incorporated 1855. Number of corporators, 76.

JOEL RUSSELL, *President.* *Treasurer,* R. B. JOHNSON.

STATEMENT.

LIABILITIES.		ASSETS.	
Deposits . . .	$1,391,423 98	Public funds . . .	$181,100 00
Earnings undivided .	32,637 06	Bank stock	186,949 67
Guaranty fund . .	18,000 00	Loans on bank stock . .	16,100 00
		Loan to Chicopee Savings Bank	10,000 00
		Railroad bonds . . .	36,000 00
		Loans on real estate . .	722,450 00
		Loans on personal security,	135,880 00
		Deposit in banks on interest,	111,223 77
		Expense account . . .	1,390 37
		Premium account . .	9,400 00
		Cash on hand . . .	31,567 23
	$1,442,061 04		$1,442,061 04

Loans on Bank Stock, amount on each: —

On 162 shares Holyoke National Bank, Holyoke	$15,500 00
On 6 shares Franklin County National Bank, Greenfield . .	600 00

Cash on Deposit in Banks, amount in each: —

Holyoke National Bank, Holyoke	$36,862 37
Franklin County National Bank, Greenfield	45,000 00
Maverick National Bank, Boston	29,361 40

Whole amount of interest or profits received or earned		$79,846 72
Rate and amount of each semi-annual dividend for previous year	{ 2¼ per cent . { 2 per cent .	27,771 12 25,760 71

Times for the dividends fixed by the by-laws: January and July.

The total amount of loans, with each specified rate of interest: $46,600, 4½ per cent; $827,830, 6 per cent.

Number of outstanding loans which are of an amount not exceeding $3,000 each	229	
Aggregate amount of the same		275,145 00
Number of open accounts	4,272	
Number and amount of deposits received for previous year,	6,980	408,299 00
Number and amount of deposits of and exceeding $300 at any one time for the previous year	221	128,370 00
Number and amount of withdrawals	3,363	377,960 19
Number of accounts opened the previous year . . .	1,118	
Number of accounts closed the previous year	714	
Amount of expenses of the corporation during previous year . .		3,782 79
Amount of treasurer's bond		25,000 00

Date of examination by commisioner: July 11.

PUBLIC FUNDS.

	Par Value.	Estimated Market Value.	Amount Invested.
United States 3½s	$111,000	$112,000 00	$111,000 00
" " 6s, currency	10,000	13,000 00	10,000 00
" " 4s	700	812 00	700 00
" " 4½s	400	450 00	400 00
State, city, and town bonds: —			
State of Massachusetts	$17,000	$19,890 00	$17,000 00
City of Holyoke 6s	5,000	5,600 00	5,000 00
of Fall River 6s	3,000	3,600 00	3,000 00
of Boston 6s	3,000	3,700 00	3,000 00
of Boston 5s	4,000	4,320 00	4,000 00
of Boston 4s	25,000	25,750 00	25,000 00
of Chelsea 6s	1,000	1,185 00	1,000 00
Town of Fair Haven, Vt., 5s	1,000	1,035 00	1,000 00
	$181,100	$191,342 00	$181,100 00

BANK STOCK.

Holyoke Nat'l Bank, Holyoke	$35,600	$39,872 00	$36,062 00
Hadley Falls Nat'l Bank, Holyoke	13,200	21,120 00	19,519 67
Agawam Nat'l Bank, Springfield	5,000	6,000 00	6,687 00
First Nat'l Bank, Springfield	11,900	17,850 00	14,964 59
Second Nat'l Bank, Springfield	5,000	8,000 00	9,302 00
Third Nat'l Bank, Springfield	13,500	21,600 00	20,678 41
Chicopee Nat'l Bank, Springfield	3,100	4,650 00	4,935 00
John Hancock Nat'l B'k, Springfield,	8,700	10,015 00	9,997 00
First Nat'l Bank, Northampton	10,000	13,500 00	13,327 50
Northampton Nat'l B'k, North'ton	7,600	11,400 00	11,670 00
Hampshire Co. Nat'l B'k, North'n	2,000	2,400 00	2,400 00
First Nat'l Bank, Easthampton	4,200	5,040 00	4,910 00
Railroad Nat'l Bank, Lowell	3,400	4,420 00	4,128 00
Townsend Nat'l Bank, Townsend	9,700	12,610 00	12,713 00
Shelburne Falls Nat'l Bank, Shelburne Falls	300	405 00	369 50
Conway Nat'l Bank, Conway	5,700	6,555 00	6,570 00
First Nat'l Bank, Westfield	400	560 00	412 00
First Nat'l Bank, South Adams	2,200	2,860 00	2,800 00
Pittsfield Nat'l Bank, Pittsfield	1,100	1,540 00	1,139 00
Monson Nat'l Bank, Monson	900	1,350 00	900 00
Franklin Co. Nat'l B'k, Greenfield	1,000	1,500 00	1,000 00
First Nat'l Bank, Newburyport	1,000	1,700 00	1,500 00
Miller's River Nat'l Bank, Athol	800	1,440 00	800 00
Merrimack Nat'l Bank, Haverhill	100	165 00	165 00
	$146,400	$196,552 00	$186,949 67

Railroad Bonds.

	Par Value.	Estimated Market Value.	Amount Invested.
Boston and Albany 6s . . .	$5,000	$5,700 00	$5,000 00
Boston and Lowell 5s . . .	5,000	5,250 00	5,000 00
Boston, Revere Beach, and Lynn 6s .	5,000	5,750 00	5,000 00
Nashua and Lowell 6s . . .	8,000	9,000 00	8,000 00
Old Colony 6s	8,000	8,800 00	8,000 00
Boston and Maine 7s . . .	5,000	5,500 00	5,000 00
	$36,000	$40,000 00	$36,000 00

HOME SAVINGS BANK — BOSTON.

Incorporated 1869. Number of corporators 61.

CHARLES H. ALLEN, *President*. *Treasurer*, B. N. BULLOCK.

STATEMENT.

LIABILITIES.		ASSETS.	
Deposits . . .	$1,846,541 98	Public funds . . .	$107,250 00
Earnings undivided .	237,827 09	Loans on public funds .	800 00
Guaranty fund . .	15,000 00	Bank stock	384,918 44
		Loans on bank stock . .	24,100 00
		Real estate by foreclosure .	195,750 00
		Loans on real estate . .	967,381 04
		Loans on personal security,	252,600 00
		Loans to counties, cities, or towns	24,000 00
		Deposit in banks on interest,	133,938 15
		Expense account . . .	990 76
		Loans on Home Savings Bank books . . .	121 40
		Cash on hand . . .	7,519 28
	$2,099,369 07		$2,099,369 07

Loans on Public Funds: —

On $800 United States 4s $800 00

Loans on Bank Stock, amount on each: —

On 40 shares Central National Bank, Boston	$4,000 00
On 22 shares Boylston National Bank, Boston	2,200 00
On 50 shares Dedham National Bank, Dedham	5,000 00
On 116 shares South Reading National Bank	10,000 09
On 24 shares Bristol County National Bank and 8 shares Taunton National Bank, Taunton	2,900 00

Cash on Deposit in Banks, amount in each: —

Central National Bank, Boston	$88,938 15
Pacific National Bank, Boston	45,000 00

Amount of real estate held by foreclosure	$195,750 00
Assessed value of the same	159,150 00
Amount of income received from the same	8,755 65
Amount of municipal tax on real estate	2,213 27

Whole amount of interest or profits received or earned . . . $111,511 12

Rate and amount of each semi-annual dividend for previous year . . . . { 2 per cent . 38,192 76; 2 per cent . 34,830 82 }

Times for the dividends fixed by the by-laws: second Wednesday in April and October.

The total amount of loans, with each specified rate of interest: $13,000, 4 per cent; $79,100, $4\frac{1}{2}$ per cent; $162,571.40, 5 per cent; $72,900, $5\frac{1}{2}$ per cent; $800,562.04, 6 per cent; $64,150, $6\frac{1}{2}$ per cent; $136,869, 7 per cent; $3,700, $7\frac{3}{10}$ per cent; $24,250, $7\frac{1}{2}$ per cent; $6,900, 8 per cent.

Number of outstanding loans which are of an amount not exceeding $3,000 each 115

Aggregate amount of the same		$178,253 20
Amount of investments from which no income is received . .		14,200 00
Number of open accounts	13,931	
Number and amount of deposits received for previous year,	2,645	281,995 62
Number and amount of deposits of and exceeding $300 at any one time for the previous year	271	159,398 09
Number and amount of withdrawals	7,514	848,917 94
Number of accounts opened the previous year	898	
Number of accounts closed the previous year	4,070	
Amount of expenses of the corporation during previous year . .		15,545 72
Amount of treasurer's bond		30,000 00

Date of examination by commissioner: Feb. 7.

PUBLIC FUNDS.

	Par Value.	Estimated Market Value.	Amount Invested.
United States 4s, 1907, registered .	$52,500	$60,965 62	$52,250 00
" " 3½s (ext. 6s, 1881), reg.	50,000	50,500 00	55,000 00
	$102,500	$111,465 62	$107,250 00

BANK STOCK.

	Par Value.	Estimated Market Value.	Amount Invested.
Atlas Nat'l Bank, Boston . .	$18,000	$22,500 00	$20,700 00
Blackstone Nat'l Bank, Boston .	8,100	9,315 00	8,856 00
Boston Nat'l Bank, Boston . .	1,400	1,792 00	1,332 00
Columbian Nat'l Bank, Boston .	4,000	5,700 00	5,251 20
Eliot Nat'l Bank, Boston . .	5,200	6,253 00	5,616 00
Everett Nat'l Bank, Boston . .	7,000	8,198 75	7,875 00
First Nat'l Bank, Boston . .	9,000	18,697 50	16,650 00
Freeman's Nat'l Bank, Boston .	9,800	11,735 50	10,584 00
Hide and Leather Nat'l B'k, Boston,	5,000	5,825 00	5,600 00
Howard Nat'l Bank, Boston . .	12,800	16,656 00	13,908 87
Hamilton Nat'l Bank, Boston . .	8,000	9,040 00	9,440 00
Market Nat'l Bank, Brighton . .	5,000	6,625 00	4,981 50
Market Nat'l Bank, Boston .	15,000	16,462 50	15,900 00
Massachusetts Nat'l Bank, Boston .	5,000	6,200 00	5,500 00
Merchants' Nat'l Bank, Boston .	10,000	14,625 00	12,593 00
New England Nat'l Bank, Boston .	20,000	29,100 00	26,800 00
North Nat'l Bank, Boston . .	20,000	28,425 00	23,400 00
North America Nat'l Bank, Boston,	5,000	5,750 00	5,400 00
Redemption Nat'l Bank, Boston .	11,300	15,269 12	14,690 00
Revere Nat'l Bank, Boston . .	15,000	18,300 00	16,800 00
Republic Nat'l Bank, Boston . .	18,000	23,580 00	22,564 87
Shawmut Nat'l Bank, Boston . .	18,000	22,950 00	21,240 00
Second Nat'l Bank, Boston . .	40,000	60,600 00	56,000 00
Shoe and Leather Nat'l B'k, Boston,	8,200	9,225 00	9,676 00
Suffolk Nat'l Bank, Boston . .	4,000	4,875 00	4,840 00
Tremont Nat'l Bank, Boston . .	18,200	22,204 00	20,020 00
Union Nat'l Bank, Boston . .	10,000	15,350 00	13,600 00
Webster Nat'l Bank, Boston . .	5,000	5,575 00	5,100 00
	$316,000	$420,828 37	$384,918 44

HOOSAC SAVINGS BANK — NORTH ADAMS.

Incorporated 1871. Number of corporators, 42.

O. A. ARCHER, *President*. *Treasurer*, C. N. INGALLS.

STATEMENT.

LIABILITIES.		ASSETS.	
Deposits	$140,006 10	Public funds	$7,805 00
Earnings undivided	575 81	Bank stock	5,020 00
Guaranty fund	1,160 00	Real estate by foreclosure	16,174 16
Individual account	30 00	Loans on real estate	64,325 09
		Loans on personal security,	24,860 04
		Expense account	414 95
		Property account	443 64
		Cash on hand	22,729 03
	$141,771 91		$141,771 91

Cash on Deposit in Bank: —
Berkshire National Bank, North Adams $21,832 97

Amount of real estate held by foreclosure		$16,174 16
Assessed value of the same		10,000 00
Amount of income received from the same		1,500 00
Amount of municipal tax on real estate		229 00
Whole amount of interest or profits received or earned		$9,331 64
Rate and amount of each semi-annual dividend for previous year	2 per cent	2,148 87
	2 per cent	2,160 53

Times for the dividends fixed by the by-laws: June and December.

Average annual per cent of dividends for the term ending at time of and including last extra dividend: 4 per cent.

The total amount of loans, with each specified rate of interest: $5,000, 5 per cent; $7,000, 5½ per cent; $77,185.13, 6 per cent.

Number of outstanding loans which are of an amount not exceeding $3,000 each	70	
Aggregate amount of the same		61,185 13
Number of open accounts	791	
Number and amount of deposits received for previous year	661	60,426 87
Number and amount of deposits of and exceeding $300 at any one time for the previous year	58	34,400 47
Number and amount of withdrawals	342	41,867 11
Number of accounts opened the previous year	176	
Number of accounts closed the previous year	100	
Amount of expenses of the corporation during previous year		1,200 00
Amount of treasurer's bond		20,000 00

Date of examination by the commissioner: Aug. 8.

PUBLIC FUNDS.

	Par Value.	Estimated Market Value.	Amount Invested.
Town of Pawtucket . . .	$7,000	$7,805 00	$7,805 00

BANK STOCK.

	Par Value.	Estimated Market Value.	Amount Invested.
Adams Nat'l Bank, North Adams .	$700	$980	$840
Berkshire Nat'l Bank . . .	3,800	4,560 00	4,180 00
	$4,500	$5,540 00	$5,020 00

HOPKINTON SAVINGS BANK — HOPKINTON.

Incorporated March 23, 1867. Number of corporators, 29.

A. A. SWEET, *President*. *Treasurer*, E. J. JENKS.

STATEMENT.

LIABILITIES.		ASSETS.	
Deposits	$291,137 51	Public funds	$41,342 50
Earnings undivided	7,475 26	Bank stock	63,388 99
Guaranty fund	5,282 01	Railroad bonds	77,247 50
Rent on real estate	108 00	Real estate by foreclosure	2,580 33
		Loans on real estate	105,278 00
		Loans on personal security,	6,804 25
		Deposit in bank on interest,	6,361 21
		Cash on hand and in bank,	1,000 00
	$304,002 78		$304,002 78

Cash on Deposit in Bank:—

Hopkinton National Bank . . . $7,361 21

Amount of real estate held by foreclosure		$2,580 33
Assessed value of the same		3,200 00
Amount of income received from the same		216 00
Amount of municipal tax on real estate		40 28
Whole amount of interest or profits received or earned		$18,891 20
Rate and amount of each semi-annual dividend for previous year	2¼ per cent	5,681 89
	2¼ per cent	6,215 49

Times for the dividends fixed by the by-laws: May 1 and Nov. 1.

Average annual per cent of dividends for the term ending at time of and including last extra dividend: 6½ per cent.

The total amount of loans, with each specified rate of interest: $15,800, 6 per cent; $96,282.25, 6½ per cent.

Number of outstanding loans which are of an amount not exceeding $3,000 each	202	
Aggregate amount of the same		103,082 25
Number of open accounts	978	
Number and amount of deposits received for previous year	766	73,870 84
Number and amount of deposits of and exceeding $300 at any one time for the previous year	51	27,606 41
Number and amount of withdrawals	188	16,398 08
Number of accounts opened the previous year	154	
Number of accounts closed the previous year	158	
Amount of expenses of the corporation during previous year		800 00
Amount of treasurer's bond		5,000 00

Date of examination by commissioner: May 23.

PUBLIC FUNDS.

	Par Value.	Estimated Market Value.	Amount Invested.
City bonds: —			
City of Belfast, Me.	$5,500	$5,610 00	$5,686 25
of Bangor, Me.	5,000	6,050 00	5,343 75
of Rockland, Me.	2,000	2,005 00	2,060 00
of Providence, R.I. . . .	5,000	5,500 00	5,150 00
of Newton	5,000	5,900 00	5,937 50
of Pawtucket, R.I. . . .	10,000	11,000 00	11,162 50
of Portland, Me.	6,000	7,440 00	6,002 50
	$38,500	$43,505 00	$41,342 50

BANK STOCK.

	Par Value.	Estimated Market Value.	Amount Invested.
Shawmut Nat'l Bank, Boston . .	$9,000	$11,317 50	$11,023 74
Hide and Leather Nat'l Bank, Boston,	1,300	1,495 00	1,404 00
Redemption Nat'l Bank, Boston .	5,000	6,756 25	6,990 00
Faneuil Hall Nat'l Bank, Boston .	1,500	1,961 20	1,965 00
Republic Nat'l Bank, Boston . .	1,500	1,871 25	1,980 00
Continental Nat'l Bank, Boston .	5,000	5,931 25	5,930 00
Atlantic Nat'l Bank, Boston . .	5,000	7,675 00	6,832 50
Revere Nat'l Bank, Boston . .	3,800	4,617 00	4,607 50
Atlas Nat'l Bank, Boston . .	6,100	7,625 00	7,505 00
North Nat'l Bank, Boston . .	3,500	4,978 75	4,657 50
Exchange Nat'l Bank, Boston. .	1,000	1,440 00	1,687 50
Everett Nat'l Bank, Boston . .	2,500	2,925 00	2,975 00
Pacific Nat'l Bank, Boston . .	5,000	5,356 25	5,331 25
Natick Nat'l Bank, Natick . .	500	575 00	500 00
	$50,700	$64,524 45	$63,388 99

RAILROAD BONDS.

	Par Value.	Estimated Market Value.	Amount Invested.
Boston and Maine Railroad . .	$5,000	$6,350 00	$5,185 00
Old Colony Railroad	8,000	9,910 00	8,515 00
Fitchburg Railroad	8,000	9,187 00	8,797 50
Boston, Fitchburg, and Clinton R.R	7,000	8,050 00	7,947 50
Boston, Fitchburg, and Clinton and New Bedford Railroad * . .	3,000	3,172 00	3,135 00
Salem and Lowell Railroad . .	10,000	11,000 00	11,100 00
Boston, Revere Beach, and Lynn R.R.	10,000	11,600 00	11,692 50
Nashua and Lowell Railroad . .	10,000	10,325 00	10,375 00
Newport and Richford Railroad .	10,000	10,200 00	10,500 00
	$71,000	$79,794 00	$77,247 50

* This bank has been notified that the investment in these bonds is illegal.

HUDSON SAVINGS BANK — HUDSON.

Incorporated 1869. Number of corporators, 44.

EDMUND M. STOWE, *President*. *Treasurer*, DANIEL W. STRATTON.

STATEMENT.

LIABILITIES.		ASSETS.	
Deposits	$267,325 67	Public funds	$34,056 78
Earnings undivided	1,284 50	Bank stock	6,106 00
Guaranty fund	2,730 77	Railroad bonds	20,375 00
		Real estate by foreclosure	800 00
		Loans on real estate	149,825 00
		Loans on personal security,	6,050 00
		Loans to counties, cities, or towns	27,500 00
		Deposit in banks on interest,	19,300 00
		Expense account	2 25
		Taxes paid	222 52
		Profit and loss	903 89
		Cash on hand and in bank,	6,199 50
	$271,340 94		$271,340 94

Cash on Deposit in Banks, amount in each:—

Blackstone National Bank, Boston	$5,000 00
Wachusett National Bank, Fitchburg	16,885 96
North National Bank, Boston	2,590 54

Amount of real estate held by foreclosure	$800 00
Assessed value of the same	800 00
Amount of income received from the same	49 77
Amount of municipal tax on real estate	13 00

Whole amount of interest or profits received or earned		$14,379 16
Rate and amount of each semi-annual dividend for previous year	2 per cent	4,456 70
	2 per cent	4,739 11

Times for the dividends fixed by the by-laws: third Wednesday in January and July.

The total amount of loans, with each specified rate of interest: $3,000, 3 per cent; $25,000, 4 per cent; $5,500, 5 per cent; $6,300, 5½ per cent; $96,700, 6 per cent; $9,250, 6½ per cent; $33,225, 7 per cent; $4,400, 7½ per cent.

Number of outstanding loans which are of an amount not exceeding $3,000 each	168	
Aggregate amount of the same		134,350 00
Number of open accounts	1,087	
Number and amount of deposits received for previous year	843	69,623 00
Number and amount of deposits of and exceeding $300 at any one time for the previous year	51	28,972 00
Number and amount of withdrawals	472	50,163 50
Number of accounts opened the previous year	200	
Number of accounts closed the previous year	107	
Amount of expenses of the corporation during previous year		635 00
Amount of treasurer's bond		40,000 00

Date of examination by commissioner: May 17.

PUBLIC FUNDS.

	Par Value.	Estimated Market Value.	Amount Invested.
United States 6s, extended . .	$10,000	$10,150 00	$10,300 00
City and town bonds : —			
City of Worcester funded loan .	$8,000	$8,560 00	$8,560 00
of Fall River water bonds .	5,000	5,700 00	5,225 00
Town of Northampton . . .	3,000	3,510 00	2,820 00
of Natick water scrip . .	2,000	2,150 00	2,064 28
of Hopkinton . . .	5,000	5,000 00	5,087 50
	$33,000	$35,070 00	$34,056 78

BANK STOCK.

State Nat'l Bank, Boston . .	$5,700	$7,125 00	$6,106 00

RAILROAD BONDS.

Eastern Railroad	$5,000	$5,475 00	$5,225 00
Salem and Lowell Railroad . .	5,000	5,750 00	5,500 00
Fitchburg Railroad 5s. . . .	9,000	9,900 00	9,650 00
	$19,000	$21,125 00	$20,375 00

HYDE PARK SAVINGS BANK — HYDE PARK.

Incorporated March 8, 1871. Number of corporators, 37.

ROBERT BLEAKIE, *President*. *Treasurer*, HENRY S. BUNTON.

STATEMENT.

LIABILITIES.		ASSETS.	
Deposits . . .	$77,392 37	Bank stock	$5,000 00
Earnings undivided .	4,665 51	Real estate by foreclosure .	3,027 45
Guaranty fund . .	607 37	Loans on real estate . .	39,165 00
		Loans on personal security,	25,625 00
		Loans to counties, cities, or towns	5,000 00
		Deposit in banks on interest,	4,052 09
		Expense account . . .	243 19
		Cash on hand . . .	552 52
	$82,665 25		$82,665 25

Cash on Deposit in Banks, amount in each: —

Maverick National Bank, Boston	$3,997 88
Commonwealth National Bank, Boston	54 21

Amount of real estate held by foreclosure . . .	$3,027 45
Assessed value of the same	3,700 00
Amount of income received from the same . . .	293 00
Amount of municipal tax on real estate	60 33

Whole amount of interest or profits received or earned		$4,286 68
Rate and amount of each semi-annual dividend for previous year	2 per cent .	778 66
	2 per cent .	1,037 14

Times for the dividends fixed by the by-laws: Jan. 1 and July 1.

The total amount of loans, with each specified rate of interest: $5,000, 5 per cent; $25,625, 6 per cent; $28,815, 7 per cent; $10,350, 8 per cent.

Number of outstanding loans which are of an amount not exceeding $3,000 each	33	
Aggregate amount of the same		34,790 00
Number of open accounts	537	
Number and amount of deposits received for previous year .	740	64,218 16
Number and amount of deposits of and exceeding $300 at any one time for the previous year	53	33,333 42
Number and amount of withdrawals	489	32,133 07
Number of accounts opened the previous year	176	
Number of accounts closed the previous year	86	
Amount of expenses of the corporation during previous year .		756 54
Amount of treasurer's bond		10,000 00

Date of examination by commissioner: March 26.

BANK STOCK.

	Par Value.	Estimated Market Value.	Amount Invested.
Commerce Nat'l Bank, Boston .	$1,000	$1,290 00	1,000 00
Freeman's Nat'l Bank, Boston .	1,300	1,547 00	1,300 00
First Nat'l Bank, Newburyport .	2,700	4,050 00	2,700 00
	$5,000	$6,887 00	$5,000 00

INSTITUTION FOR SAVINGS IN ROXBURY AND ITS VICINITY — BOSTON.

Incorporated Feb. 22, 1825. Number of corporators, 48.

ARTHUR W. TUFTS, *President*. *Treasurer*, EDWARD RICHARDS.

STATEMENT.

LIABILITIES.		ASSETS.	
Deposits	$2,683,155 91	Public funds	$279,900 00
Earnings undivided	12,737 99	Bank stock	184,639 97
Guaranty fund	53,000 00	Loans on bank stock	700 00
Profit and loss	30,960 00	Railroad bonds	57,321 73
		Real estate	2,000 00
		Real estate by foreclosure	110,956 00
		Loans on real estate	876,560 00
		Loans on personal security,	905,718 01
		Loans to counties, cities, or towns	12,000 00
		Deposit in banks on interest,	310,649 02
		Cash on hand	39,409 17
	$2,779,853 90		$2,779,853 90

Loans on Bank Stock, amount on each: —

On 10 shares People's National Bank, Boston	$500 00
On 2 shares Gloucester National Bank, Gloucester	200 00

Cash on Deposit in Banks, amount in each: —

Exchange National Bank, Boston	$179,914 07
Manufacturers' National Bank, Boston	9,542 07
Security National Bank, Boston	100,000 00
Hamilton National Bank, Boston	17,433 33
Market National Bank, Boston	3,759 55

Amount invested in real estate (for banking purposes)	$2,000 00
Estimated value of the same	29,700 00
Amount of real estate held by foreclosure	110,956 00
Assessed value of the same	86,800 00
Amount of income received from the same	3,066 00
Amount of municipal tax on real estate	1,206 52

Whole amount of interest or profits received or earned . . . $149,825 44

Rate and amount of each semi-annual dividend for previous year: 2 per cent, 48,151 04; 2 per cent, 49,979 80

Times for the dividends fixed by the by-laws: third Wednesday in April and October.

Average annual per cent of dividends for the term ending at time of and including last extra dividend: 6½ per cent.

The total amount of loans, with each specified rate of interest: $25,000, 3¼ per cent; $35,000, 3½ per cent; $204,300, 4 per cent; $290,000, 4½ per cent; $418,482.35, 5 per cent; $27,000, 5½ per cent; $446,115.66, 6 per cent; $107,150, 6½ per cent; $315,130, 7 per cent; $5,000, 7½ per cent; $6,100, 7$\frac{3}{10}$ per cent; $600, 8 per cent,

Number of outstanding loans which are of an amount not exceeding $3,000 each . . . 76

Aggregate amount of the same		$134,478 01
Number of open accounts	7,351	
Number and amount of deposits received for previous year,	7,527	559,259 00
Number and amount of deposits of and exceeding $300 at any one time for the previous year	446	261,331 00
Number and amount of withdrawals , ...	5,457	456,529 20
Number of accounts opened the previous year. . . .	1,489	
Number of accounts closed the previous year	888	
Amount of expenses of the corporation during previous year .		7,945 27
Amount of treasurer's bond		20,000 00

Date of examination by commissioner: March 25.

PUBLIC FUNDS.

	Par Value.	Estimated Market Value.	Amount Invested.
United States 4½s	$190,000	$212,800 00	$195,000 00
State and city bonds: —			
State of Maine	$3,000	$3,000 00	$3,000 00
City of Boston 6s	51,000	61,200 00	51,000 00
of Boston 4s	30,000	30,900 00	30,000 00
of Boston	1,000	1,000 00	900 00
	$275,000	$308,900 00	$279,900 00

BANK STOCK.

First Nat'l Bank, Danvers, . .	$1,500	$1,900 00	$1,500 00
Atlas Nat'l Bank, Boston . .	6,000	7,500 00	6,000 00
North Nat'l Bank, Boston . .	25,700	36,494 00	25,680 47
State Nat'l Bank, Boston . .	2,300	2,875 00	2,300 00
Market Nat'l Bank, Boston . .	2,500	2,725 00	2,500 00
Second Nat'l Bank, Boston . .	5,500	8,305 00	5,500 00
Commerce Nat'l Bank, Boston . .	1,500	1,845 00	2,000 00
Atlantic Nat'l Bank, Boston . .	5,000	7,650 00	5,000 00
Revere Nat'l Bank, Boston . .	15,000	18,300 00	15,000 00
First Nat'l Bank, Boston . .	20,000	41,400 00	20,000 00
Rockland Nat'l Bank, Boston . .	17,300	24,220 00	19,430 00
People's Nat'l Bank, Boston . .	21,000	34,020 00	21,000 00
Washington Nat'l Bank, Boston .	51,000	71,400 00	58,729 50
	$174,300	$258,634 00	$184,639 97

RAILROAD BONDS.

Old Colony Railroad . . .	$16,000	$20,000 00	$17,760 39
Boston and Providence Railroad .	12,000	15,240 00	13,614 67
Boston and Albany Railroad . .	17,000	21,590 00	19,240 42
Boston and Maine Railroad . .	6,000	7,620 00	6,706 25
	$51,000	$64,450 00	$57,321 73

INSTITUTION FOR SAVINGS IN NEWBURYPORT AND ITS VICINITY —NEWBURYPORT.

Incorporated 1820. Number of corporators, 80.

EDWARD S. MOSELEY, *President*. *Treasurer*, RICHARD STONE.

STATEMENT.

LIABILITIES.		ASSETS.	
Deposits	$4,234,123 74	Public funds	$914,000 00
Earnings undivided .	26,793 04	Loans on public funds .	8,500 00
Guaranty fund . .	90,000 00	Bank stock	922,120 00
		Loans on bank stock . .	1,450 00
		Railroad bonds . . .	140,000 00
		Real estate	15,000 00
		Real estate by foreclosure .	114,820 98
		Loans on real estate . .	1,020,122 00
		Loans on personal security,	985,310 00
		Loans to counties, cities, or towns	193,500 00
		Deposit in banks on interest,	35,678 42
		Cash on hand . . .	415 38
	$4,350,916 78		$4,350,916 78

Loans on Public Funds: —

On $8,500 United States bonds . . . $8,500 00

Loans on Bank Stock, amount on each: —

On 6 shares First National Bank, Newburyport $550 00

On 10 shares First National Bank, Merrimac . 900 00

Cash on Deposit in Banks, amount in each: —

First National Bank, Newburyport	$3,615 13
Mechanics' National Bank, Newburyport	20,000 00
Ocean National Bank, Newburyport	12,000 00
National Bank of Redemption, Boston	63 29

Amount invested in real estate (for banking purposes) . . .	$15,000 00
Estimated value of the same	20,000 00
Amount of real estate held by foreclosure	114,820 98
Assessed value of the same	108,900 00
Amount of income received from the same	2,328 78
Amount of municipal tax on real estate	1,823 31

Whole amount of interest or profits received or earned $242,720 01

Rate and amount of each semi-annual dividend for previous year . . . . { 2 per cent . 79,265 98; 2 per cent . 81,147 29 }

Times for the dividends fixed by the by-laws: fourth Wednesday in April and October.

The total amount of loans, with each specified rate of interest: $155,000, 3½ per cent; $2,000, 3⅝ per cent; $50,000, 3¾ per cent; $30,000, 3⅞ per cent; $275,000, 4 per cent; $175,000, 4¼ per cent;

$496,300, 4½ per cent; $65,000, 4¾ per cent; $265,900, 5 per cent; $7,000, 5¼ per cent; $243,500, 5½ per cent; $1,262,582, 6 per cent; $67,200, 6½ per cent; $178,400, 7 per cent.

Number of outstanding loans which are of an amount not exceeding $3,000 each	342	
Aggregate amount of the same		$345,762 00
Number of open accounts	9,696	
Number and amount of deposits received for previous year,	4,683	404,583 46
Number and amount of deposits of and exceeding $300 at any one time for the previous year	398	219,463 13
Number and amount of withdrawals	4,286	440,065 45
Number of accounts opened the previous year	1,142	
Number of accounts closed the previous year	689	
Amount of expenses of the corporation during previous year		7,456 81
Amount of treasurer's bond		20,000 00

Date of examination by commissioner: June 6.

Public Funds.

	Par Value.	Estimated Market Value.	Amount Invested.
United States bonds	$300,000	$320,631 00	$300,00 00
City and town bonds: —			
City of Charlestown 6s	$35,000	$40,950 00	$35,000 00
of Holyoke 6s.	25,000	31,250 00	25,000 00
of Lynn 6s	75,000	94,500 00	75,000 00
of Springfield 7s	40,000	54,000 00	40,000 00
of Nashua, N.H., 6s	50,000	59,000 00	50,000 00
of Hartford, Conn., 6s	5,000	5,750 00	5,000 00
of Concord, N.H., 6s	35,000	40,600 00	35,000 00
of Newburyport 5s	6,000	6,120 00	6,000 00
of Newburyport 6s	183,000	206,790 00	183,000 00
of Lewiston, Me., 6s	10,000	11,200 00	10,000 00
of Worcester 5s	4,000	4,020 00	4,000 00
of Bangor, Me, 7s	25,000	31,250 00	25,000 00
of Lawrence 5½s	25,000	25,875 00	25,000 00
of Portland, Me., 6s	60,000	65,400 00	60,000 00
Town of Wakefield 6s	11,000	11,110 00	11,000 00
of Groveland 5s.	17,000	17,850 00	17,000 00
of Melrose 7s	8,000	10,080 00	8,000 00
	$914,000	$1,036,376 00	$914,000 00

Bank Stock.

Atlantic Nat'l Bank, Boston	$12,200	$18,788 00	$12,200 00
Atlas Nat'l Bank, Boston	75,000	93,750 00	75,000 00
Blackstone Nat'l Bank, Boston	4,700	5,405 00	4,700 00
Boston Nat'l Bank, Boston	3,700	4,736 00	3,700 00
Old Boston Nat'l Bank, Boston	10,000	12,200 00	10,000 00
City Nat'l Bank, Boston	10,800	13,701 00	10,800 00

BANK STOCK — Concluded.

	Par Value.	Estimated Market Value.	Amount Invested.
Columbian Nat'l Bank, Boston .	$30,000	$42,900 00	$30,000 00
Commerce Nat'l Bank, Boston .	22,100	28,509 00	22,100 00
Commonwealth Nat'l Bank, Boston,	25,000	30,125 00	25,000 00
Eagle Nat'l Bank, Boston . .	28,600	34,320 00	28,600 00
Eliot Nat'l Bank, Boston . .	7,400	8,880 00	7,400 00
Exchange Nat'l Bank, Boston .	10,000	14,400 00	10,000 00
Faneuil Hall Nat'l Bank, Boston .	24,000	31,440 00	24,000 00
First Nat'l Bank, Boston . .	10,000	20,800 00	10,000 00
Freeman's Nat'l Bank, Boston .	27,000	32,400 00	27,000 00
Globe Nat'l Bank, Boston . .	13,300	14,896 00	13,300 00
Hamilton Nat'l Bank, Boston . .	15,000	16,950 00	15,000 00
Hide and Leather Nat'l B'k, Boston,	15,000	17,475 00	15,000 00
Howard Nat'l Bank, Boston . .	26,700	34,710 00	26,700 00
Market Nat'l Bank, Boston . .	50,800	55,880 00	50,800 00
Massachusetts Nat'l Bank, Boston .	8,250	10,230 00	8,250 00
Maverick Nat'l Bank, Boston . .	20,000	50,000 00	20,000 00
Merchants' Nat'l Bank, Boston .	17,300	25,431 00	17,300 00
New England Nat'l Bank, Boston .	10,000	14,500 00	10,000 00
North Nat'l Bank, Boston . .	30,200	42,884 00	30,200 00
North America Nat'l Bank, Boston .	6,000	6,900 00	6,000 00
Redemption Nat'l Bank, Boston .	25,800	34,830 00	25,800 00
Revere Nat'l Bank, Boston . .	37,500	45,750 00	37,500 00
Second Nat'l Bank, Boston . .	48,000	72,960 00	48,000 00
Shawmut Nat'l Bank, Boston . .	20,000	25,600 00	20,000 00
Shoe and Leather Nat'l B'k, Boston,	40,000	45,200 00	40,000 00
State Nat'l Bank, Boston . .	6,900	8,625 00	6,900 00
Suffolk Nat'l Bank, Boston . .	22,500	27,450 00	22,500 00
Traders' Nat'l Bank, Boston . .	27,200	27,744 00	27,200 00
Tremont Nat'l Bank, Boston . .	45,000	54,900 00	45,000 00
Union Nat'l Bank, Boston . .	20,800	32,032 00	20,800 00
Washington Nat'l Bank, Boston .	35,300	49,420 00	35,300 00
Webster Nat'l Bank, Boston . .	20,000	22,400 00	20,000 00
Mechanics' Nat'l B'k, Newburyport,	21,500	29,240 00	21,500 00
Merchants' Nat'l B'k, Newburyport,	24,520	36,780 00	24,520 00
Ocean Nat'l Bank, Newburyport .	5,250	7,350 00	5,250 00
First Nat'l Bank, Newburyport .	2,800	4,368 00	2,800 00
Gloucester Nat'l Bank, Gloucester .	6,000	7,920 00	6,000 00
	$922,120	$1,214,779 00	$922,120 00

RAILROAD BONDS.

Eastern Railroad	$50,000	$55,000 00	$40,000 00
Providence and Worcester Railroad .	100,000	107,000 00	100,000 00
	$150,000	$162,000 00	$140,000 00

IPSWICH SAVINGS BANK — IPSWICH.

Incorporated March, 1869. Number of corporators, 29.

JOSEPH ROSS, *President*. *Treasurer*, THEODORE F. COGSWELL.

STATEMENT.

LIABILITIES.		ASSETS.	
Deposits . . .	$191,108 93	Public funds	$16,960 00
Earnings undivided .	4,018 47	Loans on public funds .	800 00
Guaranty fund . .	1,805 00	Bank stock	47,125 00
		Loans on real estate . .	98,253 00
		Loans on personal security,	20,540 00
		Loans to counties, cities, or towns	1,000 00
		Deposit in bank on interest,	10,575 00
		Cash on hand . . .	1,679 40
	$196,932 40		$196,932 40

Loans on Public Funds: —
On $1,000 City of Newton coupon bond $800 00

Cash on Deposit in Bank: —
First National Bank, Salem $11,137 45

Whole amount of interest or profits received or earned . . . $11,440 31
Rate and amount of each semi-annual dividend for previous year . . . . { 2 per cent . 3,346 75; 2 per cent . 3,594 22 }
Times for the dividends fixed by the by-laws: fourth Wednesday in January and July.
Average annual per cent of dividends for the term ending at time of and including last extra dividend: 4 per cent.
The total amount of loans, with each specified rate of interest: $4,000, 4½ per cent; $500, 5 per cent; $3,000, 6 per cent; $27,183, 6½ per cent; $85,910, 7 per cent.
Number of outstanding loans which are of an amount not exceeding $3,000 each 189
Aggregate amount of the same 116,593 00
Number of open accounts 972
Number and amount of deposits received for previous year . 836 55,811 57
Number and amount of deposits of and exceeding $300 at any one time for the previous year 46 21,293 00
Number and amount of withdrawals 570 49,298 88
Number of accounts opened the previous year 196
Number of accounts closed the previous year 108
Amount of expenses of the corporation during previous year . . 457 75
Amount of treasurer's bond 25,000 00
Date of examination by commissioner: June 8.

PUBLIC FUNDS.

	Par Value.	Estimated Market Value.	Amount Invested.
United States 4½s, registered . .	$11,000	$12,430 00	$11,000 00
City and town bonds: —			
City of Bangor, Me., 6s . . .	$1,000	$1,100 00	$930 00
of Bath, Me., 6s . . .	1,000	1,000 00	930 00
of Manchester, N.H., 6s . .	500	585 00	500 00
of Manchester, N.H., 6s . .	100	117 00	100 00
of Providence, R.I., 5s . .	2,000	2,330 00	2,000 00
of Dover, N.H., 6s . . .	500	585 00	500 00
Town of Provincetown 5s . .	1,000	1,150 00	1,000 00
	$17,100	$19,297 00	$16,960 00

BANK STOCK.

Salem Nat'l Bank, Salem . .	$2,100	$2,520 00	$2,310 00
Naumkeag Nat'l Bank, Salem .	1,900	2,945 00	2,698 00
Mercantile Nat'l Bank, Salem . .	1,900	2,375 00	2,090 00
First Nat'l Bank, Salem . . .	4,300	5,375 00	4,945 00
Asiatic Nat'l Bank, Salem . .	690	1,035 00	920 00
Merchants' Nat'l Bank, Salem .	1,800	2,520 00	2,412 00
Exchange Nat'l Bank, Salem . .	1,300	1,625 00	1,456 00
Merchants' Nat'l Bank, Boston .	3,600	5,256 00	5,004 00
Republic Nat'l Bank, Boston . .	2,500	3,125 00	3,150 00
Second Nat'l Bank, Boston .	400	606 00	580 00
Atlas Nat'l Bank, Boston . .	1,000	1,250 00	1,175 00
Commerce Nat'l Bank, Boston .	400	516 00	400 00
Union Nat'l Bank, Boston . .	2,400	3,678 00	3,360 00
Globe Nat'l Bank, Boston . .	2,500	2,787 50	2,500 00
Revere Nat'l Bank, Boston . .	800	972 00	800 00
Howard Nat'l Bank, Boston . .	2,000	2,610 00	2,400 00
Pacific Nat'l Bank, Boston . .	4,000	4,200 00	4,260 00
New England Nat'l Bank, Boston .	4,000	5,940 00	6,000 00
Gloucester Nat'l Bank, Gloucester .	500	675 00	665 00
	$36,090	$50,010 50	$47,125 00

LAWRENCE SAVINGS BANK — LAWRENCE.

Incorporated March 10, 1868. Number of corporators, 81.

MILTON BONNEY, *President*. *Treasurer*, WILLIAM R. SPALDING.

STATEMENT.

LIABILITIES.		ASSETS.	
Deposits . . .	$335,091 08	Public funds . . .	$24,000 00
Earnings undivided .	19,447 36	Bank stock . . .	73,500 00
Guaranty fund . .	4,746 04	Railroad bonds . . .	5,000 00
		Real estate by foreclosure .	23,973 36
		Loans on real estate . .	157,709 00
		Loans on personal security,	7,129 85
		Deposit in banks on interest,	56,984 73
		Expense account . . .	1,023 89
		Cash on hand . . .	9,963 65
	$359,284 48		$359,284 48

Cash on Deposit in Banks, amount in each: —

National Bank of the Commonwealth, Boston . .		$21,984 78
Pemberton National Bank, Lawrence		41,775 95
Amount of real estate held by foreclosure		$23,973 36
Assessed value of the same		18,450 00
Amount of income received from the same		2,127 59
Amount of municipal tax on real estate		295 20
Whole amount of interest or profits received or earned . . .		$20,860 55
Rate and amount of each semi-annual dividend for previous years	2 per cent .	6,329 69
	2 per cent .	6,355 23

Times for the dividends fixed by the by-laws: Jan. 1 and July 1.

The total amount of loans, with each specified rate of interest: $5,400, 5 per cent; $37,287.85, 6 per cent; $122,151, 7 per cent.

Number of outstanding loans which are of an amount not exceeding $3,000 each	168	
Aggregate amount of the same		122,188 85
Number of open accounts	1,332	
Number and amount of deposits received for previous year,	1,115	94,746 12
Number and amount of deposits of and exceeding $300 at any one time for the previous year	76	42,377 12
Number and amount of withdrawals	812	84,791 79
Number of accounts opened the previous year	291	
Number of accounts closed the previous year	313	
Amount of expenses of the corporation during previous year .		1,600 00
Amount of treasurer's bond		10,000 00

Date of examination by commissioner: March 30.

PUBLIC FUNDS.

	Par Value.	Estimated Market Value.	Amount Invested.
United States 4s	$22,000	$25,547 50	$22,000 00
" " 6s	1,000	1,300 00	1,000 00
City bonds: —			
City of Lawrence 6s . .	$1,000	$1,210 00	$1,000 00
	$24,000	$28,057 50	$24,000 00

BANK STOCK.

Commerce Nat'l Bank, Boston .	$2,700	$3,476 25	$2,700 00
North America Nat'l Bank, Boston .	2,300	2,645 00	2,300 00
Market Nat'l Bank, Boston . .	5,600	6,202 00	5,600 00
Pemberton Nat'l Bank, Lawrence .	4,000	5,400 00	4,000 00
Traders' Nat'l Bank, Boston . .	2,100	2,142 00	2,100 00
Howard Nat'l Bank, Boston . .	1,500	1,952 00	1,500 00
State Nat'l Bank, Boston . .	5,400	6,777 00	5,400 00
Webster Nat'l Bank, Boston . .	8,900	9,923 50	8,900 00
City Nat'l Bank, Boston . . .	1,000	1,270 00	1,000 00
Eliot Nat'l Bank, Boston . . .	2,400	2,886 00	2,400 00
Atlas Nat'l Bank, Boston . .	2,000	2,500 00	2,000 00
Hide and Leather Nat'l B'k, Boston .	10,300	11,999 50	10,300 00
Third Nat'l Bank, Boston . .	3,400	3,621 00	3,400 00
Merchants' Nat'l Bank, Boston .	2,000	2,920 00	2,000 00
Commonwealth Nat'l Bank, Boston,	2,700	3,361 50	2,700 00
Lawrence Nat'l Bank, Lawrence .	700	735 00	700 00
Central Nat'l Bank, Boston . .	5,500	6,600 00	5,500 00
First Ward Nat'l Bank, Boston .	1,600	1,920 00	1,600 00
Fourth Nat'l Bank, Boston . .	2,500	2,750 00	2,500 00
Blackstone Nat'l Bank, Boston .	2,900	3,335 00	2,900 00
Tremont Nat'l Bank, Boston . .	4,000	4,880 00	4,000 00
	$73,500	$87,295 75	$73,500 00

RAILROAD BONDS.

Fitchburg Railroad . .	$5,000	$5,862 50	$5,000 00

LEE SAVINGS BANK — LEE.

Incorporated March 5, 1852. Number of corporators, 75.

HARRISON GARFIELD, *President*. *Treasurer*, JOHN L. KILBON.

STATEMENT.

Liabilities.		Assets.	
Deposits . . .	$518,333 57	Public funds	$92,000 00
Earnings undivided .	9,049 00	Bank stock	110,200 00
Guaranty fund . .	10,000 00	Loans on bank stock . .	700 00
		Real estate by foreclosure .	4,821 56
		Loans on real estate . .	263,099 77
		Loans on personal security,	24,592 00
		Loans to counties, cities, or towns	20,000 00
		Expense account . .	564 32
		Premium account . . .	14,171 25
		Cash on deposit in Lee National Bank . . .	7,233 67
	$537,382 57		$537,382 57

Loans on Bank Stock: —

On 11 shares Lee National Bank, Lee $700 00

Cash on Deposit in Bank: —

Lee National Bank, Lee $7,233 67

Amount of real estate held by foreclosure	$4,821 56
Assessed value of the same	4,925 00
Amount of income received from the same	42 80
Amount of municipal tax on real estate	54 03

Whole amount of interest or profits received or earned . . . $35,277 55

Rate and amount of each semi-annual dividend for previous year . . . . { 2 per cent . 9,610 81; 2 per cent . 10,054 81 }

Times for the dividends fixed by the by-laws: May 31 and Nov. 30.

Average annual per cent of dividends for the term ending at time of and including last extra dividend: $5\frac{8}{10}$ per cent.

The total amount of loans, with each specified rate of interest: $5,000, 5 per cent; $303,391.77, 6 per cent.

Number of outstanding loans which are of an amount not exceeding $3,000 each	264	
Aggregate amount of the same		209,289 75
Number of open accounts	1,629	
Number and amount of deposits received for previous year,	1,144	81,822 43
Number and amount of deposits of and exceeding $300 at any one time for the previous year	64	33,696 91
Number and amount of withdrawals	817	87,984 20
Number of accounts opened the previous year	225	
Number of accounts closed the previous year	188	
Amount of expenses of the corporation during previous year .		1,606 25
Amount of treasurer's bond		10,000 00

Date of examination by commissioner: Aug. 1.

PUBLIC FUNDS.

	Par Value.	Estimated Market Value.	Amount Invested.
United States 4½s	$40,000	$45,200 00	$40,000 00
State, city, and town bonds: —			
State of Massachusetts 5s . .	$20,000	$23.500 00	$20,000 00
City of Springfield 7s . . .	10,000	12,100 00	10,000 00
of Boston 4s and 5s . . .	10,000	10,530 00	10,000 00
of Hartford, Conn., 4½s . .	2,000	2,140 00	2.000 00
Town of Sandisfield 7s . . .	10,000	10,000 00	10,000 00
	$92,000	$103,470 00	$92,000 00

BANK STOCK.

Lee Nat'l Bank, Lee . . .	$18,900	$22.950 00	$18,900 00
Adams Nat'l Bank, North Adams .	7,000	9,800 00	7,000 00
First Nat'l Bank, Adams . .	3,300	5.115 00	3,300 00
Pittsfield Nat'l Bank, Pittsfield .	6,000	9,360 00	6,000 00
Housatonic Nat'l B'k, Stockbridge,	5,000	7,500 00	5,000 00
Everett Nat'l Bank, Boston . .	1,500	1,740 00	1,500 00
Continental Nat'l Bank, Boston .	2,300	2,714 00	2,300 00
Massachusetts Nat'l Bank, Boston .	2.500	3,100 00	2,500 00
Hamilton Nat'l Bank, Boston . .	1,000	1.230 00	1,000 00
First Nat'l Bank, Boston . . .	10,000	20,700 00	10,000 00
Merchandise Nat'l Bank, Boston .	5,000	5,500 00	5.000 00
Atlas Nat'l Bank, Boston . .	2,800	3,500 00	2,800 00
Atlantic Nat'l Bank, Boston . .	1,000	1,535 00	1,000 00
Hide and Leather Nat'l B'k, Boston,	6,500	7,475 00	6,500 00
Eagle Nat'l Bank, Boston . .	6,800	8,160 00	6,800 00
Revere Nat'l Bank, Boston . .	4,000	4,840 00	4.000 00
State Nat'l Bank, Boston . .	1,500	1,875 00	1,500 00
Webster Nat'l Bank, Boston . .	3,500	3,920 00	3,500 00
Commerce Nat'l Bank, Boston .	5,500	7,040 00	5,500 00
Redemption Nat'l Bank, Boston .	5,000	6.250 00	5,000 00
Commonwealth Nat'l Bank, Boston,	1,000	1,200 00	1,000 00
Republic Nat'l Bank, Boston . .	1,000	1,250 00	1,000 00
North America Nat'l Bank, Boston .	9,100	10,374 00	9,100 00
	$110,200	$147,128 00	$110,200 00

LEICESTER SAVINGS BANK – LEICESTER.

Incorporated 1869. Number of corporators, 43.

LORY S. WATSON, *President*. *Treasurer*, D. E. MERRIAM.

STATEMENT.

LIABILITIES.		ASSETS.	
Deposits . . .	$300,739 73	Public funds . . .	$81,806 25
Earnings undivided .	8,125 04	Bank stock	49,849 12
Guaranty fund . .	5,245 76	Loans on bank stock . .	1,000 00
		Railroad bonds . .	3,030 00
		Real estate by foreclosure .	1,100 00
		Loans on real estate . .	140,255 38
		Loans on personal security,	11,550 00
		Deposit in bank on interest,	22,787 24
		Expense account . . .	3 00
		Premium account . .	2,729 54
	$314,110 53		$314,110 53

Loans on Bank Stock: —
On 10 shares Leicester National Bank, Leicester . . . $1,000 00

Cash on Deposit in Bank: —
Leicester National Bank, Leicester $22,787 24

Amount of real estate held by foreclosure $1,100 00
Assessed value of the same 900 00
Amount of municipal tax on real estate 15 12

Whole amount of interest or profits received or earned . . . $15,336 82
Rate and amount of each semi-annual dividend for previous year . . . . { 2 per cent . 5,520 88; 2 per cent . 5,693 68 }
Times for the dividends fixed by the by-laws: June 1 and Dec. 1.
Average annual per cent of dividends for the term ending at time of and including last extra dividend: 4 per cent.
The total amount of loans, with each specified rate of interest: $28,550, 5 per cent; $118,095.38, 6 per cent; $5,325, 7 per cent; $835, 7½ per cent; $1,100, 8 per cent.
Number of outstanding loans which are of an amount not exceeding $3,000 each 101
Aggregate amount of the same 91,605 00
Amount of investments from which no income is received . . 1,100 00
Number of open accounts 664
Number and amount of deposits received for previous year . 336 27,284 78
Number and amount of deposits of and exceeding $300 at any one time for the previous year 28 13,329 29
Number and amount of withdrawals 233 22,603 54
Number of accounts opened the previous year 65
Number of accounts closed the previous year 49
Amount of expenses of the corporation during previous year . 1,034 75
Amount of treasurer's bond 10,000 00
Date of examination by commissioner: June 9.

PUBLIC FUNDS.

	Par Value.	Estimated Market Value.	Amount Invested.
United States 4½s	$10,000	$11,200 00	$10,000 00
" " 4s	20,000	23,000 00	20,000 00
City and town bonds: —			
City of Worcester 6s	$12,000	$14,040 00	$12,000 00
of Chelsea 6s	8,000	9,840 00	8,000 00
of Lynn 6s	9,000	10,600 00	9,000 00
of Fall River 6s	1,000	1,240 00	1,000 00
of Springfield 7s	2,000	2,360 00	2,000 00
of Somerville 5s	10,000	10,800 00	10,806 25
Town of Natick 7s	9,000	9,540 00	9,000 00
	$81,000	$92,620 00	$81,806 25

BANK STOCK.

	Par Value.	Estimated Market Value.	Amount Invested.
Eliot Nat'l Bank, Boston . .	$3,000	$3,600 00	$3,610 00
Hide and Leather Nat'l B'k, Boston,	5,000	5,750 00	5,954 40
North Nat'l Bank, Boston . .	2,000	2,840 00	2,425 00
North America Nat'l Bank, Boston .	1,200	1,374 00	1,346 00
Market Nat'l Bank, Boston . .	1,500	1,650 00	1,815 40
State Nat'l Bank, Boston . .	5,000	6,250 00	5,397 50
Webster Nat'l Bank, Boston . .	3,000	3,330 00	3,162 50
Continental Nat'l Bank, Boston .	1,000	1,180 00	1,150 00
Maverick Nat'l Bank, Boston . .	1,000	2,500 00	1,178 75
Revere Nat'l Bank, Boston . .	1,500	1,815 00	1,925 00
Commonwealth Nat'l Bank, Boston,	1,000	1,200 00	1,100 00
Traders' Nat'l Bank, Boston . .	2,500	2,540 00	2,612 50
Howard Nat'l Bank, Boston . .	2,500	3,250 00	2,635 00
Leicester Nat'l Bank, Leicester .	8,700	10,005 00	10,697 57
Central Nat'l Bank, Worcester .	2,500	3,500 00	3,525 00
Millbury Nat'l Bank, Millbury .	1,100	1,375 00	1,314 50
	$42,500	$52,159 00	$49,849 12

RAILROAD BONDS.

	Par Value.	Estimated Market Value.	Amount Invested.
Eastern Railroad 4½s	$3,000	$3,300 00	$3,030 00

LEOMINSTER SAVINGS BANK — LEOMINSTER.

Incorporated 1865. Number of corporators, 35.

LEONARD BURRAGE, *President*. *Treasurer*, H. L. BURDITT.

STATEMENT.

LIABILITIES.		ASSETS.	
Deposits . . .	$615,558 92	Bank stock	$89,225 00
Earnings undivided .	2,243 09	Loans on bank stock . .	1,900 00
Guaranty fund . .	8,000 00	Real estate by foreclosure .	18,474 45
		Loans on real estate . .	352,480 00
		Loans on personal security,	82,850 00
		Loans to counties, cities, or towns	21,700 00
		Deposit in bank on interest,	47,500 00
		Expense account . . .	235 79
		Loans on depositors' books,	390 00
		Cash on hand and in bank,	11,046 77
	$625,802 01		$625,802 01

Loans on Bank Stock: —

On 37 shares First National Bank, Leominster $1,900 00

Cash on Deposit in Bank: —

First National Bank, Leominster . . . $57,500 00

Amount of real estate held by foreclosure	$18,474 45
Assessed value of the same	19,900 00
Amount of income received from the same . . .	843 00
Amount of municipal tax on real estate	235 79

Whole amount of interest or profits received or earned . . .		$33,814 69
Rate and amount of each semi-annual dividend for previous year	2 per cent .	11,784 31
	2 per cent .	11,800 69

Times for the dividends fixed by the by-laws: Jan. 1 and July 1.

Average annual per cent of dividends for the term ending at time of and including last extra dividend: 5 per cent.

The total amount of loans, with each specified rate of interest: $21,700, 4 per cent; $447,620, 6 per cent.

Number of outstanding loans which are of an amount not exceeding $3,000 each	368	
Aggregate amount of the same		303,820 00
Number of open accounts	1,921	
Number and amount of deposits received for previous year,	1,282	108,229 22
Number and amount of deposits of and exceeding $300 at any one time for the previous year	91	55,739 25
Number and amount of withdrawals	1,034	111,960 03
Number of accounts opened the previous year	339	
Number of accounts closed the previous year	275	
Amount of expenses of the corporation during previous year . .		1,820 15
Amount of treasurer's bond		40,000 00

Date of examination by commissioner: May 24.

BANK STOCK.

	Par Value.	Estimated Market Value.	Amount Invested.
First Nat'l Bank, Leominster . .	$38,100	$39,905 00	$38,125 00
Safety Fund Nat'l Bank, Fitchburg,	8,000	8,960 00	8,000 00
Webster Nat'l Bank, Boston . .	7,500	8,325 00	7,500 00
Boston Nat'l Bank, Boston . .	6,200	7,936 00	6,200 00
Traders' Nat'l Bank Boston . .	2,600	2,652 00	2,600 00
Central Nat'l Bank, Boston . .	2,700	3,240 00	2,700 00
Globe Nat'l Bank, Boston . .	6,100	6,771 00	6,100 00
Market Nat'l Bank, Boston . .	1,000	1,090 00	1,000 00
Blackstone Nat'l Bank, Boston .	500	575 00	500 00
Eliot Nat'l Bank, Boston . .	2,500	3,000 00	2,500 00
Everett Nat'l Bank, Boston . .	3,400	3,944 00	3,400 00
Continental Nat'l Bank, Boston .	2,000	2,360 00	2,000 00
Boylston Nat'l Bank, Boston . .	1,500	1,920 00	1,500 00
Eagle Nat'l Bank, Boston . .	1,700	2,040 00	1,700 00
Pacific Nat'l Bank, Boston . .	1,000	1,040 00	1,000 00
Shoe and Leather Nat'l B'k, Boston,	200	226 00	200 00
Merchandise Nat'l Bank, Boston .	200	218 00	200 00
Commonwealth Nat'l Bank, Boston,	1,000	1,200 00	1,000 00
North America Nat'l Bank, Boston,	3,000	3,420 00	3,000 00
	$89,200	$98,822 00	$89,225 00

LOWELL FIVE CENTS SAVINGS BANK—LOWELL.

Incorporated 1854. Number of corporators, 110.

HORATIO WOOD, *President*. *Treasurer*, ARTEMAS S. TYLER.

STATEMENT.

LIABILITIES.		ASSETS.	
Deposits . . .	$1,431,462 51	Public funds . . .	$72,975 00
Earnings undivided .	143,226 91	Bank stock	150,571 50
Guaranty fund . .	21,304 81	Real estate	65,000 00
Suspense . . .	2,000 00	Real estate by foreclosure .	436,661 30
		Loans on real estate . .	604,100 00
		Loans on personal security,	151,440 00
		Loans to counties, cities, or towns	42,500 00
		Deposit in banks on interest,	70,350 80
		Expense account . . .	2,603 33
		Loans on bank books . .	600 00
		Cash on hand . . .	1,192 30
	$1,597,994 23		$1,597,994 23

Cash on Deposit in Banks, amount in each:—

Prescott National Bank, Lowell	$52,867 26
Appleton National Bank, Lowell	8,644 35
National Bank of the Commonwealth, Boston	8,830 19

Amount invested in real estate (for banking purposes) . . .	$65,000 00
Estimated value of the same	65,000 00
Amount of real estate held by foreclosure	436,661 30
Assessed value of the same	310,100 00
Amount of income received from the same	13,772 15
Amount of municipal tax on real estate	4,763 29

Whole amount of interest or profits received or earned		$91,974 34
Rate and amount of each semi-annual dividend for previous year	1 per cent .	16,063 88
	2 per cent .	29,620 53

Times for the dividends fixed by the by-laws: January and July.

Average annual per cent of dividends for the term ending at time of and including last extra dividend: $4\frac{3}{5}$ per cent.

The total amount of loans, with each specified rate of interest: $4,000, 3 per cent; $9,500, $3\frac{1}{4}$ per cent; $2,000, 4 per cent; $2,000, $4\frac{1}{4}$ per cent; $49,000, $4\frac{1}{2}$ per cent; $50,000, $4\frac{3}{4}$ per cent; $162,000, 5 per cent; $6,000, $5\frac{1}{2}$ per cent; $379,340, 6 per cent; $60,400, $6\frac{1}{2}$ per cent; $66,600, 7 per cent; $1,300, $7\frac{3}{10}$ per cent; $5,700, $7\frac{1}{2}$ per cent; $800, 8 per cent.

Number of outstanding loans which are of an amount not exceeding $3,000 each	71	
Aggregate amount of the same		103,340 00
Amount of investments from which no income is received . .		50,161 30
Number of open accounts	6,901	
Number and amount of deposits received for previous year,	1,670	145,024 49
Number and amount of deposits of and exceeding $300 at any one time for the previous year	91	51,254 79

Number and amount of withdrawals	3,310	$396,579 54
Number of accounts opened the previous year	502	
Number of accounts closed the previous year . . .	1,567	
Amount of expenses of the corporation during previous year .		6,952 21
Amount of treasurer's bond		30,000 00

Date of examination by commissioner: June 21.

PUBLIC FUNDS.

	Par Value.	Estimated Market Value.	Amount Invested.
City and town bonds: —			
City of Cambridge . . .	$15,000	$16,500 00	$15,000 00
of Charlestown . .	10,000	10,900 00	10,000 00
of Lawrence . . .	10,000	10,600 00	10,000 00
of Lowell	35,000	40,250 00	32,975 00
Town of Plymouth . . .	5,000	5,350 00	5,000 00
	$75,000	$83,600 00	$72,975 00

BANK STOCK.

Atlas Nat'l Bank, Boston . .	$3,900	$4,875 00	$3,900 00
Blackstone Nat'l Bank, Boston .	4,500	5,175 00	4,500 00
Boylston Nat'l Bank, Boston . .	5,200	6,656 00	5,200 00
Continental Nat'l Bank, Boston .	7,000	8,295 00	7,000 00
City Nat'l Bank, Boston . . .	1,300	1,651 00	1,300 00
Commerce Nat'l Bank, Boston .	1,400	1,802 50	1,100 00
Commonwealth Nat'l Bank, Boston,	1,000	1,245 00	1,000 00
Eliot Nat'l Bank, Boston . .	5,000	6,012 50	5,000 00
Eagle Nat'l Bank, Boston . .	2,800	3,353 00	2,800 00
Exchange Nat'l Bank, Boston . .	1,000	1,440 00	1,000 00
Everett Nat'l Bank, Boston . .	400	468 00	400 00
Freeman's Nat'l Bank, Boston .	5,000	5,987 50	5,000 00
Globe Nat'l Bank, Boston . .	5,200	5,798 00	5,200 00
Hamilton Nat'l Bank, Boston . .	3,400	4,207 50	3,400 00
Hide and Leather Nat'l B'k, Boston,	1,500	1,747 50	1,500 00
North America Nat'l Bank, Boston .	9,000	10,350 00	9,450 00
Revere Nat'l Bank, Boston . .	2,700	3,294 00	2,700 00
Redemption Nat'l Bank, Boston .	5,600	7,588 00	5,600 00
State Nat'l Bank, Boston . .	2,000	2,510 00	2,000 00
Suffolk Nat'l Bank, Boston . .	9,200	11,201 00	9,200 00
Second Nat'l Bank, Boston . .	2,500	3,787 50	2,500 00
Shawmut Nat'l Bank, Boston . .	500	637 50	500 00
Shoe and Leather Nat'l B'k, Boston,	1,000	1,130 00	1,000 00
Tremont Nat'l Bank, Boston . .	7,100	8,662 00	7,100 00
Union Nat'l Bank, Boston . .	2,200	3,377 00	2,200 00
Washington Nat'l Bank, Boston .	900	1,260 00	900 00
First Nat'l Bank, Lowell . .	8,500	12,750 00	11,305 00
Old Lowell Nat'l Bank, Lowell .	8,300	9,960 00	10,970 50
Merchants' Nat'l Bank, Lowell .	3,500	4,655 00	3,540 00
Prescott Nat'l Bank, Lowell . .	13,500	18,225 00	16,806 00
Railroad Nat'l Bank, Lowell . .	15,000	18,150 00	16,200 00
	$140,100	$176,250 50	$150,571 50

LOWELL INSTITUTION FOR SAVINGS—LOWELL.

Incorporated 1829. Number of corporators, 64.

THEODORE EDSON, *President*. *Treasurer*, GEORGE J. CARNEY.

STATEMENT.

LIABILITIES.		ASSETS.	
Deposits . . .	$3,510,253 80	Public funds . . .	$980,000 00
Earnings undivided .	62,629 97	Bank stock . . .	344,200 00
Guaranty fund . .	67,187 15	Loans on bank stock . .	22,500 00
		Real estate	20,334 06
		Loans on real estate . .	469,630 00
		Loans to counties, cities, or towns	1,305,800 00
		Deposit in banks on interest,	497,606 86
	$3,640,070 92		$3,640,070 92

Loans on Bank Stock:—

On 250 shares Wamesit National Bank, Lowell $22,500 00

Cash on Deposit in Banks, amount in each:—

Prescott National Bank, Lowell	$3,000 00
First National Bank, Lowell	50,000 00
Wamesit National Bank, Lowell	80,000 00
Merchants' National Bank, Lowell	364,606 86

Amount invested in real estate (for banking purposes)	$20,334 06
Estimated value of the same	20,334 06
Amount of municipal tax on real estate	486 70

Whole amount of interest or profits received or earned		$190,162 20
Rate and amount of each semi-annual dividend for previous year	2 per cent .	57,017 88
	2 per cent .	63,546 07

Times for the dividends fixed by the by-laws: first Saturday in May and November.

Average annual per cent of dividends for the term ending at time of and including last extra dividend: $7\frac{307}{1000}$ per cent.

The total amount of loans, with each specified rate of interest: $65,000, 2 per cent; $100,000, $3\frac{7}{8}$ per cent; $75,000, 4 per cent; $50,000, $4\frac{29}{100}$ per cent; $85,300, $4\frac{3}{4}$ per cent; $20,000, $4\frac{9}{10}$ per cent; $125,500, 5 per cent; $691,550, 6 per cent; $1,000, $6\frac{1}{4}$ per cent; $200,000, $6\frac{1}{2}$ per cent; $229,000, $6\frac{6}{10}$ per cent; $155,580, 7 per cent.

Number of outstanding loans which are of an amount not exceeding $3,000 each.	39	
Aggregate amount of the same		60,680 00
Number of open accounts	9,867	
Number and amount of deposits received for previous year,	24,848	933,111 56
Number and amount of deposits of and exceeding $300 at any one time for the previous year	691	384,843 00
Number and amount of withdrawals	5,393	592,508 03

Number of accounts opened the previous year . . . 2,474
Number of accounts closed the previous year . . . 1,327
Amount of expenses of the corporation during previous year . $5,600 00
Amount of treasurer's bond 20,000 00
Date of examination by commissioner: Oct. 11.

Public Funds.

	Par Value.	Estimated Market Value.	Amount Invested.
United States 4½s, 1891 . . .	$65,000	$72,800 00	$65,000 00
" " 5s, extended . .	915,000	932,156 25	915,000 00
	$980,000	$1,004,956 25	$980,000 00

Bank Stock.

	Par Value.	Estimated Market Value.	Amount Invested.
Atlas Nat'l Bank, Boston . .	$15,000	$19,500 00	$15,000 00
Boylston Nat'l Bank, Boston . .	17,500	22,400 00	17,500 00
Columbian Nat'l Bank, Boston .	17,900	26,134 00	17,900 00
Eagle Nat'l Bank, Boston . .	45,000	54,450 00	45,000 00
Freeman's Nat'l Bank, Boston. .	3,600	4,572 00	3,600 00
Hamilton Nat'l Bank, Boston . .	55,000	68,200 00	55,000 00
Merchants' Nat'l Bank, Boston .	34,100	51,150 00	34,100 00
Mount Vernon Nat'l Bank, Boston .	500	635 00	500 00
New England Nat'l Bank, Boston .	16,100	24,633 00	16,100 00
Republic Nat'l Bank, Boston . .	24,500	32,340 00	24,500 00
Second Nat'l Bank, Boston . .	47,300	72,842 00	47,300 00
Tremont Nat'l Bank, Boston . .	15,200	19,152 00	15,200 00
Union Nat'l Bank, Boston . .	500	765 00	500 00
Washington Nat'l Bank, Boston .	3,200	4,480 00	3,200 00
Railroad Nat'l Bank, Lowell . .	26,000	31,200 00	26,000 00
First Nat'l Bank, Lowell. . .	16,000	24,000 00	16,000 00
Merchants' Nat'l Bank, Lowell .	6,800	8,500 00	6,800 00
	$344,200	$464,953 00	$344,200 00

LYNN FIVE CENTS SAVINGS BANK — LYNN.

Incorporated 1854. Number of corporators, 61.

HENRY A. PEVEAR, *President*. *Treasurer*, HENRY E. NEWHALL.

STATEMENT.

LIABILITIES.		ASSETS.	
Deposits	$1,559,422 67	Public funds	$122,888 53
Earnings undivided .	67,496 87	Loans on public funds .	75,500 00
Guaranty fund . .	19,300 00	Bank stock	360,588 97
		Loans on bank stock . .	6,400 00
		Railroad bonds	9,983 65
		Real estate	35,000 00
		Real estate by foreclosure .	21,883 40
		Loans on real estate . .	705,605 42
		Loans on personal security,	121,116 00
		Loans to counties, cities, or towns	79,312 50
		Deposit in banks on interest,	100,433 99
		Expense account . . .	1,288 20
		Tax titles	423 21
		Cash on hand . . .	5,795 67
	$1,646,219 54		$1,646,219 54

Loans on Public Funds, amount on each: —

On $75,000 United States 6s, currency	$75,000 00
On $500 United States 4s	500 00

Loans on Bank Stock, amount on each: —

On 85 shares First National Bank, Lynn	$5,000 00
On 6 shares Central National Bank, Lynn	500 00
On 10 shares City National Bank, Lynn	900 00

Cash on Deposit in Banks, amount in each: —

City National Bank, Lynn, ...	$27,920 05
Maverick National Bank, Boston	2,513 94
Merchandise National Bank, Boston	30,000 00
Mount Vernon National Bank, Boston	40,000 00

Amount invested in real estate (for banking purposes)	$35,000 00
Estimated value of the same	35,000 00
Amount of real estate held by foreclosure	21,883 40
Assessed value of the same	27,850 00
Amount of income received from the same	1,196 00
Amount of municipal tax on real estate	1,560 78

Whole amount of interest or profits received or earned	$95,393 45
Rate and amount of each semi-annual dividend for previous year . . . . 2 per cent .	26,843 30
2 per cent .	27,873 85

Times for the dividends fixed by the by-laws: Jan. 1 and July 1.

The total amount of loans, with each specified rate of interest: $9,500, 3 per cent; $29,000, $3\frac{1}{2}$ per cent; $94,400, 4 per cent; $10,500, $4\frac{1}{4}$ per cent; $75,300, $4\frac{1}{2}$ per cent; $25,500, 5 per cent; $1,200, $5\frac{1}{2}$ per cent; $540,022.97, 6 per cent; $149,898.45, $6\frac{1}{2}$ per cent; $28,250, 7 per cent; $2,050, $7\frac{3}{10}$ per cent; $22,300, $7\frac{1}{2}$ per cent.

Number of outstanding loans which are of an amount not exceeding $3,000 each	408	
Aggregate amount of the same		$423,109 00
Number of open accounts	9,046	
Number and amount of deposits received for previous year,	11,050	452,360 43
Number and amount of deposits of and exceeding $300 at any one time for the previous year	206	134,489 00
Number and amount of withdrawals	6,918	395,053 42
Number of accounts opened the previous year	2,120	
Number of accounts closed the previous year	1,493	
Amount of expenses of the corporation during previous year		5,221 42
Amount of treasurer's bond		30,000 00

Date of examination by commissioner: May 27.

Public Funds.

	Par Value.	Estimated Market Value.	Amount Invested.
United States 6s, currency	$50,000	$66,500 00	$43,127 04
" " 4s	20,000	23,200 00	19,913 89
State, city, and town bonds:—			
State of New Hampshire 6s	$1,000	$1,060 00	$1,000 00
of Maine 6s	7,000	8,120 00	7,000 00
City of Cambridge 5s	2,000	2,010 00	2,000 00
of Chelsea 6s	2,000	2,360 00	2,000 00
of Cambridge 6s	1,000	1,015 00	1,072 50
of Lynn 6s	5,000	5,375 00	5,000 00
of Augusta, Me., 6s	2,000	2,120 00	2,000 00
of Providence, R.I., 5s	3,000	3,075 00	3,187 50
Town of Brookline, 7s	10,000	13,300 00	10,000 00
of Plymouth 7s	26,000	27,820 00	26,587 60
	$129,000	$155,955 00	$122,888 53

Bank Stock.

City Nat'l Bank, Lynn	$32,800	$49,200 00	$47,122 50
Central Nat'l Bank, Lynn	9,300	13,578 00	11,863 97
First Nat'l Bank, Lynn	4,400	5,500 00	5,150 00
North Nat'l Bank, Boston	3,000	4,290 00	4,150 25
Exchange Nat'l Bank, Boston	47,000	67,680 00	65,440 37
First Nat'l Bank, Boston	23,500	48,880 00	41,576 75
Globe Nat'l Bank, Boston	8,800	9,856 00	11,500 00
Redemption Nat'l Bank, Boston	25,300	33,902 00	34,000 00
Hide and Leather Nat'l Bank, Boston,	700	833 00	682 50
Revere Nat'l Bank, Boston	6,900	8,418 00	7,031 63
Freeman's Nat'l Bank, Boston	2,500	2,975 00	2,500 00
Shoe and Leather Nat'l B'k, Boston,	1,500	1,710 00	1,500 00
Continental Nat'l Bank, Boston	15,400	18,172 00	21,816 50
Traders' Nat'l Bank, Boston	13,000	13,260 00	13,649 00
Boylston Nat'l Bank, Boston	1,400	1,750 00	1,900 00
Columbian Nat'l Bank, Boston	1,700	2,448 00	2,450 00

BANK STOCK — Concluded.

	Par Value.	Estimated Market Value.	Amount Invested.
Union Nat'l Bank, Boston . .	$12,700	$19,431 00	$18,000 00
Blackstone Nat'l Bank, Boston .	5,600	6,496 00	7,512 50
Merchants' Nat'l Bank, Boston .	13,000	19,110 00	19,325 00
Republic Nat'l Bank, Boston . .	3,000	3,720 00	4,000 00
Tremont Nat'l Bank, Boston . .	12,700	15,494 00	17,000 00
Commonwealth Nat'l Bank, Boston,	5,000	6,350 00	5,000 00
Merchandise Nat'l Bank, Boston .	5,000	5,450 00	5,000 00
North America Nat'l Bank, Boston .	2,000	2,964 00	2,418 00
Georgetown Nat'l Bank, Georgetown,	10,000	9,500 00	10,000 00
	$266,800	$370,967 00	$360,588 97

RAILROAD BONDS.

Eastern Railroad	$10,500	$11,497 50	$9,983 65

LYNN INSTITUTION FOR SAVINGS — LYNN.

Incorporated 1826. Number of corporators, 61.

PHILIP A. CHASE, *President.* *Treasurer*, D. H. SWEETSER.

STATEMENT.

LIABILITIES.		ASSETS.	
Deposits . . .	$1,969,258 71	Public funds . . .	$314,500 00
Earnings undivided .	59,525 55	Loans on public funds .	3,850 00
Guaranty fund . .	46,000 00	Bank stock	214,832 00
		Loans on bank stock . .	44,050 00
		Railroad bonds . . .	19,700 00
		Loans on railroad bonds .	1,000 00
		Real estate	45,000 00
		Real estate by foreclosure .	4,765 68
		Loans on real estate . .	924,998 00
		Loans on personal security,	343,200 00
		Loans to counties, cities, or towns	81,500 00
		Deposit in banks on interest,	67,299 18
		Tax titles	625 20
		Cash on hand . . .	9,464 20
	$2,074,784 26		$2,074,784 26

Loans on Public Funds, amount on each:—

On $3,000 Town of Brookline 7s	$3,000 00
On $1,000 City of Portland 6s	850 00

Loans on Bank Stock, amount on each:—

On 80 shares City National Bank, Lynn	$7,450 00
On 73 shares First National Bank, Lynn	87,200 00
On 250 shares Maverick National Bank, Boston	25,000 00
On 16 shares First National Bank, Lynn . . . . On 18 shares Central National Bank, Lynn . . . . . . On 10 shares Exchange National Bank, Boston	4,400 00

Loans on Railroad Bonds:—

On $1,000 Boston, Revere Beach, and Lynn Railroad . .	$1,000 00

Cash on Deposit in Banks, amount in each:—

Maverick National Bank, Boston	$1,146 11
First National Bank, Lynn	66,153 07

Amount invested in real estate (for banking purposes)	$45,000 00
Estimated value of the same	50,000 00
Amount of real estate held by foreclosure	4,765 68
Assessed value of the same	4,550 00
Amount of income received from the same	270 00
Amount of municipal tax on real estate	609 87

Whole amount of interest or profits received or earned		$115,914 00
Rate and amount of each semi-annual dividend for previous year	2 per cent . 2 per cent .	34,521 76 35,811 20

Times for the dividends fixed by the by-laws: May 1 and Nov. 1.

The total amount of loans, with each specified rate of interest: $44,000, 3½ per cent; $165,300, 4½ per cent; $25,000, 4⅝ per cent; $27,000, 4¾ per cent; $177,900, 5 per cent; $7,500, 5½ per cent; $773,199, 6 per cent; $40,600, 6½ per cent; $138,099, 7 per cent.

Number of outstanding loans which are of an amount not exceeding $3,000 each	278	
Aggregate amount of the same		$380,000 00
Number of open accounts	6,126	
Number and amount of deposits received for previous year,	6,252	444,207 00
Number and amount of deposits of and exceeding $300 at any one time for the previous year	331	171,291 00
Number and amount of withdrawals	4,522	371,675 47
Number of accounts opened the previous year	1,169	
Number of accounts closed the previous year	795	
Amount of expenses of the corporation during previous year		5,328 59
Amount of treasurer's bond		50,000 00

Date of examination by commissioner: May 27.

Public Funds.

	Par Value.	Estimated Market Value.	Amount Invested.
United States 6s, extended	$5,000	$5,050 00	$5,000 00
" " 4½s	115,000	128,800 00	115,000 00
" " 4s	40,000	46,400 00	40,000 00
City and town bonds: —			
City of Cambridge 6s	$10,000	$11,800 00	$10,000 00
of Lynn 5½s	19,000	19,760 00	19,000 00
of Lynn 6s	27,000	29,160 00	27,000 00
of Lynn 6s	1,000	1,200 00	1,000 00
of Lowell 6s	10,000	11,400 00	10,000 00
of Somerville 6s	15,500	16,275 00	15,500 00
of Boston 6s	10,000	11,800 00	10,000 00
of Boston 5s	5,000	5,100 00	5,000 00
of Fall River 5s	25,000	27,500 00	25,000 00
of Lynn 5s	1,000	1,000 00	1,000 00
of Lynn 6s	3,000	3,240 00	3,000 00
Town of Natick 7s	4,000	4,200 00	4,000 00
of Saugus 5s	9,000	9,500 00	9,000 00
of Malden 6s	15,000	16,550 00	15,000 00
	$314,500	$348,735 00	$314,500 00

Bank Stock.

Atlantic Nat'l Bank, Boston	$5,300	$7,950 00	$6,625 00
Rockland Nat'l Bank, Boston	10,000	12,800 00	12,000 00
Exchange Nat'l Bank, Boston	5,500	7,700 00	6,270 00
Shoe and Leather Nat'l B'k, Boston,	6,000	6,780 00	6,000 00
New England Nat'l Bank, Boston	5,900	8,555 00	5,900 00

BANK STOCK — Concluded.

	Par Value.	Estimated Market Value.	Amount Invested.
Columbian Nat'l Bank, Boston .	$8,900	$12,905 00	$10,057 00
Market Nat'l Bank, Boston . .	2,500	2,675 00	2,500 00
Shawmut Nat'l Bank, Boston . .	2,000	2,500 00	2,000 00
Freeman's Nat'l Bank, Boston .	1,300	1,534 00	1,300 00
Traders' Nat'l Bank, Boston . .	5,000	5,250 00	5,000 00
Second Nat'l Bank, Boston . .	5,500	8,250 00	6,875 00
Continental Nat'l Bank, Boston .	3,500	4,025 00	3,500 00
Everett Nat'l Bank, Boston . .	5,400	5,940 00	5,400 00
Republic Nat'l Bank, Boston . .	10,000	13,000 00	11,000 00
Union Nat'l Bank, Boston . .	7,300	10,950 00	8,760 00
Blackstone Nat'l Bank, Boston .	5,500	6,050 00	5,500 00
First Nat'l Bank, Boston . .	2,500	5,000 00	3,750 00
Merchandise Nat'l Bank, Boston .	2,500	2,700 00	2,500 00
North America Nat'l Bank, Boston,	3,400	3,808 00	3,400 00
First Nat'l Bank, Lynn . . .	40,000	50,000 00	42,000 00
City Nat'l Bank, Lynn . . .	21,300	34,080 00	26,625 00
Central Nat'l Bank, Lynn . .	30,100	43,645 00	36,120 00
First Nat'l Bank, Lynn . . .	1,400	1,750 00	1,750 00
	$190,800	$257,847 00	$214,832 00

RAILROAD BONDS.

Eastern Railroad 4½s . . .	$21,000	$23,100 00	$19,700 00

MALDEN SAVINGS BANK — MALDEN.

Incorporated March 30, 1860. Number of corporators, 26.

CALEB WAITE, *President*. *Treasurer*, CHARLES MERRILL.

STATEMENT.

LIABILITIES.		ASSETS.	
Deposits . . .	$503,673 21	Public funds . . .	$90,500 00
Earnings undivided .	2,811 79	Bank stock	70,850 00
Guaranty fund . .	5,500 00	Loans on bank stock . .	4,550 00
		Real estate by foreclosure .	1,000 00
		Loans on real estate . .	188,575 00
		Loans on personal security,	26,500 00
		Loans to counties, cities, or towns	20,000 00
		Deposit in banks on interest,	89,805 00
		Expense account . . .	1,205 00
		Premiums	19,000 00
	$511,985 00		$511,985 00

Loans on Bank Stock, amount on each:—

On 25 shares Security National Bank, Boston	$4,000 00
On 7 shares First National Bank, Malden	550 00

Cash on Deposit in Banks, amount in each:—

First National Bank, Malden	$9,805 00
Continental National Bank, Boston	25,000 00
National Bank of Redemption, Boston	20,000 00
Pacific National Bank, Boston	10,000 00
Central National Bank, Boston	15,000 00
Maverick National Bank, Boston	10,000 00

Amount of real estate held by foreclosure	$1,000 00
Assessed value of the same	900 00
Amount of income received from the same	117 00

Whole amount of interest or profits received or earned . . .		$26,521 25
Rate and amount of each semi-annual dividend for previous year	2½ per cent .	10,316 17
	2 per cent .	8,956 59

Times for the dividends fixed by the by-laws: second Wednesday in April and October.

Average annual per cent of dividends for the term ending at time of and including last extra dividend: 5¾ per cent.

The total amount of loans, with each specified rate of interest: $9,805, 2½ per cent; $20,000, 3½ per cent; $94,000, 5 per cent; $10,000, 5½ per cent; $196,625, 6 per cent.

Number of outstanding loans which are of an amount not exceeding $3,000 each	94	
Aggregate amount of the same		139,700 00
Number of open accounts	2,210	
Number and amount of deposits received for previous year,	3,046	143,237 50

24

Number and amount of deposits of and exceeding $300 at any one time for the previous year	140	$70,951 13
Number and amount of withdrawals	1,673	131,233 53
Number of accounts opened the previous year	510	
Number of accounts closed the previous year	210	
Amount of expenses of the corporation during previous year		1,915 33
Amount of treasurer's bond		10,000 00

Date of examination by commissioner: May 2.

Public Funds.

	Par Value.	Estimated Market Value.	Amount Invested.
United States 4½s	$31,500	$35,800 00	$32,964 68
" " 6s, currency	10,000	13,400 00	10,000 00
" " 5s, extended	10,000	10,100 00	10,000 00
City and town bonds: —			
City of Newton 5s	$8,000	$9,200 00	$8,120 00
of Fall River 6s	5,000	5,900 00	5,375 00
of Bangor, Me., 6s	5,000	6,050 00	5,325 00
of Fitchburg 6s	1,000	1,180 00	1,095 00
Town of Brookline 7s	10,000	13,000 00	12,612 50
of Woburn 6s	10,000	11,800 00	10,950 00
	$90,500	$106,430 00	$96,442 18

Bank Stock.

Atlas Nat'l Bank, Boston	$2,000	$2,540 00	$2,000 00
Atlantic Nat'l Bank, Boston	2,300	3,473 00	3,490 75
Commerce Nat'l Bank, Boston	1,300	1,651 00	1,381 25
Continental Nat'l Bank, Boston	2,500	2,975 00	2,335 62
City Nat'l Bank, Boston	3,600	4,464 00	4,354 25
Eagle Nat'l Bank, Boston	2,800	3,304 00	3,143 50
Eliot Nat'l Bank, Boston	800	944 00	920 00
Exchange Nat'l Bank, Boston	6,400	9,216 00	8,953 50
Freeman's Nat'l Bank, Boston	2,500	3,100 00	2,425 00
First Nat'l Bank, Boston	1,500	3,150 00	2,745 00
Globe Nat'l Bank, Boston	2,000	2,240 00	2,045 00
Hamilton Nat'l Bank, Boston	1,000	1,210 00	1,100 00
Howard Nat'l Bank, Boston	1,100	1,408 00	1,100 00
Hide and Leather Nat'l B'k, Boston,	2,000	2,340 00	2,000 00
Massachusetts Nat'l Bank, Boston	1,000	1,240 00	1,080 00
Merchants' Nat'l Bank, Boston	3,000	4,380 00	3,834 75
Market Nat'l Bank, Boston	1,000	1,110 00	1,000 00
North America Nat'l Bank, Boston	1,200	1,536 00	1,130 50
North Nat'l Bank, Boston	1,400	1,974 00	1,778 00
Old Boston Nat'l Bank, Boston	1,050	1,315 00	1,354 75
Revere Nat'l Bank, Boston	700	868 00	707 87
Rockland Nat'l Bank, Boston	500	680 00	653 75
Redemption Nat'l Bank, Boston	5,500	7,260 00	7,361 25
State Nat'l Bank, Boston	4,700	5,875 00	5,539 00
Shawmut Nat'l Bank, Boston	1,600	1,968 00	1,710 87

BANK STOCK — Concluded.

	Par Value.	Estimated Market Value.	Amount Invested.
Security Nat'l Bank, Boston . .	$3,100	$5,797 00	$5,436 23
Suffolk Nat'l Bank, Boston . .	1,200	1,464 00	1,363 50
Traders' Nat'l Bank, Boston . .	1,500	1,545 00	1,480 00
Tremont Nat'l Bank, Boston . .	1,000	1,230 00	1,015 00
Webster Nat'l Bank, Boston . .	3,000	3,390 00	3,256 25
Malden Nat'l Bank, Boston . .	7,600	8,740 00	7,600 00
	$70,850	$92,387 00	$84,295 59

MARBLEHEAD SAVINGS BANK — MARBLEHEAD.

Incorporated 1871. Number of corporators, 41.

ISAAC C. WYMAN, *President.* *Treasurer,* WILLIAM GILLEY.

STATEMENT.

LIABILITIES.		ASSETS.	
Deposits . . .	$186,192 45	Public funds . . .	$31,816 47
Earnings undivided .	3,388 69	Bank stock	55,818 96
Guaranty fund . .	2,219 57	Real estate by foreclosure .	32,201 48
		Loans on real estate . .	48,314 00
		Loans on personal security,	10,419 70
		Loans to counties, cities, or towns	6,000 00
		Deposit in bank on interest,	4,553 27
		Expense account . . .	1,149 18
		Cash on hand . . .	1,527 63
	$191,800 71		$191,800 71

Cash on Deposit in Bank:—

Marblehead National Bank, Marblehead	$4,553 27

Amount of real estate held by foreclosure	$32,201 48
Assessed value of the same	27,400 00
Amount of income received from the same	2,144 84
Amount of municipal tax on real estate	405 23

Whole amount of interest or profits received or earned . . .		$7,290 40
Rate and amount of each semi-annual dividend for previous years	2 per cent .	3,114 78
	2 per cent .	3,272 12

Times for the dividends fixed by the by-laws: May 1 and Nov. 1.

Average annual per cent of dividends for the term ending at time of and including last extra dividend: 4 per cent.

The total amount of loans, with each specified rate of interest: $6,000, 4 per cent; $10,000, 5 per cent; $17,295.30, 6 per cent; $5,438.40, 6½ per cent; $17,450, 7 per cent; $4,000, 7 3/10 per cent; $600, 7½ per cent; $3,050, 8 per cent.

Number of outstanding loans which are of an amount not exceeding $3,000 each	33	
Aggregate amount of the same		25,800 00
Number of open accounts	1,033	
Number and amount of deposits received for previous year .	749	43,767 00
Number and amount of deposits of and exceeding $300 at any one time for the previous year	33	17,759 00
Number and amount of withdrawals	597	32,158 03
Number of accounts opened the previous year	125	
Number of accounts closed the previous year	96	
Amount of expenses of the corporation during previous year .		1,714 06
Amount of treasurer's bond		10,000 00

Date of examination by commissioner: Aug. 16.

PUBLIC FUNDS.

	Par Value.	Estimated Market Value.	Amount Invested.
United States bonds .	$1,500	$1,740 00	$1,438 13
City and town bonds: —			
City of Charlestown	$3,000	$3,570 00	$3,047 00
of Bangor, Me.	8,000	10,000 00	8,984 67
Town of Arlington	5,000	6,000 00	5,225 00
of Melrose	10,000	13,000 00	13,121 67
	$27,500	$34,310 00	$31,816 47

BANK STOCK.

Marblehead Nat'l Bank, Marblehead,	$1,200	$1,392 00	$1,344 00
Merchants' Nat'l Bank, Boston .	2,500	3,650 00	3,331 25
Shawmut Nat'l Bank, Boston . .	2,500	3,200 00	3,084 37
Shoe and Leather Nat'l Bank, Boston,	2,100	2,375 00	2,366 25
North Nat'l Bank, Boston . .	2,500	3,552 00	3,056 25
Mount Vernon Nat'l Bank, Boston .	2,000	2,560 00	2,505 20
Continental Nat'l Bank, Boston .	2,500	2,975 00	2,687 50
Blackstone Nat'l Bank, Boston .	3,000	3,450 00	3,485 00
Boylston Nat'l Bank, Boston . .	3,100	3,968 00	3,839 50
Merchandise Nat'l Bank, Boston .	1,300	1,320 00	1,297 67
State Nat'l Bank, Boston .	5,600	7,056 00	6,048 45
Hamilton Nat'l Bank, Boston . .	500	560 00	591 25
Market Nat'l Bank, Boston . .	900	990 00	999 00
Hide and Leather Nat'l B'k, Boston,	3,200	3,680 00	3,744 00
Revere Nat'l Bank, Boston . .	400	488 00	442 75
Grand Nat'l Bank, Marblehead . .	3,800	4,408 00	4,639 15
Commerce Nat'l Bank, Boston .	1,900	2,451 00	2,440 00
Redemption Nat'l Bank, Boston .	2,900	3,915 00	4,067 25
North America Nat'l Bank, Boston .	2,500	2,875 00	2,778 12
Republic Nat'l Bank, Boston . .	2,400	3,000 00	3,072 00
	$46,800	$57,865 00	$55,818 96

MARLBOROUGH SAVINGS BANK—MARLBOROUGH.

Incorporated April 3, 1860. Number of corporators, 87.

ELBRIDGE HOWE, *President.* *Treasurer*, EDWARD R. ALLEY.

STATEMENT.

LIABILITIES.		ASSETS.	
Deposits	$760,202 24	Public funds . . .	$165,484 00
Earnings undivided .	22,542 42	Bank stock	121,241 25
Guaranty fund . .	10,617 04	Real estate by foreclosure .	4,000 00
		Loans on real estate . .	411,418 50
		Loans on personal security,	76,827 50
		Deposit in banks on interest,	13,324 93
		Expense account . . .	1,065 52
	$793,361 70		$793,361 70

Cash on Deposit in Banks, amount in each: —

People's National Bank, Marlborough		$2,061 65
First National Bank, Marlborough		11,263 28
Amount of real estate held by foreclosure		$4,000 00
Assessed value of the same		8,500 00
Amount of municipal tax on real estate		175 50
Whole amount of interest or profits received or earned		$42,605 72
Rate and amount of each semi-annual dividend for previous year	2½ per cent . 2 per cent .	15,801 14 13,485 56

Times for the dividends fixed by the by-laws: third Wednesday in January and July.

The total amount of loans, with each specified rate of interest: $10,000, 4 per cent; $43,000, 5 per cent; $234,042, 6 per cent; $5,950, 6½ per cent; $118,426.50, 7 per cent.

Number of outstanding loans which are of an amount not exceeding $3,000 each	279	
Aggregate amount of the same		260,868 50
Amount of investments from which no income is received . .		4,000 00
Number of open accounts	2,551	
Number and amount of deposits received for previous year,	2,094	206,771 00
Number and amount of deposits of and exceeding $300 at any one time for the previous year	190	108,260 00
Number and amount of withdrawals	1,310	144,310 55
Number of accounts opened the previous year	614	
Number of accounts closed the previous year	374	
Amount of expenses of the corporation during previous year . .		1,635 66
Amount of treasurer's bond		10,000 00

Date of examination by commissioner: May 17.

PUBLIC FUNDS.

	Par Value.	Estimated Market Value.	Amount Invested.
United States 4½s, coupons . .	$600	$672 00	$627 00
" " 4s, coupons . .	1,100	1,276 00	1,100 00
City and town bonds:—			
City of Charlestown	$27,000	$31,980 00	$31,057 50
of Boston	21,000	24,800 00	23,090 00
of Fall River	16,000	17,960 00	16,000 00
of Lowell	12,000	14,220 00	11,920 00
of Cambridge	10,000	11,940 00	10,930 00
of Lynn	7,000	8,320 00	8,007 50
of Lewiston, Me. . . .	7,000	7,700 00	7,000 00
of Dover, N.H. . . .	4,400	5,236 00	4,752 00
of Portsmouth, N.H. . .	3,000	3,030 00	3,000 00
of Bangor, Me. . . .	2,500	2,875 00	2,500 00
Town of Marlborough . . .	20,000	21,000 00	20,000 00
of Pawtucket, R.I. . . .	10,000	11,200 00	10,700 00
of Woburn	8,000	8,160 00	8,000 00
of Southborough . . .	6,800	6,800 00	6,800 00
	$156,400	$177,169 00	$165,484 00

BANK STOCK.

Webster Nat'l Bank, Boston . .	$7,500	$8,362 50	$7,875 00
Third Nat'l Bank, Boston . .	7,000	7,455 00	7,175 00
Continental Nat'l Bank, Boston .	6,800	8,058 00	6,800 00
Globe Nat'l Bank, Boston . .	5,000	5,575 00	5,250 00
Faneuil Hall Nat'l Bank, Boston .	4,400	5,918 00	5,528 25
Market Nat'l Bank, Boston . .	4,000	4,420 00	4,000 00
Merchandise Nat'l Bank, Boston .	4,000	4,400 00	4,100 00
City Nat'l Bank, Boston . . .	4,000	5,080 00	4,200 00
North America Nat'l Bank, Boston .	3,000	3,450 00	3,150 00
State Nat'l Bank, Boston . .	3,000	3,750 00	3,150 00
Howard Nat'l Bank, Boston . .	2,000	2,600 00	2,000 00
Eliot Nat'l Bank, Boston . . .	1,600	1,920 00	1,680 00
Manufacturers' Nat'l Bank, Boston .	1,500	1,657 50	1,500 00
Atlas Nat'l Bank, Boston . .	1,500	1,875 00	1,575 00
Eagle Nat'l Bank, Boston . .	1,500	1,796 25	1,575 00
Shoe and Leather Nat'l B'k, Boston,	1,500	1,695 00	1,710 00
Commerce Nat'l Bank, Boston .	1,500	1,931 25	1,800 00
Boston Nat'l Bank, Boston . .	1,000	1,280 00	1,050 00
Blackstone Nat'l Bank, Boston .	800	920 00	878 00
Revere Nat'l Bank, Boston . .	700	854 00	735 00
Hide and Leather Nat'l B'k, Boston,	400	466 00	420 00
City Nat'l Bank, Worcester . .	1,600	1,760 00	1,600 00
First Nat'l Bank, Clinton . .	1,500	1,725 00	1,680 00
First Nat'l Bank, Lynn . . .	3,000	3,900 00	3,150 00
People's Nat'l Bank, Marlborough .	5,300	5,565 00	5,100 00
First Nat'l Bank, Marlborough .	36,300	45,375 00	43,560 00
	$110,400	$131,788 50	$121,241 25

MECHANICS' SAVINGS BANK — HOLYOKE.

Incorporated 1872. Number of corporators, 47.

JAMES H. NEWTON, *President*. *Treasurer*, C. B. PRESCOTT.

STATEMENT.

LIABILITIES.		ASSETS.	
Deposits . . .	$463,325 81	Bank Stock	$38,208 50
Earnings undivided .	8,908 47	Loans on bank stock . .	1,800 00
Guaranty fund . .	4,100 00	Loans on real estate . .	276,795 00
		Loans on personal security,	59,589 00
		Deposit in banks on interest,	91,697 15
		Expense account . . .	1,027 58
		Furniture and fixtures .	2,118 75
		Taxes	1,610 85
		Interest	1,149 34
		Cash on hand . . .	2,338 11
	$476,334 28		$476,334 28

Loans on Bank Stock: —

On 30 shares City National Bank, Holyoke . . $1,800 00

Cash on Deposit in Banks, amount in each: —

City National Bank, Holyoke $91,697 15

Hadley Falls National Bank, Holyoke 372 68

Whole amount of interest or profits received or earned $24,620 47

Rate and amount of each semi-annual dividend for previous year . . . . { 2 per cent . 7,814 87; 2 per cent . 8,405 67 }

Times for the dividends fixed by the by-laws: May and November.

The total amount of loans, with each specified rate of interest: $338,184, 6 per cent.

Number of outstanding loans which are of an amount not exceeding $3,000 each 124

Aggregate amount of the same 135,609 00

Amount of investments from which no income is received . . 18,700 00

Number of open accounts 1,570

Number and amount of deposits received for previous year. 2,403 188,966 87

Number and amount of deposits of and exceeding $300 at any one time for the previous year 136 85,414 00

Number and amount of withdrawals 1,014 155,873 42

Number of accounts opened the previous year 567

Number of accounts closed the previous year . . . 439

Amount of expenses of the corporation during previous year . . 1,454 42

Amount of treasurer's bond 20,000 00

Amount of assistant treasurer's bond 10,000 00

Date of examination by commissioner: July 11.

BANK STOCK.

	Par Value.	Estimated Market Value.	Amount Invested.
Shoe and Leather Nat'l B'k, Boston,	$2,200	$2,530 00	$3,008 50
First Nat'l Bank, Springfield . .	2,000	3,200 00	3,080 00
Third Nat'l Bank, Springfield .	5,000	8,500 00	8,500 00
Hadley Falls Nat'l Bank, Holyoke .	4,500	7,200 00	7,120 00
City Nat'l Bank, Holyoke . .	16,500	18,975 00	16,500 00
	$30,200	$40,405 00	$38,208 50

MECHANICS' SAVINGS BANK — LOWELL.

Incorporated 1861. Number of corporators, 72.

WILLIAM A. BURKE, *President*. *Treasurer*, CHARLES C. HUTCHINSON.

STATEMENT.

LIABILITIES.		ASSETS.	
Deposits	$1,391,936 17	Public funds	$87,000 00
Earnings undivided	41,170 30	Bank stock	171,050 00
Guaranty fund	25,000 00	Loans on bank stock	13,800 00
Suspense account	1,180 00	Railroad bonds	80,000 00
		Real estate	92,175 06
		Real estate by foreclosure	176,452 07
		Loans on real estate	659,325 41
		Loans on personal security,	141,900 00
		Deposit in bank on interest,	33,026 00
		Cash on hand	4,557 93
	$1,459,286 47		$1,459,286 47

Loans on Bank Stock, amount on each: —

On 70 shares National Bank of the Commonwealth, Boston	$7,000 00
On 30 shares Railroad National Bank, Lowell, and 10 shares Prescott National Bank, Lowell	2,800 00
On 20 shares Railroad National Bank, Lowell, and 20 shares Metropolitan National Bank, Boston	4,000 00

Cash on Deposit in Bank: —

Railroad National Bank, Lowell	$33,026 00

Amount invested in real estate (for banking purposes)	$92,175 06
Estimated value of the same	80,000 00
Amount of real estate held by foreclosure	176,452 07
Assessed value of the same	122,600 00
Amount of income received from the same	6,712 37
Amount of municipal tax on real estate	1,721 22

Whole amount of interest or profits received		$71,099 72
Rate and amount of each semi-annual dividend for previous year	2 per cent	25,947 67
	2 per cent	26,348 43

Times for the dividends fixed by the by-laws: first Saturday in June and December.

Average annual per cent of dividends for the term ending at time of and including last extra dividend: $5\frac{97}{100}$ per cent.

The total amount of loans, with each specified rate of interest: $25,000, 3¾ per cent; $58,400, 4 per cent; $30,000, 4½ per cent; $178,300, 5 per cent; $1,800, 5½ per cent; $386,271.84, 6 per cent; $19,500, 6½ per cent; $97,729.57, 7 per cent; $6,500, $7\frac{3}{10}$ per cent; $11,000, 7½ per cent; $524, 8 per cent.

Number of outstanding loans which are of an amount not exceeding $3,000 each	222	
Aggregate amount of the same		274,820 41
Amount of investments from which no income is received		7,000 00
Number of open accounts	3,897	

Number and amount of deposits received for previous year, 2,414 $209,612 70
Number and amount of deposits of and exceeding $300 at any one time for the previous year 404 101,645 97
Number and amount of withdrawals 2,037 208,272 47
Number of accounts opened the previous year 611
Number of accounts closed the previous year 484
Amount of expenses of the corporation during previous year . . 5,718 77
Amount of treasurer's bond 25,000 00
Date of examination by commissioner: July 25.

Public Funds.

	Par Value.	Estimated Market Value.	Amount Invested.
United States 5s, 1881 extended . .	$17,000	$17,297 50	$17,000 00
City and town bonds: —			
City of Lowell	$50,000	$59,000 00	$50,000 00
Town of Woburn	20,000	22,400 00	20,000 00
	$87,000	$98,697 50	$87,000 00

Bank Stock.

New England Nat'l Bank, Boston .	$500	$727 50	$500 00
Traders' Nat'l Bank, Boston . .	800	824 00	800 00
First Nat'l Bank, Boston . .	800	1,600 00	800 00
City Nat'l Bank, Boston . .	900	1,143 00	900 00
Mount Vernon Nat'l Bank, Boston .	1,000	1,250 00	1,000 00
Howard Nat'l Bank, Boston . .	1,300	1,690 00	1,300 00
Merchants' Nat'l Bank, Boston .	1,500	2,190 00	1,500 00
Second Nat'l Bank, Boston . .	2,000	3,030 00	2,000 00
Hide and Leather Nat'l B'k, Boston,	2,000	2,325 00	2,000 00
Eliot Nat'l Bank, Boston. . .	2,500	3,006 25	2,500 00
North America Nat'l Bank, Boston .	3,700	4,255 00	3,700 00
Shawmut Nat'l Bank, Boston . .	3,900	4,953 00	3,900 00
Eagle Nat'l Bank, Boston . .	4,000	4,780 00	4,000 00
North Nat'l Bank, Boston . .	4,300	6,106 00	4,300 00
Everett Nat'l Bank, Boston . .	9,000	10,462 50	9,000 00
Mechanics' Nat'l Bank, Boston .	5,000	6,350 00	5,000 00
Webster Nat'l Bank, Boston . .	5,000	5,575 00	5,000 00
Commerce Nat'l Bank, Boston .	4,500	5,805 00	4,500 00
Boston Nat'l Bank, Boston . .	6,300	8,064 00	6,300 00
Revere Nat'l Bank, Boston . .	16,000	19,520 00	16,000 00
Republic Nat'l Bank, Boston . .	8,300	10,624 00	8,300 00
Blackstone Nat'l Bank, Boston .	9,900	11,682 00	9,900 00
Atlas Nat'l Bank, Boston . .	10,600	13,250 00	10,600 00
Redemption Nat'l Bank, Boston .	28,100	37,935 00	28,100 00
Metropolitan Nat'l Bank, Boston .	4,000	4,810 00	4,000 00
Collateral Loan Company, Boston .	2,800	2,940 00	2,800 00
Railroad Nat'l Bank, Lowell . .	23,300	28,542 50	23,300 00
Bay State Nat'l Bank, Lawrence .	2,250	3,300 00	2,250 00
First Nat'l Bank, Malden . .	6,800	7,480 00	6,800 00
	$171,050	$214,219 75	$171,050 00

RAILROAD BONDS.

	Par Value.	Estimated Market Value.	Amount Invested.
Boston and Maine Railroad . .	$30,000	$38,550 00	$30,000 00
Old Colony Railroad . . .	50,000	62,500 00	50,000 00
	$80,000	$101,050 00	$80,000 00

MEDFORD SAVINGS BANK — MEDFORD.

Incorporated 1869. Number of corporators, 58.

HENRY HASTINGS, *President.* *Treasurer,* DANIEL W. LAWRENCE.

STATEMENT.

LIABILITIES.		ASSETS.	
Deposits	$373,252 84	Public funds	$23,440 00
Earnings undivided .	12,116 46	Loans on public funds .	17,000 00
Guaranty fund . .	5,000 00	Bank stock	23,420 00
Suspense account .	600 00	Real estate by foreclosure .	17,031 76
		Loans on real estate . .	165,175 00
		Loans on personal security,	100,550 00
		Loans to counties, cities, or towns	15,000 00
		Deposit in bank on interest,	28,944 84
		Cash on hand . . .	407 70
	$390,969 30		$390,969 30

Loans on Public Funds, amount on each: —

On $10,000 Commonwealth of Massachusetts 5s . $10,000 00

On $7,000 City of Cambridge 6s 7,000 00

Cash on Deposit in Bank: —

Exchange National Bank, Boston $28,044 84

Amount of real estate held by foreclosure $17,031 76

Assessed value of the same 17,200 00

Amount of income received from the same 787 02

Amount of municipal tax on real estate 268 32

Whole amount of interest or profits received or earned . . . $20,434 22

Rate and amount of each semi-annual dividend for previous year . . . . { $2\frac{1}{4}$ per cent . 8,217 86; 2 per cent . 6,794 51 }

Times for the dividends fixed by the by-laws: first Saturday in May and November.

Average annual per cent of dividends for the term ending at time of and including last extra dividend: $4\frac{2}{3}$ per cent.

The total amount of loans, with each specified rate of interest: $67,000, 4 per cent; $2,000, $4\frac{1}{2}$ per cent; $30,000, 5 per cent; $6,500, $5\frac{1}{4}$ per cent; $82,650, 6 per cent; $51,850, $6\frac{1}{2}$ per cent; $47,275, 7 per cent; $975, $7\frac{3}{10}$ per cent; $2,800, $7\frac{1}{2}$ per cent; $6,675, 8 per cent.

Number of outstanding loans which are of an amount not exceeding $3,000 each 110

Aggregate amount of the same 126,125 00

Number of open accounts 1,512

Number and amount of deposits received for previous year, 1,454 84,563 00

Number and amount of deposits of and exceeding $300 at any one time for the previous year 73 37,810 00

Number and amount of withdrawals 770 75,640 42

Number of accounts opened the previous year 260

Number of accounts closed the previous year 145

Amount of expenses of the corporation during previous year . . $1,000 00
Amount of treasurer's bond 20,000 00
Date of examination by commissioner: April 23.

PUBLIC FUNDS.

	Par Value.	Estimated Market Value.	Amount Invested.
City and town bonds: —			
City of Lynn	$5,000	$5,500 00	$5,000 00
Town of Melrose . . .	5,000	6,100 00	5,000 00
of Medford . . .	12,000	13,440 00	13,440 00
	$22,000	$25,040 00	$23,440 00

BANK STOCK.

	Par Value.	Estimated Market Value.	Amount Invested.
Commerce Nat'l Bank, Boston .	$1,200	$1,548 00	$1,200 00
Hamilton Nat'l Bank, Boston . .	1,500	1,755 00	1,800 00
Blackstone Nat'l Bank, Boston .	3,300	3,795 00	3,500 00
Revere Nat'l Bank, Boston . .	400	488 00	440 00
Eagle Nat'l Bank, Boston . .	1,000	1,200 00	1,120 00
Republic Nat'l Bank, Boston . .	1,500	1,875 00	1,875 00
Commonwealth Nat'l Bank, Boston,	2,000	2,400 00	2,140 00
Monument Nat'l Bank, Boston .	2,500	5,225 00	4,265 00
Market Nat'l Bank, Boston . .	1,000	1,090 00	1,050 00
Hide and Leather Nat'l B'k, Boston,	2,000	2,320 00	2,200 00
Webster Nat'l Bank, Boston . .	1,000	1,110 00	1,030 00
Boston Nat'l Bank, Boston . .	2,500	3,125 00	2,800 00
	$19,900	$25,931 00	$23,420 00

MEDWAY SAVINGS BANK — MEDWAY.

Incorporated 1871. Number of corporators, 54.

M. M. FISHER, *President*. *Treasurer*, O. A. MASON.

STATEMENT.

LIABILITIES.		ASSETS.	
Deposits . . .	$182,853 94	Bank stock	$35,113 75
Earnings undivided .	3,220 42	Loans on bank stock . .	500 00
Guaranty fund . .	4,198 18	Real estate by foreclosure .	9,948 14
		Loans on real estate . .	106,600 00
		Loans on personal security,	28,616 25
		Loans to counties, cities, or towns	6,000 00
		Deposit in bank on interest,	1,803 01
		Expense account . . .	901 63
		Cash on hand . . .	789 76
	$190,272 54		$190,272 54

Loans on Bank Stock: —

On 5 shares Eliot National Bank, Boston . . . $500 00

Cash on Deposit in Bank: —

Central National Bank, Boston $1,803 01

Amount of real estate held by foreclosure	$9,948 14
Assessed value of the same	9,115 00
Amount of income received from the same	402 00
Amount of municipal tax on real estate	127 61

Whole amount of interest or profits received or earned		$10,154 67
Rate and amount of each semi-annual dividend for previous year	2 per cent . 2 per cent .	3,196 01 3,361 66

Times for the dividends fixed by the by-laws: June and December.

Average annual per cent of dividends for the term ending at time of and including last extra dividend: $4\frac{7}{10}$ per cent.

The total amount of loans, with each specified rate of interest: $6,000, $4\frac{1}{2}$ per cent; $63,615, 6 per cent; $72,101.25, 7 per cent.

Number of outstanding loans which are of an amount not exceeding $3,000 each	195	
Aggregate amount of the same		111,716 25
Number of open accounts	788	
Number and amount of deposits received for previous year .	629	74,121 80
Number and amount of deposits of and exceeding $300 at any one time for the previous year	65	36,040 79
Number and amount of withdrawals	736	69,445 00
Number of accounts opened the previous year	104	
Number of accounts closed the previous year	91	
Amount of expenses of the corporation during previous year . .		792 30
Amount of treasurer's bond		10,000 00

Date of examination by commissioner: April 26.

BANK STOCK.

	Par Value.	Estimated Market Value.	Amount Invested.
Wrentham Nat'l Bank, Wretham .	$225	$255 00	$310 00
Merchandise Nat'l Bank, Boston .	4,200	4,704 00	4,454 50
Mount Vernon Nat'l Bank, Boston .	1,500	1,725 00	1,623 75
Market Nat'l Bank, Boston . .	1,000	1,100 00	1,030 00
S. Framingham N'l B'k, S. Fram'm,	2,000	2,000 00	2,000 00
Franklin Nat'l Bank, Franklin .	1,700	1,989 00	1,972 00
Dedham Nat'l Bank, Dedham . .	3,200	3,840 00	3,841 00
Holliston Nat'l Bank, Holliston .	4,200	5,040 00	5,040 00
Central Nat'l Bank, Boston . .	6,500	7,800 00	6,667 50
First Ward Nat'l Bank, Boston .	3,000	3,480 00	3,075 00
Manufacturers' Nat'l Bank, Boston,	5,000	5,300 00	5,100 00
	$32,525	$37,233 00	$35,113 75

MELROSE SAVINGS BANK — MELROSE.

Incorporated April 3, 1872. } Number of corporators, 24.
Organized Aug. 5, 1874. }

DANIEL RUSSELL, *President*. *Treasurer*, E. H. GOSS.

STATEMENT.

LIABILITIES.		ASSETS.	
Deposits . . .	$117,931 81	Public funds . . .	$30,227 50
Earnings undivided .	1,409 49	Bank stock	8,676 50
Guaranty fund . .	812 67	Real estate by foreclosure .	2,680 38
		Loans on real estate . .	59,060 00
		Deposit in banks on interest,	19,248 64
		Expense account . . .	213 08
		Cash on hand . . .	47 87
	$120,153 97		$120,153 97

Cash on Deposit in Bank: —
Everett National Bank . . . $19,248 64

Amount of real estate held by foreclosure . . . $2,680 38
Assessed value of the same 2,500 00
Amount of income received from the same . . . 180 00
Amount of municipal tax on real estate 34 50

Whole amount of interest or profits received or earned . . . $5,823 13
Rate and amount of each semi-annual dividend for previous year . . . . { $2\frac{1}{4}$ per cent . 2,067 89; 2 per cent . 1,792 93 }
Times for the dividends fixed by the by-laws: Jan. 1 and July 1.
The total amount of loans, with each specified rate of interest: $28,500, 6 per cent; $4,700, $6\frac{1}{2}$ per cent; $2,700, $6\frac{3}{4}$ per cent; $23,160, 7 per cent.
Number of outstanding loans which are of an amount not exceeding $3,000 each 41
Aggregate amount of the same 41,060 00
Number of open accounts 761
Number and amount of deposits received for previous year, 1,192 68,697 56
Number and amount of deposits of and exceeding $300 at any one time for the previous year 46 31,262 40
Number and amount of withdrawals 517 42,553 68
Number of accounts opened the previous year 203
Number of accounts closed the previous year 100
Amount of expenses of the corporation during previous year . . 495 82
Amount of treasurer's bond 5,000 00
Date of examination by commissioner: Dec. 1.

PUBLIC FUNDS.

	Par Value.	Estimated Market Value.	Amount Invested.
City and town bonds : —			
City of Dover 6s	$3,000	$3,180 00	$3,150 00
of Portsmouth 6s	1,000	1,060 00	1,048 75
of Portland 6s	5,000	6,150 00	5,218 75
of Lewiston 6s	3,000	3,090 00	3,150 00
of Bangor 6s	1,000	1,015 00	1,020 00
of Brockton 5s	8,000	8,640 00	8,640 00
of Boston 4s	7,000	7,140 00	7,000 00
Town of Gardiner 6s	1,000	1,030 00	1,000 00
	$29,000	$31,305 00	$30,227 50

BANK STOCK.

	Par Value.	Estimated Market Value.	Amount Invested.
Everett Nat'l Bank, Everett . .	$2,400	$2,760 00	$2,698 50
Freeman's Nat'l Bank, Boston .	5,000	6,250 00	5,978 00
	$7,400	$9,010 00	$8,676 50

MERRIMAC SAVINGS BANK — MERRIMAC.

Incorporated 1871. Number of corporators, 36.

WILLIAM H. HASKELL, *President.* *Treasurer*, DANIEL J. POORE.

STATEMENT.

LIABILITIES.		ASSETS.	
Deposits	$230,712 21	Bank stock	$2,000 00
Earnings undivided .	2,465 08	Railroad bonds . . .	8,000 00
Guaranty fund . .	2,530 03	Loans on real estate . .	122,185 00
		Loans on personal security,*	85,256 83
		Loans to counties, cities, or towns	2,325 00
		Deposit in banks on interest,	14,300 00
		Cash on hand . . .	1,040 49
	$235,707 32		$235,707 32

Cash on Deposit in Bank:—
First National Bank, Merrimac $15,340 49

Whole amount of interest or profits received or earned . . . $13,145 63
Rate and amount of each semi-annual dividend for previous year . . . . { 2 per cent . 3,815 24; 2 per cent . 4,212 48 }
Times for the dividends fixed by the by-laws: third Wednesday in April and October.
Average annual per cent of dividends for the term ending at time of and including last extra dividend: 5½ per cent.
The total amount of loans, with each specified rate of interest: $41,050, 5 per cent; $13,000, 5½ per cent; $82,331.83, 6 per cent; $10,900, 6½ per cent; $60,085, 7 per cent; $1,500, 7½ per cent.
Number of outstanding loans which are of an amount not exceeding $3,000 each 97
Aggregate amount of the same 95,516 83
Number of open accounts 754
Number and amount of deposits received for previous year . 680 60,117 31
Number and amount of deposits of and exceeding $300 at any one time for the previous year 41 18,762 60
Number and amount of withdrawals 285 23,898 64
Number of accounts opened the previous year 181
Number of accounts closed the previous year 73
Amount of expenses of the corporation during previous year . . 811 34
Amount of treasurer's bond 10,000 00
Date of examination by commissioner: June 13.

* This bank has been notified that these loans have exceeded the legal limit.

BANK STOCK.

	Par Value.	Estimated Market Value.	Amount Invested.
First Nat'l Bank, Merrimac . .	$2,000	$2,600 00	$2,000 00

RAILROAD BONDS.

West Amesbury Branch R.R. Co. .	$8,600	$9,460 00	$8,600 00

MERRIMACK RIVER SAVINGS BANK — LOWELL.

Incorporated Feb. 24, 1871. Number of corporators, 39.

J. G. PEABODY, *President*. *Treasurer*, N. G. LAMSON.

STATEMENT.

LIABILITIES.		ASSETS.	
Deposits	$334,722 87	Public funds	$7,000 00
Earnings undivided .	12,524 95	Bank stock	27,419 12
Guaranty fund . .	3,428 97	Loans on bank stock . .	14,500 00
		Loan on railroad bond .	1,000 00
		Real estate by foreclosure .	26,500 00
		Loans on real estate . .	183,481 25
		Loans on personal security,	75,850 00
		Loans to counties, cities, or towns	3,000 00
		Deposit in banks on interest,	11,625 32
		Cash on hand	301 10
	$350,676 79		$350,676 79

Loans on Bank Stock: —

On 151 shares Wamesit National Bank $14,500 00

Loan on Railroad Bonds: —

On $1,000 Boston and Lowell Railroad . . $1,000 00

Cash on Deposit in Banks, amount in each: —

Wamesit National Bank, Lowell $11,557 13

Maverick National Bank, Boston 68 19

Amount of real estate held by foreclosure $26,500 00

Assessed value of the same 26,650 00

Amount of income received from the same 1,809 45

Amount of municipal tax on real estate 573 20

Whole amount of interest or profits received or earned $17,937 22

Rate and amount of each semi-annual dividend for previous year . . . . } 2 per cent . 5,150 32; 2 per cent . 5,645 98

Times for the dividends fixed by the by-laws: first Saturday in May and November.

Average annual per cent of dividends for the term ending at time of and including last extra dividend: 5 per cent.

The total amount of loans, with each specified rate of interest: $17,000, 5½ per cent; $137,975, 6 per cent; $700, 6½ per cent; $26,806.25, 7 per cent; $1,000, 8 per cent.

Number of outstanding loans which are of an amount not exceeding $3,000 each 59

Aggregate amount of the same 73,531 25

Number of open accounts 863

Number and amount of deposits received for previous year . 755 108,564 10

Number and amount of deposits of and exceeding $300 at any one time for the previous year	112	$63,902 10
Number and amount of withdrawals	348	43,702 57
Number of accounts opened the previous year	246	
Number of accounts closed the previous year	121	
Amount of expenses of the corporation during previous year		572 14
Amount of treasurer's bond		15,000 00

Date of examination by commissioner: July 19.

Public Funds.

	Par Value.	Estimated Market Value.	Amount Invested.
Town bonds: —			
Town of Natick	$3,000	$3,200 00	$3,000 00
of Provincetown	4,000	4,300 00	4,000 00
	$7,000	$7,500 00	$7,000 00

Bank Stock.

	Par Value.	Estimated Market Value.	Amount Invested.
Tremont Nat'l Bank, Boston	$4,500	$5,715 00	$4,955 62
Blackstone Nat'l Bank, Boston	2,500	2,875 00	2,899 50
Atlantic Nat'l Bank, Boston	1,000	1,570 00	1,351 50
Atlas Nat'l Bank, Boston	3,000	3,780 00	3,525 00
Hide and Leather Nat'l B'k, Boston,	2,100	2,478 00	2,320 50
Howard Nat'l Bank, Boston	1,000	1,260 00	1,130 25
North Nat'l Bank, Boston	900	1,296 00	1,086 75
Metropolitan Nat'l Bank, Boston	1,600	1,964 00	1,600 00
Boston Nat'l Bank, Boston	5,000	6,500 00	5,750 00
Redemption Nat'l Bank, Boston	2,000	2,720 00	2,800 00
	$23,600	$30,158 00	$27,419 12

MIDDLEBOROUGH SAVINGS BANK — MIDDLEBOROUGH.

Incorporated March 15, 1873. Number of corporators, 36.

EVERETT ROBINSON, *President*. *Treasurer*, CORNELIUS B. WOOD.

STATEMENT.

LIABILITIES.		ASSETS.	
Deposits	$410,508 74	Bank stock	$13,140 00
Earnings undivided	6,410 45	Loans on bank stock	5,400 00
Guaranty fund	3,562 00	Railroad bonds	5,112 50
Interest paid in advance	2,548 12	Loans on real estate	229,889 24
		Loans on personal security,	126,175 14
		Loans to counties, cities, or towns	23,143 61
		Deposit in banks on interes	19,333 69
		Cash on hand	835 13
	$423,029 31		$423,029 31

Loans on Bank Stock: —

On 55 shares Pacific National Bank $5,400 00

Cash on Deposit in Banks, amount in each: —

Maverick National Bank, Boston $18,086 54

New England Trust Company * 1,247 15

Whole amount of interest or profits received or earned . . . $24,039 74

Rate and amount of each semi-annual dividend for previous year { $2\frac{1}{4}$ per cent . 8,028 35; 2 per cent . 7,669 16 }

Times for the dividends fixed by the by-laws: April and October.

Average annual per cent of dividends for the term ending at time of and including last extra dividend: $4\frac{1}{4}$ per cent.

The total amount of loans, with each specified rate of interest: $39,352.50, 4 per cent; $11,000, $4\frac{1}{2}$ per cent; $39,900, 5 per cent; $1,000, $5\frac{1}{2}$ per cent; $293,355, 6 per cent.

Number of outstanding loans which are of an amount not exceeding $3,000 each	367	
Aggregate amount of the same		257,227 99
Number of open accounts	1,500	
Number and amount of deposits received for previous year,	1,065	114,091 93
Number and amount of deposits of and exceeding $300 at any one time for the previous year	87	47,661 27
Number and amount of withdrawals	605	60,970 55
Number of accounts opened the previous year	316	
Number of accounts closed the previous year	137	
Amount of expenses of the corporation during previous year		670 69
Amount of treasurer's bond		10,000 00

Date of examination by commissioner: July 7.

* The Attorney-General has given an opinion that deposits by savings banks in this trust company are illegal.

BANK STOCK.

	Par Value.	Estimated Market Value.	Amount Invested.
Commerce Nat'l B'k, New Bedford,	$3,000	$4,050 00	$3,540 00
Webster Nat'l Bank, Boston . .	5,000	5,575 00	4,961 00
Tremont Nat'l Bank, Boston . .	2,200	2,684 00	2,329 00
Suffolk Nat'l Bank, Boston . .	2,100	2,541 00	2,310 00
	$12,300	$14,850 00	$13,140 00

RAILROAD BONDS.

Old Colony Railroad . . .	$5,000	$5,875 00	$5,112 50

MIDDLESEX INSTITUTION FOR SAVINGS — CONCORD.

Incorporated 1835. Number of corporators, 22.

GEORGE M. BROOKS, *President*. *Treasurer*, GEORGE HEYWOOD.

STATEMENT.

LIABILITIES.		ASSETS.	
Deposits . . .	$1,016,469 88	Public funds	$70,000 00
Earnings undivided .	33,574 50	Bank stock	270,500 00
Guaranty fund . .	10,500 00	Railroad bonds . . .	140,000 00
		Real estate by foreclosure .	22,950 00
		Loans on real estate . .	357,018 80
		Loans on personal security,	108,200 00
		Loans to towns . . .	59,350 00
		Expense account . . .	844 45
		Cash in bank . . .	31,681 13
	$1,060,544 38		$1,060,544 38

Cash on Deposit in Bank: —
Concord National Bank, Concord $31,681 13

Amount of real estate held by foreclosure		$22,950 00
Assessed value of the same		19,400 00
Amount of income received from the same		247 00
Amount of municipal tax on real estate		113 22
Whole amount of interest or profits received or earned . . .		$56,352 12
Rate and amount of each semi-annual dividend for previous year	2 per cent / 2 per cent	18,731 78 / 18,946 16
Times for the dividends fixed by the by-laws: second Tuesday in June and December.		
Average annual per cent of dividends for the term ending at time of and including last extra dividend: 7 per cent.		
The total amount of loans, with each specified rate of interest: $44,368.80, 5 per cent; $233,550, 6 per cent; $171,150, 6½ per cent; $55,450, 7 per cent; $43,000, 7½ per cent.		
Number of outstanding loans which are of an amount not exceeding $3,000 each	149	
Aggregate amount of the same		206,700 00
Amount of investments from which no income is received . .		35,000 00
Number of open accounts	2,961	
Number and amount of deposits received for previous year,	1,541	157,239 77
Number and amount of deposits of and exceeding $300 at any one time for the previous year	130	65,382 16
Number and amount of withdrawals	987	132,807 64
Number of accounts opened the previous year	403	
Number of accounts closed the previous year	230	
Amount of expenses of the corporation during previous year .		3,037 01
Amount of treasurer's bond		10,000 00

Date of examination by commissioner: June 15.

PUBLIC FUNDS.

	Par Value.	Estimated Market Value.	Amount Invested.
United States bonds . . .	$50,000	$50,625 00	$50,000 00
State bonds: —			
State of Maine	$6,000	$6,600 00	$6,000 00
of Rhode Island . . .	14,000	16,800 00	14,000 00
	$70,000	$74,025 00	$70,000 00

BANK STOCK.

Blackstone Nat'l Bank, Boston .	$10,600	$12,190 00	$10,600 00
Boston Nat'l Bank, Boston . .	13,300	17,024 00	13,300 00
Central Nat'l Bank, Boston . .	5,000	6,000 00	5,000 00
City Nat'l Bank, Boston . . .	10,000	12,325 00	10,000 00
Columbian Nat'l Bank, Boston .	6,700	9,547 50	6,700 00
Commerce Nat'l Bank, Boston .	11,300	14,577 00	11,300 00
Continental Nat'l Bank, Boston .	2,700	3,213 00	2,700 00
Eagle Nat'l Bank, Boston . .	15,000	17,925 00	15,000 00
Eliot Nat'l Bank, Boston . .	16,700	20,081 75	16,700 00
Faneuil Hall Nat'l Bank, Boston .	10,000	13,100 00	10,000 00
First Nat'l Bank, Boston . .	2,800	5,817 00	2,800 00
Hamilton Nat'l Bank, Boston . .	2,100	2,457 00	2,100 00
Hide and Leather Nat'l B'k, Boston,	7,200	8,388 00	7,200 00
Howard Nat'l Bank, Boston . .	20,000	26,000 00	20,000 00
Market Nat'l Bank, Boston . .	5,600	6,146 00	5,600 00
Merchants' Nat'l Bank, Boston .	15,000	22,005 00	15,000 00
North America Nat'l Bank, Boston .	10,000	11,500 00	10,000 00
Old Boston Nat'l Bank, Boston .	600	744 00	600 00
Revere Nat'l Bank, Boston . .	22,500	27,337 50	22,500 00
Second Nat'l Bank, Boston . .	4,500	6,817 50	4,500 00
Shawmut Nat'l Bank, Boston . .	10,000	12,600 00	10,000 00
Shoe and Leather Nat'l B'k, Boston,	10,000	11,250 00	10,000 00
State Nat'l Bank, Boston . .	13,800	17,319 00	13,800 00
Third Nat'l Bank, Boston . .	1,000	1,070 00	1,000 00
Traders' Nat'l Bank, Boston . .	5,700	5,814 00	5,700 00
Tremont Nat'l Bank, Boston . .	10,000	12,200 00	10,000 00
Webster Nat'l Bank, Boston . .	15,000	16,725 00	15,000 00
Concord Nat'l Bank, Concord . .	10,000	12,000 00	10,000 00
Old Lowell Nat'l Bank, Lowell .	900	1,125 00	900 00
Framingham Nat'l B'k, Framing'm,	500	755 00	500 00
First Nat'l Bank, Marlborough .	2,000	2,400 00	2,000 00
	$270,500	$336,453 25	$270,500 00

RAILROAD BONDS.

Eastern Railroad	$42,000	$46,200 00	$40,000 00
Boston and Albany Railroad . .	100,000	128,000 00	100,000 00
	$142,000	$174,200 00	$140,000 00

MILFORD SAVINGS BANK—MILFORD.

Incorporated April 24, 1851. Number of corporators, 42.

O. UNDERWOOD, *President.* *Treasurer*, JAMES E. WALKER.

STATEMENT.

LIABILITIES.		ASSETS.	
Deposits	$768,614 57	Public funds	$127,810 00
Earnings undivided .	8,611 24	Loans on public funds .	1,400 00
Guaranty fund . .	9,004 02	Bank stock	167,892 74
		Loans on bank stock . .	8,530 00
		Railroad bonds . . .	11,440 00
		Loan on railroad bonds .	6,000 00
		Real estate	27,000 00
		Real estate by foreclosure .	1,780 22
		Loans on real estate . .	238,000 36
		Loans on personal security,	147,244 32
		Loans to counties, cities, or towns	25,000 00
		Deposit in banks on interest,	10,791 65
		Loan on bank book . .	50 00
		Cash in bank . . .	13,290 54
	$786,229 83		$786,229 83

Loans on Public Funds, amount on each:—

On $800 United States bonds	$400 00
On $1,000 Town of Milford bonds	1,000 00

Loans on Bank Stock, amount on each:—

On 20 shares First National Bank, Barre	$1,200 00
On 126 shares Milford National Bank, Milford	7,330 00

Loan on Railroad Bonds:—

On $6,000 New York and New England Railroad 7s* . . .	$6,000 00

Cash on Deposit in Banks, amount in each:—

Maverick National Bank, Boston	$5,251 56
Manufacturers' National Bank, Boston	5,540 09
Milford National Bank, Milford	13,290 54

Amount invested in real estate (for banking purposes)	$27,000 00
Estimated value of the same	27,000 00
Amount of real estate held by foreclosure	1,780 22
Assessed value of the same	1,675 00
Amount of income received from the same	174 00
Amount of municipal tax on real estate	397 49

Whole amount of interest or profits received or earned		$40,009 39
Rate and amount of each semi-annual dividend for previous year	2 per cent .	13,274 95
	2 per cent .	14,080 26

Times for the dividends fixed by the by-laws: second Saturday in April and October.

* This bank was notified that this loan was illegal, and it has since been paid.

Average annual per cent of dividends for the term ending at time of and including last extra dividend: $6\frac{1}{2}\frac{1}{0}$ per cent.

The total amount of loans, with each specified rate of interest: $33,630.56, 4 per cent; $31,484.79, $4\frac{1}{4}$ per cent; $15,000, $4\frac{3}{4}$ per cent; $92,184.74, 5 per cent; $23,994.23, $5\frac{1}{4}$ per cent; $5,000, $5\frac{1}{2}$ per cent; $157,507.36, 6 per cent; $9,085, $6\frac{1}{2}$ per cent; $63,338, 7 per cent; $300, $7\frac{3}{10}$ per cent; $1,600, $7\frac{1}{2}$ per cent; $3,100, 8 per cent.

Number of outstanding loans which are of an amount not exceeding $3,000 each	209	
Aggregate amount of the same		$216,754 56
Number of open accounts	2,773	
Number and amount of deposits received for previous year,	2,351	398,330 03
Number and amount of deposits of and exceeding $300 at any one time for the previous year	160	83,642 68
Number and amount of withdrawals	1,603	245,528 89
Number of accounts opened the previous year	562	
Number of accounts closed the previous year	341	
Amount of expenses of the corporation during previous year		1,893 01
Amount of treasurer's bond		10,000 00

Date of examination by commissioner: June 10.

Public Funds.

	Par Value.	Estimated Market Value.	Amount Invested.
United States 4s	$16,500	$19,160 62	$16,500 00
" " $4\frac{1}{2}$s	42,000	47,460 00	43,310 00
City and town bonds:—			
City of Portland 6s, 1907	$2,000	$2,300 00	$2,000 00
Town of Beverly 6s, Note, 1886	10,000	10,800 00	10,000 00
of Milford 6s, 1887	10,000	11,000 00	10,000 00
of Milford 6s, 1897	10,000	12,400 00	10,000 00
of Milford 5s, 1893	36,000	39,240 00	36,000 00
	$126,500	$142,360 62	$127,810 00

Bank Stock.

	Par Value.	Estimated Market Value.	Amount Invested.
Central Nat'l Bank, Boston	$15,000	$18,000 00	$15,000 00
Revere Nat'l Bank, Boston	3,000	3,660 00	3,000 00
Blackstone Nat'l Bank, Boston	2,300	2,645 00	2,300 00
Howard Nat'l Bank, Boston	4,200	5,465 25	4,496 00
Webster Nat'l Bank, Boston	700	780 50	700 00
Maverick Nat'l Bank, Boston	500	1,250 00	1,000 00
Eliot Nat'l Bank, Boston	4,800	5,772 00	5,682 99
Hide and Leather Nat'l B'k, Boston,	10,000	11,650 00	10,659 50
Shawmut Nat'l Bank, Boston	10,000	12,750 00	12,057 50
Freeman's Nat'l Bank, Boston	4,000	4,790 00	5,360 00
Union Nat'l Bank, Boston	4,700	7,214 50	7,496 50
Continental Nat'l Bank, Boston	2,500	2,962 50	2,955 25

Bank Stock — Concluded.

	Par Value.	Estimated Market Value.	Amount Invested.
Redemption Nat'l Bank, Boston .	$11,000	$14,850 00	$15,655 00
Shoe and Leather Nat'l B'k, Boston,	200	225 00	274 50
Boylston Nat'l Bank, Boston . .	700	896 00	1,070 12
North Nat'l Bank, Boston . .	7,800	11,076 00	10,766 63
Exchange Nat'l Bank, Boston . .	2,500	3,600 00	3,581 25
Atlantic Nat'l Bank, Boston . .	1,000	1,535 00	1,530 00
Eagle Nat'l Bank, Boston . .	500	598 75	588 75
Washington Nat'l Bank, Boston .	4,000	5,600 00	5,505 00
Atlas Nat'l Bank, Boston . .	5,000	6,250 00	6,500 00
Hopkinton Nat'l Bank, Hopkinton .	2,700	3,240 00	2,700 00
Home Nat'l Bank, Brockton . .	10,000	11,300 00	10,000 00
Milford Nat'l Bank, Milford . .	25,300	32,890 00	29,013 75
Home Nat'l Bank, Milford . .	7,000	7,700 00	7,000 00
First Nat'l Bank, Barre . . .	3,000	3,000 00	3,000 00
	$142,400	$179,700 50	$167,892 74

Railroad Bonds.

Boston and Albany Railroad 7s .	$3,000	$3,810 00	$3,600 00
Boston and Albany Railroad 6s .	7,000	8,260 00	7,840 00
	$10,000	$12,070 00	$11,440 00

MILLBURY SAVINGS BANK — MILLBURY.

Incorporated 1854. Number of corporators, 41.

WILLIAM R. HILL, *President.* *Treasurer*, DAVID ATWOOD.

STATEMENT.

LIABILITIES.		ASSETS.	
Deposits . . .	$539,210 09	Public funds . . .	$69,500 00
Earnings undivided .	15,122 54	Bank stock	135,900 00
Guaranty fund . .	6,000 00	Railroad bonds . . .	20,000 00
		Real estate	18,000 00
		Real estate by foreclosure .	598 58
		Loans on real estate . .	219,900 00
		Loans on personal security,	300 00
		Loans to counties, cities, or towns	62,500 00
		Deposit in bank on interest,	12,706 38
		Expense account . . .	785 59
		Premium account . .	16,751 75
		Safe and furniture . .	2,265 58
		Suspense	100 00
		Cash on hand . . .	1,024 75
	$560,332 63		$560,332 63

Cash on Deposit in Bank:—

Millbury National Bank		$12,706 38
Amount invested in real estate (for banking purposes)		$18,000 00
Estimated value of the same		18,000 00
Amount of real estate held by foreclosure		598 58
Assessed value of the same		750 00
Amount of municipal tax on real estate		183 77
Whole amount of interest or profits received or earned		$31,158 79
Rate and amount of each semi-annual dividend for previous year	2 per cent .	9,744 95
	2 per cent .	10,128 76

Times for the dividends fixed by the by-laws: January and July.

The total amount of loans, with each specified rate of interest: $15,000, 4½ per cent; $35,000, 5 per cent; $167,050, 6 per cent; $65,650, 7 per cent.

Number of outstanding loans which are of an amount not exceeding $3,000 each	123	
Aggregate amount of the same		98,600 00
Number of open accounts	1,354	
Number and amount of deposits received for previous year,	1,196	98,905 32
Number and amount of deposits of and exceeding $300 at any one time for the previous year	84	48,360 35
Number and amount of withdrawals	733	83,679 72
Number of accounts opened the previous year	258	
Number of accounts closed the previous year	160	
Amount of expenses of the corporation during previous year . .		1,278 90
Amount of treasurer's bond		20,000 00

Date of examination by commissioner: May 6.

PUBLIC FUNDS.

	Par Value.	Estimated Market Value.	Amount Invested.
United States 6s of '81, extended	$5,500	$5,548 00	$5,500 00
" " 5s, extended	30,000	30,487 00	30,000 00
" " 4½s	10,000	11,300 00	10,000 00
City and town bonds: —			
City of Portland 7s	$6,000	$6,900 00	$6,000 00
of Bath 6s	6,000	6,600 00	6,000 00
of Lawrence 6s	3,000	3,450 00	3,000 00
Town of Westborough 5s	3,000	3,210 00	3,000 00
of Hopkinton 4s	6,000	6,180 00	6.000 00
	$69,500	$73,675 00	$69,500 00

BANK STOCK.

Atlas Nat'l Bank, Boston	$5,000	$6,250 00	$5,000 00
Blackstone Nat'l Bank, Boston	6,300	7,245 00	6,300 00
Boston Nat'l Bank, Boston	4,900	6,272 00	4,900 00
Commerce Nat'l Bank, Boston	5,700	7,296 00	5,700 00
Commonwealth Nat'l B'k, Boston	10,000	12,400 00	10,000 00
Continental Nat'l Bank, Boston	2,000	2,380 00	2,000 00
Eagle Nat'l Bank, Boston	1,200	1,428 00	1,200 00
Eliot Nat'l Bank, Boston	10,000	12,000 00	10,000 00
First Ward Nat'l Bank, Boston	5,000	6,000 00	5,000 00
Globe Nat'l Bank, Boston	4,200	4,662 00	4,200 00
Hamilton Nat'l Bank, Boston	2,500	3,100 00	2,500 00
Hide and Leather Nat'l B'k, Boston,	5,000	5,900 00	5,000 00
Manufacturers' Nat'l Bank, Boston	2,500	2,750 00	2,500 00
Merchandise Nat'l Bank, Boston	2,500	2,750 00	2,500 00
Merchants' Nat'l Bank, Boston	2,300	3,381 00	2,300 00
North Nat'l Bank, Boston	4,000	5,680 00	4,000 00
North America Nat'l Bank, Boston,	1,500	1,725 00	1,500 00
Old Boston Nat'l Bank, Boston	300	366 00	300 00
Second Nat'l Bank, Boston	3,500	5,285 00	3,500 00
Shawmut Nat'l Bank, Boston	2,500	3,175 00	2,500 00
Shoe and Leather Nat'l B'k, Boston,	7,400	8,362 00	7,400 00
State Nat'l Bank, Boston	5,000	6,250 00	5,000 00
Suffolk Nat'l Bank, Boston	2,000	2,420 00	2,000 00
Third Nat'l Bank, Boston	2,000	2,120 00	2,000 00
Traders' Nat'l Bank, Boston	7,000	7,140 00	7,000 00
Central Nat'l Bank, Worcester	3,600	4,680 00	3,600 00
Citizens' Nat'l Bank, Worcester	500	600 00	500 00
City Nat'l Bank, Worcester	2,700	3,132 00	2,700 00
Quinsigamond Nat'l B'k, Worcester,	2,500	2,900 00	2,500 00
Worcester Nat'l Bank, Worcester	900	1,125 00	900 00
Oxford Nat'l Bank, Oxford	600	780 00	600 00
First Nat'l Bank, Grafton	4,000	5,000 00	4,000 00
Millbury Nat'l Bank, Millbury	16,800	21,840 00	16,800 00
	$135,900	$166,394 00	$135,900 00

RAILROAD BONDS.

Providence and Worcester R.R. 6s	$20,000	$24,000 00	$20,000 00

MINERS' SAVINGS BANK — WEST STOCKBRIDGE.

Incorporated Feb. 28, 1872. Number of corporators, 29.

GEORGE W. KNIFFIN, *President.* *Treasurer,* WILLIAM C. SPAULDING.

STATEMENT.

LIABILITIES.		ASSETS.	
Deposits . . .	$53,018 48	Public funds . . .	$23,368 71
Earnings undivided .	1,391 61	Bank stock	7,715 00
Guaranty fund . .	500 00	Loans on real estate . .	20,800 00
		Loans on personal security,	675 00
		Loans to counties, cities, or towns	1,100 00
		Cash on hand . . .	1,251 38
	$54,910 09		$54,910 09

Cash on Deposit in Bank: —
Housatonic National Bank $1,251 38

Whole amount of interest or profits received or earned . . . $2,494 00

Rate and amount of each semi-annual dividend for previous year . . . . { 2 per cent . 812 89; 2 per cent . 924 75 }

Times for the dividends fixed by the by-laws: first Wednesday in January and July.

The total amount of loans, with each specified rate of interest: $22,575, 6 per cent.

Number of outstanding loans which are of an amount not exceeding $3,000 each 33

Aggregate amount of the same 18,575 00

Number of open accounts 260

Number and amount of deposits received for previous year . 310 14,843 40

Number and amount of deposits of and exceeding $300 at any one time for the previous year 3 1,540 00

Number and amount of withdrawals 119 8,321 54

Number of accounts opened the previous year 66

Number of accounts closed the previous year 36

Amount of expenses of the corporation during previous year . . 343 54

Amount of treasurer's bond 5,000 00

Date of examination by commissioner: Aug. 2.

PUBLIC FUNDS.

	Par Value.	Estimated Market Value.	Amount Invested.
United States 4½s	$3,000	$3,360 00	$3,288 75
" " 4s	13,200	15,312 00	14,375 12
City and town bonds: —			
City of Fall River 6s . .	$3,000	$3,810 00	$3,810 00
Town of Lee 6s . . .	2,000	2,000 00	1,894 84
	$21,200	$24,482 00	$23,368 71

BANK STOCK.

	Par Value.	Estimated Market Value.	Amount Invested.
Housatonic Nat'l Bank, Stockbridge,	$3,100	$4,650 00	$4,650 00
Mahaiwe Nat'l B'k, Gt. Barrington,	500	725 00	725 00
Pittsfield Nat'l Bank, Pittsfield .	1,500	2,340 00	2,340 00
	$5,100	$7,715 00	$7,715 00

MONSON SAVINGS BANK — MONSON.

Incorporated 1872. Number of corporators, 18.

C. H. MERRICK, *President.* *Treasurer*, E. F. MORRIS.

STATEMENT.

LIABILITIES.		ASSETS.	
Deposits . . .	$443,987 34	Public funds . . .	$75,710 00
Earnings undivided .	6,413 03	Loans on public funds .	2,000 00
Guaranty fund . .	5,410 00	Bank stock . . .	43,355 25
		Loans on bank stock . .	14,300 00
		Railroad bonds . . .	4,144 65
		Real estate by foreclosure .	31,413 82
		Loans on real estate . .	215.005 00
		Loans on personal security,	20,095 00
		Deposit in banks on interest,	45,000 00
		Taxes paid	475 00
		Cash on hand . . .	4,311 65
	$455,810 37		$455,810 37

Loans on Public Funds: —

On $2,000 United States 4s $2,000 00

Loans on Bank Stock, amount on each: —

On 67 shares Monson National Bank $5,300 00

On 10 shares Third National Bank, Springfield . . 1,000 00

On 90 shares City National Bank, Springfield . . . 8,000 00

Cash on Deposit in Banks, amount in each: —

Pacific National Bank, Boston $30,000 00

City National Bank, Springfield 15,000 00

Amount of real estate held by foreclosure $31,413 82

Assessed value of the same 24,400 00

Amount of income received from the same 1,703 62

Amount of municipal tax on real estate 315 10

Whole amount of interest or profits received or earned . . . $24,443 55

Rate and amount of each semi-annual dividend for previous year . . . . { 2 per cent . . 8,128 62; 2 per cent . . 8,355 81 }

Times for the dividends fixed by the by-laws: first Monday in April and October.

The total amount of loans, with each specified rate of interest: $50,000, 4 per cent; $112.550, 5 per cent; $2,400, 5½ per cent; $166,425. 6 per cent; $5,900, 7 per cent.

Number of outstanding loans which are of an amount not exceeding $3,000 each 107

Aggregate amount of the same 142,755 00

Amount of investments from which no income is received . . 3,200 00

Number of open accounts 1,198

Number and amount of deposits received for previous year . 858 93,354 82

Number and amount of deposits of and exceeding $300 at any one time for the previous year 65 35,870 96

Number and amount of withdrawals	531	$61,477
Number of accounts opened the previous year	208	
Number of accounts closed the previous year	130	
Amount of expenses of the corporation during previous year		980 75
Amount of treasurer's bond		10,000 00

Date of examination by commissioner: July 6.

Public Funds.

	Par Value.	Estimated Market Value.	Amount Invested.
United States 4s	$50,000	$58,000 00	$50,000 00
State, city, and town bonds:—			
Massachusetts 5s	$2,000	$2,350 00	$2,210 00
City of Worcester 5s	13,000	15,000 00	13,950 00
Town of Westfield 6s	10,000	10,700 00	9,550 00
	$75,000	$86,050 00	$75,710 00

Bank Stock.

North Nat'l Bank, Boston	$2,000	$2,880 00	$2,465 00
Eagle Nat'l Bank, Boston	2,000	2,400 00	2,260 00
North America Nat'l Bank, Boston	2,000	2,300 00	2,290 00
Redemption Nat'l Bank, Boston	2,500	3,500 00	3,576 50
Blackstone Nat'l Bank, Boston	1,500	1,740 00	1,440 00
Eliot Nat'l Bank, Boston	2,500	3,000 00	2,800 00
Massachusetts Nat'l Bank, Boston	500	625 00	641 50
Suffolk Nat'l Bank, Boston	4,000	4,900 00	5,070 00
Tremont Nat'l Bank, Boston	1,000	1,220 00	1,150 00
Merchants' Nat'l Bank, Boston	3,000	4,410 00	3,946 25
State Nat'l Bank, Boston	500	625 00	577 75
Webster Nat'l Bank, Boston	1,000	1,125 00	1,065 00
Hide and Leather Nat'l B'k, Boston,	1,000	1,175 00	1,162 75
Commerce Nat'l Bank, Boston	2,500	3,250 00	3,859 50
Revere Nat'l Bank, Boston	1,100	1,342 00	1,277 25
Exchange Nat'l Bank, Boston	500	725 00	881 25
City Nat'l Bank, Springfield	2,000	2,600 00	2,000 00
Ware Nat'l Bank, Ware	300	375 00	382 50
Monson Nat'l Bank, Monson	5,200	7,280 00	6,510 00
	$35,100	$45,472 00	$43,355 25

Railroad Bonds.

Eastern Railroad	$5,000	$5,500 00	$4,144 65

NANTUCKET INSTITUTION FOR SAVINGS — NANTUCKET.

Incorporated 1834. Number of corporators, 37.

THOMAS G. FOLGER, *President*. *Treasurer*, MATTHEW BARNEY.

STATEMENT.

LIABILITIES.		ASSETS.	
Deposits . . .	$365,058 80	Loan on public funds . .	$200 00
Earnings undivided .	36,423 48	Bank stock	1,400 00
Guaranty fund . .	3,797 09	Loan on savings bank book,	50 00
		Real estate	3,575 00
		Real estate by foreclosure .	56,706 52
		Loans on real estate . .	237,542 35
		Loans on personal security,	26,035 64
		Loans to counties, cities, or towns	1,000 00
		Deposit in banks on interest,	71,177 04
		Expense account . . .	646 71
		Cash on hand and in bank .	6,946 11
	$405,279 37		$405,279 37

Loan on Public Fund: —

On $500 United States 4½s . . .	$200 00

Cash on Deposit in Banks, amount in each: —

North National Bank, Boston	$21,919 11
Maverick National Bank, Boston	17,236 97
National Bank of Redemption, Boston	16,009 86
Revere National Bank, Boston	16,011 10
Pacific National Bank, Boston	4,046 07

Amount invested in real estate (for banking purposes)		$3,575 00
Estimated value of the same		3,575 00
Amount of real estate held by foreclosure		56,706 52
Assessed value of the same		48,600 00
Amount of income received from the same		3,379 67
Amount of municipal tax on real estate		1,033 65
Whole amount of interest or profits received or earned		$21,317 34
Rate and amount of semi-annual dividend for previous year, in July, 2 per cent		7,518 99
Time for the dividends fixed by the by-laws: first Monday in January and July.		
The total amount of loans, with each specified rate of interest: $1,000, 4½ per cent; $21,850, 5½ per cent; $163,952.35, 6 per cent; $56,102.60, 6½ per cent; $5,810, 7 per cent.		
Number of outstanding loans which are of an amount not exceeding $3,000 each	82	
Aggregate amount of the same		94,534 35
Amount of investments from which no income is received . .		16,113 14
Number of open accounts	1,191	
Number and amount of deposits received for previous year,	1,644	66,545 71

Number and amount of deposits of and exceeding $300 at any one time for the previous year	61	$31,909 32
Number and amount of withdrawals	1,112	137,885 09
Number of accounts opened the previous year	130	
Number of accounts closed the previous year	437	
Amount of expenses of the corporation during previous year . .		1,770 01
Amount of treasurer's bond		10,000 00

Date of examination by commissioner: Aug. 25.

Bank Stock.

	Par Value.	Estimated Market Value.	Amount Invested.
Commerce Nat'l B'k, New Bedford,	$1,400	$1,722 00	$1,400 00

NATICK FIVE CENTS SAVINGS BANK — NATICK.

Incorporated April 5, 1859. Number of corporators, 52.

JOHN O. WILSON, *President*. *Treasurer*, JAMES WHITNEY.

STATEMENT.

LIABILITIES.		ASSETS.	
Deposits	$658,095 80	Public funds	$59,550 97
Earnings undivided	18,936 20	Loans on public funds	5,025 00
Guaranty fund	6,089 93	Bank stock	100,436 87
		Loans on bank stock	15,410 00
		Real estate by foreclosure	5,300 00
		Loans on real estate	327,987 69
		Loans on personal security,	56,175 00
		Loans to counties, cities, or towns	11,000 00
		Deposit in banks on interest,	90,000 00
		Furniture and fixtures	583 99
		Cash on hand and in bank,	11,652 41
	$683,121 93		$683,121 93

Loans on Public Funds: —

On $5,050 United States 4s . . . $5,025 00

Loans on Bank Stock, amount on each: —

On 30 shares Wachusett National Bank $3,000 00

On 20 shares Dedham National Bank and 5 shares Eliot National Bank 2,410 00

On 38 shares Natick National Bank and 6 shares Rollstone National Bank, 6 shares Second National Bank, and 50 shares Commonwealth National Bank 10,000 00

Cash on Deposit in Banks, amount in each: —

Natick National Bank, Natick	$54,348 88
Wachusett National Bank, Fitchburg	5,000 00
Exchange National Bank, Boston	25,000 00
Central National Bank, Boston	15,000 00

Amount of real estate held by foreclosure	$5,300 00
Assessed value of the same	3,825 00
Amount of income received from the same	253 20
Amount of municipal tax on real estate	50 40

Whole amount of interest or profits received or earned . . . $38,760 24

Rate and amount of each semi-annual dividend for previous year . . . 2½ per cent . 13,447 50; 2½ per cent . 15,036 24

Times for the dividends fixed by the by-laws: first Saturday in May and November.

Average annual per cent of dividends for the term ending at time of and including last extra dividend: 5 per cent.

The total amount of loans, with each specified rate of interest: $5,000, 3½ per cent; $31,410, 4 per cent; $95,000, 5 per cent; $130,230, 6 per cent; $223,197, 6½ per cent; $17,940, 7$\frac{3}{10}$ per cent; $2,820.69, 7½ per cent.

Number of outstanding loans which are of an amount not exceeding $3,000 each	252	
Aggregate amount of the same		$238,052 69
Number of open accounts	2,958	
Number and amount of deposits received for previous year,	3,208	213,270 19
Number and amount of deposits of and exceeding $300 at any one time for the previous year	170	97,279 34
Number and amount of withdrawals	1,708	123,749 44
Number of accounts opened the previous year	669	
Number of accounts closed the previous year	345	
Amount of expenses of the corporation during previous year		1,395 10
Amount of treasurer's bond		30,000 00

Date of examination by commissioner: July 27.

Public Funds.

	Par Value.	Estimated Market Value.	Amount Invested.
United States 4s	$10,000	$11,662 50	$10,000 00
" " 3½s	3,000	3,037 50	3,026 25
City and town bonds: —			
City of Boston 4s	$10,000	$10,350 00	$10,132 22
of Fall River 5s, water bonds	16,000	16,960 00	16,720 00
of Cambridge 6s, sewer loan	4,000	4,800 00	4,780 00
Town of Natick 7s, water bonds	1,000	1,092 50	1,092 50
of Brookline 7s, water bonds	10,000	13,800 00	13,800 00
	$54,000	$61,702 50	$59,550 97

Bank Stock.

Atlas Nat'l Bank, Boston	$2,600	$3,250 00	$3,180 00
Boston Nat'l Bank, Boston	11,500	14,720 00	13,886 25
Boylston Nat'l Bank, Boston	700	896 00	845 25
Central Nat'l Bank, Boston	2,700	3,246 75	2,693 00
Continental Nat'l Bank, Boston	500	593 12	581 25
Columbian Nat'l Bank, Boston	1,300	1,852 50	1,855 75
Commonwealth Nat'l Bank, Boston,	2,100	2,530 50	2,654 75
Commerce Nat'l Bank, Boston	4,600	5,790 48	5,684 50
Dedham Nat'l Bank, Dedham	3,300	3,900 00	3,926 50
Eliot Nat'l Bank, Boston	1,400	1,683 50	1,715 00
Everett Nat'l Bank, Boston	7,000	8,120 00	8,210 00
Exchange Nat'l Bank, Boston	1,500	2,160 00	2,160 00
First Nat'l Bank, Chelsea	3,200	4,000 00	3,976 00
Home Nat'l Bank, Brockton	5,500	6,325 00	5,575 00
Howard Nat'l Bank, Boston	6,200	8,168 75	7,779 37
Metropolitan Nat'l Bank, Boston	400	491 00	400 00
Merchandise Nat'l Bank, Boston	3,200	3,512 00	3,501 25
Merchants' Nat'l Bank, Boston	4,600	6,704 50	6,393 75
Monument Nat'l Bank, Boston	1,500	3,138 75	2,775 00
Natick Nat'l Bank, Natick	2,000	2,400 00	2,000 00
Newton Nat'l Bank, Newton	2,000	2,300 00	2,230 00

BANK STOCK — Concluded.

	Par Value.	Estimated Market Value.	Amount Invested.
North Nat'l Bank, Boston . .	$400	$569 00	$516 00
North America Nat'l Bank, Boston,	4,100	4,704 75	4,716 50
Redemption Nat'l Bank, Boston .	1,400	1,891 68	2,135 00
Republic Nat'l Bank, Boston . .	3,000	3,742 50	3,825 00
Second Nat'l Bank, Boston . .	1,000	1,512 50	1,560 00
State Nat'l Bank, Boston . .	700	878 50	771 75
Traders' Nat'l Bank, Boston . .	500	510 00	530 00
Wachusett Nat'l Bank, Fitchburg .	3,700	7,696 00	4,360 00
	$82,600	$107,287 78	100,436 87

THE NEW BEDFORD FIVE CENTS SAVINGS BANK—NEW BEDFORD.

Incorporated May 5, 1855. Number of corporators, 133.

GEORGE HOWLAND, Jun., *President*. *Treasurer*, B. RICKETSON, Jun.

STATEMENT.

LIABILITIES.		ASSETS.	
Deposits	$2,947,163 23	Public funds	$1,337,000 00
Earnings undivided	53,912 08	Loans on public funds	209,500 00
Guaranty fund	37,318 54	Bank stock	177,900 00
		Loans on bank stock	229 11
		Railroad bonds	161,000 00
		Loans on bank books	450 00
		Loans on real estate	294,520 64
		Loans on personal security,	790,511 40
		Loans to counties, cities, or towns	4,000 00
		Deposit in banks on interest,	13,167 82
		Fixture account	2,500 00
		Loan to Citizens' National Bank	40,000 00
		Cash on hand	7,614 88
	$3,038,393 85		$3,038,393 85

Loans on Public Funds:—

On $210,000 United States 4s $209,500 00

Loans on Bank Stock:—

On 7 shares Mechanics' National Bank, New Bedford $229 11

Cash on Deposit in Banks, amount in each:—

Merchants' National Bank	$1,507 18
Citizens' National Bank	1,062 67
National Bank of Commerce	981 52
Mechanics' National Bank	3,663 79
First National Bank	1,377 83
National Bank of Redemption, Boston	4,574 83

Whole amount of interest or profits received or earned . . . $150,592 48

Rate and amount of each semi-annual dividend for previous year: 2 per cent, 49,808 86; 2 per cent, 54,359 39

Times for the dividends fixed by the by-laws: second Wednesday in April and October.

Average annual per cent of dividends for the term ending at time of and including last extra dividend: 6½ per cent.

The total amount of loans, with each specified rate of interest: $35,000, 3½ per cent; $50,000, 3¾ per cent; $270,000, 4 per cent; $75,000, 4¼ per cent; $135,000, 4½ per cent; $346,715, 5 per cent; $11,600, 5½ per cent; $366,896.15, 6 per cent.

Number of outstanding loans which are of an amount not exceeding $3,000 each 255

Aggregate amount of the same 207,695 70

Number of open accounts 11,679

Number and amount of deposits received for previous year, 7,997 735,952 64

Number and amount of deposits of and exceeding $300 at any one time for the previous year 731 484,036 20

Number and amount of withdrawals	4,695	$398,955 49
Number of accounts opened the previous year . . .	1,725	
Number of accounts closed the previous year	803	
Amount of expenses of the corporation during previous year. .		7,676 91
Amount of treasurer's bond		15,000 00

Date of examination by commissioner: Aug. 18.

PUBLIC FUNDS.

	Par Value.	Estimated Market Value.	Amount Invested.
Funded loan, 4½s, 1881 . . .	$83,500	$94,355 00	$83,500 00
United States 4s, 1891 . . .	104,500	121,350 00	104,500 00
Funded loan, 5s, extended 3½, 1881,	124,000	126,480 00	124,000 00
United States 6s, old, ext. 3½s, 1881,	1,000	1,010 00	1,000 00
Currency 6s due 1895 . . .	175,000	227,500 00	175,000 00
City and town bonds:—			
City of Norwich	$13,000	$13,910 00	$13,000 00
of Portland, Me. . . .	99,000	103,950 00	99,000 00
of New Bedford 5s . . .	23,000	23,000 00	23,000 00
of New Bedford, water . .	95,000	111,150 00	95,000 00
of Cambridge	30,000	32,100 00	30,000 00
of Newport	10,000	10,400 00	10,000 00
of Chelsea	95,000	108,300 00	95,000 00
of Bangor	66,000	72,600 00	66,000 00
of New Haven . . .	47,000	49,350 00	47,000 00
of Charlestown . . .	25,000	25,750 00	25,000 00
of Lowell	25,000	27,250 00	25,000 00
of Hartford, Conn. . . .	2,000	2,180 00	2,000 00
of Salem	25,000	27,250 00	25,000 00
of Fall River	73,000	74,460 00	73,000 00
of Boston	10,000	10,100 00	10,000 00
Town of Northampton . . .	111,000	116,550 00	111,000 00
of North Bridgewater . .	40,000	40,400 00	40,000 00
of New Haven . . .	10,000	10,500 00	10,000 00
of Holyoke	50,000	55,500 00	50,000 00
	$1,337,000	$1,485,395 00	$1,337,000 00

BANK STOCK.

Third Nat'l Bank, Springfield .	$10,000	$16,000 00	$10,000 00
Franklin Nat'l Bank, Franklin .	6,000	6,000 00	6,000 00
Merchants' Nat'l Bank, New Bedford,	49,400	80,028 00	49,400 00
First Nat'l Bank, New Bedford .	19,100	25,671 00	19,100 00
Citizens' Nat'l Bank, New Bedford.	20,000	23,450 00	20,000 00
Commerce Nat'l Bank, New Bedford,	24,400	34,099 00	24,400 00
First Nat'l Bank, Boston . .	10,000	19,900 00	10,000 00
Monument Nat'l Bank, Boston .	10,000	17,325 00	10,000 00
Revere Nat'l Bank, Boston . .	12,000	14,520 00	12,000 00
State Nat'l Bank, Boston . .	2,000	2,415 00	2,000 00
Tremont Nat'l Bank, Boston . .	2,500	3,012 00	2,500 00
Merchandise Nat'l Bank, Boston .	2,500	2,687 00	2,500 00
Merchants' Nat'l Bank, Boston .	10,000	14,000 00	10,000 00
	$177,900	$259,107 00	$177,900 00

RAILROAD BONDS.

	Par Value.	Estimated Market Value.	Amount Invested.
Boston and Albany 6s	$10,000	$11,400 00	$10,000 00
Eastern Railroad	52,500	52,434 00	52,500 00
Old Colony 6s	30,000	33,900 00	30,000 00
Old Colony 7s	20,000	23,950 00	20,000 00
Boston and Maine Railroad . .	15,000	18,637 00	15,000 00
Mansfield and Framingham R.R. .	33,500	25,627 00	33,500 00
	$161,000	$165,948 00	$161,000 00

NEW BEDFORD INSTITUTION FOR SAVINGS — NEW BEDFORD.

Incorporated 1825. Number of corporators, 119.

WILLIAM WATKINS, *President*. *Treasurer*, CHARLES H. PEIRCE.

STATEMENT.

LIABILITIES.		ASSETS.	
Deposits	$9,315,018 11	Public funds	$2,848,862 50
Earnings undivided	95,668 38	Loans on public funds	100,500 00
Guaranty fund	163,000 00	Bank stock	1,410,360 00
		Loans on bank stock	25,550 00
		Railroad bonds	760,000 00
		Real estate	30,000 00
		Loans on real estate	715,260 00
		Loans on personal security,	3,186,055 36
		Loans to counties, cities, or towns	42,300 00
		Deposit in banks on interest,	443,649 08
		Expense account	643 95
		Loans on deposits	950 00
		Cash on hand	9,555 60
	$9,573,686 49		$9,573,686 49

Loans on Public Funds, amount on each:—

On $100,000 United States 4s	$100,000 00
On 500 United States 3½s	500 00

Loans on Bank Stock, amount on each:—

On 20 shares Merchants' National Bank, New Bedford	$1,650 00
On 40 shares Mechanics' National Bank, New Bedford	2,600 00
On 35 shares National Bank of Commerce, New Bedford	2,000 00
On 9 shares First National Bank, 15 shares Mechanics' National Bank, and 22 shares National Bank of Commerce	2,000 00
On 15 shares Falmouth National Bank	1,000 00
On 63 shares Third National Bank, Springfield	6,300 00
On 100 shares Franklin County National Bank	10,000 00

Cash on Deposit in Banks, amount in each:—

Merchants' National Bank, New Bedford	$52,664 00
First National Bank, New Bedford	1,035 46
National Bank of Commerce, New Bedford	56,758 29
Mechanics' National Bank, New Bedford	41,092 30
Citizens' National Bank, New Bedford	1,517 82
Massachusetts National Bank, Boston	3,854 24
National Bank of Republic, Boston	25,848 97
National Bank of Redemption, Boston	30,462 21
Exchange National Bank, Boston	40,000 00
Maverick National Bank, Boston	40,415 79
Chapin National Bank, Springfield	150,000 00

Amount invested in real estate (for banking purposes)	$30,000 00
Estimated value of the same	30,000 00
Amount of municipal tax on real estate	315 90

Whole amount of interest or profits received or earned		$519,834 76
Rate and amount of each semi-annual dividend for previous year	2 per cent	176,832 80
	2 per cent	180,312 19

Times for the dividends fixed by the by-laws: April and October.

The total amount of loans, with each specified rate of interest: $20,000, 3 per cent; $50,000, 3½ per cent; $1,951,200, 4 per cent; $467,000, 4½ per cent; $50,000, 4¾ per cent; $954,175.70, 5 per cent; $58,000, 5½ per cent; $392,839.66, 6 per cent; $127,400, 7 per cent.

Number of outstanding loans which are of an amount not exceeding $3,000 each	162	
Aggregate amount of the same		$149,152 12
Number of open accounts	18,504	
Number and amount of deposits received for previous year,	9,367	1,337,343 28
Number and amount of deposits of and exceeding $300 at any one time for the previous year	1,107	686,325 78
Number and amount of withdrawals	10,758	1,347,755 89
Number of accounts opened the previous year	2,292	
Number of accounts closed the previous year	1,762	
Amount of expenses of the corporation during previous year		16,571 54
Amount of treasurer's bond		20,000 00

Date of examination by commissioner: Aug. 17.

Public Funds.

	Par Value.	Estimated Market Value.	Amount Invested.
United States 4½s	$700,000	$791,000 00	$721,000 00
" " 4s	805,500	934,000 00	820,812 50
State, city, and town bonds:—			
City of New Bedford 6s	$336,000	$389,000 00	$336,000 00
of New Bedford 5s	1,000	1,000 00	1,000 00
of New Bedford 7s	50,000	56,000 00	50,000 00
of Charlestown 5s	100,000	110,000 00	100,000 00
of Springfield 6s	5,000	5,500 00	5,000 00
of Manchester, N.H., 6s	20,000	21,200 00	20,000 00
of Middletown, Conn., 6s	70,500	77,500 00	70,500 00
of Northampton 6s	13,000	14,000 00	13,000 00
of Norwalk, Conn., 7s	10,000	12,000 00	10,000 00
of Bangor, Me., 6s	100,000	110,000 00	100,000 00
of Meriden, Conn., 7s	50,000	57,500 00	50,000 00
of Hartford, Conn., 6s	20,000	21,800 00	20,000 00
of Salem 6s	50,000	54,000 00	50,000 00
of Burlington, Vt., 6s	29,050	31,000 00	29,050 00
of Chelsea 6s	85,000	96,900 00	85,000 00
of Augusta, Me., 6s	4,500	4,700 00	4,500 00
of Dover, N.H., 6s	17,000	17,800 00	17,000 00
of Bath, Me., 6s (municipal)	39,000	41,700 00	39,000 00
of Newport, R.I., 6s	3,000	3,000 00	3,000 00
of Concord, N.H., 6s	5,000	5,100 00	5,000 00
Town of Greenfield 6s	5,000	5,600 00	5,000 00
of Buckland 6s	5,000	5,500 00	5,000 00
of Shelburne 6s	6,000	6,600 00	6,000 00
of Adams 6s	3,000	3,200 00	3,000 00
of Malden 5s	17,000	17,800 00	17,000 00
of Malden 6s	50,000	55,000 00	50,000 00
of Medford 6s	50,000	55,000 00	50,000 00

PUBLIC FUNDS — Concluded.

	Par Value.	Estimated Market Value.	Amount Invested.
Town of Melrose	$50,000	$55,000 00	$50,000 00
of Harwich 7s . . .	4,000	4,000 00	4,000 00
of Edgartown 6s . . .	40,000	42,800 00	40,000 00
of Attleborough water 7s .	50,000	60,000 00	50,000 00
County of Sagadahoc, Me., 6s .	19,000	20,000 00	19,000 00
	$2,812,550	$3,185,200 00	$2,848,862 50

BANK STOCK.

Merchants' Nat'l B'k, New Bedford,	$109,600	$175,360 00	$109,600 00
First Nat'l Bank, New Bedford .	135,600	183,060 00	135,600 00
Commerce Nat'l Bank, New Bedford,	136,600	187,140 00	136,600 00
Mechanics' Nat'l B'k, New Bedford,	100,000	150,000 00	100,000 00
Citizens' Nat'l Bank, New Bedford,	100,000	115,000 00	100,000 00
First Nat'l Bank, Chelsea . .	20,000	24,000 00	20,000 00
So. Reading Nat'l Bank, Wakefield,	7,000	8,150 00	7,000 00
Fall River Nat'l Bank, Fall River .	20,000	27,000 00	20,000 00
Metacomet Nat'l Bank, Fall River .	25,000	31,250 00	25,000 00
First Nat'l Bank, Malden . .	15,000	17,550 00	15,000 00
Fairhaven Nat'l Bank, Fairhaven .	1,760	1,650 00	1,760 00
Railroad Nat'l Bank, Lowell . .	9,000	10,800 00	9,000 00
Third Nat'l Bank, Springfield .	20,000	32,000 00	20,000 00
Wachusett Nat'l Bank, Fitchburg .	5,000	9,500 00	5,000 00
Hide and Leather Nat'l B'k, Boston,	19,700	22,860 00	19,700 00
Boston Nat'l Bank, Boston . .	14,300	18,300 00	14,300 00
Howard Nat'l Bank, Boston . .	13,300	17,290 00	13,300 00
Exchange Nat'l Bank, Boston . .	2,000	2,880 00	2,000 00
Commerce Nat'l Bank, Boston .	45,600	57,000 00	45,600 00
Second Nat'l Bank, Boston . .	52,600	78,900 00	58,500 00
North America Nat'l Bank, Boston .	38,000	43,700 00	38,000 00
Maverick Nat'l Bank, Boston . .	10,000	23,000 00	10,000 00
Republic Nat'l Bank, Boston . .	48,500	63,000 00	48,500 00
First Nat'l Bank, Boston . .	23,000	47,600 00	34,500 00
Merchants' Nat'l Bank, Boston .	22,500	32,800 00	22,500 00
Eliot Nat'l Bank, Boston . .	8,300	9,960 00	8,300 00
North Nat'l Bank, Boston . .	22,100	31,380 00	22,100 00
City Nat'l Bank, Boston . . .	2,700	3,380 00	2,700 00
Tremont Nat'l Bank, Boston . .	34,300	41,800 00	34,300 00
Hamilton Nat'l Bank, Boston . .	8,300	9,300 00	8,300 00
Shawmut Nat'l Bank, Boston . .	13,500	17,100 00	13,500 00
Continental Nat'l Bank, Boston .	25,000	29,500 00	25,000 00
Eagle Nat'l Bank, Boston . .	16,800	19,900 00	16,800 00
Massachusetts Nat'l Bank, Boston .	43,500	53,900 00	43,500 00
Atlas Nat'l Bank, Boston . .	36,000	45,000 00	36,000 00
Union Nat'l Bank, Boston . .	12,400	18,900 00	12,400 00
State Nat'l Bank, Boston . .	8,200	10,250 00	8,200 00
Traders' Nat'l Bank, Boston . .	13,000	13,250 00	13,000 00
Columbian Nat'l Bank, Boston .	26,000	36,900 00	26,000 00
Revere Nat'l Bank, Boston . .	49,100	59,900 00	49,100 00
Washington Nat'l Bank, Boston .	13,000	18,200 00	13,000 00

BANK STOCK — Concluded.

	Par Value.	Estimated Market Value.	Amount Invested.
Shoe and Leather Nat'l B'k, Boston,	$13,600	$15,230 00	$13,600 00
New England Nat'l Bank, Boston .	3,200	4,640 00	3,200 00
Commonwealth Nat'l Bank, Boston .	10,000	12,000 00	10,000 00
Redemption Nat'l Bank, Boston .	20,000	27,000 00	25,000 00
Everett Nat'l Bank, Boston . .	2,500	2,900 00	2,500 00
Merchandise Nat'l Bank, Boston .	2,400	2,640 00	2,400 00
Monument Nat'l B'k, Charlestown .	10,000	20,000 00	10,000 00
	$1,387,960	$1,882,810 00	$1,410,360 00

RAILROAD BONDS.

Boston and Albany 7s	$450,000	$560,000 00	$450,000 00
Boston and Albany 6s	50,000	57,500 00	50,000 00
New Bedford 7s	75,000	90,000 00	75,000 00
Worcester and Nashua 5s . .	125,000	125,000 00	125,000 00
Boston and Providence 5s . .	60,000	61,000 00	60,000 00
	$760,000	$893,500 00	$760,000 00

NEWBURYPORT FIVE CENTS SAVINGS BANK — NEWBURYPORT.

Incorporated April 24, 1854. Number of corporators, 45.

EBEN SUMNER, *President*. *Treasurer*, JOHN A. MAYNARD.

STATEMENT.

LIABILITIES.		ASSETS.	
Deposits . . .	$642,566 24	Public funds . . .	$45,000 00
Earnings undivided .	92,899 92	Bank stock	111,600 00
Guaranty fund . .	6,701 78	Loans on bank stock . .	2,000 00
		Railroad bonds . . .	5,000 00
		Real estate	43,942 46
		Real estate by foreclosure .	167,749 69
		Loans on real estate . .	290,164 00
		Loans on personal security,	29,829 00
		Deposit in banks on interest,	41,866 80
		Expense account . . .	133 33
		Cash on hand . . .	4,882 66
	$742,167 94		$742,167 94

Loans on Bank Stock: —

On 20 shares Ocean National Bank and 14 shares Mechanics' National Bank, Newburyport $2,000 00

Cash on Deposit in Banks, amount in each: —

First National Bank, Newburyport $31,935 95
Maverick National Bank, Boston 9,930 85

Amount invested in real estate (for banking purposes) $43,942 46
Estimated value of the same 40,000 00
Amount of real estate held by foreclosure 167,749 69
Assessed value of the same 163,320 00
Amount of income received from the same 2,313 29
Amount of municipal tax on real estate 3,396 33
Whole amount of interest or profits received or earned 39,571 53

Rate and amount of semi-annual dividend for previous year, 2 per cent in November $13,282 86

Times for the dividends fixed by the by-laws: first Monday in May and November.

The total amount of loans, with each specified rate of interest: $8,000, 3 per cent; $2,000, 4½ per cent; $28,000, 5 per cent; $16,700, 5½ per cent; $199,218, 6 per cent; $13,450, 6½ per cent; $47,775, 7 per cent; $2,050, 7 3/10 per cent; $2,600, 7½ per cent; $2,200, 8 per cent.

Number of outstanding loans which are of an amount not exceeding $3,000 each 179
Aggregate amount of the same 173,093 00
Amount of investments from which no income is received . . 109,817 95
Number of open accounts 3,102
Number and amount of deposits received for previous year . 418 59,009 06
Number and amount of deposits of and exceeding $300 at any one time for the previous year 54 29,303 14

Number and amount of withdrawals	1,890	$293,547 95
Number of accounts opened the previous year	150	
Number of accounts closed the previous year	1,154	
Amount of expenses of the corporation during previous year		1,768 12
Amount of treasurer's bond		20,000 00

Date of examination by commissioner: June 6.

PUBLIC FUNDS.

	Par Value.	Estimated Market Value.	Amount Invested.
United States 6s, currency	$30,000	$39,900 00	$30,000 00
City bonds: —			
City of Bangor, Me., 6s	$10,000	$11,200 00	$10,000 00
of Springfield 6s	5,000	5,300 00	5,000 00
	$45,000	$56,400 00	$45,000 00

BANK STOCK.

Atlantic Nat'l Bank, Boston	$1,000	$1,535 00	$1,000 00
Atlas Nat'l Bank, Boston	6,000	7,500 00	6,000 00
Boylston Nat'l Bank, Boston	800	1,024 00	800 00
Boston Nat'l Bank, Boston	1,700	2,176 00	1,700 00
Blackstone Nat'l Bank, Boston	3,300	3,795 00	3,300 00
Columbian Nat'l Bank, Boston	1,300	1,852 50	1,300 00
Commerce Nat'l Bank, Boston	1,800	2,317 50	1,800 00
Continental Nat'l Bank, Boston	4,200	4,982 25	4,200 00
Commonwealth Nat'l Bank, Boston,	5,000	6,025 00	5,000 00
City Nat'l Bank, Boston	8,000	10,160 00	8,000 00
Exchange Nat'l Bank, Boston	500	720 00	500 00
Eliot Nat'l Bank, Boston	3,300	3,968 25	3,300 00
Eagle Nat'l Bank, Boston	7,400	8,880 00	7,400 00
Everett Nat'l Bank, Boston	5,000	5,856 00	5,000 00
Howard Nat'l Bank, Boston	1,500	1,951 87	1,500 00
Hamilton Nat'l Bank, Boston	1,000	1,130 00	1,000 00
Hide and Leather Nat'l B'k, Boston,	2,500	2,912 50	2,500 00
Market Nat'l Bank, Boston	800	878 00	800 00
Maverick Nat'l Bank, Boston	4,000	10,000 00	4,000 00
North America Nat'l Bank, Boston,	1,000	1,150 00	1,000 00
New England Nat'l Bank, Boston	1,000	1,455 00	1,000 00
Republic Nat'l Bank, Boston	2,300	3,013 00	2,300 00
Revere Nat'l Bank, Boston	3,700	4,514 00	3,700 00
Shawmut Nat'l Bank, Boston	1,000	1,275 00	1,000 00
Suffolk Nat'l Bank, Boston	1,200	1,462 50	1,200 00
Tremont Nat'l Bank, Boston	3,300	4,026 00	3,300 00
Third Nat'l Bank, Boston	10,400	11,076 00	10,400 00
Union Nat'l Bank, Boston	2,400	3,684 00	2,400 00
Webster Nat'l Bank, Boston	5,600	6,244 00	5,600 00
First Nat'l Bank, Newburyport	10,500	16,380 00	10,500 00
Ocean Nat'l Bank, Newburyport	1,000	1,400 00	1,000 00
Mechanics' Nat'l Bank, Newburyp't,	9,100	12,922 00	9,100 00
	$111,600	$146,265 37	$111,600 00

RAILROAD BONDS.

Old Colony and Newport 7s	$5,000	$6,350 00	$5,000 00

NEWTON SAVINGS BANK — NEWTON.

Incorporated June 17, 1831. Number of corporators, 16.

GEORGE HYDE, *President*. *Treasurer*, SUSANNA M. DUNCKLEE.

STATEMENT.

LIABILITIES.		ASSETS.	
Deposits	$942,328 07	Public funds	$112,354 70
Earnings undivided	14,096 10	Loans on public funds	6,500 00
Guaranty fund	10,241 00	Bank stock	39,725 00
		Loans on bank stock	3,600 00
		Railroad bonds	53,838 98
		Real estate by foreclosure	43,442 37
		Loans on real estate	490,739 94
		Loans on personal security,	143,100 00
		Deposit in banks on interest,	71,200 00
		Expense account	909 07
		Cash on hand	1,256 01
	$966,666 07		$966,666 07

Loans on Public Funds: —

On $34,000 United States 6s, extended $6,500 00

Loans on Bank Stock, amount on each: —

On 25 shares Newton National Bank, Newton $2,000 00

On 65 shares Old Boston National Bank, Boston 1,600 00

Cash on Deposit in Banks, amount in each: —

Wachusett National Bank $35,200 00

Pacific National Bank, Boston 22,000 00

Central National Bank, Boston 14,000 00

Amount of real estate held by foreclosure $43,442 37

Assessed value of the same 42,500 00

Amount of income received from the same 2,077 35

Amount of municipal tax on real estate 595 00

Whole amount of interest or profits received or earned $57,429 98

Rate and amount of each semi-annual dividend for previous year . . . { 2 per cent . . 15,822 09; 2 per cent . . 16,784 70 }

Times for the dividends fixed by the by-laws: Jan. 1 and July 1.

The total amount of loans, with each specified rate of interest: $38,500, 5 per cent; $6,000, 5½ per cent; $467,305.50, 6 per cent; $25,300, 6½ per cent; $102,634.44, 7 per cent; $1,500, 7½ per cent; $2,700, 8 per cent.

Number of outstanding loans which are of an amount not exceeding $3,000 each 130

Aggregate amount of the same 195,739 94

Amount of investments from which no income is received . . . 3,080 00

Number of open accounts 3,867

Number and amount of deposits received for previous year, 3,583 239,478 97

Number and amount of deposits of and exceeding $300 at any one time for the previous year 160 107,627 15

Number and amount of withdrawals 1,806 $160,665 40
Number of accounts opened the previous year . . . 638
Number of accounts closed the previous year 225
Amount of expenses of the corporation during previous year . 3,541 18
Amount of treasurer's bond 20,000 00
Date of examination by commissioner: July 12.

PUBLIC FUNDS.

	Par Value.	Estimated Market Value.	Amount Invested.
City bonds: —			
City of Boston 4s	$20,000	$21,000 00	$20,000 00
of Lawrence 6s, water loan .	12,000	14,040 00	13,279 23
of Lowell 6s, water loan . .	6,000	7,020 00	6,545 46
of Newton 5s, water loan . .	50,000	56,500 00	51,358 88
of Worcester 5s, municipal .	20,000	21,400 00	21,171 13
	$108 000	$119,960 00	$112,354 70

BANK STOCK.

Brighton Nat'l Bank, Boston . .	$700	$749 00	$700 00
Commonwealth Nat'l Bank, Boston,	3,000	3,615 00	3,000 00
First Nat'l Bank, Cambridge . .	1,000	1,620 00	1,000 00
Merchandise Nat'l Bank, Boston .	2,400	2,640 00	2,400 00
Natick Nat'l Bank, Natick . .	2,500	3,000 00	2,500 00
Newton Nat'l Bank, Newton . .	1,500	1,725 00	1,500 00
Pacific Nat'l Bank, Boston . .	10,000	10,500 00	10,000 00
S. Framingham Nat'l B'k, S. Fram.	5,000	5,075 00	5,000 00
Union Market Nat'l B'k, Watertown,	7,300	8,030 00	7,300 00
Wachusett Nat'l Bank, Fitchburg .	2,500	5,125 00	2,500 00
Waltham Nat'l Bank, Waltham .	225	240 00	225 00
State Nat'l Bank, Boston . .	600	753 00	600 00
Revere Nat'l Bank, Boston . .	3,000	3,660 00	3,000 00
	$39,725	$46,732 00	$39,725 00

RAILROAD BONDS.

Boston and Albany 7s	$40,000	$50,800 00	$43,838 98
Mansfield and Framingham 7s .	10,000	10,800 00	10,000 00
	$50,000	$61,600 00	$53,838 98

NORTHAMPTON INSTITUTION FOR SAVINGS—NORTHAMPTON.

Incorporated 1842. Number of corporators, 18.

H. G. KNIGHT, *President.* *Treasurer*, L. MALTBY.

STATEMENT.

LIABILITIES.		ASSETS.	
Deposits . . .	$1,865,867 44	Public funds . . .	$464,890 63
Earnings undivided .	25,613 25	Bank stock	45,800 00
Guaranty fund . .	31,000 00	Loans on bank stock . .	13,538 70
		Railroad bonds . . .	361,875 00
		Real estate	27,582 40
		Real estate by foreclosure .	15,471 75
		Loans on real estate . .	574,794 81
		Loans on personal security,	81,135 00
		Loans to counties, cities, or towns	7,300 00
		Deposit in banks on interest,	325,395 11
		Cash on hand . . .	4,697 29
	$1,922,480 69		$1,922,480 69

Loans on Bank Stock, amount on each:—

On 3 shares Hampshire County National Bank	$300 00
On 99 shares First National Bank, Northampton	8,225 00
On 66 shares Northampton National Bank, Northampton . .	5,013 70

Cash on Deposit in Banks, amount in each:—

Northampton National Bank, Northampton	$265,395 11
City National Bank. Springfield	50,000 00
Hampshire County National Bank	10,000 00

Amount invested in real estate (for banking purposes) . . .	$27,582 40
Estimated value of the same	25,000 00
Amount of real estate held by foreclosure	15,471 75
Assessed value of the same	14,250 00
Amount of income received from the same	761 50
Amount of municipal tax on real estate	386 38

Whole amount of interest or profits received or earned . . . $103,098

Rate and amount of each semi-annual dividend for previous year . . . . { 2 per cent . 34,775 44 ; 2 per cent . 35,590 41 }

Times for the dividends fixed by the by-laws: first Wednesday in April and October.

Average annual per cent of dividends for the term ending at time of and including last extra dividend: 7 per cent.

The total amount of loans, with each specified rate of interest: $500, 4 per cent; $87,200, 5 per cent; $589,068.51, 6 per cent.

Number of outstanding loans which are of an amount not exceeding $3,000 each 327

Aggregate amount of the same 289,538 96

Number of open accounts 5,178

Number and amount of deposits received for previous year, 3,625 313,723 71

Number and amount of deposits of and exceeding $300 at any one time for the previous year	280	$164,071 89
Number and amount of withdrawals	2,705	293,590 79
Number of accounts opened the previous year	1,185	
Number of accounts closed the previous year	945	
Amount of expenses of the corporation during previous year		4,634 78
Amount of treasurer's bond		25,000 00

Date of examination by commissioner: July 12.

Public Funds.

	Par Value.	Estimated Market Value.	Amount Invested.
United States bonds	$361,000	$394,600 00	$388,890 63
City bonds:—			
City of Meriden, Conn.	$76,000	$81,600 00	$76,000 00
	$437,000	$476,200 00	464,890 63

Bank Stock.

Northampton Nat'l B'k, Northam'n,	$10,000	$16,500 00	$10,000 00
First Nat'l Bank, Northampton	1,600	2,080 00	1,600 00
City Nat'l Bank, Worcester	4,000	4,500 00	4,000 00
Atlantic Nat'l Bank, Boston	1,000	1,530 00	1,000 00
Boston Nat'l Bank, Boston	5,300	6,784 00	5,300 00
Commerce Nat'l Bank, Boston	1,500	1,920 00	1,500 00
Exchange Nat'l Bank, Boston	1,000	1,440 00	1,000 00
First Nat'l Bank, Boston	3,000	6,210 00	3,000 00
Merchants' Nat'l Bank, Boston	2,000	2,920 00	2,000 00
North America Nat'l Bank, Boston	2,700	3,105 00	2,700 00
Second Nat'l Bank, Boston	3,400	5,134 00	3,400 00
Shawmut Nat'l Bank, Boston	2,600	3,300 00	2,600 00
State Nat'l Bank, Boston	1,700	2,125 00	1,700 00
Traders' Nat'l Bank, Boston	2,000	2,040 00	2,000 00
Washington Nat'l Bank, Boston	2,000	2,800 00	2,000 00
Webster Nat'l Bank, Boston	2,000	2,220 00	2,000 00
	$45,800	$64,608 00	$45,800 00

Railroad Bonds.

Boston and Albany 6s	$40,000	$47,200 00	$41,000 00
Boston and Albany 7s	200,000	254,000 00	207,250 00
Boston and Maine 7s	70,000	88,900 00	71,275 00
Boston and Lowell 7s	40,000	49,800 00	42,350 00
	$350,000	$439,900 00	$361,875 00

NORTH ADAMS SAVINGS BANK — NORTH ADAMS.

Incorporated 1848. Number of corporators, 42.

C. T. SAMPSON, *President*. *Treasurer*, V. A. WHITAKER.

STATEMENT.

LIABILITIES.		ASSETS.	
Deposits	$900,917 79	Public funds	$93,193 75
Earnings undivided .	8,000 00	Loans on public funds .	3,550 00
Guaranty fund . .	11,000 00	Bank stock	40,661 01
State tax accrued .	2,700 00	Loans on bank stock . .	10,100 00
Other liabilities . .	684 07	Loans on bank books . .	500 00
		Real estate	5,000 00
		Real estate by foreclosure .	3,531 26
		Loans on real estate . .	486,269 05
		Loans on personal security,	229,887 51
		Loans to counties, cities, or towns	10,000 00
		Deposit in banks on interest,	21,440 04
		Expense account . . .	332 84
		Interest account . . .	14,084 02
		Cash on hand . . .	4,752 38
	$923,301 86		$923,301 86

Loans on Public Funds, amount on each: —

On $600 United States bonds	$550 00
On $3,000 North Adams water bonds	3,000 00

Loans on Bank Stock, amount on each: —

On 99 shares Adams National Bank, Adams	$9,900 00
On 5 shares Pittsfield National Bank, Pittsfield . . .	200 00

Cash on Deposit in Banks, amount in each: —

Maverick National Bank, Boston	$1,440 04
Adams National Bank, Adams	3,345 89
Berkshire National Bank, North Adams	20,000 00

Amount invested in real estate (for banking purposes) . . .	$5,000 00
Estimated value of the same	7,000 00
Amount of real estate held by foreclosure	3,531 26
Assessed value of the same	4,100 00
Amount of income received from the same	268 00
Amount of municipal tax on real estate	182 58

Whole amount of interest or profits received or earned	$46,313 53
Rate and amount of each semi-annual dividend for previous year . . . . { 2 per cent .	15,337 83
2 per cent .	16,203 86

Times for the dividends fixed by the by-laws: April 1 and Oct. 1.

The total amount of loans, with each specified rate of interest: $35,000, 4½ per cent; $37,400, 5 per cent; $548,697.51, 6 per cent; $81,234.05, 6½ per cent; $5,400, 7 per cent; $22,575, 7$\frac{3}{10}$ per cent.

Number of outstanding loans which are of an amount not exceeding $3,000 each 238

Aggregate amount of the same		$267,647 51
Number of open accounts	3,204	
Number and amount of deposits received for previous year,	3,688	269,782 64
Number and amount of deposits of and exceeding $300 at any one time for the previous year	236	124,057 23
Number and amount of withdrawals	2,070	192,420 75
Number of accounts opened the previous year	810	
Number of accounts closed the previous year	452	
Amount of expenses of corporation during previous year . .		3,994 85
Amount of treasurer's bond		20,000 00

Date of examination by commissioner: Aug. 8.

Public Funds.

	Par Value.	Estimated Market Value.	Amount Invested.
United States 4s	$50,500	$59,085 00	$55,693 75
" " 4½s	5,000	5,650 00	5,000 00
City and town bonds: —			
City of Lynn	$1,000	$1,150 00	$1,000 00
of Cambridge	5,000	5,750 00	5,000 00
of New Bedford	1.000	1,150 00	1,000 00
of Fall River	11,000	12,650 00	11,000 00
of Bangor, Me.	5,000	5,750 00	5,000 00
of Portland, Me.	5,000	5,750 00	5,000 00
Town of Adams	3,000	3,450 00	3,000 00
of North Adams . . .	1,500	1,725 00	1,500 00
	$88,000	$102,110 00	$93,193 75

Bank Stock.

	Par Value.	Estimated Market Value.	Amount Invested.
Adams Nat'l Bank, Adams . .	$24,000	$31,200 00	$26,200 92
Lee Nat'l Bank, Lee . . .	1,400	1,820 00	1,400 00
Pittsfield Nat'l Bank, Pittsfield .	5,000	7,500 00	6,254 01
First Nat'l Bank, Adams . .	6,000	7,800 00	6,806 08
	$36,400	$48,320 00	$40,661 01

NORTH AVENUE SAVINGS BANK – CAMBRIDGE.

Incorporated March 7, 1872. Number of corporators, 37.

SAMUEL F. WOODBRIDGE, *President*. *Treasurer*, MILTON L. WALTON.

STATEMENT.

LIABILITIES.		ASSETS.	
Deposits . . .	$72,068 78	Public funds . . .	$4,986 04
Earnings undivided .	1,180 72	Bank stock	6,500 00
Guaranty fund . .	994 13	Real estate by foreclosure .	4,221 39
		Loans on real estate . .	48,165 00
		Loans on personal security,	5,500 00
		Deposit in bank on interest,	4,640 28
		Suspense account . .	25 00
		Cash on hand . . .	205 92
	$74,243 63		$74,243 63

Cash on Deposit in Bank: —

Howard National Bank, Boston		$4,640 28
Amount of real estate held by foreclosure		$4,221 39
Assessed value of the same		3,300 00
Amount of income received from the same		300 00
Amount of municipal tax on real estate		52 80
Whole amount of interest or profits received or earned . . .		$4,072 58
Rate and amount of each semi-annual dividend for previous year	2 per cent .	1,228 97
	2 per cent .	1,242 30

Times for the dividends fixed by the by-laws: Jan. 10 and July 10.

Average annual per cent of dividends for the term ending at time of and including last extra dividend: 5 per cent.

The total amount of loans, with each specified rate of interest: $20,340, 6 per cent; $18,200, 6½ per cent; $11,025, 7 per cent; $3,500, 7½ per cent.

Number of outstanding loans which are of an amount not exceeding $3,000 each	20	
Aggregate amount of the same		24,165 00
Number of open accounts	510	
Number and amount of deposits received for previous year .	497	19,734 09
Number and amount of deposits of and exceeding $300 at any one time for the previous year	12	6,213 00
Number and amount of withdrawals	240	15,363 09
Number of accounts opened the previous year	73	
Number of accounts closed the previous year	40	
Amount of expenses of the corporation during previous year .		479 69
Amount of treasurer's bond		5,000 00

Date of examination by commissioner: May 28.

PUBLIC FUNDS.

	Par Value.	Estimated Market Value.	Amount Invested.
United States 4s, 1901, consols .	$5,000	$5,800 00	$4,986 04

BANK STOCK.

	Par Value.	Estimated Market Value.	Amount Invested.
Brighton Nat'l Bank, Brighton .	$6,000	$6,000 00	$6,500 00

31

NORTH BROOKFIELD SAVINGS BANK — NORTH BROOKFIELD.

Incorporated 1854. Number of corporators, 26.

SAMUEL S. EDMANDS, *President*. *Treasurer*, BONUM NYE.

STATEMENT.

LIABILITIES.		ASSETS.	
Deposits	$361,429 30	Public funds	$115,000 00
Earnings undivided	1,892 90	Bank stock	11,400 00
Guaranty fund	7,425 77	Railroad bonds	87,000 00
Real estate rent	209 85	Real estate by foreclosure	870 00
		Loans on real estate	144,134 00
		Deposit in banks on interest,	11,986 36
		Expense account	11 24
		Furniture	189 35
		Cash on hand	366 87
	$370,957 82		$370,957 82

Cash on Deposit in Bank: —

Maverick National Bank, Boston		$11,986 36
Amount of real estate held by foreclosure		$870 00
Assessed value of the same		600 00
Amount of income received from the same		52 56
Amount of municipal tax on real estate		9 48
Whole amount of interest or profits received or earned		$19,487 91
Rate and amount of each semi-annual dividend for previous year	2½ per cent	7,755 20
	2 per cent	6,513 50
Times for the dividends fixed by the by-laws: Jan. 1 and July 1.		
Average annual per cent of dividends for the term ending at time of and including last extra dividend: 5½ per cent.		
The total amount of loans, with each specified rate of interest: $144,134, 6 per cent.		
Number of outstanding loans which are of an amount not exceeding $3,000 each	140	
Aggregate amount of the same		118,834 00
Number of open accounts	1,400	
Number and amount of deposits received for previous year,	1,025	75,083 65
Number and amount of deposits of and exceeding $300 at any one time for the previous year	49	22,397 56
Number and amount of withdrawals	532	50,256 74
Number of accounts opened the previous year	271	
Number of accounts closed the previous year	163	
Amount of expenses of the corporation during previous year		950 46
Amount of treasurer's bond		14,000 00

Date of examination by commissioner: July 5.

PUBLIC FUNDS.

	Par Value.	Estimated Market Value.	Amount Invested.
United States bonds .	$17,000	$19,082 50	$17,000 00
State, city, and town bonds: —			
State of Maine	$15,000	$17,400 00	$15,000 00
of New Hampshire . .	1,500	1,762 50	1,500 00
City of Springfield	8,000	8,120 00	8,000 00
of Boston	23,000	26,735 00	23,000 00
of Providence, R.I. . . .	7,000	7,980 00	7,000 00
of Manchester	9,500	9,852 50	9,500 00
of Portsmouth, N.H. . .	5,000	5,700 00	5,000 00
of Portland, Me. . . .	5,000	6,150 00	5,000 00
of Cambridge	2,000	2,435 00	2,000 00
Town of Beverly	10,000	10,275 00	10,000 00
of Woburn	12,000	14,100 00	12,000 00
	$115,000	$129,592 50	$115,000 00

BANK STOCK.

	Par Value.	Estimated Market Value.	Amount Invested.
Ware Nat'l Bank, Ware . . .	$400	$492 00	$400 00
Eliot Nat'l Bank, Boston . .	1,000	1,202 50	1,000 00
Commonwealth Nat'l Bank, Boston,	10,000	12,050 00	10,000 00
	$11,400	$13,744 50	$11,400 00

RAILROAD BONDS.

	Par Value.	Estimated Market Value.	Amount Invested.
Boston and Albany	$31,000	$39,440 00	$31,000 00
Eastern	27,000	29,700 00	27,000 00
Boston and Providence . . .	8,000	10,140 00	8,000 00
Boston and Maine	13,000	16,517 50	13,000 00
Old Colony	8,000	9,240 00	8,000 00
	$87,000	$105,037 50	$87,000 00

NORTH EASTON SAVINGS BANK — EASTON.

Incorporated Feb. 8, 1864. Number of corporators, 30.

FRED. L. AMES, *President*. *Treasurer*, P. A. GIFFORD.

STATEMENT.

LIABILITIES.		ASSETS.	
Deposits . . .	$306,433 14	Public funds . . .	$28,330 00
Earnings undivided .	12,862 26	Loans on public funds .	100 00
Guaranty fund . .	4,400 00	Bank stock	120,161 77
		Loans on bank stock . .	5,250 00
		Real estate by foreclosure .	14,262 88
		Loans on real estate . .	130,719 01
		Loans on personal security,	12,245 19
		Expense account . . .	6 45
		Cash on hand and in bank .	12,620 10
	$323,695 40		$323,695 40

Loans on Public Funds: —

On $100 United States 4s . . . $100 00

Loans on Bank Stock: —

On 54 shares First National Bank, Easton $5.250 00

Cash on Deposit in Bank: —

First National Bank, Easton . . . $11,970 39

Amount of real estate held by foreclosure .		$14.262 88
Assessed value of the same		13,550 00
Amount of income received from the same .		552 91
Amount of municipal tax on real estate . .		242 75
Whole amount of interest or profits received or earned		$13,151 69
Rate and amount of each semi-annual dividend for previous year . . .	2 per cent .	5,392 94
	2 per cent .	5,745 76

Times for the dividends fixed by the by-laws: April 15 and Oct. 15.

The total amount of loans, with each specified rate of interest: $16,000, 5 per cent; $98,465, 6 per cent; $9,900, 6½ per cent; $17,016, 7 per cent; $4,025, 7½ per cent; $1.300, 8 per cent.

Number of outstanding loans which are of an amount not exceeding $3,000 each	97	
Aggregate amount of the same		75,506 00
Amount of investments from which no income is received . .		1.608 20
Number of open accounts	1,022	
Number and amount of deposits received for previous year .	803	77,879 08
Number and amount of deposits of and exceeding $300 at any one time for the previous year	54	28,696 55
Number and amount of withdrawals	433	49,167 27
Number of accounts opened the previous year	182	
Number of accounts closed the previous year	121	
Amount of expenses of the corporation during previous year .		600 00
Amount of treasurer's bond		10,000 00

Date of examination by commissioner: Aug. 17.

PUBLIC FUNDS.

	Par Value.	Estimated Market Value.	Amount Invested.
City and town bonds: —			
City of Bath, Me.	$2,000	$2,000 00	$2,000 00
of Bangor, Me.	8,000	8,200 00	6,960 00
of Springfield.	10,000	12,300 00	11,250 00
Town of Stoughton	8,000	8,120 00	8,120 00
	$28,000	$30,620 00	$28,330 00

BANK STOCK.

	Par Value.	Estimated Market Value.	Amount Invested.
City Nat'l Bank, Lynn	$6,600	$9,570 00	$9,578 25
Neponset Nat'l Bank, Canton	7,500	9,600 00	8,100 00
Bristol County Nat'l B'k, Taunton	3,800	5,700 00	4,560 00
Taunton Nat'l Bank, Taunton	700	1,050 00	920 50
First Nat'l Bank, Easton	10,000	13,000 00	10,690 00
Traders' Nat'l Bank, Boston	3,600	3,672 00	3,632 75
Shoe and Leather Nat'l B'k, Boston,	2,500	2,812 00	3,395 00
Tremont Nat'l Bank, Boston	2,500	3,050 00	3,137 50
State Nat'l Bank, Boston	2,500	3,150 00	2,693 75
City Nat'l Bank, Boston	2,500	3,150 00	2,765 63
Market Nat'l Bank, Boston	2,500	2,700 00	2,750 00
Atlas Nat'l Bank, Boston	2,500	3,100 00	2,878 13
Eagle Nat'l Bank, Boston	2,000	2,375 00	2,255 00
New England Nat'l Bank, Boston	2,500	3,625 00	3,450 00
North Nat'l Bank, Boston	11,300	16,000 00	15,074 63
Revere Nat'l Bank, Boston	5,700	6,950 00	7,178 50
Everett Nat'l Bank, Boston	7,800	9,200 00	10,135 00
Shawmut Nat'l Bank, Boston	5,000	6,300 00	6,500 00
Atlantic Nat'l Bank, Boston	2,500	3,825 00	3,750 00
Hamilton Nat'l Bank, Boston	2,500	2,825 00	3,450 00
Manufacturers' Nat'l Bank, Boston	2,500	2,700 00	2,753 13
Redemption Nat'l Bank, Boston	3,800	5,100 00	4,789 00
Hide and Leather Nat'l B'k, Boston,	5,000	5,800 00	5,725 00
	$97,800	$125,254 00	$120,161 77

NORTH END SAVINGS BANK — BOSTON.

Incorporated Feb. 17, 1870. Number of corporators, 25.

THOMAS L. JENKS, *President*. *Treasurer*, GEORGE C. TRUMBULL.

STATEMENT.

LIABILITIES.		ASSETS.	
Deposits	$380,910 40	Public funds	$18,117 50
Earnings undivided	20,012 26	Bank stock	56,157 17
Guaranty fund	6,480 00	Railroad bonds	20,212 50
		Real estate by foreclosure	56,759 95
		Loans on real estate	219,990 74
		Deposit in bank	31,322 86
		Expense account	1,284 62
		Vault furniture, etc.	2,494 40
		Suspense account	15 80
		Cash on hand	1,047 12
	$407,402 66		$407,402 66

Cash on Deposit in Bank: —

National Security Bank $31,322 86

Amount of real estate held by foreclosure $56,759 95
Assessed value of the same 54,500 00
Amount of income received from the same 3,647 10
Amount of municipal tax on real estate 830 18

Whole amount of interest or profits received or earned $24,694 23
Rate and amount of each semi-annual dividend for previous year . . . . { 2 per cent . 7,507 59; 2 per cent . 7,218 64 }
Times for the dividends fixed by the by-laws: Jan. 1 and July 1.
The total amount of loans, with each specified rate of interest: $68,288.74, 6 per cent; $17,200, $6\frac{1}{2}$ per cent; $73,004, 7 per cent; $5,850, $7\frac{3}{10}$ per cent; $15,700, $7\frac{1}{2}$ per cent; $39,948, 8 per cent.
Number of outstanding loans which are of an amount not exceeding $3,000 each 83
Aggregate amount of the same 122,880 37
Amount of investments from which no income is received . . 838 25
Number of open accounts 1,325
Number and amount of deposits received for previous year . 671 57,474 40
Number and amount of deposits of and exceeding $300 at any one time for the previous year 48 26,022 98
Number and amount of withdrawals 805 79,231 19
Number of accounts opened the previous year 162
Number of accounts closed the previous year 222
Amount of expenses of the corporation during previous year . 4,698 77
Amount of treasurer's bond 44,000 00
Date of examination by commissioner: Feb. 10.

PUBLIC FUNDS.

	Par Value.	Estimated Market Value.	Amount Invested.
United States 6s, extended $3\frac{1}{2}$s .	$7,600	$7,676 00	$8,417 50
City bonds, —			
City of Cambridge	$10,000	$10,350 00	$9,700 00
	$17,600	$18,026 00	$18,117 50

BANK STOCK.

	Par Value.	Estimated Market Value.	Amount Invested.
City Nat'l Bank, Boston . . .	$6,600	$8,382 00	$7,394 62
Revere Nat'l Bank, Boston . .	3,400	4,148 00	4,390 12
Shoe and Leather Nat'l B'k, Boston,	2,600	2,925 00	3,782 00
Tremont Nat'l Bank, Boston . .	2,600	3,172 00	3,360 25
First Nat'l Bank, Chelsea . .	5,000	6,250 00	5,767 42
Atlas Nat'l Bank, Boston . .	5,000	6,250 00	5,787 50
Eagle Nat'l Bank, Boston . .	7,100	8,502 25	8,012 75
Traders' Nat'l Bank, Boston . .	3,000	3,060 00	3,237 76
North Nat'l Bank, Boston . .	5,000	7,125 00	6,762 50
Suffolk Nat'l Bank, Boston . .	300	365 62	375 00
Market Nat'l Bank, Boston . .	1,000	1,097 50	1,131 25
Commonwealth Nat'l Bank, Boston,	500	602 50	660 00
Commerce Nat'l Bank, Boston .	1,000	1,297 50	1,308 50
Third Nat'l Bank, Boston . .	500	532 50	544 37
Pacific Nat'l Bank, Boston . .	3,500	3,635 00	3,643 13
	$47,100	$57,344 87	$56,157 17

RAILROAD BONDS.

	Par Value.	Estimated Market Value.	Amount Invested.
Boston and Maine 7s	$20,000	$25,450 00	$20,212 50

ORANGE SAVINGS BANK — ORANGE.

Incorporated 1871. Number of corporators, 151.

A. J. CLARK, *President*. *Treasurer*, JAMES H. WAITE.

STATEMENT.

LIABILITIES.		ASSETS.	
Deposits	$250,587 64	Public funds	$43,548 21
Earnings undivided .	1,134 23	Bank stock	39,606 60
Guaranty fund . .	2,850 00	Loans on bank stock . .	5,400 00
		Railroad bonds	16,950 00
		Real estate	1,745 02
		Loans on real estate . .	79,663 70
		Loans on personal security,	32,247 88
		Deposit in bank on interest,	35,393 66
		Taxes	16 80
	$254,571 87		$254,571 87

Loans on Bank Stock, amount on each: —

On 50 shares Franklin County National Bank	$5,000 00
On 9 shares Orange National Bank	400 00

Cash on Deposit in Bank: —

Orange National Bank, Orange	$35,393 66

Amount of real estate held by foreclosure . .	$1,745 02
Assessed value of the same	1,600 00
Amount of income received from the same . .	67 00
Amount of municipal tax on real estate . . .	32 41

Whole amount of interest or profits received or earned		$11,583 48
Rate and amount of each semi-annual dividend for previous year	2 per cent .	3,940 56
	2 per cent .	4,339 21
Times for the dividends fixed by the by-laws: February and August.		
Average annual per cent of dividends for the term ending at time of and including last extra dividend: 4 per cent.		
The total amount of loans, with each specified rate of interest: $5,400, 4 per cent; $111,911.58, 6 per cent.		
Number of outstanding loans which are of an amount not exceeding $3,000 each	160	
Aggregate amount of the same		93,698 32
Number of open accounts	1,272	
Number and amount of deposits received for previous year,	1,055	96,058 17
Number and amount of deposits of and exceeding $300 at any one time for the previous year	66	15,566 70
Number and amount of withdrawals	821	49,539 40
Number of accounts opened the previous year	340	
Number of accounts closed the previous year	100	
Amount of expenses of the corporation during previous year . .		363 15
Amount of treasurer's bond		20,000 00

Date of examination by commissioner: Aug. 11.

PUBLIC FUNDS.

	Par Value.	Estimated Market Value.	Amount Invested.
City and town bonds: —			
City of Manchester, N.H. . .	$15,000	$15,900 00	$15,458 21
of Lynn	3,000	3,520 00	3,425 00
of Fall River	2,000	2,310 00	2,290 00
of Bangor, Me. . . .	1,000	1,150 00	1,115 00
of Cambridge	1,000	1,190 00	1,180 00
of Brockton	5,000	5,400 00	5,400 00
of Auburn	1,600	1,760 00	1,680 00
Town of Sheldon, Vt. . . .	8,000	8,400 00	8,000 00
of Hyde Park . . .	5,000	5,200 00	5,000 00
	$41,600	$44,860 00	$43,548 21

BANK STOCK.

	Par Value.	Estimated Market Value.	Amount Invested.
First Nat'l Bank, Springfield . .	$1,000	$1,400 00	$1,470 00
Third Nat'l Bank, Springfield .	1,000	1,700 00	1,750 00
Union Market N'l B'k, Watertown .	700	784 00	823 62
Orange Nat'l Bank, Orange . .	10,000	11,500 00	10,000 00
First Nat'l Bank, Chelsea . .	400	460 00	460 00
Eliot Nat'l Bank, Boston . .	6,500	7,781 42	7,781 42
Hide and Leather Nat'l B'k, Boston,	500	596 25	596 25
Central Nat'l Bank, Boston . .	300	360 00	328 50
North Nat'l Bank, Boston . .	1,000	1,392 50	1,392 50
Tremont Nat'l Bank, Boston . .	3,000	3,720 00	3,720 00
Manufacturers' Nat'l Bank, Boston,	2,000	2,200 00	2,200 00
Webster Nat'l Bank, Boston . .	2,500	2,925 00	2,820 75
First Ward Nat'l Bank, Boston .	2,000	2,100 00	1,882 06
North America Nat'l Bank, Boston .	1,100	1,254 00	1,309 00
Everett Nat'l Bank, Boston . .	400	460 00	529 00
Atlas Nat'l Bank, Boston . .	1,500	1,935 00	1,935 00
Boylston Nat'l Bank, Boston . .	500	608 50	608 50
	$34,400	$11,176 67	$39,606 60

RAILROAD BONDS.

	Par Value.	Estimated Market Value.	Amount Invested.
Fitchburg	$15,000	$16,950 00	$16,950 00

PALMER SAVINGS BANK — PALMER.

Incorporated 1870. Number of corporators, 42.

JAMES B. SHAW, *President*. *Treasurer*, WILLIAM C. DEWEY.

STATEMENT.

LIABILITIES.		ASSETS.	
Deposits . . .	$527,420 63	Public funds . . .	$27,600 00
Earnings undivided .	2,340 03	Bank stock	28,300 00
Guaranty fund . .	5,500 00	Loans on bank stock . .	1,100 00
		Railroad bonds . . .	10,000 00
		Real estate	12,500 00
		Real estate by foreclosure .	10,500 00
		Loans on real estate . .	228,890 00
		Loans on personal security,*	190,304 39
		Loans to counties, cities, or towns	2,550 00
		Deposit in banks on interest,	15,500 00
		Expense account . . .	863 45
		Premium account . .	5,000 00
		Loan on savings bank book †	900 00
		Cash on hand . . .	1,252 82
	$535,260 66		$535,260 66

Loans on Bank Stock, amount on each:—

On 12 shares Palmer National Bank	$1,000 00
On 10 shares First National Bank, Chicopee . .	100 00

Loan on savings bank book (Providence Institution for Savings) † . $900 00

Cash on Deposit in Bank:—

Palmer National Bank $15,500 00

Amount invested in real estate (for banking purposes)	$12,500 00
Estimated value of the same	15,000 00
Amount of real estate held by foreclosure	10,500 00
Assessed value of the same	9,000 00
Amount of income received from the same	650 00
Amount of municipal tax on real estate	174 00

Whole amount of interest or profits received or earned $27,404 03

Rate and amount of each semi-annual dividend for previous year . . . . { $2\frac{1}{4}$ per cent . 9,780 42; 2 per cent . 9,424 46 }

Times for the dividends fixed by the by-laws: Jan. 1 and July 1.

Average annual per cent of dividends for the term ending at time of and including last extra dividend: 4.46 per cent.

The total amount of loans, with each specified rate of interest: $147,650, 5 per cent; $246,309.39, 6 per cent; $20,940, $6\frac{1}{2}$ per cent; $8,845, 7 per cent.

Number of outstanding loans which are of an amount not exceeding $3,000 each 265

Aggregate amount of the same 224,500 00

* This bank has been notified that these loans exceed the legal limit.

† This bank has been notified that this loan is illegal.

Number of open accounts	1,835	
Number and amount of deposits received for previous year,	1,520	$169,588 61
Number and amount of deposits of and exceeding $300 at any one time for the previous year	125	79,434 26
Number and amount of withdrawals	832	99,445 45
Number of accounts opened the previous year	387	
Number of accounts closed the previous year	212	
Amount of expenses of the corporation during previous year .		3,098 94
Amount of treasurer's bond		15,000 00

Date of examination by commissioner: July 6.

Public Funds.

	Par Value.	Estimated Market Value.	Amount Invested.
United States 4s	$100	$116 00	$100 00
City and town bonds: —			
City of Boston 6s, 1894	$5,000	$6,000 00	$5,000 00
of Worcester 6s, 1892 . .	6,000	7,000 00	6,000 00
of Fall River 6s, 1899 . .	5,000	5,860 00	5,000 00
of Fall River 5s, 1908 . .	3,000	3,360 00	3,000 00
of Bath, Me., 6s, 1891 . .	1,000	1,000 00	1,000 00
of Rockland, Me., 6s, 1891 .	2,500	2,500 00	2,500 00
Town of Waltham 5s, 1882 . .	5,000	5,000 00	5,000 00
	$27,600	$30,836 00	$27,600 00

Bank Stock.

Palmer Nat'l Bank, Palmer . .	$7,500	$9,825 00	$7,500 00
Monson Nat'l Bank, Monson . .	3,300	5,148 00	3,300 00
Agawam Nat'l Bank, Springfield .	3,700	4,550 00	3,700 00
State Nat'l Bank, Boston . .	2,500	3,125 00	2,500 00
Suffolk Nat'l Bank, Boston . .	2,000	2,440 00	2,000 00
Commerce Nat'l Bank, Boston .	2,300	2,944 00	2,300 00
North America Nat'l Bank, Boston .	1,000	1,150 00	1,000 00
Eliot Nat'l Bank, Boston . .	5,000	6,000 00	5,000 00
Brockton Nat'l Bank, Brockton .	1,000	1,060 00	1,000 00
	$28,300	$36,242 00	$28,300 00

Railroad Bonds.

Eastern 4s	$10,000	$11,000 00	$9,640 00

PEOPLE'S SAVINGS BANK — WORCESTER.

Incorporated May 13, 1864. Number of corporators, 192.

L. J. KNOWLES, *President*. *Treasurer*, C. M. BENT.

STATEMENT.

LIABILITIES.		ASSETS.	
Deposits	$3,470,166 94	Public funds	$353,500 00
Earnings undivided	42,157 17	Bank stock	658,600 00
Guaranty fund	53,093 89	Loans on bank stock	400 00
Dividends unpaid	57,343 29	Railroad bonds	134,500 00
Suspense account	5,309 88	Real estate	65,000 00
		Real estate by foreclosure	53,529 01
		Loans on real estate	1,297,595 00
		Loans on personal security,	635,150 00
		Loans to counties, cities, or towns	148,900 00
		Deposit in banks on interest,	100,937 67
		Expense account	2,096 75
		Rents	540 15
		Premium account	132,278 51
		Interest accrued	35,109 34
		Cash on hand	9,934 74
	$3,628,071 17		$3,628,071 17

Loans on Bank Stock:—

On 5 shares First National Bank, Barre . $400 00

Cash on Deposit in Banks, amount in each:—

Wachusett National Bank	$25,000 00
Central National Bank	75,937 67

Amount invested in real estate (for banking purposes)	$65,000 00
Estimated value of the same	65,000 00
Amount of real estate held by foreclosure	53,529 01
Assessed value of the same	40,600 00
Amount of income received from the same	1,910 47
Amount of municipal tax on real estate	1,324 95

Whole amount of interest or profits received or earned $175,514 93

Rate and amount of each semi-annual dividend for previous year . . . 2 per cent . 62,620 31; 2 per cent . 65,047 53

Times for the dividends fixed by the by-laws: February and August.

The total amount of loans, with each specified rate of interest: $63,000, 3½ per cent; $86,000, 3¾ per cent; $312,400, 4 per cent; $159,000, 4½ per cent; $667,465, 5 per cent; $781,080, 6 per cent; $8,000, 7 per cent.

Number of outstanding loans which are of an amount not exceeding $3,000 each 449

Aggregate amount of the same 592,025 00

Number of open accounts 9,888

Number and amount of deposits received for previous year, 7,929 653,783 70

Number and amount of deposits of and exceeding $300 at any one time for the previous year	550	$307,236 00
Number and amount of withdrawals	5,767	519,867 22
Number of accounts opened the previous year . . .	1,609	
Number of accounts closed the previous year . . .	1,196	
Amount of expenses of the corporation during previous year .		8,946 20
Amount of treasurer's bond		30,000 00

Date of examination by commissioner: June 2.

Public Funds.

	Par Value.	Estimated Market Value.	Amount Invested.
United States 5s and 6s, 1881, ext'd,	$230,500	$234,743 12	$230,500 00
" " 4½s	115,000	129,750 00	115,000 00
City bonds: —			
City of Boston 5s . .	$8,000	$8,480 00	$8,000 00
	$353,500	$372,973 12	$353,500 00

Bank Stock.

Market Nat'l Bank, Boston . .	$18,700	$21,177 75	$18,700 00
Shawmut Nat'l Bank, Boston . .	10,000	12,562 50	10,000 00
Atlas Nat'l Bank, Boston . .	11,200	14,000 00	11,200 00
Webster Nat'l Bank, Boston . .	10,000	11,125 00	10,000 00
Redemption Nat'l Bank, Boston .	39,700	53,644 62	39,700 00
Commerce Nat'l Bank, Boston .	10,000	12,875 00	10,000 00
North America Nat'l Bank, Boston .	16,400	18,860 00	16,400 00
Union Nat'l Bank, Boston . .	2,000	3,070 00	2,000 00
Washington Nat'l Bank, Boston .	10,800	14,931 00	10,800 00
Merchants' Nat'l Bank, Boston .	5,000	7,300 00	5,000 00
North Nat'l Bank, Boston . .	5,000	7,112 50	5,000 00
Tremont Nat'l Bank, Boston . .	25,200	30,681 00	25,200 00
Globe Nat'l Bank, Boston . .	31,700	35,345 50	31,700 00
New England Nat'l Bank, Boston .	4,000	5,940 00	4,000 00
Eagle Nat'l Bank, Boston . .	18,800	22,466 00	18,800 00
State Nat'l Bank, Boston . .	5,000	6,237 50	5,000 00
Hamilton Nat'l Bank, Boston . .	22,600	25,538 00	22,600 00
Blackstone Nat'l Bank, Boston .	49,000	56,550 00	49,000 00
Traders' Nat'l Bank, Boston . .	6,300	6,426 00	6,300 00
City Nat'l Bank, Boston . . .	3,900	4,806 75	3,900 00
Revere Nat'l Bank, Boston . .	10,100	12,322 00	10,100 00
Continental Nat'l Bank, Boston .	10,000	11,875 00	10,000 00
Suffolk Nat'l Bank, Boston . .	9,700	11,821 88	9,700 00
Hide and Leather Nat'l B'k, Boston,	30,000	35,475 00	30,000 00
Republic Nat'l Bank, Boston . .	19,800	24,700 50	19,800 00
Eliot Nat'l Bank, Boston. . .	33,200	41,002 00	33,200 00
Faneuil Hall Nat'l Bank, Boston .	5,000	6,525 00	5,000 00
Shoe and Leather Nat'l B'k, Boston,	28,000	31,500 00	28,000 00
Freeman's Nat'l Bank, Boston .	21,500	26,445 00	21,500 00
Manufacturers' Nat'l Bank, Boston,	8,200	9,020 00	8,200 00
Second Nat'l Bank, Boston . .	8,100	12,532 25	8,100 00

BANK STOCK — Concluded.

	Par Value.	Estimated Market Value.	Amount Invested.
Third Nat'l Bank, Boston . .	$30,000	$32,100 00	$30,000 00
Massachusetts Nat'l Bank, Boston .	4,000	4,960 00	4,000 00
Atlantic Nat'l Bank, Boston . .	10,000	15,350 00	10,000 00
Old Boston Nat'l Bank, Boston .	2,200	2,684 00	2,200 00
Citizens' Nat'l Bank, Worcester .	4,400	5,060 00	4,400 00
City Nat'l Bank, Worcester . .	24,500	26,460 00	24,500 00
Central Nat'l Bank, Worcester .	15,400	21,560 00	15,400 00
Quinsigamond Nat'l B'k, Worcester,	13,300	15,960 00	13,300 00
Mechanics' Nat'l Bank, Worcester .	13,500	16,200 00	13,500 00
Worcester Nat'l Bank, Worcester .	52,400	66,548 00	52,400 00
	$658,600	$800,349 75	$658,600 00

RAILROAD BONDS.

	Par Value.	Estimated Market Value.	Amount Invested.
Eastern 4½s	$22,500	$24,750 00	$22,500 00
Worcester and Nashua 5s .	12,000	12,180 00	12,000 00
Boston and Maine 7s . .	40,000	51,000 00	40,000 00
Boston and Albany 6s . .	35,000	42,000 00	35,000 00
Old Colony 7s	25,000	32,125 00	25,000 00
	$134,500	$162,055 00	$134,500 00

PLYMOUTH FIVE CENTS SAVINGS BANK — PLYMOUTH.

Incorporated April 6, 1855. Number of corporators, 70.

WILLIAM R. DREW, *President*. *Treasurer*, WILLIAM W. BREWSTER.

STATEMENT.

LIABILITIES.		ASSETS.	
Deposits	$563,320 44	Public funds	$159,400 00
Earnings undivided	13,419 12	Bank stock	29,600 00
Guaranty fund	6,476 32	Loans on bank stock	1,000 00
Suspense account	123 15	Railroad bonds	20,000 00
		Real estate	2,900 00
		Real estate by foreclosure	14,884 79
		Loans on real estate	265,207 00
		Loans on personal security,	48,605 00
		Loans to counties, cities, or towns	18,510 00
		Expense account	538 43
		Cash on hand and in banks,	22,693 81
	$583,339 03		$583,339 03

Loans on Bank Stock, amount on each: —

On 3 shares Old Colony National Bank, Plymouth	$300 00
On 7 shares Merchants' National Bank, Boston	700 00

Cash on Deposit in Banks, amount in each: —

National Bank of the Commonwealth, Boston	$9,888 84
Plymouth National Bank, Plymouth	5,862 46
Old Colony National Bank, Plymouth	6,290 41

Amount invested in real estate (for banking purposes)	$2,900 00
Estimated value of the same	3,000 00
Amount of real estate held by foreclosure	14,884 79
Assessed value of the same	13,200 00
Amount of income received from the same	864 04
Amount of municipal tax on real estate	281 70

Whole amount of interest or profits received or earned		$30,962 24
Rate and amount of each semi-annual dividend for previous year	2 per cent	10,317 70
	2 per cent	10,727 04

Times for the dividends fixed by the by-laws: second Tuesday of January and July.

The total amount of loans, with each specified rate of interest: $12,000, 4 per cent; $6,000, 4½ per cent; $42,000, 5 per cent; $3,950, 5½ per cent; $163,715, 6 per cent; $52,030, 6½ per cent; $45,317, 7 per cent; $3,315, 7 3/10 per cent; $4,845, 7½ per cent; $150, 8 per cent.

Number of outstanding loans which are of an amount not exceeding $3,000 each	314	
Aggregate amount of the same		211,372 00
Number of open accounts	2,304	

Number and amount of deposits received for previous year,	1,212	$75,210 94
Number and amount of deposits of and exceeding $300 at any one time for the previous year	67	37,599 84
Number and amount of withdrawals	688	59,883 73
Number of accounts opened the previous year	253	
Number of accounts closed the previous year	166	
Amount of expenses of the corporation during previous year		1,746 43
Amount of treasurer's bond		10,000 00

Date of examination by commisioner: Oct. 4.

PUBLIC FUNDS.

	Par Value.	Estimated Market Value.	Amount Invested.
United States 4½s, registered	$10,000	$11,300 00	$10,000 00
" " 3½s, registered	10,000	10,187 00	10,000 00
" " 4s, coupons	2,000	2,360 00	2,000 00
State, city, and town bonds:—			
State of Maine 6s	$14,000	$16,240 00	$14,000 00
of New Hampshire 6s	5,900	6,782 00	5,900 00
City of Lynn 6s	1,000	1,100 00	1,000 00
of Portland, Me., 6s	10,000	11,000 00	10,000 00
of Bath, Me., 6s	3,000	3,030 00	3,000 00
of Cambridge 6s	9,000	9,710 00	9,000 00
of New London, Conn., 7s	12,000	15,600 00	12,000 00
of New Bedford 7s	10,000	13,200 00	10,000 00
of Somerville 6½s	5,000	5,250 00	5,000 00
of Manchester, N.H., 6s	1,500	1,680 00	1,500 00
of Springfield 6s	5,000	6,450 00	5,000 00
of Bangor, Me., 6s	9,000	10,890 00	9,000 00
of Belfast, Me., 6s	2,000	2,010 00	2,000 00
of Lewiston, Me., 6s	2,000	2,200 00	2,000 00
of Providence, R.I., 5s	3,000	3,257 00	3,000 00
of Lawrence 5s	5,000	6,087 00	5,000 00
of Brockton 4s	10,000	10,000 00	10,000 00
of Northampton 6s	10,000	11,300 00	10,000 00
of Boston 5s	3,000	3,060 00	3,000 00
Town of Methuen 6s	3,000	3,630 00	3,000 00
of Natick 7s	1,000	1,070 00	1,000 00
of Plymouth 7s	13,000	16,185 00	13,000 00
	$159,400	$183,608 00	$159,400 00

BANK STOCK.

Commonwealth Nat'l Bank, Boston,	$5,000	$6,225 00	$5,000 00
Atlas Nat'l Bank, Boston	2,500	3,125 00	2,500 00
Webster Nat'l Bank, Boston	2,500	2,787 00	2,500 00
Pacific Nat'l Bank, Boston	2,500	2,625 00	2,500 00
First Ward Nat'l Bank, Boston	2,100	2,520 00	2,100 00
Revere Nat'l Bank, Boston	1,500	1,830 00	1,500 00
Republic Nat'l Bank, Boston	1,500	1,965 00	1,500 00

BANK STOCK — Concluded.

	Par Value.	Estimated Market Value.	Amount Invested.
Merchants' Nat'l Bank, Boston .	$1,000	$1,460 00	$1,000 00
Metropolitan Nat'l Bank, Boston .	1,000	1,200 00	1,000 00
City Nat'l Bank, Boston . . .	1,000	1,270 00	1,000 00
Commerce Nat'l Bank, Boston .	800	1,030 00	800 00
North Nat'l Bank, Boston . .	600	850 00	600 00
Shoe and Leather Nat'l B'k, Boston,	500	565 00	500 00
Third Nat'l Bank, Springfield .	1,000	1,450 00	1,000 00
Brockton Nat'l Bank, Brockton .	2,000	2,120 00	2,000 00
Plymouth Nat'l Bank, Plymouth .	1,600	1,760 00	1,600 00
Old Colony Nat'l Bank, Plymouth .	2,500	3,375 00	2,500 00
	$29,600	$36,157 00	$29,600 00

RAILROAD BONDS.

	Par Value.	Estimated Market Value.	Amount Invested.
Old Colony 6s	$5,000	$5,875 00	$5,000 00
Cheshire 6s	4,000	4,360 00	4,000 00
Boston and Maine 7s	1,000	1,265 00	1,000 00
Eastern 4½s	10,000	10,975 00	10,000 00
	$20,000	$22,475 00	$20,000 00

PLYMOUTH SAVINGS BANK – PLYMOUTH.

Incorporated 1829. Number of corporators, 50.

WILLIAM H. NELSON, *President*. *Treasurer*, JOHN J. RUSSELL.

STATEMENT.

LIABILITIES.		ASSETS.	
Deposits	$2,110,107 44	Public funds	$386,471 25
Earnings undivided	68,878 47	Bank stock	426,541 00
Guaranty fund	50,000 00	Loans on bank stock	8,300 00
Suspense account	200 97	Railroad bonds	135,000 00
		Real estate	7,000 00
		Real estate by foreclosure	40,807 58
		Loans on real estate	631,491 00
		Loans on personal security,	389,830 00
		Loans to counties, cities, or towns	182,500 00
		Deposit in banks on interest,	15,275 28
		Cash on hand	5,970 77
	$2,229,186 88		$2,229,186 88

Loans on Bank Stock, amount on each:—

On 42 shares Old Colony National Bank	$2,900 00
On 20 shares Plymouth National Bank and 13 shares Old Colony National Bank	3,300 00
On 18 shares Plymouth National Bank	1,800 00
On 5 shares New England National Bank	300 00

Cash on Deposit in Banks, amount in each:—

Boston National Bank, Boston	$4,868 93
Plymouth National Bank. Plymouth	3,690 91
Old Colony National Bank, Plymouth	4,470 39
National Bank of the Commonwealth, Boston	2,245 05

Amount invested in real estate (for banking purposes)	$7,000 00
Estimated value of the same	7,000 00
Amount of real estate held by foreclosure	40,807 58
Assessed value of the same	78,025 00
Amount of income received from the same	4,432 83
Amount of municipal tax on real estate	1,130 43

Whole amount of interest or profits received or earned	110,586 18
Rate and amount of each semi-annual dividend for previous year: 2½ per cent	50,544 68
2 per cent	41,282 11

Times for the dividends fixed by the by-laws: January and July.

The total amount of loans, with each specified rate of interest: $178,000, 4 per cent; $104,700, 4½ per cent; $273,700, 5 per cent; $88,350, 5½ per cent; $394,385, 6 per cent; $45,856, 6½ per cent; $127,130, 7 per cent.

Number of outstanding loans which are of an amount not exceeding $3,000 each . . . 231

Aggregate amount of the same . . . 245,621 00

Number of open accounts	6,349	
Number and amount of deposits received for previous year,	2,258	$183,485 50
Number and amount of deposits of and exceeding $300 at any one time for the previous year	153	74,437 00
Number and amount of withdrawals	2,809	230,328 57
Number of accounts opened the previous year	458	
Number of accounts closed the previous year	442	
Amount of expenses of the corporation during previous year .		6,000 00
Amount of treasurer's bond		20,000 00

Date of examination by commissioner: Oct. 4.

PUBLIC FUNDS.

	Par Value.	Estimated Market Value.	Amount Invested.
United States 6s, 1881	$70,000	$70,700 00	$70,000 00
State, city, and town bonds: —			
State of Maine	$18,000	$19,620 00	$17,705 00
of Rhode Island	12,000	12,840 00	12,000 00
City of Salem	10,000	11,400 00	10,000 00
of Cambridge	7,000	7,560 00	7,000 00
of Hartford, Conn.	5,000	5,700 00	4,662 50
of Portland, Me.	12,000	12,840 00	11,100 00
of Meriden, Conn.	25,000	28,750 00	25,000 00
of New London, Conn. . . .	50,000	63,000 00	50,000 00
of Newburyport	5,000	5,350 00	5,000 00
of Holyoke	50,000	58,500 00	46,750 00
of Fall River	10,000	11,500 00	7,845 00
of Lawrence	30,000	34,500 00	28,425 00
of New Bedford	10,000	13,000 00	10,000 00
of Lynn	13,000	14,950 00	12,983 75
of Bangor, Me.	6,000	7,200 00	6,000 00
of Brockton	16,000	16,320 00	16,000 00
Town of Plymouth	11,000	11,440 00	11,000 00
of Franklin	10,000	10,500 00	10,000 00
of West Springfield . . .	25,000	26,000 00	25,000 00
	$395,000	$441,670 00	$386,471 25

BANK STOCK.

State Nat'l Bank, Boston . .	$13,000	$16,250 00	$13,000 00
Merchants' Nat'l Bank, Boston .	22,500	32,025 00	22,500 00
Plymouth Nat'l Bank, Plymouth .	17,400	19,140 00	17,400 00
Old Colony Nat'l Bank, Plymouth .	26,200	35,370 00	26,200 00
Bristol County Nat'l B'k, Taunton .	17,100	24,795 00	17,100 00
Hingham Nat'l Bank, Hingham .	4,200	4,200 00	4,200 00
Market Nat'l Bank, Boston . .	12,800	13,952 00	10,240 00
Traders' Nat'l Bank, Boston . .	8,000	8,160 00	6,000 00
City Nat'l Bank, Boston . . .	8,400	10,500 00	8,400 00
Suffolk Nat'l Bank, Boston . .	6,200	7,440 00	6,200 00
North Nat'l Bank, Boston . .	900	1,260 00	900 00
Massachusetts Nat'l Bank, Boston .	8,500	10,200 00	8,500 00

Bank Stock — Concluded.

	Par Value.	Estimated Market Value.	Amount Invested.
Second Nat'l Bank, Boston . .	$27,000	$40,500 00	$27,000 00
Tremont Nat'l Bank, Boston . .	19,500	23,400 00	17,745 00
Atlantic Nat'l Bank, Boston . .	4,100	6,150 00	4,100 00
Eagle Nat'l Bank, Boston . .	8,000	9,040 00	8,000 00
Old Boston Nat'l Bank, Boston .	5,450	6,649 00	5,450 00
New England Nat'l Bank, Boston .	8,600	12,728 00	8,600 00
Boylston Nat'l Bank, Boston . .	7,000	8,750 00	7,000 00
Exchange Nat'l Bank, Boston . .	10,600	15,052 00	10,600 00
Abington Nat'l Bank, Abington .	1,500	1,875 00	1,500 00
Commerce Nat'l Bank, Boston .	10,800	12,960 00	9,180 00
North America Nat'l Bank, Boston .	12,000	13,560 00	10,800 00
Railroad Nat'l Bank, Lowell . .	11,000	12,100 00	11,000 00
Globe Nat'l Bank, Boston . .	2,900	3,190 00	2,494 00
Freeman's Nat'l Bank, Boston .	2,800	3,304 00	2,380 00
Shawmut Nat'l Bank, Boston . .	9,300	11,625 00	8,950 00
Union Nat'l Bank, Weymouth .	10,000	15,000 00	10,000 00
Atlas Nat'l Bank, Boston . .	23,400	29,016 00	23,400 00
Hamilton Nat'l Bank, Boston . .	5,300	6,466 00	5,300 00
Boston Nat'l Bank, Boston . .	13,900	17,375 00	12,788 00
Webster Nat'l Bank, Boston . .	11,200	12,320 00	10,080 00
Blackstone Nat'l Bank, Boston .	4,800	5,472 00	3,712 00
Columbian Nat'l Bank, Boston .	4,200	5,880 00	4,200 00
Howard Nat'l Bank, Boston . .	5,400	7,020 00	5,022 00
Revere Nat'l Bank, Boston . .	12,000	14,400 00	10,800 00
Republic Nat'l Bank, Boston . .	18,800	24,440 00	18,800 00
Commonwealth Nat'l Bank, Boston .	10,000	12,300 00	8,500 00
Third Nat'l Bank, Springfield . .	10,000	14,500 00	10,000 00
Manufacturers' Nat'l Bank, Boston .	10,000	10,900 00	6,500 00
First Ward Nat'l Bank, Boston .	10,000	11,800 00	7,000 00
Home Nat'l Bank, Brockton . .	10,000	10,000 00	9,000 00
Brockton Nat'l Bank, Brockton .	6,000	6,000 00	6,000 00
	$450,750	$567,664 00	$426,541 00

Railroad Bonds.

	Par Value.	Estimated Market Value.	Amount Invested.
Old Colony	$20,000	$23,200 00	$20,000 00
Eastern	10,500	11,550 00	5,000 00
Boston and Albany	50,000	63,000 00	50,000 00
Boston and Lowell	25,000	25,000 00	25,000 00
Salem and Lowell	25,000	30,000 00	25,000 00
Boston and Maine	10,000	12,600 00	10,000 00
	$140,500	$165,350 00	$135,000 00

PROVIDENT INSTITUTION FOR SAVINGS IN THE TOWN OF BOSTON — BOSTON.

Incorporated December, 1816. Number of corporators, 127.

JAMES S. AMORY, *President*. *Treasurer*, CHARLES J. MORRILL.

STATEMENT.

LIABILITIES.		ASSETS.	
Deposits	$23,975,481 37	Public funds . .	$4,853,000 00
Earnings undivided .	150,063 98	Loans on public funds .	550,000 00
Guaranty fund . .	210,000 00	Bank stock	1,134,625 00
Suspense account .	11,749 68	Loans on bank stock . .	1,300 00
Taxes on estates . .	18,547 26	Railroad bonds . . .	584,000 00
		Real estate	80,000 00
		Real estate by foreclosure .	133,261 04
		Loans on real estate . .	5,924,514 00
		Loans on personal security,*	9,206,928 66
		Loans to counties, cities, or towns	803,800 00
		Deposit in banks on interest,	1,042,286 97
		Expense account . . .	14,533 15
		Cash on hand	37,593 47
	$24,365,842 29		$24,365,842 29

Loans on Public Funds: —

On $550,000 United States 5s, extended at 3½ per cent $550,000 00

Loans on Bank Stock: —

On 30 shares Merchants' National Bank, New Bedford, and 10 shares National Bank of Commerce, New Bedford $1,300 00

Cash on Deposit in Banks, amount in each: —

Merchants' National Bank	$340,808 31
Exchange National Bank	395,732 57
Webster National Bank	51,161 01
Market National Bank	52,675 87
Merchandise National Bank	103,263 96
Suffolk National Bank	14,113 83
Atlas National Bank	12,623 65
Third National Bank	51,907 77
Framingham National Bank	20,000 00

Amount invested in real estate (for banking purposes)	$80,000 00
Estimated value of the same	217,000 00
Amount of real estate held by foreclosure	133,261 04
Assessed value of the same	141,000 00
Amount of income received from the same	3,672 42
Amount of municipal tax on real estate	5,001 22

Whole amount of interest or profits received		$1,069,783 41
Rate and amount of each semi-annual dividend for previous year	1½ per cent	331,782 74
	1½ per cent	338,979 03

* This institution has been notified that these loans exceed the legal limit.

Times for the dividends fixed by the by-laws: third Wednesday in January and July.

Average annual per cent of dividends for the term ending at time of and including last extra dividend: 4 per cent.

The total amount of loans, with each specified rate of interest: $90,000, 3 per cent; $50,000, 3¼ per cent; $5,779,000, 3½ per cent; $470,000, 3¾ per cent; $2,377,266.66, 4 per cent; $30,000, 4¼ per cent; $5,059,000, 4½ per cent; $4,058,700, 5 per cent; $779,900, 5½ per cent; $386,000, 5¾ per cent; $2,538,701, 6 per cent; $341,175, 7 per cent.

Number of outstanding loans which are of an amount not exceeding $3.000 each	50	
Aggregate amount of the same		$106,620 00
Number of open accounts	61,496	
Number and amount of deposits received for previous year,	61,597	5,145,211 84
Number and amount of deposits of and exceeding $300 at any one time for the previous year	3,161	1,649,216 00
Number and amount of withdrawals	42,484	4,491,981 24
Number of accounts opened the previous year	10,795	
Number of accounts closed the previous year	7,760	
Amount of expenses of the corporation during previous year		45,081 50
Amount of treasurer's bond		20,000 00

Date of examination by commissioner: Dec. 9.

PUBLIC FUNDS.

	Par Value.	Estimated Market Value.	Amount Invested.
United States 6s, extended 3½	$1,353,000	$1,364,838 75	$1,353,000 00
" " 5s, " "	1,900,000	1,928,500 00	1,900,000 00
" " 4½s	1,300,000	1,467,375 00	1,300,000 00
" " 4s	300,000	348,000 00	300,000 00
	$4,853,000	$5,108,713 75	$4,853,000 00

BANK STOCK.

Atlantic Nat'l Bank, Boston	$21,500	$33,002 50	$21,500 00
Atlas Nat'l Bank, Boston	67,500	84,375 00	67,500 00
Old Boston Nat'l Bank, Boston	35,000	42,700 00	35,000 00
Columbian Nat'l Bank, Boston	42,800	60,990 00	42,800 00
Continental Nat'l Bank, Boston	66,800	79,241 50	66,800 00
City Nat'l Bank, Boston	31,500	40,005 00	31,500 00
Eagle Nat'l Bank, Boston	45,000	53,887 50	45,000 00
Globe Nat'l Bank, Boston	31,500	35,122 50	31,500 00
Hamilton Nat'l Bank, Boston	33,700	41,703 75	33,700 00
Hide and Leather Nat'l B'k, Boston,	22,500	26,212 50	22,500 00
Massachusetts Nat'l Bank, Boston	22,500	27,900 00	22,500 00
Market Nat'l Bank, Boston	54,300	60,137 25	54,300 00
Merchants' Nat'l Bank, Boston	90,400	131,984 00	90,400 00
New England Nat'l Bank, Boston	23,900	35,611 00	23,900 00

BANK STOCK — Concluded.

	Par Value.	Estimated Market Value.	Amount Invested.
North Nat'l Bank, Boston . .	$43,000	$60,952 50	$43,000 00
Revere Nat'l Bank, Boston . .	33,200	40,504 00	33,200 00
Second Nat'l Bank, Boston . .	64,000	96,960 00	64,000 00
State Nat'l Bank, Boston . .	48,200	60,491 00	48,200 00
Suffolk Nat'l Bank, Boston . .	45,000	54,843 75	45,000 00
Shoe and Leather Nat'l B'k, Boston,	50,000	56,500 00	50,000 00
Traders' Nat'l Bank, Boston . .	3,000	3,060 00	2,625 00
Tremont Nat'l Bank, Boston . .	90,000	109,800 00	90,000 00
Union Nat'l Bank, Boston . .	31,200	47,892 00	31,200 00
Webster Nat'l Bank, Boston . .	100,000	111,500 00	100,000 00
Washington Nat'l Bank, Boston .	38,500	53,900 00	38,500 00
	$1,135,000	$1,449,275 75	$1,134,625 00

RAILROAD BONDS.

	Par Value.	Estimated Market Value.	Amount Invested.
Old Colony 6s	$250,000	$293,750 00	$250,000 00
Eastern 4½s	265,000	294,150 00	234,000 00
Boston and Albany 6s . . .	100,000	117,500 00	100,000 00
	$615,000	$705,400 00	$584,000 00

PROVIDENT INSTITUTION FOR SAVINGS IN THE TOWNS OF SALISBURY AND AMESBURY—SALISBURY.

Incorporated 1828. Number of corporators, 16.

S. WOODMAN, *President*. *Treasurer*, ALFRED C. WEBSTER.

STATEMENT.

LIABILITIES.		ASSETS.	
Deposits	$1,289,525 98	Public funds	$418,500 00
Earnings undivided	58,496 20	Bank stock	141,325 00
Guaranty fund	31,975 11	Loans on bank stock	500 00
		Railroad bonds	51,500 00
		Real estate	2,500 00
		Real estate by foreclosure	5,659 55
		Loans on real estate	218,000 00
		Loans on personal security,	110,400 00
		Loans to counties, cities, or towns	115,000 00
		Deposit in banks on interest,	309,766 54
		Expense account	1,020 96
		Cash on hand	5,825 24
	$1,379,997 29		$1,379,997 29

Loans on Bank Stock:—

On 5 shares Powow River National Bank, Salisbury . $500 00

Cash on Deposit in Banks, amount in each:—

Powow River National Bank, Salisbury	$141,155 56
Maverick National Bank, Boston	43,051 00
Blackstone National Bank, Boston	125,559 98

Amount invested in real estate (for banking purposes)	$2,500 00
Estimated value of the same	5,000 00
Amount of real estate held by foreclosure	5,659 55
Assessed value of the same	3,100 00
Amount of income received from the same	275 00
Amount of municipal tax on real estate	56 34

Whole amount of interest or profits received or earned . . . $64,268 13

Rate and amount of each semi-annual dividend for previous year: 2 per cent . 24,256 71; 2 per cent . 24,850 88

Times for the dividends fixed by the by-laws: third Wednesday in April and October.

Average annual per cent of dividends for the term ending at time of and including last extra dividend: $6\frac{3}{16}$ per cent.

The total amount of loans, with each specified rate of interest: $20,000, 4½ per cent; $17,500, 4¾ per cent; $73,200, 5 per cent; $1,300, 5½ per cent; $173,900, 6 per cent; $16,500, 6¼ per cent; $134,700, 7 per cent; $6,800, 7½ per cent.

Number of outstanding loans which are of an amount not exceeding $3,000 each . . . 263

Aggregate amount of the same . . . 241,400 00

Number of open accounts	3,912	
Number and amount of deposits received for previous year,	2,113	$144,784 00
Number and amount of deposits of and exceeding $300 at any one time for the previous year	101	50,528 00
Number and amount of withdrawals	1,583	156,733 07
Number of accounts opened the previous year	452	
Number of accounts closed the previous year	308	
Amount of expenses of the corporation during previous year .		2,126 84
Amount of treasurer's bond		20,000 00

Date of examination by commissioner: June 11.

PUBLIC FUNDS.

	Par Value.	Estimated Market Value.	Amount Invested.
United States 6s, currency . .	$20,000	$26,000 00	$20,000 00
State, city, and town bonds: —			
State of New Hampshire . .	$10,000	$10,500 00	$10,000 00
of Maine	21,000	23,000 00	21,000 00
of Rhode Island . . .	10,000	10,600 00	10,000 00
City of Augusta, Me. . . .	10,000	10,600 00	10,000 00
of Lewiston, Me. . . .	10,000	10,100 00	10,000 00
of Springfield	10,000	12,000 00	10,000 00
of Portsmouth, N.H. . .	5,000	5,600 00	5,000 00
of Bangor, Me. . . .	45,000	50,000 00	45,000 00
of Lawrence	5,000	5,500 00	5,000 00
of Belfast, Me. . . .	15,000	15,000 00	15,000 00
of Fall River 6s . . .	20,000	22,000 00	20,000 00
of Fall River 5s . . .	10,000	10,500 00	10,000 00
of Somerville	40,000	41,600 00	40,000 00
of Portland, Me. . . .	40,000	45,000 00	40,000 00
of Manchester, N.H. . .	17,000	19,000 00	17,000 00
of Chelsea	54,000	60,000 00	54,000 00
of Cambridge	27,000	29,900 00	27,000 00
of Dover, N.H. . . .	4,000	4,200 00	4,000 00
of Charlestown . . .	30,000	33,500 00	30,000 00
of Holyoke	5,000	6,000 00	5,000 00
Town of Amesbury . . .	10,500	10,500 00	10,500 00
	$418,500	$461,100 00	$418,500 00

BANK STOCK.

First Ward Nat'l Bank, Boston .	$5,000	$5,750 00	$5,000 00
Shawmut Nat'l Bank, Boston . .	4,900	6,125 00	4,900 00
Second Nat'l Bank, Boston . .	1,800	2,700 00	1,800 00
State Nat'l Bank, Boston . .	3,500	4,375 00	3,500 00
Tremont Nat'l Bank, Boston . .	4,900	5,880 00	4,900 00
Commonwealth Nat'l Bank, Boston,	5,000	6,000 00	5,000 00
Columbian Nat'l Bank, Boston .	3,500	4,900 00	3,500 00
Exchange Nat'l Bank, Boston .	5,000	7,000 00	5,000 00

BANK STOCK — Concluded.

	Par Value.	Estimated Market Value.	Amount Invested.
Atlas Nat'l Bank, Boston . .	$7,500	$9,375 00	$7,500 00
Globe Nat'l Bank, Boston . .	2,500	2,750 00	2,500 00
Redemption Nat'l Bank, Boston .	5,000	6,750 00	5,000 00
Hide and Leather Nat'l B'k, Boston,	7,500	8,625 00	7,500 00
Howard Nat'l Bank, Boston . .	4,000	5,200 00	4,000 00
Eagle Nat'l Bank, Boston . .	3,500	3,850 00	3,500 00
Suffolk Nat'l Bank, Boston . .	5,700	6,840 00	5,700 00
Merchants' Nat'l Bank, Boston .	3,500	5,075 00	3,500 00
Commerce Nat'l Bank, Boston .	3,000	3,600 00	3,000 00
Atlantic Nat'l Bank, Boston . .	2,200	3,300 00	2,200 00
New England Nat'l Bank, Boston .	1,500	2,172 00	1,500 00
Republic Nat'l Bank, Boston . .	3,000	3,900 00	3,000 00
Traders' Nat'l Bank, Boston . .	1,800	1,800 00	1,800 00
City Nat'l Bank, Boston . . .	1,000	1,250 00	1,000 00
Shoe and Leather Nat'l B'k, Boston,	2,500	2,750 00	2,500 00
Webster Nat'l Bank, Boston . .	4,000	4,400 00	4,000 00
Maverick Nat'l Bank, Boston . .	2,000	4,800 00	2,000 00
Eliot Nat'l Bank, Boston . .	4,200	5,040 00	4,200 00
First Nat'l Bank, Boston . .	1,500	3,000 00	1,500 00
Boylston Nat'l Bank, Boston . .	3,500	4,375 00	3,500 00
Revere Nat'l Bank, Boston . .	7,500	9,000 00	7,500 00
Blackstone Nat'l Bank, Boston .	6,000	6,900 00	6,000 00
Old Boston Nat'l Bank, Boston .	2,150	2,623 00	2,150 00
Faneuil Hall Nat'l Bank, Boston .	2,600	3,380 00	2,600 00
Union Nat'l Bank, Boston . .	2,500	3,750 00	2,500 00
Bay State Nat'l Bank, Lawrence .	3,375	4,000 00	3,375 00
Railroad Nat'l Bank, Lowell . .	4,200	4,500 00	4,200 00
Powow River Nat'l B'k, Salisbury .	5,000	8,000 00	5,000 00
Georgetown Nat'l Bank, Georgetown,	5,000	5,000 00	5,000 00
	$141,325	$178,735 00	$141,325 00

RAILROAD BONDS.

Eastern $4\frac{1}{2}$s	$42,000	$45,500 00	$31,500 00
Boston and Albany 7s . . .	10,000	12,500 00	10,000 00
Boston and Maine 7s . . .	5,000	6,200 00	5,000 00
West Amesbury Branch 7s . .	5,000	6,000 00	5,000 00
	$62,000	$70,200 00	$51,500 00

QUINCY SAVINGS BANK—QUINCY.

Incorporated 1845. Number of corporators, 45.

CHARLES MARSH, *President*. *Treasurer*, GEORGE L. GILL.

STATEMENT.

Liabilities.		Assets.	
Deposits	$1,044,920 73	Public funds	$55,500 00
Earnings undivided	3,574 13	Bank stock	99,406 49
Guaranty fund	17,500 00	Loans on bank stock	4,800 00
		Railroad bonds	60,000 00
		Real estate by foreclosure	147,618 83
		Loans on real estate	498,899 03
		Loans on personal security,	146,900 00
		Deposit in banks on interest,	18,838 33
		Expense account	219 60
		Premium account	14,386 04
		Interest account	16,772 80
		Taxes, etc.	611 06
		Cash on hand	2,042 68
	$1,065,994 86		$1,065,994 86

Loans on Bank Stock:—

On 47 shares Mount Wollaston National Bank, Quincy $4,800 00

Cash on Deposit in Bank:—

Granite National Bank, Quincy $18,838 33

Amount of real estate held by foreclosure	$147,618 83
Assessed value of the same	129,500 00
Amount of income received from the same	7,300 00
Amount of municipal tax on real estate	1,834 09

Whole amount of interest or profits received or earned $48,387 77

Rate and amount of each semi-annual dividend for previous year . . . . { 1½ per cent . . 14,899 98; 2 per cent . . 19,089 19 }

Times for the dividends fixed by the by-laws: first Tuesday in April and October.

Average annual per cent of dividends for the term ending at time of and including last extra dividend: 7½ per cent.

The total amount of loans, with each specified rate of interest: $64,000, 4 per cent; $140,700, 5 per cent; $15,000, 5½ per cent; $212,150, 6 per cent; $5,600, 6¼ per cent; $185,449.03, 7 per cent; $21,200, 7$\frac{3}{10}$ per cent; $6,500, 7½ per cent.

Number of outstanding loans which are of an amount not exceeding $3,000 each	213	
Aggregate amount of the same		265,705 03
Number of open accounts	3,090	
Number and amount of deposits received for previous year,	2,438	184,143 95
Number and amount of deposits of and exceeding $300 at any one time for the previous year	145	81,476 00
Number and amount of withdrawals	2,286	209,872 71

Number of accounts opened the previous year	450	
Number of accounts closed the previous year	289	
Amount of expenses of the corporation during previous year		$3,012 49
Amount of treasurer's bond		30,000 00

Date of examination by commissioner: May 6.

PUBLIC FUNDS.

	Par Value.	Estimated Market Value.	Amount Invested.
City and town bonds: —			
City of Lawrence 6s	$5,000	$5,500 00	$5,000 00
of Providence, R.I., 5s	5,000	5,900 00	5,000 00
of Somerville 5s	40,500	45,360 00	40,500 00
Town of Pawtucket 5s	5,000	5,500 00	5,000 00
	$55,500	$62,260 00	$55,500 00

BANK STOCK.

Washington Nat'l Bank, Boston	$800	$1,120 00	$844 00
Hide and Leather Nat'l B'k, Boston,	1,500	1,770 00	1,500 00
Eliot Nat'l Bank, Boston	1,700	2,040 00	1,706 20
Exchange Nat'l Bank, Boston	2,000	2,880 00	2,475 33
Webster Nat'l Bank, Boston	2,000	2,240 00	2,000 00
Boston Nat'l Bank, Boston	3,300	4,224 00	3,338 08
Atlas Nat'l Bank, Boston	6,200	7,750 00	6,909 25
Merchants' Nat'l Bank, Boston	2,500	3,675 00	2,657 50
State Nat'l Bank, Boston	2,600	3,250 00	2,800 00
North Nat'l Bank, Boston	3,000	4,260 00	3,450 00
Traders' Nat'l Bank, Boston	3,500	3,605 00	3,555 00
North America Nat'l Bank, Boston	6,700	7,705 00	6,925 00
Republic Nat'l Bank, Boston	7,500	9,825 00	9,600 00
Manufacturers' Nat'l Bank, Boston,	25,500	28,050 00	26,205 00
Revere Nat'l Bank, Boston	1,800	2,196 00	1,991 75
City Nat'l Bank, Boston	1,900	2,413 00	2,244 00
Granite Nat'l Bank, Quincy	10,000	13,000 00	10,605 38
Mount Wollaston Nat'l B'k, Quincy,	10,000	13,000 00	10,600 00
	$92,500	$113,003 00	$99,406 49

RAILROAD BONDS.

Salem and Lowell 6s	$10,000	$11,500 00	$10,000 00
Boston, Clinton, Fitchburg, and New Bedford 5s *	50,000	52,500 00	50,000 00
	$60,000	$64,000 00	$60,000 00

* This bank has been notified that the investment in these bonds is illegal.

RANDOLPH SAVINGS BANK—RANDOLPH.

Incorporated 1851. Number of corporators, 61.

J. WHITE BELCHER, *President*. *Treasurer*, SETH TURNER.

STATEMENT.

LIABILITIES.		ASSETS.	
Deposits	$714,320 96	Public funds	$157,000 00
Earnings undivided	2,828 31	Bank stock	252,400 00
Guaranty fund	18,116 24	Railroad bonds	107,500 00
		Loans on railroad stock	500 00
		Real estate by foreclosure	15,414 68
		Loans on real estate	117,960 00
		Loans on personal security,	26,550 00
		Loans to counties, cities, or towns	15,000 00
		Deposit in bank on interest,	39,849 92
		Cash on hand	3,090 91
	$735,265 51		$735,265 51

Loans on Railroad Stock:—

On 5 shares Old Colony Railroad $500 00

Cash on Deposit in Bank:—

Randolph National Bank, Randolph $39,849 92

Amount of real estate held by foreclosure		$15,414 68
Assessed value of the same		15,800 00
Amount of income received from the same		571 13
Amount of municipal tax on real estate		172 90
Whole amount of interest or profits received or earned		$43,036 86
Rate and amount of each semi-annual dividend for previous year	2 per cent	13,301 31
	2 per cent	13,704 96

Times for the dividends fixed by the by-laws: April and October.

Average annual per cent of dividends for the term ending at time of and including last extra dividend: 6½ per cent.

The total amount of loans, with each specified rate of interest: $10,000, 4 per cent; $19,000, 5 per cent; $12,500, 5½ per cent; $46,920, 6 per cent; $21,450, 6½ per cent; $34,400, 7 per cent; $440, 7 3/10 per cent; $9,550, 7½ per cent; $5,750, 8 per cent.

Number of outstanding loans which are of an amount not exceeding $3,000 each	66	
Aggregate amount of the same		67,140 00
Number of open accounts	2,096	
Number and amount of deposits received for previous year	922	92,230 86
Number and amount of deposits of and exceeding $300 at any one time for the previous year	88	41,552 74
Number and amount of withdrawals	746	79,454 21
Number of accounts opened the previous year	269	
Number of accounts closed the previous year	179	
Amount of expenses of the corporation during previous year		1,603 26
Amount of treasurer's bond		15,000 00

Date of examination by commissioner: May 19.

PUBLIC FUNDS.

	Par Value.	Estimated Market Value.	Amount Invested.
United States bonds	$105,000	$111,290 00	$105,000 00
State and city bonds:—			
State of New Hampshire . .	$1,000	$1,100 00	$1,000 00
City of Portland, Me. . . .	10,000	11,000 00	10,000 00
of Springfield	15,000	19,500 00	15,000 00
of Brockton	10,000	11,500 00	10,000 00
of Lawrence	16,000	19,200 00	16,000 00
	$157,000	$183,490 00	$157,000 00

BANK STOCK.

	Par Value.	Estimated Market Value.	Amount Invested.
Atlantic Nat'l Bank, Boston . .	$9,700	$14,890 00	$12,562 50
Atlas Nat'l Bank, Boston . .	5,000	6,250 00	5,000 00
Blackstone Nat'l Bank, Boston .	9,700	11,155 00	12,000 00
Boston Nat'l Bank, Boston . .	5,000	6,400 00	5,000 00
Blue Hill Nat'l Bank, Boston . .	1,600	1,764 00	1,600 00
Central Nat'l Bank, Boston . .	5,200	6,240 00	5,200 00
City Nat'l Bank, Boston . . .	5,000	6,162 00	5,365 00
Commonwealth Nat'l Bank, Boston,	6,300	7,590 00	6,569 75
Continental Nat'l Bank, Boston .	5,000	5,925 00	5,000 00
Commerce Nat'l Bank, Boston .	6,600	8,598 00	8,060 12
Eagle Nat'l Bank, Boston . .	5,000	5,988 00	5,336 38
Eliot Nat'l Bank, Boston . .	2,000	2,405 00	2,000 00
Everett Nat'l Bank, Boston . .	10,300	12,177 00	11,604 75
Exchange Nat'l Bank, Boston . .	2,700	3,888 00	4,064 00
Freeman's Nat'l Bank, Boston .	2,500	2,993 00	3,346 00
Hamilton Nat'l Bank, Boston . .	5,000	5,650 00	6,762 50
Hide and Leather Nat'l B'k, Boston,	10,000	11,500 00	10,269 88
Howard Nat'l Bank, Boston . .	4,600	5,980 00	4,993 75
Merchandise Nat'l Bank, Boston .	2,400	2,634 00	2,400 00
Market Nat'l Bank, Boston . .	7,500	8,232 00	7,500 00
Metropolitan Nat'l Bank, Boston .	500	600 00	500 00
Merchants' Nat'l Bank, Boston .	15,000	21,900 00	19,962 62
New England Nat'l Bank, Boston .	5,000	7,412 00	6,300 00
North Nat'l Bank, Boston . .	7,000	9,958 00	8,034 13
North America Nat'l Bank, Boston .	5,000	5,738 00	5,000 00
Revere Nat'l Bank, Boston . .	3,700	4,496 00	4,700 00
Redemption Nat'l Bank, Boston .	15,000	20,250 00	19,888 00
Shawmut Nat'l Bank, Boston . .	3,000	3,825 00	3,245 25
Shoe and Leather Nat'l B'k, Boston,	10,500	11,812 00	10,500 00
State Nat'l Bank, Boston . .	4,600	5,773 00	4,876 00
Third Nat'l Bank, Boston . .	5,000	5,350 00	5,000 00
Tremont Nat'l Bank, Boston . .	5,000	6,138 00	5,000 00
Traders' Nat'l Bank, Boston . .	2,500	2,550 00	2,500 00
Union Nat'l Bank, Boston . .	2,500	3,838 00	3,681 25
Webster Nat'l Bank, Boston . .	1,000	1,140 00	1,000 00
Home Nat'l Bank, Brockton . .	5,000	6,000 00	5,000 00
Central Nat'l Bank, Lynn . .	9,700	12,028 00	9,700 00
City Nat'l Bank, Lynn . . .	3,500	5,005 00	5,078 12
Union Nat'l Bank, Weymouth . .	1,300	1,495 00	1,300 00
Taunton Nat'l Bank, Taunton .	2,500	3,375 00	2,500 00
Manufacturers' Nat'l Bank, Boston,	4,000	4,410 00	4,000 00
	$222,400	$279,514 00	$252,400 00

RAILROAD BONDS.

	Par Value.	Estimated Market Value.	Amount Invested.
Old Colony	$60,000	$69,600 00	$60,000 00
Boston and Maine	10,000	12,800 00	10,000 00
Eastern	37,500	41,250 00	37,500 00
	$107,500	$123,650 00	$107,500 00

ROCKLAND SAVINGS BANK — ROCKLAND.

Incorporated 1868. Number of corporators, 47.

R. J. LANE, *President*. *Treasurer*, E. R. STUDLEY.

STATEMENT.

LIABILITIES.		ASSETS.	
Deposits	$366,667 39	Public funds	$20,000 00
Earnings undivided	7,676 83	Bank stock	81,176 05
Guaranty fund	5,000 00	Railroad bonds	12,000 00
		Real estate by foreclosure	4,600 00
		Loans on real estate	210,285 62
		Loans on personal security,	24,851 12
		Loans to counties, cities, or towns	9,000 00
		Deposit in bank on interest,	16,556 42
		Expense account	320 33
		Insurance account	369 76
		Cash on hand	184 92
	$379,344 22		$379,344 22

Cash on Deposit in Bank: —

Abington National Bank, Abington $16,556 42

Amount of real estate held by foreclosure $4,600 00
Assessed value of the same 2,900 00
Amount of income received from the same 50 00
Amount of municipal tax on real estate 40 31

Whole amount of interest or profits received or earned $20,829 60
Rate and amount of each semi-annual dividend for previous year . . . { 2 per cent . 6,641 66; 2 per cent . 6,956 30 }
Times for the dividends fixed by the by-laws: January and July.
Average annual per cent of dividends for the term ending at time of and including last extra dividend: $7\frac{1}{8}$ per cent.
The total amount of loans, with each specified rate of interest; $9,000, 4 per cent; $234,186, 6 per cent; $5,000, 7 per cent.
Number of outstanding loans which are of an amount not exceeding $3,000 each 281
Aggregate amount of the same 174,186 00
Amount of investments from which no income is received . . . 2,900 00
Number of open accounts 1,370
Number and amount of deposits received for previous year . 946 76,149 28
Number and amount of deposits of and exceeding $300 at any one time for the previous year 51 26,736 94
Number and amount of withdrawals 651 68,042 09
Number of accounts opened the previous year 260
Number of accounts closed the previous year 144
Amount of expenses of the corporation during previous year . 1,000 00
Amount of treasurer's bond 10,000 00
Date of examination by commissioner: Oct. 8.

PUBLIC FUNDS.

	Par Value.	Estimated Market Value.	Amount Invested.
City bonds: —			
City of Bangor, Me.	$8,000	$9,600 00	$8,000 00
of Rockland, Me.	5,000	5,000 00	5,000 00
of Middletown, Conn. . .	3,000	3,240 00	3,000 00
of Fall River	4,000	4,600 00	4,000 00
	$20,000	$22,440 00	$20,000 00

BANK STOCK.

Atlantic Nat'l Bank, Boston . .	$4,000	$6,140 00	$5,400 25
Continental Nat'l Bank, Boston .	6,700	7,906 00	7,675 00
Eliot Nat'l Bank, Boston . .	1,000	1,180 00	1,112 75
Everett Nat'l Bank, Boston . .	1,500	1,740 00	1,831 87
Freeman's Nat'l Bank, Boston .	2,500	2,993 00	3,125 00
Manufacturers' Nat'l Bank, Boston,	3,500	3,850 00	3,640 00
Metropolitan Nat'l Bank, Boston .	1,000	1,227 50	960 00
Market Nat'l Bank, Boston . .	4,800	5,268 00	5,577 25
Hide and Leather Nat'l B'k, Boston,	4,500	5,175 00	4,832 50
Howard Nat'l Bank, Boston . .	6,700	8,576 00	7,428 50
State Nat'l Bank, Boston . .	8,500	10,275 00	9,369 25
Traders' Nat'l Bank, Boston . .	6,600	6,732 00	7,074 50
Revere Nat'l Bank, Boston . .	7,300	10,242 75	8,673 75
Merchandise Nat'l Bank, Boston .	3,400	3,738 00	3,481 33
Webster Nat'l Bank, Boston . .	2,000	2,230 00	2,186 60
Pacific Nat'l Bank, Boston . .	5,000	5,000 00	5,537 50
Abington Nat'l Bank, Abington .	600	787 00	750 00
Granite Nat'l Bank, Quincy . .	2,100	2,782 00	2,520 00
	$71,700	$85,842 25	$81,176 05

RAILROAD BONDS.

Boston, Lynn, and Revere Beach .	$12,000	$14,160 00	$12,000 00

SALEM FIVE CENTS SAVINGS BANK — SALEM.

Incorporated May, 1855. Number of corporators, 145.

JOHN KINSMAN, *President*. *Treasurer*, CHARLES H. HENDERSON.

STATEMENT.

Liabilities.		Assets.	
Deposits . . .	$2,252,636 04	Public funds . . .	$374,200 00
Earnings undivided .	50,905 47	Bank stock . . .	550,830 00
Guaranty fund . .	50,000 00	Real estate by foreclosure .	50,850 00
		Loans on real estate . .	691,380 00
		Loans on personal security,	575,000 00
		Loans to counties, cities, or towns	60,000 00
		Deposit in bank on interest,	47,000 00
		Cash on hand . . .	4,281 51
	$2,353,541 51		$2,353,541 51

Cash on Deposit in Bank: —
Asiatic National Bank, Salem . . . $47,000 00

Amount of real estate held by foreclosure $50,850 00
Assessed value of the same 48,750 00
Amount of income received from the same 4,524 35
Amount of municipal tax on real estate 745 95

Whole amount of interest or profits received or earned . . . $127,190 29
Rate and amount of each semi-annual dividend for previous year . . . . { 2 per cent . { 40,414 43; 2 per cent . { 41,983 36 }
Times for the dividends fixed by the by-laws: February and August.
The total amount of loans, with each specified rate of interest: $20,000, $3\frac{1}{2}$ per cent; $50,000. $3\frac{3}{4}$ per cent; $50,000, 4 per cent; $25,000, $4\frac{1}{4}$ per cent; $290,000, $4\frac{1}{2}$ per cent; $25,000, $4\frac{3}{4}$ per cent; $115,000, 5 per cent; $156,250, 6 per cent; $77,700, $6\frac{1}{2}$ per cent; $366,100, 7 per cent; $151,330, $7\frac{3}{10}$ per cent.
Number of outstanding loans which are of an amount not exceeding $3,000 each 249
Aggregate amount of the same 349,930 00
Amount of investments from which no income is received . . . 8,300 00
Number of open accounts 7,606
Number and amount of deposits received for previous year, 4,548 381,179 73
Number and amount of deposits of and exceeding $300 at any one time for the previous year 349 212,838 44
Number and amount of withdrawals 3,175 302,214 27
Number of accounts opened the previous year 990
Number of accounts closed the previous year 658
Amount of expenses of the corporation during previous year . 6,658 89
Amount of treasurer's bond 25,000 00
Date of examination by commissioner: June 7.

PUBLIC FUNDS.

	Par Value.	Estimated Market Value.	Amount Invested.
United States 6s, ext. 1881, new 3½s,	$10,000	$10,100 00	$9,800 00
" " 4½s	40,000	45,200 00	41,400 00
City bonds: —			
City of Portland, Me. . . .	$5,000	$5,080 00	$5,000 00
of Meriden, Conn. . . .	65,000	74,540 00	65,000 00
of Waterbury, Conn. . .	20,000	25,400 00	20,000 00
of Lewiston, Me. . . .	30,000	34,500 00	30,000 00
of Gardiner, Me. . . .	10,000	10,000 00	10,000 00
of Portsmouth, N.H. . .	3,000	3,390 00	3,000 00
of Hartford, Conn. . . .	10,000	11,300 00	10,000 00
of Salem	19,000	20,690 00	19,000 00
of Fall River	25,000	29,800 00	25,000 00
of Lawrence	35,000	39,550 00	35,000 00
of Haverhill	10,000	12,000 00	10,000 00
of Springfield	41,000	52,380 00	41,000 00
of Somerville	20,000	21,300 00	20,000 00
of Lynn	20,000	23,000 00	20,000 00
of Chelsea	5,000	5,650 00	5,000 00
of Fitchburg	5,000	5,800 00	5,000 00
	$373,000	$429,680 00	$374,200 00

BANK STOCK.

Atlantic Nat'l Bank, Boston . .	$10,000	$15,300 00	$11,600 00
Atlas Nat'l Bank, Boston . .	10,000	12,500 00	10,700 00
Blackstone Nat'l Bank, Boston .	15,000	17,250 00	15,000 00
Boston Nat'l Bank, Boston . .	7,900	10,112 00	7,900 00
Boylston Nat'l Bank, Boston . .	20,000	25,600 00	22,000 00
City Nat'l Bank, Boston . . .	8,300	10,541 00	9,100 00
Columbian Nat'l Bank, Boston .	15,000	21,450 00	20,000 00
Commerce Nat'l Bank, Boston .	16,500	21,120 00	16,500 00
Commonwealth Nat'l Bank, Boston,	8,500	10,540 00	9,000 00
Continental Nat'l Bank, Boston .	11,400	13,452 00	12,000 00
Eagle Nat'l Bank, Boston . .	10,000	11,900 00	10,800 00
Eliot Nat'l Bank, Boston . .	13,300	15,960 00	14,600 00
Everett Nat'l Bank, Boston . .	7,300	8,541 00	7,300 00
Faneuil Hall Nat'l Bank, Boston .	3,500	4,690 00	4,000 00
First Nat'l Bank, Boston . .	2,500	5,175 00	2,500 00
Freeman's Nat'l Bank, Boston .	9,100	10,829 00	10,000 00
Globe Nat'l Bank, Boston . .	20,000	22,200 00	21,000 00
Hamilton Nat'l Bank, Boston . .	7,000	8,610 00	7,900 00
Hide and Leather Nat'l B'k, Boston,	8,500	10,030 00	9,300 00
Howard Nat'l Bank, Boston . .	9,700	12,610 00	10,800 00
Manufacturers' Nat'l Bank, Boston,	10,000	11,000 00	10,000 00
Market Nat'l Bank, Boston . .	2,200	2,420 00	2,200 00
Massachusetts Nat'l Bank, Boston .	15,500	19,220 00	17,000 00
Merchandise Nat'l Bank, Boston .	6,000	6,600 00	6,000 00
Merchants' Nat'l Bank, Boston .	33,300	48,951 00	38,800 00

BANK STOCK — Concluded.

	Par Value.	Estimated Market Value.	Amount Invested.
Mount Vernon Nat'l Bank, Boston .	$5,000	$6,350 00	$5,000 00
New England Nat'l Bank, Boston .	9,100	13,559 00	12,400 00
North Nat'l Bank, Boston . .	20,000	28,400 00	21,600 00
North America Nat'l Bank, Boston .	11,700	13,455 00	11,700 00
Old Boston Nat'l Bank, Boston .	6,350	7,747 00	7,500 00
Redemption Nat'l Bank, Boston .	2,000	2,700 00	2,500 00
Revere Nat'l Bank, Boston . .	20,400	24,888 00	20,400 00
Second Nat'l Bank, Boston . .	7,200	10,872 00	7,600 00
Shawmut Nat'l Bank, Boston . .	5,700	7,239 00	6,600 00
Shoe and Leather Nat'l B'k, Boston .	9,500	10,735 00	10,500 00
Suffolk Nat'l Bank, Boston . .	7,500	9,075 00	8,100 00
Third Nat'l Bank, Boston . .	15,000	15,900 00	15,000 00
Traders' Nat'l Bank, Boston . .	10,000	10,200 00	10,000 00
Tremont Nat'l Bank, Boston . .	10,000	12,200 00	11,000 00
Union Nat'l Bank, Boston . .	4,400	6,732 00	6,000 00
Webster Nat'l Bank, Boston . .	5,000	5,600 00	5,000 00
Asiatic Nat'l Bank, Salem . .	10,530	15,444 00	10,530 00
Exchange Nat'l Bank, Salem . .	10,000	12,300 00	10,000 00
First Nat'l Bank, Salem . . .	900	1,116 00	900 00
Mercantile Nat'l Bank, Salem . .	15,300	18,819 00	16,000 00
Merchants' Nat'l Bank, Salem .	8,400	11,760 00	8,700 00
Naumkeag Nat'l Bank, Salem . .	10,900	16,895 00	11,900 00
Salem Nat'l Bank, Salem . .	25,900	31,080 00	25,900 00
	$511,280	$649,667 00	$550,830 00

SALEM SAVINGS BANK — SALEM.

Incorporated January, 1818. Number of corporators, 193.

PETER SILVER, *President.* *Treasurer,* WILLIAM H. SIMONDS, Jun.

STATEMENT.

LIABILITIES.		ASSETS.	
Deposits	$6,252,034 40	Public funds	$2,094,000 00
Earnings undivided	20,338 39	Loans on public funds	107,500 00
Guaranty fund	136,000 00	Bank stock	560,436 00
		Loans on bank stock	8,300 00
		Real estate	75,000 00
		Real estate by foreclosure	109,803 85
		Loans on real estate	863,240 00
		Loans on personal security,	1,962,000 00
		Loans to counties, cities, or towns	542,450 00
		Deposit in banks on interest,	65,794 01
		Cash on hand	19,848 93
	$6,408,372 79		$6,408,372 79

Loans on Public Funds, amount on each: —

On $100,200 United States 4s	$100,200 00
On $5,500 United States 4½s	5,300 00
On $2,000 Boston 5s	2,000 00

Loans on Bank Stock, amount on each: —

On 40 shares Natick National Bank, Natick	$4,000 00
On 120 shares Asiatic National Bank, Salem	300 00
On 40 shares First National Bank, Newburyport	4,000 00

Cash on Deposit in Banks, amount in each: —

First National Bank, Boston	$50,794 01
Merchants' National Bank, Salem	15,000 00

Amount invested in real estate (for banking purposes)	$75,000 00
Estimated value of the same	75,000 00
Amount of real estate held by foreclosure	109,803 85
Assessed value of the same	88,250 00
Amount of income received from the same	6,136 44
Amount of municipal tax on real estate	1,912 53

Whole amount of interest or profits received or earned		$318,284 16
Rate and amount of each semi-annual dividend for previous year	2 per cent	118,722 23
	1¾ per cent	105,495 83

Times for the dividends fixed by the by-laws: third Wednesday in April and October.

Average annual per cent of dividends for the term ending at time of and including last extra dividend: 7 per cent.

The total amount of loans, with each specified rate of interest: $544,000, 3½ per cent; $25,000, 3⅝ per cent; $104,000, 3¾ per cent; $50,000, 3⅞ per cent; $753,000, 4 per cent; $593,350, 4½ per cent; $29,300, 4¾ per cent; $391,450, 5 per cent; $30,000, 5¼ per cent; $30,000, 5⅜ per cent; $123,400, 5½ per cent; $535,220, 6 per cent; $129,570, 6½ per cent; $28,400, 7 per cent; $100,800, 7 3/10 per cent.

Number of outstanding loans which are of an amount not exceeding $3,000 each 161
Aggregate amount of the same $240,790 00
Amount of investments from which no income is received . . 16,000 00
Number of open accounts 15,884
Number and amount of deposits received for previous year, 8,526 746,685 00
Number and amount of deposits of and exceeding $300 at any one time for the previous year 637 363,936 00
Number and amount of withdrawals 7,910 805,513 30
Number of accounts opened the previous year 1,654
Number of accounts closed the previous year 1,334
Amount of expenses of the corporation during previous year . 12,178 93
Amount of treasurer's bond 30,000 00
Date of examination by commissioner: June 2.

PUBLIC FUNDS.

	Par Value.	Estimated Market Value.	Amount Invested.
United States $3\frac{1}{2}$s, continued . .	$359,000	$366,180 00	$359,000 00
" " 4s, registered . .	170,000	197,200 00	170,000 00
" " $4\frac{1}{2}$s, registered . .	250,000	282,500 00	265,000 00
State, city, and town bonds: —			
State of Maine	$7,000	$7,280 00	$7,000 00
of New Hampshire . .	1,000	1,080 00	1,000 00
of Massachusetts . . .	5,000	5,200 00	5,000 00
City of Bath, Me.	9,000	9,000 00	9,000 00
of Boston	100,000	114,000 00	100,000 00
of Bangor, Me.	20,000	22,600 00	20,000 00
of Cambridge	15,000	16,050 00	15,000 00
of Charlestown	50,000	58,500 00	50,000 00
of Chelsea	17,000	19,880 00	17,000 00
of Fall River	60,000	72,400 00	60,000 00
of Holyoke	65,000	80,600 00	65,000 00
of Lynn	70,000	76,300 00	70,000 00
of Lowell	50,000	58,500 00	50,000 00
of Lawrence	71,000	82,425 00	71,000 00
of Malden	50,000	58,000 00	50,000 00
of Manchester, N.H. . . .	100,000	119,000 00	100,000 00
of New Bedford	17,000	17,260 00	17,000 00
of Providence, R.I.	200,000	230,000 00	200,000 00
of Salem	115,000	131,250 00	115,000 00
of Somerville	119,000	123,930 00	119,000 00
Town of Arlington	10,000	11,600 00	10,000 00
of Everett	2,000	2,320 00	2,000 00
of Marblehead	22,000	26,180 00	22,000 00
of Milford	15,000	17,100 00	15,000 00
of Waltham	75,000	79,125 00	75,000 00
of Winchester	35,000	41,650 00	35,000 00
	$2,079,000	$2,327,110 00	$2,094,000 00

BANK STOCK.

	Par Value.	Estimated Market Value.	Amount Invested.
Atlantic Nat'l Bank, Boston . .	$10,000	$15,350 00	$10,000 00
Atlas Nat'l Bank, Boston . .	1,000	1,250 00	1,100 00
Blackstone Nat'l Bank, Boston .	7,300	8,395 00	8,700 00
Boylston Nat'l Bank, Boston . .	2,500	3,200 00	3,000 00
City Nat'l Bank, Boston . . .	20,500	26,035 00	22,400 00
Columbian Nat'l Bank, Boston .	28,000	39,900 00	28,000 00
Commerce Nat'l Bank, Boston .	50,200	64,632 00	50,200 00
Freeman's Nat'l Bank, Boston .	11,400	13,651 00	12,500 00
Hamilton Nat'l Bank, Boston . .	12,000	14,760 00	14,550 00
Merchandise Nat'l Bank, Boston .	12,400	13,640 00	12,400 00
Merchants' Nat'l Bank, Boston .	58,300	85,118 00	77,300 00
North Nat'l Bank, Boston . .	27,400	38,839 00	28,400 00
Redemption Nat'l Bank, Boston .	12,500	16,875 00	17,500 00
Republic Nat'l Bank, Boston . .	16,500	21,615 00	21,600 00
Revere Nat'l Bank, Boston . .	49,800	60,756 00	50,300 00
Second Nat'l Bank, Boston . .	17,300	26,123 00	18,100 00
Shawmut Nat'l Bank, Boston . .	7,500	9,562 00	9,000 00
Suffolk Nat'l Bank, Boston . .	10,000	12,200 00	12,100 00
Tremont Nat'l Bank, Boston . .	20,000	24,400 00	20,000 00
Hide and Leather Nat'l B'k, Boston .	7,800	9,087 00	8,736 00
State Nat'l Bank, Boston . .	4,000	5,020 00	4,600 00
Asiatic Nat'l Bank, Salem . .	15,330	23,506 00	16,110 00
Exchange Nat'l Bank, Salem . .	8,500	10,200 00	8,900 00
First Nat'l Bank, Salem . . .	8,100	10,125 00	8,840 00
Mercantile Nat'l Bank, Salem .	500	625 00	500 00
Merchants' Nat'l Bank, Salem .	48,150	67,410 00	48,150 00
Naumkeag Nat'l Bank, Salem .	7,300	11,680 00	9,650 00
Salem Nat'l Bank, Salem . .	7,500	9,000 00	7,600 00
Home Nat'l Bank, Brockton . .	10,000	11,000 00	10,000 00
Beverly Nat'l Bank, Beverly . .	700	812 00	700 00
Marblehead Nat'l B'k, Marblehead .	2,000	2,320 00	2,000 00
Grand Nat'l Bank, Marblehead .	4,500	5,220 00	5,000 00
First Nat'l Bank, Chelsea . .	10,000	12,525 00	12,500 00
	$508,980	$674,831 00	$560,436 00

SEAMEN'S SAVINGS BANK — PROVINCETOWN.

Incorporated April 14, 1851. Number of corporators, 85.

LYSANDER N. PAINE, *President*. *Treasurer*, JOSEPH H. DYER.

STATEMENT.

LIABILITIES.		ASSETS.	
Deposits . . .	$321,730 11	Bank stock	$108,824 62
Earnings undivided .	9,895 18	Loans on bank stock . .	1,000 00
Guaranty fund . .	5,823 14	Real estate	1,330 29
		Real estate by foreclosure .	82,254 90
		Loans on real estate . .	37.058 74
		Loans on personal security,	37,548 20
		Loans to counties, cities, or towns	15,000 00
		Deposit in banks on interest,	49,865 70
		Furniture and safes . .	2,623 49
		Cash on hand . . .	1,942 49
	$337,448 43		$337,448 43

Loans on Bank Stock:—

On 8 shares Freeman's National Bank, Boston, and 4 shares Shawmut National Bank, Boston $1,000 00

Cash on Deposit in Banks, amount in each:—

Freeman's National Bank, Boston . . .	$9,749 03
Union Market National Bank, Watertown .	40,116 67

Amount invested in real estate (for banking purposes) . .		$1,330 29
Estimated value of the same		1,000 00
Amount of real estate held by foreclosure		82,254 90
Assessed value of the same		75,273 00
Amount of income received from the same		3,779 37
Amount of municipal tax on real estate		1,170 00
Whole amount of interest or profits received or earned . . .		$18,589 41
Rate and amount of each semi-annual dividend for previous year	2 per cent 2 per cent	6,412 25 6,193 12

Times for the dividends fixed by the by-laws: January and July.

Average annual per cent of dividends for the term ending at time of and including last extra dividend: 3 per cent.

The total amount of loans, with each specified rate of interest: $27,555.43, 6 per cent; $35,076.68, 6½ per cent; $11.465.83, 7 per cent; $594, 7½ per cent; $540, 8 per cent.

Number of outstanding loans which are of an amount not exceeding $3,000 each	64	
Aggregate amount of the same		53,731 94
Amount of investments from which no income is received . .		23,828 61
Number of open accounts	1,676	
Number and amount of deposits received for previous year .	376	41,494 35
Number and amount of deposits of and exceeding $300 at any one time for the previous year	40	16,793 62

Number and amount of withdrawals	657	$61,918 60
Number of accounts opened the previous year	115	
Number of accounts closed the previous year	217	
Amount of expenses of the corporation during previous year . .		2,100 00
Amount of treasurer's bond		20,000 00

Date of examination by commissioner: Aug. 5.

BANK STOCK.

	Par Value.	Estimated Market Value.	Amount Invested.
Atlas Nat'l Bank, Boston . .	$2,500	$3,125 00	$3,175 00
Blackstone Nat'l Bank, Boston .	2,000	2,300 00	2,500 00
Blue Hill Nat'l Bank, Boston . .	1,000	1,102 50	1,000 00
Boston Nat'l Bank, Boston . .	7,600	9,728 00	7,600 00
City Nat'l Bank, Boston . . .	1,000	1,232 50	1,000 00
Central Nat'l Bank, Boston . .	5,000	6,000 00	5,432 50
Continental Nat'l Bank, Boston .	2,500	2,965 62	3,131 25
Eliot Nat'l Bank, Boston. . .	5,000	6,012 50	6,000 00
Everett Nat'l Bank, Boston . .	5,000	5,856 25	6,575 00
Freeman's Nat'l Bank, Boston .	8,000	9,580 00	8,000 00
Globe Nat'l Bank, Boston . .	2,500	2,787 50	3,562 50
Howard Nat'l Bank, Boston . .	1,500	1,963 12	1,500 00
Home Nat'l Bank, Brockton . .	500	550 00	540 00
Mount Vernon Nat'l Bank, Boston .	5,000	6,387 50	6,250 00
Market Nat'l Bank, Boston . .	1,000	1,092 50	1,190 00
North America Nat'l Bank, Boston.	1,300	1,491 75	1,490 88
Republic Nat'l Bank, Boston . .	5,000	6,237 50	5,541 67
Old Boston Nat'l Bank, Boston .	2,000	2,440 00	3,300 00
First Nat'l Bank, Provincetown .	5,400	7,938 00	6,820 00
Revere Nat'l Bank, Boston . .	7,900	9,598 50	8,693 02
Second Nat'l Bank, Boston . .	1,700	2,569 12	1,700 00
State Nat'l Bank, Boston . .	10,100	12,675 50	10,100 00
Suffolk Nat'l Bank, Boston . .	3,000	3,656 25	4,187 50
Tremont Nat'l Bank, Boston . .	4,500	5,478 75	5,473 42
Webster Nat'l Bank, Boston . .	1,000	1,115 00	1,190 00
Manufacturers' Nat'l Bank, Boston,	2,500	3,100 00	2,871 88
	$94,500	$116,983 36	$108,824 62

SHELBURNE FALLS SAVINGS BANK — SHELBURNE FALLS.

Incorporated 1855. Number of corporators, 60.

F. A. BALL, *President*. *Treasurer*, A. K. HAWKS.

STATEMENT.

LIABILITIES.		ASSETS.	
Deposits	$730,697 87	Public funds	$207,000 00
Earnings undivided	6,618 11	Bank stock	71,300 00
Guaranty fund	14,000 00	Loans on bank stock	2,800 00
		Real estate	4,000 00
		Real estate by foreclosure	4,000 00
		Loans on real estate	355,599 85
		Loans on personal security,	78,135 51
		Loans to counties, cities, or towns	3,250 00
		Deposit in bank on interest,	25,000 00
		Cash on hand	230 62
	$751,315 98		$751,315 98

Loans on Bank Stock:—

On 28 shares Shelburne Falls National Bank . . . $2,800 00

Cash on Deposit in Bank:—

Maverick National Bank, Boston . $25,000 00

Invested in real estate (for banking purposes)	$4,000 00
Estimated value of the same	4,000 00
Amount of real estate held by foreclosure	4,000 00
Assessed value of the same: assessed with other property.	
Amount of income received from the same	189 00
Amount of municipal tax on real estate	92 00

Whole amount of interest or profits received or earned		$41,895 83
Rate and amount of each semi-annual dividend for previous year	2½ per cent	16,889 92
	2 per cent	13,982 85

Times for the dividends fixed by the by-laws: April 10 and Oct. 10.

The total amount of loans, with each specified rate of interest: $439,785.36, 5 per cent.

Number of outstanding loans which are of an amount not exceeding $3,000 each	375	
Aggregate amount of the same		279,215 36
Number of open accounts	3,097	
Number and amount of deposits received for previous year,	1,954	135,980 08
Number and amount of deposits of and exceeding $300 at any one time for the previous year	114	60,264 86
Number and amount of withdrawals	1,141	127,172 28
Number of accounts opened the previous year	445	
Number of accounts closed the previous year	270	
Amount of expenses of the corporation during previous year		1,813 09
Amount of treasurer's bond		15,000 00

Date of examination by commissioner: Aug. 9.

PUBLIC FUNDS.

	Par Value.	Estimated Market Value.	Amount Invested
United States 3½s	$25,000	$25,000 00	$25,000 00
" " 4s	21,000	24,000 00	21,000 00
" " 4½s	60,000	67,200 00	60,000 00
City bonds: —			
City of Boston 6s	$30,000	$35,000 00	$30,000 00
of Boston 5s	10,000	11,000 00	10,000 00
of Fall River 6s	29,000	34,200 00	29,000 00
of Fall River 5s	20,000	22,000 00	20,000 00
of Lynn 6s	7,000	8,000 00	7,000 00
of Lynn 5s	5,000	5,500 00	5,000 00
	$207,000	$231,900 00	$207,000 00

BANK STOCK.

Shelburne Falls Nat'l Bank, Shelburne Falls	$29,400	$37,400 00	$29,400 00
First Nat'l Bank, Northampton .	17,000	21,600 00	17,000 00
Conway Nat'l Bank, Conway . .	11,900	13,100 00	11,900 00
Adams Nat'l Bank, North Adams .	5,000	6,275 00	5,000 00
Pittsfield Nat'l Bank, Pittsfield .	3,000	4,200 00	3,000 00
Redemption Nat'l Bank, Boston .	5,000	6,225 00	5,000 00
	$71,300	$88,000 00	$71,300 00

SOUTH ADAMS SAVINGS BANK — ADAMS.

Incorporated 1869. Number of corporators, 9.

HENRY J. BLISS, *President*. *Treasurer*, HARVEY H. WELLINGTON.

STATEMENT.

Liabilities.		Assets.	
Deposits	$472,976 28	Public funds	$59,500 00
Earnings undivided	8,309 96	Bank stock	35,650 00
Guaranty fund	8,000 00	Real estate by foreclosure	6,500 00
		Loans on real estate	206,395 00
		Loans on personal security,	159,186 50
		Deposit in bank on interest,	16,440 40
		Expense account	484 41
		Premium account	5,005 00
		Insurance account	52 68
		Cash on hand	72 25
	$489,286 24		$489,286 24

Cash on Deposit in Bank: —

First National Bank, Adams	$16,440 40

Amount of real estate held by foreclosure	$6,500 00
Assessed value of the same	4,000 00
Amount of income received from the same	200 00
Amount of municipal tax on real estate	144 87

Whole amount of interest or profits received or earned		$24,853 53
Rate and amount of each semi-annual dividend for previous year: 2½ per cent		9,641 94
2 per cent		8,551 52

Times for the dividends fixed by the by-laws: January and July.

Average annual per cent of dividends for the term ending at time of and including last extra dividend: 7 per cent.

The total amount of loans, with each specified rate of interest: $56,500, 5 per cent; $163,325, 6 per cent; $35,500, 6½ per cent; $102,831.50, 7 per cent; $7,425, 8 per cent.

Number of outstanding loans which are of an amount not exceeding $3,000 each	112	
Aggregate amount of the same		88,981 50
Amount of investments from which no income is received		4,500 00
Number of open accounts	1,390	
Number and amount of deposits received for previous year,	3,927	134,619 35
Number and amount of deposits of and exceeding $300 at any one time for the previous year	95	53,129 75
Number and amount of withdrawals	561	62,686 67
Number of accounts opened the previous year	317	
Number of accounts closed the previous year	102	
Amount of expenses of the corporation during previous year		1,705 72
Amount of treasurer's bond		50,000 00

Date of examination by commissioner: Aug. 8.

PUBLIC FUNDS.

	Par Value.	Estimated Market Value.	Amount Invested.
United States 4s, consols . .	$12,000	$13,920 00	$12,000 00
" " 5s, continued . .	12,000	12,240 00	12,000 00
" " 6s, 1881, continued .	500	505 00	500 00
City and town bonds: —			
City of Somerville	$5,000	$5,500 00	$5,000 00
Town of Adams	20,000	22,400 00	20,000 00
of Clarksburg . . .	10,000	10,100 00	10,000 00
	$59,500	$64,665 00	$59,500 00

BANK STOCK.

	Par Value.	Estimated Market Value.	Amount Invested.
First Nat'l Bank, Adams . .	$18,600	$26,040 00	$20,680 00
Adams Nat'l Bank, North Adams .	2,300	2,990 00	2,300 00
Lee Nat'l Bank, Lee . . .	1,750	2,040 00	1,750 00
Berkshire Nat'l Bank, North Adams,	7,500	8,400 00	7,500 00
Third Nat'l Bank, Pittsfield . .	500	550 00	500 00
First Nat'l Bank, Woburn . .	2,500	3,800 00	3,800 00
Franklin Co. Nat'l B'k, Greenfield .	2,500	4,125 00	4,125 00
	$35,650	$47,945 00	$40,655 00

SOUTHBRIDGE SAVINGS BANK — SOUTHBRIDGE.

Incorporated April 20, 1848. Number of corporators, 84.

ROBERT H. COLE, *President*. *Treasurer*, CHARLES D. MONROE.

STATEMENT.

LIABILITIES.		ASSETS.	
Deposits	$1,034,710 83	Public funds	$491,000 00
Earnings undivided	20,579 20	Loans on public funds	20,000 00
Guaranty fund	12,000 00	Bank stock	57,139 88
		Loans on bank stock	2,900 00
		Railroad bonds	50,000 00
		Loans on real estate	197,400 00
		Loans on personal security,	151,200 00
		Loans to counties, cities, or towns	59,000 00
		Deposit in banks on interest,	22,603 39
		Expense account	561 37
		Premiums	13,150 00
		Steel safe	1,500 00
		Cash on hand	835 39
	$1,067,290 03		$1,067,290 03

Loans on Public Funds: —

On $20,000 United States bonds $20,000 00

Loans on Bank Stock, amount on each: —

On 10 shares Southbridge National Bank, Southbridge	$700 00
On 6 shares Blackstone National Bank, Boston	600 00
On 20 shares Pacific National Bank, Boston	1,600 00

Cash on Deposit in Banks, amount in each: —

Southbridge National Bank, Southbridge	$17,000 00
Maverick National Bank, Boston	5,603 39

Whole amount of interest or profits received or earned $53,018 53

Rate and amount of each semi-annual dividend for previous year: 2 per cent . 18,524 90; 2 per cent . 19,136 99

Times for the dividends fixed by the by-laws: first Wednesday in January and July.

Average annual per cent of dividends for the term ending at time of and including last extra dividend: 5 per cent.

The total amount of loans, with each specified rate of interest: $9,000, 3½ per cent; $5,000, 4 per cent; $45,000, 4½ per cent; $150,000, 4¾ per cent; $61,300, 6 per cent; $76,000, 6½ per cent; $84,200, 7 per cent.

Number of outstanding loans which are of an amount not exceeding $3,000 each 99

Aggregate amount of the same 91,000 00

Number of open accounts 2,827

Number and amount of deposits received for previous year, 1,673 134,446 09

Number and amount of deposits of and exceeding $300 at any one time for the previous year 106 56,178 00

Number and amount of withdrawals 1,016 $113,102 34
Number of accounts opened the previous year 396
Number of accounts closed the previous year 237
Amount of expenses of the corporation during previous year . 2,497 80
Amount of treasurer's bond 30,000 00
Date of examination by commissioner: Feb. 21.

PUBLIC FUNDS.

	Par Value.	Estimated Market Value.	Amount Invested.
United States 4s, 1907	$30,000	$34,800 00	$30,000 00
" " 4½s, 1891	135,000	151,300 00	137,550 00
City and town bonds: —			
City of Cambridge 6s	$21,000	$26,540 00	$22,800 00
of Charlestown 6s	13,000	15,340 00	14,600 00
of Lynn 6s	8,000	9,360 00	8,400 00
of Newton 6s	5,000	6,500 00	5,000 00
of Salem 5s	10,000	11,900 00	10,000 00
of Somerville 6½s	15,000	15,300 00	15,000 00
of Waterbury, Conn., 7s . .	10,000	13,200 00	10,000 00
of Chelsea 6s	12,000	14,400 00	12,550 00
of Chelsea 4½s	18,000	18,900 00	18,050 00
of Holyoke 6s	20,000	25,000 00	20,000 00
of Lawrence 6s	10,000	12,100 00	10,000 00
of New Bedford 6s	5,000	6,650 00	5,000 00
of New Bedford 5s	10,000	11,400 00	10,000 00
of Newburyport 5s	4,000	4,075 00	4,075 00
of Springfield 7s	10,000	11,400 00	10,000 00
of Springfield 6s	5,000	5,000 00	5,000 00
of Worcester 6s	10,000	11,900 00	11,375 00
of Fall River 6s	26,000	30,390 00	27,750 00
of Portland 6s	9,000	9,720 00	9,000 00
of Fitchburg 6s	5,000	5,800 00	5,200 00
Town of Arlington 6s	10,000	11,800 00	10,500 00
of Brookline 7s	20,000	27,600 00	20,000 00
of Malden 6s	20,000	24,000 00	20,000 00
of Northampton 6s . . .	20,000	23,400 00	20,000 00
of Pawtucket 5s	20,000	22,400 00	22,000 00
of Woburn 6s	10,000	11,700 00	10,000 00
	$491,000	$571,875 00	$503,850 00

BANK STOCK.

	Par Value.	Estimated Market Value.	Amount Invested.
Blackstone Nat'l Bank, Boston .	$4,000	$4,600 00	$4,000 00
Boylston Nat'l Bank, Boston . .	1,800	2,304 00	1,800 00
City Nat'l Bank, Boston . .	1,200	1,524 00	1,200 00
Columbian Nat'l Bank, Boston .	500	710 00	500 00
Freeman's Nat'l Bank, Boston .	10,000	11,900 00	13,400 00
New England Nat'l Bank, Boston .	2,200	3,190 00	2,200 00
Revere Nat'l Bank, Boston . .	2,500	2,775 00	2,500 00

BANK STOCK — Concluded.

	Par Value.	Estimated Market Value.	Amount Invested.
Washington Nat'l Bank, Boston .	$2,000	$2,800 00	$2,000 00
Boston Nat'l Bank, Boston . .	1,000	1,280 00	1,150 00
Suffolk Nat'l Bank, Boston . .	5,000	6,100 00	6,050 00
Commerce Nat'l Bank, Boston .	1,000	1,280 00	1,236 25
Atlas Nat'l Bank, Boston . .	500	625 00	635 63
City Nat'l Bank, Worcester . .	1,800	2,034 00	2,016 00
Quinsigamond Nat'l B'k, Worcester,	2,000	2,400 00	2,380 00
Leicester Nat'l Bank, Leicester .	1,400	1,610 00	1,582 00
Southbridge Nat'l B'k, Southbridge .	13,800	18,630 00	14,490 00
	$50,700	$63,762 00	$57,139 88

RAILROAD BONDS.

	Par Value.	Estimated Market Value.	Amount Invested.
Boston and Albany 7s	$10,000	$12,700 00	$10,000 00
Boston and Lowell 7s	20,000	24,800 00	20,000 00
Boston and Maine 7s	10,000	12,700 00	10,000 00
Old Colony 7s	10,000	12,500 00	10,300 00
	$50,000	$62,700 00	$50,300 00

SOUTH BOSTON SAVINGS BANK — SOUTH BOSTON.

Incorporated 1863. Number of corporators, 72.

GEORGE E. ALDEN, *President*. *Treasurer*, GEORGE W. ELLIS.

STATEMENT.

LIABILITIES.		ASSETS.	
Deposits	$1,045,362 10	Public funds . . .	$227,435 75
Earnings undivided .	13,529 27	Bank stock	94,300 00
Guaranty fund . .	22,300 00	Railroad bonds . . .	1,450 00
Charges on mortgages,	18 90	Real estate	61,839 38
Earnings undivided reserved to meet estimated losses on real estate . .	20,000 00	Real estate by foreclosure .	134,413 57
		Loans on real estate . .	403,346 00
		Loans on personal security,	45,000 00
		Deposit in bank on interest,	129,263 97
		Furniture and fixtures .	500 00
		Cash on hand . . .	3,661 60
	$1,101,210 27		$1,101,210 27

Cash on Deposit in Bank: —

Maverick National Bank, Boston	$129,263 97

Amount invested in real estate (for banking purposes) . . .		$61,839 38
Estimated value of the same		61,839 38
Amount of real estate held by foreclosure		134,413 57
Assessed value of the same		119,900 00
Amount of income received from the same		8,657 86
Amount of municipal tax on real estate		2,497 14
Whole amount of interest or profits received or earned . . .		$61,406 91
Rate and amount of each semi-annual dividend for previous year	2 per cent .	19,059 74
	2 per cent .	18,964 58
Times for the dividends fixed by the by-laws: third Wednesday in April and October.		
The total amount of loans, with each specified rate of interest: $30,000, 3½ per cent; $11,000, 5 per cent; $20,000, 5½ per cent; $150,400, 6 per cent; $75,800, 6½ per cent; $106,096, 7 per cent; $28,600, 7½ per cent; $16,850, 8 per cent.		
Number of outstanding loans which are of an amount not exceeding $3,000 each	139	
Aggregate amount of the same		187,846 00
Amount of investments from which no income is received . .		5,000 00
Number of open accounts	8,249	
Number and amount of deposits received for previous year,	5,553	237,290 50
Number and amount of deposits of and exceeding $300 at any one time for the previous year	140	72,877 61
Number and amount of withdrawals	4,273	256,186 25
Number of accounts opened the previous year	916	
Number of accounts closed the previous year	975	
Amount of expenses of the corporation during previous year .		5,155 85
Amount of treasurer's bond		40,000 00

Date of examination by commissioner: Feb. 28.

PUBLIC FUNDS.

	Par Value.	Estimated Market Value.	Amount Invested.
United States bonds . . .	$108,500	$111,120 62	$108,500 00
City and town bonds: —			
City of Bangor, Me. . . .	$8,000	$9,040 00	$7,320 00
of Portland, Me. . .	15,000	18,150 00	13,775 00
of New London, Conn. . .	10,000	12,500 00	10,000 00
of Norwich, Conn. . . .	30,000	34,080 00	30,000 00
of Chelsea	7,000	8,400 00	6,860 00
of Somerville	10,000	10,800 00	10,000 00
of Fall River	10,000	12,100 00	10,000 00
of Brockton	20,000	20,400 00	20,000 00
Town of Everett	1,000	1,180 00	980 75
of Scituate	10,000	10,000 00	10,000 00
	$229,500	$247,770 62	$227,435 75

BANK STOCK.

	Par Value.	Estimated Market Value.	Amount Invested.
Atlas Nat'l Bank, Boston . .	$11,100	$13,875 00	$11,100 00
Commerce Nat'l Bank, Boston .	7,500	9,656 25	7,500 00
Columbian Nat'l Bank, Boston .	6,000	8,550 00	6,000 00
Eliot Nat'l Bank, Boston . . .	10,000	11,800 00	10,000 00
Globe Nat'l Bank, Boston . .	6,000	6,690 00	6,000 00
Massachusetts Nat'l Bank, Boston .	4,500	5,580 00	4,500 00
Merchandise Nat'l Bank, Boston .	2,300	2,524 25	2,300 00
North America Nat'l Bank, Boston .	4,500	5,163 75	4,500 00
Suffolk Nat'l Bank, Boston . .	5,000	6,075 00	5,000 00
Third Nat'l Bank, Boston . .	6,500	6,938 75	6,500 00
Traders' Nat'l Bank, Boston . .	2,600	2,652 00	2,600 00
Tremont Nat'l Bank, Boston . .	15,000	18,150 00	15,000 00
Webster Nat'l Bank, Boston . .	13,300	14,829 50	13,300 00
	$94,300	$112,484 50	94,300 00

RAILROAD BONDS.

	Par Value.	Estimated Market Value.	Amount Invested.
New Bedford	$1,000	$1,150 00	$1,000 00
Eastern	1,000	1,090 00	450 00
	$2,000	$2,240 00	$1,450 00

SOUTH SCITUATE SAVINGS BANK — SOUTH SCITUATE.

Incorporated April 2, 1834. Number of corporators, 58.

PEREZ SIMMONS, *President*. *Treasurer*, EBENEZER T. FOGG.

STATEMENT.

LIABILITIES.		ASSETS.	
Deposits	$430,460 35	Bank stock	$58,800 00
Earnings undivided	1,844 82	Real estate by foreclosure	37,257 00
Guaranty fund	5,410 00	Loans on real estate	262,201 73
		Loans on personal security,	33,675 00
		Loans to counties, cities, or towns	28,995 00
		Deposit in banks on interest,	14,830 22
		Cash on hand	1,956 22
	$437,715 17		$437,715 17

Cash on Deposit in Banks, amount in each:—

Manufacturers' National Bank	$9,075 99
Commonwealth National Bank	5,754 23

Amount of real estate held by foreclosure	$37,257 00
Assessed value of the same	37,257 00
Amount of income received from the same	1,470 00
Amount of municipal tax on real estate	302 57

Whole amount of interest or profits received or earned		$20,123 52
Rate and amount of each semi-annual dividend for previous year	2 per cent	8,440 00
	2 per cent	8,478 81

Times for the dividends fixed by the by-laws: last Saturday in August and February.

Average annual per cent of dividends for the term ending at time of and including last extra dividend: 7½ per cent.

The total amount of loans, with each specified rate of interest: $15,000, 4½ per cent; $9,975, 5 per cent; $151,655.84, 6 per cent; $148,240.80, 7 per cent.

Number of outstanding loans which are of an amount not exceeding $3,000 each	341	
Aggregate amount of the same		241,197 94
Amount of investments from which no income is received		7,200 00
Number of open accounts	1,161	
Number and amount of deposits received for previous year	317	33,011 87
Number and amount of deposits of and exceeding $300 at any one time for the previous year	29	5,761 00
Number and amount of withdrawals	405	36,217 06
Number of accounts opened the previous year	94	
Number of accounts closed the previous year	71	
Amount of expenses of the corporation during previous year		1,166 00
Amount of treasurer's bond		10,000 00

Date of examination by commissioner: Oct. 13.

BANK STOCK.

	Par Value.	Estimated Market Value.	Amount Invested.
Atlantic Nat'l Bank, Boston . .	$1,000	$1,530 00	$1,300 00
Columbian Nat'l Bank, Boston .	3,200	4,544 00	4,000 00
Eliot Nat'l Bank, Boston . .	800	928 00	800 00
Globe Nat'l Bank, Boston . .	300	333 00	300 00
Hamilton Nat'l Bank, Boston . .	1,500	1,757 00	1,500 00
Massachusetts Nat'l Bank, Boston .	500	620 00	500 00
New England Nat'l Bank, Boston .	1,000	1,450 00	1,000 00
Second Nat'l Bank, Boston . .	1,700	2,550 00	1,900 00
Traders' Nat'l Bank Boston . .	2,800	2,856 00	2,800 00
Webster Nat'l Bank, Boston . .	2,000	2,220 00	2,000 00
Washington Nat'l Bank, Boston .	1,600	2,240 00	1,600 00
Boston Nat'l Bank, Boston . .	1,800	2,286 00	2,016 00
City Nat'l Bank, Boston . . .	2,300	2,829 00	2,300 00
Eagle Nat'l Bank, Boston . .	2,300	2,737 00	2,300 00
Fourth Nat'l Bank, Boston . .	4,000	4,400 00	4,000 00
Howard Nat'l Bank, Boston . .	1,400	1,792 00	1,400 00
Merchants' Nat'l Bank, Boston .	1,500	2,175 00	1,500 00
North Nat'l Bank, Boston . .	4,500	6,390 00	4,500 00
Shawmut Nat'l Bank, Boston . .	1,300	1,638 00	1,300 00
Commerce Nat'l Bank, Boston .	3,000	3,840 00	4,000 00
Union Nat'l Bank, Boston . .	1,000	1,530 00	1,133 00
Merchandise Nat'l Bank, Boston .	1,000	1,090 00	1,000 00
Revere Nat'l Bank, Boston . .	4,800	5,808 00	4,800 00
Hingham Nat'l Bank, Hingham .	2,800	2,800 00	3,556 00
Union Nat'l Bank, Weymouth .	4,300	5,160 00	4,300 00
Union Market N'l B'k, Watertown .	2,600	2,600 00	2,995 00
	$55,000	$68,103 00	$58,800 00

SOUTH WEYMOUTH SAVINGS BANK — SOUTH WEYMOUTH.

Incorporated 1868. Number of corporators, 34.

JOSIAH REED, *President.* *Treasurer,* A. E. VINING.

STATEMENT.

Liabilities.		Assets.	
Deposits	$337,090 89	Public funds	$10,000 00
Earnings undivided	10,218 30	Bank stock	143,306 12
Guaranty fund	5,000 00	Loans on bank stock	7,300 00
		Real estate by foreclosure	22,475 00
		Loans on real estate	120,259 00
		Loans on personal security,	40,991 51
		Loans to counties, cities, or towns	6,000 00
		Deposit in bank on interest,	1,229 27
		Expense account	314 50
		Cash on hand	433 79
	$352,309 19		$352,309 19

Loans on Bank Stock: —

On 73 shares First National Bank, South Weymouth . . $7,300 00

Cash on Deposit in Bank: —

First National Bank, South Weymouth $1,229 27

Amount of real estate held by foreclosure	$22,475 00
Assessed value of the same	18,450 00
Amount of income received from the same	1,217 50
Amount of municipal tax on real estate	251 88

Whole amount of interest or profits received or earned		$20,753 46
Rate and amount of each semi-annual dividend for previous year	2½ per cent	7,674 72
	2 per cent	6,406 15

Times for the dividends fixed by the by-laws: July and January.

Average annual per cent of dividends for the term ending at time of and including last extra dividend: 7½ per cent.

The total amount of loans, with each specified rate of interest: $1,924, 4 per cent; $13,000, 5 per cent; $15,705, 5½ per cent; $125,521, 6 per cent; $15,400, 7 per cent; $3,000, 8 per cent.

Number of outstanding loans which are of an amount not exceeding $3,000 each	140	
Aggregate amount of the same		109,800 00
Amount of investments from which no income is received		3,000 00
Number of open accounts	911	
Number and amount of deposits received for previous year	464	49,090 50
Number and amount of deposits of and exceeding $300 at any one time for the previous year	49	26,184 33
Number and amount of withdrawals	303	39,614 99
Number of accounts opened the previous year	138	
Number of accounts closed the previous year	70	
Amount of expenses of the corporation during previous year		1,115 22
Amount of treasurer's bond		10,000 00

Date of examination by commissioner: Oct. 5.

PUBLIC FUNDS.

	Par Value.	Estimated Market Value.	Amount Invested.
City bonds: —			
City of Worcester 4½s . . .	$5,000	$5,450 00	$5,000 00
of Fall River 4s . . .	5,000	5,200 00	5,000 00
	$10,000	$10,650 00	$10,000 00

BANK STOCK.

	Par Value.	Estimated Market Value.	Amount Invested.
Atlantic Nat'l Bank, Boston . .	$4,000	$6,120 00	$5,540 25
Boston Nat'l Bank, Boston . .	7,500	9,600 00	8,203 99
Columbian Nat'l Bank, Boston .	3,900	5,557 50	4,994 62
Continental Nat'l Bank, Boston .	3,000	3,540 00	3,382 75
Commerce Nat'l Bank, Boston .	5,000	6,400 00	5,000 00
Eagle Nat'l Bank, Boston . .	1,500	1,792 50	1,864 00
Eliot Nat'l Bank, Boston . .	9,600	11,520 00	11,085 88
Globe Nat'l Bank, Boston . .	4,000	4,460 00	5,014 25
Hide and Leather Nat'l B'k, Boston,	3,000	3,495 00	3,352 50
Howard Nat'l Bank, Boston . .	7,000	9,100 00	7,580 00
Market Nat'l Bank, Boston . .	2,000	2,195 00	2,210 00
Manufacturers' Nat'l Bank, Boston,	7,500	8,250 00	7,238 75
Merchants' Nat'l Bank, Boston .	3,500	5,110 00	4,575 87
North America Nat'l Bank, Boston .	6,000	6,840 00	6,530 25
Shawmut Nat'l Bank, Boston . .	10,000	12,750 00	11,853 00
Second Nat'l Bank, Boston . .	2,000	3,030 00	2,915 00
Suffolk Nat'l Bank, Boston . .	1,800	2,250 00	2,184 75
New England Nat'l Bank, Boston .	4,000	5,820 00	5,450 50
Revere Nat'l Bank, Boston . .	4,500	5,490 00	5,445 00
Redemption Nat'l Bank, Boston .	7,500	10,125 00	9,541 50
Republic Nat'l Bank, Boston . .	4,000	5,240 00	5,077 50
Shoe and Leather Nat'l B'k, Boston,	5,000	5,625 00	5,925 00
Tremont Nat'l Bank, Boston . .	3,700	4,514 00	4,644 62
Webster Nat'l Bank, Boston . .	8,600	9,589 00	9,045 14
S. Weymouth N'l B'k, S. Weym'th,	4,000	5,400 00	4,651 00
	$122,600	$153,813 00	$143,306 12

SPENCER SAVINGS BANK – SPENCER.

Incorporated 1871. Number of corporators, 26.

ERASTUS JONES, *President*. *Treasurer*, WALTER L. DEMOND.

STATEMENT.

LIABILITIES.		ASSETS.	
Deposits	$297,184 40	Public funds	$36,000 00
Earnings undivided	5,574 53	Bank stock	27,700 00
Guaranty fund	2,850 00	Loans on bank stock	7,000 00
		Railroad bonds	5,000 00
		Loans on real estate	121,205 00
		Loans on personal security,	40,685 00
		Loans to counties, cities, or towns	57,750 00
		Deposit in bank on interest,	4,088 81
		Expense account	408 50
		Premiums	5,771 62
	$305,608 93		$305,608 93

Loans on Bank Stock: —

On 70 shares Spencer National Bank $7,000 00

Cash on Deposit in Bank: —

Spencer National Bank $4,088 81

Whole amount of interest or profits received or earned		$14,215 82
Rate and amount of each semi-annual dividend for previous year	2 per cent	4,862 15
	2 per cent	5,181 08

Times for the dividends fixed by the by-laws: January and July.

The total amount of loans, with each specified rate of interest: $44,500, 4½ per cent; $4,000, 5 per cent; $121,205, 6 per cent.

Number of outstanding loans which are of an amount not exceeding $3,000 each	108	
Aggregate amount of the same		100,480 00
Number of open accounts	1,162	
Number and amount of deposits received for previous year,	1,222	82,196 52
Number and amount of deposits of and exceeding $300 at any one time for the previous year	59	21,760 00
Number and amount of withdrawals	613	56,990 21
Number of accounts opened the previous year	328	
Number of accounts closed the previous year	170	
Amount of expenses of the corporation during previous year		900 00
Amount of treasurer's bond		20,000 00

Date of examination by commissioner: July 5.

PUBLIC FUNDS.

	Par Value.	Estimated Market Value.	Amount Invested.
United States 4s	$12,000	$13,920 00	$12,000 00
City and town bonds:—			
City of Lynn 5s, 1905 . . .	$10,000	$11,650 00	$10,000 00
of New Bedford 4s, 1890 . .	5,000	5,150 00	5,000 00
of Belfast, Me., 6s, 1885 . .	3,000	3,030 00	3,000 00
of Bangor, Me., 7s, 1899 . .	3,000	3,570 00	3,000 00
of Springfield, 7s, 1884 . .	2,000	2,100 00	2,000 00
Town of Northampton 6s, 1892 .	1,000	1,130 00	1,000 00
	$36,000	$40,550 00	$36,000 00

BANK STOCK.

State Nat'l Bank, Boston . .	$1,500	$1,882 50	$1,500 00
North Nat'l Bank, Boston . .	2,000	2,842 50	2,000 00
Commonwealth Nat'l Bank, Boston,	5,600	6,722 80	5,600 00
Redemption Nat'l Bank, Boston .	600	710 87	600 00
Hide and Leather Nat'l B'k, Boston,	300	347 50	300 00
Webster Nat'l Bank, Boston . .	1,100	1,226 50	1,100 00
First Nat'l Bank, Worcester . .	1,200	1,680 00	1,200 00
Mechanics' Nat'l Bank, Worcester .	2,500	2,925 00	2,500 00
Central Nat'l Bank, Worcester .	500	800 00	500 00
First Nat'l Bank, Webster . .	2,500	2,750 00	2,500 00
Spencer Nat'l Bank, Spencer . .	8,500	9,350 00	8,500 00
Leicester Nat'l Bank, Leicester .	1,400	1,580 00	1,400 00
	$27,700	$32,817 67	$27,700 00

RAILROAD BONDS.

Eastern	$5,000	$5,500 00	$5,000 00

SPRINGFIELD FIVE CENTS SAVINGS BANK — SPRINGFIELD.

Incorporated 1854. Number of corporators, 32.

JOSEPH C. PYNCHON, *President.* *Treasurer*, DANIEL J. MARSH.

STATEMENT.

LIABILITIES.		ASSETS.	
Deposits	$1,477,352 64	Public funds	$208,500 00
Earnings undivided	4,446 17	Bank stock	90,200 00
Guaranty fund	16,000 00	Loans on bank stock	7,810 00
		Real estate	139,721 94
		Real estate by foreclosure	115,975 00
		Loans on real estate	664,850 00
		Loans on personal security,	218,750 00
		Deposit in banks on interest,	25,215 43
		Personal property	6,000 00
		Premium account	4,732 50
		Profit and loss	13,698 57
		Cash on hand	2,345 37
	$1,497,798 81		$1,497,798 81

Loans on Bank Stock, amount on each: —

On 20 shares City of Springfield National Bank and 10 shares Chapin National Bank, Springfield	$3,000 00
On 34 shares First National Bank, Springfield	2,200 00
On 25 shares City of Springfield National Bank	2,500 00
On 20 shares City of Holyoke National Bank	110 00

Cash on Deposit in Banks, amount in each: —

Agawam National Bank, Springfield	$5,030 58
Second National Bank, Springfield	8,000 00
City National Bank, Springfield	5,500 00
Pynchon National Bank, Springfield	6,675 85

Amount invested in real estate (for banking purposes)	$139,721 94
Estimated value of the same	139,721 94
Amount of real estate held by foreclosure	115,975 00
Assessed value of the same	98,050 00
Amount of income received from the same	9,063 82
Amount of municipal tax on real estate	2,319 37

Whole amount of interest or profits received or earned		$66,158 51
Rate and amount of each semi-annual dividend for previous year	2 per cent	25,828 83
	2 per cent	26,816 61

Times for the dividends fixed by the by-laws: Jan. 15 and July 15.

Average annual per cent of dividends for the term ending at time of and including last extra dividend: 7 per cent.

The total amount of loans, with each specified rate of interest: $236,560, 5 per cent; $654,850, 6 per cent.

Number of outstanding loans which are of an amount not exceeding $3,000 each	166	
Aggregate amount of the same		233,810 00

Amount of investments from which no income is received . .		$15,900 00
Number of open accounts	5,827	
Number and amount of deposits received for previous year,	5,863	436,484 72
Number and amount of deposits of and exceeding $300 at any one time for the previous year	306	176,015 73
Number and amount of withdrawals	3,335	316,295 59
Number of accounts opened the previous year . . .	1,293	
Number of accounts closed the previous year	862	
Amount of expenses of the corporation during previous year . .		4,819 85
Amount of treasurer's bond		30,000 00

Date of examination by commissioner: Oct. 16.

Public Funds.

	Par Value.	Eslimated Market Value.	Amount Invested
United States 6s, 1881, registered .	$150,000	$151,500 00	$150,000 00
" " 4s, continued . .	50,200	58,232 00	50,200 00
" " 4s, registered . .	700	812 00	700 00
" " 4½s, continued . .	600	678 00	600 00
City bonds:—			
City of Springfield water bonds .	$7,000	$8,050 00	$7,000 00
	$208,500	$219,272 00	$208,500 00

Bank Stock.

Agawam Nat'l Bank, Springfield .	$12,000	$15,000 00	$12,000 00
Chapin Nat'l Bank, Springfield .	12,000	15,000 00	12,000 00
John Hancock Nat'l B'k, Springfi'd,	11,500	13,800 00	11,500 00
Pynchon Nat'l Bank, Springfield .	10,900	17,500 00	10,900 00
City Nat'l Bank, Springfield . .	5,000	6,000 00	5,000 00
Second Nat'l Bank, Springfield .	4,800	7,920 00	4,800 00
Chicopee Nat'l Bank, Springfield .	7,000	10,500 00	7,000 00
City Nat'l Bank, Worcester . .	5,600	6,440 00	5,600 00
Ware Nat'l Bank, Ware . . .	5,500	6,050 00	5,500 00
Monson Nat'l Bank, Monson . .	1,000	1,500 00	1,000 00
Hadley Falls Nat'l Bank, Holyoke .	1,500	2,250 00	1,500 90
Shoe and Leather Nat'l B'k, Boston,	2,500	2,875 00	2,500 00
Hide and Leather Nat'l B'k, Boston,	3,500	3,875 00	3,500 00
State Nat'l Bank, Boston . .	3,600	4,372 00	3,600 00
First Nat'l Bank, Chicopee . .	3,800	5,700 00	3,800 00
	$90,200	$118,782 00	$90,200 00

SPRINGFIELD INSTITUTION FOR SAVINGS—SPRINGFIELD.

Incorporated 1827. Number of corporators, 67.

JAMES M. THOMPSON, *President*. *Treasurer*, HENRY S. LEE.

STATEMENT.

LIABILITIES.		ASSETS.	
Deposits	$7,348,134 17	Public funds	$2,679,300 00
Earnings undivided	69,442 04	Loans on public funds	21,150 00
Guaranty fund	90,000 00	Bank stock	708,600 00
		Loans on bank stock	98,150 00
		Railroad bonds	363,000 00
		Loans on railroad stocks	29,400 00
		Real estate	104,500 00
		Real estate by foreclosure	79,750 00
		Loans on real estate	2,229,750 00
		Loans on personal security,	335,130 55
		Loans to counties, cities, or towns	360,500 00
		Deposit in banks on interest,	329,037 63
		Premium account	96,605 67
		Cash on hand	72,702 36
	$7,507,576 21		$7,507,576 21

Loans on Public Funds, amount on each:—

On $11,100 United States 4s, 1907	$7,850 00
On $15,300 United States 4½s, 1891	10,300 00
On $3,000 City of Portsmouth, N.H., 6s	3,000 00

Loans on Bank Stock, amount on each:—

On 318 shares First National Bank, Springfield	$24,500 00
On 71 shares Second National Bank, Springfield	7,100 00
On 50 shares Third National Bank, Springfield	5,000 00
On 49 shares Agawam National Bank, Springfield	5,500 00
On 10 shares Chapin National Bank, Springfield	1,000 00
On 164 shares Chicopee National Bank, Springfield	17,300 00
On 175 shares City National Bank, Springfield	17,550 00
On 61 shares John Hancock National Bank, Springfield	4,600 00
On 16 shares Pynchon National Bank, Springfield	1,550 00
On 30 shares Holyoke National Bank, Holyoke	3,000 00
On 8 shares Hadley Falls National Bank, Holyoke	800 00
On 20 shares Northampton National Bank, Northampton	800 00
On 10 shares Hampshire County National Bank, Northampton	1,000 00
On 10 shares First National Bank, Amherst	900 00
On 10 shares Franklin County National Bank, Greenfield	1,000 00
On 28 shares First National Bank, Westfield	2,800 00
On 25 shares Lee National Bank, Lee	1,750 00
On 20 shares National Bank of Redemption, Boston	2,000 00

Cash on Deposit in Banks, amount in each:—

Agawam National Bank, Springfield	$40,000 00
City National Bank, Springfield	90,000 00
Chicopee National Bank, Springfield	27,000 00

John Hancock National Bank, Springfield $25,000 00
Second National Bank, Springfield 5,000 00
Palmer National Bank, Palmer 5,000 00
First National Bank, Northampton 50,000 00
Hampshire County National Bank, Northampton 20,000 00
Franklin County National Bank, Greenfield 55,000 00
Wachusett National Bank, Fitchburg 10,000 00
Blackstone National Bank, Boston 554 00
Maverick National Bank, Boston 1,483 63

Amount invested in real estate (for banking purposes) . . . $104,500 00
Estimated value of the same 104,500 00
Amount of real estate held by foreclosure 79,750 00
Assessed value of the same 70,100 00
Amount of income received from the same 1,885 50
Amount of municipal tax on real estate 1,866 25

Whole amount of interest or profits received or earned . . . $382,995 86
Rate and amount of each semi-annual dividend for previous year . . . . { 2 per cent . 130,768 17; 2 per cent . 135,828 99 }
Times for the dividends fixed by the by-laws: Jan. 1 and July 1.
Average annual per cent of dividends for the term ending at time of and including last extra dividend: 7 per cent.
The total amount of loans, with each specified rate of interest: $2,000, 3¾ per cent; $98,500, 4 per cent; $10,000, 4¼ per cent; $65,000, 4½ per cent; $445,889.55, 5 per cent; $2,257,700, 6 per cent; $25,000, 6½ per cent; $170,000, 7 per cent.
Number of outstanding loans which are of an amount not exceeding $3,000 each 671
Aggregate amount of the same $38,300 00
Amount of investments from which no income is received . . . 34,450 00
Number of open accounts 18,540
Number and amount of deposits received for previous year, 18,229 1,710,986 96
Number and amount of deposits of and exceeding $300 at any one time for the previous year 1,450 956,017 58
Number and amount of withdrawals 12,042 1,358,977 93
Number of accounts opened the previous year 3,578
Number of accounts closed the previous year 2,278
Amount of expenses of the corporation during previous year . . 12,776 24
Amount of treasurer's bond 30,000 00
Date of examination by commissioner: Sept. 27.

PUBLIC FUNDS.

	Par Value.	Estimated Market Value.	Amount Invested.
United States bonds . .	$1,225,800	$1,335,799 00	$1,306,300 00
State, city, and town bonds:—			
State of Maine	$118,500	$132,720 00	$128,500 00
of New Hampshire . .	160,500	185,580 00	172,500 00
of Massachusetts . . .	89,500	102,030 00	94,000 00

PUBLIC FUNDS — Concluded.

	Par Value.	Estimated Market Value.	Amount Invested.
State of Rhode Island	$5,000	$5,300 00	$5,000 00
of C necticut . . .	17,000	18,080 00	17,000 00
City of Bangor, Me., 7s . . .	5,000	5,800 00	5,000 00
of Bangor, Me., 6s . . .	5,000	6,000 00	5,000 00
of Charlestown 6s . . .	5,000	5,900 00	5,000 00
of Boston 6s	20,000	24,000 00	20,000 00
of Cambridge 6s . . .	45,000	51,750 00	45,000 00
of Chelsea 6s	25,000	28,750 00	25,000 00
of Fitchburg 6s . . .	10,000	11,400 00	10,000 00
of Holyoke 6s	31,000	37,200 00	31,000 00
of Holyoke 7s	50,000	60,000 00	50,000 00
of Lawrence 6s . . .	10,000	12,000 00	10,000 00
of Lowell 6s	10,000	11,700 00	10,000 00
of Lynn 6s	20,000	23,400 00	20,000 00
of New Bedford 6s . . .	6,000	7,200 00	6,000 00
of New Bedford 7s . . .	50,000	65,000 00	55,000 00
of Newburyport 6s . . .	5,000	5,350 00	5,000 00
of Newton 6s	35,000	42,000 00	35,000 00
of Newton 5s	5,000	5,600 00	5,000 00
of Springfield 6s . . .	43,000	46,440 00	43,000 00
of Springfield 7s . . .	167,000	212,090 00	167,000 00
of Taunton 6s	20,000	23,400 00	20,000 00
of Worcester 6s . . .	35,000	42,000 00	35,000 00
of Somerville 5s . . .	10,000	10,500 00	10,000 00
of Providence, R.I., 5s . .	10,000	11,600 00	10,000 00
of Providence, R.I., 6s . .	40,000	50,000 00	44,000 00
of Hartford, Conn., 6s . .	86,000	95,460 00	86,000 00
of Meriden, Conn., 6s . .	5,000	5,600 00	5,000 00
of Middletown, Conn., 6s .	7,000	7,490 00	7,000 00
of New Haven, Conn., 5s .	11,000	11,550 00	11,000 00
of New Haven, Conn., 6s .	5,000	5,600 00	5,000 00
of New Haven, Conn., 7s .	22,000	28,600 00	22,000 00
of Norwich, Conn., 5s . .	5,000	5,250 00	5,000 00
of Norwich, Conn., 7s . .	20,000	25,000 00	20,000 00
of Waterbury, Conn., 7s .	14,000	16,240 00	14,000 00
Town of Pittsfield 4½s . . .	30,000	31,200 00	30,000 00
of Brookline 5s . . .	15,000	16,200 00	15,000 00
of Brookline 6s . . .	5,000	5,700 00	5,000 00
of Brookline 7s . . .	10,000	13,000 00	10,000 00
of Greenfield 5s . . .	50,000	52,000 00	50,000 00
	$2,563,300	$2,897,479 00	$2,679,300 00

BANK STOCK.

First Nat'l Bank, Springfield . .	$43,600	$65,400 00	$53,300 00
Second Nat'l Bank, Springfield .	30,800	53,900 00	38,000 00
Third Nat'l Bank, Springfield . .	34,700	62,460 00	49,700 00
Agawam Nat'l Bank, Springfield .	23,000	29,900 00	23,000 00
Chapin Nat'l Bank, Springfield .	15,000	18,000 00	15,000 00
Chicopee Nat'l Bank, Springfield .	48,500	72,750 00	58,300 00

BANK STOCK — Concluded.

	Par Value.	Estimated Market Value.	Amount Invested.
City Nat'l Bank, Springfield . .	$17,000	$22,100 00	$17,000 00
John Hancock Nat'l B'k, Springfi'd,	15,700	18,055 00	15,700 00
Pynchon Nat'l Bank, Springfield .	30,000	51,000 00	43,500 00
Franklin Co. Nat'l B'k, Greenfield .	4,600	8,188 00	4,600 00
First Nat'l Bank, Adams . .	1,700	2,499 00	1,700 00
First Nat'l Bank, Chicopee . .	21,000	32,550 00	25,000 00
First Nat'l Bank, Easthampton .	1,500	1,875 00	1,500 00
Wachusett Nat'l Bank, Fitchburg .	5,000	10,000 00	5,000 00
Hadley Falls Nat'l Bank, Holyoke .	3,400	5,100 00	3,400 00
Holyoke Nat'l Bank, Holyoke . .	3,000	3,450 00	3,000 00
First Nat'l Bank, Leominster . .	10,000	11,000 00	10,000 00
Monson Nat'l Bank, Monson . .	3,900	5,655 00	3,900 00
First Nat'l Bank, Northampton .	2,000	2,500 00	2,000 00
Hampshire Co. N'l B'k, Northam'n,	3,000	3,450 00	3,000 00
Northampton N'l B'k, Northam'n .	4,500	8,100 00	4,500 00
Palmer Nat'l Bank, Palmer . .	5,000	6,000 00	5,000 00
Ware Nat'l Bank, Ware . . .	2,500	3,000 00	2,500 00
Hampden Nat'l Bank, Westfield .	2,500	3,750 00	2,500 00
Phœnix Nat'l B'k, Hartford, Conn.	1,300	2,184 00	1,300 00
Exchange N'l B'k, Hartford, Conn.	500	700 00	500 00
First Nat'l Bank, Boston . .	5,000	10,400 00	5,000 00
Second Nat'l Bank, Boston . .	20,000	30,200 00	20,000 00
Atlantic Nat'l Bank, Boston . .	10,000	15,300 00	10,000 00
Atlas Nat'l Bank, Boston . .	15,000	18,750 00	15,000 00
Blackstone Nat'l Bank, Boston .	15,000	17,250 00	15,000 00
Columbian Nat'l Bank, Boston .	10,000	14,300 00	10,000 00
Eliot Nat'l Bank, Boston . .	3,000	3,600 00	3,000 00
Freeman's Nat'l Bank, Boston .	20,000	24,000 00	20,000 00
Hamilton Nat'l Bank, Boston . .	15,000	18,600 00	15,000 00
Howard Nat'l Bank, Boston . .	13,300	17,290 00	13,300 00
Merchants' Nat'l Bank, Boston .	15,000	22,050 00	15,000 00
Mount Vernon Nat'l Bank, Boston .	2,500	3,175 00	2,500 00
Commerce Nat'l Bank, Boston .	3,700	4,736 00	3,700 00
Commonwealth Nat'l Bank, Boston,	2,000	2,480 00	2,000 00
North America Nat'l Bank, Boston,	17,500	20,125 00	17,500 00
Redemption Nat'l Bank, Boston .	25,000	33,750 00	25,000 00
City Nat'l Bank, Boston . . .	15,000	19,050 00	15,000 00
Eagle Nat'l Bank, Boston . .	5,000	6,000 00	5,000 00
Exchange Nat'l Bank, Boston . .	2,000	2,880 00	2,000 00
Hide and Leather Nat'l B'k, Boston,	3,400	4,012 00	3,400 00
Revere Nat'l Bank, Boston . .	15,000	18,300 00	15,000 00
Union Nat'l Bank, Boston . .	4,300	6,579 00	4,300 00
North Nat'l Bank, Boston . .	20,000	28,400 00	24,000 00
Old Boston Nat'l Bank, Boston .	7,000	8,540 00	7,000 00
Shawmut Nat'l Bank, Boston . .	10,000	12,700 00	10,000 00
State Nat'l Bank, Boston . .	7,500	9,375 00	7,500 00
Suffolk Nat'l Bank, Boston . .	5,000	6,050 00	5,000 00
Tremont Nat'l Bank, Boston . .	15,000	18,300 00	15,000 00
Washington Nat'l Bank, Boston .	3,000	4,200 00	3,000 00
Webster Nat'l Bank, Boston . .	7,500	8,400 00	7,500 00
	$645,400	$912,418 00	$708,600 00

RAILROAD BONDS.

	Par Value.	Estimated Market Value.	Amount Invested.
Boston and Albany 6s	$140,000	$161,000 00	$140,000 00
Boston and Albany 7s	60,000	76,200 00	63,000 00
Boston and Maine 7s	25,000	31,750 00	30,000 00
Connecticut River	130,000	130,000 00	130,000 00
	$355,000	$398,950 00	$363,000 00

STOCKBRIDGE SAVINGS BANK — STOCKBRIDGE.

Incorporated 1871. Number of corporators, 17.

MASON VAN DEUSEN, *President*. *Treasurer*, C. H. WILLIS.

STATEMENT.

LIABILITIES.		ASSETS.	
Deposits	$104,381 75	Public funds	$1,820 00
Earnings undivided	776 83	Loans on public funds	200 00
Guaranty fund	705 59	Bank stock	8,332 50
Premium	62 13	Real estate by foreclosure	2,645 00
		Loans on real estate	72,296 13
		Loans on personal security	9,552 00
		Deposit in bank	4,302 50
		Cash on hand	6,778 17
	$105,926 30		$105,926 30

Loans on Public Funds: —

On $200 United States 6s $200 00

Cash on Deposit in Bank: —

Housatonic National Bank . . $4,302 50

Amount of real estate held by foreclosure	$2,645 00
Assessed value of the same	1,350 00
Amount of income received from the same	212 50
Amount of municipal tax on real estate	14 45

Whole amount of interest or profits received or earned $5,281 44

Rate and amount of each semi-annual dividend for previous year: 2½ per cent, 1,477 15; 2½ per cent, 1,906 97

Times for the dividends fixed by the by-laws: first Thursday in April and October.

Average annual per cent of dividends for the term ending at time of and including last extra dividend: 5 per cent.

The total amount of loans, with each specified rate of interest: $37,587.13, 6 per cent; $13,842, 7 per cent; $30,619, 7 3/10 per cent.

Number of outstanding loans which are of an amount not exceeding $3,000 each	142	
Aggregate amount of the same		62,048 13
Number of open accounts	334	
Number and amount of deposits received for previous year	371	55,967 73
Number and amount of deposits of and exceeding $300 at any one time for the previous year	64	38,828 77
Number and amount of withdrawals	156	14,440 40
Number of accounts opened the previous year	130	
Number of accounts closed the previous year	47	
Amount of expenses of the corporation during previous year		$66 83
Amount of treasurer's bond		15,000 00

Date of examination by commissioner: Aug. 2.

PUBLIC FUNDS.

	Par Value.	Estimated Market Value.	Amount Invested.
Town bonds:—			
Town of Adams	$2,000	$2,360 00	$1,820 00

BANK STOCK.

	Par Value.	Estimated Market Value.	Amount Invested.
First Nat'l Bank, Adams . .	$2,500	$3,625 00	$2,970 00
First Nat'l Bank, Woburn . .	3,500	5,362 50	5,362 50
	$6,000	$8,987 50	$8,332 50

STONEHAM FIVE CENTS SAVINGS BANK — STONEHAM.

Incorporated 1855. Number of corporators, 47.

LYMAN DIKE, *President.* *Treasurer*, ONSLOW GILMORE.

STATEMENT.

LIABILITIES.		ASSETS.	
Deposits . . .	$330,997 08	Public funds . . .	$95,000 00
Earnings undivided .	9,760 34	Railroad bonds . . .	10,000 00
Guaranty fund . .	5,611 85	Real estate by foreclosure .	20,598 00
		Loans on real estate . .	132,564 73
		Loans on personal security,	3,100 00
		Loans to counties, cities, or towns	72,000 00
		Deposit in bank on interest,	10,781 39
		Expense account . . .	1,768 53
		Cash on hand . . .	556 62
	$346,369 27		$346,369 27

Cash on Deposit in Bank: —

Blackstone National Bank, Boston . .	$10,781 39

Amount of real estate held by foreclosure .		$20,598 00
Assessed value of the same		28,150 00
Amount of income received from the same .		800 00
Amount of municipal tax on real estate . .		434 15
Whole amount of interest or profits received or earned . . .		$16,392 02
Rate and amount of each semi-annual dividend for previous year — $2\frac{1}{4}$ per cent .		5,888 27
— 2 per cent .		5,598 37

Times for the dividends fixed by the by-laws: May and November.

Average annual per cent of dividends for the term ending at time of and including last extra dividend: $4\frac{1}{8}$ per cent.

The total amount of loans, with each specified rate of interest: $105,000, 4 per cent; $10,000. $4\frac{1}{2}$ per cent; $32,000, 5 per cent; $50,700, 6 per cent; $5,000, $6\frac{1}{2}$ per cent; $109,964.73, 7 per cent.

Number of outstanding loans which are of an amount not exceeding $3,000 each	130	
Aggregate amount of the same		108,264 73
Amount of investments from which no income is received . .		525 00
Number of open accounts	1,487	
Number and amount of deposits received for previous year,	1,695	119,857 75
Number and amount of deposits of and exceeding $300 at any one time for the previous year	90	50,350 00
Number and amount of withdrawals	941	88,326 51
Number of accounts opened the previous year	332	
Number of accounts closed the previous year	220	
Amount of expenses of the corporation during previous year . .		1,120 00
Amount of treasurer's bond		15,000 00

Date of examination by commissioner: May 9.

PUBLIC FUNDS.

	Par Value.	Estimated Market Value.	Amount Invested.
City bonds: —			
City of Somerville 6½s	$5,000	$5,500 00	$5,100 00
of Haverhill 6s . . .	5,000	5,650 00	5,500 00
of Boston 4s	45,000	46,800 00	45,000 00
of New Bedford 4s . . .	20,000	20,500 00	20,500 00
Town of Arlington 6s . . .	10,000	11,300 00	11,000 00
of Sheldon, Vt., 4½s . .	10,000	10,400 00	10,400 00
	$95,000	$100,150 00	$97,500 00

RAILROAD BONDS.

Boston, Clinton, and Fitchburg .	$10,000	$11,700 00	$11,487 00

SUFFOLK SAVINGS BANK FOR SEAMEN AND OTHERS — BOSTON.

Incorporated 1833. Number of corporators, 168.

THOMAS LAMB, *President*. *Treasurer*, CHARLES HENRY PARKER.

STATEMENT.

LIABILITIES.		ASSETS.	
Deposits	$15,009,648 25	Public funds	$1,042,000 00
Earnings undivided	73,816 46	Loans on public funds	260,000 00
Guaranty fund	157,825 41	Bank stock	658,345 24
Note payable	30,000 00	Loans on bank stock	2,000 00
Rents	4,409 53	Railroad bonds	625,968 00
Premium account	19,201 67	Real estate	180,000 00
		Real estate by foreclosure	121,434 21
		Loans on real estate	4,657,262 25
		Loans on personal security,*	6,583,250 00
		Loans to counties, cities, or towns	90,000 00
		Deposit in banks on interest,	953,867 74
		Deposit in banks without interest	27,215 64
		Expense account	2,086 83
		Cash on hand	91,471 41
	$15,294,901 32		$15,294,901 32

Loans on Public Funds, amount on each: —

On $17,000 United States 4s On $31,000 United States 4½s On $142,000 United States 3½s On $50,000 certificates of deposit, temporary	$240,000 00
On $20,000 City of Boston 6s	20,000 00

Loans on Bank Stock: —

On 25 shares Mechanics' National Bank, Boston	$2,000 00

Cash on Deposit in Banks, amount in each: —

Revere National Bank	$125,879 06
Shawmut National Bank	109,060 64
Exchange National Bank	338,928 04
First National Bank, Newburyport	40,000 00
Wachusett National Bank, Fitchburg	50,000 00
Market National Bank,	100,000 00
Columbian National Bank	105,195 31
New England National Bank	112,020 33

Amount invested in real estate (for banking purposes)	$180,000 00
Estimated value of the same	180,000 00
Amount of real estate held by foreclosure	121,431 21
Assessed value of the same	145,400 00
Amount of income received from the same	6,764 21
Amount of municipal tax on real estate	5,421 01

Whole amount of interest or profits received or earned	$670,446 90

* This bank has been notified that these loans have exceeded the legal limit.

Rate and amount of each semi-annual dividend for previous year	2 per cent .	$264,432 52
	1½ per cent . .	206,793 68

Times for the dividends fixed by the by-laws: second Wednesday in April and October.

Average annual per cent of dividends for the term ending at time of and including last extra dividend: $5\frac{5}{100}$ per cent.

The total amount of loans, with each specified rate of interest: $240,000, 2½ per cent; $340,000, 3 per cent; $1,385,000, 3½ per cent; $200,000, 3¾ per cent; $1,923,800, 4 per cent; $1,955,962.25, 4½ per cent; $30,000, 4¾ per cent; $2,387,700, 5 per cent; $668,500, 5½ per cent; $2,086,600, 6 per cent; $64,500, 6½ per cent; $310,450, 7 per cent.

Number of outstanding loans which are of an amount not exceeding $3,000 each	75	
Aggregate amount of the same		177,500 00
Amount of investments from which no income is received . .		22,197 50
Number of open accounts	35,924	
Number and amount of deposits received for previous year,	36,716	3,737,274 24
Number and amount of deposits of and exceeding $300 at any one time for the previous year	3,309	1,836,741 00
Number and amount of withdrawals	24,074	2,778,741 11
Number of accounts opened the previous year . . .	7,513	
Number of accounts closed the previous year . . .	4,055	
Amount of expenses of the corporation during previous year . .		25,874 86
Amount of treasurer's bond		20,000 00

Date of examination by commissioner: Nov. 25.

Public Funds.

	Par Value.	Estimated Market Value.	Amount Invested.
United States 4s	$500,000	$580,625 00	500,000 00
" " 4½s	300,000	339,000 00	300,000 00
" " 5s, extended 3½s .	200,000	204,000 00	200,000 00
City bonds: —			
City of Worcester 6s	$20,000	$21,650 00	$20,000 00
of New Bedford 6s	10,000	12,400 00	10,000 00
of Manchester, N.H., 5s . .	12,000	12,270 00	12,000 00
	$1,042,000	$1,169,945 00	$1,042,000 00

Bank Stock.

Atlantic Nat'l Bank, Boston . .	$8,500	$13,047 50	$12,601 25
Atlas Nat'l Bank, Boston . .	65,400	81,750 00	66,112 50
Bay State Nat'l Bank, Lawrence .	13,125	21,175 00	13,125 00
Boylston Nat'l Bank, Boston . .	3,000	3,840 00	3,375 00
City Nat'l Bank, Boston . . .	21,100	26,797 00	22,199 87
Columbian Nat'l Bank, Boston .	49,200	70,110 00	49,200 00
Commerce Nat'l Bank, Boston .	16,900	21,758 75	17,289 50

BANK STOCK — Concluded.

	Par Value.	Estimated Market Value.	Amount Invested.
Continental Nat'l Bank, Boston .	$13,800	$16,370 25	$15,750 00
Eagle Nat'l Bank, Boston . .	46,100	55,204 75	47,525 00
Freeman's Nat'l Bank, Boston .	4,800	5,748 00	5,698 87
Hamilton Nat'l Bank, Boston . .	15,000	16,950 00	15,000 00
Hide and Leather Nat'l B'k, Boston,	21,100	24,581 50	24,064 25
Howard Nat'l Bank, Boston . .	15,000	19,518 75	17,650 00
Market Nat'l Bank, Boston . .	15,000	16,462 50	15,000 00
Merchants' Nat'l Bank, Boston .	65,800	96,227 50	71,143 50
Massachusetts Nat'l Bank, Boston .	5,000	6,200 00	5,000 00
New England Nat'l Bank, Boston .	1,100	1,600 50	1,100 00
Railroad Nat'l Bank, Lowell . .	5,000	6,137 50	5,000 00
Redemption Nat'l Bank, Boston .	15,000	20,268 75	19,962 50
Republic Nat'l Bank, Boston . .	10,000	13,100 00	12,750 00
Revere Nat'l Bank, Boston . .	40,000	48,800 00	41,893 75
Shawmut Nat'l Bank, Boston . .	24,400	31,110 00	26,721 25
Shoe and Leather Nat'l B'k, Boston,	11,100	12,487 50	11,221 00
State Nat'l Bank, Boston . .	13,300	16,691 50	13,648 00
Suffolk Nat'l Bank, Boston . .	13,600	16,575 00	16,348 75
Tremont Nat'l Bank, Boston . .	18,700	22,814 00	20,481 00
Union Nat'l Bank, Boston . .	10,000	15,350 00	10,000 00
Washington Nat'l Bank, Boston .	15,000	21,000 00	15,000 00
Webster Nat'l Bank, Boston . .	61,700	68,795 50	63,484 25
	$617,725	$790,471 75	$658,345 24

RAILROAD BONDS.

	Par Value.	Estimated Market Value.	Amount Invested.
Old Colony 6s	$200,000	$235,000 00	$200,000 00
Fitchburg 5s	384,000	409,440 00	425,968 00
	$584,000	$644,440 00	$625,968 00

TAUNTON SAVINGS BANK — TAUNTON.

Incorporated 1869. Number of corporators, 112.

JOHN E. SANFORD, *President*. *Treasurer*, HENRY R. WOOD.

STATEMENT.

LIABILITIES.		ASSETS.	
Deposits	$1,173,358 52	Public funds	$240,013 74
Earnings undivided	60,553 33	Loans on public funds	500 00
Guaranty fund	16,899 59	Bank stock	100,208 12
Suspense account	5,353 55	Loans on bank stock	100 00
Manufacturing stock,*	3,685 00	Loans on railroad stock	150 00
		Real estate by foreclosure	42,561 86
		Loans on real estate	533,659 47
		Loans on personal security,	334,354 96
		Deposit in banks on interest,	666 12
		Expense account	1,225 09
		Furniture account	3,173 89
		Loans on bank books	500 00
		Cash on hand	2,736 74
	$1,259,849 99		$1,259,849 99

Loans on Public Funds: —

On $500 United States 4s, registered bonds $500 00

Loans on Bank Stock: —

On 1 share Taunton National Bank, Taunton . . . $100 00

Loans on Railroad Stock: —

On 2 shares Boston and Providence Railroad $150 00

Cash on Deposit in Banks, amount in each: —

Taunton National Bank, Taunton	$717 74
Maverick National Bank, Boston	666 12

Amount of real estate held by foreclosure	$42,561 86
Assessed value of the same	31,410 00
Amount of income received from the same	2,136 50
Amount of municipal tax on real estate	426 76

Whole amount of interest or profits received or earned $67,503 39

Rate and amount of each semi-annual dividend for previous year: 2 per cent, 23,012 95; 2 per cent, 22,502 07

Times for the dividends fixed by the by-laws: January and July.

The total amount of loans, with each specified rate of interest: $25,000, 4 per cent; $50,000, 4¼ per cent; $110,000, 4½ per cent; $137,500, 5 per cent; $10,000, 5¼ per cent; $27,100, 5½ per cent; $451,119.43, 6 per cent; $27,270, 6½ per cent; $18,450, 7 per cent; $8,835, 7½ per cent; $3,900, 8 per cent.

Number of outstanding loans which are of an amount not exceeding $3,000 each 235

Aggregate amount of the same 246,834 47

Number of open accounts 3,390

Number and amount of deposits received for previous year, 1,228 171,583 88

* This is a liability on account of stock of the Sagamore and Border City Mills, Fall River, taken to secure personal indebtedness.

Number and amount of deposits of and exceeding $300 at any one time for the previous year	176	$108,388 23
Number and amount of withdrawals	1,936	219,380 47
Number of accounts opened the previous year	394	
Number of accounts closed the previous year	428	
Amount of expenses of the corporation during previous year .		3,835 17
Amount of treasurer's bond		30,000 00

Date of examination by commissioner: June 20.

Public Funds.

	Par Value.	Estimated Market Value.	Amount Invested.
United States 4½s	$173,000	$195,490 00	$177,544 49
" " 6s, currency . .	15,000	19,500 00	18,006 25
State and city bonds: —			
State of Maine 6s	$1,000	$1,135 00	$1,135 00
of New Hampshire 6s . .	1,000	1,200 00	1,165 00
of Massachusetts 5s . .	3,000	3,383 10	3,330 00
City of Taunton 5s	19,900	22,487 00	21,003 00
of Taunton 5s	4,500	4,860 00	4,680 00
of Taunton 6s	2,000	2,440 00	2,290 00
of Taunton 6s	500	500 00	510 00
of New Bedford 4s	10,000	10,350 00	10,350 00
	$229,900	$261,345 10	$240,013 74

Bank Stock.

Merchants' Nat'l B'k, New Bedford,	$20,000	$32,400 00	$27,200 00
Commerce Nat'l B'k, New Bedford,	10,200	14,178 00	12,311 00
First Nat'l Bank, New Bedford .	1,700	2,278 00	2,211 01
Atlas Nat'l Bank, Boston . .	5,500	6,875 00	6,208 61
City Nat'l Bank, Boston . . .	10,000	12,300 00	11,362 50
Pacific Nat'l Bank, Boston . .	20,000	21,000 00	21,000 00
Taunton Nat'l Bank, Taunton .	10,900	16,895 00	14,250 00
Bristol Co. Nat'l Bank, Taunton .	3,400	5,270 00	4,405 00
Machinists' Nat'l Bank, Taunton .	900	1,440 00	1,260 00
	$82,600	$112,636 00	$100,208 12

TEMPLETON SAVINGS BANK — TEMPLETON.

Incorporated April 19, 1871. Number of corporators, 59.

CHARLES A. PERLEY, *President*. *Treasurer*, ASA HOSMER.

STATEMENT.

LIABILITIES.		ASSETS.	
Deposits . . .	$134,552 01	Bank stock	$4,680 00
Earnings undivided .	735 75	Loans on real estate . .	74,234 00
Guaranty fund . .	1,206 24	Loans on personal security,	15,225 00
		Loans to counties, cities, or towns.	35,000 00
		Deposit in banks on interest,	7,000 00
		Cash on hand . . .	355 00
	$136,494 00		$136,494 00

Cash on Deposit in Banks, amount in each: —

National Bank of the Commonwealth, Boston		$7,000 00
Miller's River National Bank, Athol		163 28
Whole amount of interest or profits received or earned . . .		$6,279 23
Rate and amount of each semi-annual dividend for previous year	2½ per cent .	2,354 84
	2 per cent .	2,157 46

Times for the dividends fixed by the by-laws: Jan. 1 and July 1.

Average annual per cent of dividends for the term ending at time of and including last extra dividend: 5 per cent.

The total amount of loans, with each specified rate of interest: $5,000, 3¾ per cent; $10,000, 4 per cent; $25,000, 5 per cent; $84,459, 6 per cent.

Number of outstanding loans which are of an amount not exceeding $3,000 each	121	
Aggregate amount of the same		74,359 00
Number of open accounts	526	
Number and amount of deposits received for previous year .	409	55,563 06
Number and amount of deposits of and exceeding $300 at any one time for the previous year	49	31,380 07
Number and amount of withdrawals	162	20,472 05
Number of accounts opened the previous year	141	
Number of accounts closed the previous year	46	
Amount of expenses of the corporation during previous year .		367 32
Amount of treasurer's bond		10,000 00

Date of examination by commissioner: June 24.

BANK STOCK.

	Par Value.	Estimated Market Value.	Amount Invested.
First Nat'l Bank, Orange . .	$3,000	$3,300 00	$3,000 00
First Nat'l Bank, Gardner . .	1,200	1,680 00	1,680 00
	$4,200	$4,980 00	$4,680 00

UNION INSTITUTION FOR SAVINGS IN THE CITY OF BOSTON — BOSTON.

Incorporated 1865. Number of corporators, 38.

HUGH O'BRIEN, *President*. *Treasurer*, GEORGE F. EMERY.

STATEMENT.

LIABILITIES.		ASSETS.	
Deposits	$2,533,840 34	Public funds	$352,616 25
Earnings undivided	38,825 64	Real estate	278,601 06
Guaranty fund	45,191 00	Real estate by foreclosure	522,056 91
Mortgage and interest suspense	253 26	Loans on real estate	1,198,739 00
		Loans on personal security,	240,640 72
		Deposit in banks on interest,	20,369 56
		Cash on hand	5,086 74
	$2,618,110 24		$2,618,110 24

Cash on Deposit in Banks, amount in each: —

Exchange National Bank	$13,216 64
Central National Bank	1,399 94
Boston Safe Deposit and Trust Company *	2,544 04
International Trust Company *	3,208 94

Amount invested in real estate (for banking purposes)	$278,601 06
Estimated value of the same	300,000 00
Amount of real estate held by foreclosure	522,056 91
Assessed value of the same	488,660 00
Amount of income received from the same	34,863 88
Amount of municipal tax on real estate	10,276 83

Whole amount of interest or profits received or earned		$135,331 77
Rate and amount of each semi-annual dividend for previous year	1½ per cent	38,134 07
	1½ per cent	37,073 26

Times for the dividends fixed by the by-laws: second Wednesday in May and November.

The total amount of loans, with each specified rate of interest: $300,000, 4½ per cent; $211,984, 5 per cent; $10,000, 5½ per cent; $460,845.72, 6 per cent; $19,225, 6½ per cent; $413,700, 7 per cent; $23,625, 8 per cent.

Number of outstanding loans which are of an amount not exceeding $3,000 each	380	
Aggregate amount of the same		484,150 00
Amount of investments from which no income is received		30,574 91
Number of open accounts	7,284	
Number and amount of deposits received for previous year.	5,253	535,666 03
Number and amount of deposits of and exceeding $300 at any one time for the previous year	379	237,533 00
Number and amount of withdrawals	6,289	638,288 74

* The Attorney-General has given an opinion, that under the provisions of sect. 3, chap. 214 of the Acts of 1881, deposits by savings banks in these trust companies are legal.

Number of accounts opened the previous year 859
Number of accounts closed the previous year 1,267
Amount of expenses of the corporation during previous year . . $9,245 68
Amount of treasurer's bond 15,000 00
Date of examination by commissioner: Feb. 15.

PUBLIC FUNDS.

	Par Value.	Estimated Market Value.	Amount Invested.
United States 4½s	$50,000	$56,437 50	$54,312 50
" " 3½s	6,700	6,767 00	6,700 00
City bonds:—			
City of Boston 5s	$225,000	$265,500 00	$251,812 50
of Chelsea 6s	9,000	10,640 00	10,625 00
of Lowell 6s	2,000	2,280 00	2,325 00
of Springfield 7s	2,000	2,600 00	2,600 00
of Hartford, Conn., 6s . .	1,000	1,160 00	1,170 00
of Newton 6s	4,000	5,040 00	4,920 00
of Somerville 5s	17,000	17,840 00	18,151 25
	$316,700	$368,264 50	$352,616 25

UNION SAVINGS BANK — FALL RIVER.

Incorporated 1869. Number of corporators, 32.

AUGUSTUS CHACE, *President*. *Treasurer*, D. A. CHAPIN.

STATEMENT.

LIABILITIES.		ASSETS.	
Deposits . . .	$624,589 94	Bank stock	$72,296 50
Earnings undivided .	23,868 12	Real estate	38,000 00
Guaranty fund . .	9,000 00	Real estate by foreclosure .	5,906 84
		Loans on real estate . .	290,487 00
		Loans on personal security,	203,818 00
		Deposit in bank on interest,	41,500 00
		Expense account . . .	760 40
		Cash on hand . . .	4,689 32
	$657,458 06		$657,458 06

Cash on Deposit in Bank: —

Union National Bank, Fall River		$41,500 00
Amount invested in real estate (for banking purposes) . . .		$38,000 00
Estimated value of the same		40,000 00
Amount of real estate held by foreclosure		5,906 84
Assessed value of the same		4,300 00
Amount of income received from the same		500 00
Amount of municipal tax on real estate		395 20
Whole amount of interest or profits received or earned . . .		$34,633 77
Rate and amount of each semi-annual dividend for previous year	2 per cent .	11,405 88
	2 per cent .	11,806 87

Times for the dividends fixed by the by-laws: May 15 and Nov. 15.

The total amount of loans, with each specified rate of interest: $213,810, 5 per cent; $251,022, 6 per cent.

Number of outstanding loans which are of an amount not exceeding $3,000 each	105	
Aggregate amount of the same		127,432 00
Amount of investments from which no income is received . .		29,473 00
Number of open accounts	1,380	
Number and amount of deposits received for previous year,	1,160	130,705 76
Number and amount of deposits of and exceeding $300 at any one time for the previous year	75	44,925 34
Number and amount of withdrawals	1,068	105,850 66
Number of accounts opened the previous year	307	
Number of accounts closed the previous year	251	
Amount of expenses of the corporation during previous year . .		2,000 00
Amount of treasurer's bond		25,000 00

Date of examination by commissioner: July 20.

BANK STOCK.

	Par Value.	Estimated Market Value.	Amount Invested.
Union Nat'l Bank, Fall River . .	$22,500	$25,425 00	$24,850 00
Metacomet Nat'l Bank, Fall River .	31,800	44,520 00	40,397 50
Pocasset Nat'l Bank, Fall River .	3,000	4,200 00	3,750 00
Massasoit Nat'l Bank, Fall River .	700	1,295 00	1,274 00
Fall River Nat'l Bank, Fall River .	1,500	2,100 00	2,025 00
	$59,500	$77,540 00	$72,296 50

UXBRIDGE SAVINGS BANK — UXBRIDGE.

Incorporated June 3, 1870. Number of corporators, 68.

MOSES TAFT, *President.* *Treasurer*, C. A. TAFT.

STATEMENT.

LIABILITIES.		ASSETS.	
Deposits	$287,609 46	Bank stock	$139,430 87
Earnings undivided	7,123 34	Real estate by foreclosure	28,830 48
Guaranty fund	3,850 00	Loans on real estate	92,041 90
Checks outstanding	314 80	Loans on personal security,	29,055 00
		Deposit in bank on interest,	8,799 44
		Expense account	739 91
	$298,897 60		$298,897 60

Cash on Deposit in Bank: —

Blackstone National Bank, Uxbridge	$8,799 44

Amount of real estate held by foreclosure	$28,830 48
Assessed value of the same	20,400 00
Amount of income received from the same	1,400 00
Amount of municipal tax on real estate	294 80

Whole amount of interest or profits received or earned		$15,040 74
Rate and amount of each semi-annual dividend for previous year	2 per cent	5,360 19
	2 per cent	5,509 05

Times for the dividends fixed by the by-laws: January and July.

Average annual per cent of dividends for the term ending at time of and including last extra dividend: 5½ per cent.

The total amount of loans, with each specified rate of interest: $5,000, 5 per cent; $98,061.90, 6 per cent; $3,000, 6½ per cent; $14,835, 7 per cent.

Number of outstanding loans which are of an amount not exceeding $3,000 each	76	
Aggregate amount of the same		68,371 00
Number of open accounts	1,005	
Number and amount of deposits received for previous year	478	51,329 57
Number and amount of deposits of and exceeding $300 at any one time for the previous year	38	20,893 21
Number and amount of withdrawals	377	39,106 29
Number of accounts opened the previous year	103	
Number of accounts closed the previous year	79	
Amount of expenses of the corporation during previous year		825 00
Amount of treasurer's bond		20,000 00

Date of examination by commissioner: May 2.

BANK STOCK.

	Par Value.	Estimated Market Value.	Amount Invested.
Redemption Nat'l Bank, Boston .	$8,000	$10,880 00	$11,270 00
Suffolk Nat'l Bank, Boston . .	6,100	7,625 00	7,945 00
Hide and Leather Nat'l B'k, Boston,	13,000	15,600 00	15,259 12
Revere Nat'l Bank, Boston . .	8,000	10,000 00	9,795 00
Howard Nat'l Bank, Boston . .	11,200	14,560 00	12,919 00
North Nat'l Bank, Boston . .	6,000	8,640 00	7,494 50
Tremont Nat'l Bank, Boston . .	5,800	7,076 00	7,280 00
Eliot Nat'l Bank, Boston . .	11,000	13,200 00	13,148 75
Webster Nat'l Bank, Boston . .	6,900	7,659 00	7,516 75
State Nat'l Bank, Boston . .	7,800	9,750 00	8,974 75
Mount Vernon Nat'l Bank, Boston .	1,800	2,304 00	2,223 75
Atlas Nat'l Bank, Boston . .	3,300	4,191 00	4,134 25
Eagle Nat'l Bank, Boston . .	3,000	3,630 00	3,777 75
Blackstone Nat'l Bank, Uxbridge .	1,700	2,260 00	2,260 00
Grafton Nat'l Bank, Grafton . .	500	540 00	540 00
First Nat'l Bank, Clinton . .	2,000	2,480 00	2,480 00
Wachusett Nat'l Bank, Fitchburg .	2,500	5,000 00	5,000 00
Franklin Nat'l Bank, Franklin . .	5,900	7,090 00	7,090 00
Central Nat'l Bank, Boston . .	4,000	4,800 00	4,240 00
Millbury Nat'l Bank, Millbury .	1,700	2,006 00	2,006 00
Manufacturers' Nat'l Bank, Boston,	4,000	4,400 00	4,076 25
	$114,200	$143,691 00	$139,430 87

WAKEFIELD SAVINGS BANK — WAKEFIELD.

Incorporated 1869. Number of corporators, 59.

JAMES F. EMERSON, *President*. *Treasurer*, RICHARD BRITTON.

STATEMENT.

LIABILITIES.		ASSETS.	
Deposits . . .	$91,528 74	Public funds . . .	$12,000 00
Guaranty fund . .	948 93	Bank stock	13,500 00
		Railroad bonds . . .	1,000 00
		Real estate by foreclosure .	11,174 59
		Loans on real estate . .	43,645 05
		Loans on personal security,	1,500 00
		Deposit in bank on interest,	3,825 22
		Expense account . . .	132 00
		Premiums	5,082 18
		Interest account . . .	135 01
		Tax account	8 03
		Cash on hand . . .	475 59
	$92,477 67		$92,477 67

Cash on Deposit in Bank: —

South Reading National Bank, South Reading . . $3.825 22

Amount of real estate held by foreclosure		$11.174 59
Assessed value of the same		11,500 00
Amount of income received from the same		538 73
Amount of municipal tax on real estate		161 19
Whole amount of interest or profits received or earned		$5.135 21
Rate and amount of each semi-annual dividend for previous year	2 per cent / 2 per cent	1,441 94 / 1,559 78

Times for the dividends fixed by the by-laws: February and August.

Average annual per cent of dividends for the term ending at time of and including last extra dividend: 6⅓ per cent.

The total amount of loans, with each specified rate of interest: $29,700, 6 per cent; $32,395.05, 7 per cent; $1,800, 7$\frac{3}{10}$ per cent; $2,250, 8 per cent; $5,500, 9 per cent.

Number of outstanding loans which are of an amount not exceeding $3,000 each	45	
Aggregate amount of the same		45,145 05
Amount of investments from which no income is received . .		529 07
Number of open accounts	682	
Number and amount of deposits received for previous year .	723	33,706 12
Number and amount of deposits of and exceeding $300 at any one time for the previous year	20	11.608 74
Number and amount of withdrawals	430	21,464 75
Number of accounts opened the previous year.	149	
Number of accounts closed the previous year	98	
Amount of expenses of the corporation during previous year .		584 84
Amount of treasurer's bond		10,000 00

Date of examination by commissioner: May 4.

PUBLIC FUNDS.

	Par Value.	Estimated Market Value.	Amount Invested.
City bonds: —			
City of Bath, Me., 6s	$5,000	$5,000 00	$5,225 00
of Rockland, Me., 6s . .	2,000	2,000 00	2,085 00
of Boston 6s	2,000	2,620 00	2,457 50
of Lowell 6s	2,000	2,300 00	2,330 00
of Boston 6s	1,000	1,310 00	1,230 00
	$12,000	$13,230 00	$13,327 50

BANK STOCK.

S. Reading Nat'l Bank, S. Reading,	$5,000	$7,000 00	$6,500 00
Faneuil Hall Nat'l Bank, Boston .	2,500	3,275 00	3,281 25
Boston Nat'l Bank, Boston . .	1,000	1,310 00	1,310 00
Boston Nat'l Bank, Boston . .	5,000	6,550 00	6,500 00
	$13,500	$18,135 00	$17,591 25

RAILROAD BONDS.

New York and New England 7s * .	$1,000	$1,160 00	$1,210 00

* This bank has been notified that this investment is illegal.

WALES SAVINGS BANK—WALES.

Incorporated 1870. Number of corporators, 76.

ELIJAH SHAW, *President.* *Treasurer,* H. A. MCFARLAND.

STATEMENT.

LIABILITIES.		ASSETS.	
Deposits . . .	$20,322 51	Bank stock	$6,172 50
Earnings undivided .	725 77	Loans on real estate . .	10,899 00
Guaranty fund . .	255 00	Loans on personal security,	2,931 96
		Expense account . . .	1 81
		Office furniture . . .	240 00
		Interest	4 89
		Cash on hand and in bank .	1,053 12
	$21,303 28		$21,303 28

Cash on Deposit in Bank:—

Palmer National Bank, Palmer $769 18

Whole amount of interest or profits received or earned . . . $981 94

Rate and amount of each semi-annual dividend for previous year . . . . { $2\frac{1}{4}$ per cent . 384 91; $2\frac{1}{4}$ per cent . 413 16 }

Times for the dividends fixed by the by-laws: January and July.

Average annual per cent of dividends for the term ending at time of and including last extra dividend: $4\frac{1}{2}$ per cent.

The total amount of loans, with each specified rate of interest: $1,100, 6 per cent; $12,730.96, $6\frac{1}{2}$ per cent.

Number of outstanding loans which are of an amount not exceeding $3,000 each	37	
Aggregate amount of the same		13,830 96
Number of open accounts	122	
Number and amount of deposits received for previous year .	306	4,891 26
Number and amount of deposits of and exceeding $300 at any one time for the previous year	1	300 00
Number and amount of withdrawals	35	2,564 38
Number of accounts opened the previous year	16	
Number of accounts closed the previous year	14	
Amount of expenses of the corporation during previous year .		65 95
Amount of treasurer's bond		10,000 00

Date of examination by commissioner: July 6.

BANK STOCK.

	Par Value.	Estimated Market Value.	Amount Invested.
Market Nat'l Bank, Boston . .	$500	$523 75	$523 75
Webster Nat'l Bank, Boston . .	500	558 75	558 75
Southbridge Nat'l B'k, Southbr'ge,	700	924 00	875 00
Monson Nat'l Bank, Monson . .	500	660 00	625 00
Continental Nat'l Bank, Boston .	1,000	1,130 00	1,090 00
Hamilton Nat'l Bank, Boston . .	1,000	1,250 00	1,000 00
Revere Nat'l Bank, Boston . .	1,500	1,600 00	1,500 00
	$5,700	$6,646 50	$6,172 50

WALTHAM SAVINGS BANK — WALTHAM.

Incorporated March 13, 1853. Number of corporators, 30.

HORATIO MOORE, *President*. *Treasurer*, F. M. STONE.

STATEMENT.

LIABILITIES.		ASSETS.	
Deposits	$1,263,163 26	Public funds	$88,475 00
Earnings undivided	35,060 25	Bank stock	105,625 00
Guaranty fund	28,000 00	Loans on bank stock	3,600 00
		Railroad bonds	70,500 00
		Real estate by foreclosure	16,500 00
		Loans on real estate	644,857 00
		Loans on personal security,	298,156 95
		Loans to counties, cities, or towns	80,000 00
		Deposit in banks on interest,	16,423 85
		Cash on hand	2,085 71
	$1,326,223 51		$1,326,223 51

Loans on Bank Stock, amount on each: —

On 18 shares First National Bank, Yarmouth	$1,600 00
On 25 shares Waltham National Bank, Waltham	2,000 00

Cash on Deposit in Banks, amount in each: —

Waltham National Bank, Waltham	$6,000 00
Boston Safe Deposit and Trust Company *	10,423 85

Amount of real estate held by foreclosure	$16,500 00
Assessed value of the same	18,000 00
Amount of income received from the same	750 00
Amount of municipal tax on real estate	250 00

Whole amount of interest or profits received or earned		$67,693 05
Rate and amount of each semi-annual dividend for previous year	2 per cent	22,680 36
	2 per cent	23,491 78

Times for the dividends fixed by the by-laws: second Wednesday in April and October.

The total amount of loans, with each specified rate of interest: $89,400, 4 per cent; $56,000, 4½ per cent; $192,526, 5 per cent; $50,000, 5½ per cent; $684,687, 6 per cent.

Number of outstanding loans which are of an amount not exceeding $3,000 each	219	
Aggregate amount of the same		257,606 00
Number of open accounts	4,529	
Number and amount of deposits received for previous year,	4,989	373,566 84
Number and amount of deposits of and exceeding $300 at any one time for the previous year	204	114,195 30
Number and amount of withdrawals	2,819	249,119 84
Number of accounts opened the previous year	1,041	
Number of accounts closed the previous year	572	
Amount of expenses of the corporation during previous year		2,900 00
Amount of treasurer's bond		20,000 00

Date of examination by commissioner: Nov. 28.

* The Attorney-General has given an opinion, that by the provisions of sect. 3, chap. 214 of the Acts of 1881, deposits by savings banks in this trust company are legal.

PUBLIC FUNDS.

	Par Value.	Estimated Market Value.	Amount Invested.
United States bonds	$42,500	$43,000 00	$42,475 00
Town bonds: —			
Town of Waltham 4½s	$46,000	$47,380 00	$46,000 00
	$88,500	$90,380 00	$88,475 00

BANK STOCK.

	Par Value.	Estimated Market Value.	Amount Invested.
Revere Nat'l Bank, Boston	$3,800	$4,636 00	$3,800 00
Mount Vernon Nat'l Bank, Boston	5,000	6,350 00	5,000 00
Third Nat'l Bank, Boston	5,000	5,350 00	5,000 00
Boston Nat'l Bank, Boston	7,300	9,284 00	7,300 00
Hide and Leather Nat'l B'k, Boston,	3,000	3,480 00	3,000 00
Market Nat'l Bank, Boston	4,000	4,360 00	4,000 00
Commerce Nat'l Bank, Boston	2,200	2,816 00	2,200 00
Traders' Nat'l Bank, Boston	6,000	6,120 00	6,000 00
Suffolk Nat'l Bank, Boston	5,300	6,413 00	5,300 00
North Nat'l Bank, Boston	7,700	10,934 00	7,700 00
Everett Nat'l Bank, Boston	4,600	5,382 00	4,600 00
Shawmut Nat'l Bank, Boston	5,000	6,350 00	5,000 00
Central Nat'l Bank, Boston	5,000	6,000 00	5,000 00
Continental Nat'l Bank, Boston	5,000	5,900 00	4,850 00
Metropolitan Nat'l Bank, Boston	2,000	2,400 00	2,000 00
Commonwealth Nat'l Bank, Boston,	3,000	3,000 00	3,000 00
Eliot Nat'l Bank, Boston	1,500	1,800 00	1,500 00
Waltham Nat'l Bank, Waltham	30,375	40,500 00	30,375 00
	$105,775	$131,075 00	$105,625 00

RAILROAD BONDS.

	Par Value.	Estimated Market Value.	Amount Invested.
Boston and Lowell	$30,500	$37,820 00	$30,500 00
Old Colony	10,000	12,500 00	10,000 00
Boston and Maine	5,000	6,350 00	5,000 00
Salem and Lowell	25,000	27,500 00	25,000 00
	$70,500	$84,170 00	$70,500 00

WARE SAVINGS BANK — WARE.

Incorporated 1850. Number of corporators, 40.

WILLIAM HYDE, *President*. *Treasurer*, OTIS LANE.

STATEMENT.

LIABILITIES.		ASSETS.	
Deposits	$1,868,599 28	Public funds	$609,000 00
Earnings undivided	22,936 50	Bank stock	302,900 00
Guaranty fund	12,211 43	Loans on bank books	2,000 00
		Railroad bonds	238,000 00
		Real estate	4,799 61
		Loans on real estate	554,163 62
		Loans on personal security,	99,217 41
		Loans to counties, cities, or towns	42,500 00
		Deposit in bank on interest,	10,366 60
		Deposit in bank not on interest	7,500 00
		Expense account	1,637 00
		Premium account	29,912 63
		Cash on hand	1,750 34
	$1,903,747 21		$1,903,747 21

Cash on Deposit in Banks, amount in each: —

National Bank of the Commonwealth, Boston	$10,366 60
Ware National Bank, Ware	7,500 00

Amount invested in real estate (for banking purposes)	$4,799 61
Estimated value of the same	4,799 61

Whole amount of interest or profits received or earned		$103,962 16
Rate and amount of each semi-annual dividend for previous year	2½ per cent	42,287 00
	2 per cent	35,253 97

Times for the dividends fixed by the by-laws: Jan. 1 and July 1.

Average annual per cent of dividends for the term ending at time of and including last extra dividend: 4¾ per cent.

The total amount of loans, with each specified rate of interest: $42,500, 4½ per cent; $140,000, 5 per cent; $65,000, 5½ per cent; $450,381.03, 6 per cent.

Number of outstanding loans which are of an amount not exceeding $3,000 each	245	
Aggregate amount of the same		241,616 53
Number of open accounts	4,277	
Number and amount of deposits received for previous year,	2,086	308,830 79
Number and amount of deposits of and exceeding $300 at any one time for the previous year	233	125,110 77
Number and amount of withdrawals	1,761	255,542 19
Number of accounts opened the previous year	726	
Number of accounts closed the previous year	445	
Amount of expenses of the corporation during previous year		4,408 21
Amount of treasurer's bond		25,000 00

Date of examination by commissioner: July 7.

Public Funds.

	Par Value.	Estimated Market Value.	Amount Invested.
United States 6s, currency . .	$50,000	$65,000 00	$50,000 00
" " Pacific 6s . . .	50,000	65,000 00	50,000 00
" " 5s, 1881, extended 3½s,	100,000	101,500 00	100,000 00
" " 4½s, funded loan .	200,000	225,000 00	200,000 00
City and town bonds: —			
City of Springfield 6s . . .	$1,000	$1,000 00	$1,000 00
of Fall River 6s . . .	20,000	25,000 00	20,000 00
of Boston 6s	30,000	36,000 00	30,000 00
of Boston 4s	40,000	44,000 00	40,000 00
of Somerville 5s . . .	20,000	22,000 00	20,000 00
of Holyoke 7s	40,000	49,600 00	40,000 00
of Brockton 5s . . .	30,000	34,500 00	30,000 00
Town of Pawtucket, R.I., 5s . .	5,000	5,600 00	5,000 00
of Pawtucket, R.I., 6s . .	23,000	28,175 00	23,000 00
	$609,000	$702,375 00	$609,000 00

Bank Stock.

	Par Value.	Estimated Market Value.	Amount Invested.
Atlantic Nat'l Bank, Boston . .	$1,000	$1,530 00	$1,000 00
Atlas Nat'l Bank, Boston . .	10,000	12,500 00	10,000 00
Boston Nat'l Bank, Boston . .	20,500	26,240 00	20,500 00
Blackstone Nat'l Bank, Boston .	1,200	1,380 00	1,200 00
Commerce Nat'l Bank, Boston .	7,500	9,375 00	7,500 00
City Nat'l Bank, Worcester . .	5,000	5,500 00	5,000 00
Continental Nat'l Bank, Boston .	13,600	16,048 00	13,600 00
Eliot Nat'l Bank, Boston . .	6,000	7,200 00	6,000 00
Easthampton Nat'l B'k, Eastham'n,	15,000	18,000 00	15,000 00
Exchange Nat'l Bank, Boston .	4,000	5,760 00	4,000 00
First Nat'l Bank, Boston . .	10,000	20,700 00	10,000 00
Globe Nat'l Bank, Boston . .	5,000	5,550 00	5,000 00
Leicester Nat'l Bank, Leicester	2,100	2,310 00	2,100 00
Monson Nat'l Bank, Monson .	4,700	6,110 00	4,700 00
Merchants' Nat'l Bank, Boston .	10,500	15,330 00	10,500 00
Mechanics' Nat'l Bank, Boston .	900	1,170 00	900 00
North America Nat'l Bank, Boston .	13,600	15,640 00	13,600 00
North Nat'l Bank, Boston . .	10,000	14,100 00	10,000 00
People's Nat'l Bank, Boston . .	600	972 00	600 00
Republic Nat'l Bank, Boston . .	15,000	19,650 00	15,000 00
Revere Nat'l Bank, Boston . .	15,000	18,300 00	15,000 00
Redemption Nat'l Bank, Boston .	10,000	13,500 00	10,000 00
Second Nat'l Bank, Boston . .	15,000	22,650 00	15,000 00
Southbridge Nat'l B'k, Southbridge,	1,500	2,250 00	1,500 00
State Nat'l Bank, Boston . .	16,200	20,250 00	16,200 00
Suffolk Nat'l Bank, Boston . .	3,000	3,630 00	3,000 00
Tremont Nat'l Bank, Boston . .	7,100	8,662 00	7,100 00
Traders' Nat'l Bank, Boston . .	15,400	15,708 00	15,400 00
Union Nat'l Bank, Boston . .	2,600	3,978 00	2,600 00
Ware Nat'l Bank, Ware . . .	37,900	46,996 00	37,900 00
Webster Nat'l Bank, Boston . .	20,000	22,200 00	20,000 00
Washington Nat'l Bank, Boston .	3,000	4,200 00	3,000 00
	$302,900	$387,389 00	$302,900 00

Railroad Bonds.

	Par Value.	Estimated Market Value.	Amount Invested.
Boston and Maine 7s	$75,000	$95,250 00	$75,000 00
Boston and Albany 7s . . .	60,000	76,200 00	60,000 00
Boston and Albany 6s . . .	50,000	57,000 00	50,000 00
Eastern, new loan	53,000	58,300 00	53,000 00
	$238,000	$286,750 00	$238,000 00

WAREHAM SAVINGS BANK — WAREHAM.

Incorporated 1847. Number of corporators, 29.

GERARD C. TOBEY, *President*. *Treasurer*, THOMAS R. MILES.

STATEMENT.

LIABILITIES.		ASSETS.	
Deposits	$495,663 35	Bank stock	$176,096 85
Earnings undivided	4,331 37	Real estate by foreclosure	176,647 62
Guaranty fund	5,764 00	Loans on real estate	88,677 54
		Loans on personal security,	58,828 63
		Expense account	1,330 17
		Municipal taxes on real estate	194 45
		Cash in bank	3,983 46
	$505,758 72		$505,758 72

Cash on Deposit in Bank: —
Wareham National Bank, Wareham $3,983 46

Amount of real estate held by foreclosure		$176,647 62
Assessed value of the same		139,351 00
Amount of income received from the same		10,111 01
Amount of municipal tax on real estate		194 45
Whole amount of interest or profits received or earned		$27,059 78
Rate and amount of each semi-annual dividend for previous year	2 per cent	9,359 74
	2 per cent	9,714 15

Times for the dividends fixed by the by-laws: first Monday in January and July.

The total amount of loans, with each specified rate of interest: $10,793.81, 4½ per cent; $40,095.11, 5 per cent; $2,500, 5½ per cent; $53,519.42, 6 per cent; $29,612.83, 7 per cent; $475, 7½ per cent; $10,500, 8 per cent.

Number of outstanding loans which are of an amount not exceeding $3,000 each	53	
Aggregate amount of the same		40,752 29
Number of open accounts	1,450	
Number and amount of deposits received for previous year	557	58,918 98
Number and amount of deposits of and exceeding $300 at any one time for the previous year	46	27,606 81
Number and amount of withdrawals	492	58,075 62
Number of accounts opened the previous year	154	
Number of accounts closed the previous year	113	
Amount of expenses of the corporation during previous year		1,330 17
Amount of treasurer's bond		5,000 00

Date of examination by commissioner: April 4.

BANK STOCK.

	Par Value.	Estimated Market Value.	Amount Invested.
Eagle Nat'l Bank, Boston . .	$10,000	$12,000 00	$11,068 14
Webster Nat'l Bank, Boston . .	10,000	11,200 00	11,015 59
Commerce Nat'l Bank, Boston .	5,000	6,450 00	7,053 50
North America Nat'l Bank, Boston .	7,500	8,625 00	6,993 68
City Nat'l Bank, Boston . . .	5,000	6,200 00	5,225 00
Revere Nat'l Bank, Boston . .	4,500	5,490 00	5,196 78
Exchange Nat'l Bank, Boston . .	700	1,036 00	731 50
Republic Nat'l Bank, Boston . .	3,000	3,840 00	3,135 00
First Nat'l Bank, Boston . .	2,000	4,000 00	2,090 00
Second Nat'l Bank, Boston . .	7,400	11,248 00	7,572 32
Shoe and Leather Nat'l B'k, Boston,	6,600	7,458 00	6,897 00
Blackstone Nat'l Bank, Boston .	10,000	11,500 00	13,574 81
Atlas Nat'l Bank, Boston . .	10,000	12,500 00	11,838 01
Atlantic Nat'l Bank, Boston . .	4,100	6,355 00	4,679 26
Shawmut Nat'l Bank, Boston . .	10,000	12,700 00	10,450 00
Merchants' Nat'l Bank, Boston .	10,000	14,600 00	10,949 84
Suffolk Nat'l Bank, Boston . .	10,000	12,100 00	12,147 46
Boylston Nat'l Bank, Boston . .	13,100	16,768 00	11,737 70
Andover Nat'l Bank, Andover .	500	600 00	522 50
Falmouth Nat'l Bank, Falmouth .	5,000	6,250 00	5,428 28
Merchants' Nat'l B'k, New Bedford,	2,500	3,750 00	2,612 50
Wareham Nat'l Bank, Wareham .	24,000	31,200 00	25,177 98
	$160,900	$205,870 00	$176,096 85

WARREN FIVE CENTS SAVINGS BANK — PEABODY.

Incorporated April 28, 1854. Number of corporators, 56.

RUFUS H. BROWN, *President*. *Treasurer*, ALBERT H. MERRILL.

STATEMENT.

LIABILITIES.		ASSETS.	
Deposits . . .	$1,344,826 10	Public funds . . .	$70,000 00
Earnings undivided .	58,083 55	Bank stock . . .	169,589 62
Guaranty fund . .	17,000 00	Loans on bank stock . .	1,300 00
		Railroad bonds . . .	19,750 00
		Real estate by foreclosure .	79,450 53
		Loans on real estate . .	505,774 00
		Loans on personal security,	190,533 20
		Loans to counties, cities, or towns	328,540 00
		Deposit in bank on interest,	25,939 26
		Expense account . . .	594 50
		Cash on hand . . .	28,438 54
	$1,419,909 65		$1,419,909 65

Loans on Bank Stock: —

On 7 shares Naumkeag National Bank, Salem, and 6 shares Mercantile National Bank, Salem $1,300 00

Cash on Deposit in Bank: —

Maverick National Bank, Boston $25,939 26

Amount of real estate held by foreclosure		$79,450 53
Assessed value of the same		68,275 00
Amount of income received from the same		4,742 46
Amount of municipal tax on real estate		1,147 50
Whole amount of interest or profits received or earned		$87,299 18
Rate and amount of each semi-annual dividend for previous year	2 per cent 2 per cent	24,730 86 25,025 02
Times for the dividends fixed by the by-laws: third Wednesday in May and November.		
The total amount of loans, with each specified rate of interest: $8,228.25, 3 per cent; $25,000, 3¾ per cent; $9,623.57, 4 per cent; $104,922.20, 4½ per cent; $30,623.85, 5 per cent; $232,362.48, 6 per cent; $188,769, 6½ per cent; $52,025, 7 per cent; $4,800, 7 3/10 per cent; $33,490, 7½ per cent; $19,350, 8 per cent.		
Number of outstanding loans which are of an amount not exceeding $3,000 each	164	
Aggregate amount of the same		207,175 00
Amount of investments from which no income is received . .		3,647 70
Number of open accounts	3,763	
Number and amount of deposits received for previous year,	2,398	193,329 63
Number and amount of deposits of and exceeding $300 at any one time for the previous year	172	99,433 33
Number and amount of withdrawals	1,626	171,711 23
Number of accounts opened the previous year	527	
Number of accounts closed the previous year	345	

Amount of expenses of the corporation during previous year . . $2,977 14
Amount of treasurer's bond 20,000 00
Date of examination by commissioner: June 3.

PUBLIC FUNDS.

	Par Value.	Estimated Market Value.	Amount Invested.
United States 6s, currency . .	$40,000	$53,200 00	$40,000 00
" " 4½s, registered . .	15,000	16,950 00	15,000 00
" " 4½s, coupon . .	12,000	13,560 00	12,000 00
State bonds:—			
State of Massachusetts 5s . .	$3,000	$3,060 00	$3,000 00
	$70,000	$86,770 00	$70,000 00

BANK STOCK.

	Par Value.	Estimated Market Value.	Amount Invested.
Warren Nat'l Bank, Peabody . .	$2,900	$4,205 00	$2,900 00
Howard Nat'l Bank, Boston . .	4,700	6,125 67	4,689 00
Exchange Nat'l Bank, Boston . .	8,000	11,520 00	8,000 00
Webster Nat'l Bank, Boston . .	14,100	15,721 50	14,100 00
Atlantic Nat'l Bank, Boston . .	4,500	6,907 50	4,500 00
Suffolk Nat'l Bank, Boston . .	2,500	3,050 00	2,500 00
Shoe and Leather Nat'l B'k, Boston,	5,100	5,737 50	5,100 00
Hide and Leather Nat'l B'k, Boston,	10,000	11,650 00	9,950 00
Exchange Nat'l Bank, Salem . .	900	1,035 00	900 00
Asiatic Nat'l Bank, Salem . .	2,250	3,375 00	2,250 00
Grand Nat'l Bank, Marblehead .	4,800	5,376 00	4,595 00
Atlas Nat'l Bank, Boston . .	16,500	20,625 00	16,500 00
Revere Nat'l Bank, Boston . .	4,800	5,856 00	4,800 00
Eliot Nat'l Bank, Boston . .	9,500	11,423 75	9,500 00
Blackstone Nat'l Bank, Boston .	10,000	11,500 00	10,000 00
Washington Nat'l Bank, Boston .	500	700 00	500 00
Tremont Nat'l Bank, Boston . .	10,100	12,322 00	10,100 00
Faneuil Hall Nat'l Bank, Boston .	6,000	7,845 00	6,000 00
Hamilton Nat'l Bank, Boston . .	2,300	2,599 00	2,300 00
Shawmut Nat'l Bank, Boston . .	5,200	6,030 00	5,200 00
South Danvers Nat'l Bank, Peabody,	1,000	1,500 00	1,000 00
Manufacturers' Nat'l Bank, Boston .	10,000	11,025 00	9,909 37
Merchandise Nat'l Bank, Boston .	4,500	4,950 00	4,500 00
North America Nat'l Bank, Boston,	6,000	6,900 00	6,000 00
City Nat'l Bank, Boston . . .	1,000	1,270 00	1,000 00
Market Nat'l Bank, Boston . .	8,100	8,889 75	8,100 00
Mount Vernon Nat'l Bank, Boston .	2,200	2,810 50	2,200 00
New England Nat'l Bank, Boston .	2,500	3,637 50	2,500 00
Continental Nat'l Bank, Boston .	2,500	2,962 50	2,500 00
Traders' Nat'l Bank, Boston . .	2,500	2,550 00	2,500 00
Commonwealth Nat'l Bank, Boston,	2,500	3,012 50	2,496 25
Globe Nat'l Bank, Boston . .	2,500	2,787 50	2,500 00
	$169,950	$206,499 17	$169,589 62

RAILROAD BONDS.

	Par Value.	Estimated Market Value.	Amount Invested.
Boston and Maine	$5,000	$6,350 00	$5,000 00
Old Colony	10,000	11,600 00	10,000 00
Eastern 4½s	5,000	5,487 50	4,750 00
	$20,000	$23,437 50	$19,750 00

WARREN INSTITUTION FOR SAVINGS — BOSTON.

Incorporated 1829. Number of corporators, 135.

TIMOTHY T. SAWYER, *President*. *Treasurer*, GEORGE F. TUFTS.

STATEMENT.

LIABILITIES.		ASSETS.	
Deposits . . .	$4,414,035 14	Public funds . . .	$641,000 00
Earnings undivided .	155,356 98	Loans on public funds . .	9,000 00
Guaranty fund . .	71,500 00	Bank stock . . .	199,906 00
		Loans on bank stock . .	7,750 00
		Railroad bonds . . .	200,000 00
		Real estate	50,000 00
		Real estate by foreclosure .	160,822 25
		Loans on real estate . .	1,649,581 70
		Loans on personal security,	1,517,500 00
		Loans to counties, cities, or towns	10,000 00
		Deposit in bank on interest,	181,199 05
		Expense account . . .	7,321 53
		Cash on hand . . .	6,811 59
	$4,640,892 12		$4,640,892 12

Loans on Public Funds, amount on each: —

On $8,000 City of Newton $8,000 00
On $1,000 United States 4½s 1,000 00

Loans on Bank Stock, amount on each: —

On 50 shares Maverick National Bank $5,500 00
On 8 shares Lechmere National Bank 200 00
On 10 shares Monument National Bank 150 00
On 14 shares Bunker Hill National Bank 1,000 00
On 24 shares Blackstone National Bank 900 00

Cash on Deposit in Bank; —

Bunker Hill National Bank $181,199 05

Amount invested in real estate (for banking purposes) $50,000 00
Estimated value of the same 52,800 00
Amount of real estate held by foreclosure 160,822 25
Assessed value of the same 202,570 00
Amount of income received from the same 14,600 00
Amount of municipal tax on real estate 3,256 12

Whole amount of interest or profits received or earned . . . $227,983 52
Rate and amount of each semi-annual dividend for previous year . . . . { 2 per cent . 80,786 66; 2 per cent . 85,526 44 }
Times for the dividends fixed by the by-laws: third Wednesday in April and October.
Average annual per cent of dividends for the term ending at time of and including last extra dividend: 4 per cent.

The total amount of loans, with each specified rate of interest: \$155,000, 3½ per cent; \$225,000, 3¾ per cent; \$649,500, 4 per cent; \$50,000, 4⅛ per cent; \$150,000, 4¼ per cent; \$105,000, 4½ per cent; \$160,000, 4¾ per cent; \$85,500, 5 per cent; \$44,500, 5½ per cent; \$950,570, 6 per cent; \$289,995, 6½ per cent; \$239,050, 7 per cent; \$26,000, 7 3/10 per cent; \$48,016.70, 7½ per cent; \$5,700, 8 per cent.

Number of outstanding loans which are of an amount not exceeding \$3,000 each	425	
Aggregate amount of the same		\$685,611 70
Amount of investments from which no income is received		10,350 00
Number of open accounts	12,059	
Number and amount of deposits received for previous year,	9,831	717,130 00
Number and amount of deposits of and exceeding \$300 at any one time for the previous year	624	324,432 00
Number and amount of withdrawals	5,581	494,528 45
Number of accounts opened the previous year	1,517	
Number of accounts closed the previous year	755	
Amount of expenses of the corporation during previous year		8,916 42
Amount of treasurer's bond		20,000 00

Date of examination by commissioner: Nov. 14.

Public Funds.

	Par Value.	Estimated Market Value.	Amount Invested.
United States 4½s	\$300,000	\$339,000 00	\$300,000 00
" " 4s	250,000	290,312 50	250,000 00
City and town bonds: —			
City of Charlestown 6s	\$40,000	\$47,800 00	\$40,000 00
of Somerville 6s	46,000	50,140 00	46,000 00
Town of Everett 6s	5,000	5,950 00	5,000 00
	\$641,000	\$733,202 50	\$641,000 00

Bank Stock.

Bunker Hill Nat'l Bank, Boston	\$20,000	\$36,000 00	\$20,000 00
City Nat'l Bank, Boston	2,000	2,540 00	2,000 00
Eagle Nat'l Bank, Boston	7,500	8,981 25	7,500 00
Shoe and Leather Nat'l B'k, Boston,	5,000	5,625 00	5,000 00
Hide and Leather Nat'l B'k, Boston,	15,000	17,475 00	15,000 00
Massachusetts Nat'l Bank, Boston	5,500	6,820 00	5,500 00
Traders' Nat'l Bank, Boston	10,000	10,200 00	10,000 00
Third Nat'l Bank, Boston	10,000	10,650 00	10,000 00
New England Nat'l Bank, Boston	11,600	16,878 00	11,600 00
Union Nat'l Bank, Boston	20,000	30,700 00	20,000 00
Everett Nat'l Bank, Boston	6,000	7,027 50	6,000 00
Naumkeag Nat'l Bank, Salem	4,200	6,342 00	4,200 00
Merchandise Nat'l Bank, Boston	5,000	5,500 00	5,000 00
Webster Nat'l Bank, Boston	10,000	11,150 00	10,000 00

BANK STOCK — Concluded.

	Par Value.	Estimated Market Value.	Amount Invested.
Eliot Nat'l Bank, Boston . . .	$15,800	$18,999 50	$15,800 00
State Nat'l Bank, Boston . .	11,800	14,809 00	12,836 00
Tremont Nat'l Bank, Boston . .	10,800	13,176 00	12,300 00
Atlas Nat'l Bank, Boston . .	9,000	11,250 00	10,170 00
Howard Nat'l Bank, Boston . .	10,000	13,050 00	11,000 00
Second Nat'l Bank, Boston . .	4,300	6,498 37	6,000 00
	$193,500	$253,671 62	$199,906 00

RAILROAD BONDS.

Boston and Albany 6s	$50,000	$60,000 00	$50,000 00
Old Colony 7s	50,000	62,500 00	50,000 00
Old Colony 6s	50,000	58,750 00	50,000 00
Worcester and Nashua 5s . .	50,000	52,500 00	50,000 00
	$200,000	$233,750 00	$200,000 00

WATERTOWN SAVINGS BANK — WATERTOWN.

Incorporated 1870. Number of corporators, 18.

CHARLES J. BARRY, *President*. *Treasurer*, TILDEN G. ABBOTT.

STATEMENT.

Liabilities.		Assets.	
Deposits	$238,353 93	Public funds	$28,125 00
Earnings undivided	893 12	Bank stock	32,210 50
Guaranty fund	2,320 00	Loans on bank stock	800 00
		Railroad bonds	12,590 00
		Loans on real estate	132,915 00
		Loans to counties, cities, or towns	5,793 00
		Deposit in bank on interest,	29,000 00
		Cash on hand	133 55
	$241,567 05		$241,567 05

Loans on Bank Stock: —

On 10 shares Union Market National Bank, Watertown . . $800 00

Cash on Deposit in Bank; —

Union Market National Bank $29,000 00

Whole amount of interest or profits received or earned		$12,159 05
Rate and amount of each semi-annual dividend for previous year	$2\frac{1}{4}$ per cent	4.237 21
	$2\frac{1}{4}$ per cent	4,699 34

Times for the dividends fixed by the by-laws: April and October.

Average annual per cent of dividends for the term ending at time of and including last extra dividend: $4\frac{85}{100}$ per cent.

The total amount of loans, with each specified rate of interest: $4,000, 4 per cent; $15,793, 5 per cent; $25.000, $5\frac{1}{2}$ per cent; $61,290, 6 per cent; $1,900, $6\frac{1}{2}$ per cent; $57,025, 7 per cent; $11,400, 8 per cent.

Number of outstanding loans which are of an amount not exceeding $3,000 each	62	
Aggregate amount of the same		64,708 00
Number of open accounts	907	
Number and amount of deposits received for previous year,	1,163	76,672 98
Number and amount of deposits of and exceeding $300 at any one time for the previous year	62	30.062 17
Number and amount of withdrawals	442	41.397 21
Number of accounts opened the previous year	275	
Number of accounts closed the previous year	113	
Amount of expenses of the corporation during previous year		836 37
Amount of treasurer's bond		5,000 00

Date of examination by commissioner: April 18.

PUBLIC FUNDS.

	Par Value.	Estimated Market Value.	Amount Invested.
City and town bonds: —			
City of Lewiston, Me., 6s . . .	$1,000	$1,100 00	$1,030 00
of Bangor, Me., 6s, municipal .	2,000	2,420 00	2,100 00
of Newburyport 6s	1,000	1,120 00	1,050 00
of Charlestown 6s	3,000	3,510 00	3,300 00
of Fitchburg 6s	1,000	1,190 00	1,125 00
of Newton 6s	1,000	1,300 00	1,195 00
of Cambridge 6s	6,000	7,620 00	7,155 00
of Boston 6s	1,000	1,300 00	1,190 00
Town of Arlington 6s	4,000	4,720 00	4,280 00
of Watertown 5s . . .	5,000	5,250 00	5,100 00
of Brookline 7s . . .	500	685 00	600 00
	$25,500	$30,215 00	$28,125 00

BANK STOCK.

	Par Value.	Estimated Market Value.	Amount Invested.
Commonwealth Nat'l Bank, Boston,	$2,000	$2,480 00	$2,000 00
Blackstone Nat'l Bank, Boston .	2,500	2,875 00	2,745 00
Metropolitan Nat'l Bank, Boston .	800	960 00	800 00
Market Nat'l Bank, Boston . .	2,200	2,431 00	2,310 00
Exchange Nat'l Bank, Boston . .	1,000	1,440 00	1,375 00
Continental Nat'l Bank, Boston .	2,000	2,370 00	2,100 00
Webster Nat'l Bank, Boston . .	1,900	2,137 50	2,014 00
North America Nat'l Bank, Boston .	2,000	2,300 00	2,155 00
Third Nat'l Bank, Boston . .	4,000	4,260 00	4,000 00
Boston Nat'l Bank, Boston . .	2,500	3,200 00	2,800 00
Central Nat'l Bank, Boston . .	2,000	2,400 00	2,105 00
Traders' Nat'l Bank, Boston . .	1,500	1,530 00	1,569 00
Manufacturers' Nat'l Bank, Boston,	1,000	1,100 00	1,037 50
Massachusetts Nat'l Bank, Boston .	2,250	2,790 00	2,700 00
Union Market Nat'l B'k, Watertown,	2,500	2,800 00	2,500 00
	$30,150	$35,073 50	$32,210 50

RAILROAD BONDS.

	Par Value.	Estimated Market Value.	Amount Invested.
Boston and Maine 7s	$2,000	$2,540 00	$2,200 00
Vermont and Massachusetts 6s .	400	412 00	400 00
Fitchburg 5s	9,000	10,170 00	9,990 00
	$11,400	$13,122 00	$12,590 00

WEBSTER FIVE CENTS SAVINGS BANK — WEBSTER.

Incorporated March 16, 1868. Number of corporators, 52.

F. D. BROWN, *President*. *Treasurer*, EDWIN MAY.

STATEMENT.

LIABILITIES.		ASSETS.	
Deposits	$395,295 33	Public funds	$11,405 00
Earnings undivided .	1,888 53	Bank stock	68,500 00
Guaranty fund . .	3,721 53	Railroad bonds	41,587 50
		Real estate by foreclosure .	4,400 00
		Loans on real estate . .	203,365 00
		Loans on personal security,	10,872 00
		Loans to counties, cities, or towns	14,000 00
		Deposit in bank on interest,	38,367 90
		Expense account . . .	335 98
		Premium account . .	7,400 50
		Cash on hand	671 51
	$400,905 39		$400,905 39

Cash on Deposit in Bank:—

First National Bank, Webster		$38,367 90
Amount of real estate held by foreclosure		$4,400 00
Assessed value of the same		3,000 00
Amount of income received from the same		217 50
Amount of municipal tax on real estate		38 92
Whole amount of interest or profits received or earned . . .		$20,748 76
Rate and amount of each semi-annual dividend for previous year	2 per cent . 2 per cent .	6,299 43 6,910 55
Times for the dividends fixed by the by-laws: Jan. 1 and July 1.		
The total amount of loans, with each specified rate of interest: $6,000, 4 per cent; $8,000, 4½ per cent; $17,500, 5½ per cent; $193,565, 6 per cent; $3,172, 7 per cent.		
Number of outstanding loans which are of an amount not exceeding $3,000 each	181	
Aggregate amount of the same		153,437 00
Number of open accounts	2,115	
Number and amount of deposits received for previous year,	1,653	110,267 46
Number and amount of deposits of and exceeding $300 at any one time for the previous year	76	37,903 00
Number and amount of withdrawals	702	68,317 03
Number of accounts opened the previous year	269	
Number of accounts closed the previous year	177	
Amount of expenses of the corporation during previous year .		1,154 34
Amount of treasurer's bond		20,000 00

Date of examination by commissioner: April 11.

Public Funds.

	Par Value.	Estimated Market Value.	Amount Invested.
United States bonds	$4,000	$4,645 00	$3,960 00
City and town bonds: —			
City of Rockland, Me. . . .	$2,000	$2,120 00	$2,120 00
Town of Pawtucket, R.I., water .	5,000	5,325 00	5,325 00
	$11,000	$12,090 00	$11,405 00

Bank Stock.

	Par Value.	Estimated Market Value.	Amount Invested.
Quinsigamond Nat'l B'k, Worcester,	$6,100	$7,442 00	$6,100 00
Worcester Nat'l Bank, Worcester .	8,000	10,160 00	8,000 00
Mechanics' Nat'l Bank, Worcester .	700	868 00	700 00
First Nat'l Bank, Worcester . .	1,200	1,860 00	1,200 00
City Nat'l Bank, Worcester . .	2,000	2,200 00	2,000 00
Southbridge Nat'l Bank, Southb'dge,	500	660 00	500 00
Oxford Nat'l Bank, Oxford . .	2,000	2,640 00	2,000 00
Grafton Nat'l Bank, Grafton . .	1,000	1,070 00	1,000 00
Webster Nat'l Bank, Webster .	5,600	6,272 00	5,600 00
Barre Nat'l Bank, Barre . . .	2,300	2,852 00	2,300 00
Revere Nat'l Bank, Boston . .	3,600	4,392 00	3,600 00
Boylston Nat'l Bank, Boston . .	1,900	2,432 00	1,900 00
Shoe and Leather Nat'l B'k, Boston,	7,400	8,362 00	7,400 00
State Nat'l Bank, Boston . .	1,000	1,260 00	1,000 00
Merchants' Nat'l Bank, Boston .	1,000	1,480 00	1,000 00
Webster Nat'l Bank, Boston . .	6,400	7,232 00	6,400 00
Blackstone Nat'l Bank, Boston .	4,800	5,520 00	4,800 00
Atlas Nat'l Bank, Boston .	3,400	4,250 00	3,400 00
Hide and Leather Nat'l B'k, Boston,	400	476 00	400 00
Old Boston Nat'l Bank, Boston .	2,500	3,050 00	2,500 00
Eliot Nat'l Bank, Boston . .	1,000	1,200 00	1,000 00
Eagle Nat'l Bank, Boston . .	500	600 00	500 00
City Nat'l Bank, Boston . . .	200	254 00	200 00
Uncas Nat'l Bank, Norwich, Conn. .	2,500	3,150 00	2,500 00
First Nat'l Bank, Norwich, Conn. .	2,500	2,925 00	2,500 00
	$68,500	$82 607 00	$68,500 00

Railroad Bonds.

	Par Value.	Estimated Market Value.	Amount Invested.
Boston and Albany	$5,000	$6,350 00	$6,050 00
Old Colony	10,000	12,950 00	11,937 50
Old Colony	10,000	12,950 00	11,900 00
Revere Beach and Lynn . . .	10,000	11,700 00	11,700 00
	$35,000	$43,950 00	$41,587 50

WELLFLEET SAVINGS BANK — WELLFLEET.

Incorporated 1863. Number of corporators, 61.

RICHARD R. FREEMAN, *President*. *Treasurer*, THOMAS KEMP.

STATEMENT.

LIABILITIES.		ASSETS.	
Deposits	$317,280 00	Bank stock	$232,968 78
Earnings undivided	10,086 30	Real estate	2,000 00
Guaranty fund	8,994 58	Loans on real estate	86,127 50
Bills payable	310 69	Loans on personal security,	5,825 10
		Loans to counties, cities, or towns	2,435 00
		Deposit in bank on interest,	6,854 20
		Expense account	286 83
		Cash on hand	174 16
	$336,671 57		$336,671 57

Cash on Deposit in Bank: —

Blackstone National Bank, Boston		$6,854 20
Amount invested in real estate (for banking purposes)		$2,000 00
Estimated value of the same		3,500 00
Amount of municipal tax on real estate		48 80
Whole amount of interest or profits received or earned		$21,297 28
Rate and amount of each semi-annual dividend for previous year	2 per cent 2 per cent	5,953 55 6,013 48

Times for the dividends fixed by the by-laws: January and July.

Average annual per cent of dividends for the term ending at time of and including last extra dividend: $5\frac{3}{4}$ per cent.

The total amount of loans, with each specified rate of interest: $8,000, 5 per cent; $65,037.60, 6 per cent; $13,350, 7 per cent; $8,000, 8 per cent.

Number of outstanding loans which are of an amount not exceeding $3,000 each	51	
Aggregate amount of the same		43,887 60
Amount of investments from which no income is received		500 00
Number of open accounts	994	
Number and amount of deposits received for previous year	252	33,641 52
Number and amount of deposits of and exceeding $300 at any one time for the previous year	32	16,714 15
Number and amount of withdrawals	421	37,727 32
Number of accounts opened the previous year	88	
Number of accounts closed the previous year	116	
Amount of expenses of the corporation during previous year		1,399 47
Amount of treasurer's bond		20,000 00

Date of examination by commissioner: Aug. 4.

BANK STOCK.

	Par Value.	Estimated Market Value.	Amount Invested.
State Nat'l Bank, Boston . .	$9,100	$11,397 75	$9,810 75
Commerce Nat'l Bank, Boston .	3,000	3,877 50	4,618 10
Republic Nat'l Bank, Boston . .	13,700	17,947 00	14,579 38
Revere Nat'l Bank, Boston . .	1,800	2,250 00	1,998 00
Hamilton Nat'l Bank, Boston . .	8,600	10,642 50	10,222 25
Union Nat'l Bank, Boston . .	2,300	3,536 25	2,773 25
Hide and Leather Nat'l B'k, Boston,	10,000	11,875 00	12,214 51
Central Nat'l Bank, Boston . .	7,500	9,000 00	7,608 75
Tremont Nat'l Bank, Boston . .	10,000	12,200 00	12,923 25
North Nat'l Bank, Boston . .	3,500	5,040 00	4,210 62
Freeman's Nat'l Bank, Boston .	8,500	10,178 75	10,126 50
Mount Vernon Nat'l Bank, Boston .	2,000	2,555 00	2,540 00
Globe Nat'l Bank, Boston . .	4,200	4,704 00	5,469 25
New England Nat'l Bank, Boston .	2,500	3,781 25	4,318 75
Suffolk Nat'l Bank, Boston . .	3,000	3,630 00	3,612 50
Old Boston Nat'l Bank, Boston .	2,500	3,050 00	3,675 00
Third Nat'l Bank, Boston . .	20,000	21,300 00	21,501 92
Second Nat'l Bank, Boston . .	2,200	3,333 00	3,195 50
Manufacturers' Nat'l Bank, Boston,	6,100	6,725 25	6,939 00
Webster Nat'l Bank, Boston . .	3,500	3,902 50	3,500 00
Blackstone Nat'l Bank, Boston .	10,000	11,500 00	10,000 00
Atlas Nat'l Bank, Boston . .	13,500	17,145 00	13,500 00
Continental Nat'l Bank, Boston .	14,500	17,218 75	13,500 00
Shawmut Nat'l Bank, Boston . .	9,000	11,475 00	9,000 00
Eliot Nat'l Bank, Boston . .	15,600	18,759 00	15,600 00
Eagle Nat'l Bank, Boston . .	10,000	11,750 00	10,000 00
Faneuil Hall Nat'l Bank, Boston .	4,000	5,380 00	4,000 00
Boylston Nat'l Bank, Boston . .	3,600	4,527 00	3,600 00
Shoe and Leather Nat'l B'k, Boston,	800	904 00	800 00
Boston Nat'l Bank, Boston . .	1,000	1,280 00	1,000 00
Traders' Nat'l Bank, Boston . .	1,100	1,146 75	1,100 00
Howard Nat'l Bank, Boston . .	1,500	1,951 87	1,500 00
First Nat'l Bank, Provincetown .	2,400	3,600 00	2,531 50
	$211,000	$257,563 12	$232,968 78

WESTBOROUGH SAVINGS BANK — WESTBOROUGH.

Incorporated Feb. 9, 1869. Number of corporators, 66.

CYRUS FAY, *President.* *Treasurer*, GEORGE O. BRIGHAM.

STATEMENT.

Liabilities.		Assets.	
Deposits	$453,203 33	Public funds	$12,500 00
Earnings undivided	5,483 78	Bank stock	48,100 00
Guaranty fund	5,000 00	Railroad bonds	3,000 00
Suspense account	1,083 85	Real estate by foreclosure	11,174 30
		Loans on real estate	288,390 52
		Loans on personal security,	55,383 00
		Loans to counties, cities, or towns	8,500 00
		Deposit in bank on interest,	29,864 00
		Cash on hand	7,859 14
	$464,770 96		$464,770 96

Cash on Deposit in Bank: —

Commonwealth National Bank, Boston	$29,864 00

Amount of real estate held by foreclosure		$11,174 30
Assessed value of the same		10,345 00
Amount of income received from the same		522 00
Amount of municipal tax on real estate		109 45
Whole amount of interest or profits received or earned		$26,982 98
Rate and amount of each semi-annual dividend for previous year	2½ per cent	9,722 40
	2 per cent	8,230 16

Times for the dividends fixed by the by-laws: February and August.

Average annual per cent of dividends for the term ending at time of and including last extra dividend: 4½ per cent.

The total amount of loans, with each specified rate of interest: $1,500, 4 per cent; $6,000, 5 per cent; $79,000, 6 per cent; $265,773.52, 6½ per cent.

Number of outstanding loans which are of an amount not exceeding $3,000 each	212	
Aggregate amount of the same		238,173 52
Number of open accounts	1,507	
Number and amount of deposits received for previous year,	1,356	128,021 01
Number and amount of deposits of and exceeding $300 at any one time for the previous year	85	44,967 09
Number and amount of withdrawals	874	78,314 76
Number of accounts opened the previous year	338	
Number of accounts closed the previous year	209	
Amount of expenses of the corporation during previous year		929 48
Amount of treasurer's bond		20,000 00

Date of examination by commissioner: May 19.

Public Funds.

	Par Value.	Estimated Market Value.	Amount Invested.
City and town bonds:—			
City of Rockland	$2,500	$2,400 00	$2,500 00
Town of Westborough, water . .	10,000	11,000 00	10,000 00
	$12,500	$13,400 00	$12,500 00

Bank Stock.

Traders' Nat'l Bank, Boston . .	$5,500	$5,610 00	$5,500 00
Tremont Nat'l Bank, Boston . .	3,000	4,350 00	3,000 00
Globe Nat'l Bank, Boston . .	1,600	1,776 00	1,600 00
Commerce Nat'l Bank, Boston .	800	1,024 00	800 00
Redemption Nat'l Bank, Boston .	2,000	2,800 00	2,000 00
Everett Nat'l Bank, Boston . .	3,000	3,480 00	3,000 00
Merchants' Nat'l Bank, Boston .	4,200	6,090 00	4,200 00
New England Nat'l Bank, Boston .	600	870 00	600 00
Hide and Leather Nat'l B'k, Boston,	1,900	2,185 00	1,900 00
Republic Nat'l Bank, Boston . .	1,000	1,250 00	1,000 00
First Nat'l Bank, Westborough .	16,400	17,712 00	16,400 00
Millbury Nat'l Bank, Millbury .	2,000	2,400 00	2,000 00
Grafton Nat'l Bank, Grafton . .	500	550 00	500 00
Marlborough Nat'l Bank, Marlboro',	3,000	3,750 00	3,000 00
Northborough Nat'l B'k, Northboro',	2,000	2,200 00	2,000 00
	$48,100	$56,053 00	$48,100 00

Railroad Bonds.

Boston, Clinton, and Fitchburg .	$2,000	$2,140 00	$2,000 00
Fitchburg	1,000	1,100 00	1,000 00
	$3,000	$3,240 00	$3,000 00

WESTFIELD SAVINGS BANK — WESTFIELD.

Incorporated 1853. Number of corporators, 53.

SAMUEL FOWLER, *President*. *Treasurer*, V. W. CROWSON.

STATEMENT.

LIABILITIES.		ASSETS.	
Deposits	$757,196 11	Public funds	$193,000 00
Earnings undivided	19,505 55	Bank stock	54,200 00
Guaranty fund	8,919 13	Loans on bank stock	3,150 00
Rent received on real estate held under foreclosure	1,520 39	Real estate by foreclosure	25,260 66
		Loans on real estate	388,218 56
		Loans on personal security,	46,940 90
		Loans to counties, cities, or towns	38,000 00
		Deposit in bank on interest,	5,119 94
		Expense account	1,280 66
		Premium on public funds	14,531 56
		Premium on bank stock	15,545 25
		Taxes and expenses on real estate	356 55
		Cash on hand	1,537 10
	$787,141 18		$787,141 18

Loans on Bank Stock: —

On 38 shares First National Bank, Westfield $3,150 00

Cash on Deposit in Bank: —

First National Bank, Westfield $5,119 94

Amount of real estate held by foreclosure		$25,260 66
Assessed value of the same		24,300 00
Amount of income received from the same		1,432 56
Amount of municipal tax on real estate		317 44
Whole amount of interest or profits received or earned		$40,047 80
Rate and amount of each semi-annual dividend for previous year	2 per cent	14,433 31
	2 per cent	14,717 00

Times for the dividends fixed by the by-laws: Jan. 10 and July 10.

The total amount of loans, with each specified rate of interest: $63,000, 5 per cent; $413,309.46, 6 per cent.

Number of outstanding loans which are of an amount not exceeding $3,000 each	208	
Aggregate amount of the same		217,875 00
Number of open accounts	2,571	
Number and amount of deposits received for previous year,	6,554	165,822 97
Number and amount of deposits of and exceeding $300 at any one time for the previous year	115	58,870 47
Number and amount of withdrawals	1,395	135,812 33
Number of accounts opened the previous year	344	
Number of accounts closed the previous year	310	
Amount of expenses of the corporation during previous year		1,395 66
Amount of treasurer's bond		10,000 00

Date of examination by commissioner: July 13.

Public Funds.

	Par Value.	Estimated Market Value.	Amount Invested.
United States 6s, currency . .	$40,000	$52,205 00	$47,463 15
" " $4\frac{1}{2}$s	20,000	22,400 00	20,000 00
" " 4s	57,000	66,120 00	59,324 48
" " $3\frac{1}{2}$s	56,000	56,560 00	57,111 43
City bonds: —			
City of Providence, R. I., water .	$10,000	$11,912 00	$11,912 50
of Charlestown, water . .	3,000	3,555 00	3,555 00
of Chelsea	3,000	3,705 00	3,705 00
of Portland, Me.	4,000	4,460 00	4,460 00
	$193,000	$220,917 00	$207,531 56

Bank Stock.

	Par Value.	Estimated Market Value.	Amount Invested.
First Nat'l Bank, Westfield . .	$42,200	$57,392 00	$56,973 25
Hampden Nat'l Bank, Westfield .	800	1,160 00	1,100 00
Hampshire Co. N'l B'k, Northamp'n,	3,000	3,900 00	3,000 00
Agawam Nat'l Bank, Springfield .	3,200	4,160 00	3,672 00
City Nat'l Bank, Springfield . .	5,000	6,000 00	5,000 00
	$54,200	$72,612 00	$69,745 25

WEYMOUTH SAVINGS BANK — WEYMOUTH.

Incorporated 1833. Number of corporators, 72.

EBEN DENTON, *President.* *Treasurer*, CHARLES T. CRANE.

STATEMENT.

LIABILITIES.		ASSETS.	
Deposits . . .	$560,293 79	Public funds . . .	$26,782 65
Earnings undivided .	37,394 01	Bank stock	68,400 00
Guaranty fund . .	11,150 00	Railroad bonds . . .	11,800 00
		Real estate by foreclosure .	135,546 00
		Loans on real estate . .	282,711 00
		Loans on personal security,	51,294 00
		Loans to counties, cities, or towns	5,000 00
		Suspense account * . .	25,700 00
		Cash on hand and in bank .	1,604 15
	$608,837 80		$608,837 80

Cash on Deposit in Bank: —
Union National Bank, Weymouth $1,353 45

Amount of real estate held by foreclosure $135,546 00
Assessed value of the same 95,500 00
Amount of income received from the same 6,001 79
Amount of municipal tax on real estate 1,340 03

Whole amount of interest or profits received or earned . . . $36,367 43
Rate and amount of each semi-annual dividend for previous year . . . . 2 per cent . 13,189 09; 2 per cent . 11,434 17
Times for the dividends fixed by the by-laws: January and July.
Average annual per cent of dividends for the term ending at time of and including last extra dividend: 7½ per cent.
The total amount of loans, with each specified rate of interest: $30,000, 4 per cent; $5,000, 4½ per cent; $6,900, 5 per cent; $70,110, 6 per cent; $88,690, 6½ per cent; $49,755, 7 per cent; $4,900, 7$\frac{3}{10}$ per cent; $41,102, 7½ per cent; $42,548, 8 per cent.
Number of outstanding loans which are of an amount not exceeding $3,000 each 208
Aggregate amount of the same 203,005 00
Number of open accounts 1,794
Number and amount of deposits received for previous year . 274 23,046 63
Number and amount of deposits of and exceeding $300 at any one time for the previous year 19 8,350 72
Number and amount of withdrawals 1,171 155,696 56
Number of accounts opened the previous year 81
Number of accounts closed the previous year 522
Amount of expenses of the corporation during previous year . . 2,750 72
Amount of treasurer's bond 17,500 00
Date of examination by commissioner: May 23.

* This amount is made up of indebtedness in suspense, but from which there is a possibility that something may be realized.

PUBLIC FUNDS.

	Par Value.	Estimated Market Value.	Amount Invested.
United States 4s	$27,000	$31,363 75	$26,782 65

BANK STOCK.

	Par Value.	Estimated Market Value.	Amount Invested.
Union Nat'l Bank, Weymouth .	$36,400	$43,680 00	$36,400 00
Hide and Leather Nat'l B'k, Boston,	7,500	8,737 00	7,500 00
Washington Nat'l Bank, Boston .	4,000	5,600 00	4,000 00
Traders' Nat'l Bank, Boston . .	4,000	4,080 00	4,000 00
Webster Nat'l Bank, Boston . .	2,700	3,011 00	2,700 00
Boston Nat'l Bank, Boston . .	2,700	3,456 00	2,700 00
Republic Nat'l Bank, Boston . .	3,000	3,930 00	3,000 00
Exchange Nat'l Bank, Boston .	1,500	2,160 00	1,500 00
Merchants' Nat'l Bank, Boston .	1,200	1,752 00	1,200 00
North Nat'l Bank, Boston . .	1,400	1,988 00	1,400 00
Metropolitan Nat'l Bank, Boston .	2,000	2,400 00	2,000 00
Merchandise Nat'l Bank, Boston .	2,000	2,200 00	2,000 00
	$68,400	$82,994 00	$68,400 00

RAILROAD BONDS.

	Par Value.	Estimated Market Value.	Amount Invested.
Boston, Revere Beach, and Lynn 6s .	$10,000	$11,800 00	$11,800 00

WHITINSVILLE SAVINGS BANK — WHITINSVILLE.

Incorporated 1872. Number of corporators, 58.

JOHN C. WHITIN, *President*. *Treasurer*, H. A. GOODELL.

STATEMENT.

LIABILITIES.		ASSETS.	
Deposits . . .	$222,739 64	Public funds . . .	$9,000 00
Earnings undivided .	6,298 05	Bank stock	76,398 79
Guaranty fund . .	2,076 24	Railroad bonds . . .	26,640 00
		Loans on real estate . .	63,340 01
		Loans on personal security,	41,000 00
		Deposit in bank on interest,	11,209 30
		Expense account . .	802 05
		Cash in bank . . .	2,723 78
	$231,113 93		$231,113 93

Cash on Deposit in Banks, amount in each: —

Commonwealth National Bank, Boston		$11,209 30
Whitinsville National Bank		2,723 78
Whole amount of interest or profits received or earned . . .		$11,765 98
Rate and amount of each semi-annual dividend for previous year	2 per cent . 2 per cent .	3,767 66 4,049 19

Times for the dividends fixed by the by-laws: May and November.

The total amount of loans, with each specified rate of interest: $22,500, 4 per cent; $9,000, 4½ per cent; $10,300, 5 per cent; $65,205, 6 per cent; $1,450, 6½ per cent; $2,850, 7 per cent; $2,035.01, 7½ per cent.

Number of outstanding loans which are of an amount not exceeding $3,000 each	43	
Aggregate amount of the same		42,740 01
Number of open accounts	820	
Number and amount of deposits received for previous year .	770	59,849 25
Number and amount of deposits of and exceeding $300 at any one time for the previous year	37	16,122 25
Number and amount of withdrawals	384	41,233 30
Number of accounts opened the previous year	191	
Number of accounts closed the previous year	105	
Amount of expenses of the corporation during previous year . .		419 50
Amount of treasurer's bond		20,000 00

Date of examination by commissioner: May 2.

PUBLIC FUNDS.

	Par Value.	Estimated Market Value.	Amount Invested.
City bonds: —			
City of Norwich, Conn. . .	$1,000	$1,140 00	$1,000 00
of Fall River . . .	5,000	6,250 00	5,000 00
of Manchester, N.H. .	3,000	3,480 00	3,000 00
	$9,000	$10,870 00	$9,000 00

Bank Stock.

	Par Value.	Estimated Market Value.	Amount Invested.
Atlantic Nat'l Bank, Boston . .	$3,900	$5,986 50	$5,640 75
Atlas Nat'l Bank, Boston . .	2,000	2,540 00	2,492 50
Blackstone Nat'l Bank, Boston .	2,000	2,350 00	2,651 17
Boylston Nat'l Bank, Boston . .	2,000	2,560 00	2,998 00
Boston Nat'l Bank, Boston . .	300	393 00	323 25
Columbian Nat'l Bank, Boston .	1,600	2,292 00	2,225 00
Commonwealth Nat'l Bank, Boston,	3,000	3,720 00	3,752 50
Commerce Nat'l Bank, Boston .	1,100	1,432 75	1,334 00
City Nat'l Bank, Worcester . .	4,000	4,500 00	4,500 00
Everett Nat'l Bank, Boston . .	3,000	3,513 75	3,735 00
Eliot Nat'l Bank, Boston . .	1,000	1,202 50	1,167 50
Exchange Nat'l Bank, Boston . .	1,000	1,482 50	1,740 00
Faneuil Hall Nat'l Bank, Boston .	1,000	1,345 00	1,398 75
Freeman's Nat'l Bank, Boston .	2,500	3,137 50	3,360 25
Massachusetts Nat'l Bank, Boston .	3,000	3,825 00	3,760 62
Merchants' Nat'l Bank, Boston .	4,200	6,300 00	6,055 75
Millbury Nat'l Bank, Millbury .	3,000	3,600 00	3,541 75
Northborough Nat'l B'k, Northboro',	1,600	2,000 00	2,080 00
New England Nat'l Bank, Boston .	1,000	1,520 00	1,485 00
North Nat'l Bank, Boston . .	2,500	3,000 00	3,243 75
North America Nat'l Bank, Boston .	3,000	3,607 50	3,287 50
Redemption Nat'l Bank, Boston .	4,000	5,410 00	6,027 50
Revere Nat'l Bank, Boston . .	1,900	2,375 00	2,369 75
Republic Nat'l Bank, Boston . .	2,800	3,668 00	3,578 50
Union Nat'l Bank, Boston . .	1,000	1,512 50	1,372 50
Webster Nat'l Bank, Boston . .	2,000	2,275 00	2,277 50
	$58,400	$76,148 50	$76,398 79

Railroad Bonds.

	Par Value.	Estimated Market Value.	Amount Invested.
Providence and Worcester . .	$12,000	$14,400 00	$13,340 00
Old Colony	7,000	8,120 00	7,000 00
Worcester and Nashua	1,000	1,000 00	1,000 00
Salem and Lowell	3,000	3,300 00	3,300 00
Connecticut and Passumsic Rivers .	2,000	2,320 00	2,000 00
	$25,000	$29,140 00	$26,640 00

WINCHENDON SAVINGS BANK — WINCHENDON.

Incorporated 1854. Number of corporators, 125.

ORLANDO MASON, *President*. *Treasurer*, C. L. BEALS.

STATEMENT.

LIABILITIES.		ASSETS.	
Deposits	$482,631 58	Public funds	$8,000 00
Earnings undivided .	17,706 70	Bank stock	89,100 00
Guaranty fund . .	10,370 74	Loans on bank stock . .	20,234 04
		Railroad bonds . . .	21,000 00
		Real estate by foreclosure .	2,700 00
		Loans on real estate . .	244,479 60
		Loans on personal security,	96,033 12
		Loans to counties, cities, or towns	8,000 00
		Deposit in bank on interest,	16,210 80
		Furniture account . .	200 00
		Cash on hand . . .	4,751 46
	$510,709 02		$510,709 02

Loans on Bank Stock, amount on each:—

On 205 shares First National Bank, Winchendon	$20,054 54
On 2 shares Quinsigamond National Bank, Worcester	179 50

Cash on Deposit in Bank:—

First National Bank, Winchendon	$16,210 80

Amount of real estate held by foreclosure	$2,700 00
Assessed value of the same	2,775 00
Amount of income received from the same	174 00
Amount of municipal tax on real estate	40 24

Whole amount of interest or profits received or earned		$25,923 04
Rate and amount of each semi-annual dividend for previous year	2 per cent .	8,817 94
	2 per cent .	9,013 07

Times for the dividends fixed by the by-laws: May and November.

Average annual per cent of dividends for the term ending at time of and including last extra dividend: 7 per cent.

The total amount of loans, with each specified rate of interest: $20,000, 4 per cent; $3,000, 4½ per cent; $44,954.54, 5 per cent; $4,000, 5½ per cent; $200,292.22, 6 per cent; $1,500, 6½ per cent; $7,700, 7 per cent.

Number of outstanding loans which are of an amount not exceeding $3,000 each	175	
Aggregate amount of the same		137,892 22
Number of open accounts	1,806	
Number and amount of deposits received for previous year .	789	73,727 61
Number and amount of deposits of and exceeding $300 at any one time for the previous year	48	22,289 28
Number and amount of withdrawals	633	56,348 10
Number of accounts opened the previous year	207	

Number of accounts closed the previous year 133
Amount of expenses of the corporation during previous year . . $995 49
Amount of treasurer's bond 50,000 00
Date of examination by commissioner: June 24.

PUBLIC FUNDS.

	Par Value.	Estimated Market Value.	Amount Invested.
United States 3½s	$8,000	$8,040 00	$8,000 00

BANK STOCK.

	Par Value.	Estimated Market Value.	Amount Invested.
First Nat'l Bank, Winchendon .	$31,600	$39,500 00	$31,600 00
First Nat'l Bank, Leominster . .	8,500	8,500 00	8,500 00
First Nat'l Bank, Boston . .	1,600	3,200 00	1,600 00
Mechanics' Nat'l Bank, Boston .	3,400	4,250 00	3,400 00
Eliot Nat'l Bank, Boston . .	6,700	7,638 00	6,700 00
Faneuil Hall Nat'l Bank, Boston .	4,800	5,856 00	4,800 00
Merchants' Nat'l Bank, Boston .	10,000	13,900 00	10,000 00
Commonwealth Nat'l Bank, Boston .	2,500	2,800 00	2,500 00
Redemption Nat'l Bank, Boston .	10,000	12,800 00	10,000 00
Rollstone Nat'l Bank, Fitchburg .	9,000	13,950 00	9,000 00
Fitchburg Nat'l Bank, Fitchburg .	1,000	1,350 00	1,000 00
	$89,100	$113,744 00	$89,100 00

RAILROAD BONDS.

	Par Value.	Estimated Market Value.	Amount Invested.
Cheshire	$6,000	$6,180 00	$6,000 00
Fitchburg	15,000	15,900 00	15,000 00
	$21,000	$22,080 00	$21,000 00

WINCHESTER SAVINGS BANK — WINCHESTER.

Incorporated 1871. Number of corporators, 30.

THOMAS P. AYER, *President*. *Treasurer*, JOHN T. MANNY.

STATEMENT.

LIABILITIES.		ASSETS.	
Deposits	$229,688 15	Public funds	$46,385 00
Earnings undivided	975 76	Bank stock	14,510 75
Guaranty fund	2,429 53	Railroad bonds	15,511 25
Premium fund	1,635 00	Real estate by foreclosure	2,027 05
		Loans on real estate	111,217 22
		Loans on personal security,	17,250 00
		Deposit in banks on interest,	27,151 48
		Safe and fixtures	500 00
		Cash on hand	175 69
	$234,728 44		$234,728 44

Cash on Deposit in Banks, amount in each: —

Exchange National Bank	$24,000 00
Eliot National Bank	3,151 48

Amount of real estate held by foreclosure	$2,027 05
Assessed value of the same	2,150 00
Amount of income received from the same	180 00
Amount of municipal tax on real estate	25 37

Whole amount of interest or profits received or earned		$11,884 00
Rate and amount of each semi-annual dividend for previous year	2½ per cent	4,260 37
	2½ per cent	5,024 06

Times for the dividends fixed by the by-laws: third Wednesday in April and October.

Average annual per cent of dividends for the term ending at time of and including last extra dividend: 5 per cent.

The total amount of loans, with each specified rate of interest: $5,000, 4 per cent; $34,000, 5 per cent; $3,500, 5½ per cent; $73,892.22, 6 per cent; $8,000, 6½ per cent; $48,525, 7 per cent; $9,350, 7½ per cent; $200, 8 per cent.

Number of outstanding loans which are of an amount not exceeding $3,000 each	29	
Aggregate amount of the same		34,975 00
Number of open accounts	890	
Number and amount of deposits received for previous year,	1,229	86,660 22
Number and amount of deposits of and exceeding $300 at any one time for the previous year	67	30,043 65
Number and amount of withdrawals	513	43,861 70
Number of accounts opened the previous year	232	
Number of accounts closed the previous year	118	
Amount of expenses of the corporation during previous year		791 67
Amount of treasurer's bond		5,000 00

Date of examination by commissioner: May 7.

PUBLIC FUNDS.

	Par Value.	Estimated Market Value.	Amount Invested.
State, city, and town bonds:—			
State of New Hampshire . . .	$2,000	$2,400 00	$2,170 00
of Maine	1,000	1,020 00	1,030 00
City of Chelsea	3,000	3,420 00	3,270 00
of Portland, Me. . . .	2,000	2,210 00	2,140 00
of Lynn	2,000	2,320 00	2,340 00
of Cambridge	1,000	1,160 00	1,180 00
Town of Woburn	3,000	3,420 00	3,255 00
of Winchester . . .	30,000	32,050 00	31,000 00
	$44,000	$48,000 00	$46,385 00

BANK STOCK.

Metropolitan Nat'l Bank, Boston .	$2,000	$2,400 00	$2,000 00
Eliot Nat'l Bank, Boston . .	3,000	3,600 00	3,240 00
Atlas Nat'l Bank, Boston . .	2,200	2,750 00	2,583 00
Woburn Nat'l Bank, Woburn . .	2,000	3,000 00	3,000 00
Eagle Nat'l Bank, Boston . .	1,300	1,560 00	1,472 25
State Nat'l Bank, Boston . .	700	875 00	844 25
North America Nat'l Bank, Boston,	500	575 00	570 00
Hamilton Nat'l Bank, Boston . .	400	452 00	496 00
Commerce Nat'l Bank, Boston .	300	384 00	305 25
	$12,400	$15,596 00	$14,510 75

RAILROAD BONDS.

Boston and Lowell	$6,000	$6,655 00	$6,368 75
Old Colony	4,000	4,600 00	4,800 00
Boston and Albany	2,000	2,320 00	2,162 50
Fitchburg	2,000	2,200 00	2,180 00
	$14,000	$15,775 00	$15,511 25

WOBURN FIVE CENTS SAVINGS BANK—WOBURN.

Incorporated April 11, 1854. Number of corporators, 11.

JOHN CUMMINGS, *President*. *Treasurer*, E. E. THOMPSON.

STATEMENT.

LIABILITIES.		ASSETS.	
Deposits	$440,461 71	Bank stock	$204,140 88
Earnings undivided	28,993 65	Real estate by foreclosure	37,353 50
Guaranty fund	2,617 95	Loans on real estate	124,082 90
		Loans on personal security,	63,350 00
		Loans to counties, cities, or towns	36,676 43
		Deposit in bank on interest,	6,118 70
		Cash on hand	350 90
	$472,073 31		$472,073 31

Cash on Deposit in Bank:—
First National Bank, Woburn $6,118 70

Amount of real estate held by foreclosure $37,353 50
Assessed value of the same 49,870 00
Amount of income received from the same 2,710 00
Amount of municipal tax on real estate 738 43

Whole amount of interest or profits received or earned . . . $22,481 82
Rate and amount of each semi-annual dividend for previous year . . . . { 2½ per cent . 7,970 72; 2 per cent . 7,091 78 }
Times for the dividends fixed by the by-laws: January and July.
Average annual per cent of dividends for the term ending at time of and including last extra dividend: 4½ per cent.
The total amount of loans, with each specified rate of interest: $6,118.70, 2½ per cent; $48,700, 4 per cent; $20,976.43, 4½ per cent; $38,590, 5 per cent; $18,792.90, 6 per cent; $23,600, 6½ per cent; $37,515, 7 per cent; $200, 7$\frac{3}{10}$ per cent; $5,875, 8 per cent.
Number of outstanding loans which are of an amount not exceeding $3,000 each 88
Aggregate amount of the same 76,790 00
Amount of investments from which no income is received . . 1,200 00
Number of open accounts 2,205
Number and amount of deposits received for previous year, 1,982 153,119 89
Number and amount of deposits of and exceeding $300 at any one time for the previous year 129 76,791 85
Number and amount of withdrawals 812 49,678 15
Number of accounts opened the previous year 484
Number of accounts closed the previous year 199
Amount of expenses of the corporation during previous year . . 2,206 32
Amount of treasurer's bond 20,000 00
Date of examination by commissioner: April 9.

BANK STOCK.

	Par Value.	Estimated Market Value.	Amount Invested.
Atlas Nat'l Bank, Boston . .	$13,000	$16,250 00	$15,208 13
Blackstone Nat'l Bank, Boston .	10,500	12,075 00	14,738 50
Boston Nat'l Bank, Boston . .	2,000	2,560 00	3,252 50
Continental Nat'l Bank, Boston .	6,700	7,947 87	9,070 75
Commerce Nat'l Bank, Boston .	1,200	1,545 00	1,515 00
Eliot Nat'l Bank, Boston . .	4,500	5,411 25	5,373 75
Faneuil Hall Nat'l Bank, Boston .	5,500	7,191 25	7,125 25
Hide and Leather Nat'l B'k, Boston,	12,800	14,720 00	13,642 25
Howard Nat'l Bank, Boston . .	2,500	3,252 92	2,831 25
New England Nat'l Bank, Boston .	16,500	24,502 50	23,452 50
Old Boston Nat'l Bank, Boston .	1,000	1,220 00	1,260 00
Revere Nat'l Bank, Boston . .	15,000	18,225 00	18,012 50
Shawmut Nat'l Bank, Boston . .	25,000	31,875 00	30,118 75
Shoe and Leather Nat'l B'k, Boston,	17,000	19,125 00	22,638 75
Second Nat'l Bank, Boston . .	2,000	3,030 00	3,205 00
Suffolk Nat'l Bank, Boston . .	3,900	4,753 13	4,912 00
Webster Nat'l Bank, Boston . .	1,000	1,115 00	1,050 00
Woburn Nat'l Bank, Woburn .	20,000	29,000 00	26,734 00
	$160,100	$203,798 92	$204,140 88

WORCESTER COUNTY INSTITUTION FOR SAVINGS—WORCESTER.

Incorporated Feb. 5, 1828. Number of corporators, 187.

ALEXANDER H. BULLOCK, *President*. *Treasurer*, CHARLES A. CHASE.

STATEMENT.

LIABILITIES.		ASSETS.	
Deposits	$8,118,000 85	Public funds	$1,898,800 00
Earnings undivided	220,076 55	Loans on public funds	25,000 00
Guaranty fund	133,000 00	Bank stock	791,050 00
Suspense account	10,597 71	Loans on bank stock	65,500 00
		Railroad bonds	738,000 00
		Real estate by foreclosure	121,240 35
		Loans on real estate	2,430,681 00
		Loans on personal security,	1,164,595 70
		Loans to counties, cities, or towns	556,200 00
		Deposit in banks on interest,	681,260 56
		Expense account	5,043 91
		Cash on hand	4,303 59
	$8,481,675 11		$8,481,675 11

Loans on Public Funds:—

On $25,000 United States 4s $25,000 00

Loans on Bank Stock, amount on each:—

On 550 shares First National Bank, Worcester	$55,000 00
On 100 shares Franklin County National Bank, Greenfield	10,000 00
On 5 shares Central National Bank, Worcester	500 00

Cash on Deposit in Banks, amount in each:—

First National Bank, Worcester	$113,000 00
Citizens' National Bank, Worcester	50,000 00
City National Bank, Worcester	120,000 00
Quinsigamond National Bank, Worcester	60,000 00
Worcester National Bank, Worcester	115,260 56
Exchange National Bank, Boston	65,000 00
National Bank of the Commonwealth, Boston	73,000 00
Wachusett National Bank, Fitchburg	75,000 00
Westminster National Bank, Westminster	10,000 00

Amount of real estate held by foreclosure	$121,240 35
Assessed value of the same	111,840 00
Amount of income received from the same	4,038 00
Amount of municipal tax on real estate	1,864 00

Whole amount of interest or profits received or earned		$427,410 43
Rate and amount of each semi-annual dividend for previous year	2 per cent	147,143 42
	2 per cent	151,719 49

Times for the dividends fixed by the by-laws: Jan. 1 and July 1.

The total amount of loans, with each specified rate of interest: $150,000, 3⅜ per cent; $493,500, 3½ per cent; $100,000, 3¾ per cent; $335,700, 4 per cent; $165,500, 4¼ per cent; $84,500, 4½ per cent; $12,000, 4¾ per cent; $1,587,500, 5 per cent; $60,000, 5½ per cent; $1,223,681, 6 per cent; $4,500, 7 per cent.

Number of outstanding loans which are of an amount not exceeding $3,000 each	592	
Aggregate amount of the same		$901,245 70
Number of open accounts	19,009	
Number and amount of deposits received for previous year,	13,208	1,196,430 26
Number and amount of deposits of and exceeding $300 at any one time for the previous year	1,052	600,111 21
Number and amount of withdrawals	9,868	1,014,690 75
Number of accounts opened the previous year	2,828	
Number of accounts closed the previous year	2,008	
Amount of expenses of the corporation during previous year		13,797 39
Amount of treasurer's bond		50,000 00

Date of examination by commissioner: June 1.

Public Funds.

	Par Value.	Estimated Market Value.	Amount Invested.
United States 4½s	$50,000	$56,000 00	$50,000 00
" " 4s	553,800	642,400 00	553,800 00
State, county, city, and town bonds:—			
State of Maine 6s	$20,000	$23,000 00	$20,000 00
of Rhode Island 6s	77,000	78,540 00	77,000 00
County of Merrimack, N.H., 6s	1,500	1,590 00	1,500 00
City of Worcester 6s	102,500	112,750 00	102,500 00
of Worcester 5s	105,000	115,500 00	105,000 00
of Worcester 4s	500,000	540,000 00	500,000 00
of Roxbury 5s	20,000	20,250 00	20,000 00
of Charlestown 6s	5,000	5,750 00	5,000 00
of Newton 6s	40,000	53,600 00	40,000 00
of Lawrence 6s	5,000	5,750 00	5,000 00
of Lynn 6s	50,000	62,000 00	50,000 00
of Lowell 6s	36,000	42,120 00	36,000 00
of New Bedford 6s	5,000	5,850 00	5,000 00
of New London, Conn., 7s	25,000	36,000 00	25,000 00
of Meriden, Conn., 7s	26,000	31,200 00	26,000 00
of Manchester, N.H., 6s	38,500	46,200 00	38,500 00
of Nashua, N.H., 6s	33,000	39,270 00	33,000 00
of Fitchburg 6s	35,000	41,300 00	35,000 00
of Somerville 6½s	10,000	10,450 00	10,000 00
of Providence, R.I., 4½s	50,000	54,250 00	50,000 00
of Chelsea 4½s	46,000	47,800 00	46,000 00
of Concord, N.H., 6s	500	610 00	500 00
Town of Brookline 7s	20,000	27,500 00	20,000 00
of Natick 7s	10,000	10,800 00	10,000 00
of Northampton 6s	13,000	15,400 00	13,000 00
of Westborough 5s	21,000	24,360 00	21,000 00
	$1,898,800	$2,150,240 00	$1,898,800 00

BANK STOCK.

	Par Value.	Estimated Market Value	Amount Invested.
Atlantic Nat'l Bank, Boston	$5,400	$8,262 00	$5,400 00
Atlas Nat'l Bank, Boston	37,500	46,875 00	37,500 00
Blackstone Nat'l Bank, Boston	13,800	15,870 00	13,800 00
Boylston Nat'l Bank, Boston	1,400	1,792 00	1,400 00
Columbian Nat'l Bank, Boston	5,400	7,722 00	5,400 00
Continental Nat'l Bank, Boston	12,000	14,160 00	12,000 00
Eliot Nat'l Bank, Boston	9,000	10,800 00	9,000 00
Faneuil Hall Nat'l Bank, Boston	2,000	2,680 00	2,000 00
First Nat'l Bank, Boston	25,000	51,750 00	25,000 00
Freeman's Nat'l Bank, Boston	17,200	20,468 00	17,200 00
Globe Nat'l Bank, Boston	3,100	3,441 00	3,100 00
Hamilton Nat'l Bank, Boston	18,000	22,140 00	18,000 00
Howard Nat'l Bank, Boston	15,000	19,500 00	15,000 00
Market Nat'l Bank, Boston	7,400	8,140 00	7,400 00
Massachusetts Nat'l Bank, Boston	11,000	13,640 00	11,000 00
Merchants' Nat'l Bank, Boston	12,500	18,375 00	12,500 00
Commerce Nat'l Bank, Boston	18,000	23,040 00	18,000 00
North America Nat'l Bank, Boston,	7,800	8,970 00	7,800 00
Redemption Nat'l Bank, Boston	9,300	12,555 00	9,300 00
Republic Nat'l Bank, Boston	21,000	27,510 00	21,000 00
City Nat'l Bank, Boston	20,800	26,416 00	20,800 00
Eagle Nat'l Bank, Boston	11,000	13,090 00	11,000 00
Exchange Nat'l Bank, Boston	4,900	7,056 00	4,900 00
Hide and Leather Nat'l B'k, Boston,	30,800	36,314 00	30,800 00
Revere Nat'l Bank, Boston	37,500	45,750 00	37,500 00
Union Nat'l Bank, Boston	7,100	10,863 00	7,100 00
Webster Nat'l Bank, Boston	30,000	33,750 00	30,000 00
New England Nat'l Bank, Boston	19,900	29,250 00	19,900 00
North Nat'l Bank, Boston	4,700	6,674 00	4,700 00
Old Boston Nat'l Bank, Boston	3,250	3,965 00	3,250 00
Second Nat'l Bank, Boston	35,200	53,150 00	35,200 00
Shawmut Nat'l Bank, Boston	17,300	21,970 00	17,300 00
Shoe and Leather Nat'l B'k, Boston,	13,400	15,140 00	13,400 00
State Nat'l Bank, Boston	11,300	14,125 00	11,300 00
Suffolk Nat'l Bank, Boston	3,400	4,114 00	3,400 00
Tremont Nat'l Bank, Boston	15,600	19,032 00	15,600 00
Washington Nat'l Bank, Boston	19,000	26,600 00	19,000 00
Blackstone Nat'l Bank, Uxbridge	1,000	1,250 00	1,000 00
Fitchburg Nat'l Bank, Fitchburg	5,100	7,905 00	5,100 00
Grafton Nat'l Bank, Grafton	4,500	4,950 00	4,500 00
Lancaster Nat'l Bank, Lancaster	2,300	2,875 00	2,300 00
Leicester Nat'l Bank, Leicester	5,500	6,050 00	5,500 00
Millbury Nat'l Bank, Millbury	10,800	12,960 00	10,800 00
Oxford Nat'l Bank, Oxford	4,800	5,760 00	4,800 00
Southbridge Nat'l B'k, Southbridge,	3,000	4,050 00	3,000 00
Third Nat'l Bank, Springfield	20,000	33,000 00	20,000 00
Ware Nat'l Bank, Ware	800	960 00	800 00
Central Nat'l Bank, Worcester	28,100	37,935 00	28,100 00
Citizens' Nat'l Bank, Worcester	24,800	28,520 00	24,800 00
City Nat'l Bank, Worcester	29,500	33,335 00	29,500 00
Mechanics' Nat'l Bank, Worcester	13,300	15,428 00	13,300 00
Quinsigamond Nat l B'k, Worcester,	20,600	23,072 00	20,600 00
Worcester Nat'l Bank, Worcester	80,000	102,400 00	80,000 00
	$791,050	$1,025,429 00	$791,050 00

RAILROAD BONDS.

	Par Value.	Estimated Market Value.	Amount Invested.
Boston and Albany	$200,000	$245,300 00	$200,000 00
Boston and Maine	30,000	38,100 00	30,000 00
Fitchburg	30,000	39,300 00	30,000 00
Old Colony	154,000	192,500 00	154,000 00
Providence and Worcester . .	64,000	78,080 00	64,000 00
Worcester and Nashua . . .	260,000	262,600 00	260,000 00
	$738,000	$855,880 00	$738,000 00

WORCESTER FIVE CENTS SAVINGS BANK — WORCESTER.

Incorporated April 1, 1854. Number of corporators, 303.

CLARENDON HARRIS, *President*. *Treasurer*, GEORGE W. WHEELER.

STATEMENT.

LIABILITIES.		ASSETS.	
Deposits	$2,301,853 95	Public funds	$387,500 00
Earnings undivided	24,511 45	Loans on public funds	3,900 00
Guaranty fund	25,000 00	Bank stock	273,600 00
		Loans on bank stock	6,825 00
		Railroad bonds	29,000 00
		Real estate by foreclosure	10,350 00
		Loans on real estate	1,112,900 00
		Loans on personal security,	2,150 00
		Loans to counties, cities, or towns	84,500 00
		Deposit in banks on interest,	412,061 71
		Expense account	2,089 60
		Premium account	25,000 00
		Cash on hand	1,489 09
	$2,351,365 40		$2,351,365 40

Loans on Public Funds, amount on each: —

On $3,000 United States bonds	$3,000 00
On $1,000 City of Norwich bonds	900 00

Loans on Bank Stock, amount on each: —

On 8 shares Central National Bank, Worcester	$600 00
On 15 shares Quinsigamond National Bank, Worcester	1,500 00
On 30 shares Worcester National Bank, Worcester	2,500 00
On 15 shares Grafton National Bank, Grafton	1,225 00
On 5 shares Millbury National Bank, Millbury	500 00
On 5 shares Shawmut National Bank, Boston	500 00

Cash on Deposit in Banks, amount in each: —

City National Bank, Worcester	$112,061 71
Quinsigamond National Bank, Worcester	110,000 00
Maverick National Bank, Boston	125,000 00
Security National Bank, Boston	40,000 00
Wachusett National Bank, Fitchburg	25,000 00

Amount of real estate held by foreclosure	$10,350 00
Assessed value of the same	6,100 00
Amount of income received from the same	373 12
Amount of municipal tax on real estate	102 69

Whole amount of interest or profits received or earned		$115,750 41
Rate and amount of each semi-annual dividend for previous year	2 per cent	41,060 98
	2 per cent	42,401 85

Times for the dividends fixed by the by-laws: Jan. 1 and July 1.

Average annual per cent of dividends for the term ending at time of and including last extra dividend: 5½ per cent.

The total amount of loans, with each specified rate of interest: $347,061.71, 4 per cent; $67,000, 4½ per cent; $55,000, 4 7/10 per cent; $505,975, 5 per cent; $557,300, 6 per cent.

Number of outstanding loans which are of an amount not exceeding $3,000 each	481	
Aggregate amount of the same		$586,975 00
Number of open accounts	9,914	
Number and amount of deposits received for previous year,	7,799	403,686 18
Number and amount of deposits of and exceeding $300 at any one time for the previous year	354	196,941 78
Number and amount of withdrawals	4,257	332,661 28
Number of accounts opened the previous year	1,564	
Number of accounts closed the previous year	987	
Amount of expenses of the corporation during previous year		5,279 29
Amount of treasurer's bond		20,000 00

Date of examination by commissioner: June 2.

PUBLIC FUNDS.

	Par Value.	Estimated Market Value.	Amount Invested.
United States 4s	$39,000	$45,288 75	$43,256 00
" " 4½s	65,000	73,450 00	72,825 00
" " 5s, continued	70,000	71,400 00	71,221 00
" " 6s, continued	51,000	51,510 00	51,510 62
City and town bonds:—			
City of Cambridge 6s	$25,000	$25,750 00	$25,000 00
of Lowell 6s	27,000	30,510 00	27,000 00
of Lynn 5s	5,000	5,050 00	5,000 00
of New London, Conn., 7s	14,000	18,900 00	14,000 00
of Newton 6s	25,000	31,250 00	25,000 00
of Salem 5s	3,000	3,030 00	3,000 00
of Springfield 7s	12,000	16,680 00	12,000 00
of Worcester 5s and 6s	46,500	50,775 00	46,500 00
Town of Brookline 7s	5,000	6,650 00	5,000 00
	$387,500	$430,243 75	$401,312 62

BANK STOCK.

Atlas Nat'l Bank, Boston	$5,000	$6,250 00	$5,000 00
Blackstone Nat'l Bank, Boston	8,800	10,120 00	9,693 75
City Nat'l Bank, Boston	2,500	3,175 00	3,003 13
Commerce Nat'l Bank, Boston	4,400	5,665 00	4,400 00
Commonwealth Nat'l Bank, Boston,	8,000	9,960 00	9,103 75
Eagle Nat'l Bank, Boston	10,000	11,975 00	10,000 00
Eliot Nat'l Bank, Boston	12,200	14,670 50	12,593 75
First Nat'l Bank, Boston	6,700	13,919 25	6,700 00
Fourth Nat'l Bank, Boston	2,500	2,750 00	2,683 13
Globe Nat'l Bank, Boston	10,000	11,150 00	11,000 00
Hamilton Nat'l Bank, Boston	5,000	6,187 50	5,000 00
Hide and Leather Nat'l B'k, Boston,	16,400	19,106 00	17,983 25

BANK STOCK — Concluded.

	Par Value.	Estimated Market Value.	Amount Invested.
Howard Nat'l Bank, Boston . .	$10,000	$13,125 00	$10,000 00
Market Nat'l Bank, Boston . .	1,200	1,329 00	1,296 00
Merchants' Nat'l Bank, Boston .	5,000	7,300 00	5,000 00
North Nat'l Bank, Boston . .	800	1,134 00	800 00
North America Nat'l Bank, Boston .	18,500	21,275 00	21,121 50
Pacific Nat'l Bank, Boston . .	10,000	10,550 00	10,601 25
Shawmut Nat'l Bank, Boston . .	5,000	6,375 00	5,000 00
Shoe and Leather Nat'l B'k, Boston,	6,300	7,119 00	7,072 50
State Nat'l Bank, Boston . .	5,000	6,275 00	5,000 00
Third Nat'l Bank, Boston . .	1,600	1,704 00	1,712 00
Traders' Nat'l Bank, Boston . .	15,700	16,014 00	16,195 87
Webster Nat'l Bank, Boston . .	11,000	12,265 50	11,817 50
Central Nat'l Bank, Worcester .	7,000	9,100 00	7,000 00
Citizens' Nat'l Bank, Worcester .	700	770 00	700 00
City Nat'l Bank, Worcester . .	26,800	29,480 00	26,800 00
Mechanics' Nat'l Bank, Worcester .	6,400	7,040 00	6,400 00
Quinsigamond Nat'l B'k, Worcester,	13,900	15,568 00	13,900 00
Worcester Nat'l Bank, Worcester .	2,000	2,240 00	2,000 00
First Nat'l Bank, Leominster .	5,000	5,750 00	5,000 00
Grafton Nat'l Bank, Grafton .	5,000	6,000 00	5,000 00
Leicester Nat'l Bank, Leicester .	3,000	3,600 00	3,000 00
Millbury Nat'l Bank, Millbury .	10,700	13,375 00	10,700 00
Northborough Nat'l B'k, Northboro',	3,000	3,450 00	3,000 00
Spencer Nat'l Bank, Spencer . .	5,000	5,400 00	5,000 00
Wachusett Nat'l Bank, Fitchburg .	2,500	5,000 00	2,500 00
Westminster Nat'l B'k, Westminster,	1,000	1,000 00	1,000 00
	$273,600	$327,166 75	$284,787 38

RAILROAD BONDS.

Worcester and Nashua 5s . .	$29,000	$30,200 00	$29,000 00

WORCESTER MECHANICS' SAVINGS BANK – WORCESTER.

Incorporated April 15, 1851. Number of corporators, 102.

HARRISON BLISS, *President*. *Treasurer*, HENRY WOODWARD.

STATEMENT.

LIABILITIES.		ASSETS.	
Deposits . . .	$3,202,293 77	Public funds	$639,000 00
Earnings undivided .	38,427 79	Bank stock	265,200 00
Guaranty fund . .	38,388 18	Loans on bank stock . .	3,795 00
		Railroad bonds . . .	71,500 00
		Real estate by foreclosure .	51,309 97
		Loans on real estate . .	1,260,412 56
		Loans on personal security,	365,447 34
		Loans to counties, cities, or towns	54,000 00
		Deposit in banks on interest,	509,494 46
		Expense account . . .	3,120 16
		Suspense account . .	7,712 13
		Premium account . .	40,249 89
		Cash on hand . . .	7,868 23
	$3,279,109 74		$3,279,109 74

Loans on Bank Stock, amount on each:—

On 15 shares City National Bank, Worcester	$495 00
On 4 shares Leicester National Bank	300 00
On 4 shares Central National Bank, Worcester, and 5 shares Leicester National Bank	500 00
On 28 shares First National Bank, Worcester	2,500 00

Cash on Deposit in Banks, amount in each:—

National Bank of Commerce, Boston	$5 33
Mechanics' National Bank, Worcester	272,142 40
Maverick National Bank, Boston	117,346 73
City National Bank, Worcester	45,000 00
Quinsigamond National Bank, Worcester	50,000 00
Wachusett National Bank, Fitchburg	25,000 00

Amount of real estate held by foreclosure	$51,309 97
Assessed value of the same	49,500 00
Amount of income received from the same	1,320 00
Amount of municipal tax on real estate	764 96

Whole amount of interest or profits received or earned . . .		$159,470 15
Rate and amount of each semi-annual dividend for previous year	2 per cent .	58,273 66
	2 per cent .	60,032 12

Times for the dividends fixed by the by-laws: January and July.

The total amount of loans, with each specified rate of interest: $150,000, 3½ per cent; $88,798.09, 4 per cent; $50,000, 4½ per cent; $462,180, 5 per cent; $932,676.81, 6 per cent.

Number of outstanding loans which are of an amount not exceeding $3,000 each	479	
Aggregate amount of the same		618,208 20

Number of open accounts	6,571	
Number and amount of deposits received for previous year,	3,613	$467,366 76
Number and amount of deposits of and exceeding $300 at any one time for the previous year	493	282,283 62
Number and amount of withdrawals	3,426	393,643 08
Number of accounts opened the previous year	918	
Number of accounts closed the previous year	642	
Amount of expenses of the corporation during previous year		8,107 59
Amount of treasurer's bond		20,000 00

Date of examination by commissioner: June 3.

PUBLIC FUNDS.

	Par Value.	Estimated Market Value.	Amount Invested.
United States 4½s	$155,000	$173,600 00	$155,000 00
" " 4s	188,000	217,080 00	188,000 00
City and town bonds: —			
City of Worcester 5s	$100,000	$109,000 00	100,000 00
of Providence 4½s	79,000	84,925 00	79,000 00
of Springfield 7s	34,000	47,600 00	34,000 00
of Cambridge 6s	25,000	27,500 00	25,000 00
of New London 7s	20,000	27,000 00	20,000 00
of Fitchburg 6s	10,000	12,000 00	10,000 00
of Augusta, Me., 6s	11,000	12,110 00	11,000 00
of Portsmouth, N.H., 6s	5,000	5,000 00	5,000 00
of Norwich, Conn., 5s	5,000	5,500 00	5,000 00
Town of Brookline 7s	7,000	9,450 00	7,000 00
	$639,000	$730,765 00	$639,000 00

BANK STOCK.

Boylston Nat'l Bank, Boston	$4,000	$5,120 00	$4,000 00
Revere Nat'l Bank, Boston	16,000	18,300 00	16,000 00
North Nat'l Bank, Boston	10,000	14,212 50	10,000 00
Hide and Leather Nat'l B'k, Boston,	17,100	19,921 50	17,100 00
Boston Nat'l Bank, Boston	11,300	14,464 00	11,300 00
Eliot Nat'l Bank, Boston	8,600	10,341 50	8,600 00
Redemption Nat'l Bank, Boston	5,000	6,750 00	5,000 00
City Nat'l Bank, Boston	10,000	12,700 00	10,000 00
Traders' Nat'l Bank, Boston	5,500	5,610 00	5,500 00
Republic Nat'l Bank, Boston	3,400	4,454 00	3,400 00
Market Nat'l Bank, Boston	10,000	10,975 00	10,000 00
Suffolk Nat'l Bank, Boston	5,900	7,198 00	5,900 00
Merchants' Nat'l Bank, Boston	7,000	10,237 50	7,000 00
Commerce Nat'l Bank, Boston	17,000	21,887 50	17,000 00
Mechanics' Nat'l Bank, Worcester	35,400	40,710 00	35,400 00
Worcester Nat'l Bank, Worcester	9,500	11,875 00	9,500 00
Citizens' Nat'l Bank, Worcester	11,500	12,880 00	11,500 00
Central Nat'l Bank, Worcester	8,400	11,920 00	8,400 00
City Nat'l Bank, Worcester	18,000	19,080 00	18,000 00

BANK STOCK — Concluded.

	Par Value.	Estimated Market Value.	Amount Invested.
First Nat'l Bank, Worcester . .	$1,200	$1,680 00	$1,200 00
Quinsigamond Nat'l B'k, Worcester,	1,600	1,840 00	1,600 00
First Nat'l Bank, Leominster . .	10,000	11,200 00	10,000 00
Westminster Nat'l B'k, Westminster,	2,000	2,000 00	2,000 00
Grafton Nat'l Bank, Grafton . .	11,400	12,540 00	11,400 00
Millbury Nat'l Bank, Millbury .	4,300	5,375 00	4,300 00
Southbridge Nat'l B'k, Southbridge,	3,500	4,725 00	3,500 00
Franklin Nat'l Bank, Franklin .	5,100	5,355 00	5,100 00
First Nat'l Bank, Clinton . .	1,000	1,120 00	1,000 00
Wachusett Nat'l Bank, Fitchburg .	11,500	21,275 00	11,500 00
	$265,200	$325,746 50	$265,200 00

RAILROAD BONDS.

Boston and Albany 7s . . .	$20,000	$25,400 00	$20,000 00
Worcester and Nashua 5s . .	51,500	51,500 00	51,500 00
	$71,500	$76,900 00	$71,500 00

WORCESTER NORTH SAVINGS INSTITUTION — FITCHBURG.

Incorporated May 26, 1868. Number of corporators, 102.

BENJAMIN SNOW, *President*. *Treasurer*, HENRY A. WILLIS.

STATEMENT.

LIABILITIES.		ASSETS.	
Deposits	$1,779,593 13	Public funds	$309,623 86
Earnings undivided	15,525 50	Loans on public funds	500 00
Guaranty fund	24,566 63	Bank stock	103,790 37
		Loans on bank stock	16,000 00
		Railroad bonds	34,408 29
		Real estate by foreclosure	23,397 54
		Loans on real estate	780,273 92
		Loans on personal security,	367,035 03
		Loans to counties, cities, or towns	158,022 95
		Deposit in banks on interest,	24,000 00
		Expense account	1,438 19
		Cash on hand	1,195 11
	$1,819,685 26		$1,819,685 26

Loans on Public Funds: —

On $500 United States 4s, consols, 1907 . . $500 00

Loans on Bank Stock, amount on each: —

On 13 shares Rollstone National Bank, Fitchburg	$1.300 00
On 90 shares Wachusett National Bank, Fitchburg, and other collateral	10.000 00
On 25 shares Fitchburg National Bank	2,000 00
On 10 shares Safety Fund National Bank, Fitchburg	800 00
On 8 shares Agricultural National Bank, Pittsfield, and 11 shares Pittsfield National Bank	1.900 00

Cash on Deposit in Banks, amount in each: —

Rollstone National Bank, Fitchburg	$9.000 00
First National Bank, Leominster	15.000 00

Amount of real estate held by foreclosure	$23,397 54
Assessed value of the same	23.100 00
Amount of income received from the same	1.481 32
Amount of municipal tax on real estate	415 80

Whole amount of interest or profits received or earned $92,453 89

Rate and amount of each semi-annual dividend for previous year { $2\frac{1}{4}$ per cent . 34,156 01; 2 per cent . 32,728 85 }

Times for the dividends fixed by the by-laws: Jan. 1 and July 1.

The total amount of loans, with each specified rate of interest: $86,500, 4 per cent; $52,000, $4\frac{1}{4}$ per cent; $89,500, $4\frac{1}{2}$ per cent; $43,000, $4\frac{3}{4}$ per cent; $230,054.20, 5 per cent; $36,400, $5\frac{1}{2}$ per cent; $666,177.70, 6 per cent; $93,825, $6\frac{1}{2}$ per cent; $39,375, 7 per cent.

Number of outstanding loans which are of an amount not exceeding $3,000 each . . . 330

Aggregate amount of the same 368.248 92

Amount of investments from which no income is received . . 1,846 07

Number of open accounts 4,644

Number and amount of deposits received for previous year,	3,609	$309,627 05
Number and amount of deposits of and exceeding $300 at any one time for the previous year	385	224,914 56
Number and amount of withdrawals	2,180	261,841 69
Number of accounts opened the previous year	1,002	
Number of accounts closed the previous year	496	
Amount of expenses of the corporation during previous year .		4,766 47
Amount of treasurer's bond		20,000 00

Date of examination by commissioner: June 24.

Public Funds.

	Par Value.	Estimated Market Value.	Amount Invested.
United States 6s, continued . .	$15,000	$15,450 00	$16,668 43
" " 5s, continued . .	55,000	55,975 00	57,193 43
City and town bonds: —			
City of Boston	$30,000	$32,700 00	$31,400 00
of Springfield	20,000	23,640 00	22,600 00
of New Bedford	20,000	25,000 00	21,300 00
of Norwich, Conn.	20,000	27,000 00	22,400 00
of Providence, R.I.	20,000	20,400 00	20,262 00
of Fall River	20,000	22,500 00	20,650 00
of Portland, Me.	15,000	17,750 00	15,593 00
of Fitchburg	10,000	11,600 00	11,000 00
of Lewiston, Me.	10,000	10,800 00	10,000 00
of Lynn	10,000	11,000 00	10,300 00
Town of Danvers	10,000	11,100 00	10,107 00
of Wayland	10,000	10,900 00	10,150 00
	$295,000	$325,815 00	$309,623 86

Bank Stock.

	Par Value.	Estimated Market Value.	Amount Invested.
Rollstone Nat'l Bank, Fitchburg .	$11,500	$18,400 00	$16,996 00
Boston Nat'l Bank, Boston . .	10,000	12,800 00	9,000 00
First Nat'l Bank, Leominster . .	10,000	11,000 00	10,000 00
City Nat'l Bank, Boston . . .	10,000	12,700 00	10,689 00
Atlas Nat'l Bank, Boston . .	10,000	12,500 00	10,902 62
Commerce Nat'l Bank, Boston .	10,000	12,800 00	10,487 50
Webster Nat'l Bank, Boston . .	5,000	5,587 50	5,000 00
Merchants' Nat'l Bank, Boston .	5,000	7,300 00	6,390 25
Eagle Nat'l Bank, Boston . .	5,000	5,987 50	5,200 00
Blackstone Nat'l Bank, Boston .	5,000	5,750 00	5,406 25
Continental Nat'l Bank, Boston .	5,000	5,925 00	5,687 50
Tremont Nat'l Bank, Boston . .	5,000	6,125 00	6,100 00
Faneuil Hall Nat'l Bank, Boston .	1,500	2,017 50	1,871 25
	$93,000	$118,892 50	$103,790 37

Railroad Bonds.

	Par Value.	Estimated Market Value.	Amount Invested.
Vermont and Massachusetts . .	$33,000	$38,260 00	$34,408 29

WORONOCO SAVINGS BANK — WESTFIELD.

Incorporated 1871. Number of corporators, 26.

SAMUEL HORTON, *President*. *Treasurer*, CHARLES L. WELLER.

STATEMENT.

LIABILITIES.		ASSETS.	
Deposits	$656,236 90	Public funds	$199,138 44
Earnings undivided	13,999 59	Loans on public funds	1,000 00
Guaranty fund	7,534 26	Bank stock	5,995 00
		Loans on bank stock	1,325 00
		Real estate by foreclosure	2,100 00
		Loans on real estate	299,337 22
		Loans on personal security,	38,068 74
		Loans to counties, cities, or towns	42,000 00
		Deposit in banks on interest,	75,838 94
		Expense account	6,233 20
		Cash in bank	6,734 21
	$677,770 75		$677,770 75

Loans on Public Funds: —

On $1,000 United States 4s $1,000 00

Loans on Bank Stock: —

On 24 shares Hampden National Bank $1,325 00

Cash on Deposit in Banks, amount in each: —

Suffolk National Bank, Boston	$75,838 94
Hampden National Bank, Westfield	6,734 21

Amount of real estate held by foreclosure		$2,100 00
Assessed value of the same		1,900 00
Amount of income received from the same		131 00
Amount of municipal tax on real estate		49 82
Whole amount of interest or profits received or earned		$33,993 72
Rate and amount of each semi-annual dividend for previous year	2 per cent	12,613 50
	1¾ per cent	11,066 69

Times for the dividends fixed by the by-laws: January and July.

The total amount of loans, with each specified rate of interest: $44,400, 5 per cent; $337,330.96, 6 per cent.

Number of outstanding loans which are of an amount not exceeding $3,000 each	160	
Aggregate amount of the same		104,006 46
Number of open accounts	1,587	
Number and amount of deposits received for previous year,	1,140	130,567 52
Number and amount of deposits of and exceeding $300 at any one time for the previous year	106	85,033 75
Number and amount of withdrawals	878	126,987 40
Number of accounts opened the previous year	253	
Number of accounts closed the previous year	234	
Amount of expenses of the corporation during previous year		950 30
Amount of treasurer's bond		15,000 00

Date of examination by commisioner: July 13.

PUBLIC FUNDS.

	Par Value.	Estimated Market Value.	Amount Invested.
United States 4s	$56,000	$65,030 00	$56,831 25
" " $4\frac{1}{2}$s	105,000	118,650 00	110,441 57
" " 5s, continued . .	30,000	30,600 00	31,865 62
	$191,000	$214,280 00	$199,138 44

BANK STOCK.

Hampden Nat'l Bank, Westfield .	$4,000	$5,800 00	$5,995 00

AGGREGATE STATEMENT.

Liabilities.		Assets.	
Deposits . .	$230,444,479 10	Public Funds: —	
Surplus . .	4,890,600 67	United States bonds . .	$22,025,197 16
Guaranty fund .	3,341,062 35	State, county, city, and town bonds	17,407,423 68
Sundries . .	260,596 66	Loans on public funds . .	1,558,780 00
		Bank stock	24,937,671 02
		Loans on bank stock . .	1,003,430 53
		Railroad bonds . . .	7,802,403 05
		Real estate by foreclosure .	8,052,450 79
		Real estate for banking purposes	2,546,902 85
		Loans on mortgage of real estate	82,518,068 04
		Loans on personal security .	48,349,666 59
		Loans to counties, cities, or towns	8,684,666 39
		Deposits in banks on interest,	11,770,415 27
		Sundries *	1,218,003 35
		Cash on hand	1,061,651 06
	$238,936,738 78		$238,936,738 78

Whole amount of interest or profits received or earned . . . $12,285,345 35
Percentage of earnings to total assets 5⅐

Rate of Ordinary Dividends paid by 162 Banks: —

2 at 2 per ct.† (1 dividend each).	110 at 4 per ct.	1 at 4¾ per ct.
4 at 3 per ct.	8 at 4¼ per ct.	7 at 5 per ct.
3 at 3½ per ct.	23 at 4½ per ct.	3 banks paid no dividend.‡
4 at 3¾ per ct.		

Amount of loans, with specified rates of interest: —

$65,000.00, 2 per ct.	$50,000.00, 4 62/100 per ct.	$53,637,622.57, 6 per ct.
256,941.24, 2½ per ct.	20,000.00, 4 6/10 per ct.	44,600.00, 6¼ per ct.
738,177.00, 3 per ct.	13,790,607.74, 4½ per ct,	40,000.00, 6 45/100 per ct.
389,500.00, 3¼ per ct.	25,000.00, 4⅝ per ct.	5,132,949.18, 6½ per ct.
150,000.00, 3⅜ per ct.	55,000.00, 4 7/10 per ct.	220,000.00, 6 6/10 per ct.
9,431,500.00, 3½ per ct.	1,222,100.00, 4¾ per ct.	2,700.00, 6¾ per ct.
27,000.00, 3⅝ per ct.	30,137,838.29, 5 per ct.	11,199,082.19, 7 per ct.
1,662,000.00, 3¾ per ct.	206,294.23, 5¼ per ct.	483,069.00, 7 3/10 per ct.
180,000.00, 3⅞ per ct.	30,000.00, 5⅜ per ct.	616,459.19, 7½ per ct.
13,499,615.52, 4 per ct.	4,311,225.79, 5½ per ct.	415,172.72, 8 per ct.
50,000.00, 4⅛ per ct.	391,000.00, 5¾ per ct.	51,500.00, 9 per ct.
1,095,484.79, 4¼ per ct.		

* This item includes loans on railroad stock, accrued interest, premium and expense accounts, etc.

† Of these banks one was temporarily enjoined, and in one payments to depositors were limited.

‡ Of these banks two were temporarily enjoined, and one was organized during the previous year.

Aggregate amount of ordinary dividends for the previous year .		$8,203,774 37
Average rate of ordinary dividends for the previous year: 4 per cent.		
Number of outstanding loans which are of an amount not exceeding $3,000 each	32,777	
Aggregate amount of the same		34,020,584 95
Number of open accounts	738,951	
Number and amount of deposits received for previous year	615,514	48,223,496 86
Number and amount of deposits of and exceeding $300 at any one time for the previous year	36,604	20,753,979 53
Number and amount of withdrawals	419,959	40,212,786 44
Number of accounts opened the previous year . .	118,381	
Number of accounts closed the previous year . .	86,991	
Amount of expenses of the corporations the previous year .		617,672 51

COMPARATIVE AGGREGATES.

	1880. One hundred and sixty-four Savings Banks.	1881. One hundred and sixty-five Savings Banks.	Increase.	Decrease.
Number of open accounts	706,395	738,951	32,556	–
Amount of deposits	$218,047,922 37	$230,444,479 10	$12,396,556 73	–
Number of deposits during the year preceding	532,594	615,514	82,920	–
Amount of the same	$42,751,557 43	$48,223,496 86	$5,471,939 43	–
Number of deposits received during the year of and exceeding $300 at one time	32,570	36,604	4,034	–
Amount of the same	$18,301,375 81	$20,753,979 53	$2,452,603 72	–
Number of withdrawals during the year	389,775	419,959	30,184	–
Amount of the same	$34,403,428 23	$40,212,786 44	$5,809,358 21	–
Number of accounts opened during the year	109,030	118,381	9,351	–
Number of accounts closed during the year	75,573	86,991	11,418	–
Amount of surplus on hand	$4,758,194 88	$4,890,600 67	$132,405 79	–
Amount of guaranty fund	2,670,152 85	3,341,062 35	670,909 50	–
Public funds	37,865,057 83	39,432,620 84	1,567,563 01	–
Loan on public funds	2,160,783 00	1,558,780 00	–	$602,003 00
Bank stock	24,078,448 84	24,937,671 02	859,222 18	–
Loans on bank stock	894,822 70	1,003,439 53	108,616 83	–
Deposits in banks bearing interest	16,256,776 98	11,770,415 27	–	4,486,361 71
Railroad bonds	7,011,550 72	7,802,403 05	790,852 33	–
Invested in real estate	2,584,022 44	2,546,902 85	–	37,119 59
Real estate by foreclosure	9,222,345 71	8,052,450 79	–	1,169,894 92
Loans on mortgage of real estate	82,431,984 23	82,518,068 04	86,083 81	–
Loans to counties, cities, or towns	9,248,848 62	8,684,666 39	–	564,182 23
Loans on personal security	30,737,205 39	48,349,666 59	17,612,461 20	–
Cash on hand	1,664,490 95	1,061,651 06	–	602,839 89
Average rate of ordinary dividends for last year	3.93 per cent.	4 per cent.	07 per cent,	–
Aggregate amount of earnings	$11,894,710 60	$12,285,345 35	$390,634 75	–
Aggregate amount of ordinary dividends	7,957,887 09	8,293,774 37	335,887 28	–
Number of outstanding loans not exceeding $3,000	32,320	32,777	457	–
Amount of the same	$34,203,951 81	$34,020,584 95	–	183,366 86
Annual expenses of the institutions	581,274 35	617,672 51	36,398 16	–

[illegible]

3,311,044 43	[illegible]	229,928,216 74	20,482,520 85	1,596,260 00	229,817,071 08	[illegible]	77,892,165 05	69,023,150 79	2,646,923 53	242,815,686 91	148,348,050 16	10,004,869 38	411,770,186 77	5,091,804 00	6,218,005 55	[illegible] 70

181 182 183 184 185

* Amount received by United States [illegible], amount [illegible] by State, County, City, and Town [illegible]

ALPHABETICAL LIST OF THE SAVINGS BANKS, WITH STATEMENTS OF THEIR LIABILITIES AND ASSETS AT THE CLOSE OF BUSINESS OCT. 31, 1881.

No.	Name of Bank	[illegible]	[illegible]	[illegible]	[illegible]	[illegible]	[illegible]	[illegible]	[illegible]	[illegible]	[illegible]	[illegible]	[illegible]	[illegible]	[illegible]	[illegible]	[illegible]	[illegible]	[illegible]	[illegible]
1	Abington Savings Bank	[illegible]	[illegible]	[illegible]	[illegible]	[illegible]	[illegible]	[illegible]	[illegible]	[illegible]	[illegible]	[illegible]	[illegible]	[illegible]	[illegible]	[illegible]	[illegible]	[illegible]	[illegible]	[illegible]
2	Amherst Savings Bank	[illegible]	[illegible]	[illegible]	[illegible]	[illegible]	[illegible]	[illegible]	[illegible]	[illegible]	[illegible]	[illegible]	[illegible]	[illegible]	[illegible]	[illegible]	[illegible]	[illegible]	[illegible]	[illegible]
3	Andover Savings Bank	[illegible]	[illegible]	[illegible]	[illegible]	[illegible]	[illegible]	[illegible]	[illegible]	[illegible]	[illegible]	[illegible]	[illegible]	[illegible]	[illegible]	[illegible]	[illegible]	[illegible]	[illegible]	[illegible]
4	Arlington Five Cents Savings Bank	[illegible]	[illegible]	[illegible]	[illegible]	[illegible]	[illegible]	[illegible]	[illegible]	[illegible]	[illegible]	[illegible]	[illegible]	[illegible]	[illegible]	[illegible]	[illegible]	[illegible]	[illegible]	[illegible]
5	Athol Savings Bank	[illegible]	[illegible]	[illegible]	[illegible]	[illegible]	[illegible]	[illegible]	[illegible]	[illegible]	[illegible]	[illegible]	[illegible]	[illegible]	[illegible]	[illegible]	[illegible]	[illegible]	[illegible]	[illegible]
6	Attleborough Savings Bank	[illegible]	[illegible]	[illegible]	[illegible]	[illegible]	[illegible]	[illegible]	[illegible]	[illegible]	[illegible]	[illegible]	[illegible]	[illegible]	[illegible]	[illegible]	[illegible]	[illegible]	[illegible]	[illegible]
7	Barre Savings Bank	[illegible]	[illegible]	[illegible]	[illegible]	[illegible]	[illegible]	[illegible]	[illegible]	[illegible]	[illegible]	[illegible]	[illegible]	[illegible]	[illegible]	[illegible]	[illegible]	[illegible]	[illegible]	[illegible]
8	Bass River Sav'gs B'k, S. Yarmouth	[illegible]	[illegible]	[illegible]	[illegible]	[illegible]	[illegible]	[illegible]	[illegible]	[illegible]	[illegible]	[illegible]	[illegible]	[illegible]	[illegible]	[illegible]	[illegible]	[illegible]	[illegible]	[illegible]
9	Benj. Franklin Sav'gs B'k, Franklin	[illegible]	[illegible]	[illegible]	[illegible]	[illegible]	[illegible]	[illegible]	[illegible]	[illegible]	[illegible]	[illegible]	[illegible]	[illegible]	[illegible]	[illegible]	[illegible]	[illegible]	[illegible]	[illegible]
10	Berkshire County Savings Bank	[illegible]	[illegible]	[illegible]	[illegible]	[illegible]	[illegible]	[illegible]	[illegible]	[illegible]	[illegible]	[illegible]	[illegible]	[illegible]	[illegible]	[illegible]	[illegible]	[illegible]	[illegible]	[illegible]
11	Beverly Savings Bank	[illegible]	[illegible]	[illegible]	[illegible]	[illegible]	[illegible]	[illegible]	[illegible]	[illegible]	[illegible]	[illegible]	[illegible]	[illegible]	[illegible]	[illegible]	[illegible]	[illegible]	[illegible]	[illegible]
12	Boston Five Cents Savings Bank	[illegible]	[illegible]	[illegible]	[illegible]	[illegible]	[illegible]	[illegible]	[illegible]	[illegible]	[illegible]	[illegible]	[illegible]	[illegible]	[illegible]	[illegible]	[illegible]	[illegible]	[illegible]	[illegible]
13	Boston Penny Savings Bank	[illegible]	[illegible]	[illegible]	[illegible]	[illegible]	[illegible]	[illegible]	[illegible]	[illegible]	[illegible]	[illegible]	[illegible]	[illegible]	[illegible]	[illegible]	[illegible]	[illegible]	[illegible]	[illegible]
14	Braintree Savings Bank	[illegible]	[illegible]	[illegible]	[illegible]	[illegible]	[illegible]	[illegible]	[illegible]	[illegible]	[illegible]	[illegible]	[illegible]	[illegible]	[illegible]	[illegible]	[illegible]	[illegible]	[illegible]	[illegible]
15	Bridgewater Savings Bank	[illegible]	[illegible]	[illegible]	[illegible]	[illegible]	[illegible]	[illegible]	[illegible]	[illegible]	[illegible]	[illegible]	[illegible]	[illegible]	[illegible]	[illegible]	[illegible]	[illegible]	[illegible]	[illegible]
16	Brighton Five Cents Savings Bank	[illegible]	[illegible]	[illegible]	[illegible]	[illegible]	[illegible]	[illegible]	[illegible]	[illegible]	[illegible]	[illegible]	[illegible]	[illegible]	[illegible]	[illegible]	[illegible]	[illegible]	[illegible]	[illegible]
17	Bristol Co. Savings Bank, Taunton	[illegible]	[illegible]	[illegible]	[illegible]	[illegible]	[illegible]	[illegible]	[illegible]	[illegible]	[illegible]	[illegible]	[illegible]	[illegible]	[illegible]	[illegible]	[illegible]	[illegible]	[illegible]	[illegible]
18	Broadway Savings Bank, Lawrence	[illegible]	[illegible]	[illegible]	[illegible]	[illegible]	[illegible]	[illegible]	[illegible]	[illegible]	[illegible]	[illegible]	[illegible]	[illegible]	[illegible]	[illegible]	[illegible]	[illegible]	[illegible]	[illegible]
19	Brockton Savings Bank, Brockton	[illegible]	[illegible]	[illegible]	[illegible]	[illegible]	[illegible]	[illegible]	[illegible]	[illegible]	[illegible]	[illegible]	[illegible]	[illegible]	[illegible]	[illegible]	[illegible]	[illegible]	[illegible]	[illegible]
20	Brookfield Savings Bank	[illegible]	[illegible]	[illegible]	[illegible]	[illegible]	[illegible]	[illegible]	[illegible]	[illegible]	[illegible]	[illegible]	[illegible]	[illegible]	[illegible]	[illegible]	[illegible]	[illegible]	[illegible]	[illegible]
21	Brookline Savings Bank	[illegible]	[illegible]	[illegible]	[illegible]	[illegible]	[illegible]	[illegible]	[illegible]	[illegible]	[illegible]	[illegible]	[illegible]	[illegible]	[illegible]	[illegible]	[illegible]	[illegible]	[illegible]	[illegible]
22	Cambridgeport Savings Bank	[illegible]	[illegible]	[illegible]	[illegible]	[illegible]	[illegible]	[illegible]	[illegible]	[illegible]	[illegible]	[illegible]	[illegible]	[illegible]	[illegible]	[illegible]	[illegible]	[illegible]	[illegible]	[illegible]
23	Cambridge Savings Bank	[illegible]	[illegible]	[illegible]	[illegible]	[illegible]	[illegible]	[illegible]	[illegible]	[illegible]	[illegible]	[illegible]	[illegible]	[illegible]	[illegible]	[illegible]	[illegible]	[illegible]	[illegible]	[illegible]
24	Canton Institution for Savings	[illegible]	[illegible]	[illegible]	[illegible]	[illegible]	[illegible]	[illegible]	[illegible]	[illegible]	[illegible]	[illegible]	[illegible]	[illegible]	[illegible]	[illegible]	[illegible]	[illegible]	[illegible]	[illegible]
25	Cape Ann Savings Bank, Gloucester	[illegible]	[illegible]	[illegible]	[illegible]	[illegible]	[illegible]	[illegible]	[illegible]	[illegible]	[illegible]	[illegible]	[illegible]	[illegible]	[illegible]	[illegible]	[illegible]	[illegible]	[illegible]	[illegible]
26	Cape Cod Five Cts. Sav. B'k, Harwich	[illegible]	[illegible]	[illegible]	[illegible]	[illegible]	[illegible]	[illegible]	[illegible]	[illegible]	[illegible]	[illegible]	[illegible]	[illegible]	[illegible]	[illegible]	[illegible]	[illegible]	[illegible]	[illegible]
27	Central Savings Bank	[illegible]	[illegible]	[illegible]	[illegible]	[illegible]	[illegible]	[illegible]	[illegible]	[illegible]	[illegible]	[illegible]	[illegible]	[illegible]	[illegible]	[illegible]	[illegible]	[illegible]	[illegible]	[illegible]
28	Charlestown Five Cents Savings B'k	[illegible]	[illegible]	[illegible]	[illegible]	[illegible]	[illegible]	[illegible]	[illegible]	[illegible]	[illegible]	[illegible]	[illegible]	[illegible]	[illegible]	[illegible]	[illegible]	[illegible]	[illegible]	[illegible]
29	Chelsea Savings Bank	[illegible]	[illegible]	[illegible]	[illegible]	[illegible]	[illegible]	[illegible]	[illegible]	[illegible]	[illegible]	[illegible]	[illegible]	[illegible]	[illegible]	[illegible]	[illegible]	[illegible]	[illegible]	[illegible]
30	Chicopee Falls Savings Bank	[illegible]	[illegible]	[illegible]	[illegible]	[illegible]	[illegible]	[illegible]	[illegible]	[illegible]	[illegible]	[illegible]	[illegible]	[illegible]	[illegible]	[illegible]	[illegible]	[illegible]	[illegible]	[illegible]
31	Chicopee Savings Bank	[illegible]	[illegible]	[illegible]	[illegible]	[illegible]	[illegible]	[illegible]	[illegible]	[illegible]	[illegible]	[illegible]	[illegible]	[illegible]	[illegible]	[illegible]	[illegible]	[illegible]	[illegible]	[illegible]
32	Citizens' Savings Bank, Fall River	[illegible]	[illegible]	[illegible]	[illegible]	[illegible]	[illegible]	[illegible]	[illegible]	[illegible]	[illegible]	[illegible]	[illegible]	[illegible]	[illegible]	[illegible]	[illegible]	[illegible]	[illegible]	[illegible]
33	City Five Cts. Sav'gs B'k, Haverhill	[illegible]	[illegible]	[illegible]	[illegible]	[illegible]	[illegible]	[illegible]	[illegible]	[illegible]	[illegible]	[illegible]	[illegible]	[illegible]	[illegible]	[illegible]	[illegible]	[illegible]	[illegible]	[illegible]
34	City Institution for Savings, Lowell	[illegible]	[illegible]	[illegible]	[illegible]	[illegible]	[illegible]	[illegible]	[illegible]	[illegible]	[illegible]	[illegible]	[illegible]	[illegible]	[illegible]	[illegible]	[illegible]	[illegible]	[illegible]	[illegible]
35	Clinton Savings Bank	[illegible]	[illegible]	[illegible]	[illegible]	[illegible]	[illegible]	[illegible]	[illegible]	[illegible]	[illegible]	[illegible]	[illegible]	[illegible]	[illegible]	[illegible]	[illegible]	[illegible]	[illegible]	[illegible]
36	Cohasset Savings Bank	[illegible]	[illegible]	[illegible]	[illegible]	[illegible]	[illegible]	[illegible]	[illegible]	[illegible]	[illegible]	[illegible]	[illegible]	[illegible]	[illegible]	[illegible]	[illegible]	[illegible]	[illegible]	[illegible]
37	Crocker Inst. for Sav'gs, Turner's F'ls	[illegible]	[illegible]	[illegible]	[illegible]	[illegible]	[illegible]	[illegible]	[illegible]	[illegible]	[illegible]	[illegible]	[illegible]	[illegible]	[illegible]	[illegible]	[illegible]	[illegible]	[illegible]	[illegible]
38	Danvers Savings Bank	[illegible]	[illegible]	[illegible]	[illegible]	[illegible]	[illegible]	[illegible]	[illegible]	[illegible]	[illegible]	[illegible]	[illegible]	[illegible]	[illegible]	[illegible]	[illegible]	[illegible]	[illegible]	[illegible]
39	Dedham Institution for Savings	[illegible]	[illegible]	[illegible]	[illegible]	[illegible]	[illegible]	[illegible]	[illegible]	[illegible]	[illegible]	[illegible]	[illegible]	[illegible]	[illegible]	[illegible]	[illegible]	[illegible]	[illegible]	[illegible]
40	East Boston Savings Bank	[illegible]	[illegible]	[illegible]	[illegible]	[illegible]	[illegible]	[illegible]	[illegible]	[illegible]	[illegible]	[illegible]	[illegible]	[illegible]	[illegible]	[illegible]	[illegible]	[illegible]	[illegible]	[illegible]
41	East Bridgewater Savings Bank	[illegible]	[illegible]	[illegible]	[illegible]	[illegible]	[illegible]	[illegible]	[illegible]	[illegible]	[illegible]	[illegible]	[illegible]	[illegible]	[illegible]	[illegible]	[illegible]	[illegible]	[illegible]	[illegible]
42	E. Cambridge Five Cts. Savings B'k	[illegible]	[illegible]	[illegible]	[illegible]	[illegible]	[illegible]	[illegible]	[illegible]	[illegible]	[illegible]	[illegible]	[illegible]	[illegible]	[illegible]	[illegible]	[illegible]	[illegible]	[illegible]	[illegible]
43	[illegible] Savings Bank	[illegible]	[illegible]	[illegible]	[illegible]	[illegible]	[illegible]	[illegible]	[illegible]	[illegible]	[illegible]	[illegible]	[illegible]	[illegible]	[illegible]	[illegible]	[illegible]	[illegible]	[illegible]	[illegible]
44	[illegible] Weymouth Savings Bank	[illegible]	[illegible]	[illegible]	[illegible]	[illegible]	[illegible]	[illegible]	[illegible]	[illegible]	[illegible]	[illegible]	[illegible]	[illegible]	[illegible]	[illegible]	[illegible]	[illegible]	[illegible]	[illegible]
45	[illegible] Five Cents Savings Bank	[illegible]	[illegible]	[illegible]	[illegible]	[illegible]	[illegible]	[illegible]	[illegible]	[illegible]	[illegible]	[illegible]	[illegible]	[illegible]	[illegible]	[illegible]	[illegible]	[illegible]	[illegible]	[illegible]
46	Emigrant Savings Bank,* Boston	[illegible]	[illegible]	[illegible]	[illegible]	[illegible]	[illegible]	[illegible]	[illegible]	[illegible]	[illegible]	[illegible]	[illegible]	[illegible]	[illegible]	[illegible]	[illegible]	[illegible]	[illegible]	[illegible]
47	[illegible]	[illegible]	[illegible]	[illegible]	[illegible]	[illegible]	[illegible]	[illegible]	[illegible]	[illegible]	[illegible]	[illegible]	[illegible]	[illegible]	[illegible]	[illegible]	[illegible]	[illegible]	[illegible]	[illegible]
48	Fairhaven Institution for Savings	[illegible]	[illegible]	[illegible]	[illegible]	[illegible]	[illegible]	[illegible]	[illegible]	[illegible]	[illegible]	[illegible]	[illegible]	[illegible]	[illegible]	[illegible]	[illegible]	[illegible]	[illegible]	[illegible]
49	Fall River Five Cents Savings Bank	[illegible]	[illegible]	[illegible]	[illegible]	[illegible]	[illegible]	[illegible]	[illegible]	[illegible]	[illegible]	[illegible]	[illegible]	[illegible]	[illegible]	[illegible]	[illegible]	[illegible]	[illegible]	[illegible]
50	Fall River Savings Bank	[illegible]	[illegible]	[illegible]	[illegible]	[illegible]	[illegible]	[illegible]	[illegible]	[illegible]	[illegible]	[illegible]	[illegible]	[illegible]	[illegible]	[illegible]	[illegible]	[illegible]	[illegible]	[illegible]
51	Fitchburg Savings Bank	[illegible]	[illegible]	[illegible]	[illegible]	[illegible]	[illegible]	[illegible]	[illegible]	[illegible]	[illegible]	[illegible]	[illegible]	[illegible]	[illegible]	[illegible]	[illegible]	[illegible]	[illegible]	[illegible]
52	Florence Savings Bank	[illegible]	[illegible]	[illegible]	[illegible]	[illegible]	[illegible]	[illegible]	[illegible]	[illegible]	[illegible]	[illegible]	[illegible]	[illegible]	[illegible]	[illegible]	[illegible]	[illegible]	[illegible]	[illegible]
53	Foxborough Savings Bank*	[illegible]	[illegible]	[illegible]	[illegible]	[illegible]	[illegible]	[illegible]	[illegible]	[illegible]	[illegible]	[illegible]	[illegible]	[illegible]	[illegible]	[illegible]	[illegible]	[illegible]	[illegible]	[illegible]
54	Framingham Savings Bank	[illegible]	[illegible]	[illegible]	[illegible]	[illegible]	[illegible]	[illegible]	[illegible]	[illegible]	[illegible]	[illegible]	[illegible]	[illegible]	[illegible]	[illegible]	[illegible]	[illegible]	[illegible]	[illegible]
55	Franklin Savings Bank, Boston	[illegible]	[illegible]	[illegible]	[illegible]	[illegible]	[illegible]	[illegible]	[illegible]	[illegible]	[illegible]	[illegible]	[illegible]	[illegible]	[illegible]	[illegible]	[illegible]	[illegible]	[illegible]	[illegible]
56	Franklin Savings Inst., Greenfield	[illegible]	[illegible]	[illegible]	[illegible]	[illegible]	[illegible]	[illegible]	[illegible]	[illegible]	[illegible]	[illegible]	[illegible]	[illegible]	[illegible]	[illegible]	[illegible]	[illegible]	[illegible]	[illegible]
57	Gardner Savings Bank	[illegible]	[illegible]	[illegible]	[illegible]	[illegible]	[illegible]	[illegible]	[illegible]	[illegible]	[illegible]	[illegible]	[illegible]	[illegible]	[illegible]	[illegible]	[illegible]	[illegible]	[illegible]	[illegible]
58	Georgetown Savings Bank	[illegible]	[illegible]	[illegible]	[illegible]	[illegible]	[illegible]	[illegible]	[illegible]	[illegible]	[illegible]	[illegible]	[illegible]	[illegible]	[illegible]	[illegible]	[illegible]	[illegible]	[illegible]	[illegible]
59	Grafton Savings Bank	[illegible]	[illegible]	[illegible]	[illegible]	[illegible]	[illegible]	[illegible]	[illegible]	[illegible]	[illegible]	[illegible]	[illegible]	[illegible]	[illegible]	[illegible]	[illegible]	[illegible]	[illegible]	[illegible]
60	Great Barrington Savings Bank	[illegible]	[illegible]	[illegible]	[illegible]	[illegible]	[illegible]	[illegible]	[illegible]	[illegible]	[illegible]	[illegible]	[illegible]	[illegible]	[illegible]	[illegible]	[illegible]	[illegible]	[illegible]	[illegible]
61	Greenfield Savings Bank	[illegible]	[illegible]	[illegible]	[illegible]	[illegible]	[illegible]	[illegible]	[illegible]	[illegible]	[illegible]	[illegible]	[illegible]	[illegible]	[illegible]	[illegible]	[illegible]	[illegible]	[illegible]	[illegible]
62	Groveland Savings Bank	[illegible]	[illegible]	[illegible]	[illegible]	[illegible]	[illegible]	[illegible]	[illegible]	[illegible]	[illegible]	[illegible]	[illegible]	[illegible]	[illegible]	[illegible]	[illegible]	[illegible]	[illegible]	[illegible]
63	Hampden Savings Bank	[illegible]	[illegible]	[illegible]	[illegible]	[illegible]	[illegible]	[illegible]	[illegible]	[illegible]	[illegible]	[illegible]	[illegible]	[illegible]	[illegible]	[illegible]	[illegible]	[illegible]	[illegible]	[illegible]
64	Hampshire Savings Bank	[illegible]	[illegible]	[illegible]	[illegible]	[illegible]	[illegible]	[illegible]	[illegible]	[illegible]	[illegible]	[illegible]	[illegible]	[illegible]	[illegible]	[illegible]	[illegible]	[illegible]	[illegible]	[illegible]
65	Haverhill Savings Bank	[illegible]	[illegible]	[illegible]	[illegible]	[illegible]	[illegible]	[illegible]	[illegible]	[illegible]	[illegible]	[illegible]	[illegible]	[illegible]	[illegible]	[illegible]	[illegible]	[illegible]	[illegible]	[illegible]
66	Haydenville Savings Bank	[illegible]	[illegible]	[illegible]	[illegible]	[illegible]	[illegible]	[illegible]	[illegible]	[illegible]	[illegible]	[illegible]	[illegible]	[illegible]	[illegible]	[illegible]	[illegible]	[illegible]	[illegible]	[illegible]
67	Hingham Institution for Savings	[illegible]	[illegible]	[illegible]	[illegible]	[illegible]	[illegible]	[illegible]	[illegible]	[illegible]	[illegible]	[illegible]	[illegible]	[illegible]	[illegible]	[illegible]	[illegible]	[illegible]	[illegible]	[illegible]
68	Holliston Savings Bank	[illegible]	[illegible]	[illegible]	[illegible]	[illegible]	[illegible]	[illegible]	[illegible]	[illegible]	[illegible]	[illegible]	[illegible]	[illegible]	[illegible]	[illegible]	[illegible]	[illegible]	[illegible]	[illegible]
69	Holyoke Savings Bank	[illegible]	[illegible]	[illegible]	[illegible]	[illegible]	[illegible]	[illegible]	[illegible]	[illegible]	[illegible]	[illegible]	[illegible]	[illegible]	[illegible]	[illegible]	[illegible]	[illegible]	[illegible]	[illegible]
70	Home Savings Bank	[illegible]	[illegible]	[illegible]	[illegible]	[illegible]	[illegible]	[illegible]	[illegible]	[illegible]	[illegible]	[illegible]	[illegible]	[illegible]	[illegible]	[illegible]	[illegible]	[illegible]	[illegible]	[illegible]
71	Hoosac Savings Bank	[illegible]	[illegible]	[illegible]	[illegible]	[illegible]	[illegible]	[illegible]	[illegible]	[illegible]	[illegible]	[illegible]	[illegible]	[illegible]	[illegible]	[illegible]	[illegible]	[illegible]	[illegible]	[illegible]
72	Hopkinton Savings Bank	[illegible]	[illegible]	[illegible]	[illegible]	[illegible]	[illegible]	[illegible]	[illegible]	[illegible]	[illegible]	[illegible]	[illegible]	[illegible]	[illegible]	[illegible]	[illegible]	[illegible]	[illegible]	[illegible]
73	Hudson Savings Bank	[illegible]	[illegible]	[illegible]	[illegible]	[illegible]	[illegible]	[illegible]	[illegible]	[illegible]	[illegible]	[illegible]	[illegible]	[illegible]	[illegible]	[illegible]	[illegible]	[illegible]	[illegible]	[illegible]
74	Hyde Park Savings Bank	[illegible]	[illegible]	[illegible]	[illegible]	[illegible]	[illegible]	[illegible]	[illegible]	[illegible]	[illegible]	[illegible]	[illegible]	[illegible]	[illegible]	[illegible]	[illegible]	[illegible]	[illegible]	[illegible]
75	Institution for Savings in Roxbury	[illegible]	[illegible]	[illegible]	[illegible]	[illegible]	[illegible]	[illegible]	[illegible]	[illegible]	[illegible]	[illegible]	[illegible]	[illegible]	[illegible]	[illegible]	[illegible]	[illegible]	[illegible]	[illegible]
76	Inst. for Savings in Newburyport	[illegible]	[illegible]	[illegible]	[illegible]	[illegible]	[illegible]	[illegible]	[illegible]	[illegible]	[illegible]	[illegible]	[illegible]	[illegible]	[illegible]	[illegible]	[illegible]	[illegible]	[illegible]	[illegible]
77	Ipswich Savings Bank	[illegible]	[illegible]	[illegible]	[illegible]	[illegible]	[illegible]	[illegible]	[illegible]	[illegible]	[illegible]	[illegible]	[illegible]	[illegible]	[illegible]	[illegible]	[illegible]	[illegible]	[illegible]	[illegible]
78	Lawrence Savings Bank	[illegible]	[illegible]	[illegible]	[illegible]	[illegible]	[illegible]	[illegible]	[illegible]	[illegible]	[illegible]	[illegible]	[illegible]	[illegible]	[illegible]	[illegible]	[illegible]	[illegible]	[illegible]	[illegible]
79	Lee Savings Bank	[illegible]	[illegible]	[illegible]	[illegible]	[illegible]	[illegible]	[illegible]	[illegible]	[illegible]	[illegible]	[illegible]	[illegible]	[illegible]	[illegible]	[illegible]	[illegible]	[illegible]	[illegible]	[illegible]
80	Leicester Savings Bank	[illegible]	[illegible]	[illegible]	[illegible]	[illegible]	[illegible]	[illegible]	[illegible]	[illegible]	[illegible]	[illegible]	[illegible]	[illegible]	[illegible]	[illegible]	[illegible]	[illegible]	[illegible]	[illegible]
81	Leominster Savings Bank	[illegible]	[illegible]	[illegible]	[illegible]	[illegible]	[illegible]	[illegible]	[illegible]	[illegible]	[illegible]	[illegible]	[illegible]	[illegible]	[illegible]	[illegible]	[illegible]	[illegible]	[illegible]	[illegible]
82	Lowell Five Cents Savings Bank	[illegible]	[illegible]	[illegible]	[illegible]	[illegible]	[illegible]	[illegible]	[illegible]	[illegible]	[illegible]	[illegible]	[illegible]	[illegible]	[illegible]	[illegible]	[illegible]	[illegible]	[illegible]	[illegible]

Name of Bank	Figures
Lawrence Savings Bank	[illegible]
Lowell Five Cents Savings Bank	[illegible]
Lowell Institution for Savings	[illegible]
Lynn Five Cents Savings Bank	[illegible]
Lynn Institution for Savings	[illegible]
Malden Savings Bank	[illegible]
Marblehead Savings Bank	[illegible]
Marlborough Savings Bank	[illegible]
Mechanics' Savings Bank, Holyoke	[illegible]
Mechanics' Savings Bank, Lowell	[illegible]
Medford Savings Bank	[illegible]
Medway Savings Bank	[illegible]
Melrose Savings Bank	[illegible]
Merchants' Savings Bank, Merrimac	[illegible]
Merrimack River Sav'gs B'k, Lowell	[illegible]
Middleborough Savings Bank	[illegible]
Middlesex Inst. for Savings, Concord	[illegible]
Milford Savings Bank	[illegible]
Millbury Savings Bank	[illegible]
Monson Savings B'k, W. Stockbridge	[illegible]
Monson Savings Bank	[illegible]
Nantucket Institution for Savings	[illegible]
Natick Five Cents Savings Bank	[illegible]
New Bedford Five Cts. Savings Bank	[illegible]
New Bedford Institution for Savings	[illegible]
Newburyport Five Cts. Savings Bank	[illegible]
Newton Savings Bank	[illegible]
Northampton Institution for Savings	[illegible]
North Adams Savings Bank	[illegible]
N. Avenue Savings B'k, Cambridge	[illegible]
North Brookfield Savings Bank	[illegible]
North Easton Savings Bank	[illegible]
North End Savings Bank, Boston	[illegible]
Orange Savings Bank	[illegible]
Palmer Savings Bank	[illegible]
People's Savings Bank, Worcester	[illegible]
Plymouth Five Cents Savings Bank	[illegible]
Plymouth Savings Bank	[illegible]
Provident Inst. for Savings, Boston	[illegible]
Prov. Inst. Sav., Salisb'y & Amesb'y	[illegible]
Quincy Savings Bank	[illegible]
Randolph Savings Bank	[illegible]
Rockland Savings Bank	[illegible]
Salem Five Cents Savings Bank	[illegible]
Salem Savings Bank	[illegible]
Seamen's Savings Bank	[illegible]
Shelburne Falls Savings Bank	[illegible]
South Adams Savings Bank	[illegible]
Southbridge Savings Bank	[illegible]
South Boston Savings Bank	[illegible]
South Scituate Savings Bank	[illegible]
South Weymouth Savings Bank	[illegible]
Spencer Savings Bank	[illegible]
Springfield Five Cts. Savings Bank	[illegible]
Springfield Institution for Savings	[illegible]
Stockbridge Savings Bank	[illegible]
Stoneham Five Cents Savings Bank	[illegible]
Suffolk Savings Bank	[illegible]
Taunton Savings Bank	[illegible]
Templeton Savings Bank	[illegible]
Union Inst. for Savings, Boston	[illegible]
Union Savings Bank, Fall River	[illegible]
Uxbridge Savings Bank	[illegible]
Wakefield Savings Bank	[illegible]
Wales Savings Bank	[illegible]
Waltham Savings Bank	[illegible]
Ware Savings Bank	[illegible]
Wareham Savings Bank	[illegible]
Warren Five Cts. Sav. B'k, Peabody	[illegible]
Warren Inst. for Savings, Boston	[illegible]
Watertown Savings Bank	[illegible]
Webster Five Cents Savings Bank	[illegible]
Wellfleet Savings Bank	[illegible]
Westborough Savings Bank	[illegible]
Westfield Savings Bank	[illegible]
Weymouth Savings Bank	[illegible]
Whitinsville Savings Bank	[illegible]
Winchendon Savings Bank	[illegible]
Winchester Savings Bank	[illegible]
Woburn Five Cents Savings Bank	[illegible]
Worcester County Inst. for Savings	[illegible]
Worcester Five Cents Savings Bank	[illegible]
Worcester Mechanics' Savings Bank	[illegible]
Worcester North Savings Institution	[illegible]
Woronoco Savings Bank, Westfield	[illegible]
Total of 143 Banks	[illegible]

* Temporarily enjoined.

† Amount invested in United States bonds, [illegible]; amount invested in State, County, City, and Town bonds, [illegible].

BANKS IN THE HANDS OF RECEIVERS.

BARNSTABLE SAVINGS BANK — BARNSTABLE.

Incorporated Jan. 29, 1831; perpetually enjoined by decree of Supreme Judicial Court May 23, 1878.

GUSTAVUS A. HINCKLEY, SAMUEL SNOW, *Receivers.*

STATEMENT.

LIABILITIES.		ASSETS.	
Deposits . . .	$429,791 52	Real estate	$4,000 00
		Real estate acquired by foreclosure . . .	142,620 87
		Mortgage loans . . .	180 43
		Personal loans	63,416 79
		Profit and loss	172,713 48
		Deposits in national banks,	35,568 57
		Cash on hand . . .	11,291 38
	$429,791 52		$429,791 52

Amount of assets delivered to the receivers $1,274,040 81
Date of delivery: June 11, 1878.
Amount due depositors at time the bank was placed in hands of receivers 1,291,302 05
Corrected amount 1,287,614 04
Further corrected (by amount set off under statute, 1878, chap. 261) 1,286,407 94
Date, percentage, and amount of dividends allowed by the Supreme Judicial Court: Oct. 15, 1878, 25 per cent, $321,893.72; July 2, 1879, 25 per cent, $321,893.72; Oct. 11, 1880, 10 per cent, $128,749.88; September, 1881, 10 per cent, $128,629.28.
Amount of each dividend paid to date . . . . { 320,924 58; 320,500 51; 125,645 30; 89,544 91 }
Number of open accounts 3,228
Number and amount of open accounts on which no dividend has been claimed or paid 38 2,670 52
Estimated amount to be realized from remaining assets applicable to payment of dividends 160,000 00
Amount of each class of assets disposed of to date, and amount of profit or loss on each: bank stock, $249,065, profit, $564.54; city and town bonds and notes, $47,553.12, loss, $271.87; real estate, $248,276.33, loss, $29,163.78; mortgage loans, $554,013.82, loss, $131,803.47; personal loans, $163,747.10, loss, $12,709.80.
Amount of expenses of receivership to date 10,155 53
Date of examination by commissioner: July 1.

DORCHESTER SAVINGS BANK — BOSTON.

Incorporated 1853; perpetually enjoined by decree of Supreme Judicial Court Feb. 26, 1878.

RICHARD C. HUMPHREYS, J. FRANK POPE, *Receivers.*

STATEMENT.

Amount of assets delivered to receivers		$412,124 27
Date of delivery: March 1, 1878.		
Amount due depositors at time the bank was placed in hands of receivers		398,161 65
Percentage and amount of dividends allowed by Supreme Judicial Court*	$92\frac{65}{100}$	368,883 87
Balance now due depositors†		1,038 29

* Final dividend allowed Oct. 1, 1880.

† This balance has since been deposited with the treasurer of the Commonwealth agreeably to the provisions of chap. 70 of the Acts of 1881.

HYANNIS SAVINGS BANK — HYANNIS.

Incorporated April, 1868; perpetually enjoined by decree of Supreme Judicial Court, Sept. 11, 1878.

JOSEPH R. HALL, FRANK THACHER, *Receivers.*

STATEMENT.

LIABILITIES.		ASSETS.	
Deposits . . .	$200,596 97	Mortgage loans . . .	$14,391 88
		Real estate acquired by foreclosure . . .	45,386 12
		Personal loans . . .	4,104 89
		Suspense account . .	300 00
		Profit and loss . . .	74,956 67
		Shawmut National Bank .	40,065 30
		First National Bank . .	20,556 92
		Cash	835 19
	$200,596 97		$200,596 97

Amount of assets delivered to the receivers	$529,058 64
Date of delivery: Sept. 16, 1878.	
Amount due depositors at time the bank was placed in hands of receivers	524,617 05
Date, percentage, and amount of dividends allowed by Supreme Judicial Court: Jan. 8, 1879, 25 per cent, $131,154.26; Sept. 25, 1879, 25 per cent, $131,154.26; May 22, 1880, 12½ per cent, $65,577.13.	
Amount of each dividend paid to date	130,055 56 129,948 56 64,020 08

Number of open accounts	1,584	
Number and amount of open accounts on which no dividend has been claimed or paid	44	$1,410 04
Estimated amount to be realized from remaining assets applicable to payment of dividends, etc.		82,000 00
Amount of each class of assets disposed of to date, and amount of profit or loss on each: bank stock, $125,210.50, loss, $32,551.51; bonds, $31,301.25, profit, $254.07; personal loans, $100,381.80, loss, $21,938.43; mortgage, $121,371.17, loss, $5,471.61; real estate, $82,623.01, loss, $35,385.55.		
Amount of expenses of receivership to date		6,269 93
Date of examination by commissioner: July 1.		

LANCASTER SAVINGS BANK — LANCASTER.

Incorporated 1845; perpetually enjoined by decree of Supreme Judicial Court Dec. 30, 1875.

William H. McNeil, Elisha Brimhall, Benjamin Snow, *Receivers.*

Statement.

Liabilities.		Assets.	
Deposits . . .	$451,417 50	Loans on real estate . .	$18,000 00
Dividends unpaid .	3,392 24	Real estate acquired . .	245,400 00
		Profit and loss . . .	168,429 40
		Cash	22,980 34
	$454,809 74		$454,809 74

Amount of assets delivered to the receivers		$1,030,523 27
Date of delivery: Jan. 1, 1876.		
Amount due depositors at time the bank was placed in hands of receivers		973,390 36
Date, percentage, and amount of dividends allowed by the Supreme Judicial Court: June 10, 1876, 33⅓ per cent, $324,463.45; Nov. 19, 1877, 10 per cent, $96,732.32; Oct. 29, 1878, 10 per cent, $96,732.32.		
Amount of each dividend paid to date		323,514 89 95,948 13 95,072 83
Number of open accounts	2,397	
Number and amount of open accounts on which no dividend has been claimed or paid	28	2,765 68
Estimated amount to be realized from remaining assets applicable to payment of dividends		75,000 00
Amount of each class of assets disposed of to date, and amount of profit or loss on each: bank stock, $76,300, profit, $15,559.50; loans on bank stock, $2,000; loans on public		

fund, $1,075; loans on railroad stock, $1,092, loss, $366.75; loans on mortgage of real estate, $338,706.27, loss, $70,604.18; loans on personal security, $290,850, loss, $126,889.37; loans on railroad bonds, $31,500, loss, $20,326.92.

Amount of expenses of receivership to date: viz., receivers, $10,757.99; advertising, $529.09; stationery, $171.37; rent, $250; commissions, $600.53; insurance, $1,033.63; engineers, experts, etc., $171.43; expenses of real estate, $4,206.34; clerical expenses, $2,964.66; taxes, $9,135.42; recording and conveyancing, $256.80; legal expenses, $2,474.41 . . . . $33,151 67

Date of examination by commissioner: Dec. 6.

LEXINGTON SAVINGS BANK — LEXINGTON.

Incorporated March, 1871; perpetually enjoined by decree of Supreme Judicial Court Dec. 13, 1878.

GEORGE W. ROBINSON, *Receiver*.

STATEMENT.

LIABILITIES.		ASSETS.	
Due depositors . .	$24,443 17	Mortgage loans . . .	$3,000 00
Surplus . . .	7,891 15	Loans on personal security,	39 79
		Real estate acquired by foreclosure . . .	21,100 00
		Real estate acquired by purchase	431 89
		Cash on hand and in bank .	7,162 64
	$32,334 32		$32,334 32

Amount of assets delivered to the receiver $101,209 89

Date of delivery: Dec. 24, 1878.

Amount due depositors at time the bank was placed in hands of receiver 95,222 52

Date, percentage, and amount of dividends allowed by the Supreme Judicial Court: December, 1878, 25 per cent, $23,805.63; August, 1879, 25 per cent, $23,805.63; February, 1880, 25 per cent, $23,805.63.

Amount of each dividend paid to date . . . { 23,667 57 / 23,633 55 / 23,478 23

Number of open accounts 473

Number and amount of open accounts on which no dividend has been claimed or paid 61 487 28

Estimated amount to be realized from remaining assets applicable to payment of dividends 29,562 64

Amount of each class of assets disposed of to date, and amount of profit or loss on each: mortgage loans, $30,700, at par; loans on personal security, $21,750, profit, $200; on sales of real estate acquired by foreclosure, profit, $150.

Amount of expenses of receivership to date . . . 365 82

Date of examination by commissioner: Aug. 15.

MECHANICS' SAVINGS BANK — BOSTON.

Incorporated March 30, 1874; perpetually enjoined by decree of Supreme Judicial Court Feb. 1, 1877.

GEORGE R. DWELLEY, JOHN F. COLBY, *Receivers*.

STATEMENT.

Amount of assets delivered to the receivers	$421,960 33
Date of delivery: Feb. 21, 1877.	
Amount due depositors at time the bank was placed in hands of the receivers	428,934 92
Percentage and amount of dividends allowed by Supreme Judicial Court: 72⅓ per cent*	309,502 45
Balance now due depositors	833 50

* Final dividend allowed May 9, 1879.

MERCANTILE SAVINGS INSTITUTION — BOSTON.

Incorporated 1861; perpetually enjoined by decree of Supreme Judicial Court Feb. 20, 1878.

ALVAH A. BURRAGE, HENRY G. CROWELL, ALPHONSO J. ROBINSON, *Receivers*.

STATEMENT.

LIABILITIES.		ASSETS.	
To depositors, after fourth dividend .	$1,154,321 18	Balance J. A. McNabb's note, new	$7 60
To balance first dividend unpaid . .	2,657 74	Summer-street lease acc't,*	20,071 39
To balance second dividend unpaid .	1,569 38	Bank furniture . . .	530 16
To balance third dividend unpaid .	3,092 95	Estates owned by the institution	131,121 30
To balance fourth dividend unpaid . .	8,363 74	Expenses on mortgaged estates account . . .	19 63
To persons at present unknown . . .	330 60	Expenses in suits account .	5 72
To excess from sales of mortgaged estates,	135 92	Profit and loss account .	683,456 33
To suspense account .	5,425 00	Cash on hand . . .	547,758 87
To capital stock . .	205,200 00		
To dividends on capital stock . . .	1,793 79		
To rent account . .	80 70		
	$1,382,971 00		$1,382,971 00

Amount of assets delivered to receivers	$3,519,294 70
Date of delivery: Feb. 27, 1878.	
Amount due depositors at time the bank was placed in hands of receivers	3,208,060 66

* Held to apply on this account: $12,000 ten per cent bonds of Lowe Township, Moultrie County, Ill.; $14,000 ten per cent bonds of Unity Township, Platt County, Ill. In process of collection.

Date, percentage, and amount of dividends allowed by Supreme Judicial Court: May 13, 1878, 20 per cent, $659,612.15; Jan. 1, 1879, 10 per cent, $329,806.08; Nov. 10, 1879, 15 per cent, $494,709.11; Nov. 10, 1880, 20 per cent, $659,612.14.

Amount of each dividend paid to date . . { $656,954 41; 328,236 70; 491,616 16; 651,248 40 }

Number of open accounts 9,792

Number and amount of open accounts on which no dividend has been claimed or paid . . . . 702 | 13,128 25

Estimated amount to be realized from remaining assets applicable to payment of dividends 577,000 00

Amount of each class of assets disposed of to date, and amount of profit or loss on each: mortgages, $1,448,539.27, loss, $137,392.54; estates in possession, $572,230.73, loss, $190,676.42; estates owned, $276,328.33, loss, $116,780.13; personal securities, $58,965.17, loss, $25,115.66; railroad bonds, $187,700, profit, $5,496.46; public funds, $429,500, profit, $32,633.43; loans to towns, $33,225, profit, $601.78; bank stock, $12,600, loss, $1,821.63; pianos, $5,348.79, loss, $1,566.76; suspense account, $1,012.50, profit, $153.69; bank building, $176,725.81, loss, $68,516.46.

Amount of expenses of receivership to date . . . 56,682 04

Date of examination by commissioner: July 30.

NEEDHAM SAVINGS BANK — NEEDHAM.

Incorporated April 7, 1874; perpetually enjoined by decree of Supreme Judicial Court March 4, 1879.

EMERY GROVER, *Receiver*.

STATEMENT.

LIABILITIES.		ASSETS.	
Due depositors . .	$6,252 02	Real estate	$1,100 00
Interest collected .	1,632 60	Loans on real estate . .	850 00
		Loans on personal securities,	1,650 00
		Judgment	735 00
		Furniture	519 36
		Cash on hand and in bank .	3,030 26
	$7,884 62		$7,884 62

Amount of assets delivered to the receiver . . . $23,623 37

Date of delivery: March 4, 1879.

Amount due depositors at time the bank was placed in hands of receiver 23,354 17

Date, percentage, and amount of dividends allowed by Supreme Judicial Court: July 23, 1879, 25 per cent, $5,837.86; Feb. 4, 1880, 25 per cent, $5,837.86; June 17, 1881, 25 per cent, $5,837.86.

Amount of each dividend paid to date		$5,802 72 5,756 28 5,543 15
Number of open accounts	209	
Number and amount of open accounts on which no dividend has been claimed or paid	32	141 08
Estimated amount to be realized from remaining assets applicable to payment of dividends		7,000 00

Amount of each class of assets disposed of to date, and amount of profit or loss on each: bank stock, $1,680.50, loss, $445.50; mortgages on real estate, $16,550, loss, $120; loans on personal securities, $1,785.

Amount of expenses of receivership to date	260 34

Date of examination by commissioner: Dec. 31.

NORTH BRIDGEWATER SAVINGS BANK — BROCKTON.

Incorporated April 24, 1851; perpetually enjoined by decree of Supreme Judicial Court Nov. 13, 1877.

RUFUS P. KINGMAN, ELLIS AMES, *Receivers.*

STATEMENT.

LIABILITIES.		ASSETS.	
Due depositors	$110,272 05	Mortgage loan	$31,608 23
Suspense account	6,055 57	Personal loan	26,654 39
Profit and loss	16,765 80	Real estate	1,900 00
Interest	57,083 90	Bank stock	2,385 24
Dividends unpaid	8,832 42	E. Southworth	68,091 84
		Dunbar & Co.	2,852 51
		Furniture and fixtures	208 55
		Expense	16,666 48
		Cash in bank	47,415 20
		Cash on hand	1,227 30
	$199,009 74		$199,009 74

Amount of assets delivered to receivers	$450,840 40

Date of delivery: Nov. 19, 1877.

Amount due depositors at time the bank was placed in hands of receivers	553,000 21

Date, percentage, and amount of dividends allowed by Supreme Judicial Court: Jan. 22, 1878, 25 per cent, $137.840.08; Oct. 8, 1878, 25 per cent, $137,840.07; Aug. 22, 1879, 15 per cent, $82,704.04; July 8, 1880, 15 per cent, $82,704.04.

Amount of each dividend paid to date		35,694 10 135,421 31 80,898 51 80,241 89
Number of open accounts	2,297	
Number and amount of open accounts on which no dividend has been claimed or paid	88	8,571 04
Estimated amount to be realized from remaining assets applicable to the payment of dividends		60,000 00

Amount of each class of assets disposed of to date, and amount of profit or loss on each: bonds, $17,152.50, profit, $150.32; bank stock, $25,088.50, loss, $525.50; mortgage loan, $241,171.23, loss, $1,670; personal loan, $96,181.70, loss, $3,922.80.

Amount of expenses of receivership to date $16,666 48

Date of examination by commissioner: July 6.

READING SAVINGS BANK — READING.

Incorporated July 14, 1869; perpetually enjoined by decree of Supreme Judicial Court April 11, 1879.

WILLIAM J. HOLDEN, SOLON BANCROFT, *Receivers.*

STATEMENT.

LIABILITIES.		ASSETS.	
Due depositors . .	$136,042 96	Mortgage loans	$41,805 00
Interest account .	6,178 29	Personal loans	8,374 00
The depositors' account has been increased by the allowance, by the Supreme Judicial Court, of a claim made upon a book which represented no actual deposit. Other contested claims to a large amount were submitted to the full Court in March last, and now await its decision. Until a decision is made, it is impossible to tell upon what amount dividends should be paid.		United States bonds . .	1,000 00
		Bank stock	2,900 00
		Due from late treasurer .	38,387 74
		Expense	4,412 51
		Note of E. Wight . .	409 41
		Real estate	13,293 31
		Profit and loss . . .	283 12
		Cash	31,356 16
	$142,221 25		$142,221 25

Amount of assets delivered to the receivers $108,962 81

Date of delivery: April 23, 1879.

Assets afterwards recovered by the receivers 4,250 00

Amount due depositors at time the bank was placed in hands of receivers 155,345 69

Date, percentage, and amount of dividend allowed by Supreme Judicial Court: Nov. 3, 1879, 12½ per cent* 19,418 21

Amount of dividend paid to date 19,302 73

Number of open accounts 681

Number and amount of open accounts on which no dividend has been claimed or paid 33 936 16

Estimated amount to be realized from remaining assets applicable to payment of dividends 16,545 00

Amount of each class of assets disposed of to date, and amount of profit or loss on each: real estate and mortgages, $35,448, loss, $231.36; personal notes, $8,290.80, — all at par.

* Another dividend of fifteen per cent allowed Nov. 23, 1881.

Amount of expenses of receivership to date $4,412 51
Date of examination by commissioner: Dec. 3.

The amount of assets as given above includes notes and mortgages which are claimed by other parties, the ownership of which is to be determined by judicial proceedings.

ROCKPORT SAVINGS BANK — ROCKPORT.

Incorporated 1853; perpetually enjoined by decree of Supreme Judicial Court Feb. 26, 1878.

CHARLES P. THOMPSON, JOSEPH MANNING, *Receivers.*

STATEMENT.

LIABILITIES.		ASSETS.	
Amount due depositors	$55,676 73	Profit and loss	$24,584 69
		Cash on hand and in bank .	31,092 04
	$55,676 73		$55,676 73

Amount of assets delivered to the receivers $194,459 71
Date of delivery: Feb. 26, 1878.
Amount due depositors at time the bank was placed in hands of receivers 182,415 58
Corrected amount 182,320 88
Date, percentage, and amount of dividends allowed by Supreme Judicial Court:* Oct. 23, 1878, 25 per cent, $45,580.22; Oct. 3, 1879, 20 per cent, $36,464.17; Aug. 18, 1880, 25 per cent, $45,580.22,
Amount of each dividend paid to date . . . . { 45,403 32 / 36,128 38 / 45,019 36 }
Number of open accounts 882
Number and amount of open accounts on which no dividend has been claimed or paid 12 175 63
Amount of each class of assets disposed of to date, and amount of profit or loss on each: mortgages, $100,822.11, loss, $22,340.89; real estate, $24,207, loss, $16,037.14; bank stock, $22,255.12, loss, $1,610.93; personal notes, $3,370, loss, $125.
Amount of expenses of receivership to date 6,422 26
Date of examination by commissioner: Sept. 15.

* Final dividend of fourteen and seven-tenths per cent allowed since this report was compiled.

SANDWICH SAVINGS BANK — SANDWICH.

Incorporated 1866; perpetually enjoined by decree of Supreme Judicial Court Jan. 29, 1878.

H. G. O. Ellis, *Receiver.*

Statement.

Liabilities.		Assets.	
Due depositors . .	$29,691 34	Personal loans . . .	$740 00
Due G. C. Hoag . .	58 51	Mortgage loans . . .	11,840 89
		Real estate held by foreclosure	1,050 00
		Cash (dividends unpaid) .	2,653 80
		Cash on hand . . .	2,191 77
		Deficit	11,273 39
	$29,749 85		$29,749 85

Amount of assets delivered to the receivers $109,586 22

Date of delivery: April 1, 1878,

Amount due depositors at time the bank was placed in hands of receivers 108,145 35

Date, percentage, and amount of dividends allowed by Supreme Judicial Court: Aug. 23, 1878, 30 per cent. $32,442.95; Oct. 22, 1879, 15 per cent, $16,221.62; Sept. 24, 1880, 15 per cent, $16,221.62; June 14, 1881, 15 per cent, $16,221.62.

Amount of each dividend paid to date . . . { 32,249 85; 16,016 09; 15,722 25; 14,465 82 }

Number of open accounts 517

Number and amount of open accounts on which no dividend has been claimed or paid 17 193 10

Estimated amount to be realized from remaining assets applicable to payment of dividends 6,000 00

Amount of each class of assets disposed of to date, and amount of profit or loss on each: mortgage loans, $56,872.11, loss, $17,775; personal loans, $23,973, loss, $198; bonds, $14,000, profit. $1,630.

Interest received from all sources 11,477 52

Amount of expenses of receivership to date 4,624 47

Date of examination by commissioner: July 31.

SCITUATE SAVINGS BANK — SCITUATE.

Incorporated May 31, 1851; perpetually enjoined by decree of Supreme Judicial Court July 9, 1880.

EBENEZER T. FOGG, WILLARD TORREY, *Receivers.*

STATEMENT.

LIABILITIES.		ASSETS.	
Deposits . . .	$101,555 79	Loans on mortgages of real estate	$26,886 00
Unpaid dividends .	148 11	Loans on personal securities,	3,564 90
		Real estate by foreclosure .	36,850 00
		Due on bond . . .	3,250 00
		Profit and loss . . .	4,604 81
		Cash on hand . . .	26,548 19
	$101,703 90		$101,703 90

Amount of assets delivered to the receivers		$125,486 44
Date of delivery: July 23, 1880.		
Amount due depositors at time the bank was placed in hands of receivers, being $80.24 less than Oct. 31, 1880, occasioned by errors in books		127,181 29
Date, percentage, and amount of dividends allowed by Supreme Judicial Court:* Sept. 11, 1880, 20 per cent, $25,625.50.		
Amount of dividend paid to date		25,477 39
Number of open accounts	341	
Number and amount of open accounts on which no dividend has been claimed or paid	9	148 11
Estimated amount to be realized from remaining assets applicable to payment of dividends		55,550 00
Amount of each class of assets disposed of to date, and amount of profit or loss on each: real estate, $15,800, loss, $4,235; mortgages, $12,169.50, loss, $50; notes, $2,885.43, at par value; bank stock, $4,200, loss, $170.		
Amount of expenses of receivership to date		467 96
Date of examination by commissioner: Oct. 13.		

* Another dividend of twenty per cent allowed Nov. 15, 1881.

WEST BOSTON SAVINGS BANK — BOSTON.

Incorporated 1867; perpetually enjoined by decree of Supreme Judicial Court Jan. 9, 1878.

LYMAN P. FRENCH, CLEMENT WILLIS, *Receivers.*

STATEMENT.

LIABILITIES.		ASSETS.	
Deposits . . .	$471,240 64	Profit and loss . . .	$251,591 83
		Cash	219,648 81
	$471,240 64		$471,240 64

Amount of assets delivered to the receivers . . . $1,930,897 59

Date of delivery: Jan. 12, 1878.

Amount due depositors at time the bank was placed in hands of receivers 1,822,015 83

Date, percentage, and amount of dividends allowed by Supreme Judicial Court:* June 10, 1878, 25 per cent, $455,503.96; Feb. 17, 1879, 15 per cent, $273,302.37; April 21, 1879, 10 per cent, $182,201.58; Oct. 6, 1879, 15 per cent, $273,302.37; June 23, 1880, 10 per cent, $182,201.58.

Amount of each dividend paid to date . . { 453,410 44; 271,753 27; 180,988 11; 270,245 74; 174,377 63 }

Number of open accounts 5,451

Number and amount of open accounts on which no dividend has been claimed or paid 634 2,093 52

Amount of each class of assets disposed of to date, and amount of profit or loss on each: real estate and loans on real estate, $1,533,315.71, loss, $343,042.41; loans on personal security, $71,825.10, loss, $60,107.86; bank stocks, $208,753.26, loss, $46,004.62; public funds, $48,855, loss, $948.75; railroad bonds, $3,165, profit, $135; loans on bank stock, $700; loan to town of Braintree, $20,000, at par value.

Expenses of receivership to date: repairs on real estate, $13,593.21; taxes, including corporation tax, $27,278.50; auction, commission, and registry expenses, $8,056.69; cancelling lease, $1,600; legal expenses, $4,514.86; clerical expense, $7,464.50; receivers' allowance, $12,000; rent of rooms, $2,271.57; stationery and printing, $520.70; miscellaneous expenses, including postage and revenue stamps, $1,178.38 . . . . 78,478 41

Date of examination by commissioner: Oct. 19.

* Final dividend of ten per cent allowed Nov. 29, 1881.

AGGREGATE STATEMENT OF BANKS IN THE HANDS OF RECEIVERS—1881.

Liabilities.		Assets.	
Deposits . . .	$3,171,301 87	Public funds . . .	$1,000 00
Sundries . . .	336,688 41	Bank stock	5,285 24
		Real estate	20,293 31
		Real estate by foreclosure .	247,438 88
		Loans on real estate . .	394,562 43
		Loans on personal security,	108,544 76
		Profit and loss . . .	1,380,620 33
		Sundries	290,243 00
		Cash on hand and in banks,	1,048,728 94
		Deficit	11,273 39
	$3,507,990 28		$3,507,990 28

AGGREGATE STATEMENT OF BANKS IN THE HANDS OF RECEIVERS—1880.

Liabilities.		Assets.	
Deposits . . .	$4,046,122 09	Bank stock	$12,611 24
Sundries . . .	123,531 79	Railroad bonds . . .	31,500 00
		Real estate	174,345 63
		Real estate by foreclosure .	1,118,539 19
		Loans on real estate . .	594,314 40
		Loans on personal security,	257,713 62
		Profit and loss . . .	548,416 40
		Sundries	181,902 33
		Cash on hand and in banks,	992,305 90
		Deficit	258,005 17
	$4,169,653 88		$4,169,653 88

TABLE exhibiting the Number, Condition, and Progress of the Savings Banks of Massachusetts in each Year from 1834 to 1881 inclusive.
(Returns first required by Acts 1834, Chap. 190.)

YEAR.	No. of Banks.	Number of Deposit Accounts.	Increase in Number of Accounts over Previous Year.	Percentage of Increase.	Amount of Deposits.	Increase in Am't of Deposits over Previous Year.	Percentage of Increase.	Average to each Account.	Population of Massachusetts.	Deposits to each Person of Population.	Expense of Management.	Percentage of Expense to Total Deposits.
1834 .	22	24,256	–	–	$3,407,773 00	–	–	$140 09	614,408*	$5 58	$10,968 00	
1835 .	27	27,232	2,976	12	3,921,370 00	$513,597 00	15	143 99	–	–	12,066 00	
1836 .	28	29,786	2,554	9	4,374,578 00	453,208 00	11½	146 19	–	–	14,413 00	.0033
1837 .	30	32,564	2,778	9⅓	4,781,426 00	406,848 00	9⅓	146 51	–	–	17,504 00	
1838 .	30	33,063	499	1½	4,869,393 00	87,967 00	2	147 27	–	–	18,329 00	
1839 .	30	36,686	3,623	11	5,608,159 00	738,766 00	15¼	152 86	–	–	17,204 00	
1840 .	31	37,470	784	2	5,819,554 00	211,395 00	3¾	157 98	737,609	7 88	17,952 00	
1841 .	30	41,423	3,953	10½	6,714,182 00	894,628 00	15½	162 08	–	–	19,248 00	
1842 .	–	42,587	1,164	2⅔	6,900,451 00	186,270 00	2¾	162 03	–	–	–	
1843 .	31	43,217	630	1½	6,935,547 00	35,095 00	½	160 40	–	–	20,777 00	
1844 .	31	49,699	6,482	15	8,261,345 00	1,325,798 00	19	166 23	–	–	22,688 00	
1845 .	33	58,178	8,479	17	9,813,288 00	1,551,943 00	18 2/7	168 66	–	–	27,017 00	.0029
1846 .	38	62,893	4,715	8	10,680,933 00	867,645 00	⅞	169 82	–	–	29,307 00	
1847 .	39	68,312	5,419	8½	11,780,813 00	1,099,880 00	10	172 45	–	–	34,490 00	
1848 .	41	69,894	1,582	2	11,970,448 00	189,635 00	1¼	171 26	–	–	36,405 00	
1849 .	43	71,629	1,735	2½	12,111,554 00	141,106 00	1	169 08	–	–	37,361 00	
1850 .	45	78,823	7,194	10	13,660,024 00	1,548,471 00	13	174 57	994,514	13 73	41,681 00	
1851 .	45	86,537	7,715	9⅔	15,554,089 00	1,894,065 00	14	179 73	–	–	43,707 00	
1852 .	53	97,353	10,816	12½	18,401,308 00	2,847,219 00	12	189 01	–	–	49,380 00	.0026
1853 .	60	117,404	20,051	20½	23,370,102 00	4,968,794 00	27	199 05	–	–	59,071 00	
1854 .	73	136,654	19,250	16½	25,936,858 00	2,566,756 00	11	189 88	–	–	63,471 00	
1855 .	80	148,263	11,609	8½	27,296,217 00	1,257,359 00	4⅔	184 10	1,132,369	24 12	77,757 00	.0028
1856 .	81	165,484	17,221	11½	30,373,447 00	3,077,231 00	10¾	184 15	–	–	89,309 00	

1857 .	86	177,375	11,891	8	33,015,757 00	2,642,310 00	8⅔	186 13	–	–	102,027 00	.0028
1858 .	86	182,655	5,280	3	33,914,972 00	899,215 00	2⅔	185 67	–	–	105,339 00	
1859 .	86	205,409	22,754	12½	39,424,419 00	5,509,647 00	16	191 93	–	–	107,951 00	
1860 .	89	230,068	24,659	12¼	45,054,236 00	5,629,817 00	14⅓	195 83	1,232,065	35 59	112,264 00	
1861 .	93	225,058	5,010†	2⅙†	44,785,439 00	268,797 09†	⅗†	198 99	–	–	120,886 00	.0027
1862 .	93	248,900	23,842	10½	50,403,674 00	5,618,235 00	12½	202 50	–	–	135,783 00	
1863 .	95	272,219	23,319	9⅓	56,883,828 00	6,480,154 00	12⅘	208 92	–	–	140,713 00	
1864 .	97	291,616	19,397	7	62,557,604 30	5,673,775 75	10‡	214 52	–	–	184,739 77	.0029
1865 .	102	291,488	128†	–	59,936,482 52	2,621,121 78	4⅙†	205 62	1,267,329	47 29	203,348 56	.0033
1866 .	102	316,853	25,365	8⅔	67,732,264 31	7,795,281 79†	13	213 76	–	–	219,257 03	.0032
1867 .	108	348,593	31,740	10	80,431,583 71	12,699,319 40	18⅔	230 73	–	–	254,225 79	.0031
1868 .	115	383,094	34,501	10‡	94,838,336 54	14,406,752 83	18‡	247 55	–	–	297,527 60	
1869 .	130	431,769	48,675	12¾‡	112,119,016 64	17,280,680 10	18⅙	259 67	–	–	339,271 57	.0030
1870 .	139	488,797	57,028	13	135,745,097 54	23,626,080 90	21	277 71	1,457,352	93 14	375,734 09	.0027
1871 .	160	561,201	72,404	14	163,704,077 54	27,958,980 00	20⅐	291 52	–	–	429,080 09	.0026
1872 .	172	630,246	69,045	12⅓	184,797,313 92	21,093,236 38	12⅞	293 21	–	–	469,681 80	.0025
1873 .	175	666,229	35,983	5⅖‡	202,195,343 70	17,398,029 78	8½	303 49	–	–	547,518 83	.0026
1874 .	179	702,099	35,870	5⅖	217,452,120 84	15,256,777 14	7⅓	309 71	–	–	644,682 68	.0029
1875 .	180	720,639	18,540	2 64/100‡	237,848,963 21	20,396,842 37	9⅖	330 05	1,651,652	144 00	661,503 92	.00277
1876 .	180	739,289	18,650	2½	243,340,642 75	5,491,679 54	2¼	329 15	–	–	657,858 72	.0027
1877 .	179	739,757	468	–	244,596,614 18	1,255,971 43	½	330 64	–	–	671,728 23	.00275
1878 .	168	674,251	65,506†	9⅙†	209,860,631 18	34,735,983 00†	14⅕†	311 25	–	–	606,550 23	.00289
1879 .	166	675,555	1,304	⅕	206,378,709 53	3,481,921 65†	1⅔†	305 50	–	–	590,820 18	.00286
1880 .	164	706,395	30,840	4⅓	218,047,922 37	11,669,212 84	5⅓	308 68	1,783,086	122 29	581,274 35	.00271
1881 .	165	738,951	32,556	4 4/7	230,444,479 10	12,396,556 73	5⅜	311 85	–	–	617,672 51	.00268

* In 1830. † Decrease. ‡ Nearly.

Statements were made by the following-named companies in accordance with the provisions of their charters: —

AMERICAN LOAN AND TRUST COMPANY — BOSTON.

Nov. 5, 1881.

Liabilities.		
Capital	. . . .	$1,000,000 00
Deposits subject to check	$513,964 21	
Certificates of deposit	3,421 80	
Bills payable on demand	84,900 00	
Bills payable on time	491,467 19	
		1,093,753 20
Undivided profits	. . . .	23,451 98
		$2,117,205 18
Assets.		
Loans payable on time	. . . .	$1,047,520 70
Loans payable on demand	. . . .	382,130 00
State bonds	$4,470 67	
Municipal bonds	38,208 62	
Railroad stocks	69,003 75	
Railroad bonds	287,987 57	
		399,670 61
Furniture and fixtures	. . . .	6,842 70
Expenses	. . . .	8,805 67
Cash in national banks	. . . .	269,943 43
Bills, specie, and cash items	. . . .	2,292 07
		$2,117,205 18

Date of examination by commissioner: Dec. 19.

BOSTON SAFE DEPOSIT AND TRUST COMPANY — BOSTON.

Nov. 14, 1881.

Liabilities.		
Capital stock	. . . .	$400,000 00
Profit and loss	. . . .	66,937 62
Interest	$18,299 15	
Commissions	3,641 89	
Safe, rental, and storage	10,618 86	
Discount	20,321 45	
		52,881 35
Deposits	. . . .	2,648,103 57
Trust funds	. . . .	32,079 78
		$3,200,002 32
Assets.		
United States Government bonds	$200,206 63	
City (New England) bonds	30,710 00	
Town (Massachusetts) bonds	41,350 00	
Railway (New England) bonds	197,852 50	
		$470,119 13
Loans: —		
Payable on demand, with collaterals or sureties	$686,900 00	
Payable on time, with collaterals or sureties	1,545,814 32	
Payable on time, with mortgages of real estate	159,800 00	
		2,392,514 32
Amount carried forward	. . . .	$2,862,633 45

BOSTON SAFE DEPOSIT AND TRUST COMPANY — Concluded.

Amount brought forward	. . . .	$2,862,633 45
Expenses: —		
General expense account	$12,874 87	
United States taxes	2,193 92	
State taxes	3,384 96	
		18,453 75
Safes and fixtures	. . . .	40,000 00
Cash: —		
In banks	$266,821 79	
In office	12,093 33	
		278,915 12
		$3,200,002 32

TRUST DEPARTMENT.

Liabilities.

In trust: —		
Under wills	$651,643 36	
Other trusts	71,000 00	
		$722,643 36
Income	. . . .	3,247 97
		$725,891 33

Assets.

United States Government bonds	. . . .	$172,327 50
Mortgages of real estate	. . . .	130,444 73
Railroad stock	. . . .	18,686 00
City bonds	. . . .	28,750 00
Railroad bonds	. . . .	115,475 00
Bank stocks	. . . .	74,289 00
Manufacturing company stock	. . . .	40,350 00
Estates occupied by beneficiaries	. . . .	17,425 00
Boston Music Hall Association	. . . .	200 00
Massachusetts Hospital Life Insurance Company, annuities in trust	. . . .	70,000 00
Town notes	. . . .	5,000 00
Massachusetts savings bank deposits	. . . .	4,000 00
Loans on personal security	. . . .	16,864 32
Cash: —		
Principal	$28,831 81	
Income	3,247 97	
		32,079 78
		$725,891 33

Date of examination by commissioner: Nov. 22.

COLLATERAL LOAN COMPANY — BOSTON.

Nov. 30, 1881.

Liabilities.

Capital stock paid in	$150,000 00
Reserve account, No. 43	315 57
Notes payable	22,858 72
Dividend	829 00
Undivided profits	11,594 57
	$185,597 86

Resources.

Cash on hand	$5,850 38
Loan account	176,747 48
Furniture	3,000 00
	$185,597 86

Date of examination by commissioner: Dec. 31.

INTERNATIONAL TRUST COMPANY — BOSTON.

OCT. 31, 1881.

Liabilities.	
Capital stock	$300,000 00
Deposits	793,973 95
Undivided profits	17,476 29
Bills payable	100,000 00
Dividends unpaid	1,715 42
Deposits for payment of coupons	5,337 50
	$1,218,503 16
Assets.	
United States bonds	$4,479 75
City and town bonds	90,208 75
Railway and steamboat bonds and stocks	197,427 32
International Trust Company stock, held for distribution under by-laws	5,000 00
Demand loans	356,636 16
Time loans	431,887 50
Furniture and fixtures	2,164 66
Expenses and taxes paid	6,130 72
Deposits in national banks	121,728 00
Cash in office	2,840 30
	$1,218,503 16

Date of examination by commissioner: Oct. 6.

MASSACHUSETTS LOAN AND TRUST COMPANY — BOSTON.

OCT. 31, 1881.

Capital stock actually paid in	$500,000 00
Investments in railroad bonds (Atlantic and Pacific)	27,000 00
Investments in R.R. stocks (Ohio and Mississippi, preferred)	20,000 00
Cash on hand	143,515 85
Dividend paid Aug. 15, 1881, since last report: 3 per cent.	

This corporation takes no deposits, and has never opened or done any business under its Trust Department, and has therefore no returns to make, as provided by its charter, other than those given herein.

Date of examination by commissioner: Nov. 30.

NEW ENGLAND TRUST COMPANY — BOSTON.

Oct. 31, 1881.

Liabilities.		
Capital stock	$500,000 00	
Deposits	7,171,271 64	
Interest	132,382 06	
Profit and loss account	12,333 88	
Guaranty	200,000 00	
Commissions	1,612 85	
For payment of bonds, coupons, dividends, etc.	29,206 48	
Sinking funds of railroad companies	26,713 39	
United States tax	16,729 12	
		$8,090,249 42
Assets.		
United States Government bonds		$1,029,000 00
City of Charlestown bonds		12,000 00
Railroad bonds		234,000 00
Loans on time notes, with collateral or sureties	$2,960,963 10	
Loans on time notes to states, counties, cities, and towns in New England	117,000 00	
Loans on time notes to corporations in Massachusetts,	882,301 32	
		3,960,264 42
Loans on call, with collateral or sureties	$800,850 00	
Loans on call to corporations in Massachusetts	696,762 39	
		1,497,612 39
Cash in banks in Boston	$1,310,120 97	
Cash in office	16,503 36	
		1,326,624 33
Expense account		30,748 28
		$8,090,249 42
Trust Department.		
Liabilities.		
Trust accounts	$528,974 89	
Income	5,421 08	
Dividends	1,491 02	
		$535,886 99
Assets.		
United States Government bonds		$123,661 22
City bonds (in Massachusetts)		25,027 57
State bonds (in New England)		24,219 82
Railroad bonds	$148,111 03	
Railroad stocks	40,012 74	
		188,123 77
Manufacturing stocks (special trust)		7,500 00
Insurance stocks (special trust)		2,500 00
Mortgage notes	$122,000 87	
Real estate	12,500 00	
		134,500 87
Stock in national banks in Boston		17,545 50
Notes secured by collateral		4,500 00
Cash in banks in Boston		8,308 24
		$535,886 99

Date of examination by commisioners: Nov. 3.

WORCESTER SAFE DEPOSIT AND TRUST COMPANY — WORCESTER.

Oct. 31, 1881.

Liabilities.		
Capital stock		$200,000 00
Deposits		1,573,777 21
Profit and loss	$14,423 11	
Undivided profits	4,897 37	
Surplus fund	20,000 00	
		39,320 48
Dividends unpaid		231 00
Trust funds		1,118 49
		$1,814,447 18
Assets.		
Cash: —		
In office	$104,549 68	
In banks	131,533 35	
		$236,083 03
Bonds: —		
United States	$2,050 00	
Vt. Central and Vt. and Canada equipment 8s	152,000 00	
Worcester Street Railway	20,000 00	
		174,050 00
Stocks: —		
Central National Bank, New York		13,400 00
Loans: —		
Notes of corporations	$1,144,353 84	
To individuals, with collaterals	170,339 00	
On mortgage of real estate	23,700 00	
		1,338,392 84
Expenses: —		
General expenses		703 70
Furniture and fixtures	$10,000 00	
Premium account	5,019 18	
Clearing-house fund	1,000 00	
Real estate	33,000 00	
Real estate by foreclosure	2,798 43	
		51,817 61
		$1,814,447 18

Trust Department.

Liabilities.		
In trust: —		
Under wills	$62,235 00	
Other trusts	4,900 00	
Income	80 99	
		$67,215 99
Assets.		
United States bonds	$17,912 50	
Railroad bonds	44,285 00	
Railroad stock	1,000 00	
Bank stock	2,400 00	
Gas-light companies stock	400 00	
Express companies stock	100 00	
Cash: —		
Principal	1,037 50	
Income	80 99	
		$67,215 99

Dividend Oct. 1, 1881 (3 per cent)	$6,000
Number of accounts	1,704

Date of examination by commissioner: June 6.

MASSACHUSETTS HOSPITAL LIFE INSURANCE COMPANY — BOSTON.

DEC. 31, 1881.

Liabilities.	
Deposits	$14,717,391 76
Earnings undivided	137,335 44
Insurance on lives	8,174 49
Annuities on lives	433,614 72
Capital stock	500,000 00
Surplus	172,043 24
	$15,968,559 65
Assets.	
Mortgages	$8,415,637 83
Real estate	90,000 00
Personal and collateral loans	4,817,700 00
United States bonds	750,000 00
Municipal bonds	95,000 00
Railroad bonds	985,918 75
Railroad stocks	414,000 00
Bank stock	128,579 13
Cash on hand	271,723 94
	$15,968,559 65

Date of examination by commissioner: Dec. 28.

STATEMENTS

OF THE

CO-OPERATIVE SAVING-FUND

AND

LOAN ASSOCIATIONS.

MADE IN CONFORMITY TO THE REQUIREMENTS OF CHAPTER 129 OF THE ACTS OF 1879.

CAMBRIDGE CO-OPERATIVE SAVING-FUND AND LOAN ASSOCIATION — EAST CAMBRIDGE.

Incorporated Sept. 5, 1877. Commenced business Sept. 12, 1877.

Capital to be accumulated, $500,000.

RUFUS R. WADE, *President*. *Secretary*, ROBERT L. SAWIN.

JOHN LOUGHREY, *Treasurer*.

STATEMENT.

LIABILITIES.		ASSETS.	
37 shares of stock, first series, at $56.48	$2,089 76	Loans on real estate	$4,165 00
12 shares of stock, second series, at $51.91	622 92	Loans on shares	823 00
15 shares of stock, third series, at $48.81	732 15	Unpaid dues	63 00
4 shares of stock, fourth series, at $45.18	180 72	Balance of permanent expense account	109 13
14 shares of stock, sixth series, at $38.40	537 60	Other assets	63 31
5 shares of stock, ninth series, at $26.52	132 60	Cash on hand	1,061 75
5 shares of stock, tenth series, at $23 07	115 35		
21 shares of stock, eleventh series, at $19.60	411 60		
17 shares of stock, twelfth series, at $16.16	274 72		
33 shares of stock, thirteenth series, at $12.60	415 80		
15 shares of stock, fourteenth series, at $9.38	140 70		
70 shares of stock, fifteenth series, at $6.22	435 40		
48 shares of stocks, sixteenth series, at $3.06	146 88		
Surplus	10		
Forfeited share account	11 12		
Interest on dues paid in advance	1 22		
Other liabilities	36 55		
	$6,285 19		$6,285 19

Number of shares issued during the year	227	
Number of shares now in force	296	
Number of shares now borrowed upon	61	
Amount of dues received during the year		$3,474 00
Highest premium received during the year		35
Lowest premium received during the year		5
Fine for non-payment of dues		2
Transfer fee		25
Number of members withdrawn during the year	24	
Present number of members	50	
Present number of borrowers	14	
Present number of non-borrowers	36	

Amount of loans at date		$4,988 00
Number and amount of loans on real estate	9	4,165 00
Number and amount of loans secured by first mortgage of real estate	9	4,165 00
Number and amount of loans on shares	5	823 00
Largest loan to any one member		1,000 00
Smallest loan to any one member		25 00
Largest number of shares held by any one member . .	20	
Amount of expenses of the corporation for previous year (not including interest)		96 23
Value of shares at last report		5,819 38
Total value of unpledged shares (including unpaid dues) . .		4,036 91
Number of shares forfeited during the year	2	
Amount of interest credited to shares during the year . . .		319 47
Number of shares withdrawn during the year	165	
Number and amount of loans repaid during the year . .	11	635 00
Geographical limit: Massachusetts.		
Amount of cash received during the year		4,087 22
Amount of cash paid during the year		3,254 35
Secretary's salary		40 00
Treasurer's bond		1,000 00
Secretary's bond		500 00
Date of examination by commissioner: Sept. 3.		

CAMPELLO CO-OPERATIVE SAVING-FUND AND LOAN ASSOCIATION — BROCKTON.

Incorporated Oct. 3, 1877. Commenced business Oct. 8, 1877.

Capital to be accumulated, $1,000,000.

ALBERT KEITH, *President*. *Secretary*, WARREN T. COPELAND.

ZIBA C. KEITH, *Treasurer*.

STATEMENT.

LIABILITIES.		ASSETS.	
588 shares of stock, first series, at $58.44 . . .	$34,362 72	Loans on real estate . .	$54,750 00
238 shares of stock, second series, at $42.31 . . .	10,069 78	Loans on shares . . .	3,050 00
386 shares of stock, third series, at $27.36 . . .	10,560 96	Unpaid dues . . .	263 00
408 shares of stock, fourth series, at $13.59 . . .	5,544 72	Balance of permanent expense account . . .	338 20
362 shares of stock, fifth series, at $1.00 . . .	362 00	Balance of temporary expense account . . .	31 50
Dues paid in advance . .	963 00	Fines	5 91
Interest	194 32	Cash on hand . . .	3,774 05
Premium	52 55		
Transfer fees	1 00		
Surplus	51 40		
Withdrawal profits . .	50 21		
	$62,212 66		$62,212 66

Number of shares issued during the year	558	
Number of shares now in force	1,982	
Number of shares now borrowed upon	399	
Amount of dues received during the year		$21,277 00
Highest premium received during the year		60
Lowest premium received during the year		5
Fine for non-payment of dues: 2 per cent per month.		
Transfer fee		25
Number of members withdrawn during the year	56	
Present number of members	412	
Present number of borrowers	72	
Present number of non-borrowers	340	
Amount of loans at date		57,800 00
Number and amount of loans on real estate	62	54,750 00
Number and amount of loans secured by first mortgage of real estate	62	54,750 00
Number and amount of loans on shares	10	3,050 00
Largest loan to any one member		2,100 00
Smallest loan to any one member		50 00
Largest number of shares held by any one member	25	
Amount of expenses of the corporation for previous year (not including interest)		552 49
Value of shares at last report: first series, $41.84; second series, $27.15; third series, $13.54; fourth series, $1.00.		
Total value of unpledged shares (including unpaid dues)		44,820 04
Amount of interest credited to shares during the year		4,511 97
Number of shares withdrawn during the year	297	
Number and amount of loans repaid during the year	28	13,730 00
Geographical limit: Massachusetts.		
Amount of cash received during the year		40,613 62
Amount of cash paid during the year		36,989 47
Secretary's salary		250 00
Treasurer's bond		1,500 00
Secretary's bond		1,500 00
Date of examination by commissioner: July 7.		

EQUITABLE CO-OPERATIVE SAVING-FUND AND LOAN ASSOCIATION — LYNN.

Incorporated Oct. 2, 1877. Commenced business Oct. 8, 1877.

Capital to be accumulated, $1,000,000.

JAMES H. RICHARDS, *President*. *Secretary*, BENJAMIN E. PORTER.

WILLIAM A. ESTES, *Treasurer*.

STATEMENT.

LIABILITIES.		ASSETS.	
130 shares of stock, first series, at $53.67	$6,977 10	Loans on real estate	$12,550 00
53 shares of stock, second series, at $39.60	2,098 80	Loans on shares	345 00
56 shares of stock, third series, at $26 17	1,465 52	Unpaid dues	640 92
59 shares of stock, fourth series, at $19.69	1,161 71	Balance of permanent expense account	21 70
80 shares of stock, fifth series, at $13.31	1,064 80	Balance of temporary expense account	4 00
173 shares of stock, sixth series, at $7.09	1,226 57	Interest account	188 56
107 shares of stock, seventh series, at $4.02	430 14	Cash on hand	792 64
94 shares of stock, eighth series, at $1.00	94 00		
Surplus	3 08		
Forfeited share account	21 10		
	$14,542 82		$14,542 82

Number of shares issued during the year	457	
Number of shares now in force	752	
Number of shares now borrowed upon	76	
Amount of dues received during the year		$6,699 83
Highest premium received during the year		19
Lowest premium received during the year		05
Fine for non-payment of dues: 2 per cent per month.		
Transfer fee		25
Number of members withdrawn during the year	31	
Present number of members	176	
Present number of borrowers	26	
Present number of non-borrowers	150	
Amount of loans at date		12,895 00
Number and amount of loans on real estate	22	12,550 00
Number and amount of loans secured by first mortgage of real estate	22	12,550 00
Number and amount of loans on shares	5	345 00
Largest loan to any one member		2,200 00
Smallest loan to any one member		20 00
Largest number of shares held by any one member	25	
Amount of expenses of the corporation for previous year (not including interest)		158 03

Value of shares at last report: first series, $52.67; second series, $38.60; third series, $25.17; fourth series, $18.69; fifth series, $12.31; sixth series, $6.09; seventh series, $3.02.

Total value of unpledged shares (including unpaid dues)		$12,019 87
Amount of interest credited to shares during the year		523 94
Number of shares withdrawn during the year	134	
Number and amount of loans repaid during the year	3	100 00

Geographical limit: Massachusetts.

Amount of cash received during the year	7,231 80
Amount of cash paid during the year	6,774 47
Secretary's salary	50 00
Treasurer's salary	25 00
Treasurer's bonds	2,000 00
Secretary's bonds	1,000 00

Date of examination by commissioner: Aug. 9.

FITCHBURG CO-OPERATIVE SAVING-FUND AND LOAN ASSOCIATION — FITCHBURG.

Incorporated Oct. 27, 1877. Commenced business Nov. 8, 1877.

Capital to be accumulated, $1,000,000.

Jabez Fisher, *President*. *Secretary*, Joseph F. Simonds.

George E. Clifford, *Treasurer*.

Statement.

Liabilities.		Assets.	
317 shares of stock, first series, at $53.92	$17,092 64	Loans on real estate	$48,222 00
231 shares of stock, second series, at $46.50	10,741 50	Loans on shares	4,680 00
107 shares of stock, third series, at $39.28	4,202 96	Unpaid dues, interest, premiums, and fines	1,403 25
151 shares of stock, fourth series, at $32.23	4,866 73	Balance of permanent expense account	199 13
169 shares of stock, fifth series, at $25.38	4,289 22	Other assets	61 25
298 shares of stock, sixth series, at $18.74	5,584 52	Cash on hand	416 63
388 shares of stock, seventh series, at $12.36	4,795 68		
463 shares of stock, eighth series, at $6.09	2,819 67		
Dues paid in advance	434 00		
Forfeited share account	29 01		
Interest on dues paid in advance	44 76		
Other liabilities	81 57		
	$54,982 26		$54,982 26

Number of shares issued during the year	878	
Number of shares now in force	2,124	
Number of shares now borrowed upon	432	
Amount of dues received during the year		$10,173 44

Highest premium received during the year: $2\frac{16}{100}$ per cent.
Lowest premium received during the year: $\frac{12}{100}$ per cent.
Fine for non-payment of dues: 1 per cent per month.

Transfer fee		$0 25
Number of members withdrawn during the year	15	
Present number of members	282	
Present number of borrowers	78	
Present number of non-borrowers	204	
Amount of loans at date		52,902 00
Number and amount of loans on real estate	65	48,222 00
Number and amount of loans secured by first mortgage of real estate	65	48,222 00
Number and amount of loans on shares	27	4,680 00
Largest loan to any one member		2,000 00
Smallest loan to any one member		20 00
Largest number of shares held by any one member	25	
Amount of expenses of the corporation for previous year (not including interest)		386 96
Value of shares at last report		32,702 89
Total value of unpledged shares (including unpaid dues)		41,359 59
Number of shares forfeited during the year	1	
Amount of interest credited to shares during the year		2,390 39
Number of shares withdrawn during the year	159	
Number and amount of loans repaid during the year	21	4,845 00

Geographical limit: Massachusetts.

Amount of cash received during the year	28,578 37
Amount of cash paid during the year	29,045 77
Treasurer's salary	50 00
Secretary's salary	180 00
Treasurer's bonds	2,000 00
Secretary's bonds	1,000 00

Date of examination by commissioner: Oct. 3.

HAVERHILL CO-OPERATIVE SAVING-FUND AND LOAN ASSOCIATION — HAVERHILL.

Incorporated Aug. 20, 1877. Commenced business Sept. 3, 1877.

Capital to be accumulated, $1,000,000.

AMOS W. DOWNING, *President*. *Secretary*, WILLIAM H. PAGE.

J. W. BENNETT, *Treasurer*.

STATEMENT.

LIABILITIES.		ASSETS.	
169 shares of stock, first series, at $56.03	$9,469 07	Loans on real estate	$21,200 00
49 shares of stock, second series, at $46.25	2,266 25	Loans on shares	150 00
124 shares of stock, third series, at $29.73	3,686 52	Unpaid dues	320 00
265 shares of stock, fourth series, at $16.46	4,361 90	Balance of permanent expense account	250 00
174 shares of stock, fifth series, at $10.09	1,755 66	Balance of temporary expense account	120 02
253 shares of stock, sixth series, at $4	1,012 00	Cash on hand	944 78
Surplus	57 67		
Forfeited share account	4 80		
Withdrawal profits	9 25		
Other liabilities	361 68		
	$22,984 80		$22,984 80

Number of shares issued during the year	519	
Number of shares now in force	1,034	
Number of shares now borrowed upon	116	
Amount of dues received during the year		$10,793 00
Highest premium received during the year		30
Lowest premium received during the year		15
Fine for non-payment of dues: 2 per cent per month.		
Transfer fee		25
Number of members withdrawn during the year	59	
Present number of members	255	
Present number of borrowers	31	
Present number of non-borrowers	224	
Amount of loans at date		21,350 00
Number and amount of loans on real estate	29	21,200 00
Number and amount of loans secured by first mortgage of real estate	29	21,200 00
Number and amount of loans on shares	2	150 00
Largest loan to any one member		2,000 00
Smallest loan to any one member		50 00
Largest number of shares held by any one member	25	
Amount of expenses of the corporation for previous year (not including interest)		431 67
Value of shares at last report		14,396 91

Total value of unpledged shares (including unpaid dues) . . .		$10,140 79
Number of shares forfeited during the year	3	
Amount of interest credited to shares during the year . . .		947 93
Number of shares withdrawn during the year	236	
Number and amount of loans repaid during the year . .	4	950 00
Geographical limit: Massachusetts.		
Amount of cash received during the year		13,746 97
Amount of cash paid during the year		12,119 77
Secretary's salary: 1½ per cent of gross receipts.		
Treasurer's bonds		2,000 00
Secretary's bonds		2,000 00
Date of examination by commissioner: Nov. 22.		

HOLYOKE CO-OPERATIVE SAVING-FUND AND LOAN ASSOCIATION — HOLYOKE.

Incorporated July 24, 1880. Commenced business Aug. 22, 1880.

Capital to be accumulated, $1,000,000.

WILLIAM GROVER, *President*. *Secretary*, FREDERICK DRUCE.

JOSEPH METCALF, *Treasurer*.

STATEMENT.

LIABILITIES.		ASSETS.	
370 shares of stock, first series, at $15.25 . . .	$5,642 50	Loans on real estate . .	$3,600 00
200 shares of stock, second series, at $10.07 . .	2,014 00	Loans on shares . .	50 00
142 shares of stock, third series, at $4 . . .	568 00	Unpaid dues . . .	187 00
Interest	128 50	Balance of permanent expense account . . .	161 32
Premium	27 22	Balance of temporary expense account . . .	47 00
Fines	16 22	Cash on hand . . .	4,378 00
Transfer	50		
Dues in advance . . .	10 00		
Surplus	2 62		
Forfeited share account .	2 90		
Withdrawal profits . .	1 73		
Forfeiture profits . .	1 75		
Other liabilities . . .	7 38		
	$8,423 32		$8,423 32

Number of shares issued during the year	367	
Number of shares now in force	717	
Number of shares now borrowed upon	25	
Amount of dues received during the year		$7,415 00
Highest premium received during the year		1 00
Lowest premium received during the year		10
Fines for non-payment of dues		32 27
Transfer fees		50
Number of members withdrawn during the year	12	
Present number of members	120	
Present number of borrowers	4	
Present number of non-borrowers	116	

Amount of loans at date		$3,650 00
Number and amount of loans on real estate	3	3,600 00
Number and amount of loans secured by first mortgage of real estate	3	3,600 00
Number and amount of loans on shares	1	50 00
Largest loan to any one member		2,000 00
Smallest loan to any one member		50 00
Largest number of shares held by any one member	25	
Amount of expenses of the corporation for previous year (not including interest)		115 00
Value of shares at last report		5,843 25
Total value of unpledged shares (including unpaid dues)		7,895 00
Number of shares forfeited during the year	7	
Amount of interest credited to shares during the year		115 25
Number of shares withdrawn during the year	83	

Geographical limit: Massachusetts.

Amount of cash received during the year	7,783 21
Amount of cash paid during the year	4,523 83

Secretary's salary: $10 per month.

Treasurer's bonds	3,000 00
Secretary's bonds	1,000 00

Date of examination by commissioner: Oct. 18.

HOMESTEAD CO-OPERATIVE SAVING-FUND AND LOAN ASSOCIATION — BOSTON.

Incorporated Sept. 11, 1877. Commenced business Sept. 12, 1877.

Capital to be accumulated, $1,000,000.

JOSEPH S. ROPES, *President*. *Secretary*, DANIEL ELDREDGE.

THOMAS SWADKINS, Jun., *Treasurer*.

STATEMENT.

LIABILITIES.		ASSETS.	
84 shares of stock, first series, at $57.50	$4,830 00	Loans on real estate	$53,750 00
232 shares of stock, second series, at $49.88	11,572 16	Loans on shares	2,650 00
150 shares of stock, third series, at $42.22	6,333 00	Unpaid dues	1,140 00
122 shares of stock, fourth series, at $34.87	4,254 14	Balance of permanent expense account	300 00
340 shares of stock, fifth series, at $27.79	9,448 60	Balance of temporary expense account	83 34
226 shares of stock, sixth series, at $20.98	5,580 68	Cash on hand	985 83
609 shares of stock, seventh series, at $14.43	8,787 87		
809 shares of stock, eighth series, at $8.11	6,560 99		
521 shares of stock, ninth series, at $2.00	1,042 00		
Surplus	20 43		
Forfeited share account	13 98		
Withdrawal profits	59 21		
Other liabilities	406 11		
	$58,909 17		$58,909 17

Number of shares issued during the year	1,597	
Number of shares now in force	3,133	
Number of shares now borrowed upon	416	
Amount of dues received during the year		$32,385 00
Highest premium received during the year		1 00
Lowest premium received during the year		05
Fine for non-payment of dues: 2 per cent per month.		
Transfer fee		25
Number of members withdrawn during the year	179	
Present number of members	600	
Present number of borrowers	66	
Present number of non-borrowers	534	
Amount of loans at date		56,400 00
Number and amount of loans on real estate	49	53,750 00
Number and amount of loans secured by first mortgage of real estate	48	52,550 00
Number and amount of loans secured by other mortgage of real estate	1	1,200 00
Number and amount of loans on shares	17	2,650 00
Largest loan to any one member		2,600 00
Smallest loan to any one member		50 00
Largest number of shares held by any one member	25	
Amount of expenses of the corporation for previous year (not including interest) *		1,035 22
Value of shares at last report		34,966 72
Total value of unpledged shares (including unpaid dues)		47,203 47
Number of shares forfeited during the year	18	
Amount of interest credited to shares during the year *		2,845 22
Number of shares withdrawn during the year	796	
Number and amount of loans repaid during the year	21	11,350 00
Geographical limit: Massachusetts.		
Amount of cash received during the year		47,617 37
Amount of cash paid during the year		50,405 64
Secretary's salary		500 00
Treasurer's salary		25 00
Treasurer's bonds		1,000 00
Secretary's bonds		3,000 00
Date of examination by commissioners: July 27.		

* For year ending Aug. 31.

MECHANICS' CO-OPERATIVE SAVING-FUND AND LOAN ASSOCIATION — TAUNTON.

Incorporated Sept. 14, 1877. Commenced business Sept. 17, 1877.

Capital to be accumulated, $1,000,000.

ELIJAH TOLMAN, *President*. *Secretary*, EDWARD S. HERSEY.

CHARLES L. LOVERING, *Treasurer*.

STATEMENT.

LIABILITIES.		ASSETS.	
232 shares of stock, first series, at $54.56	$12,657 92	Loans on real estate	$68,271 00
378 shares of stock, second series, at $47.42	17,924 76	Loans on shares	5,750 00
397 shares of stock, third series, at $35.84	14,228 48	Unpaid dues	375 60
678 shares of stock, fourth series, at $22.60	15,322 80	Balance of permanent expense account	289 84
1,380 shares of stock, fifth series, at $10.12	13,965 60	Balance of temporary expense account	98 88
Advance payments	771 87	Unpaid interest	93 83
Interest (profit since July 1),	1,496 00	Unpaid premium	14 62
Premium (profit since July 1),	202 63	Unpaid fines	12 04
Fines	62 37	Other assets	45 44
Surplus	26 55	Cash on hand	1,856 05
Forfeited share account	5 94		
Other liabilities	142 38		
	$76,807 30		$76,807 30

Number of shares issued during the year	1,500	
Number of shares now in force	3,065	
Number of shares now borrowed upon	710	
Amount of dues received during the year		$37,655 45
Highest premium received during the year		35
Lowest premium received during the year		05
Fines for non-payment of dues		152 92
Transfer fees		6 25
Number of members withdrawn during the year	144	
Present number of members	481	
Present number of borrowers	105	
Present number of non-borrowers	376	
Amount of loans at date		74,021 00
Number and amount of loans on real estate	77	68,271 00
Number and amount of loans secured by first mortgage of real estate	77	68,271 00
Number and amount of loans on shares	40	5,750 00
Largest loan to any one member		3,700 00
Smallest loan to any one member		25 00
Largest number of shares held by any one member	25	
Amount of expenses of the corporation for previous year (not including interest)		480 95

Value of shares at last report: first series, $40.89; second series, $34; third series, $22.82; fourth series, $10.05.

Total value of unpledged shares (including unpaid dues) . .		$55,447 52
Number of shares forfeited during the year	3	
Amount of interest credited to shares during the year . . .		4,757 51
Number of shares withdrawn during the year	1,130	
Number and amount of loans repaid during the year . .	49	26,200 00
Geographical limit: Massachusetts.		
Amount of cash received during the year.		62,245 41
Amount of cash paid during the year		60,389 36
Secretary's salary		240 00
Treasurer's bonds		5,000 00
Secretary's bonds		1,000 00
Date of examination by commissioner: Sept. 9.		

NEW BEDFORD CO-OPERATIVE SAVING-FUND AND LOAN ASSOCIATION — NEW BEDFORD.

Incorporated July 8, 1881. Commenced business Aug. 19, 1881.

Capital to be accumulated, $1,000,000.

ISAAC W. BENJAMIN, *President*. *Secretary*, CHARLES R. PRICE.
GIDEON B. WRIGHT, *Treasurer*.

STATEMENT.

LIABILITIES.		ASSETS.	
826 shares of stock, first series, at $3	$2,478 00	Loans on real estate . .	$2,600 00
Interest account . . .	10 34	Unpaid dues . . .	57 00
Premium account . .	1 79	Balance of permanent expense account . .	68 24
Fines account . . .	20 36	Balance of temporary expense account . . .	5 79
Transfer fee account . .	25	Cash on hand . . .	64 71
Advance dues . . .	285 00		
	$2,795 74		$2,795 74

Number of shares issued during the year.	826	
Number of shares now in force	826	
Number of shares now borrowed upon	15	
Amount of dues received during the year		$2,706 00
Highest premium received during the year		30
Lowest premium received during the year		15
Fine for non-payment of dues: 2 per cent per month.		
Transfer fee		25
Number of members withdrawn during the year	1	
Present number of members	137	
Present number of borrowers	5	
Present number of non-borrowers	132	
Amount of loans at date		2,600 00
Number and amount of loans on real estate	5	2,600 00
Number and amount of loans secured by first mortgage of real estate	5	2,600 00

Largest loan to any one member		$800 00
Smallest loan to any one member		300 00
Largest number of shares held by any one member	25	
Total value of unpledged shares (including unpaid dues)		2,433 00
Number and amount of loans repaid during the year	1	347 00
Geographical limit: Massachusetts.		
Amount of cash received during the year		2,738 74
Amount of cash paid during the year		2,674 03
Secretary's salary for current six months		100 00
Treasurer's salary for current six months		25 00
Treasurer's bonds		2,000 00
Secretary's bonds		1,000 00
Date of examination by commissioner: Sept. 19.		

PIONEER CO-OPERATIVE SAVING-FUND AND LOAN ASSOCIATION — BOSTON.

Incorporated July 26, 1877. Commenced business Aug. 6, 1877.

Capital to be accumulated, $1,000,000.

JOSIAH QUINCY, *President*. *Secretary*, DANIEL ELDREDGE.

A. J. MERCER, *Treasurer*.

STATEMENT.

LIABILITIES.		ASSETS.	
706 shares of stock, first series, at $59.53	$42,028 18	Loans on real estate	$75,900 00
313 shares of stock, second series, at $49.02	15,343 26	Loans on shares	5,050 00
194 shares of stock, third series, at $33.99	6,594 06	Unpaid dues	1,311 00
640 shares of stock, fourth series, at $20.03	12,819 20	Balance of permanent expense account	250 00
634 shares of stock, fifth series, at $13.45	8,527 30	Balance of temporary expense account	66 67
1,038 shares of stock, sixth series, at $7.11	7,380 18	Other assets	126 79
512 shares of stock, seventh series, at $1	512 00	Cash on hand	10,874 97
Surplus	338 05		
Forfeited share account	10 64		
Withdrawal profits	26 31		
Other liabilities	25		
	$93,579 43		$93,579 43

Number of shares issued during the year	1,913	
Number of shares now in force	4,037	
Number of shares now borrowed upon	595	
Amount of dues received during the year		$40,444 00
Highest premium received during the year		1 00
Lowest premium received during the year		05
Fine for non-payment of dues: 2 per cent per month.		
Transfer fee		25
Number of members withdrawn during the year	161	
Present number of members	794	
Present number of borrowers	96	
Present number of non-borrowers	698	

Amount of loans at date		$80,950 00
Number and amount of loans on real estate	64	75,900 00
Number and amount of loans secured by first mortgage of real estate	62	73,900 00
Number and amount of loans secured by other mortgage of real estate	2	2,000 00
Number and amount of loans on shares	32	5,050 00
Largest loan to any one member		5,000 00
Smallest loan to any one member		50 00
Largest number of shares held by any one member	25	
Amount of expenses of the corporation for previous year (not including interest) *		1,677 67
Value of shares at last report		62,834 30
Total value of unpledged shares (including unpaid dues)		75,484 11
Number of shares forfeited during the year	3	
Amount of interest credited to shares during the year *		5,244 74
Number of shares withdrawn during the year	700	
Number and amount of loans repaid during the year	40	42,850 00
Geographical limit: Massachusetts.		
Amount of cash received during the year		89,714 36
Amount of cash paid during the year		81,693 80
Secretary's salary		800 00
Treasurer's salary		25 00
Treasurer's bonds		3,000 00
Secretary's bonds		3,000 00
Date of examination by commissioner: July 27.		

* For year ending Sept. 30.

SECURITY CO-OPERATIVE SAVING-FUND AND LOAN ASSOCIATION — BROCKTON.

Incorporated Dec. 17, 1877. Commenced business Dec. 17, 1877.

Capital to be accumulated, $1,000,000.

H. H. Packard, *President*. *Secretary*, F. B. Washburn.
C. D. Fullerton, *Treasurer*.

Statement.

Liabilities.		Assets.	
475 shares of stock, first series, at $50.93	$24,191 75	Loans on real estate	$42,805 00
123 shares of stock, second series at $36.68	4,511 64	Loans on shares	875 00
323 shares of stock, third series at $23.42	7,564 66	Unpaid dues	288 00
681 shares of stock, fourth series at $11	7,491 00	Balance of permanent expense account	286 78
Surplus	502 57	Balance of temporary expense account	341 60
Forfeited share account	2 90	Cash on hand	5,279 64
Withdrawal profits	131 30		
Interest on dues paid in advance	92 76		
Other liabilities	5,387 44		
	$49,876 02		$49,876 02

Number of shares issued during the year	674	
Number of shares now in force	1,602	
Number of shares now borrowed upon	290	
Amount of dues received during the year		$18,130 00
Highest premium received during the year		50
Lowest premium received during the year		10
Fine for non-payment of dues: 2 per cent per month.		
Transfer fee		25
Number of members withdrawn during the year	64	
Present number of members	324	
Present number of borrowers	53	
Present number of non-borrowers	271	
Amount of loans at date		43,680 00
Number and amount of loans on real estate	46	42,805 00
Number and amount of loans secured by first mortgage of real estate	46	42,805 00
Number and amount of loans on shares	7	875 00
Largest loan to any one member		3,000 00
Smallest loan to any one member		50 00
Largest number of shares held by any one member	25	
Amount of expenses of the corporation for previous year (not including interest)		388 57
Value of shares at last report: first series, $36.76; second series, $23.42; third series, $11.		
Total value of unpledged shares (including unpaid dues)		35,887 70
Amount of interest credited to shares during the year		1,611 00
Number of shares withdrawn during the year	386	
Number and amount of loans repaid during the year	12	10,016 00
Geographical limit: Provincetown and Newton.		
Amount of cash received during the year		37,720 26
Amount of cash paid during the year		33,720 30
Secretary's salary		250 00
Treasurer's salary		25 00
Security Committee, each		25 00
Treasurer's bonds		5,000 00
Secretary's bonds		2,500 00
Date of examination by commissioner: Aug. 31.		

SOMERVILLE CO-OPERATIVE SAVING-FUND AND LOAN ASSOCIATION — SOMERVILLE.

Incorporated May 4, 1880. Commenced business June 7, 1880.

Capital to be accumulated, $1,000,000.

CHARLES S. LINCOLN, *President.* *Secretary,* GEORGE I. VINCENT.

WILLIAM H. BRINE, *Treasurer.*

STATEMENT.

LIABILITIES.		ASSETS.	
215 shares of stock, first series, at $17.52 . . .	$3,766 80	Loans on real estate . .	$7,800 00
307 shares of stock, second series, at $11.23 . .	3,447 61	Loans on shares . . .	50 00
172 shares of stock, third series, at $7.11 . . .	1,222 92	Unpaid dues . . .	162 00
34 shares of stock, fourth series, at $1	34 00	Balance of permanent expense account . . .	177 56
Interest account . . .	36 75	Balance of temporary expense account . . .	8 33
Premium account . .	3 82	Interest and premium charged to shareholder .	5 31
Fines account . . .	7 68	Cash on hand . . .	586 31
Advance payments . .	254 00		
Surplus	1 81		
Forfeited share account .	2 01		
Interest on dues paid in advance	12 11		
	$8,789 51		$8,789 51

Number of shares issued during the year	559	
Number of shares now in force	728	
Number of shares now borrowed upon	48	
Amount of dues received during the year		$7,804 00
Highest premium received during the year		35
Lowest premium received during the year		05
Fine for non-payment of dues: 2 per cent per month.		
Transfer fee		25
Number of members withdrawn during the year . . .	30	
Present number of members	174	
Present number of borrowers	7	
Present number of non-borrowers	167	
Amount of loans at date		7,850 00
Number and amount of loans on real estate	13	7,800 00
Number and amount of loans secured by first mortgage of real estate	13	7,800 00
Number and amount of loans on shares	1	50 00
Largest loan to any one member		2,600 00
Smallest loan to any one member		50 00
Largest number of shares held by any one member . . .	25	
Amount of expenses of the corporation for previous year (not including interest)		137 11
Value of shares at last report		1,305 00
Total value of unpledged shares (including unpaid dues) . .		7,914 00

Number of shares forfeited during the year	3	
Amount of profit credited to shares during the year		$215 33
Number of shares withdrawn during the year	92	
Number and amount of loans repaid during the year	1	900 00
Geographical limit: Massachusetts.		
Amount of cash received during the year		9,041 90
Amount of cash paid during the year		8,455 59
Secretary's salary		100 00
Treasurer's bonds		1,000 00
Secretary's bonds		1,000 00
Date of examination by commissioner: Sept. 30.		

TAUNTON CO-OPERATIVE SAVING-FUND AND LOAN ASSOCIATION — TAUNTON.

Incorporated March 2, 1880. Commenced business March 17, 1880.

Capital to be accumulated, $1,000,000.

HENRY M. LOVERING, *President*. *Secretary*, HERBERT O. MORSE.

CHARLES FOSTER, *Treasurer*.

STATEMENT.

LIABILITIES.		ASSETS.	
2,304 shares of stock, first series, at $20.54	$47,324 16	Loans on real estate	$51,650 00
665 shares of stock, second series, at $6	3,990 00	Loans on shares	600 00
Surplus	1,561 33	Unpaid dues	656 93
Forfeited share account	17 30	Balance of permanent expense account	178 84
Dues paid in advance	439 75	Balance of temporary expense account	205 62
		Cash on hand	41 15
	$53,332 54		$53,332 54

Number of shares issued during the year	680	
Number of shares now in force	2,969	
Number of shares now borrowed upon	264	
Amount of dues received during the year		$34,067 00
Highest premium received during the year		20
Lowest premium received during the year		05
Fine for non-payment of dues: 2 per cent per month.		
Transfer fee		25
Number of members withdrawn during the year	96	
Present number of members	480	
Present number of borrowers	44	
Present number of non-borrowers	436	
Amount of loans at date		52,250 00
Number and amount of loans on real estate	37	51,650 00
Number and amount of loans secured by first mortgage of real estate	37	51,650 00
Number and amount of loans on shares	7	600 00

Largest loan to any one member		$4,000 00
Smallest loan to any one member		50 00
Largest number of shares held by any one member	25	
Amount of expenses of the corporation for previous year (not including interest)		419 63
Value of shares at last report		20,886 80
Total value of unpledged shares (including unpaid dues)		47,235 60
Number of shares forfeited during the year	7	
Amount of interest credited to shares during the year		1,153 22
Number of shares withdrawn during the year	296	
Number and amount of loans repaid during the year	6	7,700 00
Geographical limit: Massachusetts.		
Amount of cash received during the year		36,789 03
Amount of cash paid during the year		37,435 78
Secretary's salary		300 00
Treasurer's salary		50 00
Treasurer's bonds		3,000 00
Secretary's bonds		3,000 00

Date of examination by commissioner: Sept. 9.

TROY CO-OPERATIVE SAVING-FUND AND LOAN ASSOCIATION—FALL RIVER.

Incorporated July 10, 1880. Commenced business July 20, 1880.

Capital to be accumulated, $1,000,000.

Spencer Borden, *President*. *Secretary*, C. C. Rounseville.
Henry T. Buffington, *Treasurer*.

Statement.

Liabilities.		Assets.	
539 shares of stock, first series, at $16.71	$9,006 69	Loans on real estate	$22,500 00
670 shares of stock, second series, at $13.48	9,031 60	Loans on shares	50 00
543 shares of stock, third series, at $7.15	3,882 45	Unpaid dues	272 00
500 shares of stock, fourth series, at $1	500 00	Balance of permanent expense account	107 49
Forfeited share account	41 52	Other assets	32 41
Other liabilities	1,050 29	Cash on hand	550 65
	$23,512 55		$23,512 55

Number of shares issued during the year	1,536	
Number of shares now in force	2,252	
Number of shares now borrowed upon	134	
Amount of dues received during the year		$19,655 00
Highest premium received during the year		62
Lowest premium received during the year		10
Fine for non-payment of dues: 2 per cent per month.		
Transfer fee		25

Number of members withdrawn during the year	25	
Present number of members	434	
Present number of borrowers	21	
Present number of non-borrowers	413	
Amount of loans at date		$22,550 00
Number and amount of loans on real estate	20	22,500 00
Number and amount of loans secured by first mortgage of real estate	20	22,500 00
Number and amount of loans on shares	1	50 00
Largest loan to any one member		3,300 00
Smallest loan to any one member		50 00
Largest numbers of shares held by any one member	25	
Amount of expenses of the corporation for previous year (not including interest)		308 09
Value of shares at last report		2,028 68
Total value of unpledged shares (including unpaid dues)		20,811 28
Number of shares forfeited during the year	22	
Amount of interest credited to shares during the year		794 22
Number of shares withdrawn during the year	149	
Number and amount of loans repaid during the year	3	1,440 00
Geographical limit: no limit.		
Amount of cash received during the year		23,022 72
Amount of cash paid during the year		23,360 17
Secretary's salary		180 00
Treasurer's bonds		2,000 00
Secretary's bonds		2,000 00
Date of examination by commissioner: Nov. 17.		

WALTHAM CO-OPERATIVE SAVING-FUND AND LOAN ASSOCIATION — WALTHAM.

Incorporated Oct. 13, 1880. Commenced business Oct. 21, 1880.

Capital to be accumulated, $1,000,000.

Manley U. Adams, *President*. *Secretary*, Daniel F. Viles.

G. Frank Frost, *Treasurer*.

Statement.

Liabilities.		Assets.	
2,054 shares of stock, first series, at $13.45	$27,626 30	Loans on real estate	$31,750 00
969 shares of stock, second series, at $7.12	6,899 28	Loans on shares	100 00
342 shares of stock, third series, at $1	342 00	Unpaid dues	298 00
Dues paid in advance	205 00	Balance of permanent expense account	281 78
Surplus	204 06	Other assets	8 88
Other liabilities	39 17	Cash on hand	2,877 15
	$35,315 81		$35,315 81

Number of shares issued during the year	1,509
Number of shares now in force	3,365
Number of shares now borrowed upon	174

Amount of dues received during the year		$34,679 00
Highest premium received during the year		50
Lowest premium received during the year		05
Fine for non-payment of dues: 2 per cent per month.		
Transfer fee		25
Number of members withdrawn during the year	53	
Present number of members	474	
Present number of borrowers	26	
Present number of non-borrowers	448	
Amount of loans at date		31,850 00
Number and amount of loans on real estate	31	31,750 00
Number and amount of loans secured by first mortgage of real estate	24	26,350 00
Number and amount of loans secured by other mortgage of real estate (in all cases they hold the first also)	7	5,400 00
Number and amount of loans on shares	2	100 00
Largest loan to any one member		3,500 00
Smallest loan to any one member		50 00
Largest number of shares held by any one member	25	
Amount of expenses of the corporation for previous year (not including interest, and including expense of organization) . .		574 07
Value of shares at last report (Oct. 1, 1881): first series, $12.45; second series, $6.12.		
Total value of unpledged shares (including unpaid dues) . .		32,952 03
Amount of interest credited to shares during the year . . .		1,040 58
Number of shares withdrawn during the year	406	
Number and amount of loans repaid during the year . . .		4,950 00
Geographical limit: Massachusetts.		
Amount of cash received during the year		41,229 36
Amount of cash paid during the year		40,684 21
Secretary's salary		200 00
Treasurer's bonds		1,000 00
Secretary's bonds		3,000 00
Date of visitation by commissioner: Nov. 29.		

WEST ROXBURY CO-OPERATIVE SAVING-FUND AND LOAN ASSOCIATION — BOSTON.

Incorporated Feb. 1, 1881. Commenced business March, 1881.
Capital to be accumulated, $1,000,000.

JOHN PEARCE, *President*. *Secretary*, THEODORE B. MOSES.
DANIEL A. BROWN, *Treasurer*.

STATEMENT.

LIABILITIES.		ASSETS.	
264 shares of stock, first series, at $8.32 . . .	$2,196 48	Loans on real estate . .	$2,400 00
188 shares of stock, second series, at $2.08 . . .	391 04	Unpaid dues . . .	84 00
		Balance of permanent expense account . . .	22 55
		Balance of temporary expense account . . .	80 97
	$2,587 52		$2,587 52

Number of shares issued during the year	469	
Number of shares now in force	452	
Number of shares now borrowed upon	12	
Amount of dues received during the year		$2,425 00
Highest premium received during the year		50
Lowest premium received during the year		05
Fines for non-payment of dues		11 00
Number of members withdrawn during the year	3	
Present number of members	109	
Present number of borrowers	3	
Present number of non-borrowers	106	
Amount of loans at date		2,400 00
Number and amount of loans on real estate	3	2,400 00
Number and amount of loans secured by first mortgage of real estate	3	2,400 00
Largest loan to any one member		1,500 00
Smallest loan to any one member		400 00
Largest number of shares held by any one member	20	
Amount of interest credited to shares during the year		48 00
Number of shares withdrawn during the year	17	
Geographical limit: Massachusetts.		
Amount of cash received during the year		2,498 87
Treasurer's bonds		1,000 00
Secretary's bonds		1,000 00
Date of examination by commissioner: Dec. 24.		

WORCESTER CO-OPERATIVE SAVING-FUND AND LOAN ASSOCIATION — WORCESTER.

Incorporated Oct. 19, 1877. Commenced business October, 1877.

Capital to be accumulated, $1,000,000.

D. S. Goddard, *President*. *Secretary*, T. J. Hastings.

T. M. Lamb, *Treasurer*.

Statement.

Liabilities.		Assets.	
402 shares of stock, first series, at $55.28	$22,222 56	Loans on real estate	$53,700 00
237 shares of stock, second series, at $40.51	9,600 87	Loans on shares	1,740 00
427 shares of stock, third series, at $26.57	11,345 39	Unpaid dues	491 00
936 shares of stock, fourth series, at $13.39	12,533 04	Balance of temporary expense account	152 37
635 shares of stock, fifth series, at $1	635 00	Safe	50 00
Dues paid in advance	2,541 00	Balance of permanent expense account	284 13
Interest account	260 05	Suspense account	471 62
Premium account	24 64	Cash on hand	2,293 03
Fines account	11 61		
Transfer fee account	25		
Forfeited share account	7 74		
	$59,182 15		$59,182 15

Number of shares issued during the year	1,205	
Number of shares now in force	2,637	
Number of shares now borrowed upon	385	
Amount of dues received during the year		$26,938 00
Highest premium received during the year: $\frac{15}{100}$ per cent per month.		
Lowest premium received during the year: $\frac{1}{100}$ per cent per month.		
Fine for non-payment of dues: 2 per cent per month.		
Transfer fee		25
Number of members withdrawn during the year	62	
Present number of members	479	
Present number of borrowers	68	
Present number of non-borrowers	411	
Amount of loans at date		55,440 00
Number and amount of loans on real estate	56	53,700 00
Number and amount of loans secured by first mortgage of real estate	45	47,950 00
Number and amount of loans secured by other mortgage of real estate	11	5,750 00
Number and amount of loans on shares	25	1,740 00
Largest loan to any one member		3,600 00
Smallest loan to any one member		25 00
Largest number of shares held by any one member	25	
Amount of expenses of the corporation for previous year (not including interest)		697 00
Value of shares at last report: first series, $54.28; second series, $39.51; third series, $25.57; fourth series, $12.39.		
Total value of unpledged shares (including unpaid dues)		45,562 60
Number of shares forfeited during the year	3	
Amount of interest credited to shares during the year		2,517 46
Number of shares withdrawn during the year	318	
Number and amount of loans repaid during the year	16	8,430 00
Geographical limit: Massachusetts.		
Amount of cash received during the year		38,373 45
Amount of cash paid during the year		38,273 80
Secretary's salary		350 00
Treasurer's salary		100 00
Treasurer's bonds		2,500 00
Secretary's bonds		500 00
Date of examination by commissioner: Sept. 13.		

WORKINGMEN'S CO-OPERATIVE SAVING-FUND AND LOAN ASSOCIATION — BOSTON.

Incorporated June 9, 1880. Commenced business June 11, 1880.

Capital to be accumulated, $1,000,000.

ROBERT TREAT PAINE, Jun., *President*. *Secretary*, DANIEL ELDREDGE.

CHARLES W. DEXTER, *Treasurer*.

STATEMENT.

LIABILITIES.		ASSETS.	
611 shares of stock, first series, at $17.36	$10,606 96	Loans on real estate	$14,600 00
504 shares of stock, second series, at $11.09	5,589 36	Loans on shares	50 00
459 shares of stock, third series, at $5	2,295 00	Unpaid dues	801 00
Surplus	12 86	Balance of permanent expense account	240 00
Forfeited share account	4 06	Balance of temporary expense account	9 23
Withdrawal profits	9 81	Cash on hand	3,323 78
Other liabilities	505 96		
	$19,024 01		$19,024 01

Number of shares issued during the year	1,134	
Number of shares now in force	1,574	
Number of shares now borrowed upon	83	
Amount of dues received during the year		$16,339 00
Highest premium received during the year (for one month only)		1 10
Lowest premium received during the year		05
Fine for non-payment of dues: 2 per cent per month.		
Transfer fee		25
Number of members withdrawn during the year	78	
Present number of members	284	
Present number of borrowers	12	
Present number of non-borrowers	272	
Amount of loans at date		14,650 00
Number and amount of loans on real estate	11	14,600 00
Number and amount of loans secured by first mortgage of real estate	11	14,600 00
Number and amount of loans on shares	1	50 00
Largest loan to any one member		2,700 00
Smallest loan to any one member		50 00
Largest number of shares held by any one member	25	
Amount of expenses of the corporation for previous year (not including interest) *		283 12
Value of shares at last report		4,065 00
Total value of unpledged shares (including unpaid dues)		17,564 54
Number of shares forfeited during the year	12	
Amount of interest credited to shares during the year *		314 19
Number of shares withdrawn during the year	361	
Number and amount of loans repaid during the year	4	4,000 00

* For year ending May 31.

Geographical limit: Massachusetts.

Amount of cash received during the year	$21,316 80
Amount of cash paid during the year	18,058 94
Secretary's salary	150 00
Treasurer's bonds	1,000 00
Secretary's bonds	1,000 00

Date of examination by commissioner: July 27.

INDEX.

INDEX TO THE ANNUAL REPORTS.

SAVINGS BANKS.

TRUST COMPANIES.

CO-OPERATIVE SAVING-FUND AND LOAN ASSOCIATIONS.